WORLD COMMUNICATIONS

ENDORSED BY
THE U.S. COUNCIL FOR
WORLD COMMUNICATIONS YEAR 1983

ANNENBERG / LONGMAN COMMUNICATION BOOKS

George Gerbner and Marsha Siefert, Editors

The Annenberg School of Communications

University of Pennsylvania

WORLD COMMUNICATIONS

A Handbook

GEORGE GERBNER and
MARSHA SIEFERT, Editors

Longman

New York & London

World Communications
A Handbook

Longman Inc., 1560 Broadway, New York, N.Y. 10036
Associated companies, branches, and representatives throughout the world.

Developmental Editor: Gordon T. R. Anderson
Editorial and Design Supervisor: Joan Matthews
Production Supervisor,: Ferne Y. Kawahara
Manufacturing Supervisor: Marion Hess

Grateful acknowledgment is made to The Annenberg School of Communications for permission to use the following articles from the *Journal of Communication:* "The Many Worlds of the World's Press" by George Gerbner and George Márványi, Winter 1977: 52-66. Copyright © 1977 by The Annenberg School of Communications. "Global Traffic in Television Programming" by Tapio Varis, Winter 1974: 102-109. Copyright © 1974 by The Annenberg School of Communications. An updated version of "Transborder Data Flow: An International Policy Survey" by G. Russell Pipe (originally "National Policies, International Debates"), Spring 1979: 114-123. Copyright © 1979 by The Annenberg School of Communications. An updated version of "Direct Satellite Broadcasting: Definitions and Prospects" by Rolf T. Wigand, Spring 1980: 140-146. Copyright © 1980 by The Annenberg School of Communications. An updated version of "Satellite Broadcasting: Cooperative Ventures" by Edward W. Ploman (originally "Western Europe: International Ambiguity"), Spring 1980: 178-185. Copyright © 1980 by The Annenberg School of Communications. An updated version of "Telecommunications Alternatives for Developing Countries" by Ronald E. Rice and Edwin B. Parker, Autumn 1979: 125-136. Copyright © 1979 by The Annenberg School of Communications. "Mass Media Reform and Social Change: The Peruvian Experience" by Rita Atwood and Sérgio Mattos, Spring 1982: 33-45. Copyright © 1982 by The Annenberg School of Communications. "Communication as Complement to Development" by Robert C. Hornik, Spring 1980: 10-24. Copyright © 1980 by The Annenberg School of Communications. An updated version of "INTELSAT: An International Satellite System" by Marcellus S. Snow, Spring 1980: 147-156. Copyright © 1980 by The Annenberg School of Communications. "The MacBride Report: The Results and Response" by Kusum Singh and Bertram Gross, Autumn 1981: 104-117. Copyright © 1981 by The Annenberg School of Communications. "UNESCO and the International Program for the Development of Communications" by William G. Harley (originally "The U.S. Stake in the IPDC"), Autumn 1981: 150-158. Copyright © 1981 by The Annenberg School of Communications. "Instituting the International Program for the Development of Communications" by Clifford H. Block (originally "Promising Step at Acapulco: A U.S. View"), Summer 1982: 60-70. Copyright © 1982 by The Annenberg School of Communications. "Information Exchange between Developing and Industrial Countries" by V. A. Vinogradov et al. is excerpted from "Toward an International Information System," *International Social Science Journal*, UNESCO, 33(1), 1981, pp. 10-49. Reprinted by permission of UNESCO. Copyright © 1981 by UNESCO. "Toward an International Data Network" by V. A. Vinogradov et al. is excerpted from "Toward an International Information System," *International Social Science Journal*, UNESCO, 33(1), 1981, pp. 10-49. Reprinted by permission of UNESCO. Copyright © 1981 by UNESCO. "Global Statellite Systems" is reprinted by permission of Joseph N. Pelton.

Library of Congress Cataloging in Publication Data

Main entry under title:

World communications, a handbook.

(Annenberg/Longman communication books)
Bibliography: p
Includes index.
1. Communication, International — Addresses, essays,
lectures. 2. Underdeveloped areas — Communication — Addresses,
essays, lectures. 3. Communication policy —
Addresses, essays, lectures. I. Gerbner, George.
II. Siefert, Marsha, 1949–   . III. Series.
P96.15W67 1983   001.51   82-24963

Manufactured in the United States of America
Printing: 9 8 7 6 5 4 3 2 1   Year 92 91 90 89 88 87 86 85 84

ISBN 0-582-28457-0

Contents

APPENDIXES

Editors' Preface

The time has long passed since the West could speak for the whole world. Genuine international discourse requires authentic voices from all "three worlds." Authenticity and candor are especially important in a handbook intended to be a guide for governments, corporations, scholars, students, and policy makers. That has been a guiding principle behind the organization of this handbook. Speaking for themselves are scholars and policy makers from the U.S., Western Europe, the socialist countries, including the U.S.S.R. and Eastern Europe, and the developing world, including Africa, Asia, and Latin America. Over 25 countries are represented. This multiplicity of views and actors is the essence of world communications. Our goal was not to orchestrate the voices but to select papers that are well-argued and representative of the diversity of opinion on various issues.

On many international issues, dividing the globe into First, Second, and Third Worlds, or into North-South and East-West is convenient for delineating interests and views. But developing world communications ties and infrastructures creates other patterns of cooperation and conflict as well. Thus, we have also included case studies of individual countries or regions, when their situations illustrated common world communications concerns.

The selection of articles for this handbook reflects a joining of research and policy. When possible we have provided studies that assess communications situations, along with policy statements or informed views on these same issues. Different skills are called upon by the researcher and the policy maker, although the position of the latter may also inform the inquiry of the former. But interpretation is essential to both, and we hope that bringing them together in one volume will enhance their value.

Part 1, "Global Perspectives on Information," sets out the assumptions and rationales for information policies of various world constituencies. In addition to presenting the views of professional policy makers from the United States, Western Europe, the Socialist countries, and the Third

World, we have also included the now classic paper by Mustapha Masmoudi in which the call for a New World Information Order was first presented.

Part 2, "Transnational Communications: The Flow of News and Images," addresses a concern expressed by Third World countries as to whom is controlling that flow. We have included chapters on news reports, television programs, film, advertising, and cultural stereotypes, along with benchmark assessments of many world media systems.

"Telecommunications" is the subject of Part 3. Technological developments in satellite and computer systems have minimized geographical obstacles and challenged the salience of political boundaries in the global flow of information. The physical limitations of spectrum space and the capital required for participating in telecommunications networks have intensified competition over markets for hardware and software. Developing countries, in particular, have a sense of urgency in terms of participation and access.

Part 4, "Mass Communications: Development within National Contexts," contains articles particularly concerned with how communications systems have been used to meet national goals. Case studies focus on the use of mass communications for radical social change, for unifying large nations and for governing small ones, and for coping with language differences and providing education. The variety of issues addressed by these authors exemplifies the diversity and innovation inherent in the uses and functions of mass communications.

Part 5 describes the structures and functions of "Intergovernmental Systems." These systems and organizations represent some of the main forums in which world communications issues are debated and in which cooperation is forged. Also included in this section are discussions of some of the most important meetings and organs of UNESCO, a prime organization in the global discourse on communications issues. The closing articles recount the formation and activities of the International Program for the Development of Communication which aims to pump money as well as words into the enhancement of world communications.

A project like *World Communications: A Handbook* must of necessity involve many people. We are forunate in that the Trustees of The Annenberg School of Communications at the University of Pennsylvania provided funds that allowed for a face-to-face meeting of most of the contributors to this project. The realization of the book could not been possible without the assistance of Janice Fisher, Madeline Sann, Suzy Glazer, Anne Evans, Cathy Kirkland, and Laura Wawrzaszek. The support of Longman Inc., especially Gordon T. R. Anderson and Joan Matthews, has also been invaluable. We thank them all.

We are pleased that this book is being published during World Communications Year and dedicate it to all those who have worked toward global understanding.

About the Authors

Binod C. Agrawal, Scientist and Coordinator, Educational Resources Cell, Space Applications Centre, Indian Space Research Organization, Ahmedabad, India.

Sarath L. B. Amunugama, Director, International Program for the Development of Communications (IPDC), UNESCO, Paris; former Director, Asian Mass Communication Research and Information Center (AMIC); former Secretary of the Ministry of State, Sri Lanka.

T. V. Andrianova, Researcher, Institute of Scientific Information on Social Sciences, U.S.S.R. Academy of Sciences (INION), Moscow.

Paul A. V. Ansah, Director, School of Journalism and Communication, University of Ghana; President, the African Council on Communication Education.

Rita Atwood, Faculty, College of Communications, University of Texas, Austin.

Clifford H. Block, Associate Director, Research and Development Program, Agency for International Development, Washington, D.C.; U.S. delegate to the IPDC meeting at Acapulco.

Nolan A. Bowie, Assistant Attorney General, Attorney General's Office (Civil Rights Bureau), The New York State Department of Law; former Executive Director, the Citizens Communications Center, Washington, D.C.

Anne Branscomb, Attorney specializing in communications law; Chairman of the Communications Division of the Science and Technology Section, the American Bar Association.

Chen C. Chimutengwende, Senior Lecturer, Zimbabwe Institute of Mass

Communication; UNESCO Regional Office for Africa; Secretary General of the Pan African Association of Writers and Journalists; formerly at the University of Nairobi, Kenya.

Forrest Chisman, Communications Consultant, Alexandria, Virginia; former Deputy Associate Administrator, Office of Policy Analysis and Development at the National Telecommunications and Information Administration, U.S. Department of Commerce, Washington, D.C.

Hastings Mawola Sanderson Chunga, Undersecretary, the Ministry of Transport and Communications, Lilongwe, Malawi.

Daniel Dayan, University of Paris; formerly at Communications Institute, Hebrew University, Jerusalem.

Herbert S. Dordick, Director, Center for Communication Policy and Research, The Annenberg School of Communications, University of Southern California, Los Angeles.

John M. Eger, Vice President, Strategic Planning and International Development and Head, CBS Broadcast International, CBS Broadcast Group, New York; former Director of the White House Office of Telecommunications Policy.

Kamal El Menoufi, Faculty of Economics and Political Science, Cairo University, Egypt; also Faculty of Commerce, Department of Political Science, Kuwait University, Kuwait.

Guido Fauconnier, Professor of Communications, Catholic University, Leuven, Belgium.

George Gerbner, Professor and Dean, The Annenberg School of Communications, University of Pennyslvania; Editor, *Journal of Communication.*

Luis Gonzaga Motta, Centro Internacional de Estudios Superiores de Comunicacion para America Latina (CIESPAL), Quito, Ecuador.

Stephen Gorove, Professor of Law, the University of Mississippi Law Center; Corresponding Member, the International Academy of Astronautics; Vice President of Programs, Association of U.S. Members of the International Institute of Space Law.

Bertram Gross, Distinguished Professor Emeritus, Hunter College, City University of New York, New York City; Visiting Professor-at-Large, Saint Mary's College of California, Moraga, California.

Thomas Guback, Research Professor, Institute of Communications Research, University of Illinois, Urbana-Champaign.

Cees J. Hamelink, Institute of Social Studies, The Hague, The Netherlands.

William G. Harley, U.S. National Commission for UNESCO, Washington, D.C.; member of the U.S. delegations to the four General Conferences of UNESCO; U.S. delegate to the initial meeting of the IPDC Council.

Robert C. Hornik, Faculty, The Annenberg School of Communications, University of Pennsylvania.

Zoltán Jakab, Head, Mass Communication Research Center, Hungarian Radio and Television; specialist in long-range planning of mass communications policies in Budapest.

Noreene Janus, Research Coordinator, Instituto Latinoamericano de Estudios Transnacionales (ILET), Mexico City.

Elihu Katz, Communications Institute, Hebrew University, Jerusalem; The Annenberg School of Communications, University of Southern California, Los Angeles.

V. R. Khisamutdinov, Department Head, Institute of Scientific Information on Social Sciences, U.S.S.R. Academy of Sciences (INION), Moscow.

David C. King, Staff Associate, Global Perspectives in Education, Inc.; freelance curriculum writer.

L. S. Kiouzadjan, Deputy-Director, Institute of Scientific Information on Social Sciences, U.S.S.R. Academy of Sciences (INION), Moscow.

G. B. Kossov, Department Head, Institute of Scientific Information on Social Sciences, U.S.S.R. Academy of Sciences (INION), Moscow.

A. M. Kul'kin, Department Head, Institute of Scientific Information on Social Sciences, U.S.S.R. Academy of Sciences (INION), Moscow.

James F. Larson, Faculty, College of Communications, University of Texas, Austin.

Harvey J. Levin, Weller Professor of Economics, Hofstra University; Senior Associate, the Center for Policy Research, New York City.

Sergei Losev, Director-General, TASS, Moscow; member of the MacBride Commission.

George Márványi, Editor in Chief of Programs, Hungarian Radio and Television, Budapest, Hungary.

Mustapha Masmoudi, Ambassador and Permanent Delegate from Tunisia to UNESCO; former Secretary of State for Information for Tunisia.

Sérgio Mattos, Faculty, Federal University of Bahia, Brazil.

R. R. Mdivani, Department Head, Institute of Scientific Information on Social Sciences, U.S.S.R. Academy of Sciences (INION), Moscow.

William H. Melody, Professor of Communication Studies, Simon Fraser University, Burnaby, British Columbia, Canada.

Pierre Motyl, Communications Institute, Hebrew University, Jerusalem.

Hamid Mowlana, Director, School of International Service, American University, Washington, D.C.

Kaarle Nordenstreng, Professor and Chairman, Department of Journalism and Mass Communications, University of Tampere, Finland; President, International Organization of Journalists.

Rita Cruise O'Brien, Fellow, Institute of Development Studies, University of Sussex, England.

Edwin B. Parker, Vice President, Equatorial Communications Company, Mountain View, California.

Joseph N. Pelton, Executive Assistant to the Director-General, International Telecommunications Satellite Organization, Washington, D.C.

G. Russell Pipe, President and Editorial Director, Transnational Data Reporting Service, Amsterdam and Washington, D.C.

Walery Pisarek, Director, Press Research Center, Cracow; Head, Journalism Department, Jagiellonian University, Cracow, Poland.

Edward W. Ploman, Vice Rector, Global Learning, United Nations University, Tokyo; former Executive Director, International Institute of Communications, London.

Sarah Goddard Power, Regent, University of Michigan; former U.S. Deputy Assistant Secretary for Human Rights and Social Affairs, Bureau of International Organizational Affairs, U.S. Department of State.

Syed A. Rahim, Research Associate, Communications Policy and Planning, East-West Communication Institute, East-West Center, Honolulu, Hawaii.

A. I. Rakitov, Department Head, Institute of Scientific Information on Social Sciences, U.S.S.R. Academy of Sciences (INION), Moscow.

Fernando Reyes Matta, Director, Division of Communication Studies, Instituto Latinoamericano de Estudios Transnacionales (ILET), Mexico City.

Ronald E. Rice, Faculty, The Annenberg School of Communications, University of Southern California, Los Angeles.

John Richardson, Jr., President, Youth for Understanding (International Student Exchange), Washington, D.C.; President, Freedom House, New York; Chairman, American Council, the United Nations University.

Herbert I. Schiller, Professor of Communications, University of California, San Diego.

Jorge A. Schnitman, Faculty, Center for Latin American Studies, Stanford University.

L. V. Shemberko, Senior Researcher, Institute of Scientific Information on Social Sciences, U.S.S.R. Academy of Sciences (INION), Moscow.

Benno Signitzer, Faculty, Institute for Journalism and Mass Communication Theory, Salzburg, Austria.

Kusum J. Singh, Faculty, Department of Communications, Saint Mary's College of California, Moraga, California.

Marcellus S. Snow, Faculty, Department of Economics, University of Hawaii, Honolulu.

Humphrey Tonkin, Director, International Programs, University of Pennsylvania, Philadelphia.

Frank Okwu Ugboajah, Head, Department of Mass Communication, University of Lagos, Nigeria; Editor, *UNILAG Communication Review*.

Tapio Varis, Director, Peace Research Institute, Tampere, Finland; Institute of Journalism and Mass Communication, University of Tampere.

S. K. Vilenskaya, Department Head, Institute of Scientific Information on Social Sciences, U.S.S.R. Academy of Sciences (INION), Moscow.

V. A. Vinogradov, Director of the Institute of Scientific Information on Social Sciences, U.S.S.R. Academy of Sciences (INION).

Robert A. White, Research Director, Centre for the Study of Communication and Culture, London, England.

Rolf T. Wigand, Professor of Public Affairs and Communication, Arizona State University, Tempe, Arizona.

Yassen Zassoursky, Dean, Faculty of Journalism, Moscow State University, U.S.S.R.

PART 1

Global Perspectives
on Information

One

Grounds for a United States International Information Policy

Forrest Chisman

It is generally agreed that the United States government does not have, and perhaps cannot have, an overall international telecommunications and information (T & I) policy. Certainly it addresses a great number of T & I issues on an individual basis, including issues of international facilities, spectrum planning, mass media, technology transfer, and sales of goods and services. In many cases, these issues are addressed effectively and with a view to both national and global interests. Yet the federal government has not thus far developed an overall intellectual framework, a set of basic guiding principles, or an organizational unity linking T & I activities in a variety of international arenas. The growing realization that T & I issues are as interdependent economically, technically, politically, and culturally as the burgeoning T & I technologies to which they apply has prompted calls for this fact to be recognized and reflected in the framework of U.S. policy.

To some extent such calls suggest intellectual naivete. While there can be no doubt that international T & I issues are increasingly interdependent, one cannot assume that, for practical purposes, policies that address these issues on a partial basis are deficient. One is tempted to say that the United States will have an international information policy as soon as it has an overall policy linking the rest of its international concerns or, for that matter, an overall domestic policy, or overall policies on health care, defense, and taxation. Only in times of great emergency or opportunity has the United States had comprehensive and consistent policies in any of these areas, and it is not clear that we are any worse off without them.

Regrettably, however, this comfortable partial approach to policy-making in the international T & I sphere is being eroded by events. For example, it is becoming clear that planning for satellite and cable facilities must be coordinated, with each other and with planning of radio frequency use. At the same time, international debate on cultural issues raised under rubrics like *informatique*, the New World Information Order, DBS, and transborder data flows has increasingly been tied to major international political issues, and these political issues, in turn, are impinging upon the domains of trade and international spectrum management, which were once largely the reserve of experts.

This is not to deny that many aspects of international T & I issues still are best addressed on a partial basis. Spectrum management and facilities are a case in point and, on the whole, the United States has done well in addressing them. The U.S. is experiencing difficulties, however, in dealing with the growing number of issues where technological convergence has forced the need for a convergence of policy as well.

By contrast, other nations have not been at all hesitant to begin developing overall information policies. In Japan, in the various nations of Europe, and in the European Parliament, broad-gauged studies have been undertaken to guide and coordinate the growth of information systems. Similar policy programs have been discussed at meetings of the IBI (International Bureau of Informatique). The United States is being forced to look at difficult issues of convergence in international communications business because other nations are our partners in it and their planning activity forces us to share at least some of their concerns. To take a crude example, European nations could force the United States to take account of their concerns about the introduction of value-added services simply by refusing to interconnect with American companies until the rules for providing services have been worked out to their satisfaction.

THE NEED FOR AN INTERNATIONAL POLICY

The growing number of convergence issues and other nations' policies toward them make the call for an overall U.S. international information policy of more than academic interest. In order to maintain an effective dialogue with its partners, the United States must develop at least the outlines of a more comprehensive approach to emerging issue areas. In the absence of such an approach, the U.S. will increasingly find itself arguing at cross-purposes with other nations. It will lack a common ground on which to agree or disagree with them constructively and a framework of common assumptions within which to bargain and settle.

Without such commonalities, there is a real danger that the growing number of convergence issues could pose a serious threat to the growth and effectiveness of international information systems in which all nations have a vital stake. These systems are not only important economic, political, and social engines in themselves, but they are also the life blood of international economic growth. Without them, international banking, insurance, construction, and a great variety of other industries that are central to late twentieth century economies would simply be impossible. In a world that is increasingly short on energy and other raw materials, economic security for all is coming to depend to a large extent on the efficiencies achieved by interdependent international information systems. To live well in the coming decades we must increasingly replace fuel power with brain power, but the brains are more and more "artificial" brains— information machines—and they are world-wide systems, not discrete boxes. The success of these systems depends to a large extent upon international cooperation, and misunderstandings among nations that block their efficient and most socially useful development can, therefore, pose a severe threat to global well-being.

THE BROADER FRAMEWORK

To be effective in meeting this threat, a broader approach to United States T & I policy in the international area must satisfy several criteria. It must (a) bridge a variety of issue areas, (b) indicate what is at stake in those areas, (c) provide grounds for action, (d) provide the basis for effective dialogue with our international partners, and (e) be consistent with our basic goals and national values.

How can the U.S. begin to develop such a broad approach? A critical first step must be the construction of a strong economic agenda to parallel the technical, political, and social agendas on which T & I issues traditionally have been placed. Although economics has always been an important consideration for T & I policymakers, the primary determinants of the partial U.S. policies that do exist have been technical, political, and social considerations.

A parallel economic emphasis can significantly advance discussions with other nations for several reasons. First, economics is a major concern, possibly *the* major concern, underlying convergence issues. Policymakers have difficulty dealing with the development of new international information systems to a large extent because economic disagreements overshadow possible areas of consensus or stable compromise. For example, almost everyone in free nations believes in the right to personal privacy, and no one would oppose almost any kind of regulations to protect that right, were it not for the fact that unwise restrictions on T & I systems could severely undermine their economic efficiency. The same is true of facilities issues. No one would question the analyses of engineers about the most efficient way to introduce value-added international services were it not for the economic competition that they create and their effects on the differing economic goals of nations that they link. A stronger economic emphasis in U.S. international information policy would, therefore, at least focus attention more directly on some of the major barriers to resolving disputes.

A second reason for developing an economic emphasis in policy-making is that other nations have increasingly placed economic considerations at the center of their information policies. The Japanese and the French, as well as the European Economic Community, all have concluded that national economic development is heavily dependent on the rapid growth of domestic information industries and, consequently, that such growth requires planning in an integrated fashion. It is no wonder, then, that the United States finds itself talking past other nations when it deals with these issues piecemeal or assumes that at heart they are technical, political, or social issues outside the economic context.

A third reason for suggesting an economic emphasis is that economics is an international language that all nations understand and an area of policy which they take very seriously. We know how to agree and disagree, how to emphasize and condition, how to analyze and act in terms of domestic and international economic concerns. Disagreements about economic issues allow for the possibility of bargaining. Indeed bargaining is inherent in them. Disputes about technical and social issues often become stalemated because they are fundamentally disagreements about facts and values on which parties find it difficult to compromise. Economic disputes, however, often can be resolved more readily because they give parties greater freedom to make deals and seek a middle ground.

What would adopting an economic focus on international information issues mean in terms of U.S. policy? First, it would clearly establish at least two of the basic goals of our international information activities: free trade and fair opportunities for competition. The U.S. believes that these goals are essential both to its own well-being and to the well-being of the rest of the world. An economic emphasis would make it clear that these goals will be lasting cornerstones of our policy.

Second, an economic emphasis would unify our analysis of information issues from a known and practiced perspective. For example, we could analyze, set objectives, and develop policies concerning proposed restrictions on transborder data flows in terms of their impact on our own and other nation's economies as well as on the overall efficiency of international information systems. To the extent that our perceptions of the world and our own self-interest in these cases may differ from those of others, we could bargain. Such an approach provides the prospect of more rapid resolution of many issues on terms that are reasonably satisfactory to all parties.

Third, an economic approach would allow us to integrate into U.S. international information policy concerns that have been notoriously neglected—the concerns of trade policy narrowly construed. Trade in telecommunications and information goods constitutes one of our largest export sectors, approaching $20 billion per year, and contributing heavily to remedying our balance of payments situation. Trade in services is difficult to measure, but such areas as telephony and value added remote data processing amount to hundreds of millions of dollars and their growth rate is extremely rapid. Technically, functionally, politically, and socially, whether we can sell computers or telephone equipment to Germany or Egypt has a major impact upon whether and how we or anyone else will be able to communicate effectively with those countries for either private or public purposes. In adopting an economic perspective, the U.S. would be placing T & I trade issues on center stage, where they belong, rather than waiting in the wings, where they have too often been found.

THE SOCIAL GOALS OF AN ECONOMIC APPROACH

It is important not to misconstrue the implications of an economic emphasis in relation to U.S. economic goals. The United States does not have and never has had an international economic policy that is based purely on gain. Economic policy has always been responsive to and founded upon considerations of national sovereignty, cultural diversity, political necessity, and hopefully, technical rationality. Moreover, given our traditional economic principles and current policy approaches, we are unlikely to adopt economic measures such as cartels and major subsidies that are available to other nations. Neither would adopting an economic emphasis mean postponing international T & I issues until broader international economic issues are resolved. While the relation of T & I issues to broader economic concerns cannot be ignored, they can be dealt with on their own to a significant degree.

The issue, therefore, is not whether cultural and social issues are important or economic considerations are unbridled. Rather, it is whether or not we can discover the basic, underlying problems that cause us concern about the growth of information systems and can deal with them in an intelligent and focused manner. In many cases, economic gains must be set aside because the price for the resolution of some issues may be exhorbitantly high. But an economic agenda would at least force the United States and other nations to focus on whether particular political, technical, or social stakes are as high as the common stake we hold in vigorous world-wide information systems.

How would we deal with any particular issue differently by adopting an economic perspective of this sort? Take the New World Information Order as an example. I would not have us set aside cultural and technical dialogues on the issues raised. I would, rather, have us develop at the same time an economic dialogue about how, realistically, cultural goals can be met. To be realistic, such a dialogue would go beyond mass media to the needs of nations for a variety of interrelated information systems. It would stress the national and world economic implications of alternative ways of achieving them. It would look at hard facts of economic interdependence, capital formation, and growth, and it would count the cost of alternative proposals in a hard-headed way. I do not know what the outcome of such a dialogue would be, but I believe that it would at least shift the center of gravity of discussion to grounds where a constructive resolution is possible.

In conclusion, viewing U.S. information policy as an aspect of international economic policy meets the criteria for an integrated T & I policy perspective. Economic concerns bridge most issue areas and lie at the heart of international interdependence. Economic analyses allow grounds for action, or at least for conditioning action, as well as for effective dialogue. Finally, an economic policy, properly balanced, is consistent with U.S. traditions of fairness and openness and the goals of international well-being.

Two

Information: Predicates for International Regulation

John M. Eger

The meaning of the word "information" has become very broad. Information·no longer refers only to conventional bodies of statistics, facts, academic knowledge, scientific data, or daily news; it now includes electronic sensing and computer analysis of the human heartbeat, electrical impulses measuring physical phenomena in outer space or beneath the sea, and numeric digits holding passengers' airplane seats or transferring funds to and from bank accounts. No matter how information is stored or recorded—whether on film, paper, or magnetic tape or in books, magazines, movies, or computer memories—it is part of a growing industry.

Today we are increasingly dependent upon these various forms of information for the health and growth of the economy, the smooth functioning of institutions, and the preservation of the quality of life. In simple terms, information has become a marketable, transferable, exportable commodity—a commodity for production, sale, and consumption with which more and more of us are engaged every day.

A 1977 U.S. Commerce Department study by Marc Porat revealed that over 70 percent of the U.S. work force is employed within an information-based sector, representing 65 percent of the GNP and approximately 25 percent of total U.S. exports, a bright spot in our balance of trade. West Germany, Japan, France, and other industrialized countries exhibit the same trend, and they, like us, are analyzing these developments, attempting to ascertain probable impacts on national infrastructures, formulating responsive national policies to accommodate and foster the orderly and healthy introduction of new information technologies, and assessing the need for increased government intervention and—possibly a promising occurrence—denationalization, or privatization as it has been coined in the United Kingdom, of telephone and telegraph monopolies.

Significantly, such awareness is not limited to the developed countries.

Already in 1978 the Director-General of the Intergovernmental Bureau for Informatics, Fermin Bernasconi, told the 1st International Conference on Transnational Data Regulation that "well over 50 countries have adopted . . . comprehensive national informatics plans." Bernasconi defined informatics as the "national management and exploitation of information resources, according to an overall strategy implemented by appropriate policies." He also noted that "the recognition that information is a powerful resource with political, economic, social and cultural dimensions is motivating governments to consider regulatory or other control policies to protect or promote their national interests."

Clearly, the economic importance of information is secure throughout the world. Less certain, unfortunately, is the role of information and of computer, telecommunications, and other information technologies in the New World Economic Order or the New World Information Order. In Europe, Japan, and Canada, for example, privacy and data protection laws, taxes on information, and increased tariffs and restrictions on telecommunication facilities are now emerging; more direct control of international information flow everywhere appears likely as tensions rise over trade, unemployment, and inflation. Faced with the barriers to the free flow of information erected by the Soviet Union and many less developed countries—not for protectionist reasons but out of genuine fear of electronic inundation, or, in the words of a Third World official, "electronic colonization"—the United States and all other nations dependent upon global information flows must tackle what may be one of the most complicated issues of this century.

Censorship, data protection laws, tariffs, standards, information taxes, nationalization, and information espionage all figure in this global arena in which nations are confronting each other over the issue of information. These developments threaten the world economy, requiring us to reconsider both our approach to the human community and our approach to the formulation of international law and policy. We cannot allow the international politicization of communications technology to continue unchecked.

I would be guilty of gross misrepresentation were I to argue that national information strategies or so-called informatics plans are inherently evil or somehow contrary to international harmony. However, intellectual enchantment with the concept of a post-industrial, information-based economy and society is fostering the creation of an information elite, and with it the development of information laws, taxes, tariffs, regulations, and policies that will be difficult to repeal or amend once enshrined in national law. Such policies will serve to inhibit the orderly development of law and communications policy on an international scale that is badly needed. Consider a few comments by public officials from France, Canada, and Sweden.

France's Magistrate of Justice, Louis Joinet, stated his concern at a symposium in Vienna in September 1977.

> Information is power, and economic information is economic power. Information has an economic value and the ability to store and process certain types of data may well give one country political and technological advantage over other countries. This in turn may lead to a loss of national sovereignty through supranational data flows.

In the opening address of the 1977 conference of the International Federation of Information Processing Societies in Toronto, Hugh Faulkner, Canadian Minister for Science and Technology, spoke of the effects of the export of information from Canada.

> It creates the potential of growing dependence, rather than interdependence, the loss of employment opportunities, in addition to the balance of payments problem, the danger of loss of legitimate access to vital information, and the danger that industrial and social development will be largely governed by the decisions of interest groups residing in another country.

This perspective is shared by Jan Freese, Director of the Swedish Data Protection Board. Speaking before an OECD Conference on Privacy in 1978, Vienna, Austria, he argued for a free but balanced flow of information. Thus, according to Freese, this flow must be regulated in order to be free, a position taken by many less developed nations concerned over the transmission of news and related broadcast information.

Such statements by officials throughout the world are resulting in a redefinition of sovereignty or, more precisely, are encouraging "information sovereignty," in which view all information or data entering or leaving a country are suspect and must be closely regulated and monitored, along with the computer-communications infrastructure, which possibly should be managed directly by government.

The Clyne Committee Report of 1979, commissioned by the Canadian government to produce specific recommendations regarding Canadian telecommunications development, advocated such control.

> Canadian sovereignty in the next generation will depend heavily upon telecommunications. If we wish to have an independent culture then we will have to continue to express it through radio and television. If we wish to control our economy, then we will require a sophisticated telecommunications sector *developed and owned* in Canada to meet specific Canadian requirements. To maintain our Canadian identity and independence we must ensure an adequate measure of control over data banks, transborder data flows and the content of information services available in Canada. (Emphasis added.)

The Nora-Minc Report from France, the SARK Report from Sweden's

Ministry of Defense, and a host of other official documents voice similar fears and argue, with minimal empirical support, for a new era of regulation and control.

A NEW DIRECTION IN REGULATION

The regulatory moves we already have seen and those in the offing will slow down if not entirely disrupt the free flow of information, which is a necessity in the modern world. However, international regulation is inevitable, and the only question is whether the regulations with which we end up are progressive or reactionary. The United States has a responsibility to help formulate forward-looking international policy. Our influence, whether purposefully channeled or not, is likely to increase during the rest of this century and, although the belief in a special U.S. role in world affairs has been the cause of mistakes in the past, our experience with building a national community while fostering diversity and our achievement in preserving freedom of expression provide a solid foundation on which to build a constructive approach. The United States has an obligation to assist in this international effort because it is rich in communications technology.

Of course, government can play only a limited role in this area. An equally important part must be played by universities, media, businesses, arts, and voluntary associations with the capacity to influence relationships with other societies. During the next decade we should support and join with private citizens and organizations throughout the world in a program not only of study and research but also of active participation in the debate on the social, political, and psychological impacts of the new communications capabilities—impacts that can be either good or bad. For as we saw in the Munich Olympics and witnessed daily from Iran, international terrorism is as much stimulated by new communications technology as is our consciousness of interdependence. Clearly, we need to examine a broad range of issues, such as communications and cultural integrity, education, manpower, and cultural interchange and access to, and responsibilities of, the mass media. We need also to examine and seek agreement in specific areas where the need for consistent, minimal regulation, and technological innovation exists, areas such as communication equipment and standards, communication tariffs and facilities planning, property rights in the new software technologies, and multilateral agreements to insure privacy, confidentiality, and security in information flows.

Indeed, we need agreements on compatible equipment, standards, and reciprocal certification to create an affordable yet effective interface of equipment and systems from country to country. And we need tariffs in each country to be cost based and better harmonized nation to nation, so that the cost of transmission across a national border is not ten to twenty times that of transmission over the same distance intranationally. We need also to provide a mechanism for underseas cable planning. In conjunction with our satellite planning process, such cable planning should proceed through a consultative procedure involving all parties concerned with the development of public facilities throughout the world (allowing, of course, for private design and development). Finally, we need agreements that will preserve, not terminate, the confidentiality of and proprietary rights in all international transactions. Strongly differing views on privacy, security, or enforcement of regulations can only create conflict within the international community.

Although this agenda may seem overly technical, disregarding the need for wider access to communications channels for all nations and their citizens, I am aware that communications is too often one-way—from the developed to the less developed nations, from rich to poor, large to small, elites to masses. From the northern to the southern hemisphere, the transfer of knowledge too often stresses technological and commercial advantage; it frequently overwhelms rather than stimulates. But the solution is not to impede the free flow of information. Rather, it is to guarantee that the channels be open to all; in short, that there be not only freedom for dialogue but also the capabilities for dialogue and that the channels of communications be unhampered by unnecessary technical, economic, and political constraints.

The question of the 1980s is surely no longer one of technology or technique but one of will. Until recently, however, neither the highly complex international economic system nor the ever thickening global web of communications technology has been so vulnerable, nor has the temptation to assume national control been so strong. To counter this tendency the technology of communications should be politically neutral. A stable world depends on it.

Three

The New World Information Order[1]

Mustapha Masmoudi

Information plays a paramount role in international relations, both as a means of communication between peoples and as an instrument of understanding and knowledge between nations. This role played by information is all the more important and crucial to present-day international relations in that the international community now possesses, thanks to new inventions and major technological breakthroughs, highly sophisticated and very rapid means of communication which make it possible to transmit information almost instantaneously between the different regions of the globe. . . . [However], information in the modern world is characterized by basic imbalances, reflecting the general imbalance that affects the international community. They occur in a wide range of fields, particularly in the political, legal, and technico-financial spheres.

INFORMATION IMBALANCES

The Political Sphere

In the political sphere, that is, in respect to the conception of information, these imbalances take many forms:

1. *A flagrant quantitative imbalance between North and South.* This imbalance is created by the disparity between the volume of news and information emanating from the developed world and intended for the developing countries, and the volume of the flow in the opposite direction. Almost 80 percent of the world news flow emanates from the major transnational agencies; however, these devote only 20 to 30 percent of news coverage to the developing countries, despite the fact that the latter account for almost three-quarters of mankind. This results in a veritable *de facto* monopoly on the part of the developed countries.

2. *An inequality in information resources.* The five major transnational agencies monopolize between them the essential share of material

and human potential, while almost a third of the developing countries do not yet possess a single national agency. Inequality also exists in the distribution of the radio frequency spectrum between developed and developing countries. The former control nearly 90 percent of the source of the spectrum, while the developing countries have no means of protecting themselves against foreign broadcasts. It is frequently difficult for them to compete, particularly since some of these broadcasts are transmitted from stations located within developing countries. In respect to television, not only do 45 percent of the developing countries have no television of their own, but this disparity is aggravated still further by the broadcasting in these countries of a large number of programs produced in the developed countries.

3. *A de facto hegemony and a will to dominate.* Such hegemony and domination are evident in the marked indifference of the media in the developed countries, particularly in the West, to the problems, concerns, and aspirations of the developing countries. They are founded on financial, industrial, cultural, and technological power and result in most of the developing countries being relegated to the status of mere consumers of information sold as a commodity like any other. They are exercised above all through the control of the information flow, wrested and wielded by the transnational agencies operating without let or hindrance in most developing countries and based in turn on the control of technology, illustrated by the communication systems satellites, which are wholly dominated by the major international consortia.

4. *A lack of information on developing countries.* Current events in the developing countries are reported to the world via the transnational media; at the same time, these countries are kept "informed" of what is happening abroad through the same channels. By transmitting to the developing countries only news processed by them, that is, news which they have filtered, cut, and distorted, the transnational media impose their own way of seeing the world upon the developing countries. . . . Moreover, [they often] present these communities—when indeed they do show interest in them—in the most unfavorable light, stressing crises, strikes, street demonstrations, putsches, etc., or even holding them up to ridicule. If and when the press in the industrialized countries does present the Third World's problems, achievements, and aspirations in an objective light, it does so in the form of special supplements or issues, for which high rates of payment are charged.

5. *Survival of the colonial era.* The present-day information system enshrines a form of political, economic, and cultural colonialism which is reflected in the often tendentious interpretation of news concerning the developing countries. This consists in highlighting events whose significance, in certain cases, is limited or even non-existent; in collecting isolated facts and presenting them as a "whole"; in setting out facts in such

a way that the conclusion to be drawn from them is necessarily favorable to the interests of the transnational system: in amplifying small-scale events so as to arouse justified fears; in keeping silent on situations unfavorable to the interests of the countries of origin of these media. In this way, world events are covered only insofar as it suits the interests of certain societies. . . .

Likewise, information is distorted by reference to moral, cultural, or political values peculiar to certain stages, in defiance of the values and concerns of other nations. The criteria governing selection are consciously or unconsciously based on the political and economic interests of the transnational system and of the countries in which this system is established. The use of labels and persuasive epithets and definitions, chosen with the intention of denigrating, should also be stressed.

6. *An alienating influence in the economic, social, and cultural spheres.* In addition to dominating and manipulating the international news flow, the developed countries practice other forms of hegemony over the communications institutions of the Third World. First of all, they have possession of the media through direct investment. Then, there is another form of control, one which today is far more decisive, namely, the near-monopoly on advertising throughout the world exercised by the major advertising agencies, which operate like the media transnationals and which earn their income by serving the interests of the transnational industrial and commercial corporations, which themselves dominate the business world. A further form of domination is represented by the influence used to oppose social evolution; this is practiced quite openly by the institutions engaging in propaganda. Moreover, advertising, magazines and television programs are today so many instruments of cultural domination and acculturation, transmitting to the developing countries messages which are harmful to their cultures, contrary to their values, and detrimental to their development aims and efforts.

7. *Messages ill-suited to the areas in which they are disseminated.* Even important news may be deliberately neglected by the major media in favor of other information of interest only to public opinion in the country to which the media in question belong. Such news is transmitted to the client countries and is indeed practically imposed on them, despite the fact that readers and listeners in these countries have no interest therein. The major mass media and those who work for them take no account of the real relevance of their messages. Their news coverage is designed to meet the national needs of their countries of origin. They also disregard the impact of their news beyond their own frontiers. They even ignore the important minorities and foreign communities living in their national territory, whose needs in matters of information are different from their own. . . . All such political and conceptual shortcomings are worsened— when they are not actually justified—by inadequate international legal structures.

The Legal Sphere

The present international legal framework is defective and even non-existent in certain fields. Moreover, the application of present-day legislation is arbitrary. It favors a small number of countries at the expense of the majority, thanks to a conception of liberty peculiar to those who own or control the communication media and who are frequently the very same people who own or control the means of production. In this context, questions need to be raised on many issues:

1. *Individual rights and community rights*. The philosophy which has prevailed to date has given prominence to the rights of a small number of persons or bodies specializing in this field. As a result, the rights and concerns of groups have been more or less disregarded. Yet, if it is true that the right to information is intrinsic to the human condition, it is nonetheless a natural right of every human community, in the sense that each people feels an overpowering urge to communicate with "the other," not only in order to come to terms with and to preserve its own personality but also in order to know and understand other peoples better; and so, through the communication channels established in this way, to create conditions likely to foster a climate of mutual understanding and respect, and cooperative relations that will be beneficial to all.

2. *Freedom of information or freedom to inform*. Freedom of information is presented as the corollary of freedom of opinion and freedom of expression, but was in fact conceived as the "freedom of the informing agent." As a result, it has become an instrument of domination in the hands of those who control the media. In legal terms, it has resulted in the enshrining of the rights of the communicator, while disregarding his duties and responsibilities towards those to whom he is communicating.

3. *Right of access to information sources*. This right is understood in a one-sided manner, and essentially benefits those who have the resources to obtain and impart information. This *de facto* situation has allowed certain major transnational corporations to turn this right into a prerogative, and enabled the wealthy powers to establish their domination over the information channels.

4. *The ineffectiveness of the right of correction*. In contrast to the domestic law of certain countries, the right of correction is regulated very ineffectively by international law. With the exception of the convention of 1952, no valid means exist of enabling states to have false or inaccurate information concerning them corrected. Moreover, the 1952 convention is itself not very effective (cf. Articles 3 and 4). Regulations in this area are in fact restrictive and unfavorable to developing countries.

5. *The absence of an international deontology and the defective character of the regulations governing the profession*. In this context, the imbalance is also fostered by the absence of an international deontology. Attempts made to date by UNESCO and the United Nations to institute

an international code of ethics suited to the needs of the individual and the community have proved ineffectual.

6. *Imbalance in the field of copyright.* Matters of copyright have long been regulated by the Berne Convention of 1886, which is protectionist in its scope of application, in the duration of the validity of copyright, and in the fewness of the waivers that may be applied to these provisions. The Universal Convention of 1952, revised in 1971 and administered by UNESCO, provides for a less rigorous degree of protection. As regards the Florence convention, because of the protectionist effects which it may generate while at the same time fostering the circulation of intellectual works from the industrialized countries to developing countries, it has benefitted the latter not at all. Altogether, the international publishing and distribution system operating today has led, on pretext of protecting copyright, to the predominance of certain commercial interests in the developed countries and has indirectly contributed to the cultural and political domination of these countries over the international community as a whole.

7. *Imbalance in the distribution of the source of the spectrum.* The objective must be to denounce the provisions of Article 9 of the Radio Regulations, which enshrine vested interests in respect of the distribution of the spectrum, and so deprive in particular recently independent countries of satisfactory means of making their voices heard.

8. *Disorder and lack of coordination in telecommunications and in the use of satellites, compounded with flagrant inequalities between states in this field.* In the absence of any effective regulation, the present inequalities in this field are likely to increase, while the rights of the more powerful will become consolidated in a manner beyond remedy. It hardly needs stressing that such great progress has been made in this field that, without adequate regulation, a veritable invasion of radio broadcasts and television programs must be expected, amounting to a violation of national territories and private homes and a veritable form of mental rape. . . .

The Technico-Financial Sphere

The developed countries' technological lead and the tariff system for international communications which they have instituted have enabled them to benefit from monopoly situations and prerogatives. [This has occurred] both in fixing the rates for transport of publications and telecommunications and in the use of communications and information technology. The advent of satellites is likely to intensify this imbalance if decisive international action is not taken and if technological aid is not furnished to the developing countries. This imbalance is particularly apparent in the following fields:

1. *Telecommunications.* The present structures and patterns of tele-

communications networks between developing countries are based solely on criteria of profitability and volume of traffic, and so constitute a serious handicap to the development of information and communication. This handicap affects both the infrastructure and the tariff system.

With regard to the infrastructure, in addition to the absence of direct links between developing countries, a concentration of communication networks is to be observed in the developed countries. The planning of the infrastructure devised by the former colonial powers precludes, for certain developing countries, all possibility of transmitting information beyond their frontiers (earth stations allowing only reception of television programs produced in the industrialized countries, with no possibility of broadcasting towards these countries).

With regard to tariffs the situation is even more striking and in certain respects quite irrational. Designed so as to disadvantage small outputs, the present tariff system perpetuates the stranglehold of the rich countries on the information flow. It is strange, to say the least, that, over the same distance, communications should cost more between two points within developing countries than between two others situated in developed countries.

Similarly, nothing can justify the fact that the same communication should cost less when transmitted from a developed to a developing country than in the opposite direction. The survival of anachronistic practices is in itself sufficient to explain certain operating norms: why, for example, a telegraphic press circuit sometimes costs as much as or even more than a telephone circuit. How can we accept the privileges enjoyed by the major news agencies, which secure, thanks to the density of their traffic, fulltime use of circuits at a cost that in certain cases does not exceed that of a daily average use of one hour? The situation is aggravated still further in certain countries by the leasing of the telecommunications network to foreign companies whose *raison d'être* is profiteering, and the channeling of international traffic to the country of origin.

2. *Satellites.* Although the 1977 Geneva conference endeavored to establish main heads of a procedure designed to prevent abuses in the rational use of satellites, the developing countries are still threatened by the anarchic use of extra-atmospheric space, which is liable to worsen the imbalance affecting the present telecommunications system.

3. *Distribution of radio frequencies.* The problem of allocating the frequency spectrum, which is a universal but limited natural resource, arises today with particular urgency. The developing countries are in fact more determined than ever to challenge vigorously the rights that the developed countries have arrogated to themselves in the use of the frequency spectrum. They are also determined to secure an equitable sharing out of this spectrum.

It is common knowledge that almost 90 percent of the source of the spectrum is controlled by a few developed countries, and that the developing countries, although covering far more extensive areas, possess fewer channels than the developed countries. The power density per square kilometer is four times less in the developing countries than in the developed.

4. *Transport of publications*. The imbalance observed in the telecommunications field also occurs in the flow of newspapers and publications:

—tariffs and distribution rates for newspapers are governed, as are those for all other mail, by the Universal Postal Convention, and all member countries of the Universal Postal Union are obliged to respect them;
—with regard to newspapers, and bearing in mind their role as a means of information, culture, and education, the Universal Postal Convention allows member countries the option of granting a maximum 50 percent reduction in the tariff applicable to printed materials in respect both of newspapers and periodicals, books and pamphlets;
—in addition to the optional nature of this reduction, air mail is subject to a bottom rate which does not favor the transport of small-circulation publications, i.e., precisely those produced in the developing countries. . . .

NEW WORLD INFORMATION ORDER

The Political Viewpoint

. . . It should be emphasized that this new order entails a thorough-going readjustment. It is no ready-made recipe, which could enable an unjust situation to be transformed overnight into one less unjust. Because it is the product of a long history, the present situation cannot be put right quickly. The aim must be rather to initiate a process at the national, regional, and international levels. Effective, concrete measures are called for, rather than academic discussion. . . .

The new world information order founded on democratic principles seeks to establish relations of equality in the communications field between developed and developing nations and aims at greater justice and greater balance. Far from calling in question the freedom of information, it proposes to ensure that this principle is applied fairly and equitably for all nations and not only in the case of the more developed among them. . . .

From the political viewpoint, the hopes, concerns, and struggles of communities, groups, and nations must be treated on equal terms and with complete honesty and objectivity, while avoiding provocations, supporting the causes of liberty and justice, defending human rights in their full, universal dimension, and making every effort to eliminate the sequels of colonialism, racialism, apartheid, and all other discriminatory practices and serving the cause of peace in the world. Such measures should be taken at three levels, and concern each of the different media.

In respect to developing countries, the aims must be:

—to define national communications policies, as being necessary to each country's economic and social development and of a nature to motivate its citizens on behalf of such development;

—to make provision, in the formulation of such national communications policies, for measures favoring optimum exchanges of news programs at the regional or sub-regional level, and fostering active and determined participation on the part of all developing countries in the operation of international communications and information centers and networks;

—to multiply exchange agreements between information bodies, training and research institutes, and national, regional, and international organizations directly or indirectly involved in the communications sector. In this context, the exchange of journalists and technicians should be intensified with a view to fostering better mutual understanding;

—to consolidate and develop the established structures, particularly among the non-aligned countries, while at the same time, helping, in cooperation with the developed countries and the international organizations concerned, to establish communications media, to train qualified personnel, and to acquire suitable materials and equipment in a spirit of collective self-reliance;

—to institute and strengthen assistance to the least developed countries;

—to pay particular attention to the information supplied by the national news collection centers or news pools of the developing countries, on the problems which concern their respective regions or countries;

—to alert the media of the developed countries to the imbalances, deficiencies, and imperfections of the present communications system, by arranging for meetings (conferences, seminars, or symposia) between those responsible for the different media in the developed and developing countries.

—to launch a wide-ranging campaign in the field of communications in the universities of both developing and developed countries, aimed at training or retraining professionals and inculcating the values of the new international economic order and the new world information order;

—to democratize information resources and structures. At the horizontal level, this implies setting up national news agencies and machinery for cooperation and mutual assistance between developing countries, such as the Press Agency Pool of the Non-Aligned Countries or the regional unions (African, Arab, Asian, Latin American), and on the vertical plane, curtailing the monopolies of the major press agencies by promoting the conclusion of international agreements aimed at equal and

fair utilization of all communications media, including satellites;
—to establish a system fostering a free and equitable flow between developed and developing countries, from the point of view of content, volume, and intensity;
—to implement a national policy to promote literary and artistic creation by instituting a tax system that is as favorable as possible;
—to encourage the setting up or development of national societies of authors aimed at ensuring optimum management for the countries concerned of the resources deriving from the exploitation of intellectual works in all their diversity.

In respect to the developed countries the aims must be:

—to call public attention to the action taken by the developing countries, emphasizing the ever-increasing interdependence of the different nations of the world. It is indeed unthinkable that public opinion in the developed countries should continue to be unaware of the widening gap between these and the deprived countries, or to adopt an attitude of indifference to the matter;
—to help "decolonize" information by taking a more objective approach to the aspirations and concerns of the developing nations, while at the same time eschewing all incitement to hatred or racial, religious, political, or any other kinds of discrimination, and all initiatives liable to misrepresent, distort, or show in an unfavorable light the measures taken by the developing countries.
—to help establish a balance in the information flow by devoting more space in newspapers and in radio and television programs to news concerning developing countries as well as to news concerning immigrants working for the development and well-being of host countries;
—to promote better mutual understanding by encouraging the media in the industrialized countries to devote greater attention to the content of their transmissions in order to better satisfy the needs of listeners, viewers, and subscribers both in and outside their national territory as also to make the cultures and civilizations of other peoples, especially those to whom the transmissions are addressed, more widely known;
—to ensure that journalists and writers show the utmost prudence and themselves verify the reliability and authenticity of all material, data, or arguments used by them which might tend to intensify the arms race;
—to ensure that journalists respect the laws of country and the cultural values of the different peoples, and acknowledge that the right of peoples to make known their own concerns and to learn about those of other peoples is as important as respect for individuals;
—to put an end to the pernicious activities of foreign stations established outside national frontiers;
—to give particular attention to information supplied by national news-

gathering centers or news pools in the developing countries on events concerning their respective regions or countries, and to encourage the mass media to subscribe to these pools and to the main news gathering centers, with a view to balancing and diversifying the news concerning these countries and in general increasing the space allotted thereto;
—to ensure that, prior to each mission, special correspondents acquire as comprehensive a knowledge as possible of the countries to which they are sent, so as to be able to assess problems and concerns correctly and not see merely the sensational or anecdotal aspect of events, refrain from hasty judgments, free themselves of any distorting ideological lens through which they might be tempted to judge events and people, guard against all bias or prejudice, and endeavor to ensure that their conclusions correspond to reality.

In respect to the international organizations, efforts should be aimed at:

—enlarging and diversifying the scope of the aid given by UNESCO and the other international organizations to developing countries and supplying means for linking up multilateral and bilateral assistance to these countries so as to step up such assistance and render it more effective;
—helping to promote the development of the media in developing countries both at the national and regional levels, in a spirit of collective self-sufficiency;
—enabling the developing countries to take advantage of the forums open to them in the international organizations in order to make known their demands and to bring about the establishment of a new world information order;
—supporting the efforts of developing countries to formulate and adopt national communications policies, to promote research, particularly on the implications of transfers of technology, and to set up documentation centers on communications;
—instituting a tax in the developed countries which are exporters of literary and artistic works of all kinds, the proceeds from which would help to finance the international copyright fund which is to be administered by UNESCO;
—enlarging and diversifying the range of the aid granted to developing countries, and helping them to use the communication sciences to promote social evolution by undertaking studies based on assumptions and methods which reflect the realities and correspond to the needs of the developing countries;
—granting maximum technical and financial assistance to institutions carrying out research on communications, in accordance with the needs emerging in each country and each region;
—implementing with all due dispatch and in collaboration with the mass

communications training centers which exist in all developing countries, a program to draw up and coordinate the curricula of mass communications institutes and departments and special vocational training courses in this field. The essential purpose of this program would be to adapt studies to the specific practical needs of each country and each region in respect of communications. To this end, a board or consultative panel should be set up on which directors of institutes, departments, or university courses in mass communications would serve;

—promoting, through the grant of fellowships and similar measures, an advanced university training course in the communication sciences. Such training should be given in accordance with the needs, objectives and potentialities of developing countries; . . .

—helping to formulate research programs and to establish training centers so as to enable developing countries to produce radio and television programs designed to serve the aims of the New International Economic Order;

—granting the mass communications sector a status that corresponds to its undoubted importance and to its evident influence on all other sectors of activity, so as to develop an easy and harmonious relationship not only with the cultural sector but also with the education sector and with others that are today less closely linked thereto;

—devising a clear-cut policy on the use of satellites transmission systems, respecting in all cases the sovereign rights of individual states;

—encouraging the testing, evaluation, and dissemination of new, low-priced, and easy-to-use communications technology so as to enable the message of development to reach the masses at present cut off from all such information;

—helping to establish historical documentation and archives centers in the developing countries.

The Legal Viewpoint

From the legal viewpoint, there can be no justice in international communications unless and until rights in this field are redefined and applied on an extensive scale. Information must be understood as a social good and a cultural product, and not as a material commodity or merchandise. Seen in this perspective, all countries should enjoy the same opportunities of access to sources of information as well as to participate in the communication process. Sociocultural considerations should prevail over individual, materialistic, and mercantile considerations. . . .

Information is not the prerogative of a few individuals or entities that command the technical and financial means enabling them to control communications; rather, it must be conceived as a social function intrinsic to the various communities, cultures, and different conceptions of civilization. . . .

The need to establish an international deontology governing information and communications is becoming ever more strongly felt. The self-regulation of professional media organizations must, to be sure, be given recognition in such a deontology. However, it cannot replace a more wide-ranging formula, since no social group should have the prerogative of not being held accountable to the community to which it belongs. . . .

The protection of journalists is a key element in the world communications and information system. Such protection should extend to the relations between the journalists and employers and should enable them to safeguard freedom of thought and analysis against all potential pressures. It must cover the journalist in the performance of professional duties. . . .

This right of correction should be reinforced by calling to account the individual or legal entity guilty of violating the principles of professional deontology or of propagating false or biased information before an international tripartite body grouping together representatives of states, representatives of the profession, and neutral figures known for their moral integrity and competence in matters of information.

As has been pointed out by the international organizations responsible for the assignment of frequencies, the natural resources of both the electromagnetic spectrum and the geostationary orbits are limited. This limitation makes it essential to revise the present allocation of the resources of the spectrum and to regulate the use of extra-atmospheric space for telecommunications purposes. This task is all the more urgent in that direct broadcasting by satellite is, according to present forecasts, likely to come into operation in the next decade.

For this purpose, it is essential to provide for:

—the safeguarding of the rights of countries still under domination to equitable access to the frequency spectrum;
—the revision of Article 9 of the Radio Regulations and the reappraisal of the rule of "first-come, first-served" where the frequency spectrum is concerned;
—a "moratorium" on the free-for-all use of extra-atmospheric space pending the conclusion of an international agreement which satisfactorily guarantees the supply and use of modern telecommunications technical resources in general; the Final Acts of the World Satellite-Broadcasting Administrative Radio Conference, held in Geneva in 1977, should serve as a basis for the drafting of this agreement. . . .

The developing countries must coordinate their action within the overall framework of the United Nations system so that matters lying within the competence of the ITU may be given a significance which transcends the purely technical context.

The Technical and Financial Viewpoints

From the technical and financial viewpoints, . . . the steps to be taken include the following:

—rethinking the present pattern of the international telecommunication network;

—fostering the establishment of centers or nodes of communication in developing countries and setting up direct links whenever possible between developing countries;

—working for the lowering of communication tariffs between developing countries;

—ensuring that satellites are seen primarily as a means of alleviating certain telecommunications functions hitherto discharged by point-to-point, short-wave transmission;

—using satellites for transmitting radio and television programs of developing countries which have hitherto been unable to ensure their adequate diffusion solely by conventional means;

—assigning a predominant role to the developing countries at the World Administrative Radio Conference (WARC) in October 1979.

—ensuring equitable redistribution of the spectrum, without taking any *faits accomplis* into consideration, on the basis of a balanced allocation between all regions of the globe;

—taking joint action in order to obtain new favorable terms for newspapers at the congress of the Universal Postal Union;

—doing away with the minimum tariff and inducing air transport companies and postal administrations to take joint action in order to reduce the air freight surtax on publications;

—formulating an international code of conduct governing the transfer of technology which corresponds to the specific needs and conditions of developing countries.

The technical advances achieved during the recent decades in all sectors of economic activity have not been equitably distributed between members of the economic community. The income of the developing countries, in which 75 percent of the world's population is concentrated, at present represents only 30 percent of world income. Average per capita income in the industrialized countries today stands at $2400 per annum, whereas that of the developing countries, in which three-quarters of the world's population live, is a mere $180. More serious still, the 24 poorest countries have an annual per capita income not exceeding $100. This disparity is bound to increase: it is estimated that [by 1988] these figures will be $3400 and $280 respectively.

The developing countries' share in world trade, already limited to 32 percent in 1950, has continued to diminish, dropping to a mere 17 percent. . . . The deterioration in [trade] . . . has been attended by a considerable increase in the Third World's debt, which rose to $233,000 million in 1977. These phenomena were perceived by the developing countries as a continuation of political hegemony and an expression of the will to pursue neo-colonialist exploitation. Conscious of the grave implications of this ever-widening gulf between Third World countries and industrialized countries, the United Nations proclaimed on May 1, 1974, their common determination to undertake the urgent task of establishing a new international economic order founded on equity and capable of redressing the flagrant inequalities of the present system.

However, the failure of these appeals for equity to produce a response or to gain a hearing has soon proved their essential inefficacy. The media have even conditioned public opinion in the developed countries to such an extent as to render it allergic to all claims and demands emanating from the Third World.

Accordingly, the establishment of a new world information order must be considered as the essential corollary of the new international economic order. In order to give concrete reality to this new approach and to enable the media to fulfil their task of educating and informing, measures must be taken both by the industrialized and the developing countries, as well as by the international organizations concerned. . . .

The process initiated is a complex one, and transformations will take time. What is essential is to familiarize public opinion with change and to promote a responsive awareness of it. For the developing countries, self-reliance must be the watchword; this they can achieve by developing cooperation at the horizontal level so as to enable them to establish a balanced flow with the developed countries.

NOTE

1. This chapter is excerpted from the document presented to the International Commission for the Study of Communication Problems (the "MacBride Commission") established by the General Conference of UNESCO at its nineteenth session.

Four

Defining the New International Information Order

Kaarle Nordenstreng

Several works have documented the developments, events, and debates that have brought us the notion of the New International Information Order from various points of view (2, 5, 7). Along with the discussions of a new order has emerged a new brand of quasi-scientific writing in which events throughout the world diplomatic arena are reported rather than analyzed as a coherent, sociologically and historically meaningful picture. I would like to raise two fundamental points that may assist such an analysis.

First, the call for the New International Information Order was articulated within the movement of nonaligned countries as a *particular reflection of the movement's general anti-imperialist effort to achieve decolonization*. This was evident in the first statements on information endorsed by the fourth summit of the movement in Algiers (1973) (see 2, pp. 46–47) and there could be no doubt about such an orientation in the documents on information endorsed by the fifth summit in Colombo (1976). Let us recall a few paragraphs of one of these documents, the New Delhi Declaration.

1. The present global information flows are marked by a serious inadequacy and imbalance. The means of communicating information are concentrated in a few countries. The great majority of countries are reduced to being passive recipients of information which is disseminated from a few centers.

2. This situation perpetuates the colonial era of dependence and domination. It confines judgments and decisions on what should be known, and how it should be made known, into the hands of a few. . . .

4. Just as political and economic dependence are legacies of the era of colonialism, so is the case of dependence in the field of information which in turn retards the achievement of political and economic growth.

5. In a situation where the means of information are dominated and monopolized by a few, freedom of information really comes to mean the freedom of these few to propagate information in the manner of their choosing and the virtual denial to the rest of the right to inform and be informed objectively and accurately.

This document not only advocated political pressure against the "imperialist forces" dominating the "free world" information structures and flows but also implied a fundamental philosophical challenge. The New Delhi Declaration rejected the traditional "libertarian theory of the press" in at least three different respects. First, it implied that laissez-faire will lead to monopolization and create neocolonial dependence. Second, it noted how insufficient it is merely to guarantee abstractly the right to freedom of information without insuring the material means to put that right into practice. Third, the information being moved through the media was given explicit content qualifications: it should be objective and accurate.

The second fundamental point I want to make in putting the New International Information Order into perspective is that *little in this new order is genuinely new*. Just as the overall process of decolonization is a well-established and indeed a traditional concept, most of what has been included under the umbrella of the New International Information Order can in fact be found in earlier political, professional, and academic exercises. Take, for example, the problem of news values and distorted coverage of the developing countries in the Western media. Most of the criticism, analytical conceptualizations, and guidelines for change voiced over the past few years were articulated in the 1960s by Johan Galtung and Mari Holmboe Ruge (1).

Consider also the overall problem of global imbalance and assistance to developing countries in the field of information and mass media. The U.N. General Assembly expressed concern more than twenty years ago over the fact that "70 percent of the population of the world lack adequate information facilities and are thus denied effective enjoyment of the right to information" and invited the governments of developed countries "to cooperate with less developed countries with a view to meeting the urgent needs of the less developed countries in connexion with this programme for the development of independent national information media, with due regard for the culture of each country" (United Nations General Assembly Resolution 1778, December 7, 1962). The same kind of U.N. resolutions were issued in the 1950s, inviting UNESCO, for example, "to formulate concrete proposals to assist in meeting the needs of less developed countries in building up adequate media of information" (United Nations General Assembly Resolution 1313, December 12, 1958). In fact, as early as 1952 a General Assembly resolution declared "it is essential for a proper development of public opinion in under-developed countries that independent domestic information enterprises should be given facilities and assistance in order that they may be enabled to contribute to the spread of information, to the development of national culture and to international understanding," adding that "the time has arrived for the elaboration of a concrete programme and plan of action in this respect" (United Nations General Assembly Resolution 633, December 16, 1952).

Nevertheless, it took nearly thirty years for the U.N. system, notably UNESCO, to react to this diplomatic lip service by launching a major program for the development of communications (such a program was outlined by an intergovernmental conference at UNESCO in April 1980). Why the delay? And, more significant to this discussion, why did the phrase "New International Information Order" galvanize the world community? A proper reply to these questions cannot be found by looking exclusively at the field of information and communications; we must look also at changes in the relations of broader socioeconomic and political forces (see 5).

We are back to my first point: the call for a New International Information Order is a reflection of the decolonization process. And by the early seventies this process had reached a critical stage wherein national liberation from colonial and neocolonial domination was supported by such instruments as the U.N. Declaration on the New International Economic Order. This situation had put the system of Western domination, including the transnational corporations, sharply on the defensive. Consequently, the new order became an issue not because of the introduction of dramatically new phenomena (such as new technology) into the field of information but fundamentally because a sufficiently strong coalition of social forces had accumulated to enforce a new order, at least as a political program if not as an immediate reality.

The same pattern marked the history of the Mass Media Declaration of UNESCO. This instrument only appeared to place qualitatively new elements on the agenda of international communications and politics; in fact, it was only a collection of norms and principles, most of which already had been enunciated in U.N. documents and indeed in international law. The only major innovation to the credit of UNESCO was that the declaration brought together the various standards scattered throughout earlier instruments. Thus, the battle over the declaration was largely symbolic.

OLD ELEMENTS OF THE NEW ORDER: INTERNATIONAL STANDARDS FOR MASS MEDIA

This section summarizes a study made at the University of Tampere concerning the moral and, in some cases, legal obligations of the mass media as prescribed by conventions and similar instruments of international law, as well as other less legally binding instruments such as declarations and resolutions of the United Nations and its agencies (above all UNESCO, which has a particular mandate in the field of culture and communications). Forty-four documents, comprising twelve conventions, fourteen declarations, and eighteen resolutions, were analyzed. Each document was coded for the presence or absence of seven themes: (1) peace and security, (2) war propaganda, (3) friendship and mutual understanding among nations, (4) objectivity and truthfulness, (5) racial equality, (6) other standards on contents of reporting, and (7) free flow of information.[1] We coded each mention according to whether it was a direct reference to "mass media," or an indirect reference to "public opinion," etc. Table 4.1 summarizes the results.

International law sets significant standards for the performance of the mass media, especially in matters directly concerning international relations, for example, the promotion of friendly relations between states and peoples and the prevention of war propaganda (categories 1–4). A similarly significant set of standards focuses on matters concerning primarily the national context, above all, prevention of propaganda for racial or other discrimination (categories 5–6). Free flow of information (7) has not been defined in international law to be more central than standards relating to the six preceding content categories. More specifically, in the view of international law, the principle of freedom of information must be subordinated to such obligations as the promotion of peace and security and the prevention of propaganda for war or racism. Finally, five conventions out of twelve not only provide standards for the performance of the mass media but also touch upon such fundamental issues of the journalistic profession as truthfulness and objectivity, honesty, and freedom from prejudice.

The instruments studied make direct references in all of the content categories under consideration to the mass media at the level of both conventions and less binding declarations and resolutions. Also, whereas these documents indicate that states have an *obligation* to promote the standards concerning peaceful and friendly relations among nations, in matters of primarily national concern they usually have just a *right* (but not a binding commitment) to place standards on the performance of the mass media.

Clearly, the UNESCO Mass Media Declaration and other manifestations of the New International Information Order contain little beyond the rich material provided by earlier instruments of international law and diplomacy. Indeed, one of the first tasks for anyone interested in the substance of the new order is to get acquainted with international law on communications. It is noteworthy that the United Nations machinery has produced so many laudable documents that have to be repackaged as the fashionable New International Information Order before receiving serious attention from media professionals and political leaders.[2]

Table 4.1 Themes Referred to in International Documents by Type of Reference

Type of Reference in	Content Categories						
	Peace and Security	War Propaganda	Friendship	Objectivity	Racial Equality	Reporting Standards	Free Flow
Conventions (N = 12)							
Direct	3	3	5	5	1	5	5
Indirect	1	5	1	0	7	3	3
None	8	4	6	7	4	4	4
Declarations (N = 14)							
Direct	7	1	6	6	5	9	7
Indirect	4	6	4	2	1	0	2
None	3	7	4	6	8	5	5
Resolutions (N = 18)							
Direct	9	1	10	6	3	12	8
Indirect	4	2	5	0	0	2	0
None	5	15	3	12	15	4	10
Total references (N = 44) (direct + indirect)	28	18	31	19	17	31	25

RADICAL AND CONSERVATIVE IMPLICATIONS
OF THE NEW ORDER

Although the New International Information Order represents a renaissance of old ideas, some qualitatively new elements have entered the field of information only in the seventies, such as problems of informatics (transborder data flows, computer-telecommunication systems, etc.) and to some extent problems of access and participation, as well as problems concerning the contribution of the mass media to international conflict resolution and disarmament.

It would be very misleading, however, to understand the New International Information Order as a package of mainly old and some new ammunition to be automatically directed against the existing order. On the contrary, the old struggle among different socioeconomic and political forces simply has been raised to a new level using new semantics (5). Making the same point, Cees Hamelink warned in his contribution to the MacBride Commission (Document 34, p. 9) that unless the concepts and principles of the New International Economic Order are used to determine the shape and substance of the new information order, the latter may become "yet another mechanism to subtly integrate the dependent countries in an international order which perpetuates their dependence." Therefore, special care is needed when approaching this topic. Clearly, a scientifically satisfactory definition of the parameters, principles, and indeed terminology of the new order would require a comprehensive, in-depth analysis of a variety of problems, from the structure of the international economic system to the nature of information. My ambition here is only to identify some crucial points.

First, the new order is primarily a matter of international relations. This point was made by the context in which the new order was discussed in various U.N. resolutions and other multinational statements. In December 1978 (right after the adoption in UNESCO of the Mass Media Declaration) the order was mentioned under the title "International Relations in the Sphere of Information and Mass Communications" (United Nations General Assembly Resolution 33/115B, December 1978); in the next General Assembly in 1979 it appeared in a resolution on "Implementation of the Declaration on the Strengthening of International Security" (United Nations General Assembly Resolution 34/100, 1979). In a subchapter on "The Co-operation in the Field of Information and Mass Communication Media," the final declaration of the sixth summit of nonaligned nations pointed out: "The Conference takes note with gratification of the fact that non-aligned and other developing countries have made notable progress along the path of emancipation and development of national information media and stresses that the co-operation in the field of information is an integral part of the struggle of non-aligned and other developing countries for the creation of new international relations in general, and a new international information order in particular" (4).

Note that the documents of the nonaligned movement regularly refer to "international order" whereas the United Nations and UNESCO resolutions mostly use the phrase "world order." Evidently, this departure from the formulation of the nonaligned movement does not represent a significant strategic move. However, the theory of international relations and established diplomatic phraseology teaches that in this connection the word "international" should be used although "world" may sound more elegant. Furthermore, the phrase "world order" may be used as a device to dissociate the concept of New International Information Order from the concept of New International Economic Order (see 5). "World order" also implies the theory of an interdependent world, which in many instances has become a conceptual tool in co-opting the interests of the developing countries so that they collaborate with, rather than challenge, the Western "transnational-corporate order." Faced with the expression "increasingly interdependent world" we may ask whether developments such as the liberation of Vietnam, the abolishing of the Portuguese colonial system, and the overthrow of Somoza have brought about a higher level of interdependence or whether the opposite is true. As suggested by Hamelink, we might better use the word "interindependence"; in any case, there are no reasons faithful to the cause of developing countries to substitute "world" for "international" in speaking about the new order.

Second, the new order has a national dimension. It is impossible totally to separate national and international levels in social theory any more than in political practice. Let me quote what was said about the New International Information Order in this respect in the final statement issued by an international seminar meeting in Tashkent under the auspices of UNESCO (September 1979).

> On the national plane a new information order presupposes the establishment of democratic social structures on the basis of which an independent and endogenous national system of mass media can be built, which will enable developing countries effectively to participate in international exchange of information as equal members of the world community (3).

Third, the cornerstones of the New International Information Order are decolonization and democratization. A third "D" might be added to this list with a view of the concentration of national and international capital: demonopolization. Development could be identified as a fourth cornerstone.

The idea of democratization applies not only to the national level but also to the nature of international relations (in the field of information as well as in general). In fact, the essence of the New International Information Order is contained by the idea of democratization of the system of international relations in the field of information. Another way to characterize the same kind of objective is the well-known concept of peaceful coexistence, enunciated by Lenin and incorporated in the fundamental principles of the nonaligned movement as well as in U.N. philosophy.

It is vital to recognize that all these dimensions of the information order refer to both the structure and the contents of communication; at the same time, they refer to the underlying principles that determine the overall terms of operation of communication systems.

As to "information" and "communication," vagueness and confusion surround their meanings and implications in general as well as vis-à-vis the New International Information Order. The original sponsor of the new order, the nonaligned movement, uses the term "information," sometimes accompanied by "mass media" or "mass communications." Similarly, the language of international politics and diplomacy favors "information" as a generic term referring to all kinds of media and their uses, all types of messages, etc. (the term is used in this sense in the Helsinki Final Act, for example). On the other hand, there are those—especially from the Spanish-speaking hemisphere—who consider "information" both very limited and opposed to the democratic idea of participatory, two-way communication. Finally, it can be argued that the word "communication" diverts attention from the message communicated to the technical means of communicating and thus dilutes the objectives of changing the performance of the mass media. A tentative solution has been to use both terms: "new international information and communication order" or, as in the sixth summit document, "new international order in the field of information and mass media."

Fourth, the phrasing of the new order that was inserted first in the preamble of the UNESCO declaration and thereafter in a number of U.N. resolutions provides a classic example of how substance is maneuvered by means of language. This compromise formulation (strongly influenced by U.S. diplomacy) reads as follows: "a new, more just and more effective world information and communication order."

Little in this formulation would bluntly contradict the line determined by the four cornerstones of the order, identified earlier—if only there were a solid theoretical and political basis to determine the conceptualization in keeping with the original principles and objectives of the nonaligned movement. But today we do not have such a basis, and especially in the United Nations and UNESCO the formulations are virtually hanging in air or, to be more specific, floating in the ether of diplomatic-political tactics. Thus, there is an urgent need for scientifically based contributions to the continual building of the New International Information Order. Absence of conceptual and theoretical understanding of the issues will be functional to those who are interested in maintaining the old order under a smoke-screen of new rhetoric.

NOTES

1. These categories were further divided into 8 to 10 subcategories each, which will not be reported here (for details, see 6).

2. The journalistic community has seriously started to do its homework in this area, as indicated by the Mexican Declaration, adopted in 1980 by the meeting of international and regional organizations of professional journalists (for details, see 6).

REFERENCES

1. Galtung, Johan and Mari Holmboe Ruge. "The Structure of Foreign News." *Journal of Peace Research*, 1965.

2. Gunter, Jonathan F. *et al. The United States and the Debate on the World "Information Order."* Washington, D.C.: Academy for Educational Development, 1978.

3. International Seminar of Journalists in Tashkent. *Final Statement.* Moscow: Novosti Press Agency Publishing House, 1980, p. 134.

4. Non-Aligned Nations. *Final Declaration* of the Sixth Summit of Non-Aligned Nations. Reprinted in *Review of International Affairs* (Yugoslavia) 707, September 20, 1979, p. 20.

5. Nordenstreng, Kaarle. "Behind the Semantics—A Strategic Design." *Journal of Communication* 29(2), Spring 1979, pp. 195–198.

6. Nordenstreng, Kaarle. *The Mass Media Declaration of UNESCO.* Norwood, N.J.: Ablex, 1981.

7. Van Dinh, Tran. "Nonalignment and Cultural Imperialism." In K. Nordenstreng and H. Schiller (Eds.) *National Sovereignty and International Communication.* Norwood, N.J.: Ablex, 1979.

Five

The Political Economy of Information: A North-South Perspective

Rita Cruise O'Brien

The central focus of economic activity in post-industrial society is shifting from the manufacturing of objects to the handling of information and knowledge.[1] The power of major transnational firms now rests as much upon their capacity to marshal information and knowledge as on their traditional role in directly productive activities. There is every indication that the sharpest aspect of competition in the future may be based more on the efficient use of both specialized information and new communications technology than on more traditional factors. Information handling capacity already offers industrialized countries and firms considerable economic and political leverage in North-South interactions.

The information accessible to firms and governments in industrialized countries about resources, weather, technology, and market conditions, for example, far exceeds such knowledge in developing countries. A great deal of these data, which are gathered and systematized for retrieval, are not available outside their storage point. Universities and research institutions, as well as privately financed research and development activities, enhance the capacity of public and private decisionmakers in the North to profit from world market participation and to bargain internationally. Negotiators and market participants from developing countries are accordingly at a serious relative disadvantage; their information difficulties derive not only from data scarcity and access in "on-off" situations, but also from the absence of expertise at either the national or the intergovernmental level.

NORTH-SOUTH NEGOTIATIONS: THE POLITICS OF INFORMATION

Expansion of and cost reduction in facilities for communication, transportation, financial transactions, and travel have intensified global interaction and thereby altered the environment of politics. The question of information access, which was formerly distinct from political calculation, has acquired major political importance in the new environment. But the literature on international politics and the relevant social science literature on information still examine the effects of increased communication and information flow as though they were simply accelerating the creation of global interdependence, without considering the implications of unequal information access either for the efficiency and equity of international market functioning or for the creation of new international bargaining capacities (see 7, 9, 11).

Political independence and even partial delinking from the transnational economic system through nationalization and other measures have radically changed the environment of information needs and access. Countries of the South, pursuing economic policies based on their own interests, have new requirements that demand new sources of information and expertise, new information systems, and new means of codification and use. These countries and their major economic institutions often have engaged in bilateral or multilateral bargaining in which their lack of information and expertise has added to their vulnerability in the search for alternate markets and sources of supply. In no part of the current debate over global political and economic problems is the importance of information more dramatically evident than in the search for new forms of mutually agreeable relations—new contracts—between transnational corporations and developing countries.[2]

The new agenda item of information in world politics suggests the necessity for analytical distinction according to the capacity of the actors in an interdependent situation. The inequality of access to information adds another factor to an asymmetry originally based on political and economic divergence, since it adds a disparity in the bargaining capacity of the parties involved. Having better access to and control of information in a negotiating situation is an important factor of power; having poor access to information tends to incur present and future costs for the more vulnerable parties. Some specific examples will situate the problem.

The manpower and expertise that can be marshaled by industrialized countries in preparation for international negotiations such as those of the General Agreement on Tariffs and Trade (GATT), the Law of the Sea, or the World Administrative Radio Conference (WARC) far outstrip those available to developing countries.[3] This international form of inequality may be detrimental to the global interest, not just to that of the Third World. There is a growing concern that the lack of information enabling developing countries to adequately prepare for intergovernmental negotiations makes the bargaining process unworkable. In the absence of adequate technical analysis, it may lead to the politicization of issues. The resulting incapacity to specify and sustain negotiating positions may jeopardize results previously achieved.[4] Discussions on the reform of the international monetary system or on the allocation of sea and space resources are thus often preempted by the industrialized nations, leaving the developing countries with only a "yes, but . . ." role or encouraging them to politicize issues as a substitute for the technical arguments which they lack.[5] Such a stance has been regarded as obstructionist by the more powerful actors in international bargaining, but the hindsight of nearly a decade of new forms of North-South bargaining may reveal it to have been astute. Might this not be a (variably effective) delaying tactic to give much needed time for assembling a better informed and hence more persuasive negotiating team?

Interdependence may be accepted as inevitable by developing countries, but the specific terms on which it is to be achieved are still at issue. Those who argue from a technocratic perspective that interdependence is an inexorable trend may be regarded with skepticism by the South.

> Sociospheres, econospheres and technospheres are the complex and interwoven network of institutions, organisations and interdependent technological systems which begin to show potential as a unified network of human service systems around the planet—depending for its integrated functions on a swift availability of and access to, shared information and communication (9, p. 106).

Politicians of the rich countries who both argue that interdependence will benefit all and resort to symbolism that suggests the obsolescence of conflicts of interest may be regarded with mistrust (2, pp. 20–21). But, above all, the promotion of interdependence as a functional approach to solving the problems of a new information era in the interests of the already information-rich states[6] is likely to be resisted.

TECHNOLOGICAL CHANGES IN INFORMATION: PROBLEMS FOR THE SOUTH

The most important effects of current technological advances in the information sector are cost reduction through miniaturization based on microprocessors; increased volume and specificity of computer systems; and enhanced speed of global transmission through telecommunication systems relying on optical fibers and satellites. The latest high growth area in the industry is the convergence of electronic information processing, data banks, and telecommunication networks in a single system known as *telematics*. Digital data networks and reliance on video channels also have expanded.

The basic question that must be raised in relation to technological innovation in the information industry is whether these new developments will either *increase* the already substantial potential for centralization and control of information in traditional world centers, thus enhancing their power, or be used by developing countries (individually or collectively by region, or in commodity groups) to *decrease* their present information disadvantage. An adequate response must take account of both the time horizon and the capacity of systems to relate available information to specific requirements.

In the short run, technological developments may increase the power of data-rich countries and firms. For the present, commercial incentives dictate the design of new equipment and systems geared to large markets: private firms, carriers, and governments in industrialized countries. Transnational corporations are dependent on multinational computer systems to facilitate their relationships with suppliers and customers. The business literature acknowledges that the wider use of such systems will enhance the transnationals' power and influence in relation to governments and widen the gap between rich and poor.[7]

Far ahead even of Western governments in their utilization of the most modern information systems, major transnational corporations have long since overcome the principal difficulty of market exchange by internalizing their information (and other) flows. These firms have the capacity not only to use the new hardware of the data processing industry but also to develop or to encourage others to develop the even more important (and often industry- or form-specific) software.[8] Market incentives are, as always, guiding technological innovation in information processing.

> The large multinational firms with widely scattered operations represent the most attractive customers [for computer firms], so that enormous investments are being made to develop new applications and capabilities that would appeal to these firms. Further, the computer industry itself is becoming more unified worldwide through the use of common procedures, systems and software (10, p. 21).

Modern telecommunication systems have evolved under U.S. leadership, specifically in response to the needs of transnational corporations (and defense surveillance). Transnational enterprise depends on a system of free flow of information and open borders. The reduction of nontechnical barriers (like tariffs on alternative voice-data circuits) has led to the immense growth of private carriers, upon which many forms of transnational enterprise (and business consortia) depend.[9] These tendencies have prompted some analysts to ask whether the international information policymaking process has been able to deal adequately with technological breakthroughs that promote increased interdependence (3, 11). Few have asked the basic question—in whose interests and at what cost?

In the longer run, technological innovations may result in cost reductions that enable Third World countries to reduce their data dependency and marshal information resources commensurate with their needs. There is a growing literature on the development and uses of information technology (see, e.g., 13), but not in relation to the critical area of international negotiation. Questions about information production and transmission must be related to the efficient satisfaction of specific needs. As in the case of information generally, the greatest problem in the improvement of information access through electronic means may be the creation of the knowledge and organizational supports required in making use of the information system. The substantial reduction in hardware costs may mean that electronically produced software, whether imported or developed locally, will henceforth be the dominant cost in communications. Are there enough incentives for software to be made commercially in forms suited to the needs of developing countries? Can software be adapted for Third World use from other systems? Can it be obtained from noncommercial sources?

The rapid accumulation of information systems in developing countries is encouraged by efforts to promote self-sufficiency in computer technology (12) and to add *informatics*—the rational and systematic application of information to economic, social, and political problems (8)—to the agenda for international discussion. The potential danger of such general initiatives is that they mistakenly assume that telecommunication and information systems in themselves will promote growth and development and that the only problem is their rapid acquisition (14, pp. 290–291). However, the use of high technology in other sectors frequently has produced new forms of dependence rather than increased independence and even has generated new dimensions of inequality and poverty by diverting investment away from other sectors. Developing countries cannot ignore advances in information production, but will they enter this field with the care that experience in other sectors would suggest is required?

CONCLUSION

Information is both a key intermediate input (which can be acquired for a price) and an important factor of power in international bargaining. Differential access to information can therefore be a major element in the distribution of the world's income. Research on present information stocks and flows, including new technological capacity for data collection, storage, transmission, and use, cannot be postponed.

The new international division of labor assumes that high technology industries, especially those contained in the information economy, will predominate in the industrialized countries. Yet those sectors of the world economy producing raw materials or manufactured goods remain dependent on the means of information and telecommunication to enhance their range and capacity for commercial exchange. Studies are required on information access in specific types of negotiation, including those among firms and governments and in sectors including minerals, commodities, manufactured goods, and finance. Empirical categorization is required on stocks and flows of information within these sectors and types of negotiation. The interface between knowledge and information must be understood in sound analytical terms before applying this understanding to different contexts or countries. Above all, analysis of the context and application of enhanced information capacity must precede the analysis of technological change in the field.

Recent discussions on the prospects of creating an intergovernmental secretariat, like the OECD, for Third World countries (17) increase the need to consider strengthening the information sharing and expertise among developing nations. There may be ways to take advantage of externalities, scale economies, and information exchange so as to overcome the edge enjoyed at present by large, experienced commercial firms. The stimulation of competition among sellers and of cooperation among buyers will improve information flow and may regularize the current market for expertise. Improved conceptualizations of information questions in political-economic terms and detailed research at the level of sectors and countries will make it possible to analyze the enlarging range of information policy issues confronting the developing nations.

NOTES

1. Knowledge has therefore become a major factor of production: "As a consequence, the 'knowledge industries'—education, information processing and research and development—have become the most important sectors of advanced industrial societies" (6, p. 166; see also 16). Porat's nine-volume report for the U.S. Commerce Department (15) estimated that in 1967 46 percent of the U.S. GNP was in information related activities, accounted for more than 40 percent of the work force (1970), and earned 53 percent of all wages (1970). Daniel Bell's argument that society is now postindustrial (1), is based on the growing importance of the tertiary sector. A recent critical review of Bell, Dahrendorf, and other "modern improvement theorists" may be found in (5).

2. "A key consideration in bargaining power rests with the extent of information available so as to detect and evaluate the practices of transnational enterprises" (22, p. 31).

3. The professional team backing the U.S. negotiations in GATT numbered about 160; that preparing the U.S. position for WARC was conservatively estimated at 930 (including only government employees). The latter estimate was made by the FCC chairman in 1977 (21, p. 29).

4. Recent examples of this particularly acute political problem, especially the

hiatus between declared demands and coherent negotiating power, may be found in the UNCTAD negotiations in Manila in 1979 and the Lomé II negotiations between the ACP states and the European Economic Community, also in 1979.

5. An important feature of multilateral negotiation is information handling, reflected in the complexity of items on the agenda at most international conferences (23, p. 199). In advance of WARC, *Business Week* noted that "the presence of so many Third World newcomers and their assertiveness in the planning stages had many observers worried that this conference may abandon its traditional technical approach and turn into an explosion of political and economic rhetoric between the LDCs and the industrial nations" (4, pp. 40D–40E). In the end result, it did not but the advance discussions make interesting retrospective reading.

6. Brzezinski called for a bloc of developed nations to deal with technological breakthroughs in a negotiated manner (3, p. 308).

7. B. Nanus (10, p. 24) outlined the problem succinctly: "There is some reason to suspect that the widespread use of multinational computer systems may aggravate the present tensions that exist between nation states and MNCs [multinational corporations]. It is unlikely, for example, that multinational management information systems could be made effective without contributing to the homogenization of problem-solving behaviors, cultural values and public attitudes on a worldwide basis. Moreover, multinational computer systems are likely to enhance the power and influence of multinational organizations whose interests transcend national ones."

8. An excellent paper recently prepared for a meeting of the Organization for Economic Cooperation and Development (OECD) on business information gives a thorough idea of the sources and services of data banks available to private enterprise in industrialized countries. The enormous gap between these types of services and the as yet rudimentary organization of information available to Third World governments, state corporations, and private firms is apparent (20).

9. For example, 250 European and North American banks are served by the Society for Worldwide Interbank Financial Telecommunications (SWIFT) (see 18, pp. 197–200).

REFERENCES

1. Bell, Daniel. *The Coming of Post-Industrial Society.* London: Heinemann, 1974.

2. Bergsten, F. J., R. O. Keohane, and J. S. Nye. "International Economics and International Politics: A Framework for Analysis." *International Organisation* 29(1), Winter 1975.

3. Brzezinski, Zbigniew. *Between Two Ages: America's Role in the Technotronic Era.* London: Penguin Books, 1976.

4. *Business Week.* "The Hassle over Sharing the Radio Waves." May 21, 1979.

5. Gershuny, J. *After Industrial Society? The Emerging Self-Service Economy.* London: Macmillan, 1978.

6. Gilpin, Robert. *U.S. Power and the Multinational Corporation.* New York: Basic Books, 1975.

7. Keohane, R. O. and J. S. Nye. *Power and Interdependence*. New York: Little Brown, 1977.

8. Intergovernmental Bureau of Informatics. *Informatics in the Service of the New International Economic Order*. Rome: IBI, July 1978.

9. McHale, John. *The Changing Information Environment*. London: Paul Elek, 1977.

10. Nanus, B. "Business, Government and the Multinational Computer." *Columbia Journal of World Business* 13(1), Spring 1978.

11. Oettinger, A. G. *et al*. *High and Low Politics of Information Resources for the 80s*. Cambridge, Mass.: Ballinger, 1977.

12. Pipe, G. R. and A. A. M. Veenhuis (Eds.). *National Planning for Informatics in Developing Countries*. The Hague: Mouton, 1976.

13. Pool, Ithiel de Sola *et al*. *Low-Cost Data and Text Communication for Less Developed Countries*. Cambridge, Mass.: MIT Research Program on Communications Policy, 1976.

14. Pool, Ithiel de Sola. "Serving the Information Needs of Developing Countries." OECD Informatics Studies 11, *Conference on Computer and Telecommunications Policy*, Paris, 1976.

15. Porat, Marc Uri. *The Information Economy: Definition and Measurement*. Washington, D. C.: U.S. Department of Commerce, Office of Telecommunications, May 1977.

16. Porat, Marc Uri. "Global Implications of the Information Society." *Journal of Communication* 28(1), Winter 1978.

17. Ramphal, S. "Not by Unity Alone: The Case for Third World Organisation." *Third World Quarterly* 1(3), London, July 1979.

18. Read, William H. "Foreign Policy: The High and Low Politics of Telecommunications." In A. G. Oettinger *et al.*, *High and Low Politics of Information Resources for the 80s*. Cambridge, Mass.: Ballinger, 1977.

19. Stigler, George. "The Economics of Information." *Journal of Political Economy* 69(3), June 1961.

20. Treille, Jean-Michel. "New Strategies for Business Information." OECD, Working Party on Information, Computer and Communication Policy. Paris, March 22, 1979, DSTI/ICCP/79.19.

21. U.S. Senate Foreign Relations Committee. "The New World Information Order." November 1977.

22. Vaitsos, C. V. "Money as a Negotiable Input in International Business Activities." New York: U.N. Center for Transnational Corporations, unpublished. 1978.

23. Winham, G. R. "The Mediation of Multilateral Negotiations." *Journal of World Trade Law* 13(3), June 1979.

Six

The New World Information Order: An Eastern European Perspective

Zoltán Jakab

The essential interest of mankind—détente—can be served only by the development and maintenance of international contacts and cooperation, especially the mutual solution of shared problems. A New World Information Order—national autonomy and sovereignty, balanced economic development, a strong cultural identity—can be built only in an atmosphere of détente, not amidst a new cold war. From this perspective, I am going to review problems of mass media investment and mass communications planning.

CHOOSING APPROPRIATE MEDIA

According to a UNESCO estimate (6), the total aid to the communication sector of the developing countries amounted to some $267 million in 1978–1979. This sum equalled approximately 1 percent of all aid commitments. Some argue that the short-term financial requirements of this sector amount to $15–20 billion. Whether these estimates are accurate or not, they illustrate rather convincingly that the communication sector of the developing countries is generally in a deplorable financial situation, particularly in Africa and Asia. Even if aid for communication skyrocketed in the coming years, a considerable number of developing countries would face a difficult period of slow development of communications. However, this period perhaps could be used to lay the foundation for cost-effective future development. To this end, decisionmakers must understand and take into account the real nature of mass media.

The most understandable political concern voiced over the fate of mass communications in developing countries reflects the widespread failure to recognize that the particular sorts of media in the developed countries are neither inevitable nor necessarily ideal. The mass communication media are the product of philosophical, ideological, economic, and political views and structures; hence, to a considerable extent the media are subject to planning and modification. This is *not* to imply that any state can hope to develop or even to survive without modern mass media, but this *is* to say that mass communication systems are *not* neutral vis-à-vis the social contexts they serve. The type of society desired in a developing country should shape the choice of media; the society should not be shaped by the alleged inevitability of technological progress in communication.

The historical evolution of mass media in the developed countries differed entirely from that of the classical inventions in the engineering or chemical industries (see 3). The latter fields grew in response to more or less clearly felt social needs, as in the case of the steam engine or of plastics, whereas the social utilization of the mass media was discovered—and needs generated and shaped—*after* the technology had been developed to a practically feasible stage. That is, the development and marketing of technological novelties such as sound broadcasting and videocassettes were rooted in the needs of the businesses manufacturing the equipment.

The developing countries cannot permit the uncritical transfer of new communication technologies to shape their socioeconomic growth and the information needs of their people. In fact, a historically new logistic seems necessary in the advance of mass communications in the Third World. The assessment of national and local, institutional and individual, communication and information requirements must be the first step. Seeking and sorting out communication technologies—or developing alternative ones—that are most appropriate to meet these needs should be the second step. The third step would be the creation of endogenous models for providing access to the communication system. This new logistic presupposes, among other things, the cutting of costs, large-scale planning, and regional cooperation (see 1, 2).

THE HIDDEN COSTS OF MEDIA SYSTEMS

When experts think about investments in mass media, whether for developed or developing countries, they concentrate on at most three elements of the system: allocation of resources for production, distribution, and, to a lesser extent, professional training of communicators. Investments in maintenance and updating are often neglected, especially in countries short on financial means. Also neglected are the investments made by audiences. Audience data are available (manufacturers show interest in them), but they are disregarded in communication system planning. This may be partly due to the fact that, in the developed countries, the cost of broadcasting communications *appears* to be incredibly cheap for individual members of the audience.

This contrasts with the situations of the daily press and of film production and distribution, in which the organizations that produce and distribute the products handle the economies at a national level. Depreciation, modernization, and operating costs are covered directly by audience receipts, advertising revenues, and in certain cases government or institution subsidies. Consequently, the economic position of these organizations depends greatly on the extent to which they are able to make the message consumption activities of potential audiences regular, especially in societies where the media markets are highly competitive. Both the press and the film industry have tried to stabilize their income by various contractual or other soft techniques, including newspaper subscriptions and the standardization of film genres.

The record player, radio, and then television brought about a radical change in the economies of mass communication. Would-be consumers must make a preliminary investment by purchasing the technology and then bear maintenance costs (as well as make further investments in the case of the record player). The sum total of consumer investments after the short ' initial period of the introduction of a medium considerably exceeds the sum invested by the production and distribution organizations. In addition, the marketing of record players and radio and TV receivers that are technologically dazzling but only marginally improved induces the public to make new investments before physical replacement is necessary.

Available statistics show that in the developed countries consumer investment is relatively lowest in the case of tape recorders, followed by radio and television, and finally by record players and amplifiers. The newer mass communication technologies such as the videotape recorder and cable television do not promise a reversal of this trend (see 4). As for satellite television with direct reception, a 1978 estimate for the Federal Republic of Germany indicated that if 10 percent of television households were to install parabolic antennae, the consumer investment would equal 2 billion marks; the total expenditure for satellites, launchings, accessory equipment, and communication links would amount to 250 million (5).

In short, the developing countries must recognize that a large part of the population, especially the rural population, cannot make the necessary consumer investments in modern communication technologies, especially television; accordingly, investment in certain message producing and distributing equipment represents dead capital at worst and serves the interests of only a small urban elite at best. Moreover, government subsidy of consumer investment in technology will aggravate budget deficits since in the absence of domestic electronics manufacturing the equipment must be imported to meet the growing demand.

CONSIDERATIONS IN MEDIA PLANNING

Comprehensive and long-range media planning is necessary whatever model of mass communications is followed. Experience with such plans in various European countries has uncovered pitfalls that the developing nations can avoid.

First, such plans (generally covering ten to fifteen years) have proven vulnerable even to minor changes in the political or economic situation of the country.

Second, in the absence of an integrated approach, that is, a plan covering all principal elements of mass communications, the policies and procedures of the communication industry itself will dictate the development of the mass media.

Third, the complex nature of communications tends to fragment responsibility for the realization of communication goals important to the whole society. The highly articulated institutional structure of communications means that even if planning is a cooperative venture, broad assessment of communication needs takes a back seat to minimizing tensions and conflicts of interest among the parties involved.

CONCLUSION

The bulk of the developing nations can acquire the appropriate technological media systems only by cooperation with the more industrialized countries: in the foreseeable future only a few Third World countries will have domestic electronics industries. On the other hand, close regional cooperation among Third World countries with cultural and political ties can facilitate mass media development through the pooling of economic resources and experts. This approach can quickly reduce software imports, and after all the message is the central element in communications.

REFERENCES

1. Jakab, Z. "The Long-Range Planning of Mass Communication: System and Practice Abroad" (in Hungarian). *Magyar Radio es Televizio Szemle* 1975(2–3), 1976(1).

2. Jakab, Z. "Who Needs Long-Range Radio and Television Planning?" Paper prepared for the 3rd Hungarian-Soviet Seminar on Mass Communication Research, Budapest, 1979.

3. Rose, H. and S. Rose. *Science and Society*. Harmondsworth: Penguin, 1970.

4. Szalai, A. "Future Implications of Recent Advances in Communications Technology." Paper prepared for the UNITAR Conference on Forecasting, London, December 1972.

5. Thiele, R. "Satelliten—Rundfunk. . . ." *Media Perspektiven*, June 1978.

6. UNESCO. Working Paper prepared by the Intergovernmental Conference for Co-operation on Activities, Needs and Programmes for Communication Development. Paris, April 14–21, 1980.

Seven

Information Exchange between Developing and Industrial Countries[1]

V. A. Vinogradov, L. S. Kiouzadjan, T. V. Andrianova,
S. K. Vilenskaya, G. B. Kossov, A. M. Kul'kin, R. R. Mdivani,
A. I. Rakitov, V. R. Khisamutdinov, and L. V. Shemberko

The positive impact of the exchange of socioeconomic information on the development of all countries can serve as a criterion for the effectiveness of information exchange. While this standpoint seems to be the only feasible one, it immediately raises a series of methodological and technical problems.

What should the notion of "development" imply? In what way can the connection between the creation and functioning of information systems and the processes of social and economic development be traced? What is a feasible correlation pattern between socioeconomic development priorities and the priorities for information systems? And finally, in what way can the effect of an information system on socioeconomic life be defined or evaluated?

Among factors to be taken into account in this context the following are important:

—The level of education in a given country. One of the indicators can be an "intellectual potential," measured by the number of people with higher education per 1,000 adult citizens.
—The level of training of national personnel, including indices of the education level of the national work force.
—The "perception threshold" of advanced science and technology as conditioned by factors relating to tradition, culture, psychological stereotypes inherent in the society, etc. The complexity of elaborating such an index is due to the fact that these factors can hardly be formalized, so that it seems expedient to make use of expert evaluations. In this connection the experience of the Soviet Central Asian republics, as well

as that of other socialist countries, may prove to be of a certain interest. Proceeding from this assumption, the most constructive approach to the problem seems to be the one which may be described as functional. The efficient functioning of information exchanges between the developing and industrial countries presupposes the successive resolution of three tasks:

First, information is accumulated by way of the exchange of data on problems of social and economic development and scientific knowledge (setting up data banks). Such information should cover statistical and other empirical data. as well as analytical and conceptual categories. Most important here is the standardization of definitions and indices and their classification, which makes data useful for evaluative analysis, i.e., sufficiently functional.

Second, the aggregate information, thus obtained, gives an objective view of the processes taking place in the developing countries and can be used as a basis for elaborating national and regional development aims (optimum development models). Since development processes affect the life of the widest sections of the population, their participation in the elaboration or discussion of such aims seems expedient. To recruit their involvement, it is necessary to inform properly not only the experts but also wide segments of the population of developing countries on development issues.

The setting of targets inevitably postulates a certain order of priority which, in turn, certainly affects information flows, their volume and content. Consequently, the elaboration of national and regional tasks on the basis of the data provided by an information system affects that system.

Third, following the elaboration of optimum development models, data on their implementation and on the inevitable adjustments will be entered into the information exchange system, which is to provide feedback. Adjustments imply an alteration of the terms originally fixed as well as an assessment of the expediency of carrying out certain tasks. Such evaluative alterations are unavoidable and inherent in the development process. Their delay usually stems from the inadequacy or tardiness of the information influx, and considerably hampers policy.

ECONOMIC INFORMATION AS A FACTOR OF ECONOMIC PROGRESS

The notions of economic and social development are interconnected and mutually conditioned. Economic development does not necessarily imply corresponding development in the social structure. Thus, for example, a chiefly export-oriented economy or luxury industries do not necessarily promote social progress. Therefore one must define these notions according to the real prevailing conditions. The structure and system of the information flow must conform to this definition and to the aims of economic policy stemming therefrom. One indispensable condition for optimum decision-making in economics is a proper information basis, normally not available in the developing countries. A low level of economic development does not provide the prerequisites for an information system's growth and this in turn hampers economic development. It is only in the sphere of information that this vicious circle can be broken at minimum expense: it is easier to build up an information system which will ensure economic progress than to proceed in reverse order.

An information system can therefore be viewed as a subsystem within the structure of economic management, which can substantiate the need to allocate resources to it.

The design of an information system should proceed from the assumption that there exists a certain spectrum of possible economic development models and each developing country should choose one alternative over a given period depending on its particular circumstances. In this connection the following considerations apply.

First, by adopting economic categories accepted in the industrial countries, political leaders and economists in the developing countries consider economic development in terms of absolute economic growth, i.e., per capita GNP increase.

This, however, is meeting with ever-growing criticism even in the Western industrial countries. It is altogether unacceptable for the developing countries. In the advanced countries mass production coupled with mass consumption is artificially stimulated by advertising; it is often irrational, excessive and has been conditioned by the patterns prevalent in the 1950s and 1960s, largely due to the prolonged uneven exchange between the industrial and developing countries. The extension of such economic growth and corresponding consumption to the other two-thirds of the human race runs up first of all against a natural obstacle—limited raw material and energy reserves. It is, therefore, highly unlikely that this model can be accepted over the long term.

A critical reappraisal of the model logically entails a revision of the set of indices of economic performance. Normally falling under this category are such indicators as the GNP, economic growth rate, share of capital investments in the national income, volume of energy consumption, employment, etc. Despite their importance, their relative value depends upon the conception of economic growth which is accepted. Incompatibility between a model and a set of economic indicators can even distort the real picture, and disorientate those engaged in the elaboration and implementation of policy, which should certainly be taken into consideration in an international system of economic information to meet needs of the developing countries.

Second, one point in the discussion relates to the utilization of advanced technology. As Western literature not infrequently submits, this is incompatible with certain conditions in developing areas and thus compounds their economic and social problems. Those who support this viewpoint argue that the advanced countries' modern technology is, on the one hand, highly capital- and energy-intensive and, on the other hand, not labor-intensive, while developing countries suffer from an acute shortage of capital and their energy resources are mostly scanty (with the exception of a small group of oil-producing and exporting countries); at the same time they possess excess labor and suffer from chronic mass unemployment. The conclusion is that it would be expedient to develop such technology as requires low expenditure of capital and energy and is rather labor-intensive.

There is no denying that such problems as shortage of capital and know-how or an excess labor force do exist. Yet the proposed solution to refuse advanced technology is, first, tantamount to a still more unequal and subordinate position in the international alignment of forces and, secondly, is simply impracticable. It would be naive to suppose that peoples who have attained political independence and taken the road of autonomous development should refuse to adopt modern civilization, scientific knowledge, advanced technology, etc. The real task therefore consists in the development of a rational, realistic economic strategy enabling the developing countries to work out an optimum model for the modernization of their national economies both in terms of its structure and the rate of construction.

Advocates of the viewpoint presented above advance another, similar argument: that the adoption of advanced technology is also hampered by archaic social and political structures, cultural backwardness, etc. They assert that the introduction of advanced technology presupposes wide-ranging modernization; yet for the most part, in the developing countries either this is not occurring, or it has not yet matured.

While in no way denying the complexity and even painfulness involved in the modernization of the archaic social and political structures, it should be stressed that this task can and is being solved by the countries undergoing progressive reorganization in close coordination with the reconstruction of the material and technical base of their economy. The conception of economic assistance held by the U.S.S.R. and other socialist countries proceeds on the assumption that the building up of modern technology and technical reconstruction of all economic branches speeds up social and cultural progress.

Third, some researchers submit that to meet the developing countries' needs implies going back to Western technology of the pre-industrial era. Since its production could not normally compete with that of industrial countries, such technology could function only under protective barriers.

Yet another model proposes "feasible technology," essentially small-scale, and with limited capital requirements, which makes use of the local resources and mainly produces for domestic consumption. Here, stress is laid on full employment and on meeting chiefly traditional demands.

Admittedly this can make better use of material and human resources and extension of production. Yet it is supplementary and should not be mistaken for a key guideline of strategy. It cannot alter the developing countries' unequal position in the international division of labor, and can result in increasing dependence on the advanced capitalist countries or on transnational corporations.

ELEMENTS OF AN ECONOMIC INFORMATION SYSTEM

In building an advanced economy the three major obstacles are lack of resources, science and technology, and skilled labor. Mutual cooperation can notably speed up matters and certain positive experiences have already been had at the regional level. Information systems should foster such cooperation and exchange of experience; they should define the most advantageous areas and patterns of economic co-operation.

A functioning economic information system would consist of the following elements:

Cooperative efforts from both industrial and developing countries to elaborate optimum models of economic development for countries, groups of countries and regions.

Improvement of economic information services in the developing countries and channelling the information flow from these countries to the scientific research centers of the industrial countries.

Analysis of the collected information, correlation of the prevailing economic situation in the developing countries with optimum models and subsequent recommendations for correcting the models, or economic policy, or both the models and policy simultaneously.

For alternative models, forecasts on different options and their implications.

Analysis of the two-way information flow for completeness and adequacy in the improvement of the information system.

Unimpeded and uninterrupted supply of information to the main users; the collection, processing, storage and dissemination of information should be centralized to a certain extent and a major information center set up in each country.

THE IMPACT OF SOCIOECONOMIC INFORMATION ON SOCIAL DEVELOPMENT

The United Nations publication *Towards a System of Social and Demographic Statistics* (1975) presents an organized combination of types of socioeconomic information. Developing countries can use the experience of advanced countries to work out their own schemes with emphasis not on social statics but on social dynamics. The interaction of social and economic processes should certainly be taken into consideration. One example is the influence of improved living standards on the growth rate. They can either bring the growth rate down or accelerate it, or in some cases have no perceptible impact on it. In other words, the same economic factors may have different social effects, and vice versa.

The major requirements for a successful exchange of information on social development are as follows:

Joint efforts in industrial and developing countries should be aimed at optimum social development models. These will depend on optimum economic development models. For developing countries, social development should imply: (1) assistance in the modernization of social structures; (2) minimizing the negative consequences of such modernization; (3) a cautious attitude towards the norms of the traditional and national system, because their destruction may result in a lowering of living standards despite economic progress.

Information on the social problems facing developing areas must regularly reach the relevant scientific research centers of industrial countries.

This information should be updated from time to time.

Scientific research centers in the industrial countries should correlate the information received with optimum models of social development. Such correlation is to correct their own scientific output which in turn guides policy in the developing countries and also orients their scientific centers.

Socioeconomic information must regularly reach users in the developing countries: scientific institutions, government, political parties, religious and public organizations, public libraries, etc.

A steady information flow from the developing countries to the industrial ones should occur, covering statistical data and works on social life and philosophical, religious and ethical traditions.

The feedback loop of information between the developed and developing countries should embrace data on the formers' information consumption and its impact, thus making it possible to evaluate the effects of this information.

NOTE

1. This chapter is excerpted from the *International Social Science Journal* 33(1). © UNESCO 1981. Reproduced by permission of UNESCO.

Eight

Communication Issues Confronting the Developing Nations

Sarath L. B. Amunugama

In the 1970s communications entered the dialogue between the developed and the developing world. Until then, this area was of concern primarily to manufacturers from industrialized countries and Third World media professionals—journalists, broadcasters, and filmmakers, who depend heavily on the West for equipment and other resources. Only the United States had recognized the study of mass communications as an academic discipline; elsewhere the emphasis was on professional training for media practitioners, which was usually available only in the colonial metropolis. The situation has now changed considerably. Governments and media institutions, particularly in developing countries, are aware of the role and potential effects of mass media. Likewise, international attention has been directed to the mass media, as evidenced by a UNESCO recommendation in the spring of 1980 to establish a mechanism within the ambit of that entity to insure assistance in communications development to the Third World. Why this new awareness?

First, the sixties and seventies saw a greater investment by the Third World in mass media, particularly radio and television. While the use of mass media is by no means spread evenly throughout the Third World and certainly does not parallel media use in the industrially developed countries, policymakers in developing nations are increasingly employing media to achieve national goals. Today, lower costs, particularly of transistorized radio receivers, are bringing rural communities within the orbit of mass media services.[1] Second, over the past several decades Third World investments in social welfare areas such as education, health, and transportation have expanded the audience for the mass media.

These two factors of course overlap: new facilities create new audi-

56

ences and vice versa. In India, for example, between the first five-year plan (beginning in 1951) and the fifth five-year plan (beginning in 1974), the amount of budget allotted to expand and strengthen mass media facilities increased by a factor of eighteen. When India became free in 1947 it had about one thousand newspapers and periodicals; in 1980 it had sixteen thousand. In 1947 only six cities had broadcasting stations—these were received by an estimated seven hundred thousand radios; in 1980 there were eighty-four broadcasting stations throughout the country and over twenty million receivers. Film production has more than doubled and the number of movie theaters more than tripled over the same period (2).

Third, while these changes are dramatic in the context of the Third World, nevertheless the gap in media resources and services is widening between the developed and the developing countries. Manufacture of media equipment and program material is heavily concentrated in a few industrialized nations: a 1980 UNESCO survey (3) showed that, while nineteen industrialized countries had 3,256 daily newspapers, eighty-three non-oil-producing developing countries had a total of 2,034 newspapers. While the developed countries had an average of 283 copies of newspapers per thousand inhabitants, the corresponding average in the developing countries was 27. In the case of radio receivers, twenty industrialized countries had an average of 910 sets per thousand inhabitants while the developing countries had 93. As regards television receivers, the average was 367 per thousand inhabitants for the developed countries against 33 for the developing countries. Telephone, telex, satellite, and computer facilities show even greater disparities. More significant is the monopolization of the so-called consciousness industry by the developed countries: the poor nations are, in effect, the dumping ground for Western programs and other communications products. They depend on material sold by the major news, radio, and TV organizations of the West to keep their mass media institutions functioning on a day-to-day basis. Hence the label "cultural imperialism."

Fourth, having recognized the complex role of media in *internal* contexts and the growing worldwide gap in media resources and facilities, the Third World is also aware that communications technology in the not so distant future will allow a new phase of social experimentation that not only will affect the social and cultural fabric of industrialized societies but also will permit the *manipulation* of social, cultural, and political values in the Third World countries economically dependent on the developed nations. Just as consumers of the future will be able to sit at home and summon news, entertainment, and intellectual programming and organize banking and shopping via computer, powerful governments of all ideological varieties, transnational agencies, and even private organizations will have the technological means to influence, and perhaps to interfere with, the cultures and eventually the politics of sovereign peoples.

THE IMPACT OF MODERN MEDIA ON TRADITIONAL CULTURES

The growing recognition of the role of media has been accompanied by a resurgence of indigenous cultural symbolism in the developing world. Such symbol systems, though derived from traditional cultures, must not be equated with traditional culture itself. If the seventies marked a further step in decolonization, they also highlighted the increasing complexity of relationships within the cultures of poor countries. Traditional values, indigenous cultural innovations in response to contemporary pressures, and assimilated metropolitan values all constitute the new mix we identify as the contemporary cultures of Third World countries.

It is simplistic and misleading to describe this situation as a clash of cultures or of values.[2] This new culture has a complex history. In most colonies the anti-imperialist struggle began as an attempt to keep the core of traditional culture from being obliterated by the values of the colonizer. Thus, traditional religion and medicine, along with indigenous educational and legal systems, produced ideologues who attempted to counterpose to the colonial value system an alternative, indigenous world view. In a large Asian arc from the Philippines through Indochina, Indonesia, Malaysia, and the Indian subcontinent to Iran, indigenous cultures were defended by traditional literati, the earliest ideologues of the anticolonial struggle.

One of the most significant phenomena in the field of communications is the creative and innovative use of both traditional and modern message systems by such literati for the diffusion of ideas that emphasize community and devalue personal identity and privatism. Gandhi and Mao followed this road. Their messages encouraged self-sufficiency as against dependence, and they opposed materialism, commercialism, and consumerism—all identified with the colonial experience. At the turn of the century the great Buddhist revivalist Anagarika Dharmapala of Sri Lanka wrote:

> We purchase Pear soap, and eat coconut biscuits manufactured by Huntley and Palmer, and sit in chairs made in Austria, drink the purified liquid known as tinned milk while our own cows are dying for want of fodder and grazing grounds and our own pottery we have given up for enamel goods manufactured in distant Austria and our own brass lamps we have melted and are paying to purchase lamps which require a supply of fragile chimneys manufactured in Belgium. Our own weavers are starving and we are purchasing cloth manufactured elsewhere (1, p. 509).

This message of revivalism was effectively carried in the early vernacular press, just as cassette recorders carried the message of Iranian revivalism in 1978–1979.

A question then arises. The elites of developing countries have accepted a model of modernization based on the historical experiences of the industrialized West. This model calls for quantitative growth, industrialization, urbanization, economic rationalism, and capital-intensive technology. But how should these modernizing elites act in a social and cultural milieu permeated by values of a different nature? Whatever values the majority of people in the developing world embrace, their leaders have set as goals economic growth, rational use of human and material resources, and enhancement of living standards and the quality of life. The People's Republic of China, for instance, has identified the need to modernize agriculture, industry, science, and technology and increase military strength. Clearly, the central communications problem in the eighties concerns the manner and means by which Third World countries will reconcile these opposed values and pressures in the context of globally distributed modern media and national development requirements.

Unlike the developed nations, which have a coherent political and cultural polity, the product of many years' evolution, most Third World countries have not yet consolidated a national identity. The transition from regional, tribal, ethnic, religious, or caste loyalty to national identity has not been completed. Ironically, the concept of the nation-state itself is a colonial legacy and the mass of Third World people are not particularly receptive to this goal. The dialogue between the developed and the developing world is conducted against this backdrop, as is evident in the following review of information flow, media infrastructure, and technology transfer, three thorny problems in this dialogue.

THE NEED FOR A FREE AND BALANCED INFORMATION FLOW

As we have seen, the manufacture of media material is concentrated in the developed world.[3] What is significant about this fact is the potential impact of the values implied by this material on the developing world. Although the West produces excellent television and radio programs, for example, alternative news sources and feature services are available to Third World media that can provide media products much closer to the immediate concerns of the developing countries. The giant information conglomerates are geared to satisfy a market that they themselves have created, and countries that find it difficult to provide even primary education fritter away their meager resources on television imports depicting violence and sex. Once audiences have been hooked on this type of programming, with its technical superiority, their preferences are nearly unshakable, and local media industries are forced to cater to Western-cultivated tastes.

The traditional intelligentsia resents this intrusion via the media of new values, perceiving them as a direct threat to the indigenous value system. Likewise, the intelligentsia regards the modernizing elites, which encourage this transfer, as antinational. This phenomenon, though best illustrated perhaps in the Middle East, is common to the Third World.

The imbalance in news flow illustrates the problem. News media throughout the world emphasize Western Europe and North America; the major transnational news agencies have relegated the developing countries to the bottom rung in terms of coverage. From the point of view of the Third World, news flow both between the developing and the developed countries and among the developing countries must become balanced, expressing the aspirations and achievements of the poorer nations.

The Western media do not take into account the complexity of problems Third World states encounter even in preserving national unity. Emphasis on dramatic events, rather than on multifaceted processes, creates new difficulties for a country that already has its hands full merely keeping the social fabric intact. Thus, the developing nations plead for perspective: individual events must be related to a process of development.

MEDIA INFRASTRUCTURE AND TECHNOLOGY TRANSFER

The need for a systemic approach to communications is increasingly felt in the Third World. Many of these countries retain strong interpersonal communications systems that belong to traditional culture; for instance, oral tradition still plays a dominant role. Experience has called into question the belief that modern mass media can be used effectively by themselves in changing attitudes and diffusing innovations. Clearly, a mix of traditional and modern communication methods is imperative.

Unfortunately, practical problems plague the coordination of media activities in the Third World. The segmentation of tasks into different departments with different lines of command, the overreliance on the media by the elite, the lack of research, and the failure to achieve a two-way flow of information tend to make the investments in mass media appear doubtful on a cost-effective basis. While in the seventies poor countries made greater investments in media than ever before, the majority of the world's population still has no access to even the most basic media. Indeed, the vast majority of our people live in primitive or peasant societies in which mass media play little or no part.

This raises the question of appropriate technology. Mass media represent a major area of technology transfer from developed to developing countries. But this transfer creates many problems of unsuitable technology, waste, and inefficiency, long-term dependency in servicing and spare parts, and lack of trained personnel to operate equipment and produce programs. The practical dimension of a new information order thus entails, among other things, the development of low cost and low maintenance media technology. The transistor revolutionized audio broadcasting in the developing world; today in most parts of India and China the most potent form of mass communication is the radio. The Satellite Instructional Television Experiment (SITE) in India yielded valuable insights into the use of low-cost technology at the village level. However, as this project demonstrated, a major problem that communicators tend to forget is how to maintain and repair radio and television receivers in rural settings. Clearly, only if sufficient heed is paid to the conditions prevailing in the developing countries will media structures and technology be functional in these varied contexts.

FUTURE PROSPECTS

Third World nations must be given the opportunity to develop their own media so that the latter can not only service national audiences but also facilitate a more equitable global exchange of information. To this end the Third World needs appropriate media technology and training facilities.

The Third World has begun to take the initiative in media development. Though imperfect, the news pooling arrangements of the nonaligned countries represent such an effort. The development of a Third World news agency like Inter Press Service is another step. Lowering or raising tariffs on information and communication flow to accommodate Third World users and protect Third World resources is yet another approach.

Obviously, the Third World itself has to look to the industrialized countries for access to the latest developments in media technology. The Third World lacks the scientific and financial infrastructure necessary to produce media innovations, and collaboration with the West to obtain new, low-cost technology is imperative. Fortunately, the more recent the technology, the less expensive (relatively speaking) it tends to be.

Of course, technology is but part of the picture. To further the interests of its people, each Third World country must safeguard freedom of expression for both local and foreign media. Public criticism can expose contradictions within developing societies, elitism, lack of planning, and inefficient implementation and help create a truly egalitarian basis for Third World societies. We can plead for better understanding, devise means of publicizing our point of view, and protest when our problems are not viewed sympathetically, but government censorship and discrimination against foreign reporters do not bring us any nearer the goal of a free and balanced news flow. In the final analysis what is important for the people of the Third World is not a good press but efficient attainment of socially desirable ends.

NOTES

1. Production costs of such technology are going down at the rate of 20 percent per year.

2. We are now witnessing the reincarnation of cultural relativism, which is a concept well known from the social sciences.

3. Third World dependence on the major news agencies of course is only a

reflection of the economic dependence of the poor countries on the industrial states.

REFERENCES

1. Dharmapala, Anagarika. *Return to Righteousness*. Ananda Guruge, Ed. Colombo: Government Press, 1965.

2. Sahgal, S. K. Paper delivered at UNESCO Intergovernmental Conference for Co-operation on Activities, Needs and Programmes for Communication Development, Paris, 1980.

3. UNESCO. *Basic Statistics for Communication Development* (cc 80/conf 212/4). Paris, 1980.

Nine

A Social View of Information

Fernando Reyes Matta

Decisions on communications issues are necessary because of the problems that were not solved during preceding decades. After World War II, representatives from approximately fifty countries met at what was to become the birth of UNESCO. Information was one of the prominent subjects on the agenda, and the problem of how to protect the individual's right to inform and be informed was an item of concern. This point of view, which is significantly different from a more current *social* view of information, was expressed in Article 19 of the Universal Declaration on Human Rights, adopted in 1948. During the conference a large number of countries, led by the United States, were simultaneously promoting the principle of the free flow of information. The political nature of this principle was evident at the conference on information held in Geneva in 1948, as well as in succeeding events of the postwar period. As John Foster Dulles, U.S. Secretary of State at the time, stated: "If I were to be granted one point of policy and no other, I would make it the free flow of information."

But the sixties marked the end of classical colonialism. Liberation movements began to proliferate. New voices, new actors, and new arguments arose that have not been fully understood by those who hold an ethnocentric view of information systems under constant transnational expansion. Various Asian and African nations began to express their will to exist, a goal that requires the recovery of the most significant values of each country's national culture. Simultaneously, Latin American countries became aware of the problems created by increasing dependency; political avant-garde movements and academicians demonstrated that Latin American development was guided mainly by an identification with the goals, methods, and forms of action of the dominant countries (see 1).

In the seventies it became evident that African, Asian, and Latin American nations, in spite of their different experiences, all needed to find a common way to overcome their colonial heritage, which constituted an obstacle to the construction of authentic independence. The increasing penetration of transnational corporations had created a situation of neo-colonialism that hampered both economic development and political and cultural autonomy. Thus, in 1975 the Third World countries pointed out that, for the New International Economic Order to be successful, it required independent information systems whose approach to reality and current events would be radically different from that of prevailing news and other communication networks. Furthermore, these systems should help create awareness among broad social sectors of the process of change in developed and developing countries. These considerations provided the basis for the New International Information Order, which many sectors, particularly in industrial countries, have adopted as their theme although the exact definition of this order is elusive.

Currently, the contents and attitudes of international information are determined in the international capitals of information; a news agenda, in which the majority of Third World countries do not feel represented, is imposed on the world from these cities. Similarly, African and Latin American nations have expressed concern over the disregard in Western-originated news reports of cultural diversity. Indeed, instead of the recognition of cultural diversity the promotion of a transnational form of culture characterizes the mass media worldwide. Accordingly, Third World countries have pointed out emphatically that information should, above all, constitute a social benefit and not be treated as merchandise.

CONFLICT WITH THE DOMINANT MODEL

By making specific demands for the reformulation of cultural and informational relations at the international level, the Third World inevitably finds itself in conflict with the dominant model of information flow and control. How is this information model perceived by the countries whose culture it affects? According to this model, the search for information is determined primarily by competition. Therefore, news is transmitted almost as reported events occur; speed and broad coverage are essential. This causes information to be perceived as a spectacle. The ongoing battle between news agencies to determine who transmitted a news item seconds ahead of other agencies often proves baffling to the people of Third World countries, where the concept of time is radically different from the Western concept. The search for new markets also affects communications by virtue of the interrelation between advertising and news, two message forms that use the same setting—namely, television screens or newspaper and magazine columns.

Observers from the Third World also are concerned over the way in which information is organized. Transborder information systems present facts and events completely out of context; the connection between events is usually concealed and facts are not presented in proper historical context. Thus in the world information system certain *events* may be followed over time but not *processes*. Only a limited number of publications, which circulate in intellectual elite circles and decisionmaking centers in various countries, produce so-called analytical journalism.

World information systems are also notoriously insular. The various media reinforce each other's messages: radio and television news spots provide the basis for magazine and newspaper stories, and technologies like TV-photos and film-news complement and combine their appeals. All these elements help define the agenda of current events and contemporary history, but is this a trustworthy process?

TELEVISION: SO MUCH AND SO LITTLE

U.S. television is one of the technically best and largest information structures in the world. Whether we like it or not, it constitutes a significant example of what this medium can be like in a highly informationalized society. But, advanced technology does not insure a well-informed public. *Excelsior*, a leading Mexican newspaper, published the following note on March 26, 1980.

> After almost twenty years of being the most trusted man in the U.S., Walter Cronkite revealed that the daily evening news is inaccurate and does not deserve the audience's confidence. "Actually, during the last twenty years my lips have been sealed," said Cronkite during a recent interview. "Television news is no more than a headline type of service. There is no time to enter into subtle details and complex situations." Cronkite, a symbol of television news in the United States, is concerned with the fact that 65 percent of North Americans obtain their information from the twenty-six minutes of evening news broadcast by CBS.

This type of news broadcasting, inadequate in the context that created it, has been adopted in many other nations, where it fails even more to reflect current needs of different social groups. Consequently, various Latin American sectors have spoken up on the need for change. (It is not coincidence that the first continental conferences on cultural and communications policies convened by UNESCO were held in Latin America.)

The proposed changes do not, as many people think, entail primarily a choice between government and private enterprise, although this is an important issue. The more pressing problem is the participation of all social sectors in communication. As Mexico's coordinator of social communication pointed out:

> At the outset of the eighties we must be aware of the fact that vertical and nonparticipatory communication cannot continue to prevail in our societies. Although superior technology is increasingly available, it also promotes con-

centration in the hands of a minority. Our task is to foster effective participation in communications, to make it feasible by creating adequate political channels and means for action. But, if individuals and social groups are to play a leading, influential, and guiding role in communications, if the public is to have its say, we must create a formative process to support public activities. We must open the doors of schools and other training centers to the subject of communications. Our best allies in modifying current forms of communication are the men and women of our society, people who care and are aware of the benefits of a new informational situation (*El Día*, May 8, 1980).

Statements of this nature demonstrate that the creation of a new area of social right is imminent. At national and international levels this task demands creativity and attitudes that look to the future rather than defend the past. Proponents of the dominant information model rarely ask themselves the crucial questions: What have we left undone? Where have we failed? Why are so many people demanding change? If the answers to these questions were approached serenely, the challenges posed by the future would be much more understandable.

PRINCIPAL AREAS FOR DECISION

Information and communication probably will be radically different when the eighties are over. Nevertheless, people have diverse views on how to achieve change in this area. Some of us think that things will be different because technology will modify human relations and the relationship between humanity and environment. Others think that it is not a question of having more—more technology, more communications, more simultaneity, more accumulation, more data—but rather of *being more*. In any case, four fundamental areas require decisions in this decade.

1. *Making Information a Public Service.* If the concept of information as a product subject to market forces is rejected, it will be possible to use information for social benefit. And if the concept of information as a public service is accepted, concern over the influence of advertising will follow naturally. In this case, whether information is controlled by private enterprise, the public, or government will not be relevant. Information is for everybody; it is created by the activities of individuals and social groups considered more or less important by others. Consequently, the production and broadcasting of information confers a permanent responsibility.

2. *Developing a New Area of Social Right.* The magnitude of information and communication in contemporary society constitutes a legal challenge because the current legal framework within which to define the right to information is proving insufficient. Communication as a social function requires specific laws to define the rights and obligations of those involved. Communication has ceased to be solely an individual right and

in becoming a social right it has become necessary to the preservation of other social as well as individual rights. National communication policies, rules for transnational corporations, the role of the state in communications, and the role of communicators in participatory communications are areas that must be addressed from this perspective.

The main objective of this new right should be the democratization of communications. Consequently, social and legal mechanisms should be created in order to eliminate political and economic authoritarianism from communications, thereby effecting greater horizontal interaction between the sectors involved. Once rights and obligations have been clearly defined, the media can be held accountable for the way in which they exercise their social function.

3. *Promoting Effective Participation in Communications.* One of the major problems confronting the mass media is the participation of individuals, groups, and large sectors of the population in the communications process. In all models of development, the issues of active participation in the creation, political orientation, organization, and forms of communication need to be resolved.

To a large extent, bureaucratic misgivings about the potential creativity of the public have foreclosed mass access to communications. Thus, even when participation is permitted, it is usually trivial in nature and thus incapable of genuinely influencing national awareness. The industrial exploitation of information also plays a part in denying the public a dynamic role in communications. The current system, based on nineteenth-century economic theories, expands by the use of neocolonial instruments of transnational power. This system creates concentrations of resources and power; decisions on what to communicate and how to inform are made by a restricted group, which never asks audiences whether these decisions are adequate.

The fundamental challenge lies in modifying this situation in order to achieve democratic communications and different forms of participation, thereby to work toward a democratic society.

4. *Humanizing Technology.* Despite claims that technology by itself can remedy contemporary information problems, awareness of the social and political dangers implicit in the expansion of technological information systems is increasing. New technology, such as remote-sensing satellites and computer-telecommunications networks, increases the capacity for prompt, coordinated, and efficient decision-making. Indeed, we can foresee a future in which each home is connected to enormous computer centers capable of providing data of every description, from news to cinema timetables to scientific essays. These data depots would constitute external reality for human beings, creating an atomized world totally disconnected from effective social practice and creative interaction. Technology thus can provide a mechanism for concealing social contradictions under seemingly

broad access to large quantities of accumulated and processed information. In short, communications technology threatens us with increasingly vertical forms of communication and curtailed participation.

The fact that individuals are connected to many computer terminals does not make communication more democratic. Democracy is achieved through social interaction—through joint activity and joint search for solutions. Therefore, technology can be either an essential tool for democratizing communications or an instrument for increasing authoritarianism. This is the fundamental choice in national and international communications.

REFERENCES

1. Reyes Matta, Fernando. "The Latin American Concept of News." *Journal of Communication* 29 (2), Spring 1979, pp. 164–171.

Ten

A Right to International Communication?

Humphrey Tonkin

When we consider international communication we are apt to think in terms of relations between states. When we consider communication rights we are inclined to look at communications technology and the prerogatives of the individual, within his or her own country, with respect to that technology. My present concern is with neither of these areas. Rather, I wish to raise some questions about the opportunities and rights enjoyed by individual citizens in their dealings with people in other countries. To what extent are the communication rights that we possess as citizens of particular states transferable to our dealings with nationals of other states? To what extent do governments have a right to regulate contacts between their own subjects and people abroad? To what extent do they have an obligation to support and facilitate such contacts?

HUMAN RIGHTS IN INTERNATIONAL LAW

We can divide the codification of human rights in the postwar era into three main periods. First came the establishment of the United Nations in 1945 and the acceptance of the Universal Declaration of Human Rights in 1948. The immediate origins of the Universal Declaration lay in the United Nations Charter, wherein the member states pledged themselves to promote and encourage "respect for human rights and for fundamental freedoms for all without distinction as to race, sex, language, or religion." But in reality the idea that there exist certain principles of human behavior that transcend particular states and take priority over the laws of those states has an extensive history and, particularly in our own century, a measure of recognition in international law.[1] In one form or another, this idea provides the starting point for most national constitutions.

The Universal Declaration of Human Rights was intended to be not only a universal declaration but also a declaration of universals. However, in recent years numerous voices have been raised to emphasize that the composition of the United Nations in 1948 was very different from what it is today and that the principles thus elevated to international recognition in fact have Western philosophical and constitutional roots.

A second phase is discernible in the expansion of the Universal Declaration through the International Covenant on Economic, Social, and Cultural Rights and the International Covenant on Civil and Political Rights, both of which were adopted by the General Assembly in 1966 and came into force in 1976, and through such instruments as the Declaration of the Rights of the Child (1959), the Genocide Convention (1948), and the Declaration on the Promotion among Youth of the Ideas of Peace, Mutual Respect, and Understanding between Peoples (1965). We can associate with this phase also the adoption of a number of regional instruments, among them the European Convention on Human Rights (1950/ 1953) and the American Convention on Human Rights (1969/1978) (see 1, 6, 12).

A third phase in thinking about human rights began in the 1970s. During this period, the vast expansion in U.N. membership changed that organization's focus and concerns in a fundamental way. In the field of human rights, above all, the United Nations made a systematic attempt to link the rights of individuals, as outlined in the Universal Declaration, to the rights of states and to establish parallels between the two. Hence the emergence of such concepts as the New International Economic Order (see 13) and the New World Information Order. We also witnessed during this period a systematic effort to strengthen education on human rights.

The expansion of human rights to embrace the rights of states has been accompanied by expansion of the scope of individuals' rights as new rights have been either "discovered" or "established." The emergence of a "right to communicate" and the efforts to define that right are very much a phenomenon of this third phase. It is sometimes pointed out that the right to communicate is still simply an idea, or not yet a right. We should pause for a moment to consider the implications of this curious formulation.

The framers of the Universal Declaration of Human Rights seem to have assumed that rights exist just as people exist. In this sense the declaration was an attempt not to invent rights but to discover them. According to this interpretation it makes little sense to refer to something as not yet a right since for something to be a right it would have to be in existence already, even if undiscovered or unformulated. Behind this view of human rights lies a belief in a set of fundamental rights inherent in an identifiable beginning of human society. This identifiable beginning might be described as one of those magnificent myths advocated in Plato's *Republic* (III, 414c) as devices for providing legitimacy to human institutions.

There is an opposite view. Though it may seem hard these days to believe in the ideas of progress, we cling to the assumption that the building of international institutions and the creation of international order *progresses*. Through this process human rights are codified and expanded. The process of expansion becomes possible as consensus grows; codification prevents slippage. According to this view, new rights are *made* and then codified by common consent.

In fact, the philosophical basis for the idea of human rights would seem to lie in a middle ground that incorporates elements from both of these views. The codification of human rights moves forward by constant redefinition of the past, by rewriting the legal fiction, in the light of present social organization. In this process we appeal to existing codifications, broadening and deepening their meaning and recognizing within them latent possibilities. At the same time we become aware of new abridgments of rights already defined, and we recognize that changing conditions, especially those brought about by technological innovation, require the definition of new principles, or rights, on which to base future efforts at international regulation. We see this process not only in discussions of the right to communicate but also in such areas as the debate over the law of the sea.

In this context it is arguable whether the need to regulate leads to the definition of new rights or whether greater consciousness of the scope of human rights leads to a desire to regulate. The latter is, of course, frequently a political and philosophical justification for the former. In any event, there is a growing feeling that changes in the world and the increasing need for international action to prevent various kinds of human catastrophe necessitate the codification of so-called new rights. Thus, at a recent meeting convened by UNESCO, experts on human rights defined four issues requiring examination in the area of "emergent" human rights: development, peace, environment, and the common heritage of mankind (14). The meeting looked particularly at the first two of these issues. The right to communicate relates to both.

INTERNATIONAL RECOGNITION OF A RIGHT TO COMMUNICATE

The history of the emergence of a right to communicate, or at least discussion of the question, is well known (see, for example, 2, 3, 8). Article 19 of the Universal Declaration of Human Rights specifies that "everyone has the right to freedom of opinion and expression; this right includes freedom to hold opinions without interference and to seek, receive and impart information and ideas through any media and regardless of frontiers."Allied with this formulation is the notion of "free flow of information"—the view that everyone, including groups of people, should be free to collect and disseminate information essentially without hindrance. This principle goes hand in hand with one of the basic beliefs of the founders of UNESCO: inhumanity and war are products of human ignorance.

But Article 19 tells us nothing about how the right to impart information has to be exercised. In an era when human beings moved only as fast as the fastest horse, when no public meeting could exceed in size the capabilities of the human larynx, when the technology of printing had advanced little beyond Gutenberg (such was the situation in the late eighteenth century, when the formulation of human rights began in earnest), ownership of the means of dissemination was an issue of relatively little importance. Today, when mass communications, with all the investment that they represent, play so dominant a role in the formation of public opinion, in education, in all aspects of political, social, and cultural life, the question of ownership, access, and control becomes all-important.

Since 1974, when the issue was first raised in the UNESCO General Conference, Article 19 has been reinterpreted and its inadequacies exposed. How can we make it possible for people to participate in two-way communication, to share in the discoveries of the new technology not as passive recipients but as active, individual participants? And how can the question of monopoly or near monopoly of means of communication be confronted?

The discussion has gone in two directions. First (and in line with the initial formulation of the problem by the Swedish delegate to UNESCO in 1974), there has been extensive discussion of individual rights within countries, that is to say, communication in the service of democratic social processes. Second, a fierce debate has taken place concerning the rights of states to take measures to create communication balance—a debate that reached a fragile consensus in the UNESCO Declaration on the Mass Media of 1978 (16). Both aspects have received attention from the International Commission for the Study of Communication Problems, the MacBride Commission, established by the Director-General of UNESCO in 1978 (see 17, and its background documents).

Neither the MacBride Commission nor the other parties to these debates have given much attention to the rights of individuals in the international, or transnational, context. In the hierarchy individual–state–international community, there has been much discussion of the rights of states in the international community and of the rights of individuals in states but little of the communication rights of the individual in the international community. Of course, the level of the individual and that of the state are potentially in conflict since, as many contend, states do have a right to limit the information flowing to their nationals— in the name of cultural integrity and social unity.[2]

There are other reasons for this relative silence on the rights of individuals to communicate with other individuals across national boundaries. Much of the discussion of individual rights has been couched in political terms, e.g., influencing political processes, making one's voice heard by one's government, which has naturally tended to focus interest on the nation-state. Furthermore, a great deal of the debate has centered on how communications technology, the mass media, imposes itself on society whether the individual wants it to or not.

THE HUMAN DIMENSION IN COMMUNICATIONS

Our preoccupation with technology in the debate on the right to communicate is in certain respects unfortunate. Technology is, after all, only an extension of the human will, and it is will that lies at the heart of all communication. Communication is not a microphone or a television camera, or even electrical impulses along a cable, any more than eating is a fork or sleeping is a bed. Communication begins in the mind and its first instruments are the human larynx, human facial expressions, human language. We sometimes forget that the most sophisticated means of communication are silent without this basic human contribution. It is here that the debate should begin (see 9, 10).

The relative lack of attention to language in discussions on the right to communicate has historical reasons associated with the development of the science of linguistics and the science of communications along essentially separate lines. Linguistics has tended, at least until recently, to give scant attention to other forms of human communication. Only lately has sociolinguistics begun to ask questions about the context of speech acts, to say nothing of other means of communication. The study of communications has concentrated on mass communication, on communication technology. Given the overwhelming dominance of the United States both in the production of hardware and in programming for mass communications, it is little wonder that the English language dominates the field and that issues of language differences seldom enter the consciousness of mass media producers and planners (see, for example, 4, 5, 11). Hence the meetings organized by UNESCO on the right to communicate have used English more or less exclusively, just as the work of the MacBride Commission was carried on largely in English. In the interests of efficiency, and on the assumption (perhaps accurate, but probably self-fulfilling) that anyone interested or competent in the topic has a mastery of English, the debate on communications balance has been carried on under linguistic rules decidedly lopsided.

Fortunately, and partly thanks to the energetic intervention of at least one international nongovernmental organization (19), the final report of the MacBride Commission (17) does give some attention to language. Its Interim Report said almost nothing on the subject. The truth, of course, is that language plays a vital, but often unrecognized, role in all aspects of human rights, in national development, in communication and communication policies, in education, in the creation of political institutions, in political participation, in decolonization, in the building of a new international order. It is at least arguable that American inability to listen to any other Iranian voices than English-speaking ones contributed to the spectacular breakdown in communications between the United States and Iran. It is possible that the violence in Liberia had a great deal to do with the fact that a small English-speaking elite has for years dominated a vast non-English-speaking majority incapable of expressing itself in the language of government and of national institutions and consequently without political power.

DOES THE RIGHT TO COMMUNICATE STOP AT NATIONAL BORDERS?

The MacBride Commission seems willing to maintain that the language factor is important in the establishment and development of a right to communicate at the national level: national minorities must have a voice and cultural pluralism must be recognized and understood. If that is the case, an ability to understand and use language is even more important at the international level. To what extent are the other elements in the debate on the right to communicate *within states* applicable· to relations across national boundaries? To what extent does the debate on free flow and balance *between states* have something to tell us about individual contacts across national boundaries?

I will not rehearse the statistics on the degree to which we are becoming interdependent—the quantity of business carried on by multinationals, the spectacular growth of tourism, the huge international programs of United Nations agencies and nongovernmental organizations, and so on. We are aware of the enormous increase in the movement of migrant labor, for example, the guest workers of Western Europe. We know that international telephone calls have multiplied in the last few years and that international correspondence has hardly decreased. To what extent is such international communication between individuals protected by the major international instruments on human rights? To what extent do states have an obligation to facilitate the international contacts of their citizens, or at least not to abridge or interfere with them? If we have a right to education, do we have a right to an education international in scope, calculated to promote human contact and understanding across the frontiers of states?

We have already examined Article 19 of the Universal Declaration of Human Rights. Five other articles have relevance to our inquiry. According to Article 12, "No one shall be subjected to arbitrary interference with his privacy, family, home or correspondence, nor to attacks upon his honour or reputation." Although in fact interference with personal correspondence and with the receipt of books and printed matter is fairly widespread, Article 12 would seem to guarantee the right to send and receive international mail, at least if such mail is solicited by the recipient.

Article 13.2 states that "everyone has the right to leave any country, including his own, and to return to his country." Again, international practice is sharply different from international principle. Frequently it is argued that foreign travel must be limited for economic reasons, though it is interesting that the corresponding article of the International Covenant on Civil and Political Rights is silent on the matter.

Article 18 refers to freedom of "thought, conscience and religion." It would surely be hard to argue that while such freedom can be exercised within a given state, it cannot be exercised in communication with a person in a different country.

Above all, Article 28 declares that "everyone is entitled to a social and international order in which the rights and freedoms set forth in this Declaration can be fully realized." And Article 29.2 adds: "In the exercise of his rights and freedoms, everyone shall be subject only to such limitations as are determined by law solely for the purpose of securing due recognition and respect for the rights and freedoms of others and of meeting the just requirements of morality, public order and the general welfare in a democratic society."

RIGHTS OF STATES VERSUS INDIVIDUAL RIGHTS

Although Article 29 places no limitation on the exercise of human rights with respect to national boundaries, the Universal Declaration of Human Rights and the two major covenants rest on a set of assumptions having to do with the essential integrity and isolation of states. Though Articles 13, 14 (on political asylum), 15 (on nationality), and 19 (on information) do allude to transnational freedoms, they pay relatively little attention to personal communication at the international level. In fact, it is Article 19, with its crucial phrase "regardless of frontier," that provides strongest justification for the view that personal communication at the international level is within the scope of, and governed by, the various provisions of the Universal Declaration.

In this connection Article 28, referring to the creation of a just social and international order, is curiously ambiguous. We may read the distinction between "social" and "international" as a further manifestation of the hierarchy already alluded to, "social" referring to the individual within society, enjoying rights in his or her own country, and "international" referring to the nation-states in an international community, building their relationships in a spirit of reciprocity. It is precisely this interpretation that leads to the philosophy of a New International Economic Order, in which states are like so many individuals with a claim on equality.

On the other hand, we may read Article 28 to suggest that we are members *as individuals* not only of a particular local or national community but also of a world community—a larger international order governed precisely by the rights of the individual laid out in the Declaration. This interpretation is implied in the long history of efforts at "education for international understanding"—a history going back to the late nineteenth century and embodied in the preamble to the UNESCO Constitution: "A peace based exclusively upon the political and economic arrangements of governments would not be a peace which could secure the unanimous, lasting and sincere support of the peoples of the world. The peace must therefore be founded, if it is not to fail, upon the intellectual and moral solidarity of mankind" (15).[3]

I do not pretend to be able to reconcile these two conflicting interpretations of Article 28. For my present purposes it is enough to recognize that a conflict exists, at least if we acknowledge that there are circumstances under which it is legitimate for states to serve as mediators between other states and their own citizens. This is just one area in which a certain murkiness surrounds the definition of the international rights of individuals. Even at the national level, the matter of communication rights is still far from clear. Though UNESCO has made some progress in establishing principles for the exchange of information from country to country through its Mass Media Declaration, it has done less well with the other half of its mission, the securing of personal rights to communicate at the local and national levels.

As for the international level, we have only the few allusions of the Universal Declaration (barely expanded in the later covenants) and UNESCO's efforts on behalf of international education to establish even the basic recognition of an international community of individuals in contact with one another across frontiers. To this we might add the occasional pronouncements of the United Nations and the specialized agencies on the role of nongovernmental organizations (though it is a constant source of complaint among such organizations that their rights and privileges are insufficiently secured).[4]

At the regional level, there is rather more evidence of concern for international communication among individuals. The Final Act of the Conference on Security and Cooperation in Europe, the Helsinki Declaration, dwells extensively on such matters as the movement of business people and of migrant workers across national boundaries, the "contribution made by international tourism to the development of mutual understanding among peoples," and, above all, the need "to facilitate freer movement and contacts, individually and collectively, whether privately or officially, among persons, institutions and organizations of the participating States, and to contribute to the solution of the humanitarian problems that arise in that connection."

The Helsinki Declaration also devotes a paragraph to the importance of language learning and gives considerable attention to international education. It is education about the world, desire to understand that world for oneself, and the knowledge of the means for communicating on an equal footing with that world (among them, language) that form the positive basis for the various safeguards to be found here and there in international instruments. If we have neither the desire nor the means to become informed, ignorance and xenophobia will govern our relations with the larger world. It is at least arguable that as members of the human race we have a right to learn about the human race and to be informed about the human race in universal terms.

Given that the desire and the means to communicate internationally exist, and that such individual communication, uninhibited by the problems of balance that beset the mass media, can do much to dispel ignorance and create a sense of solidarity and common international purpose, there is a need for more effective safeguards for such communication. While few would dispute that the Helsinki Declaration is repeatedly violated (though the text's repeated emphasis on improvement of the existing situation leaves plenty of margin for interpretation) and that the same is too often true of the Universal Declaration, an attempt to examine thoroughly international contacts between individuals could prove immensely helpful. At one end of the scale, Hungary and Austria have dropped visa requirements; at the other end, not even diplomats are exempt from harassment and incarceration. While international agreements (which exist in abundance to cover the latter issue) may prove meager protection, a clearer assessment of the rights of the individual in the world community could only help to prepare us for the integration of interests and activities on a world scale, which is a burgeoning phenomenon of our age.

Is there, in short, a right to international communication? We can discern the rudiments of such a right in a number of international agreements. However, obstacles to the exercise of that right loom up at every turn: some are rooted in prejudice and in shortcomings in education; others are the product of arbitrary acts of governments to limit the international communication of their citizens (even for nonpolitical purposes); still others spring from laws framed either without regard to, or specifically to inhibit, international contact. Greater clarity on the prerogatives of nation-states to limit the international contacts of their citizens would presumably lead to greater clarity on the rights of individuals to make contact with people in other countries. Such precision in this, as in so many other international matters, would benefit us all.

NOTES

1. The first great statement of these principles is generally acknowledged to

be the French Declaration of the Rights of Man and of the Citizen of 1789 (for historical background see 7, pp. 11–42).

2. For a rather different view, minimizing potential conflict between individual rights and collective rights, see (20, pp. 45–63).

3. This sentiment lies behind the 1974 document on education for international understanding, UNESCO's Recommendation concerning Education for International Understanding, Cooperation and Peace and Education relating to Human Rights and Fundamental Freedoms (for a commentary on the recommendation, see 1; cf. 18, esp. pp. 37–48).

4. This matter has recently returned to the agenda of the Conference of Non-governmental Organizations in Consultative Status with the United Nations Economic and Social Council. Also relevant are the statements of the International Council of Scientific Unions on access to scientific conferences.

REFERENCES

1. Buergenthal, Thomas and Judith V. Torney. *International Human Rights and International Education*. Washington, D.C.: U.S. National Commission for UNESCO, 1976.

2. Gunter, Jonathan F. "An Introduction to the Great Debate." *Journal of Communication* 28(4), 1978, pp. 142–156.

3. Harms, L. S., Jim Richstad, and Kathleen A. Kie (Eds.) *Right to Communicate: Collected Papers*. Honolulu: University of Hawaii Social Sciences and Linguistics Institute, 1977.

4. Schiller, Herbert I. *Communication and Cultural Domination*. White Plains, N.Y.: International Arts and Sciences Press, 1976.

5. Shore, Larry. "U.S. Domination of the Transnational Music Industry." Paper presented at the International Studies Association Convention, Los Angeles, March 1980.

6. Sohn, Louis and Thomas Buergenthal (Eds.) *Basic Documents on International Protction of Human Rights*. New York: Bobbs-Merrill, 1973.

7. Szabo, Imre. "Fondements historiques et développement des droits de l'homme." In Karel Vasak (Ed.) *Les dimensions internationales des droits de l'homme*. Paris: UNESCO, 1978, pp. 11–42.

8. Tonkin, Humphrey. "The Right to Communicate: A Discussion Paper." In *Language and the Right to Communicate*. Esperanto Documents, No. 13-A. Rotterdam: Universal Esperanto Association, 1978, pp. 9–13.

9. Tonkin, Humphrey. *Language and International Communication: The Right to Communicate*. Esperanto Documents, No. 15-A. Rotterdam: Universal Esperanto Association, 1979.

10. Tonkin, Humphrey. "Equalizing Language." *Journal of Communication* 29(2), 1979, pp. 124–133.

11. Tunstall, Jeremy. *The Media are American*. London: Constable, 1976.

12. United Nations. *Human Rights: A Compilation of International Instruments of the United Nations*. New York, 1973.

13. UNESCO. "Resolution on the Establishment of a New International Economic Order." *Records of the General Conference, Eighteenth Session*. Paris: UNESCO, 1975, Vol. 1, pp. 114–118.

14. UNESCO. *Final Report: Expect Meeting on Human Rights, Human Needs and the Establishment of a New International Economic Order*. Paris, June 19–23, 1978. UNESCO Doc. SS-78/CONF.630/COL.2.

15. UNESCO. *Manual of the General Conference*. Paris, 1979.

16. UNESCO. *Declaration on Fundamental Principles Concerning the Contribution of Mass Media to Strengthening Peace and International Understanding, to the Promotion of Human Rights and to Countering Racialism, Apartheid and Incitement to War*. Paris, 1979.

17. UNESCO, International Commission for the Study of Communication Problems. *Many Voices, One World: Communication and Society Today and Tomorrow*. Paris, 1980.

18. UNESCO. *The Teaching of Human Rights of Man*. Proceedings of the International Congress on the Teaching of Human Rights, Vienna, September 12–16, 1978. Paris, 1980.

19. Universal Esperanto Association. *Language Problems: Communication Problems*. Commentary and Recommendations on the Interim Report on Communication Problems in Modern Society of the International Commission for the Study of Communication Problems. Submitted to the Commission by the Universal Esperanto Association, Rotterdam, December 1978.

20. Van Boven, Theodoor C. "Les critères de distinction des droits de l'homme." In Karel Vasak (Ed.). *Les dimensions internationales des droits de l'homme*. Paris: UNESCO, 1978, pp. 45–63.

PART 2

Transnational Communications: The Flow of News and Images

Eleven

International News: Mutual Responsibilities of Developed and Developing Nations

Paul A. V. Ansah

Discussion on what has come to be known as the New International Information Order, a debate opened with some acrimony especially at UNESCO conferences, is gradually giving way to a more rational, sober, and accommodating approach on both sides to finding ways of redressing the communications imbalance. While the problem is still far from solution, headway has been made since the topic came under active discussion; for example, the transnational news agencies have admitted to certain major deficiencies in their operations vis-à-vis the Third World and media professionals and scholars in the developing world have recognized that defects in their own national media systems and policies have helped make the work of the transnational news agencies difficult.

Though some of the philosophical and ideological underpinnings of the various media systems worldwide appear irreconcilable, a new *modus vivendi*, more satisfactory than the existing situation, seems likely. If the seventies constituted a period of identifying problems and pursuing critical self-examination, the eighties should be a decade of finding concrete solutions and working out mechanisms for implementing them. In looking forward to some of these solutions, this chapter reviews current trends and positions on the issues.

TRANSNATIONAL NEWS AGENCIES AND DEVELOPING COUNTRIES

The principal complaint of the developing countries is that they have not had a fair deal from the major transnational news agencies and their media clients. First, they assert that reports about developing countries have been distorted, superficial, and inadequate, with the result that people in the industrialized states have been led to form negative images of the Third World. Furthermore, lacking adequate communication facilities themselves, the developing nations depend on the transnational news agencies for information about the Third World and thus also form negative images of each other.

In reply, the news agencies and scholars who have considered the question have offered a variety of explanations—historical, political, economic, and cultural. They argue that the transnational news agencies were set up to cater to the needs of their major clients, which were in the industrialized nations. Whether they were operating as cooperatives or as straight commercial ventures, the agencies had to provide the kind of service their members or clients wanted. The collection of news about "outsiders" was therefore secondary; such information was sought only when it touched the political or economic interests of their clients.

In truth, the transnational news agencies are not basically service organizations entrusted with serving the public interest, as are the government-financed national news agencies in the majority of African countries. They are profit-oriented, commercial enterprises and, while they do operate in regions that may yield inadequate returns on investment, losses must be made up by profitable ventures in other areas. Therefore, to the extent that the principle of free and balanced flow of information through adequate coverage of Third World countries does not fit into the commercial structure and profit ethic, it is relegated to a secondary position; that is, the present structure itself precludes international fair play.

To date, efforts to improve Third World coverage have been halfhearted at best. Agencies tend to send to developing countries young, inexperienced reporters who lack the background to perform satisfactorily. Because of costs, too, news organizations have few correspondents covering very large areas. The inevitable result is that reports sent from and about developing countries generally are episodic, perfunctory, and quite often out of context. Newspaper editors in the industrialized states contend that the average reader whose tastes and interests they consider in the selection of news shows no particular interest in foreign news from developing countries (about which a large part of the readership seems to be unaware). In fairness to these editors, it must be conceded that within the United States itself even national papers like the *New York Times* and the *Washington Post* pay as little attention to such "faraway" states as Idaho, Wyoming, or Montana as they do to exotic countries like Surinam and Burundi unless a particularly arresting event occurs therein. The point is that the neglect of news from certain areas is not so much a question of discrimination as of response to market forces in the light of consumer interests.

One can retort that readers will ask for information about events and places of which they have prior knowledge, and editors indeed have a responsibility to stimulate reader interest and to create awareness of issues in order to generate interest. The 1973 international oil crisis dramatically drew attention to the interdependence of the nations of the world, and regions once considered inconsequential now dominate the media. Similarly, the issue of pollution from toxic waste disposal demonstrates that people on the industrialized side of the Atlantic have to become sensitive to the welfare of those living along the nonindustrialized shores of that ocean. In brief, regardless of purely economic considerations there is a need for increased and regular flow of accurate and meaningful information among the peoples of the world.

Discussion about news gathering and distribution must look also at the role of the transnational news agencies in the horizontal flow of news among Third World countries. In spite of recognized deficiencies in this regard, their operations have helped over the years to reduce the isolation that otherwise would have persisted among developing countries within the same region. The national news agencies set up over the past two decades cover only domestic news because they lack the technical, financial, and personnel resources to set up offices abroad. To date only the Ghana News Agency among sub-Saharan services has correspondents outside the country (in Lagos, London, Nairobi, and New York). In general, information about neighboring countries thus has to come from the transnational services, and it may not be an exaggeration to assert that, all their deficiencies notwithstanding, if the transnational news agencies did not exist it might be necessary to invent them.

But this state of affairs has the effect of making people in the Third World see one another through the eyes of foreign reporters and editors whose viewpoints, value systems, and even prejudices often intrude in the reports. Many Western editors contend that in the absence of prior knowledge of, and interest in, foreign affairs on the part of their readers, only dramatic news about small, distant places qualifies for publication. The result is that press coverage of the Third World in the industrialized nations tends to be sensational and negative, emphasizing things that go wrong to the virtual exclusion of things that go right. The cumulative impression thereby created in the minds of readers, viewers, and listeners is one of near chaos in the Third World.

For example, the year 1979 saw the ousting of three of the most bloodthirsty leaders in Africa: Idi Amin Dada of Uganda, Nguema Macias of Equatorial Guinea, and Jean-Bedel Bokassa of the Central African Republic. These events had all the elements of drama and made good copy; the Western (and African) press devoted considerable space to a gory recapitulation of the fallen leaders' misdeeds. At the same time, however, two West African countries—Ghana and Nigeria—were preparing for elections for a return to representative civilian government after long spells of military rule; these positive developments received comparatively little attention in the media. I do not suggest that negative events in the Third World go unreported, but a proper balance must be maintained between positive and negative news.

NEWS VALUES AND CROSS-CULTURAL COMMUNICATION

The criticisms levelled against the transnational news agencies and the Western media in general by Third World communications scholars (and some Western scholars) have focused on the cross-cultural implications of news values and news selection. Whereas the Western definition of news tends to stress the bizarre or the incongruous—the "man bit dog" criterion of newsworthiness—Third World scholars prefer media emphasis on events that reflect how their peoples are trying to find solutions to enormous development problems. There may be nothing dramatic or sensational about the construction of health centers, schools, and bridges, but these efforts in social and economic development are being made in the face of great odds and deserve to be better publicized than tribal conflicts or abortive coups, which constitute an inordinately large portion of Western media offerings. In this regard, individual newspaper editors deserve much more blame than do news agencies. Editors are prone to select from the wire services dramatic, "hard" stories, which they sometimes distort in the interests of saving column space, rather than "soft" ones, which may deal with development efforts but do not sell newspapers. In trying to create a more accurate image of developing countries, therefore, the various gatekeepers have a much greater responsibility than they have been willing to shoulder so far.

A large number of newspaper editors in the developing countries are no better at selecting development related news than their counterparts in the industrialized nations. Their own training and the traditions they have inherited make them more likely to feature a story about the romantic adventures of a movie celebrity than one involving a grass-roots development effort that could give inspiration to the people. Though the transnational agencies do not supply this kind of development related news on a regular basis, the little they carry is used rather seldom. The news agencies should be encouraged to provide more of this type of news, but, equally important, Third World news editors themselves must learn to emphasize positive development news.

This new orientation, called development journalism (or developmental journalism), has been given diverse interpretations, so a definition may be useful. According to this approach, editors should endeavor to emphasize items that have a bearing on development efforts; development journalism does not mean exclusive concern with development issues that expose only positive and cohesive forces in society, precluding scrutiny of government activities. Government officials often give this interpretation. arguing that since popular mobilization and consensus are needed for development, newspaper editors should omit material critical of the government and hence possibly divisive. This view is to be rejected because in developing and industrialized countries alike the watchdog role of the press is essential in insuring the accountability of public officials. Abdication of this important press function can only help cover up government ineptitude and corruption, which foster instability and decelerate efforts toward development.

But despite the need to emphasize meaningful, development related news from Third World countries, the present structure of the international economic and trade system insures that the foreign pages of Third World newspapers will not be filled exclusively with news from that group of nations: the factors governing the selection of news include historical ties, economic and trade relations, and cultural affinities. Because of the economic dependence of the developing countries on the developed nations, events in the latter group tend to affect affairs in the former. For example, a lot of developing countries have more trade with industrialized states than they do with one another. It stands to reason, therefore, that events in developed countries that could affect local commodity prices and currencies should be reported in developing countries. In this sense a logical link is established between the call for a New International Information Order and the call for a New International Economic Order. When international trade begins to move horizontally rather than vertically, the flow of international news will also shift in the same direction.

GOVERNMENTS AND MEDIA

In an attempt to give a proper cultural perspective to news from the Third World, the transnational news agencies and individual media organizations have sometimes recruited local people as correspondents and stringers. This effort has been hampered in some cases by different perceptions of the role of media in society and by the relationship between government and media. A very crude distinction between First and Third World media systems rests on their different basis in free enterprise, on one hand, and state ownership and control, on the other.

This is only a rough distinction because the Western bloc is no more uniform in its media systems than is the Third World. For example, many Western governments are directly involved with the operation of the electronic media, but in the United States these are entirely in the hands of private corporations and the government has only regulatory power. Similarly, the Third World shows varying degrees of government control in both the print and electronic media; certain states have mixed systems in which government controlled media exist side by side with privately owned media.

These differences reflect philosophical and political perspectives that generate other divergences in the sociopolitical and economic spheres. And this is hardly surprising since a mass media or communication system reflects the political structure and ideological orientation of its society. However, it appears simplistic to depict the various media systems as different points on an authoritarian-libertarian continuum; a more useful distinction separates systems that treat the provision of information as a social service and those that treat it as a basically commercial venture in which social responsibility is subordinated to the logic of market forces.

Those who have been nurtured on the principle underlying the First Amendment to the U.S. Constitution ought to recognize that responding to a different set of historical, political, economic, and demographic circumstances, governments in many developing countries will continue to be involved with the operation of the mass media. The concept of the provision of information as a social service reinforces state involvement with the media; such involvement ranges from financial grants and subsidies to varying degrees of control. The point needs to be forcefully made that many developing countries would have virtually no media system if the government were not involved. As a French commentator observed, in many developing countries the question of the lack of press freedom is more a lack of press than a lack of freedom. In such a situation, the path of wisdom and realism leads to a recognition of the government's role in media operations and a search for means to minimize this control.

State ownership of mass media facilities need not mean total lack of freedom for the press. Considerable evidence shows that the acquisition of controlling shares in large newspapers by the military government in Nigeria did not in any appreciable way constrain the free expression of opinion through those papers. Yet, journalists in African countries are the first to recognize the extent to which excessive regulation limits their capacity to operate professionally in the national interest, and they are making gallant efforts to reduce government control. For example, there is a move to vest the supervisory powers over the press presently exercised by ministers of information and broadcasting in independent boards of trustees to insure that opposing views be given expression in the state financed media (Ghana now has such a provision).

As I noted previously, most developing countries need a certain amount of central control over the mass media if the media are to be used as tools for development. Many African countries are still striving for national integration and cohesion, which calls for the creation of national symbols. For this reason, a fragmented, freewheeling media system can easily degenerate into a force of disintegration and divisiveness. Moreover, mobilization for development depends on broad, comprehensive communication policies, which can best be formulated within a governmental framework.

To the extent that the achievement of an adequate, free, and balanced flow of information among countries with different political and media systems is possible only if there is a desire for coexistence and cooperation among those directly operating the media, the various philosophical options must be appreciated. As long as Westerners look on the Third World media as nothing more than weapons in the arsenals of authoritarian governments, such cooperation cannot come about. In the case of national news agencies, for example, there is really no alternative to government financing. Most African countries have an average of two national dailies, a single radio station, and fewer than half a dozen weeklies or other periodicals. The clientele for such a national news agency is thus extremely limited, and without government financing, the agency cannot generate enough revenue to pay even a skeleton staff. The issue, then, is not to write off Third World solutions but to understand the realities of developing countries and to help their media work in accordance with the highest professional standards and in conformity with national needs and international obligations.

NATIONAL NEWS AGENCIES AND CREDIBILITY

The transnational news services that have news exchange agreements with agencies in Third World countries have expressed skepticism about the reliability of reports from government financed and controlled news agencies. Some even consider the national news services as mere appendages of the ministries of information. While this charge may be true in certain cases, in a lot of developing countries media and government are quite separate. On the other hand, in some places where the operations are distinct, the national news agencies have not established a record of independence, reliability, and freedom of action vis-à-vis the political executive. Yet Westerners who dismiss the credibility of African national news agencies solely on the argument that they are government financed should recall that the Agence France-Presse enjoys considerable government support and that the British government is not altogether detached from the operations of Reuters. Indeed, various Western media organizations receive government subsidies without arousing suspicion that the subsidies by themselves exert undue influence on those operating the media.

But when all this is said, governments in the developing countries ought to recognize that their own policies have contributed in no small measure to the lack of credibility among Third World media. Because of the excessive controls and the poor record of media independence in most

Third World countries, foreign news agencies and media organizations are disinclined to cooperate with local services. Therefore, Third World countries must insure the independence of their mass media, which in turn will protect professional standards, attract high caliber people, and facilitate access to sources of information for both local and foreign correspondents.

The question of credibility is fundamental to solving the problem of imbalance in the flow of news both between developed and developing countries and among developing countries. As long as some Third World countries have reason to suspect that reports filed by national news agencies to the Non-Aligned News Agencies Pool, based in Belgrade, lack objectivity, they will not use them. The planned PanAfrican News Agency, to be headquartered in Dakar, also will have to address this issue.

Some Westerners have expressed the fear that Third World efforts to create news agency pools will eventually mean the exclusion of Western correspondents from developing countries. This fear is based on certain statements made by some Third World government officials. Enlightened opinion in the Third World, however, inclines toward cooperation and healthy competition rather than toward confrontation and exclusion. The multiplicity of sources can only foster balance and comprehension, and any effort to exclude reporters of one region of the world from another will be a retrograde step that will subvert rather than enhance the objective of insuring a more balanced flow of news.

CONCLUSION

Debate over a more equitable distribution of information among the nations of the world has not yet achieved spectacular results, but it certainly has focused attention on world communication problems and stimulated fresh thinking on this subject. Directors of transnational news agencies who yesterday complacently believed that they were doing their best now openly admit weaknesses in their operations and show some willingness to improve their performance. Third World leaders who complained about existing affairs without taking concrete measures to redress the situation now are willing to commit the necessary resources to establish regional organs to complement and compete with transnational agencies.

But beyond the demonstration of goodwill, there is also a need for basic change in attitudes on both sides. Western media organizations ought to recognize that it is time to dig deeper in order to present a fairer and more balanced picture of events in developing countries. While maladministration and corruption may account for some of the economic difficulties of developing countries, an incomplete and distorted picture is given, for example, when the fundamental weakness in the economy—resulting from commodity price fixing in the industrialized nations—is not taken into account. On the other hand, Third World leaders ought to recognize that as long as they constrain both local and foreign correspondents from operating freely, incomplete and skewed accounts of Third World development efforts will reach the local people as well as the outside world.

In a world operating according to different political, economic, cultural, and philosophical systems, mass media organization and functions will necessarily vary greatly from nation to nation. However, the absence of uniformity does not preclude peaceful coexistence and cooperation among the different systems.

Twelve

The Many Worlds of the World's Press[1]

George Gerbner and George Márványi

Distinctive standards of reporting reflect conditions of industrial investment (including the manufacture of news), national security, and popular support. Studies of newsroom decision making around the world (see 1) illustrate various aspects of newsroom climate resting on the real or assumed interests (or actual interventions) of publishers, stockholders, advertisers, parties, and other private or public organizations that set the terms of employment.

When the subject is foreign news, the process is even more variable; there is no effective reality check. Many different versions of the day's "world news" can be equally true and significant when judged by different standards of relevance.

This is the report of a multinational comparative study of foreign news coverage designed to explore the similarities and differences in the images of the "outside world" that each type of society projects for its members. The study included 60 daily papers published in nine countries of the capitalist, socialist and developing worlds. The countries were the United States, Great Britain, the Federal Republic of Germany (West Germany), the Soviet Union, Hungary, Czechoslovakia, Ghana, India, and the Philippines. A total of 5,866 pages and 11,437 separate foreign news items were analyzed to probe dimensions of coverage affecting different societies' views of each other and of the rest of the world.

After a discussion of the development, questions, and conduct of the study, the findings will be summarized in two parts. First, we shall discuss the amounts of foreign news coverage in the different press systems. Second, we shall describe and illustrate the distribution of news-event locations around the world, leading to some conclusions about the "worlds" of the U.S., Western and Eastern European, Soviet, and non-aligned press systems.

THE STUDY

The Sample

We decided to focus the analysis on one week's foreign news at a time when the IndoChina war still commanded major press attention in order to provide a benchmark for later trend studies. We picked the week of May 24, 1970. There were elections in Ceylon, riots in Paris, and runoffs for the world soccer championships in Mexico. Israeli aircraft raided Lebanon, U.S. troops advanced into Cambodia, bombing and fighting raged in Vietnam. NATO ministers met in Rome, Arab leaders met in Khartum, and the Komsomol Congress met in Moscow. Sudan nationalized some industries and the Queen of England dissolved Parliament in preparation for new elections. These and hundreds of minor stories made up the news of the world of that week. If it was "unique" (and which week isn't?), it fits the typical categories into which each country dips for its own news.

The newspaper samples were drawn to include various types of papers and to approximate a cross-section of news readerships. This required the selection of both elite and popular organs and of both mass-circulation and small newspapers. It was decided to divide the press of each country into five circulation classes and to select the largest circulation paper in each class. In those circulation categories in which a generally recognized elite newspaper was found, that paper was selected. Newspapers were chosen from as many different regions within the country as possible. Furthermore, when a circulation class in a country represented a much larger proportion of all newspapers than the same class in another country, more than one paper was selected from the latter class in order to give it greater weight in the total sample.

The characteristics of the samples reflect the relative circulations and sizes of the different newspapers. The United States press sample included two "elite" dailies of national circulation, the New York *Times* and the *Christian Science Monitor*. In the "popular" category of large circulation it also included the New York *Daily News*, and the medium circulation, San Francisco *Chronicle*. Three newspapers of relatively low circulation (under 50,000) were included to represent the small local newspaper, and to provide additional geographic coverage. A total of nine U.S. newspapers of a combined circulation of almost 4 million copies and over 2,000 pages were analyzed.

The British sample included the London *Times* and *Daily Telegraph* as "elite" papers. The giant *Daily Mirror* was the "popular" daily, and other smaller papers represented other circulation and regional categories. The large circulation of national dailies brought the total British sample to over 8 million copies with only 900 pages.

The West German sample included the "elite" *Frankfurter Allgemeine* and *Die Welt*, the "popular" *Bild Zeitung*, and three other smaller circulation regional papers. The combined circulation of the sample was almost 5.5 million, and its size was 924 pages.

The Soviet press sample included *Pravda* as the "elite" daily, three other papers published in Moscow, and four regional dailies. The combined circulation was nearly 14 million, but the size of the sample was 156 pages.

The Hungarian and Czechoslovakian samples each included ten papers in the respective categories, amounting to a combined circulation of less than 2 million with a total of over 50 pages each.

The non-aligned Third World was represented by three papers each in Ghana, India, and the Philippines, each including one "elite" daily, and all printed in English. Their combined circulation was over 11 million; the size of the sample was 60 pages.

We defined news as non-advertising printed matter (text, picture, or tabular information) except editorials, cartoons and comic strips, book reviews, indices and tables of contents, and Sunday magazine sections or other special supplements not part of the general weekday format of the newspaper.

The world, meaning the outside world, was defined as any territory outside of the geographical boundaries of the country in which the newspaper is published. Colonies or protectorates of the home country were to be considered foreign for purposes of our study.

The Definition of News

The general rule for the identification of a foreign news story was that the bulk of the information contained in the story had to come from abroad. Therefore, stories originating abroad (e.g., having a foreign dateline) were to be considered foreign news even if the subject matter involved domestic affairs. Second, when most of the information came from abroad or the story dealt mostly with foreign matter, or both, it was to be considered foreign news, even if it had a domestic dateline. Third, a story about foreign visitors was always to be considered foreign news. News originating in or written about international zones and their affairs (the U.N. in New York, Geneva, etc.; Berlin, East or West) was to be considered foreign in all papers.

The unit of analysis was the foreign news story or item, which we defined as a substantively and typographically distinct unit of relevant printed matter. Several items sharing the same headline were considered separate items if they were substantively and typographically distinct. Each item was to be marked, measured, and coded separately, except that a block of tabular information from abroad printed without other text, such as financial, weather, or sports statistics, was to be considered a single item.

Two coding forms were developed: one for a given issue of a newspaper *in toto*, and another for each item of foreign news within each issue. A core group of four researchers worked with two issues from each sample to compile a master list of foreign items and to develop examples of completed forms for coder training purposes.

Coders were first trained on materials which were not in the sample, then tested on the issues coded by the core group. Coders were not permitted to code newspapers on their own until they demonstrated a high degree of reliability with the core group on the materials they had coded for testing purposes. The coders worked independently on each stage. They were randomly assigned to a given stage of a given paper.

The analysis of the material was conducted simultaneously in Philadelphia and in Budapest following the procedure worked out jointly in advance. The U.S., Western European, and non-aligned press samples were analyzed in Philadelphia while the Soviet and Eastern European samples were analyzed in Budapest. Sample analyses were exchanged and recoded to improve coder reliability.

THE AMOUNT OF FOREIGN NEWS COVERAGE

The amount of attention newspapers devote to foreign news (or to anything else) depends on their physical characteristics and their policies. The United States press ranked first on the average *length* of foreign news items. As Table 12.1 shows, Western European papers carried nearly twice as many foreign news items *per day* as U.S. papers, with Eastern European papers second and the non-aligned press third. The press of Western Europe also led in the absolute amount of space per day, with non-aligned newspapers second and U.S. dailies third. In average length of foreign news items, U.S. newspapers were followed by non-aligned and Western European papers.

Large papers have more space, but much of that is devoted to advertising and other non-news features (which is why they are large in the first place). Nearly 60 percent of U.S. newspaper space, and over 40 percent of Western European newspaper space was devoted to advertising matter. Ads occupied only 15 percent of Eastern European and 2 percent of Soviet newspaper space. The average amount of non-advertising space per issue in U.S. newspapers was one-quarter larger than in Western Europe, twice as much as in the non-aligned countries, and almost four times as much as in Eastern Europe and in the Soviet Union.

The amount of foreign coverage can thus be measured in two ways. One is the absolute number of items and square inches of space devoted to foreign news. These measures are strongly influenced by physical char-

Table 12.1 Ranks (R) and Measures (M) of Foreign News Coverage

	United States		Western Europe		Soviet Union		Eastern Europe		Non-Aligned	
	R[a]	M	R	M	R	M	R	M	R	M
Number of foreign news items per newspaper per day	4	25.1	1	49.8	5	19.4	2	39.7	3	30.8
Square inches of foreign news space per newspaper per day	3	518	1	857	5	206	4	321	2	535
Square inches of foreign news space per item	1	20.7	3	17.2	4	10.6	5	8.1	2	17.4
Number of foreign news items per page	5	0.6	4	1.8	1.5	4.6	1.5	4.6	3	2.2
Square inches of foreign news per page	5	12.6	4	32.4	1	48.9	3	36.9	2	37.5
Foreign news space as percent of all nonadvertising space	5	11.1	2	23.6	4	16.5	1	24.7	3	22.8

[a] Items are ranked across rows.

acteristics. The other is the relative amount of available space or percent of the "news hole" devoted to foreign news. That is more a matter of editorial choice.

In absolute terms, the U.S. press used almost as much newsprint per issue as the other eight countries combined. While the U.S. dailies averaged 41 (mostly large-sized) pages per issue, those of Western Europe averaged 26, the non-aligned countries 14, Eastern European papers 9, and Soviet dailies 4.

Relative allocations, however, present a different picture. As Table 12.1 shows, Soviet and Eastern European papers led in the number of foreign news *items per page*. The Soviet press was also first in the amount of *space per page* devoted to foreign news, with non-aligned papers second and Eastern European dailies a close third. Eastern European newspapers devoted the largest *percentage of non-advertising space* to foreign news, with the press of Western Europe second, of non-aligned countries third, and of the U.S.S.R. fourth. The U.S. newspaper sample ranked last on all relative measures.

The U.S. press, then, ranked low in comparison with the other areas on relative measures of attention to the outside world, reflecting low priority of editorial attention. The press of Western Europe led in absolute numbers of items and amounts of space, and the daily papers of the Socialist countries led in the proportion of available space devoted to foreign news. The non-aligned countries came in second and third on all measures.

Taking the percentage allocation of non-advertising space as perhaps the most sensitive measure of editorial policy, we find that the leader is the German paper appropriately named *Die Welt*; it devoted 43.7 percent of its total non-advertising space to foreign news. Five other papers gave more than 30 percent: the Soviet *Pravda* (38.0 percent), the Hungarian *Magyar Nemzet* (37.6 percent), *Nepszábadság* (36.0 percent), and *Magyar Hirlap* (35.6 percent), and the Czechoslovakian *Lud* (30.1 percent). Another 16 dailies, including the *Christian Science Monitor* (28.7 percent), gave more than 25 percent, but no other U.S., British, or Soviet paper did. The New York *Times* used 16.4 percent of its non-advertising space for foreign news, the London *Times* 22.4 percent.

Less than 10 percent of available news space was devoted to foreign news by one Philippine, two Soviet, one British, and six U.S. daily papers. "Elite" papers gave generally more attention to foreign news than did the "popular" press.

An interesting comparison is made possible by the fact that six papers of our sample were also included in Jacques Kayser's study (2) of the news in 1951. Table 12.2 shows that three of the six papers devoted about the same percentages to foreign news in 1951 as in 1970, and that the rank order of the six papers shifted only because the *Times of India* nearly doubled its foreign coverage, perhaps as a result of independence.

Table 12.2   Foreign News Content as a Percentage of Total News Space in
1951 and 1970

	1951 %	1970 %
New York *Times*	16	16
New York *Daily News*	2	7
London *Times*	25	22
Pravda	30	38
Rude Pravo	25	29
Times of India	14	25

In general, there is an inverse relationship between commercial sponsorship (and the consequent demand for sales and localized news service) and foreign news coverage. On the whole, the publicly owned or institutionally managed press assigns higher priority to the outside world than does the strictly commercial press.

DIFFERENTIAL ATTENTION TO GEOGRAPHICAL AREAS

To make the description of the global play of attention manageable, we divided the world into 15 regions on the basis of a combination of geographical, political, and current affairs considerations. The regions are: (1) Western Europe, (2) Eastern Europe, (3) the Soviet Union, (4) the Mideast, (5) Israel, (6) North Africa, (7) Central Africa, (8) South Africa, (9) North Vietnam, (10) South Vietnam, (11) Eastern Socialist countries (China, Mongolia, North Korea), (12) South Asia and the Far East (including Burma, Cambodia, India, Indonesia, Japan, South Korea, Taiwan), (13) Australia and Oceania, (14) Latin America, and (15) North America.

Figure 12.1 illustrates the many worlds of the world's press. The first map shows the world simplified into these regions, and the others show the "worlds" of the five press systems scaled to the percentage of representation of each region in each press system.

Starting from the necessarily arbitrary assumption that each region has equal chance of newsworthiness, we first equalized the size of all regions, and then reduced each to the percentage of the equalized size that corresponds to its percentage representation in each press system (indicated on the map of each region).

Looking at the world of U.S. newspapers, we can see that foreign news events happening in Western Europe, South Asia and the Far East, North America, and the Middle East (including Israel) make up two-thirds of the U.S. foreign news map of the world. The war in Vietnam made that small region loom larger than all of Africa and China combined. The Mideast and Israel attracted more attention than the Soviet Union plus Eastern Europe.

In the world of British and West German newspapers ("Western Europe"), events in Western Europe, Latin America, and North America (in that order) occupied nearly two-thirds of all attention. These Western European papers paid less attention to Israel and to Vietnam than did the U.S., but more attention to Eastern Europe and Latin America.

Eastern European papers gave as much news to events about their own region as Western European ones did to theirs, but much more to Western Europe than vice versa. Otherwise, Eastern European press allocations followed fairly closely those of Western Europe. However, Eastern Europe devoted less attention to events in the Soviet Union than did any other press system, including that of the United States. Even Africa got more play in the press of Eastern Europe than did the Soviet Union.

The Soviet press, on the other hand, ranked Eastern Europe first and North America second (the highest rank of attention devoted to North America of all the press systems). Western Europe ranked third in the Soviet press. The three regions accounted for two-thirds of Soviet press attention to the outside world. (Yet neither the U.S. nor the Western European press paid much attention to the Soviet Union.) The percentage of Soviet attention to Israel or South Vietnam or South Asia and the Far East was about half of that devoted to these regions by the U.S. press.

The world of the Third World newspapers was the only one in which the Soviet Union loomed large, in fact the largest among all regions. Next were South Asia and the Far East, Western Europe, North America, and Latin America, in that order, together making up two-thirds of the world of the non-aligned press. In that world, the Mideast ranked lower and Central Africa ranked higher than in any of the others.

What can we conclude from these findings? Readers of all press systems know most about Western Europe. For U.S. readers, non-communist Asia and the Mideast are next. The relative blind spot of the U.S. press is Latin America, at least in comparison with the other press systems.

The Western newspapers studied have little interest in the Socialist countries. News of the Soviet Union is also kept out of the press of Eastern Europe, but gets top play in newspapers of the Third World. Soviet readers get more news about the U.S. and Western and Eastern Europe than readers of those areas get about the Soviets. The regions of Africa, Australia and Oceania, and the Eastern Socialist countries of China, Mongolia, and North Korea were barely visible in the world's press of 1970.

This study suggests some dimensions underlying the present state of communications between different social systems. Our findings indicate where the process of reciprocal information may be out of joint. But our "snapshot" of the global flow of foreign news can only serve as a starting

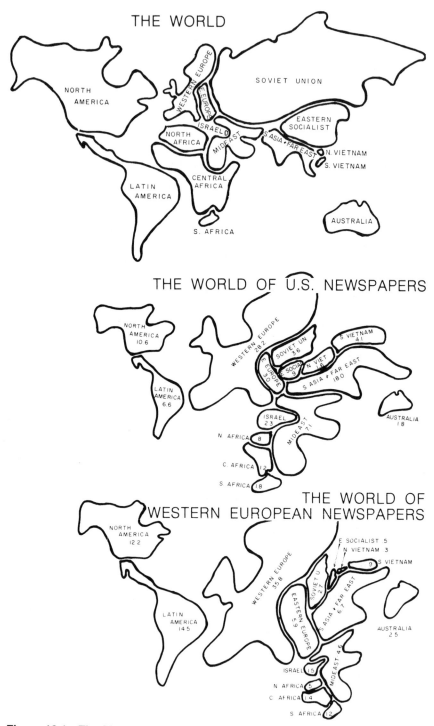

THE WORLD

THE WORLD OF U.S. NEWSPAPERS

THE WORLD OF
WESTERN EUROPEAN NEWSPAPERS

Figure 12.1 The Many Worlds of the World's Press.

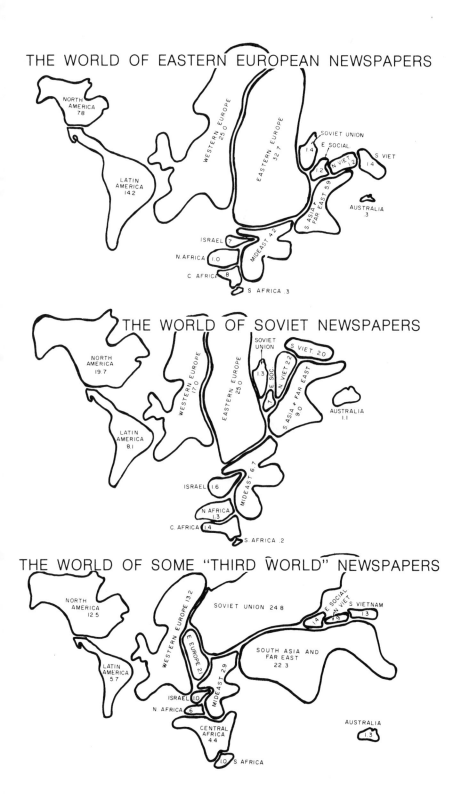

THE WORLD OF EASTERN EUROPEAN NEWSPAPERS

NORTH AMERICA 78

WESTERN EUROPE 25.0

EASTERN EUROPE 32.7

SOVIET UNION 1.4

E SOCIAL

N VIET .2

S VIET 1.4

S ASIA + FAR EAST 5.9

AUSTRALIA .3

LATIN AMERICA 14.2

ISRAEL .7

N. AFRICA 1.0

MIDEAST 4.2

C. AFRICA .8

S. AFRICA .3

THE WORLD OF SOVIET NEWSPAPERS

SOVIET UNION

S VIET 2.0

NORTH AMERICA 19.7

WESTERN EUROPE 17.0

EASTERN EUROPE 25.0

1.3

E SOC

N VIET 2.2

S ASIA + FAR EAST 9.0

.7

AUSTRALIA 1.1

LATIN AMERICA 8.1

ISRAEL 1.6

MIDEAST 6.7

N AFRICA 1.3

C. AFRICA 1.4

S. AFRICA .2

THE WORLD OF SOME "THIRD WORLD" NEWSPAPERS

NORTH AMERICA 12.5

WESTERN EUROPE 13.2

SOVIET UNION 24.8

E SOCIAL

N VIET

S VIETNAM

1.4

.3

1.3

E EUROPE 2.1

SOUTH ASIA AND FAR EAST 22.3

LATIN AMERICA 5.7

ISRAEL 1.0

MIDEAST 2.9

N AFRICA .6

CENTRAL AFRICA 4.4

AUSTRALIA 1.3

1.0 S AFRICA

point for comparative analysis. Certainly the end of the war in Southeast Asia, and the relative rise in prominence of other areas, may have altered the distribution of news attention. More comprehensive and reliable insight into the "many worlds of the world's press" will come from indicators of trends over time and of the conceptions they cultivate in the minds of readers around the world.

NOTES

1. Research assistance was provided by Robert Adels, Virginia Eaton, Doug Goldschmidt, Adrian Guidotti, Terry Hustedt, Tim McInerny, Walter Lupan, Robin Niemann, Willard Rowland, and Marjory Vandenburgh. The authors gratefully acknowledge the grant of the International Research and Exchanges Board of New York and the support of their home institutions that made the study possible.

REFERENCES

1. Gerbner, George and George Márványi. "A Bibliography of Studies on World News Flow across National Boundaries." *Journal of Communication* 27(1), Winter 1977, pp. 61–66.

2. Kayser, Jacques. *One-Week's News: Comparative Study of 17 Major Dailies for a Seven-Day Period*. Paris: UNESCO, 1953.

Thirteen

U.S. Television
Coverage of Foreign News

James F. Larson

In the United States, the trend toward greater public reliance on television as a source of international news has been convincingly documented in surveys sponsored by the television and newspaper industries (16, 19). Television is now the most widely used and credible source of international news for a majority of Americans. A similar trend may occur in numerous other countries with media systems modeled after the Anglo-American pattern (21). The available evidence already shows that television news systems around the world depend largely on the same wire services and newsfilm agencies and have adopted the same Western formats for presentation of news (11, 12, 24).

This chapter reviews a study of international news coverage on U.S. network television evening news broadcasts during the 1970s; particular attention is paid to coverage of Third World countries. I present major findings from a study of the 1972–1976 period (13) and identify related areas of inquiry to be dealt with in an expansion of my earlier study. The theoretical basis of this research was an expanded version of the chain of news communication, first presented by Johan Galtung and Marie Ruge (8).

The chapter is organized according to the three basic approaches taken in most research on television news (1). Content research establishes the extent of international news coverage on television and explores its various dimensions. Production research examines factors that influence the selection and shaping of newscast content. Finally, effects research looks at the impact of television news in such areas as politics, economics, and culture. All three of these approaches bear on the general question of how well television conveys international news and on the more particular concern over news from the Third World.

CONTENT RESEARCH

Content analysis is central to research on the international flow of news: it can identify both independent variables for effects research and dependent variables for production research (1). Properly used, content analysis is a procedure for textual coding; used by itself, this method of inquiry is inadequate (14).

Using content analysis of U.S. network television news on international events, 1972 through 1976, I looked for stable, long-term patterns in coverage, avoiding possible distortions caused by saturation events that might fill evening news broadcasts for relatively short periods (7). My definition of international news was very broad: any news story, regardless of its thematic content or dateline, that mentioned a country other than the United States was considered an international story. Such a definition is unambiguous and includes any news item that might be considered international by other possible definitions; furthermore, it produces an only slightly inflated measure of the total amount of international news when compared with other possible definitions.

After formally testing the reliability of the *Television News Index and Abstracts* (23) as a measure of international news coverage, I coded content data from that source for a random sample of approximately 13 percent of the weekday evening news broadcasts during the 1972–1976 period for each of the three U.S. networks, ABC, CBS, and NBC.

The individual news story was the basic unit of analysis. On network television the news story takes one of the following forms: the studio report, read from a New York, Washington, Chicago, or London studio by the anchor correspondent and accompanied by projections of maps, pictures, or drawings; the domestic film report, which is videotaped or filmed in Washington, D.C., New York, or another U.S. location; and the foreign film report, which is videotaped or filmed overseas, usually by a network correspondent.

I coded stories into nine thematic categories, divided into crisis and noncrisis themes. Crisis themes were unrest and dissent; war, terrorism, crime; coups and assassinations; and disasters. Noncrisis themes were politics-military; economics; environment; technology-science; and human interest. Subsequently I compared coverage of developed countries with Third World coverage by using the quantitative data on international news coverage, broken down according to story type and the categories of countries mentioned in the sampled stories. I followed the United Nations (22) classification of countries and territories: developed market economies numbered 31; developing market economies, 169; and centrally planned economies, 12. Stories mentioning only one or more of the twelve centrally planned economies were excluded from the comparisons. Finally, since network comparisons (13) showed relative extent of coverage by country

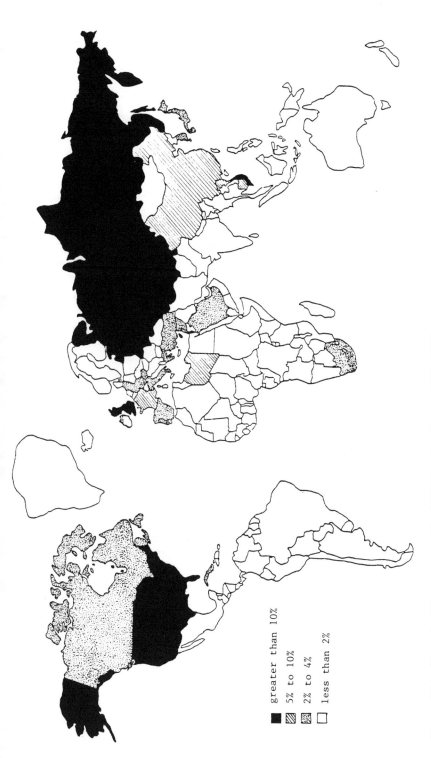

Figure 13.1   Extent of Coverage on the CBS Evening News, 1972–1976, as Indicated by Percent of Sampled Stories in Which Countries Are Mentioned.

greater than 10%

5% to 10%

2% to 4%

less than 2%

to be highly correlated during the 1972–1976 period, I based my analysis of international coverage on data for a single network, CBS.

The major findings showed that overall, Third World countries received less coverage than did developed nations (see Figure 13.1). Developed nations received more coverage both overall and within each major story type, as indicated by the mean number of mentions per country or territory.

Coverage of Third World countries contained a higher proportion of crisis stories than did coverage of developed nations. A crosstabulation of story type by categories of countries mentioned showed that the proportion of crisis stories was highest in stories that mentioned only Third World countries and generally lowest in stories that mentioned only developed countries. Of the three major story types, foreign film reports had the highest proportion of crisis themes, reflecting television's attraction to visually exciting material. Seventy-four percent of all such reports that mentioned only Third World countries concerned crises.

Third World countries appeared most often in news stories that mentioned the United States or other developed countries. Twelve percent of the sampled stories mentioned only countries from the Third World, as compared with 50 percent that mentioned both developed and developing countries. The developed nation most often mentioned in connection with Third World countries was the United States. (See Table 13.1.)

Third World countries appeared relatively less often than did developed nations in news stories that mentioned only one country. This finding suggests that stories mentioning only a single country are likely to concern news from that country in its own right, apart from international involvements and the center-periphery arrangement of the international power structure.

Table 13.1   CBS Television News Stories by Categories of Countries Mentioned, 1972–1976 (excluding centrally planned economies)

Countries Mentioned	N	%
Only developing	123	12
Developing and developed (not including U.S.)	88	9
Only developed (not including U.S.)	193	19
Only U.S. and developing	293	29
Only U.S. and other developed	184	18
U.S., other developed, and developing	117	12
Total	998	99[a]

[a] Rounding error

Visual Dimensions of International News

These findings were based entirely on data gathered from the *Television News Index and Abstracts* (23). Analysis of videotaped news broadcasts would add several dimensions to the study. In general, the visual images on network television news may be approached from three perspectives: first, those that are determined by event factors; second, those that result from production factors; and third, the interaction between visual images and the audio portion of newscasts (2).

Event factors in the visual image are not under the control of the television networks. Coverage of the Iran hostage crisis during the early months of 1980 provides numerous examples: one such example would be visual elements of the carefully prepared visits to the hostages by American clergy.

Production factors contributing to the visual image include such elements as closeups, longshots, camera angles, editing, and juxtaposition (2). Also important are the repetitive visual symbols chosen to accompany studio reports, which comprise about half of the international news stories broadcast by U.S. networks on a typical evening (13). Maps, still photos, and artists' sketches may be as consequential for the image of certain countries as is film or videotape.

Prior research has suggested that the relationship between the visual and audio portions of the television message may be crucial to understanding its impact. For example, non-voice-over film is generally thought to be more realistic, immediate, and vivid than is voice-over film (2).

In summary, empirical data on the visual dimensions of international news on the U.S. networks will allow a more complete comparison of the coverage given to Third World and developed nations. Event factors, production factors, and the relationship between audio and visual portions of the televised message all deserve attention in such a comparison.

Comparative Content Research

Comparative research designs may be used to address both the general questions regarding television as an international news medium and the particular concern over coverage of Third World nations. Cross-media comparisons and cross-national comparisons of coverage by the same medium are two major forms of comparative research.

A comparison of television with newspapers, radio, or news magazines can shed light on the limitations and strengths of televised coverage of international affairs. Since obtaining extramedia data (17, 18) is generally acknowledged to be difficult, comparison of television with a paper like the *New York Times* or with a wire service file (20) would partly indicate the universe of events not covered on the evening news.

Cross-national comparisons of television may provide empirical evidence for, and elaboration of, the thesis that media systems throughout the world tend to follow the Anglo-American pattern of development (12, 21). The comparison of how television news systems in different countries cover the same event is a particularly valuable technique. Despite the dependence of most television news systems on the same wire services and newsfilm agencies, there is considerable variation in their use of material from such sources to describe the same event (24). In the past, such comparative research focused on the print media (20). Today, with improved technology and the establishment of scholarly and historical archives, television news is more accessible to researchers.

PRODUCTION RESEARCH

Production research, as the term is used here, encompasses all possible influences on the shaping and selection of news content. Since Edward Epstein's (6) book on network television news, the organizational approach to the study of televised news has been widely accepted. However, for the study of international news, theoretically based research has been much broader in scope. Such factors as population, international trade, level of development, physical or psychological distance, technology, telecommunications traffic, and cultural affinity have all been suggested as influences on the international flow of news (4, 8, 10, 15, 18). In an earlier study (13) I examined the technical structure (9) of the international television news system, looking at such factors as communication channels and correspondent locations; elements of this structure have long been considered an influence, at least potentially, on the international flow of news. Indeed, in 1970 government experts on space communication, meeting under UNESCO auspices in Paris, recommended that communication satellites be developed in such a way as to encourage a more balanced flow of visual news in the world, "particularly with regard to providing news coverage to and from, as well as between, developing areas" (3).

All of the U.S. television networks rely on the same basic news organizations and methods for their international news coverage. They use satellite communication channels on a regular basis and often pool their transmissions through such channels. All three networks maintain overseas bureaus in the "major news centers" of the world. In addition, all rely on the same newspapers and wire services for the bulk of their nonvisual news from overseas. Since the news processes and international news coverage from the three U.S. networks are so similar, I focused the analysis on the *CBS Evening News.*

Foreign film reports and studio reports served as the dependent variables. Both dependent variables were expressed in terms of the number of film or studio reports during 1972–1976 for each country or territory. However, I quantified the reports differently. Foreign film reports were those that originated or were filmed in any country or territory of the world outside the United States, regardless of the countries or territories mentioned in the report. Studio reports, on the other hand, were those that mentioned any country or territory. I hypothesized that the amount of coverage given any country or territory would increase in proportion to the presence of one or more of the following four news systems in the country under analysis.

1. Newspaper or world news service. The major Western news agencies— AP, UPI, Reuters, and AFP—as well as the major newspaper services, such as the *New York Times* and the *Washington Post-Los Angeles Times* services, maintained a presence in fifty-four countries during the 1972–1976 period.
2. CBS bureau. From 1972 to 1976, CBS maintained news bureaus in thirteen countries. I included the Saigon bureau, which closed in mid-1975, in the analysis.
3. National news agency. Ninety sovereign countries and four territories had their own national news agencies during the five-year period under consideration.
4. INTELSAT earth station. Forty-one countries possessed INTELSAT earth stations during the entire five-year period; an additional thirty-nine countries or territories established earth stations during this period.

The remaining countries and territories had no earth stations. I used these four parts of the international news system as independent variables. All of the independent variables were categorical. The first three were dichotomous; the fourth, dealing with INTELSAT earth stations, was a continuous variable indicating the length of time that each country or territory had had an earth station. The INTELSAT variable, expressed in years, had a value from zero to five.

The major findings (see 13) showed that the presence of components of the international news system did relate to the level of coverage of a given country. Tests for differences in mean levels of news coverage showed that countries with national or international news agencies, CBS bureaus, or INTELSAT earth stations had a greater number of both studio reports and foreign film reports. All differences were statistically significant at the .01 level.

Growth in the INTELSAT global system between 1972 and 1976 was accompanied by increased foreign film coverage for two categories of countries: those that possessed INTELSAT earth stations for the entire five-year period and those that acquired earth stations during the period.

Table 13.2   Kendall Partial Rank-Order Correlation Coefficients for News System Organizations with the Number of CBS News Studio Reports from 1972–1976

	Correlation of the Number of CBS News Studio Reports with:			
	National News Agency	International Newspaper- Wire s.	CBS Bureau	INTELSAT Earth Station
Zero-order correlation:	.43	.55	.33	.39
Controlling for:				
National news agency	—	.45	.27	.30
International newspaper- wire service	.26	—	.12	.16
CBS bureau	.41	.48	—	.34
INTELSAT earth station	.36	.45	.24	—

Growth of the INTELSAT system during the same period was accompanied by increased studio report coverage for countries that acquired earth stations during 1972–1976. Such coverage remained stable for countries that either possessed earth stations or did not have them for the entire period. Partial rank-order correlations indicated that the presence of international newspaper and wire correspondents was relatively more powerful in predicting international news coverage than were the other three independent variables (see Tables 13.2 and 13.3).

Table 13.3   Kendall Partial Rank-Order Correlation Coefficients for News System Organizations with the Number of CBS News Foreign Film Reports from 1972–1976

	Correlation of the Number of CBS News Foreign Film Reports with:			
	National News Agency	International Newspaper- Wire s.	CBS Bureau	INTELSAT Earth Station
Zero-order correlation:	.37	.52	.45	.40
Controlling for:				
National news agency	—	.43	.41	.33
International newspaper- wire service	.19	—	.29	.19
CBS bureau	.32	.50	—	.31
INTELSAT earth station	.29	.40	.37	—

While the spread of satellite technology was associated with an increase in both studio reports and foreign film coverage on the *CBS Evening News*, the data did not allow an unequivocal inference that the technology caused the increased coverage. It may be that satellite earth stations are a necessary but not a sufficient condition for the flow of news. In any event, the partial correlation analysis demonstrated clearly that the presence of correspondents for major news agencies or elite newspapers was relatively the most important influence on the flow of international news through U.S. network television.

EFFECTS RESEARCH

Despite a generally heavy emphasis on effects research by mass communication scholars, there have been very few empirical studies of the effects of international news coverage. Possible effects would cover such areas as politics, culture, and economics. Of these, concern over the political impact of television news is most pronounced. Therefore, I limit the following discussion to that category of effects.

Concern over the political impact of televised news from the Third World may be found both within and outside the United States. Following Bernard Cohen's (5) landmark study of the press and foreign policy, we can ask several questions. What are the consequences of television for the foreign policymaking environment, of the way that network television defines and performs its job, and of the way that TV output is assimilated by the participants in the process? Network television coverage of Iran during the early months of 1980 provides an excellent case in point. Within the United States many questioned the political impact of such coverage on the president and other key figures in the foreign policy process, particularly in a presidential election year. Outside the United States such questions were not lost on Iran's leadership.

Coverage of the Iran crisis during the early months of 1980 raised a number of important issues concerning televised reports on the Third World, echoing the long-standing concern of developing nations over the structure and flow of international news. From that perspective, there has been a lack of balance in the flow of news and certain kinds of distortion over many years.

The present trend is toward greater involvement of television reporters and organizations in public diplomacy. The implications of this trend, both for television news gathering and for the process of diplomacy, deserve further attention. Content analysis, by suggesting independent variables for effects research, may help to illuminate the role of television in diplomacy. For example, certain elements of content, such as interviews with government officials, may be taken as indicators of a diplomatic role for the television journalist. Using such indicators, longitudinal studies of content can trace changes in the role of television news. Likewise, impact studies may point up the need for further content analysis (1).

In summary, content research, production research, and effects research all contribute to a better understanding of how television conveys news from the Third World.

Analysis of U.S. network television evening news content in the 1970s indicated that more news flows to the United States from developed than from developing nations and that proportionately more news from the Third World deals with crises. The global distribution of news agency and newspaper correspondents, INTELSAT earth stations, network bureaus, and national news agencies is reflected in the amount of news coverage given other countries on the network evening news. Of these factors, the presence of news agency and newspaper correspondents is relatively most important. Future research on the effects of televised international news should help us understand its influence on foreign policymaking and diplomacy.

REFERENCES

1. Adams, William C. "Network News Research in Perspective: A Bibliographic Essay." In William Adams and Fay Schreibman (Eds.) *Television Network News: Issues in Content Research*. Washington, D.C.: School of Public and International Affairs, George Washington University, 1978.

2. Adams, William C. "Visual Analysis of Newscasts: Issues in Social Science Research." In William Adams and Fay Schreibman (Eds.) *Television Network News: Issues in Content Research*. Washington, D.C.: School of Public and International Affairs, George Washington University, 1978.

3. *Broadcasting from Space*. UNESCO Reports and Papers on Mass Communication, No. 60. Paris: UNESCO, 1970.

4. Charles, Jeff *et al.* "The New York Times Coverage of Equatorial and Lower Africa." *Journal of Communication* 29(2), Spring 1979, pp. 148–155.

5. Cohen, Bernard C. *The Press and Foreign Policy*. Princeton, N.J.: Princeton University Press, 1963.

6. Epstein, Edward J. *News From Nowhere*. New York: Random House, 1973.

7. Frank, Robert S. *Message Dimensions of Television News*. Lexington, Mass.: D. C. Heath, 1973.

8. Galtung, Johan and Mari Holmboe Ruge. "The Structure of Foreign News." *Journal of Peace Research* 2(1), 1975, pp. 64–91.

9. Harris, Phil. "International News Media Authority and Dependence." *Instant Research on Peace and Violence* 6: 4, 1976, pp. 148–159.

10. Hester, Al. "Theoretical Considerations in Predicting Volume and Direction of International Information Flow." *Gazette* 19: 4, 1973, pp. 239–247.

11. Katz, Elihu. "Television as a Horseless Carriage." In George Gerbner and others (Eds.) *Communications Technology and Social Policy: Understanding the New "Cultural Revolution."* New York: Wiley, 1973, pp. 381–392.

12. Katz, Elihu and George Wedell. *Broadcasting in the Third World.* Cambridge, Mass.: Harvard University Press, 1977.

13. Larson, James F. "America's Window on the World: U.S. Network Television Coverage of International Affairs, 1972–1976." Unpublished Ph.D. dissertation, Stanford University, 1978.

14. Markoff, John *et al.* "Toward the Integration of Content Analysis and General Methodology." In David R. Heise (Ed.) *Sociological Methodology 1975.* San Francisco: Jossey-Bass, 1974, pp. 1–58.

15. Ostgaard, E. "Factors Influencing the Flow of News." *Journal of Peace Research* 1, 1965, pp. 39–63.

16. Roper, Burns W. *Trends in Attitudes Toward Television and Other Media: A Sixteen-Year Review.* Report to the Television Information Office, New York, April 1975.

17. Rosengren, Karl E. "International News: Intra and Extra Media Data." *Acta Sociologica* 13: 2, 1970, pp. 96–109.

18. Rosengren, Karl E. "Four Types of Tables." *Journal of Communication* 27(1), Winter 1977, pp. 67–75.

19. Sterling, Christopher H. and Timothy R. Haight. *The Mass Media: Aspen Institute Guide to Communication Industry Trends.* New York: Praeger Publishers, 1978.

20. Stevenson, Robert L. and Richard R. Cole. "News Flow Between the Americas: Are We Giving Our Own Hemisphere the Coverage it Deserves?" Paper presented at the 35th annual meeting of the Inter-American Press Association, Toronto, Ontario, Canada, October 1979.

21. Tunstall, Jeremy. *The Media Are American.* New York: Columbia University Press, 1977.

22. United Nations. *Statistical Yearbook 1975.* New York: United Nations, 1976.

23. Vanderbilt Television News Archive. "Television News Index and Abstracts: A Guide to the Videotape Collection of the Network Evening News Programs in the Vanderbilt Television News Archive." Nashville, Tennessee: Joint University Libraries (monthly).

24. "World: The Clouded Window." Television program produced for PBS by WGBH in Boston. Narrated by Daniel Schorr; produced and directed by David Kuhn; first broadcast in 1977.

Fourteen

Polish Actors in the Socialist and Capitalist Press

Walery Pisarek

Since World War II a number of researchers have analyzed press coverage of various countries in order to identify international differences in the content of communication (1, 2, 3, 4, 5, 7, 8, 10). Research on world views and on racial or national stereotypes held by various societies also has looked at how the press shapes public attitudes through subtle and not so subtle means (see 6, 9, 11).

For obvious reasons, every newspaper has to single out people worthy of becoming the object of public interest. Who and how often someone is selected as an actor in a given newspaper clearly reveals a paper's editorial policy. By knowing the actors most frequently appearing in a newspaper, one can derive a political and ideological profile of the editorial policy. This chapter examines which of the 35 million Poles appear in stories published in non-Polish newspapers, specifically, the U.S., French, West German, Soviet, Czech, and East German press.

ANALYSIS OF POLISH ACTORS IN SIX NON-POLISH NEWSPAPERS

On the following pages I review the findings of a study rather more modest in scope than the works cited above: the study was confined to the daily press, it took into account a relatively small number of newspapers, and it focused on the actors from only one country. On the other hand, the study can be viewed not only as an analysis of international press coverage of Poland but also as an example of foreign press coverage of any socialist country.

This study formed part of a series of comparative content analyses of the press of the developed capitalist and socialist countries. In this project, carried out by the Press Research Center in Cracow, we identified a number of common features in the press of both camps: political and economic news constituted the largest category of news content; foreign affairs coverage was dominated by foreign news abroad; and geopolitical factors exerted a powerful influence on international coverage—the United States and the Soviet Union dominated foreign news but alignment with one or the other superpower and proximity among nations likewise strongly affected foreign news reporting. For example, the *London Times* devotes most of its space to the United States and Western Europe; *Pravda*, to the European socialist countries; U.S. newspapers, to Western Europe; and the Polish press, to the USSR, the United States, Western Europe, and other socialist countries. Content analysis revealed superficial similarities in the world press (e.g., semantic and stylistic regularities), but more detailed categories of analysis uncovered basic differences, for instance, in the amount of space devoted to political and economic news, in word frequency, in attitudes toward the same events, in sources of information, and in the amount of attention paid to smaller countries.

Given these findings, we expected that the actors mentioned in international news would also reflect these geopolitical factors. We distinguished the actors at three levels in terms of frequency of mention. The most frequently mentioned actors of foreign news we expected to be the same individuals or to be persons occupying the same sociopolitical positions in all newspapers. The second most frequently mentioned actors, however, would differ depending upon whether the newspapers were from socialist or capitalist countries. Finally, the third most frequently mentioned actors would be people who held interest for particular newspapers or particular countries.

Using this model we looked at Polish actors in foreign news in dailies published in three socialist and three capitalist countries. The socialist press was represented by *Neues Deutschland* (East Germany), *Pravda* (USSR), and *Rude Pravo* (Czechoslovakia); the capitalist press, by *Le Monde* (France), *Frankfurter Allgemeine Zeitung* (West Germany), and *International Herald Tribune* (United States).[1] The analysis covered all issues from January 1 through December 31, 1978. In general, the socialist press was more interested in Poles than was the Western press. *Pravda* and *International Herald Tribune* were least interested in Poles; *Neues Deutschland* and *Le Monde*, most interested.[2]

All Polish actors in the foreign newspapers were divided into six broad categories: (1) government-party-administration; (2) science-culture-mass media; (3) church-religion; (4) opposition-dissent; (5) history; (6) ordinary people-citizens. When we considered the number of different persons (types) in each of these categories we found no regularities. Actors in category 1 were the most numerous in *Pravda*; actors in category 2, in *Neues Deutschland, Rude Pravo, Le Monde,* and *Frankfurter Allgemeine Zeitung*; actors in category 4, in *International Herald Tribune*. We obtained more

Figure 14.1 Rank Order of Leading Actors by Newspaper

Rank						
	All Newspapers					
1	E. Gierek					
	All Socialist Newspapers			All Western Newspapers		
2	M. Hermaszewski			S. Wyszynski		
	All Socialist Newspapers			Le Monde	FAZ	IHT
3	P. Jaroszewicz			A. Michnik	M. Rakowski	W. Gomulka
	Pravda	ND	RP			
4	W. Jaruzelski	J. Korczak	J. Mitrega	A. Wajda	W. Gomulka	A. Michnik
5	K. Olszewski	H. Jablonski	H. Jablonski	J. Korczak	P. Jaroszewicz	L. Kolakowski

interesting results when instead of comparing the number of persons in each category (types) we compared the frequency of mention of each person (tokens). The results confirmed our hypotheses about the distribution of foreign actors in various newspapers. Thus, actors in category 1. government-party-administration, were the most frequently mentioned in all the papers. The next most frequently mentioned actors belonged to category 2 in all but *International Herald Tribune*, where category 4 occupied second place. Third place in the socialist newspapers belonged to ordinary people (category 6) who were never mentioned by name in the Western press. Actors absent in the socialist press—people in categories 3 and 4—occupied third and fourth place in the French and West German newspapers; those in categories 2 and 3 represented third and fourth place in *International Herald Tribune*.

It is noteworthy that in all six newspapers actors of foreign news were almost exclusively men. As far as age is concerned, Polish actors were a little older in the Western press.

These results are graphically displayed in Figure 14.1, which shows the most frequently named Poles across the six newspapers. In lists of the twenty most frequently cited Poles for each paper, E. Gierek, then the first secretary of the party, led off. But second place distinguished socialist from Western newspapers. In the socialist press this slot was filled by M. Hermaszewski, an astronaut whose name has never appeared in the Western press; the three Western newspapers gave second place to S. Wyszynski, the Polish Primate (not found among the 20 most frequently mentioned Poles in the socialist press). Moving down the lists, third place in the three socialist newspapers was occupied by P. Jaroszewicz, then the prime minister of Poland (he appeared further down the lists of the Western newspapers); in the Western press, third place went to A. Michnik (*Le Monde*), a prominent Polish dissident, M. Rakowski (*Frankfurter Allgemeine Zeitung*), editor in chief of the weekly *Polityka*, and W. Gomulka (*International Herald Tribune*), formerly first secretary of the party (none of these people were found on the lists of the socialist newspapers). Fourth and fifth places showed no pattern.

To sum up:

- All the newspapers wrote most frequently about the individual holding the top political position in the state.
- The socialist press, showing more agreement than the Western press, wrote more often about people personifying common achievements of their countries (e.g., an astronaut).
- Newspapers from the capitalist countries emphasized people holding key positions in institutions that could form the basis for ideological or political opposition (the primate). However, the Western European newspapers resembled the socialist press more closely than they did the

International Herald Tribune in terms of the 20 most frequently named actors.

These findings confirm our expectations about the levels at which the mention of leading Polish actors would be found in international newspapers.

A BRIEF LOOK at *TRYBUNA LUDU*

In the context of these results it is interesting to review the foreign actors—from Czechoslovakia, France, West and East Germany, the United States, and the Soviet Union—appearing in the Polish press, specifically, *Trybuna Ludu*.

Accordingly, we looked at what actors from these countries were mentioned in *Trybuna Ludu* over the same periods of time (1978 and 1979) covered in our examination of Polish actors in non-Polish newspapers. A few general findings emerged.

- Soviet and U.S. actors were mentioned most frequently.
- The chief executive (president, prime minister, or first secretary of the ruling party) was the actor most often mentioned.
- While party or other state political leaders received most attention, second place in the case of the three socialist countries and the United States was held by representatives of science, culture, and the mass media; in the case of France, also by representatives of the parliamentary opposition; and in the case of West Germany, by war criminals.
- The leading categories of French, U.S., and West German actors closely paralleled those of Poles mentioned in the three socialist rather than the three Western newspapers.

CONCLUSION

It might seem less important *who* one writes about than *how* one writes about them. However, stylistic regularities go hand in hand with the identity of the actors of foreign news. Thus, it becomes important to study the sociopolitical positions of these actors and to identify those aspects of their social role accentuated by the press. Knowledge of the position and role of foreign actors presented in a newspaper makes it possible in turn to determine editorial preferences.

Our analysis of the actors of foreign news in six non-Polish newspapers indicated that the probability of writing about people who are citizens of a foreign country increases if the newspaper's country and the actor's homeland have common goals and a cooperative relationship; there is a conflict of interest between the two countries; the actor's behavior is regarded as socially or ideologically desirable by the newspaper and can be used to promote the newspaper's politics and ideology; information on an actor would prove cognitively or practically useful to readers; the actor's behavior can serve as the basis for a human interest story. As I noted previously, leaders of the superpowers receive most notice in the press worldwide. However, whereas the socialist press focuses on government or party leaders, the Western press has a clear interest in dissidents.

Without doubt, the patterns identified in this chapter reflect and in turn foster the international images of nations. The results should make us ask whether present strategies—conscious or unconscious—of selecting and presenting the actors of foreign news are consonant with the goal of peaceful coexistence. There are many indications that the revealed tendencies will not be halted but, on the contrary, will increase in the coming decade. Will international news reporting encourage the deepening divisions within the global community?

NOTES

1. All these newspapers would be considered prestige newspapers according to de Sola Pool's definition. The *International Herald Tribune* was chosen as a representative of the U.S. press because it is more oriented to Europe than are other newspapers from the United States.

2. We excluded Pope John Paul II from our analysis because press interest in him turns on his position as head of the Roman Catholic church.

REFERENCES

1. Bassow, W. "Izvestia Looks Inside USA." *Public Opinion Quarterly* 12, 1948, pp. 430–439.

2. Dallin, A. "America Through Soviet Eyes." *Public Opinion Quarterly* 11, 1947, pp. 26–39.

3. Gerbner, George. "Towards 'Cultural Indicators': The Analysis of Mass Mediated Message Systems." *AV Communication Review* 17, 1969, pp. 137–148.

4. Gerbner, George and Larry Gross. "Living With Television: The Violence Profile." *Journal of Communication* 26(1), Winter 1976, pp. 173–199.

5. Gerbner, George and G. Marvanyi. "The Many Worlds of the World's Press." *Journal of Communication* 27(4), Autumn 1974, pp. 52–66.

6. Halloran, J. D. *et al. Race as News.* Paris: UNESCO, 1974.

7. Kayser, J. *One Week's News: A Comparative Study of 17 Major Dailies for a Seven-Day Period.* Paris: UNESCO, 1953.

8. Kriesberg, M. "Soviet News in the New York Times." *Public Opinion Quarterly* 10, 1946, pp. 540–564.

9. Merrill, J. C. "How Time Stereotyped Three U.S. Presidents." *Journalism Quarterly* 42, pp. 563–570.

10. Nordenstreng, Kaarle and M. Salomaa. "Studying the Image of Foreign Countries as Portrayed by the Mass Media: A Progress Report." Paper prepared for the scientific conference of the IAMCR, Warsaw, September 4–9, 1978.

11. Quasthoff, U. *Soziales Vorurteil u. Kommunikation.* Frankfurt a/M: Athanäum Fischer, 1973.

Fifteen

Foreign News Coverage in Nigerian Media

Frank Okwu Ugboajah

International news flow has been characterized in different ways, depending upon the point of view. For example, Phil Harris (9) has described it in terms of the market for international news: "[S]ince the market for the international news media is predominantly that of the Western advanced nations, the commodity which is produced is geared primarily towards these areas [whereas] news markets in underdeveloped areas are concentrated according to metropolitan interests of former colonial powers." Peter Gould (8) has identified such an imbalance in the reporting of international news on television.

To understand how non-Western national mass media view the nature of international coverage one must also consider general trends in news coverage and a broad range of influences. For example, worldwide shortages of newsprint affect the Third World press most acutely. In the developing countries as elsewhere, the major concern of all national media is the nation; yet as Schramm stated, in these countries "a significant minority of items comes from outside" (12). An additional influence on news coverage is the editor, who has the final say on what news reaches the public. All these factors played a role, for example, in the shift from an international to a national focus in the Nigerian press between 1973 and 1975, a trend studied by Adewale Fatona (6). In this chapter I will examine sources and subjects of news in the Nigerian mass media during 1979, identifying influences on both these areas, and see how it compares to international news coverage by Western media.

SOURCES OF, AND COUNTRIES IN, INTERNATIONAL NEWS

To examine international news coverage in the Nigerian media, I did a content analysis of stories from three media—newspapers, radio, and television. I used the stories from three newspapers—*Daily Times*, the *New Nigerian*, and *Punch*—and the broadcasts from one Lagos radio station (FRCN) and one television network (NTV). To obtain my sample, I considered that at the time of this analysis, there were 15 daily newspapers in Nigeria with a total daily cumulative circulation of approximately 800,000 copies. The newspapers selected for this study accounted for over half of this circulation figure. Also, these three newspapers are national in outlook and have developed a dependable and efficient distribution system.

Although there were twenty radio stations and nineteen television stations in the country during 1979, nearly all of them were state or local stations that were not in the habit of originating foreign news broadcasts. The two broadcast stations in my sample were those that originate national network broadcasts including foreign news items which emanate from Lagos, the capital. The FRCN carries the only international service, Voice of Nigeria, which serves North Africa and overseas as well as West, Central, and Southern Africa. NTA is the only authority charged with television broadcasting and its Lagos station originates the national network programs, including newscasts.

For the study I used a composite week (excluding Sundays) for the year 1979. Sample dates were selected to span a limited period, rather than the whole year, and were selected by taking a sample Monday from the first week in April, a Tuesday two weeks after this date, a Wednesday two weeks later, and so on through the sixteenth of June. Missing dates were replaced by the nearest available issue before or after the missing day. Only the main news bulletins of the day from radio and television were analyzed for the study.

This resulted in a total of 205 international news items which comprised the sample (see Table 15.1). Of all the stories, about 53 percent were given prominence, as either front or back page stories in the newspapers or opening segments of radio and television broadcasts. As shown in Table 15.2, fifty-one countries or organizations, nearly half in Africa, were the subject of news reports.[1] Outside of Nigeria, the African coun-

Table 15.1   International News Stories in Nigerian Media during 1979

Medium	National Circulation 1975	International News Items N	%
Lagos *Daily Times*	230,000	107	52.1
New Nigerian	175,000	32	15.6
Punch	200,000	26	12.7
Radio (FRCN/Lagos)	1,500,000 sets (in Lagos)	34	16.6
Television (NTA/network)	150,000 sets	6	3.0
Total		205	100.0

Table 15.2 Countries Covered in Nigerian Media by Region

Region	Number of Stories	Percent of All Stories	Number of Different Countries Mentioned	Countries Mentioned Most	Number of Stories
North America	24	12.4	2	U.S.	23
Latin America	5	2.6	4	Brazil	2
Africa	103	53.4	23	Nigeria	17
Middle East	23	11.9	9	Israel	7
Asia	20	10.4	8	India	5
Eastern Europe	0	0.0	0	—	—
Western Europe	16	8.3	3	Great Britain	11
Other	2	1.0	2	—	—
Total	193	100.0	51	—	—

tries that received most attention were those that were in the midst of political upheaval. Uganda received the most coverage due to the notoriety of Idi Amin, and Tanzania was covered most frequently in its role in ousting that leader. Stories focused on Egypt because of the Israeli–Egyptian peace talks and on Rhodesia (now Zimbabwe) and Kenya because of their changes in leadership. Ghana's geographical and cultural proximity to Nigeria accounts for its high number of stories.

Other Third World countries, regions, or groups covered were Brazil, Cambodia, Cuba, El Salvador, India, Indonesia, Iran, Iraq, Korea (North and South), Kuwait, Lebanon, the Caribbean, and the PLO—nearly all associated with civil strife and warfare. India and Indonesia received the most coverage in this group—India because of both its long history of trade with and migration to Nigeria and Indira Gandhi's local popularity, and Indonesia because of its similar domestic political troubles.

Finally, the United Nations, NATO (but not the Organization of African Unity), and various developed nations—Canada, China, Germany, Israel, South Africa, the United Kingdom, and the United States—were mentioned in international news reports.[2] The United Kingdom and the United States received most mention—indeed, the United States was covered in more stories than was Nigeria, whose news was being analyzed. Nigeria's former colonial ties to the United Kingdom explain the frequency of articles about that country. The United States' prominence in the news was probably due to U.S. dominance in international media and most news services and Nigerian adoption in 1977 of a constitution modeled after that of the U.S.

Few of the news items analyzed originated from Nigeria. Official Nigerian sources contributed to 1.5 percent of all items, foreign media sources, mainly international radio broadcasts, 9.8 percent.[3] The News Agency of Nigeria (NAN) had only just been established and therefore had not yet developed the type of infrastructure needed to cope with international news.[4] Reuters, which used to be the major news agency serving Nigeria,[5] had been expelled by the military regime "because of political intrusions," and so contributed only 2.9 percent of the international news items used by the Nigerian media in the year under study. The Associated Press was responsible for 2.4 percent of the international news used. The French service, AFP, the only Western news agency permitted to operate in Nigeria, contributed the largest number of stories (11.7 percent). The Soviet news agency, TASS, made a minimal contribution (1.5 percent). Finally, Nigerian media's own correspondents abroad—in East Africa, West Africa, and England—contributed 6.8 percent of international news items. As expected, the largest portion of foreign news (23.4 percent) used by all media could not be traced to a source, as Nigerian news media have a tendency not to identify their sources of international news.[6]

MAIN TOPICS IN INTERNATIONAL NEWS

Economics and diplomacy were the principal concerns in the material I analyzed. Stories about diplomacy, including politics and elections, comprised 27 percent of the coverage. Stories about general economic subjects like trade negotiations, capital investments, stock market activity, cost of living increases, industrial projects, and agriculture accounted for 34.5 percent. Capital investment received the least attention, which reflects the reluctance of multinational companies to invest in Third World countries they consider unstable. Not surprisingly, discussion of monetary earnings and expenditures was prominent (24 percent) as Nigeria is the seventh largest exporter in OPEC. Finally, military matters accounted for 14.4 percent of the content of international news stories. Of course, only a thin line separates military from political themes, especially since Nigeria was under military rule until October 1979.[7]

The types of actors found in news reports reveal the ideological framework within which the mass media interpret social action. Harris (9) suggested that the most prominent actors in international news are almost always government or ruling groups, a pattern confirmed in my study. Political leaders—ceremonial heads of state, executive heads of state, government ministers, members of legislatures, members of ruling parties, recognized political opposition members, ambassadors, and military personnel—accounted for 32.2 percent of the actors named in international news during 1979. Industrial, trade union, and media personnel received no mention, and ordinary people only 1 percent (see 1). Over fifty percent of the sample had no title given in the story, however.

Several studies (7, 11) have shown that news media tend to attribute primary importance to persons rather than to social processes. This tendency was apparent in the items I analyzed, as were several related features. First, the Ugandan crisis attracted news media attention over the long term because coverage of initial events had created a familiar conceptual framework within which subsequent events could comfortably be interpreted (9). Second, the mass media emphasize various actors in international news in keeping with national or regional interests. As Fatona (6) observed, international news concerning Africa was prominent in the Nigerian media in 1973 because the Organization of African Unity was then chaired by a former Nigerian head of state, Yakubu Gowon. Another important finding is that newspapers play a more significant role than radio or television in reporting international news.

To sum up, the Nigerian mass media, like Western media, emphasize top-ranking political figures in international news reports. The mass media may not use all the items disseminated by the various sources of international news, but they do tend to select those items relating to African and other Third World countries, particularly those experiencing political conflict.

Diplomatic and economic issues dominate the Nigerian news media, reflecting, among other things, Nigeria's position in OPEC, the country's British colonial experience, and commitment to U.S.-style democracy. As the News Agency of Nigeria gains credence among domestic media and acquires the infrastructure that could enable it to compete with established international news agencies, perhaps the complexion of international news reporting in Nigeria will change. It is heartening to observe that the *Daily Times*, the country's most prosperous newspaper, now has a crop of diligent international correspondents in certain major cities of Africa and Europe. Indeed, one of these correspondents played a part in the emergence of the nation of Zimbabwe—an indication of the vital role the media can have in the developing countries.

NOTES

1. This finding supported West T. Ezekiel's (5) conclusion that Africa and the Middle East tend to receive the greatest news coverage in the Nigerian mass media.

2. Other studies of international news found a similar pattern of dominance by Western Europe and the United States. Elliot and Golden (3, 4), Schramm (12), and Harris (9) agree that the metropolitan areas of Britain, Western Europe, and the United States occupy top-ranking positions in international "news geography."

3. Fifty-two countries direct English-language broadcasts toward anglophone Africa. Boyd and MacKay (2, pp. 29–32) pointed out that these broadcasts are aimed at the African elite "because they constitute a class which is most desirable as target audience by international communicators."

4. Besides, NAN has a credibility problem created by its operational relationship with the Ministry of Information. During its first two months of operation (October to December, 1978) NAN witnessed a massive rejection of its news items, both local and foreign. The *Daily Times*, the most prominent newspaper in Nigeria, used only *two* NAN stories, which represented 1.4 percent of the paper's total news materials over this period (see 13).

5. Harris (9) observed in his study of the West African wire service of Reuters that international news agencies put the countries of Africa, Asia, and Latin America on the periphery of the international news network. He noted that financial, communications, technological, and personnel constraints keep the media of the developing countries from competing with the dominant media in the international arena.

6. Mbure (10) studied the performance of the Nigerian and Kenyan press during the October 1973 Middle East war. He found that the Kenyan press used 75 percent of all photographs printed by the press of both countries; the Nigerian press, 25 percent. Whereas the Kenyan press identified 86 percent of all identified news sources, its Nigerian counterpart credited only the remaining 14 percent.

7. Elliot and Golden (3) suggested that military events are widely regarded as newsworthy in the Third World because "they provide some of the few circum-

stances in which a developing nation surfaces into the consciousness of the developed world."

REFERENCES

1. Aborisade, Bisi. "Comparative Study of Newsmention Between Known Personalities and Unknown Personalities in the Nigerian Media." *Unilag Communication Review* 1(1), January–March 1977.

2. Boyd, Douglas and Donald MacKay. "English Radio Broadcasts to Africa." *Communication and Development Review* 2(2), Summer 1978.

3. Elliot, P. and P. Golden. "Mass Communication and Social Change: The Imagery of Development and the Development of Imagery." Paper presented at Broadcast Studies Association Conference on Development, University of York, April 12, 1972.

4. Elliot, P. and P. Golden. "The News Media and Foreign Affairs." In Boardman, R. and A. J. R. Groom (Eds.) *The Management of Britain's External Relations.* London: Macmillan, 1973.

5. Ezekiel, West T. "Foreign News in the Nigerian Press." Unpublished Honors thesis, Lagos: University of Lagos, 1975.

6. Fatona, Adewale. "Reporting Africa in the Nigerian Press—A Content Analysis." Unpublished honors thesis, University of Lagos, 1976.

7. Galtung, J. and M. Ruge. "The Structure of Foreign News." *Journal of Peace Research* 1, 1965, pp. 64–91.

8. Gould, Peter, "The Flow of Information." *Issues in Communication* (London: International Institute of Communications), 1978.

9. Harris, Phil. "An Analysis of the West African Wire Service of an International News Agency." Paper presented at the International Association for Mass Communications Research conference at University of Leicester, August 30-September 4, 1976.

10. Mbure, Geoffrey. "The Role Played by Kenyan and Nigerian Press During the First Fourteen Days of October 1973 Middle East War." Unpublished honors thesis, University of Lagos, 1974.

11. Ostgaard, E. "Factors Influencing the Flow of News." *Journal of Peace Research* 1, 1965, pp. 39–56.

12. Schramm, Wilbur, *Mass Media and National Development,* Stanford: Stanford University Press, 1964.

13. Ugboajah, Frank Okwu. "A Quest for Credibility: The First Two Months of the News Agency of Nigeria (NAN)." Paper presented at Special Meeting Number 21, International Political Science Association World Congress, Moscow, August 12–18, 1979.

Sixteen

Television Diplomacy: Sadat in Jerusalem

Elihu Katz with Daniel Dayan and Pierre Motyl

The dramatic announcement from Anwar el-Sadat in November 1977 of his intention to come to Jerusalem to address the Knesset, the parliament of the enemy, signaled the beginning of a historic event in which the mass media played an important part. Sadat's arrival in Jerusalem and most of his activities during the visit were televised live to Israel, Egypt, and much of the West, placing this event alongside the handful of other events in the history of broadcasting—the moon landings, Pope John Paul II's visits, the mourning for Kennedy, the Olympics—that have electrified the world. In this chapter we examine Sadat's visit as an extraordinary example of open diplomacy, speculating on the functions and effects of the media with regard to the participants, public opinion, the institution of diplomacy, and the media themselves. At the same time, we shall note points of similarity and difference between this case and other major media events (cf. 5).

A CHRONICLE OF THE EVENT

The stage for Sadat's visit had been set long ago—with the insistent call of each Israeli government since 1948 for talk "anywhere, anytime" with neighboring Arab countries. These calls typically had gone unanswered, though there is some debate over possible opportunities missed and over possible responses that went unnoticed. One of these was Sadat's statement in 1971 that he was prepared to recognize Israel.

In the Yom Kippur War of 1973 Sadat became the "hero of the crossing" of the Suez Canal. And while the victory militarily went to Israel, the restored honor of Egypt and the heightened stature of Sadat were important new elements in the situation. Observers then recalled that it was Sadat who had also dismissed the Russians from Egypt; the Egyptian leader looked like a winner.

In 1977, Menachem Begin's government came to power, mostly in reaction to the Labor party's domestic failings but partly in response to the unhealed wound of the war, for which the Labor leadership was held responsible. Making peace and conceding territory were the last things that anybody thought Begin would do, and yet these were his first acts in office. Following Sadat's overture and the good offices of go-betweens in Morocco and Rumania, highly secret contacts led Sadat to propose his visit, implying Egypt's willingness to effect a reconciliation with Israel. This about-face apparently prompted Begin to state his willingness to negotiate the return of the territories taken from Egypt in 1967. Some observers think that this turnabout was possible because the government of Israel no longer had to contend with the opposition of Menachem Begin.

Ten days before the visit, Sadat made public his intention in a speech to the Egyptian parliament. World attention was riveted on the Middle East. Walter Cronkite asked Sadat in a filmed telephone conversation whether "it might be as little as one week?" and Sadat replied, "You could say so, Walter." Even those in the know were surprised by the speed of events: Begin told Cronkite on a Monday that the American ambassadors in Israel and Egypt would be asked to deliver his invitation; by Wednesday, the two leaders had agreed to a meeting at Lydda airport that Saturday night at sundown.

Reporters booked every plane to, and every hotel in, Jerusalem, and in two days the municipal theater was converted into a telecommunications center of magnificent scope and capability. Israel Television mobilized for the largest and most complex operation of its history as agreements were made for a direct line-of-sight feed to Egyptian television and a satellite feed to Europe and the Americas. There were dress rehearsals (without the principals, of course). An advance party arrived from Egypt. The Israeli army band played the Egyptian national anthem by ear, and a local flag manufacturer enjoyed a windfall. The buildup in the media generated great anticipation and no little anxiety—among public and professionals—over the problems of security.

On Saturday night at sundown, people gathered in each other's homes to watch together, as they had done in the early days of television and for other great television events. The special broadcast, which began an hour before the scheduled touchdown, reviewed the preparations, readied the audience for what would happen, and showed the gathering of the elite at the airport. The most professional of television news personnel confessed that they were thrilled.

For a moment, the pregnant plane framed by the cameras was the hero. When it landed, the broadcaster at the airport said, in exhilaration, "He has arrived! Fifty-six years old! Anwar el-Sadat!" An El Al stairway kissed the hull of Egypt Air's Boeing plane. The door opened—just as it had done on the moon. Barbara Walters was one of the first to disembark.

She, Cronkite, and John Chancellor, invited to make the flight from Egypt, went directly to their microphones. "Historic" was everybody's word.

Then Sadat appeared at the door, escorted by the Israeli chief of protocol and the crew of the Egyptian plane. A thrill ran through the crowd and a cheer went up at the airport, echoed in every living room in Israel. Some say they experienced a sense of relief that this was neither a decoy, as the commander-in-chief had cautioned, nor a Trojan horse. Sadat stood at attention as the band struck up the Egyptian and Israeli national anthems; looking a little severe, he descended the stairs but soon was smiling and chatting as he made his way along the reception line meeting everybody from the chief of staff to the chief rabbi to the Armenian archbishop to cabinet ministers galore. He reviewed the honor guard of troops and altogether did everything that a head of state is expected to do on an official visit abroad. After a path was cleared through the throng of journalists and photographers, the waiting limousines set off to Jerusalem.

The road to Jerusalem and streets within the city were dotted with groups of people hoping to catch a glimpse of Sadat. But the real drama was at home, in front of the television set.

Sadat was live on television for a good portion of his total waking hours. He was seen arriving at and departing from the hotel, entering the home of the prime minister, worshipping in the holiday service at the El Aqsa mosque, visiting the memorial to the Holocaust, receiving a standing ovation at the Knesset, and delivering his speech. Sadat spoke sternly, apart from his now famous remark in which he attributed 70 percent of the Arab-Israeli problem to phobias. The conservatism of his words almost contradicted the gesture of his coming—a contradiction that the new pope has made familiar during his visits. The prime minister and the leader of the opposition replied.

The dinner that evening, also televised, featured the same cast as at the airport. The viewers saw them all, heard the menu described in detail, watched the entertainment, listened to the play-by-play commentaries about who was greeting whom. Subsequently, the two leaders were interviewed together by each of the three United States networks, and it is noteworthy that although Walters tried to get them to talk business and address the issues on which there was little chance of agreement, they preferred to act as brothers reunited and to sound optimistic.

The next day Sadat met separately with members of the Knesset from each of the parties. This, too, was televised live and came closer than any of the other public events to clarifying issues and relationships. But the highlight of the morning was surely the exchange between Sadat and Golda Meir in which Meir presented the president with a gift from a grandmother to a new grandfather; Sadat confessed that he was used to referring to her as the old lady. In the afternoon, there was a joint press conference for eight hundred reporters. Next Sadat exchanged gifts with, and took leave of, President and Mrs. Katzir and made his triumphant departure from Israel, amidst honor guard, anthems, and very warm farewells. Fifty minutes later he was back in Cairo, being mobbed and cheered all the way home, to the relief of those Israelis who had feared that something might go wrong during the visit.

THE TRADITIONAL ROLE OF MASS MEDIA IN INTERNATIONAL RELATIONS

This dramatic use of television as a stage for diplomacy recalled more traditional functions of the mass media in international relations. Before looking more closely at the unusual, however, let us have a look at the familiar.

Three such roles can be easily identified. First, the media often mediate in international conflict: they open a channel between nations that have no such link. Thus, in the Middle East nations regularly address each other through the media. Radio has played an important part in this process, Edward R. Murrow's parallel interviews with Nasser and Ben-Gurion being a good example. The danger of such mediation is that mass media tend to exacerbate rather than reduce conflict. Walters's search for irreconcilable differences between Begin and Sadat in the very midst of the honeymoon had this character. Overall, however, the media acted to bring the sides closer together in the Sadat visit. Cronkite's scoop may even have hastened the date of the rendezvous; it certainly made Sadat's intention and Begin's endorsement a matter of world record.

Second, the media are used as agents of persuasion. Most notably, they allow leaders to talk to the people of another nation over the heads of their leaders. Domestically, this technique was used by both Roosevelt and Hitler to establish a direct liaison with the people. The disadvantage of this form of communication is obvious: it emasculates parliaments and other secondary institutions that protect people against the incursions of mass society (cf. 6). In the present case one can argue that Begin invited Sadat to come to Israel to talk over Begin's head in order to persuade Israelis to release their leader from the hard line he traditionally followed. Munir Nasser has observed that Sadat was talking primarily to Americans over the heads of both Israelis and President Carter (9).

A third role of the media in international relations is to dramatize politics by emphasizing ritual, ceremony, and holiday, both national and international. Obviously, this role was at the heart of the present case. Had Sadat's visit been more routine, the speech making and the handshaking would have looked like the traditional summitry that goes on at national airports almost daily. But this occasion was not routine; it represented a heroic gesture that the whole world was able to watch because of live television. However, in speculating, as we have been doing, about the dysfunctions of the media in international relations, we are reminded of Walter Benjamin's dictum that communism politicizes art, fascism aestheticizes politics.

The issue, of course, is whether the presence of live television cameras at an event of this kind has the impact we suspect. Would Sadat's visit have been different in the era of print-only journalism or of radio? Conclusive proof is obviously impossible, but we shall try to conceptualize the problem for analysis. We shall distinguish, therefore, among the functions and effects of television for diplomacy, for public opinion, for the principals in the drama, and for the media. We shall identify effects—on cognition, affect, political integration, and status conferral. And we shall ask what makes television effective—its technology, its message, the context in which it is received, or the norms governing its deployment.

Television and Diplomacy

The most interesting of the likely effects of television is on the institutional level, that is, on diplomacy itself. On its surface Sadat's visit looked like Woodrow Wilson's dream come true: "open covenants openly arrived at." However, if a covenant was proclaimed here, it was an implicit one that was both preceded and followed by highly secret negotiations in Rumania and Morocco and at Camp David. There was certainly nothing openly arrived at to be seen on television from Jerusalem.

Abba Eban (1) may be closer to the mark than Woodrow Wilson in this case. Analyzing the character of present-day diplomacy, Eban noted three major sources of change. The first is modern transportation, which makes direct contacts among leaders—summitry—so easy. The second is international organizations, such as the United Nations and the EEC. The third is mass communications, particularly the norms that legitimate publicity and derogate secrecy. Eban suggested that these developments eclipse the function of the ambassador and transform diplomacy from a rhetoric of bargaining and exchange to the declarative, exhortatory rhetoric of parliamentarism: compromise is more difficult under the floodlights or among top leaders or in international conference rooms. Moreover, according to Eban, it is now difficult to say different things to different audiences, as leaders and diplomats once could do. Worst of all is the publicizing of negotiations, since the public on each side tends to see only what is being lost. Although Eban admitted that publicity and the right to know may have some positive functions in diplomacy (the Bay of Pigs is still everybody's favorite example), on the whole he cautioned against open diplomacy.

Even Eban's model, however, does not really fit what happened in Jerusalem. True, there was no explicit bargaining—that took place before and after—and true, the Knesset speeches did not sound conciliatory. But the point is that this was diplomacy of gesture rather than of negotiation. Indeed, Sadat made several different gestures, and if we read them right, they are the key to the role of the media at least in this diplomatic episode.

First of all, he made the gesture that Israelis had been seeking from their neighbors for thirty years. By coming, he recognized Israel's existence and its sovereignty, and he said that there would soon be a convenant to seal that recognition *de jure*. That is, Sadat gestured reconciliation. What better way to do this—what better way to signal recognition and reconciliation—than on television live to the world?

At the same time, the drama of the heroism of his coming, and the story of the personal and political risks that accompanied him on his journey, was a gesture that invoked the norm of reciprocity. By asking the world to bear witness to his sacrifice, Sadat was seeking support for demanding something grand in return. Recall that he did not immediately grant Begin's wish to visit Cairo—that would have been too easy—but instead created an expectation that Israel owed Egypt something valuable in exchange. "I pray God's guidance for Prime Minister Begin," said Sadat, "who must make hard decisions. I made mine by coming here."

Sadat tried also to gesture to the Arabs. He came not only to the Knesset, which he addressed in Arabic, but also to the Jerusalem that is holy to Islam, and he prayed effusively in one of the holiest of Moslem shrines on a day holy to Islam. The visual documentation of every genuflection, every bead of sweat, was surely as effective as the strong demands Sadat made in the Knesset on behalf of the Palestinians.

While these gestures may not have been in the normative language of diplomacy, they had important diplomatic implications. Indeed, the analysis of this case turns on the tension between the gestures of reconciliation and those of reciprocity. Begin was more interested in the former; Sadat, at least as much in the latter. The Israelis had long sought recognition from their neigbors, and Sadat brought it to them. Using the same floodlights, the Egyptian leader demanded something in return, and it was a long while before Israelis dared to ask whether the exchange were equal. That these gestures were witnessed by a global audience added to their dramatic power and helped mobilize public opinion in Egypt, Israel, and the rest of the world. One of the important effects of the existence of the live electronic media, then, is the jockeying by world leaders over the representation of events; of course, the media also have a role in this process, as we shall note below.

Sadat's attempt to gesture specifically to Arabs raises the question of whether it may not be possible, in spite of the media, to say different things to different audiences, as classical diplomacy was wont to do. Content analysis of his speech in the Knesset (3) suggested that he used a different word for peace (*salaam*) from the word he had used on previous occasions when insisting that peace (*sulkh*, forgiveness) for Israel was a very long way off. Sadat also alluded to the common ancestry of Abraham but allowed for different readings by Arabs and Jews of whether Ishmael or Isaac were the true carrier of this heritage.

To sum up, television affects the institution of diplomacy in several ways. More than the other media it personalizes politics, thereby facilitating summitry. But rather than force leaders apart, television may—as it did in the present case—create pressure for them to succeed. Indeed, in almost every episode in this drama, including the meetings at Camp David and the mutual visits of Carter, Begin, and Sadat, the media apparently put pressure on the protagonists to produce a positive statement that would withstand instant analysis. Though real openness may not exist in diplomacy, television has fostered an *expectation* of openness, which makes secret diplomacy more difficult. In an analogous way, the Kennedy-Nixon debates created an expectation that presidential candidates should confront each other publicly even though sixteen years passed before Ford and Carter did so again. Finally, television makes the ceremonial and social aspects of politics accessible to a vast audience, involving them emotionally with events of international significance.

Television and Public Opinion

Analysis of the role of television in diplomacy goes hand in hand with analysis of the effects of TV on public opinion. In all media events of international scope a hero overcomes some popular view of "natural law," which is one of the central characteristics of such events. Just as the astronauts defied the popular view of the limits of man's ability in space (see 4) and Olympic heroes defy the recorded limits of man's physical abilities, so the pope in Poland and Sadat in Jerusalem defied popular views of social and historical laws. (Interestingly, the idea of entering the enemy camp unarmed and staring one's opponent down is a familiar image in television fiction, particularly in the western.)

The story of these exploits, narrated and visually transmitted as they happen, rallies tremendous interest and support. Such events are celebrated both while they are unfolding and when they are over—provided that they succeed. The uncertainty of success is a crucial element in the electronic drama of conquest.

Television coverage produces a sense of occasion, which contemporary society often lacks. Thus, charged with excitement, friends and neighbors gathered in each other's homes to watch the moon landings. Likewise, the adoration of Sadat in Israel was overwhelming—in spite of his image as a pro-Nazi sympathizer only a few years before. Israeli women fell in love with him and, apparently, his television-based success as tall, dark, handsome, strong, wise, and fearless was almost as great (and even more important) in the United States.

The emotional aspect of public opinion should not be underestimated. Television is perhaps unique in its ability to thrill the world, but there is a cognitive dimension as well. United States opinion polls (see 7) showed, soon after Sadat's visit, that Sadat was perceived as a better negotiator than Begin. Sadat's popularity exceeded that of Egypt's, while Begin's trailed behind the image of Israel. More important, the salience of Middle East politics increased dramatically in the wake of Sadat's visit: the proportion of respondents who said that they were following affairs in the area rose from 48 to 71 percent. At the same time, support for Israel declined from 54 to 43 percent, probably not because opinions had changed, but because the issue had become newly salient for nonsupporters. In Israel, too, polls showed a sharp rise in trust of Egypt's peaceful intentions as a direct response to Sadat's visit. However, this was a highly selective reaction: Israelis did not change either their attitudes toward the acceptability of negotiations with the PLO or the desirability of a Palestinian state or their evaluation of Syria's intentions (2). We do not have opinion data for Egypt, but there seems little doubt that the masses backed Sadat's gesture enthusiastically; the elite was divided. A Western journalist has suggested that the live broadcasts from Israel were particularly effective in Egypt because of widespread illiteracy among the masses and widespread mistrust of the press among the elite.

The mechanisms that transmit an audience's reactions—emotional and cognitive—to performers have not been well studied in communications research. We suggest that the experience of starring in a historic event, attested to by the journalists, their cameras, and their telecommunications, plus the galvanization of the public, affect the behavior of the principals.

In the case of Sadat's visit, we believe that the two leaders experienced a sense of liberation, a freedom of action that released them, at least briefly, from the control of their bureaucracies, their political parties, and their traditional reference groups. There is evidence that both Begin and Sadat went beyond the boundaries that their foreign ministries would have permitted them, and there is evidence that Begin went far beyond the boundaries of his own long-standing political commitments, as could be seen in the reaction of some of his lifelong ideological partners in the party that he built. Sadat surely defied even the closest of his Arab allies. Perhaps all this—including the about-face, the disloyalty, the risk—was calculated by the two men in advance. We suggest that the occasion was so electric, the opportunity so historic, the messianic mood so pervasive that Begin and Sadat could act as they did. While the question is beyond proof, we propose that the consciousness of being live on television, acting as principals in a world drama, had something to do with their iconoclasm.

Television and Journalistic Responsibility

Media events make the day for broadcast journalism, too. Media person-nel are conspicuously part of the elite and remind us continually of their role as historians. But theirs is also very hard work and they must face difficult decisions daily.

The media must decide, first of all, whether to accept the definition of an event provided by its organizers. Is this a story of reconciliation or of the demand for reciprocity? Is this diplomacy of gestures or of cove-nants? How much weight should be given to the components of spectacle, ritual, festival, and contest? These categories of John McAloon's (8), devised for the Olympic games, pertain to all media events, and the man-agers of the media must make decisions about them. Do the organizers of the Republican and Democratic national conventions want the speeches to be seriously heeded or are they satisfied with the media emphasis on festival? Bargaining—explicit or implicit—goes on about these issues both among the organizers and between the organizers and the media.

A related question for broadcast journalists is how much reverence to show an event. In general, international media events are described in a tone of respect that we do not usually associate with journalism. In the case of the Sadat visit, we found this to be more true of the Israeli pre-sentation than that of the U.S. But even NBC and ABC, which were more analytic and less awed in their live coverage than was CBS, stood at atten-tion when the national anthems were played, did not chatter during high points in the rituals of arrival hospitality, and continually stressed the his-toric aspect of the occasion. A similar respect for the integrity of the event has greeted the moon landings, the presidential debates, and, of course, the coronations and state funerals.

But what if something goes wrong? What if an event being broadcast live does not come off as planned? Consider the protests outside the Dem-ocratic convention of 1968, the terrorist attack at the Munich Olympics, the pro-Palestinian demonstration against the signing of the Egypt-Israel peace treaty in Washington. In such instances, the media experience con-flict between commitment to the integrity of the event and commitment to journalistic norms. Different media organizations appear to have made different decisions in these cases. In the Sadat visit consider the implica-tions of depending on the feed from Israel Television.

Journalists encounter other problems in covering events of great sig-nificance. One is how to tell a story whose end is unknown. Another is how to cope with the responsibility that the television reality may come to be seen as the only reality. A third problem, far simpler, is apparent in the way in which journalists search in interviews for criteria that will allow them to judge whether an effort has succeeded or failed. On the eve of President Carter's departure from Jerusalem for Cairo, Cronkite announced that Carter's mission had failed. Some heard this assessment as an echo of United States efforts to put pressure on Israel; others, as an attempt to dramatize the success that would resound from the Egyptian airport meeting the following night. The game is a risky one for journalists, too.

REFERENCES

1. Eban, Abba. "The New Diplomacy." Unpublished manuscript, Institute for Advanced Study, Princeton, N.J., 1978.

2. Guttman, Louis. *The Impact of Sadat in Jerusalem on the Israeli Jew.* Jerusalem, Israel: Israel Institute of Applied Social Research, 1977.

3. Israeli, Raphael. *The Public Diary of President Sadat.* Leiden, The Netherlands: E. J. Brill, 1978.

4. Katz, Elihu. "Sadat and Begin: Astronauts?" *Record* of the Annenberg School of Communications at the University of Southern California, September 1978.

5. Katz, Elihu. "Media Events: The Sense of Occasion." *Studies in Visual Communication* 6, Fall 1980, pp. 84–89.

6. Kornhauser, William. *The Politics of Mass Society.* New York: Free Press, 1959.

7. Lipset, Seymour M. "The Polls on the Middle East." *Middle East Review*, Fall 1978.

8. McAloon, John. "Olympic Games and the Theory of Spectacle in Modern Societies." Unpublished manuscript, The College, University of Chicago, 1978.

9. Nasser, Munir. "Sadat's Television Diplomacy: A Model of Media Manipulation."Unpublished manuscript, University of the Pacific at Stockton, 1979.

Seventeen

Transnational Advertising: The Latin American Case

Noreene Janus

Research on the structure of Latin American media institutions has suggested an apparent paradox: the mass media show decreasing foreign ownership while the Latin American economies as a whole have experienced increasing transnational penetration over time. To resolve this paradox one must analyze the ownership and control not only of media facilities but also of complementary industries. In Latin America the media are now largely owned by nationals. In recent years, however, the media have taken on a *distribution* function separate from the *production* function. The production of media contents is still carried out largely by foreign firms. News, films, television series, records, cassettes, and advertising—the bulk of media contents—are produced almost exclusively by outside concerns that are controlled by transnational corporations. When ABC and CBS, for example, sold off their Latin American broadcast interests, foreign domination over these media did not come to an end; only the *form* of transnational control changed.

From a Latin American perspective, perhaps the most important (and least studied) of these transnational media products is advertising. Advertising is important because it is an essential part of the corporate system of global communication. Without advertising the transnational corporation would cease to exist.

This chapter addresses four questions: How much of Latin America's media consists of advertising? How is the growth of Latin American advertising related to the development of advertising in the United States? Why is advertising so important to transnational corporations? How do the growth and transnational expansion of advertising affect Latin American media?

THE EXTENT OF ADVERTISING IN LATIN AMERICAN MEDIA

In the late 1970s a study sponsored by the Instituto Latinoamericano de Estudios Transnacionales (ILET) in Mexico analyzed twenty-two of the major newspapers of thirteen Latin American countries (4). By measuring the square centimeters of advertising as opposed to other types of content, Magdalena Brockmann found that these newspapers sell approximately 50 percent of their space. In five of them the space sold exceeds 60 percent.[1] When Brockmann subtracted classified ads from these totals, the average amount of space sold to commercial interests is 30 percent.

What about magazines? An ILET study of twenty-five women's magazines (of the *Cosmopolitan* type) from all over Latin America showed that advertising space accounts for an average of 33 percent of the publications' space (7).

In Latin America, political and economic factors hastened adoption of the U.S. model of advertising supported broadcasting. But whereas network affiliated stations inside the United States limit advertising to around nine minutes per prime time hour, Mexico, for example, limits advertising to eighteen percent of total transmission time. Guatemala represents a more extreme case. Unlike Mexico, it has no regulations concerning the number of broadcast minutes that may be sold to advertisers. Therefore, a sixty-minute U.S. program when transmitted in Guatemala (and Guatemala imports far more television shows than do most other Latin American countries) may last ninety minutes in order to allow for thirty extra minutes of advertising.

THE GROWTH OF LATIN AMERICAN ADVERTISING AND THE DEVELOPMENT OF ADVERTISING IN THE UNITED STATES

The growth of advertising in Latin America to a large extent reflects developments in the U.S. advertising industry. During the 1960s the largest Madison Avenue agencies expanded to most areas of the non-Socialist world, first to Europe and Canada and then to the major markets of Latin America, Asia, and Africa. Although the initial mechanism for expansion was the opening of new offices with personnel from the home office, this method soon became too expensive and gave way to the purchasing of existing offices in the penetrated country. During the 1960s and 1970s the purchase of local European, Asian, African, and Latin American agencies by the Madison Avenue giants proceeded at an impressive rate. Even in countries, such as India and Nigeria, that had legislated limits on the foreign ownership of local business, these U.S. agencies devised ways to acquire control. Grant Advertising in Nigeria, for example, signed a management services and technical consultancy agreement with McCann-

Table 17.1 International Distribution of Major Advertising Agencies in Latin American Countries

Agency	Brazil (12)[a]	Mexico (21)	Venezuela (22)	Argentina (26)	Colombia (29)	Peru (32)
J. Walter Thompson	X	X	X	X		X
Young & Rubicam	X	X	X			
McCann-Erickson, Inc.	X	X	X	X	X	X
Leo Burnett Co.	X	X	X	X	X	
Ogilvy & Mather Int'l	X	X	X	X		
BBDO International	X					
Ted Bates & Co.						
SSC&B Inc.	X	X		X		
D'Arcy-McManus Masius		X				
Grey Advertising	X		X	X		
Foote, Cone & Belding		X				
Doyle Dane Bernbach		X				
Benton & Bowles				X		
Kenyon & Eckhardt	X		X	X	X	X
Campbell-Ewald	X					

Source: Skuba (9).
[a] Numbers in parentheses refer to GNP rank as of 1977.

139

Erickson, one of the three largest U.S. agencies. Table 17.1 shows the partial networks of the largest of these agencies.

These agencies literally took over the advertising business wherever they opened their doors. In Belgium, Italy, and Britain at least seven of the ten largest agencies are U.S. owned or affiliated (1). In West Germany the situation is even more extreme: nine of the ten largest agencies are in the hands of Madison Avenue giants. Central American advertising is dominated by a single U.S. transnational—McCann-Erickson. In Mexico, at least eight of the ten biggest agencies are partially or totally owned by foreign interests; the situation is similar in Argentina; likewise, nine of the ten leading Venezuelan agencies are controlled by foreign capital. Twenty-three of the twenty-five largest agencies in the world are U.S. owned (the other two are Japanese)—a degree of U.S. control unparalleled in other industries.

For the large U.S. agencies, international expansion represents big business. Without their international networks, they could not survive in today's competitive world: in 1978, for the ten largest U.S. agencies, international billings accounted for an average of 52 percent of total billings (an impressive increase over the average of 47 percent in 1977); McCann-Erickson and SSC & B, two U.S. agencies that have since merged, each did about 70 percent of their business overseas as of 1978 (see 6).

WHY IS ADVERTISING SO IMPORTANT TO TRANSNATIONAL CORPORATIONS?

As I noted previously, one cannot analyze Latin American advertising outside the context of the global political and economic system. Today this system is dominated by the transnational corporation, which explains the importance of global advertising. U.S. advertising agencies have expanded internationally to serve their transnational clients. For example, in many Third World countries the rapid growth of advertising has been associated with the expansion of transnational manufacturing firms. Likewise, research has shown that those products most advertised in the United States, South Korea, and Nigeria are prepared foods, soft drinks, beer, drugs and cosmetics, tobacco, and soaps—industries generally controlled by transnational firms (2).

To sell their products transnational corporations rely on the transnational advertising agencies, which over the years have become the primary source of persuasive marketing techniques. The agency offers its clients valuable information on how to overcome customer resistance to the transnational's products. Examples of persuasive campaigns carried out on behalf of global clients are illustrative. In Brazil, advertising is used to persuade people to switch from ground to instant coffee. All over Latin America, Gerber's tells mothers that commercially produced baby food is superior to food prepared in the home. And in Europe, a heavy media advertising campaign for McDonald's proclaims that "eating fast foods is fun."

On another level, advertising is increasingly used to legitimize the presence of transnational corporations—to justify their existence—especially in countries where nationalist and revolutionary movements are struggling to regulate or expel such firms. But this very important use of corporate advertising deserves a separate study.

To promote specific products, corporations, and even the free enterprise system, the transnationals rely heavily on and in fact promote certain types of media, especially television. Television is of fundamental importance to the global firms both because it is the best marketing device to reach illiterate groups and because it is one of the few successful means of advertising in countries, such as Israel, that have multiethnic and multilingual populations. The special marketing characteristics of television explain why in Mexico and Peru, for example, television is used for approximately 60 percent of all advertising placed in the mass media. By comparison, U.S. television accounts for about 30 percent of U.S. media advertising expenditures, reflecting the fact that the United States, with a highly literate population, places a great deal of advertising in magazines and newspapers (10).

HOW DO THE GROWTH AND TRANSNATIONAL EXPANSION OF ADVERTISING AFFECT LATIN AMERICAN MASS MEDIA?

Several changes or shifts in Latin American mass media may be associated either directly with the expansion of transnational firms and their agencies or indirectly with the type of development model promoted by this foreign participation. I shall briefly note some of these trends occurring in Latin America and elsewhere.

First, as advertising budgets expand they give rise to more media or, more accurately, to the expansion of existing media. In Hong Kong and Singapore, for example, as many as twenty new magazines were started in a single year; since 1960 the number of large consumer magazines in Mexico jumped from six to fifty-four (5). Similarly, television has spread rapidly across the developing world.

Second, many of these new media ventures have a distinctly international flavor that has been proudly promoted by their sponsors. Lebanon, for example, saw the beginning of new magazines copied from *Time* and *Playboy*. And Mexico produces a television newsmagazine closely modeled on *Sixty Minutes*—ticking clock and all.

Third, there is an unmistakable trend toward the commercialization of broadcasting, that is, a shift from public or state financing to private funding heavily reliant on advertising. This development may be observed even in the traditionally state supported systems of western Europe, India, and Israel. The advertising and media industries recognized this trend early:

> Generally, the short history of TV around the world indicates clearly that increasing commercialization is the great, central tendency concomitant with the medium. Odds are that henceforth new burgeoning TV systems set up by governments in Africa and Asia will profit by the experience of the more developed countries and admit commercials very early on as a way of building the TV systems (*Television Age*, Jan. 1, 1968, p. 19).

The fourth and perhaps most striking effect is the extensive use of Latin American mass media to advertise transnational corporations' products. Although data are scarce, the evidence is clear: the ILET study of major Latin American newspapers found that between 20 and 50 percent of advertising was purchased by transnational firms to promote their products. In the ILET study of Latin American women's magazines, transnational advertising accounted for an average of 50 percent of total advertising. Finally, a study of one day's television advertising in Mexico indicated that 77 percent of all ads promoted transnational products (8).[2]

CONCLUSION

The primary use of the mass media in Latin America is not the preservation of Latin American cultures and national independence. Instead, they are used as marketing tools by global corporations building world markets. Countries that have attempted to regulate transnational advertising agencies have met with little success. For the most part, these agencies have found ways to circumvent such legislation. For example, those few countries that prohibit broadcast advertising can be reached by advertising carried by stations in neighboring countries (the so-called media spill-in strategy). Advertising represents a vast amount of money (presently about $70 billion a year worldwide) spent on selling cigarettes and deodorants when so many basic needs are still unmet. Equally important, the transnationalization of advertising is creating an international consumer culture whose members eat, drink, and smoke the same products (3).

NOTES

1. Of course, a similar pattern exists in the United States. On one typical weekday (during the week of May 12, 1980) I found that 50 percent of the *Philadelphia Bulletin* (35 percent paid advertising and 15 percent classified) and 60 percent of the *New York Times* (50 percent paid advertising and 10 percent classified) was advertising.

2. This exceptionally high figure reflects the tendency for transnational firms to prefer television as an advertising medium and the fact that competition over limited television time has driven prices so high that transnational corporations are the principal buyers.

REFERENCES

1. *Advertising Age*. Annual international agency issues.
2. American Association of Advertising Agencies. *The Advertising Agency Business Around the World* (7th ed.). New York: American Association of Advertising Agencies, 1975.
3. Barnet, Richard J. and Ronald F. Muller. *Global Reach*. New York: Simon and Schuster, 1974, p. 33.
4. Brockmann, Magdalena. "Three Days in the Latin American Press." Mexico: ILET, 1978.
5. Janus, Noreene Z. "The Transnationalization of U.S. Advertising and the Mass Media in Latin America." Ph.D. Dissertation, Institute for Communication Research, Stanford University, 1980.
6. Janus, Noreene Z. and Rafael Roncagliolo. *Transnational Advertising, Media, and Dependence*. Mexico City: ILET-Neuva Imagen, in press.
7. Santa Cruz, Adriana and Viviana Erazo. *Compropolitan: El Orden Trans-nacionale y su Modelo Feminino*. Mexico City: ILET-Neuva Imagen, 1980.
8. Sahugún, Victor Bernal. *Anatomía de la Publicidad en México*. Mexico City: Editorial Nuestro Tiempo, 1974, p. 117.
9. Skuba, Charles J. "International Advertising Investment Opportunities." Mimeo, Ketchum International Advertising, New York, 1977.
10. Starch INRA Hooper. *World Advertising Expenditures*. Mamaroneck, New York, 1978.

Eighteen

Global Traffic in Television Programming[1]

Tapio Varis

Very few attempts have been made to compare the television program structures of different nations, or to measure or study the flow of information among nations via the television screen. A prevalent view emphasizes the free flow of information—an ideal system in which sovereign national networks distribute the best programs from all over the world, balanced for their own productions. This system, however, has never been shown to exist; in fact, evidence tends to show a quite different effect.

International broadcasting research has mainly dealt with radio broadcasting. The content, reception, and jamming of external radio service have been studied, although much of this research could be called "Cold War scholarship." World television has until recent years been largely unexplored.

The term "international broadcasting" as used here includes both direct broadcasts from one country to another and the use of foreign material on domestic radio and television services. International broadcasting is one form of transaction among nations—not only a social and cultural transaction, but also an economic one: television programs are produced, sold and purchased as one commercial commodity among others.

An inventory of international program structure was begun in 1971 at the University of Tampere and the Finnish Broadcasting Company with UNESCO support. The original objective was to obtain a global view of the composition of television programs, based on information from countries representing various political and cultural systems and at various stages of economic development. The television stations of nearly 50 countries were surveyed about their program schedules, the sources of their programs and the conduits through which international program transactions are conducted.

A broad summary of the survey results is presented in Figure 18.1 The results can best be discussed in terms of the production, distribution, and consumption of TV programs on a worldwide scale.

THE WORLDWIDE PRODUCTION OF TELEVISION PROGRAMS

In international TV program production the United States led markets in the mid-60's by exporting more than twice as many programs as all other countries combined. The U.S. is still the leading originator of programs, but changing production conditions and the outflow of production capital from the United States make it difficult to estimate the aggregate total of American programs sold or produced abroad and distributed to various countries.

Other major originators of TV programs for international distribution are the United Kingdom, France, and the Federal Republic of Germany. Certain countries are major producers of programs for limited international distribution: for example, programs produced in Mexico are widely distributed throughout Latin America and in Spanish-speaking areas of the United States. Lebanon and the United Arab Republic are major producers for the Middle East. Programs produced in socialist countries are used mainly in other socialist countries, although the U.S.S.R. and the German Democratic Republic originate a large number of television programs which are used outside the socialist world—for example, in some Arab countries.

The production of television programs for international distribution, unlike that of radio programs, which are often used for propaganda purposes, is primarily aimed at making money. Commercial competition in the world market has led to concentration. In the United States, for example, where more than 150 companies are active in the producing and exporting of TV programs, the nine companies which form the Motion Picture Export Association of America account for about 80 percent of the total U.S. sales abroad.

Most programs in international circulation were originally made to satisfy the tastes of audiences in the countries where they were produced and first marketed. These programs were most often made for viewers in the U.S., Canada, Australia, Japan, and Western Europe. Later, they were adapted for worldwide commercial distribution—or for "cultural distribution."

Our analysis of direct sales of television programs indicates that the exporting corporations often aim at enhancing the national image of the producing country, in order to receive financial support from that state. Thus, only part of the foreign distribution of the French ORTF, for example, is classified as commercial; the rest is called "cultural distribution." "Cultural distribution" means that only the rights for the programs are paid

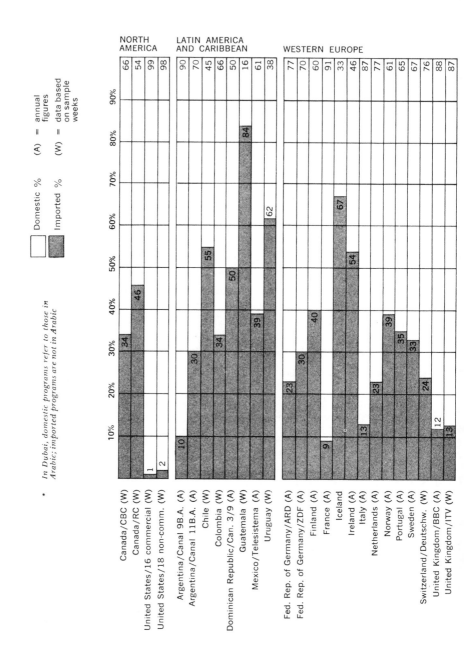

Figure 18.1   Percentage of Imported and Domestically Produced Television
Programming (Including Repeats) by Hours, 1970–1971.

EASTERN EUROPE | ASIA AND THE PACIFIC | NEAR EAST | AFRICA

Country	Top	Bars
EASTERN EUROPE		
Bulgaria (A)	55	45
German Democratic Rep. (A)	68	32
Hungary (A)	60	40
Poland (A)	83	17
Romania (A)	73	27 / 5
Soviet Union/Cent. 1st (W)	95	5
Soviet Union/Leningrad (A)	95	
Soviet Union/Estonia (A)	88	12
Yugoslavia/Beograd (A)	82	18
ASIA AND THE PACIFIC		
Australia (A)	43	57 / 1
People's Rep. China/Shanghai (W)	99	22
Rep. of China/Enterprise (A)	78	
Hongkong/RTV&HK-TVB English (W)	60	40
Hongkong/RTV&HK-TVB Chinese (W)	69	31
Japan/NHK General (A)	96	4
Japan/NHK Educational (A)	99	1
Japan/Commercial stations	90	10
Rep. of Korea/Tong-yang (A)	69	31
Malaysia (A)	29	71
New Zealand (W)	27	73
Pakistan (A)	65	35
Philippines/ABC CBV (A)	71	29
Singapore (W)	22	78
Thailand/Army TV (W)	82	18
NEAR EAST		
Dubai (A)	28	72*
Iraq (A)	48	52
Israel (A)	45	55
Kuwait (A)	44	56
Lebanon/Telibor (A)	60	40
Saudi-Arabia/Riyadh TV (W)	69	31
Saudi-Arabia/Aramco TV (W)	100	
United Arab Republic (A)	59	41
People's Rep. Yemen (W)	43	57
AFRICA		
Ghana (W)	73	27
Uganda (W)	81	19
Zambia (W)	36	64

for—either by the French foreign ministry or by the recipient nation; the distribution itself is on a nonprofit basis. This noncommercial distribution is aimed mainly at developing nations. Exporters in other Western countries report similar practices.

Governmental subsidies to program exports explain the low cost of imported programs in some countries. The prices of United States films on TV vary considerably from area to area, and it is difficult to give a meaningful range of prices charged for U.S. feature films around the world. Some of the "blockbuster" films have been sold for as much as $50,000. But the effective distribution systems in the Western countries —particularly of the U.S. film industry—make it easy for poor countries to purchase cheap programs. The lack of a similar distribution system in socialist countries makes it more difficult for the poor countries to buy programs from them.

Agencies which act as middlemen between program buyers and sellers are often located in third countries. In Finland, for example, more than one-third of the feature films imported in 1971 for television showing were purchased somewhere other than the producing country. London has been a center of traffic in United States films, and similar local centers for distribution are found elsewhere. Direct travel by program purchasers to the producing countries is an important method of acquiring programs but is too expensive for the small countries. Viewing sessions and film festivals serve as meeting places for producers and purchasers.

Conditions for effective program exchange through broadcasting unions do not yet exist in most parts of the world. Even in Europe, where the systems of program exchange are most developed, the total amount of exchanged entertainment and news programs is not very large. In 1971 Eurovision (originating in Western Europe) produced about 1,200 hours and Intervision (originating in Eastern Europe) about 1,400 hours of programming. The total outgoing exchange (multilateral, bilateral, and unilateral) of the BBC to Europe in 1970 was only 15 percent of its direct sales to Europe.

The origination of news items by Eurovision is heavily concentrated in London; almost half of all news items originate in the United Kingdom. This is partly because London is the newsfilm distribution center for American and British agencies. Worldwide distribution of newsfilm is so organized that U.S. and Central European subscribers may often receive a newsfilm of an event on the same day it occurs, while subscribers outside Europe receive the film four days after the event.

The Distribution of Television Programming

The distribution of Western news material to the socialist countries, and of those countries' news material to the West, is done through Austrian television. Because the production of television programs is expensive, television stations in most countries of the world are heavily dependent on imported material. Although the average share of imported material in many areas is one-third of total output or less, some countries import more than two-thirds of their programming.

Many of the developing countries use much imported material, but—with the exception of a number of Latin American countries and a few Middle East countries—television is still of minor importance in most parts of the developing world; when it is available, it is for the most part merely a privilege of the urban rich.

The United States and the People's Republic of China are examples of countries which currently use little foreign material—at least compared with the total amount of their own programming. Japan and the Soviet Union also produce most of their own programs. Most other nations, however, are heavy purchasers of foreign material. Even in an area as rich as Western Europe, imported programs account for about one-third of total transmission time.

Most nonsocialist countries purchase programs mainly from the United States and the United Kingdom. In Western Europe, for example, American-produced programs account for about half of all imported programs, and from 15 to 20 percent of total transmission time. The socialist countries also use American and British material, but only TV Belgrade uses as large a share of American programs as the Western European countries.

The real social and political impact of imported programs may be greater than might be inferred from the volume of imported material, because of audience viewing patterns and the placing of foreign programming. Available studies about prime-time programming in various countries tend to show that the proportion of foreign material during these hours is considerably greater than at other times.

TYPES AND AMOUNTS OF IMPORTED PROGRAMMING

For each country surveyed, we looked at the categories into which imported programs fell. Program imports are heavily concentrated on serials and series, long feature films, and entertainment programs. In importing sports programs and in the selection of most entertainment programs, ideological considerations do not play much of a role, but many countries exercise greater selectivity in purchasing information-type programs.

Comparisons of types and amounts of imported programming were especially interesting in countries with both commercial and public or non-commercial TV stations (notably the U.S., U.K., Australia, Japan). Because most commercial stations would not release data on the sources of their imported programs, they could not be systematically studied. In the United States, the TV audience has been introduced to foreign programs mainly through the noncommercial public television system, although even those stations use a minimal amount of imported material. During the test week of the study, the U.S. public broadcasting stations were showing a British documentary, the British production of *The Forsyte Saga*, and a Soviet feature film. U.S. commercial stations showed series, feature films, and drama from the U.K., Australia, the Federal Republic of Germany, Switzerland, and Scandinavia.

In the United Kingdom, 90 percent of the foreign programming used by the BBC during the test week was of U.S. origin, and all of the imported material used by the commercial ITV was American. Available data suggest that Japanese and Australian commercial stations purchase more of their foreign programs from the United States than do their noncommercial counterparts.

The Flow of Newsfilm

In the importation and exchange of newsfilm, distribution is concentrated in three worldwide agencies: Visnews (British), UPITN (joint British and American ownership), and CBS-Newsfilm (American). The fourth important newsfilm distributor is the West German DPA-ETES, but it has not gained a similar dominant role in world distribution. There are practically no other worldwide newsfilm distributors, and nearly all broadcasters in the world have to use film from these agencies.

The flow of information through television news is one-sided both between Western Europe and the developing countries and between Western Europe and the socialist countries. In the regular newsfilm exchange via satellite between Eurovision and four Latin American countries (Brazil, Colombia, Peru, and Venezuela), the flow between March 1971 and June 1972 consisted of 2,461 news items from Europe to Latin America, and only 45 news items from Latin America to Europe. Of the 252 news items dealing with the Arab world carried by Eurovision in 1971, only 16 originated in the Arab nations themselves; 209 came from the Big Three newsfilm agencies and the rest came from other European or American correspondents. The situation is much the same with news from other developing areas of the world.

The flow of information through news items between Western and Eastern Europe (through Eurovision and Intervision) is also one-sided—at least when measured in quantity. Although both Western and socialist countries have increased their offers of material to each other since the beginning of regular news exchanges in 1965, only the socialist countries have increased their reception of Western material; the Western European countries have kept their reception of material from the socialist countries

FROM WEST TO EAST

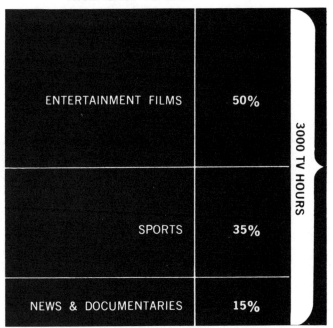

FROM EAST TO WEST

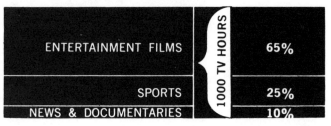

Figure 18.1   The flow of Television Programs between Eastern and Western Europe.

steadily low. The total flow of television programs (including both news and feature films) from Western to Eastern Europe amounted to roughly 3,000 hours in 1970, while the reverse flow from Eastern to Western Europe amounted to about 1,000 hours. (See Figure 18.2.)

CONCLUSION

Our survey tried to supplement plain statistics with some qualitative aspects. Our data are not sufficient for total understanding of international television. We did not, for example, examine audience exposure to imported programs. Regular audience ratings from various countries suggest that foreign programs are watched by large audiences, but these data have not been compared among countries.

The information we have gathered, however, does increase our knowledge of the present state of affairs in the flow of information among nations through television. The small and even the middle-sized nations of the world have been placed in remarkably similar positions under the pressure of foreign material.

One solution to the present imbalance in the market situation for TV programs might be new efforts on the parts of small and middle-sized producers to coproduce programs. The small producers cannot distribute packages of programs, and they are usually forced into black and white production and into high prices which make international distribution difficult. Coproductions can decrease costs and improve quality.

The technical and practical problems are important in the present-day television industry, but the basic problem has been and remains to be the social and political role of television communication: what is the real communication policy of this medium in various societies, and how much real choice is available and used in acquiring programs?

NOTE

1. This chapter summarizes a research project discussed in UNESCO's Reports and Papers on Mass Communication, No. 71, "Television Traffic: A One-Way Street?"

Nineteen

International Circulation of U.S. Theatrical Films and Television Programming

Thomas Guback

Motion pictures and television programs are widely considered to be entertainment and amusement; as part of our cultural life, they provide recreation, escape, and thrills. Television programs frequently are studied for their role in orienting behavior and providing a fictional picture of social reality. Most often, they are dissected, sorted, and classified for likely effects on their consumers. Similarly, motion pictures are studied typically as artistic statements whose meaning must be deciphered or whose production histories must be unraveled for the sake of scholarly accuracy. Genres, the work of individual filmmakers, and the internal codes of films also draw attention from researchers and teachers.

Although these studies have broadened our knowledge of communication as a social process, they generally overlook the essential nature of communication in a market-dominated society. Motion pictures and television programs are monopoly commodities. As such, these products fulfill certain functions for private capital. Basically, they constitute a way in which capital can be multiplied through investment in and acquisition of equipment, intellectual property, and labor. In a less obvious but nonetheless important way, films and television programs, through their uncritical content, serve to promote the property system that contributes to their production. The purpose of motion picture companies is not merely to produce and distribute theatrical films or television programs; their ultimate purpose is to produce surplus value for investors and to repay money borrowed from banks, insurance companies, and other creditors. Indeed, if film production were the sole objective, companies would not have moved into other lines of business.

GOVERNMENT AND THE PRIVATE SECTOR

U.S. political mythology tells us that government is an adversary of the private sector and that freedom consists in the absence of government restraint. These claims are especially true for communications media because U.S. ideological tradition calls upon government to stand aloof from media operation and content. A moment's reflection should confirm, however, that communication can be constrained and stifled by numerous forces other than government and that the marketplace itself—on which the private system is built—impinges on communication. When communication is turned into a business, whatever is said has to be said profitably. Because communication is a commodity, media output is subject ultimately to an economic and commercial test based on profit and loss.

Although government intrusion in business is resisted, government support is courted, sometimes by businesses or other groups discriminated against or shut out of the marketplace. In this respect, government becomes a vehicle through which particular industries, companies, or organizations can gain political or financial advantages. The antitrust program, for example, does not seek to demolish the institution of business or to eliminate private ownership. Often called into action by companies in the private sector, the program instead seeks to create and preserve competition so that the market test can operate without restraint. After all, there are no ineluctable economic laws that make competition self-perpetuating. If anything, competition leads to its own negation and calls itself into question as a foundation of the market economy.

Our negative beliefs about government intervention are bent continually to allow state support of business in general and of particular businesses. Indeed, we cannot afford to enforce the private enterprise system and laissez-faire because that would engender economic havoc and a loss of confidence in our institutions. It is not surprising, therefore, to see government programs supporting a chronically ill economy and keeping afloat major corporations in it. Far from being a staunch foe of business, government is the arena in which conflicting business priorities are sorted out in the tug among various pro-private enterprise forces; it is, as well, the court of appeals for enterprises dealt an unfair blow by competitors.

As businesses, communications industries are motivated by the same goals that propel the rest of the private sector. Consequently, they benefit from the same general mentality that applauds helping business because it is in the public interest to have a strong and healthy commercial environment. In addition, there have been times when the communications industries have been singled out for special assistance.

COMMUNICATION AS A POLITICAL INSTRUMENT

Communication is not merely an economic transaction; it is a political act as well. This argument seems hard to accept because movies, TV programs, comic books, recorded music, etc., as cultural commodities have the superficial gloss of inoffensive, apolitical amusement. They supposedly differ from information, which does have the potential to be persuasive even though it is "objective." This common dichotomy between cultural products and media dispensed information is necessarily false because both involve the transfer and sharing of symbols. All communication follows from selection of what to communicate, and selection is based on values and priorities. Consequently, communication, whether information or entertainment, is partisan: it has the ability to shape not only what we think but also what we think about.

This is not a radical view. Indeed, it is shared by the International Communication Agency (ICA), which carries out the functions formerly assigned to the U.S. Information Agency and the State Department's Bureau of Educational and Cultural Affairs. In 1978 the Director of the ICA explained:

> The separate existence of these two functions for so many years encouraged the artificial distinction between what is "information" and what is "cultural."
> . . .
> "Information" was "hard"; "culture" was "soft." Information was political, hard-nosed, immediate and short term. Culture was apolitical, mild, aloof from real-life problems and long-haul in its utility. The two were thought to be totally incompatible. . . .
> We have decreed the end to the largely arbitrary distinction between culture and information (2).[1]

American export of media materials, predominantly theatrical motion pictures and TV programs, as well as the resulting cultural dominance and dependency relations that frequently exist, must be construed as an economic and political manifestation of a monopolistic, market-dominated media system.

Because the United States is a powerful country, it exerts influence, sometimes quite considerable, over the cultural life of other nations. U.S. motion pictures account for only 6 or 7 percent of all feature films made annually in the world, but they occupy about half of world screen time and probably represent close to half of world box office receipts. U.S. television programs are shown in just about every country, and our news agencies dominate global news flow. Of the world's three largest music and phonograph record operations, two are American, and they probably control almost a fifth of the world market for recorded music.

Naturally, American penetration of the cultural sector abroad has not come about without opposition and resentment. In June 1977, the U.S. Senate Foreign Relations Committee held hearings on international communication (17). Even though all witnesses were friendly—that is, they supported the basic ideological commitments of the United States—it was apparent from what they said that the country was losing momentum. Time and again, they pointed out that a national communications policy was needed not only to deal with our own internal tensions but also, and perhaps more important, to come to grips with media problems confronting the United States overseas. The "free flow of information"—the official American position on international communication—was endorsed again by United States media businesses, not surprisingly, because it was in their interest to do so, i.e., they monopolize the domestic market and seek to maintain their dominance abroad. U.S. government officials expressed no concern about American films' dominance of world screens and the impact this has on foreign cultures or industries. Indeed, when the alarm was sounded by media representatives, it was because foreign trade restrictions now hinder American concerns trying to maintain or increase their foreign market shares.

THE ROLE OF GOVERNMENT IN MEDIA DEVELOPMENT AND EXPORTATION

Government assistance to business has had manifold effects upon the global flow of American motion pictures and television programs.

On the insistence of certain mineral interests, the government approved the Webb-Pomerene Export Trade Act in 1918. This legislation permits companies supposedly competitive in the American market to combine as a cartel for foreign trade, as well as to fix prices and allocate customers in overseas markets. A study by the Federal Trade Commission in 1967 revealed that the "kind of firms which have gained advantages from the act has not been the smaller firms in our economy, but rather those which are large in an absolute sense and which simultaneously have major positions in the markets they serve. . . . More often than not those exercising the right [to form export cartels] were least in need of it," the FTC concluded (4).

The Webb Act's qualified exemptions from antitrust laws were the basis for the incorporation in June 1945 of the Motion Picture Export Association of America (MPEAA), which brought together the major American companies and allowed them jointly to market their products in certain foreign countries. Although now the companies independently distribute their films abroad, the MPEAA still carries on an active campaign against trade restrictions that hamper earnings and operations. The association also is the major companies' spokesman when the federal government solicits views and information about the foreign market.

Other associations have been established under the protective umbrella of the Webb Act. In December 1959, the TV networks, some independent producers of TV programs, and the TV production-distribution subsidiaries of some major studios created the Television Program Export Association (TPEA) to stimulate sales abroad of American programming. The dissolution of the TPEA in 1970 was provoked by several things, among them the decline of independent TV production, the withdrawal of the networks from production of entertainment programming, and the existence since 1959 of a TV program export committee within the MPEAA itself. An association concerned solely with TV exportation ceased to be needed when the production and distribution of programming for American television became centralized in the Hollywood film companies, which already were members of the MPEAA.

The major motion picture companies also have established, under the Webb Act, two joint-trading associations to develop the African market for American films. The American Motion Picture Export Company (Africa), or AMPECA, was incorporated in April 1961 and chartered to operate in five English-speaking countries. Because the West African market is too small to support independent operation by each American company, centralized distribution through AMPECA offers administrative economies while eliminating competition among the association's members. Indeed, as late as 1970, "it has been AMPECA's policy [in northern Nigeria] that if any exhibitor showed another company's pictures without AMPECA's consent, supplies to this exhibitor would be stopped" (1). Such a restraint of trade would be illegal in the United States, of course, but the U.S. approves certain anti-competitive arrangements when its businesses deal abroad. In December 1969, major American film companies incorporated and licensed AFRAM Films to distribute their products in more than a dozen French-speaking countries south of the Sahara. AFRAM's functions and powers are similar to those of AMPECA. Both associations and their members also create a demand for their products by encouraging construction and modernization of theaters.

Other government support, centering specifically on communication, grew out of the cold war view of media as instruments of international power, in addition to their customary identity as commodities in global trade. In 1948, the federal government established the Informational Media Guaranty Program to encourage export of printed matter and theatrical films to soft currency areas from which companies had difficulty repatriating their revenues. The government agreed to buy with dollars certain foreign currencies earned by U.S. media companies, provided the materials exported reflected the best elements of American life. This was an important incentive to film companies because it allowed them to distribute their pictures in selected countries with complete assurance that approved amounts of revenue would be converted into dollars at attractive rates. With such government backing, American films went forward with the rank of ambassador. From the inception of this program until mid-1966, American film companies received close to $16 million under currency conversion provisions (18).

State aid to private enterprise in general, and the film industry in particular, was a prominent feature of the Revenue Act of 1971, which demonstrated the increasing collaboration between government and business. With corporate backing, Congress approved this legislation to stimulate a persistently sick economy characterized by small GNP growth, modest capital goods expenditures, high unemployment and inflation, and an adverse balance of payments. A key element of the act was a 7 percent investment tax credit. The original version of this legislation did not identify theatrical film and TV program productions as eligible to receive the government subsidy—which, after all, is what the act provided. However, the Motion Picture Association of America (MPAA) hired a lobbyist to persuade lawmakers to extend special tax advantages to film productions (14). In addition, the board of directors of the MPAA was told at its meeting in November 1971 that the group's president "was discussing with various influential Senators a way to have inserted in the Investment Credit Bill specific language which would permit the motion picture industry to take advantage of the credit and he was reasonably confident that the Association would be successful in having favorable language inserted" (11). As a result, theatrical film and TV program productions benefit from this government aid, although this industry hardly can be thought of as ailing. In fact, unprofitable ventures can be turned around, as the management of Metro-Goldwyn-Mayer reported to stockholders in January 1980: "Even the financial results of an unsuccessful [TV] series can be rewarding because of the substantial investment tax credits generated by television production" (10). Similarly, executives of Taft Broadcasting declared to a meeting of security analysts in November 1979 that the net cost of producing episodes of *Man from Atlantis* was $9.4 million after an investment tax credit of $600,000. This program, by the way, was the first U.S. show purchased by the People's Republic of China (13). MCA Inc., which through its Universal subsidiaries is one of the most important producers of TV programs and theatrical films for global consumption, realized investment tax credits of $27.8 million in 1978 and $21.1 million in 1977 (9). In short, this legislation, which amounts to subsidizing private business at public expense, obviously helps perpetuate American media dominance around the world.

Help of a more routine nature is provided the film and TV program industry by the State and Commerce departments. Although the motion picture industry prides itself as being one of the few that negotiates directly with foreign governments, American ambassadors,[2] and embassy personnel sometimes are called upon to help hammer out film trade treaties or to exert official pressure against foreign regulations and taxes. U.S. government presence in these cases authenticates the demands of private business and ratifies U.S. media positions abroad (see 5, 6). Briefings by industry trade association representatives alert foreign service personnel to restrictions on America's global film trade. Embassy staffs also prepare reports on film industries in foreign countries, outlining market structure, trade conditions, and government policies. In the early 1970s, the MPEAA applauded Department of Commerce personnel for the

> considerable interest which you have been taking to improve motion picture and television reporting in overseas areas by American embassies and [for] the substantial progress which has been achieved. . . . Reports on significant film and television developments abroad are of considerable interest and value to the American film industry. . . . Last year [1972] our industry remitted from abroad . . . a total of $342 million. Carefully prepared embassy reports . . . clearly will be helpful to us in maintaining and, hopefully, increasing these substantial foreign earnings (19).

Information flows in the opposite direction, too. Data and presentations by the industry trade association find their way into State Department negotiations and into documents published by the Commerce Department (see 15, 16).[3] In some cases, it is difficult to separate official government positions from industry declarations.

Government services typically call for expressions of gratitude. Accordingly, the film industry trade organization, high level company executives, and companies themselves have made political contributions. For example, in the 1972 campaign, the MPAA bought double-page advertisements at $20,000 each in the convention programs published by the Democratic and Republican parties (14).[4]

THE FOREIGN EXPANSION OF THE AMERICAN FILM INDUSTRY

The foreign expansion of American cinema interests can be examined historically in terms of both their structure and policy aspects.

Although initially film companies engaged solely in the exportation of their own products, business growth demanded the establishment overseas of increasing numbers of subsidiaries and branches. Subsequently, the function of some of these foreign subsidiaries was expanded to include production, so that locally made products, along with American imports, could be offered to theaters. A more complex stage began when films made (or acquired) overseas by American subsidiaries in one country were exported to third countries on a regional or worldwide basis. In a parallel development American companies acquired foreign theater interests and production studios. For these companies, it was less a case of capital exportation and more one of using foreign earnings to generate more income. Complete integration occurred when films no longer could be identified as products of particular countries by virtue of complex international financial arrangements, multinational production companies, mixed casts and technical crews, etc. The international film foreshadowed the international auto by two decades or more.

With respect to export, the 1920s and 1930s were the era of American expansion. By the end of this period, American film companies had staked out foreign fields of interest, assumed dominant positions in many markets, and virtually extinguished competition in others. Management structure for global operation was inaugurated, and the trade organization for Hollywood production and distribution interests created a foreign department to handle the industry's diplomatic work. Free trade and free markets were dominant themes of this period, as American companies fought against protectionist legislation abroad. Exportation was deemed in the national interest by industry leaders who claimed that U.S. films served as global showcases for American techniques, products, and merchandise (12).[5]

The end of World War II ushered in a second phase that lasted well into the 1960s. This era was characterized initially by the rebuilding of companies' foreign operations and later by the consolidating of American power in established areas, the creation of new theatrical markets, and the servicing of nascent television systems abroad (as I noted earlier, the Motion Picture Export Association of America was incorporated in 1945). Major policy themes of this period drew fuel from cold war propaganda needs, and although American film companies still fought vigorously for free trade where it served their interests, global distribution of American pictures was rationalized by the films' importance as ideological weapons.

Beginning around 1970, a third policy phase became apparent that paralleled the continuing U.S. domestic economic crisis and chronic international trade deficit. Film companies became aware of stagnating theatrical revenues in many foreign markets and reacted by thoroughly reorganizing their operations. A few foreign offices were closed altogether; some competing companies merged their offices in selected cities abroad; and Universal and Paramount combined their entire foreign distribution operations in Cinema International Corporation. These moves intensified concentration in a field already characterized by few global distribution channels. In this current period, a new policy theme emerged to rationalize U.S. exportation: foreign trade in films makes a positive contribution to the American balance of payments and therefore requires official support and encouragement.

CONCLUSION

The history of the industry reveals a proclivity for collusion, parallel behavior to restrain trade, and anticompetitive practices—all carried out beneath the rhetoric of private enterprise and the free market.[6] Oligopolistic market structures and concentration of ownership are only pieces of a pattern that also embraces cross-media holdings and extensive diversification into sectors beyond the media. Dominance in the domestic market is carried abroad by American companies.

Although there are about 175 distributors of theatrical motion pictures in the U.S. domestic market, most distributors handle only two or three films annually. The bulk of product is distributed by Columbia, Buena Vista (Disney), Paramount, Warner, Universal, Twentieth Century-Fox, and United Artists, which also handles releases from Metro-Goldwyn-Mayer. In 1978, these companies, all members of the Motion Picture Association of America, accounted for about 94 percent of receipts from films earning domestic rentals of $1 million or more that year. Throughout the 1970s, these companies typically captured about 85 percent of the domestic market, while the top three distributors among them consistently took about 50 percent of the domestic rentals. The same major companies all but monopolize foreign earnings of American films.

Most foreign markets are dominated by U.S. pictures. Foreign films, on the other hand, are virtually shut out of the American market, not by government trade barriers or quotas but by the structure and policies of the American industry. Decades of vertical integration, in which Hollywood production-distribution companies also owned key theater circuits, cultivated consumer tastes that persist today. The so-called art theater circuit of the 1950s and early 1960s has disintegrated, and foreign films that do achieve some distribution in the United States are not infrequently of the international genre and/or partially financed by American companies.

In television programming and theatrical films the United States is not a dependent country. Elsewhere, however, filmmaking has managed to survive only as a protected industry. Historical evidence demonstrates that American dominance has been achieved not by the interplay of competitive forces but by the initial smothering of smaller or weaker rivals. Free trade is not a solution to the problem; it is the cause.

NOTES

1. The Director went on to relate an anecdote about the visit to Eastern Europe of a modern dance troupe from the U.S. and asserted that the *real* significance of this artistic act was political.

2. A few film industry executives have become ambassadors. In the late 1930s, Joseph P. Kennedy, one of the founders of RKO Pictures, was ambassador to the United Kingdom, and in that capacity assisted American film interests in fighting legislation to protect the British film industry. In the post-war period, Stanton Griffis, a former chairman of the executive committee of Paramount Pictures, was ambassador to Poland, Egypt, Argentina, and Spain. After his tenure in Spain in 1951, exports of American films increased to that country and on better terms than had prevailed before.

The three presidents of the film industry trade association (the MPAA and its predecessor, the Motion Picture Producers and Distributors Association of America) also have had close ties with the federal government. Will Hays was a Postmaster General. He was succeeded by Eric Johnston, who handled government assignments during the Roosevelt, Truman, and Eisenhower administrations, mostly as an overseas salesman for the free enterprise system. His successor, Jack Valenti, handled the 1960 Kennedy-Johnson campaign in Texas, and later went to the White House as a special assistant to President Johnson.

3. Collaboration between the U.S. State Department and TV program production and export interests was evident in the preparation of America's position on international trade in television programs, presented in the early 1960s to working parties on the General Agreement on Tariffs and Trade. According to a confidential bulletin from the Television Film Export Committee of the Motion Picture Export Association of America, March 6, 1962, the American "proposal [was] originally worked out more than a year ago between the State Department, MPEAA and other TV industry interests." A March 27, 1963 bulletin from the Television Program Export Association declared that "the views of the member companies were incorporated in a revised text which has been sent to the State Department." Coincidentally, MPEAA vice president Griffith Johnson resigned in 1962 to become U.S. Assistant Secretary of State for Economic Affairs. In that capacity, he attended the 20th Session of the General Agreement on Tariffs and Trade, and headed U.S. delegations to important international conferences, some involving satellite communication. In 1965, Johnson left government service and returned to the Motion Picture Association of America.

4. The only other purchasers of two-page spreads for both parties were Ford Motor Company and General Motors.

5. Similar claims date to the early 1920s (see 3).

6. I have written elsewhere more extensively on the structure of the U.S. film industry (see 7, 8).

REFERENCES

1. American Motion Picture Export Company (Africa), Minutes of the Board of Directors Meeting, June 16, 1970.

2. Bray, Charles W. III. Address to the 20th annual meeting of the International Communication Association, Chicago, April 27, 1978.

3. Cromelin, Paul (Vice President, National Association of the Motion Picture Industry). Address to Motion Picture Association of America, May 4, 1921. Reported in *Official Report of the Eighth National Foreign Trade Convention*, of the National Foreign Trade Council.

4. Federal Trade Commission. *Webb-Pomerene Associations: A 50-Year Review*. Washington, D.C.: U.S. Government Printing Office, 1967, pp. 34, 59.

5. Guback, Thomas. *The International Film Industry*. Bloomington: Indiana University Press, 1969.

6. Guback, Thomas. "Hollywood's International Market." In Tino Balio (Ed.) *The American Film Industry*. Madison: University of Wisconsin Press, 1976.

7. Guback, Thomas. "Theatrical Film." In Benjamin Compaine (Ed.) *Who Owns the Media?* White Plains, N.Y.: Knowledge Industry, 1979.

8. Guback, Thomas and Dennis Dombkowski. "Television and Hollywood—Economic Relations in the 1970s." *Journal of Broadcasting* 20(4), Fall 1976.

9. MCA Inc. Annual Report, 1978.

10. Metro-Goldwyn-Mayer Inc., Report of Stockholders' Annual Meeting, January 5, 1980.

11. Motion Picture Export Association of America, Minutes of the Board of Directors Meeting, November 1, 1971.

12. Motion Picture Association of America. Annual Report, 1952.

13. Taft Broadcasting Company. Transcript of Meeting with the Entertainment Group of the New York Society of Security Analysts, November 15, 1979.

14. U.S. Congress. "Convention Financing: Corporate America's Role." *Congressional Quarterly Weekly Report*, July 8, 1972, pp. 1656–1660.

15. U.S. Department of Commerce. *U.S. Industrial Outlook* (published annually).

16. U.S. Department of Commerce. *U.S. Service Industries in World Markets*, December 1976.

17. U.S. Senate. *International Communications and Information*. Hearings before the Subcommittee on International Operations of the Committee on Foreign Relations, 95th Congress, 1st Session, 1977.

18. U.S. Senate. *U.S. Informational Media Guaranty Program*. Hearings before the Committee on Foreign Relations, 90th Congress, 1st Session, 1967.

19. Valenti, Jack (President, Motion Picture Association of America). Letter to Norris Lynch, Director, Consumer Goods and Services Division, Domestic and International Business Administration, Department of Commerce, May 24, 1973.

Twenty

International Competition and Indigenous Film Industries in Argentina and Mexico

Jorge A. Schnitman

In recent years, the debate over the degree of freedom of or restraint on mass media products and other messages crossing national borders has been one of the focal points of discussion in the policymaking and policy research forums related to international communications (6, 15). Within the broad area of study and discussion encompassed by this debate, the issue of protectionism and its role in communication policies in developing countries deserves further attention.

Generally speaking, the need for state protection for mass media industries can be predicated on four different arguments: economic, political, cultural, and professional. According to the economic argument, state protection for local mass media industries is necessary as part of a set of measures designed to curb imports and reduce either the drain on the foreign currency reserve or the debt of the country in question. The political argument stresses either the actual or potential role of the mass media as part of a system supporting development efforts or their role as contributors to national integration. According to the cultural argument, local mass media industries are necessary to preserve the cultural-ideational integrity of the various nations and peoples of the world. The professional argument affirms the need to protect local mass media industries in order to maintain a pool of highly skilled mass communications technicians in every country.

On the basis of any combination of these justifications, state protection for local production can be seen as a basic ingredient of national communications policies in developing countries. On closer analysis, however, protectionism in the area of mass communications cannot be considered a simple process of social engineering. Not enough is known about the elements that together would form a successful national communications policy in developing countries. Comparative studies on extant forms of protection for local mass media industries might be a step in acquiring the information needed for the design and implementation of such policies. To this end I present a brief comparison of protectionism for the domestic film industries in two of the largest Latin American countries, Argentina and Mexico.

THE INTERNATIONAL FILM CONTEXT

Protectionism, as any other set of measures derived from a policy formation process, can be better comprehended when viewed within the complex socioeconomic, political, and cultural context of the countries under study and of other significant actors in the world system. Derived from such a broad context, state protectionist measures interact with and influence at least some aspects of their local and international context.

For instance, both the Argentine and Mexican film industries originated in the context of domestic markets dominated by foreign films from the United States and Europe. During the period from 1908 to 1930, the film industry in the United States had evolved into what Balio (2, p. 313) called a "mature oligopoly," and by the end of the 1920s, five U.S. companies had emerged as the most powerful in the world. Utilizing their own distribution channels, these companies controlled a considerable portion of the market in the United States and in other countries.

From 1896 to 1920, local firms had distributed foreign films in Argentina and Mexico. The U.S. and other foreign countries, however, aspired to deal directly with local exhibitors so as to avoid sharing profits with local distributors. In the early 1920s, most of the large U.S. film companies established distribution branches in both Argentina and Mexico, where they encountered only relatively mild competition from European film companies and local distributors (20, p. 49; 23, p. 298).

In the 1930s and 1940s, aided by the devastating effects of both world wars on European cinematography, the U.S. film industry gained complete control of its own domestic market and of substantial portions of the markets of other countries, including Mexico and Argentina. In Argentina in 1935, 76.6 percent of the 504 films released were distributed by U.S. firms (3). In Mexico in 1938, 80.5 percent of the 1,582 films presented for censorship review were from the United States (7, p. 166). Thus, the international dominance of the U.S. film industry was one of the basic elements of the framework in which the Argentine and Mexican film industries attempted to develop.

AN OVERVIEW OF DOMESTIC FILM PRODUCTION IN ARGENTINA AND MEXICO

The 1930s

During World War I, the interruption in the flow of European films created the first opportunity for local producers to fill the gap. But no protectionist structure existed, and domestic film production in both Mexico and Argentina declined after the war as foreign films again predominated.

With the advent of sound films in 1930, Argentine and Mexican producers had a new opportunity to conquer part of their growing domestic markets. Although the more affluent sectors of society in both Argentina and Mexico preferred the products of foreign cultural industries, as they preferred foreign manufactured products in general, domestic film producers could offer a distinct local product that appealed to rural and urban low income audiences across Latin America (4, Vol. 1, p. 61; 5, Vol. 2, p. 7). Sound films encouraged the growth of both film industries (see Table 20.1), but their paths, relatively similar until 1934, increasingly diverged after that year. From 1934 onward, the two governments took clearly different positions toward the local film industry.

From 1930 to 1939 the Argentine film industry grew consistently, without any form of state protection. Argentine film producers, however, were vulnerable to local exhibitors and foreign distributors for three reasons: the absence of a distribution network in the provinces that was controlled by local producers, the absence of a distribution network to serve the Latin American market, and a chronic undercapitalization of producers (see 20, pp. 69–70).

Table 20.1   Domestic Yearly Film Production in Argentina and Mexico, 1932–1979

Decade	Average No. of Argentine Films	Average No. of Mexican Films
1930s	20.13	28
1940s	39.3	66.2
1950s	37.4	96.8
1960s	31	70.1
1970s	30.4	68.13

NOTE: Figures were not available for 1975 and 1976 in Mexico. After 1972 the figures for Mexico include some co-productions, some foreign films made in Mexico, and some Mexican films made abroad.
SOURCES: Argentine films: (8, 10, 12, 14); Mexican films: (5, 11, 12, 17, and *Variety*, March 19, 1980)

In Mexico, on the other hand, the role of the state in encouraging a local film industry was far more important than in Argentina.[1] In 1934 the state guaranteed a loan to finance the construction of the first modern film studio in Mexico City. State ministries financed the production of two feature films, and plans were made to create a comprehensive state system of film production financing (5, Vol. 1, p. 69). By 1936, however, events in Spain had reduced the Spanish-speaking competition for the local film industry, and local entrepreneurs advocating a privately owned film industry became more vocal and influential. The system that eventually prevailed incorporated state and privately owned production, distribution, and exhibition facilities.

The government of President Cárdenas (1934–1940) was the initial key to this development. Among other economic measures aimed at boosting Mexico's industrialization process, the government developed a protectionist policy for domestic film production that included tax exemption for the local film industry and the creation of a state institution (Financiadora de Peliculas) to provide loans for film production and studio construction. In October 1939, Cárdenas issued a decree that made it mandatory for all Mexican theaters to show at least one local film each month. After Cárdenas, President Ávila Camacho (1941–1946) continued and expanded the protectionist system for the local film industry. In general, the political continuity afforded by long-term majority party rule in Mexico created a better context for a consistent protectionist policy for the local film industry than did the sociopolitical discontinuities in Argentina's modern political history.

1939–1955

In the 1939–1955 period, domestic and international events were crucial for the growth of local film industries in both Argentina and Mexico. In Argentina, President Castillo (1940–1943) decided on a policy of neutrality during World War II. Argentina was an important provider of grain for the British war effort, but the country's neutrality was seen in U.S. diplomatic circles as a sign of pro-Axis sentiment. To prevent this alleged Axis sympathy from influencing the content of Argentine films, the U.S. cut its allocation of celluloid to the Argentine film industry. The remaining quota was markedly insufficient to maintain production at previous levels (4, Vol. 2, p. 49; see also *Variety*, July 7, 1943) and Argentina lost the Latin American market. Mexico, a firmly pro-Allied country, benefitted from this policy, receiving from the U.S. loans, equipment, technical advice, and a practically unlimited supply of raw film (5, Vol. 1, p. 9).

Argentine film producers then turned to the state, demanding financial support and a stronger hold on the domestic market; however, they did not receive any state support until 1944, under a government strongly influenced by Juan Perón. As president from 1946 to 1955, General Perón pursued a policy of accelerated, semi-autonomous, capitalist development. Perón's government sought to establish a social pact, under the control of the state, between industrialists and workers. The overall economic plan included the creation of a state protectionist structure that would stimulate Argentina's industrial development, expand domestic markets, and promote Argentine products in Latin American and other external markets.

Local filmmaking benefitted considerably from state protectionism, which included specific measures for this industry.

1944   Local films were distributed for a percentage of revenues rather than for a flat fee.

1947   Argentine films were allocated a minimum of 25 percent of screen time in the first-run Buenos Aires theaters and 40 percent of screen time in the rest of the country.

1948   The Industrial Bank granted special loans for local film production.

1950   Decree increasing local producers' participation in theaters' gross revenues and reducing average number of weekly spectators required for a film to be held over for an extra week in the same theater.

1952   Further increase in local producers' participation in theaters' gross revenues and additional reduction in holdover quota for local films vis-à-vis foreign films.

In general, these measures encouraged a quantitative growth in local film production, but censorship and other features of the protectionist system tended to make the films that were produced low budget and innocuous (13, p. 51).

The state never intervened directly as owner of film distribution and exhibition films, and plans to create UniArgentina, a state enterprise in charge of distributing local films abroad, were never implemented. State protectionism could not offset the lack of both a reliable external market and a supportive middle-class audience, problems compounded by television after 1951. In Mexico, on the other hand, during the forties and fifties many forms of state support aided the remarkable growth of the local film industry.[2] From 1941 to 1946, under Ávila Camacho, the Mexican government ratified and enforced the decree establishing mandatory exhibition of Mexican films in all Mexican theaters. In 1942 a film bank (privately owned with state participation) was created to support the creation of a large production and distribution company encompassing most of the larger local firms engaged in film production and distribution. By 1943, this system and U.S. support during World War II (9, p. 17) had established the preeminence of Mexican films in the Latin American market.

After World War II, film production in Mexico went through a transition period marked by a quantitative decline in 1946 and 1947; this circumstance was offset by reorganization and expansion of the state protectionist system. In 1947 the Film Bank was transformed into a national bank under full state control (9, pp. 128–9).The National Film Bank in turn supported the creation of three distribution companies to organize the domestic and foreign distribution of all Mexican films. The success of this organization, particularly in the Latin American market, is attested to by the director of the National Film Bank, who wrote that Pel-Mex, the state enterprise in charge of film distribution in Latin America, was probably "the Mexican enterprise best established and with the most ramifications abroad" (9, p. 43). This reorganization of the state protectionist system also contributed to a new growth in quantitative output that continued until the early 1960s.

State Policies After 1955

After the military coup in 1955, Argentine state policies toward local film production changed drastically, as did government policies in other economic and social areas. The protectionist structure benefiting local industries was dismantled, and foreign capital was allowed to operate under reduced controls. All restrictions on the importation of foreign films were lifted, creating an abundance of foreign productions in the domestic market that overpowered local producers. After some delay, and following considerable pressure from groups involved in domestic production, a new protectionist scheme for the local film industry was formulated by the government.

The new protectionist system announced in 1957 involved the creation of a national film institute, production loans, a government subsidy, and prizes for quality films. Revisions of the protectionist structure for the local film industry were made by subsequent governments. All the protectionist measures implemented after 1955, however, failed to boost local film production. Local producers were still faced with competition from foreign film industries, the organization of local exhibitors into chains, higher production costs, competition from television, and harsher censorship than foreign films. Thus the Argentine film industry remained at an average annual level of 29.4 productions between 1956 and 1979.

During the 1960s and 1970s the Mexican government continued expanding its participation in all aspects of local film production, distribution, and exhibition. Churubusco, Mexico's leading film studios and laboratories, was purchased by the state in 1959, and an important chain of theaters, Operadora de Teatros, was nationalized in 1960. In the early 1960s the Mexican government was involved in approximately 50 percent of local film industry activities (9, p. 93); a few years later the National Film Bank was generating 90 percent of all financing for domestic films and coordinated "companies managing the various other branches of the film industry: filmmaking, distribution, exhibition and promotion" (17, p. 288). By the early 1970s, the state owned 60 percent of the theaters, as well as the company distributing 95 percent of Mexican films.

In 1970 lack of interest on the part of private producers prompted the National Film Bank to begin acting directly as a producer, sometimes associated with local film technicians and workers (16). Following the trend of deeper state intervention and protection, the government subsequently purchased the America studios, the second best in Mexico (after the state-owned Churubusco) and created two new state production companies.

Since 1977 there has been an increase in private production, still within a framework of clear state hegemony in local filmmaking, distribution, and exhibition. The National Film Bank has been integrated into the Radio, Television, and Cinema Board (RTC), a new superstructure designed to function as a ministry in charge of all communications policies in Mexico (18). Overall, extensive state participation has resulted in a relatively high yearly output of local films and sustained employment for Mexican film workers—technicians as well as actors.

STATE PROTECTIONISM AND FILM INDUSTRY DEVELOPMENT

Comparison of the major trends in state protectionism for the domestic film industries of Argentina and Mexico makes apparent that the choice and implementation of protectionist measures for local mass media industries in developing countries is not a simple task. Protectionism originates in a complex socioeconomic, political, and cultural context, part of which consists of diverse pressure groups with contradictory demands. Protectionist measures in turn interact with and influence at least some aspects of the overall system. The final effects of protectionist measures depend on the design and implementation of the measures themselves, as well as on their interaction with other significant elements of the economic, political, and cultural environment of the society in question and with significant actors in the world system.

In both Mexico and Argentina the policies toward the film industry parallel the political evolution of the country; thus while in Mexico the role of the state in the development of a local film industry grew continually, in Argentina discontinuities in the political process were reflected in state policies toward the film industry. The general result of state protectionism for film in Argentina has been to keep all initiative in the private sector; in Mexico, the general trend has been toward decisive state participation in all phases of the local film industry, even replacing private initiative when necessary. In both countries, the local film industries were forced from the beginning to compete in domestic markets dominated by films coming from the advanced industrialized countries.

The foregoing comparative analysis highlighted the importance of state protectionism for the survival and growth of mass communications industries in developing countries. Such survival and growth can be seen as a necessary but not a sufficient condition for the social use of mass communications (as distinct from use dictated by the profit motive). The question then arises about the most effective forms of state support for local mass media industries. In the case of film, a helpful distinction can be made between restrictive and supportive protectionist policies.

A purely *restrictive* state protectionist policy would concentrate on measures designed to impede a complete takeover of the domestic film market by foreign producers or distributors (by means of screen quotas, import quotas, high import taxes, etc.). A *supportive* state protectionist policy would concentrate on different forms of assistance to the local film industry (bank loans, production subsidies, organization of a foreign distribution service for local films, scholarships and fellowships for film technicians, etc.). A *comprehensive* state protectionist policy would include both restrictive (of foreign competition) and supportive (of local production) aspects.[3]

The comparative analysis of the film industries of Mexico and Argentina illustrates some practical consequences of the four arguments in favor of protectionism for mass media industries in developing countries presented earlier. From an economic perspective, the cases of Argentina and Mexico suggest that protectionism can benefit local producers and reduce developing countries' reliance on foreign mass media products. From a political perspective, any successful protectionist policy will depend upon its broader political framework, including local protection pressure groups, government outlook, etc. Protectionism also facilitated the development in the two countries of highly trained mass communications professionals whose trade unions have consistently supported protectionism in both Argentina and Mexico.

From a cultural point of view, many observers (13, 18, 22) have pointed out that in both Argentina and Mexico some forms of state protectionism have encouraged the production of low quality films, although sometimes the problem of censorship is intertwined in this argument. If that is the case, certain forms of state protectionism may affect not only the economic interests of particular sectors of the cultural industry but also the cultural interests of some audiences.

The comparative analysis of Argentina and Mexico suggests that a carefully designed and implemented protectionist policy can certainly promote the growth of local mass media industries. The notion of development, however, encompasses qualitative as well as quantitative concerns, or at least a view of the communication process not solely in terms of production but also in terms of distribution and audience use. These factors can be accommodated only by comprehensive mass communication policies that presuppose the planning of other social aspects of mass communication besides economic protectionism.

NOTES

1. Anderson and Cockcroft (1, p. 222) identified the following "goal structure" of the Mexican political system after the Civil War: political stability, economic growth through industrialization and modernization of agriculture, public welfare, and Mexicanization, the policy of securing control over the major economic companies and activities in the country for either private Mexican citizens or public agencies. This suggests a background for Mexican state behavior toward the domestic film industry.

2. For more information on the complex organizational factors that differentiated the Argentine and Mexican film industries, see (20, pp. 86–89).

3. For a more detailed discussion of protectionist measures for film in Argentina, Mexico, and Western Europe, see (20 and 21).

REFERENCES

1. Anderson, B. and J. Cockcroft. "Control and Cooptation in Mexican Politics." In J. D. Cockcroft, A. Gunder Frank, and D. L. Johnson (Eds.). *Dependence and Underdevelopment*. New York: Doubleday, 1972.

2. Balio, T. (Ed.). *The American Film Industry*. Madison: University of Wisconsin Press, 1976.

3. Bruski, N. "Argentina." In *International Motion Pictures Almanac*, 1936.

4. Di Nubila, D. *Historia del cine argentino*, 2 vols. Buenos Aires: Cruz de Malta, 1959.

5. Garcia Riera, E. *Historia documental del cine mexicano*, 9 vols. Mexico City: Era, 1969–1970.

6. Gunter, J. "An Introduction to the Great Debate." *Journal of Communication* 28(4), Autumn 1978, pp. 142–156.

7. Harley, J. *World-Wide Influences of the Cinema*. Los Angeles: University of Southern California Press, 1940.

8. *Heraldo del cine*, Buenos Aires, April 1, 1967.

9. Heuer, F. *La industria cinematográfica mexicana*. Mexico City, 1964.

10. Instituto Nacional de Cinematografía. *Memoria*, Buenos Aires, 1973.

11. *International Film Guide*. London: Tantivity Press,

12. *International Motion Picture Almanac*. New York: Quigley,

13. Mahieu, A. *Breve historia del cine nacional*. Buenos Aires: Alzamor, 1974.

14. Martin, J. *Cine argentino*. Buenos Aires: Metrocop, 1977–1979.

15. Nordenstreng, K. and H. Schiller (Eds.). *National Sovereignty and International Communication*. Norwood, N. J.: Ablex, 1979.

16. Perez Turrent, T. and G. Turner. "Mexico." In *International Film Guide 1974*. London: Tantivity Press, 1974.

17. Perez Turrent, T. and G. Turner. "Mexico." In *International Film Guide 1977*. London: Tantivity Press, 1977.

18. Perez Turrent, T. and G. Turner. "Mexico." In *International Film Guide 1980*. London: Tantivity Press, 1980.

19. Sadoul, G. *Histoire generale du cinema*, vol. 6. Paris: Denoel, 1954.

20. Schnitman, J. "The Argentine Film Industry: A Contextual Study." Unpublished Ph.D. dissertation, Stanford University, 1979.

21. Schnitman, J. "Economic Protectionism and Mass Media Development." In E. McAnany, J. Schnitman, and N. Janus. (Eds.). *Communication and Social Structure: Critical Studies in Mass Media Research*. New York: Praeger, 1981.

22. Tabbia, A. "Argentina." In *International Film Guide 1973*. London: Tantivity Press, 1973.

23. Turner, F. *The Dynamic of Mexican Nationalism*. Chapel Hill: University of North Carolina Press, 1968.

Twenty-One

U.S. Images of Other Cultures: The Need for Education

John Richardson, Jr., and David C. King

The age of accelerating interdependence and deepening disorder in which we find ourselves demands a competent and culturally knowledgeable citizenry. Neither the United States nor any other democratic society can rely any longer on an internationally aware elite—a cadre of those equipped by exceptional education and experience to deal effectively with transnational developments. Today the farmer in the grain belt, the young professional or businessperson, the shopper, the steel-worker, the voter—all of us find our lives closely entwined in countless strands of interdependence and our sense of security menaced by conflict and upheaval in many parts of the world. The rising generation is desperately in need of new coping skills adequate to the pressures and opportunities of this international age.

The burden of providing such skills and techniques falls heavily on our educational institutions. In the United States we are, in effect, asking our schools to make a quantum leap. From training young people for a culturally pluralistic but ideologically unitary and economically self-sufficient national society, the schools must turn to preparing students for effective functioning in an interconnected, multicultural society, torn by strife not only among nations but among belief systems and economic interest groups as well.

Understandably, educators disagree as to how to proceed. In precollegiate education in this country—and to some extent also in the colleges and universities—there is serious controversy over future directions. Some are convinced that major educational reforms are essential—that, in fact, we need a new curriculum for the twenty-first century. Others argue for a return to, or a reemphasis of, what are popularly referred to as "the basics."

One hopeful sign in this debate is that both sides are in agreement on a critical point: today's young people are woefully underprepared for life

174

in the emerging global society. On the one hand, the editor of *Change* magazine, one of the journals calling for major reform, found "an awesome incongruence between educational shortsightedness and accelerating world change. . . . The future shape of the human race is not likely to be one which the current school and college generation will be able to recognize when its time comes at the helm" (6, p. 2). At the same time, the editors of the more conservative *Basic Education* wrote that "no one in his right mind could deny the pathetic and potentially tragic implications of the cultural isolation in which Americans grow up. Most of us come to voting age, middle age, and old age ignorant of many of the simplest facts of international reality" (2, p. 2).

Without doubt our schools and colleges have failed up to now to provide young people with both a cognitive map of their world and those skills and attitudes that permit constructive and flexible responses. There is even considerable suspicion that formal education is not well suited to this task. Yet we believe that through classroom education our young people must acquire an understanding of, and a degree of empathy for, people whose way of life is very different from their own. We hope, too, that they will acquire the basic tools for clear and effective communication across cultural, ideological, and national boundaries.

Our efforts in these directions are often characterized more by good intentions than by achievements. We assume, for instance, that a high school course requiring the study of another culture will build toward international understanding and empathy. At the very least, we anticipate a reduction in ethnocentric bias. Unfortunately, classroom exposure to another culture often yields disappointing results. Students may emerge with their negative stereotypes intact or reinforced and even with some new ones. One 1970 study found that stereotypes about African cultures increased among some students *after* they had completed a study of those cultures (8).

We cannot be confident either that American youths are being adequately equipped to cope with the diversity in our own country. Over the past two decades, our society has changed in remarkable ways: old divisions based on distinctions of class or status have been submerged in a new awareness of the rights and needs of many different groups—ethnic minorities, women, the young and the old, the handicapped and the poor—in what Stephen K. Bailey called "an explosive expansion in the concept of fairness" (1). Generally speaking, our schools are not doing enough to help young people develop either a sufficient awareness of the richness of this diversity or the ability to cope with it. In a recent test of seventh graders in California, 34 percent of the students, when asked to identify an ethnic group, chose the answer "people on welfare."

Just as in the United States there are great differences within other nations. For example, the media provided us with glimpses of life in Iran that dispel some misconceptions and stereotypes. But, for many, new misconceptions and even more outrageous stereotypes replace the earlier set. American power and interests are critically affected by deep divisions within Iran based on such criteria as religion, ideology, history, tradition and power. One of the key survival skills in the twenty-first century will be the ability to recognize, accept, and deal with the various elements of such diversity in other nations. And one of the key strategies in developing those skills will probably be tó teach awareness of the diversity at home.

Growing and increasingly visible diversity is characteristic of global society as well. We can no longer afford to lump nations into convenient but often inaccurate categories like east and west, north and south, developed and developing. Apart from ignoring cultural differences, for instance, it is misleading to teach students that Saudi Arabia (with a per capital GNP of $7,600) belongs on the same list of developing nations as Malawi (per capita GNP, $150).

Multinational business has begun to face one aspect of the problem of functioning in a multicultural global village. The proportion of American executives adequately equipped to transcend cultural barriers is low. According to Frederica Hoge Dunn, a consultant to multinational corporations, more than 30 percent of executives sent to overseas posts are eventually judged inadequate. She described how one young executive failed in an international assignment even though his qualifications seemed outstanding. Apparently, Dunn concluded, his "success in school and on the job arose from his extraordinary zest for competition—a zest that is common in American business, sports, and politics. In the Middle East, however, he had to work with a multinational team, and his competitive spirit alienated many of its members. Some of them represented cultures where an individual winner is regarded as having offended all those who lost" (4).

REACHING ACROSS NATIONAL BORDERS

How can we help young people of relatively self-sufficient and inward-looking nations such as the U.S., the USSR, the People's Republic of China, and Brazil to overcome the preconceptions, arrogance, and prejudices they so often bring to direct or indirect contact with other cultures? More face-to-face encounters among members of different societies is an obvious answer. But, like many other forms of communication, direct human interaction is no more likely to produce a constructive outcome than the reverse. Everything depends on psychological, cultural, and situational variables. A professional diplomat usually arrives in a new post determined to establish good personal relations with those in the host government and has been selected, trained, and motivated for success in this role. On the other hand, it is a reasonable hypothesis that an engineer sent by a rich and powerful country to a relatively deprived society for a limited time to perform a technical function is not likely to establish constructive relationships with co-workers. at least in the absence of a task requiring intensive teamwork.

As this example suggests, crucial variables include those affecting the degree of emotional identification with host country groups achieved by the sojourner. When such a feeling of belonging develops, empathy and sensitivity are also likely. Such is often the case, for instance, when a business or economic consultant works on a project over a period of time as part of a team of indigenous personnel; even in the absence of a preexisting commitment to culture learning, a dramatic increase in insight and capacity for cooperation is a probable outcome—often on both sides. In contrast, few tourists achieve such rapport and indeed too often succeed only in exacerbating preexisting prejudices among both nationalities.

A variety of exchange programs attempt to meet the need for increased international understanding. The most effective are those that not only immerse the participants in the general life of the receiving country, or simply in a particular field of study, but include as well active collaboration with indigenous groups. Thus, team research and team teaching are usually more helpful in achieving culture learning objectives than is an individual study project, everything else being equal.

One form of exchange deserves special mention for its impact both on exchange participants and on the schools and communities of the host country. An extended visit in an indigenous family, wherein hosts and visitor are committed to learning from the experience, is among the most efficacious ways to broaden horizons, reduce prejudice, and eliminate stereotypes. When, in addition, the individual visitor is young enough to want to be accepted as a member of the host family and the family is receptive to this desire, the results are often dramatic. Over many years, programs such as the Experiment in International Living, AFS International/Intercultural Programs, and Youth for Understanding have demonstrated an astonishingly high success rate, measured by transformation of participants' world view, increased empathy and sensitivity to cultural differences, superior interpersonal communication skills, and the formation of enduring, close personal relationships. All three organizations rely on carefully monitored home stays as the most significant element in the learning experience.

Collectively all such programs assure the presence of foreign students and returned American exchange students in a substantial proportion (probably one-third to one-half) of public high schools in the United States. It is well worth considering whether full advantage is taken of this unique resource by educational authorities.

A well-selected foreign student in an American high school can easily be helped to identify with classmates and the school, assume a role as a cross-cultural link, and engage in class and extra-curricular activity for educational purposes. Many returned American exchange students are also capable of serving as a focus of attention in classes learning about other cultures. This resource has so far been largely neglected, probably in the majority of American schools. So, while it is quite true that financial constraints permit only a tiny fraction of American high school students to have an exchange experience abroad, a substantial proportion of American schools have ready access to individuals ideally equipped to assist in global perspectives education.

Other human resources are often available as well. A teacher who has studied abroad, exchange students on a college campus, or a returned Peace Corps volunteer may be both willing and able to help students and the broader educational community to acquire new insights and perceptions. As Clark Kerr pointed out: "Students . . . learn from each other, and the 250,000 students from other countries who are now studying in American colleges and universities are an under-utilized resource for improved communication between cultures" (9, p. xxvii).

TEACHING INTERNATIONAL UNDERSTANDING

John I. Goodlad, Director of the ambitious Study of Schooling in the United States, has observed with distress that we emphasize understanding *other* nations, *other* cultures, *other* peoples, thus reinforcing an image of a world divided into we and they. "How," he asked, "does one come to acquire a worldwide moral landscape? How can we be assured that positive attitudes will emerge from personal contact with persons from other cultures, especially when these contacts are usually of short duration? What we know about developing human empathy for the whole of mankind is dwarfed beside our ignorance" (7, p. xvii).

However, we are beginning to appreciate what formal education can accomplish and some of this insight is being applied to new educational programs. We must view these new efforts with caution since they are still in more or less experimental stages. Nevertheless, the development of such learning activities and techniques in a formal educational setting can help young people become more competent in coping with social reality.

We have known for some time, for example, that distorted images and other barriers to effective communication come from a variety of sources. Many researchers have singled out the peer group and the mass media, especially television, as key villains in the creation of dysfunctional cultural blinders. Traditionally the role of the schools has been to try to correct the distortions—to act as an antidote to other socializing agents. However, a number of studies have suggested why these corrective measures achieve only limited success. Judith Torney, for instance, who has conducted research for UNESCO and many other organizations, noted

that "the period of middle childhood has . . . been identified by many studies as a time of relatively low rejection of groups and relatively high flexibility. . . . Once the end of this period is reached (about age 15), behavior
organized in a given pattern is extraordinarily difficult to reorganize" (10,
p. 68).

In other words, if an individual has developed a particular mind set
toward people of another culture—or perhaps toward all outsiders—by
the age of fourteen or fifteen such distorted images are very resistant to
change unless we provide an emotionally powerful experience such as living in a family in another country. The middle years of precollegiate
education, therefore, are critical. This would seem the age on which to
concentrate much of our efforts at positive attitude formation toward different cultures, provided that we have available good teaching methods
and worthwhile classroom materials—ingredients that can compete successfully with the media and other agents of attitude formation. Fortunately, a number of educational agencies are now engaged in the task of
developing the strategies and materials that can lead to a greater degree
of understanding and perhaps "empathy for the whole of humankind," in
Goodlad's words.

Some of the learning that builds toward a global perspective can be
thought of in terms of building blocks rather than the direct study of
another society or analysis of global issues. On the surface, many of the
newer learning activities look quite traditional, and they place heavy
emphasis on basic skill development. On closer examination, however, one
finds the beginnings of important innovation.

Many of the new materials are centered around basic themes or concepts. Ernest L. Boyer, former U.S. Commissioner of Education, enthusiastically endorsed this approach. In advocating a core curriculum for
American colleges and universities, Boyer identified three central themes:
communication, interdependence, and change (3). Organizations such as
Global Perspectives in Education have applied these concepts to broad
areas of the precollegiate curriculum. A number of other themes or concepts have been added, the most common being human conflict.

New programs are helping teachers and curriculum specialists use
these concepts as organizing themes in traditional subject areas—social
studies, science, language arts. The premise is deceptively simple: if young
people learn more about, say, interdependence in a wide variety of settings, they eventually will be better able to understand and deal with the
complexities of interdependence on a global scale. Much of the work of
acquiring these conceptual building blocks involves content that seems far
removed from the pressing world issues of the day. This is one important
way in which education for a global perspective differs from traditional
notions of international education. Two brief examples can help illustrate
these new trends and their potential for promoting cross-cultural understanding and acceptance.

The first case involves a class of youngsters in a California suburb—a fifth-grade class reading a story about a boy growing up in Sierra Leone. The story told about the hero's confrontation with the school bully; it included an exciting chase through the village streets and a denouement in which the hero not only avoided the violence he feared but enlisted public opinion (i.e., from people watching his desperate flight) to achieve a satisfactory resolution of the conflict. The students, ages ten and eleven, analyzed the story in terms of the conflict theme. This in itself was a little unusual since American textbooks until recently have been careful to avoid the subject of conflict. One important discovery these children were making was that conflict in another time frame (the 1920s) and another cultural setting bore remarkable similarities to conflicts they were familiar with in their own lives. In a subtle way, they were encountering human commonalities across time and space.

The second case involves the same school on the same day. A class of high school students took a trip to the inner city of San Francisco—to the neighborhood known as the Mission. The journey itself was a valuable learning experience: it was the first time most of the class crossed the cultural, ethnic, and economic boundaries separating their affluent suburb from the core city. These students had come to study wall art. They took photographs and made sketches of the huge murals splashed across the once-barren walls of stores and housing projects. The artists were Mexican, Mexican-American, black, white, and Asian-American—reflecting the diverse makeup of the Mission's population. The teenagers had already gained quite a bit of experience with the themes of conflict and interdependence, and these formed the bases for their analysis and discussion. Sometimes they argued about interpretation. One mural depicted a rapid transit system borne on the shoulders of people. Was the Mexican artist saying that the subway system was supported by the people or that they were being weighed down by the financial burden? Was the system bringing the city into closer harmony or wrenching it apart? Through such debate the students were identifying different modes of expressing conflict and many seemed to be gaining insight into ways in which perceptions can influence a conflict situation.

Testing of the results of programs in global perspectives education is still in the beginning stages. So far, the data are quite encouraging. The students in the two classes we mentioned were part of a test group whose scores were compared with national averages on standardized tests from both the Educational Testing Service and the Institute for the Development of Educational Activities. Students in the global perspective sample scored higher than the national average in such areas as understanding of human conflict and willingness to consider alternative means of resolving specific conflicts. Their knowledge of global interdependence was greater, although they showed the national tendency toward low scores in geography. And, perhaps most significant of all, the test group had positive gains in attitude questions relating to ethnocentric bias.

The movement toward a global perspective in education is still in its formative stages. It seems unlikely that these new approaches and teaching materials will be, or should be, molded into a grand redesign of curriculum. As two specialists in curriculum design cautioned: "We doubt seriously that all the competencies needed by citizens of a pluralistic democracy and a complex global society can ever be adequately identified, defined, and predicted" (5, p. 390).

While we cannot state precisely what specific learning approaches or objectives will create a generation more comfortable in an interdependent, multicultural, conflict-prone environment, there is a growing sense that we can help young people develop more flexible thought processes and greater skill in human interactions. These are among the broad goals of what is being called a global perspective in education. People involved in this effort do not discount the importance of study in such areas as world issues, foreign languages, and specific cultures. Indeed, they are working to create a context that will make such programs of study more effective. The need is as compelling as any suggested by the daily headlines.

REFERENCES

1. Bailey, Stephen K. "Education in the Eighties: The Case for Optimism." *New Ways*, Kettering Foundation, Fall 1979.

2. *Basic Education* 24(3), November 1979.

3. Boyer, Ernest L. and Martin Kaplan. *Educating for Survival*. Change Magazine Press, 1977.

4. Dunn, Frederica Hoge. "The 'Best Man' Theory and Why It Fails." *New York Times*, July 16, 1978.

5. Fischer, W. Paul and M. Frances Klein. "Challenging Simplistic Beliefs About Curriculum." *Educational Leadership*, February 1978.

6. "The Future Forsaken." *Change*, October 1978.

7. Goodlad, John I. Foreword to James M. Becker (ed.) *Schooling for a Global Age*. New York: McGraw–Hill, 1979.

8. Hicks, E. and Barry K. Beyer. "Images of Africa." *Journal of Negro Education* 39, 1970, pp. 155–170.

9. Kerr, Clark. In introduction to Barbara R. Burn, *Expanding the International Dimension of Higher Education*. San Francisco: Jossey-Bass, 1980.

10. Torney, Judith V. "Psychological and Institutional Obstacles to the Global Perspective in Education." In James M. Becker (Ed.) *Schooling for a Global Age*. New York: McGraw-Hill, 1979.

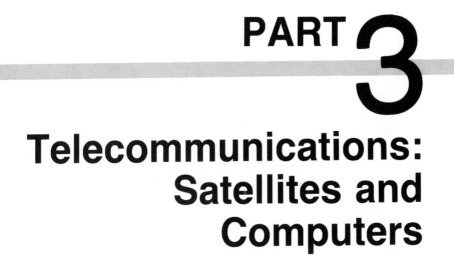

PART 3

Telecommunications: Satellites and Computers

Twenty-Two

Principles for Global Telecommunications Systems

Anne Branscomb

While political arguments proliferate concerning the right to communicate, communication systems spring up and expand at a dramatic rate. The linkup between satellite and computer technology is revolutionizing and democratizing communications by making available "real-time" interactive messages. Space has become irrelevant; time is now a matter of zone and convenience. Modes of transmission—voice, video, data—are fast converging so that senders can combine technologies to meet their needs. Moreover, the cost of both communicating and computing is fast diminishing (satellite technology on a per channel basis costs 40 percent less each year—the same price decline seen in computer storage). Thus, the marriage of computers and communications could mean in a few years' time the universal interconnection of public data networks, which would provide maximum flexibility and diversity at minimum cost.

This chapter discusses the principles that might underlie a global communications policy serving all the people of the world equitably while permitting nation-states to preserve their local and national options. These principles—availability, reliability, integrity, security, efficiency, transparency, interconnectivity, interactivity, diversity, and universality—stand apart from those fundamental to a global information policy. Semantic confusion has arisen from the interchangeable use of the words "information" and "communication": communications policy concerns the transmittal of messages from one being to another via any means available; information policy addresses message content. A fortune cookie clearly demonstrates the difference: the communications system is the cookie, the information is the fortune. Information policy issues include prior consent, free or balanced flow of information across national boundaries, quotas on importation of television programs, licensing of journalists, and the right of access. My concern here lies with communications policy.

PRINCIPLES OF A GLOBAL COMMUNICATIONS SYSTEM

Availability refers to the physical existence of communication systems. Accessibility—the guaranteed and unimpeded ability to use a desired system—is an information policy issue at heart; availability stops short of guaranteed use. Availability encompasses not only communication facilities but also the channel space and operational readiness to receive and transmit messages whenever and wherever there is a message that needs to be transmitted. Today, telecommunication facilities are concentrated (that is, widely available) in the developed world: developing countries, with 70 percent of the world's population and 20 percent of its gross national product, have only 7.3 percent of the world's telephones; 75 percent of the telephones and television sets are found in only eight countries.

Reliability means service offered on a regular and uninterrupted basis. Visual telegraphy was not very reliable because it required individuals to be physically in position to watch and transmit signals. Storms, smog, and nighttime interfered with message transmission, which was also vulnerable to human error.

Integrity denotes message clarity and accuracy. Senders want assurance that the message sent is the message received. Otherwise, business may be disrupted, troops misdirected, and lovers lost. Telegraphy was notoriously prone to distortion. Voice telephony and postal text have preserved message integrity except in cases of language incompatibility or inaccurate typing. In computer communications, two computers cooperate to confirm that the complete message is received without error; and receipt is acknowledged by the recipient. Higher speed, lower cost, and greater integrity of messages make this technology particularly attractive.

Security is the control of access to messages. Today, preventing access is desired by some senders, but by no means all. Earlier in the era of telephony operators heard all; visual telegraphers saw all; and a young telegraph operator named Andrew Carnegie is said to have learned how to succeed as a capitalist entrepreneur by paying attention to messages he sent across the wires. On the other hand, large sums of money have been spent to encode or scramble messages for military as well as business purposes, and the ability to provide security of transmission is a high-priority goal.

Efficiency dictates that the communication system be cost-effective for its purpose. Thus, some countries prefer what is called thin-route telephony, or high-powered satellites with low-powered ground stations, rather than low-powered satellites with high-powered ground stations.

Transparency means that the manner in which a message is sent should not be obvious to the user. Whether the transmission is achieved by satellite, microwave, cable, or optical fiber should be irrelevant to the user. Neither should the message be distorted or limited by incompatibility among communication systems.

Interconnectivity implies more than plug compatibility, including protocols for access to, through, and across various public and private networks. If the publics of the world are to enjoy optimum service, then public networks should not be permitted to deny certain users access to the system. At the same time, private networks should be capable of interconnection unless compelling reasons require privacy.

Interactivity refers to the potential for immediate response in real time, as with a voice circuit telephone system or face-to-face conversation. Such interactive communication is becoming more widely available in the mass media as well as in point-to-point systems. For example, television teleconferencing takes place every weeknight on the *MacNeil/Lehrer Report* and media diplomacy is increasingly common.

Diversity points to a broad choice of transmission modes—telegraph, telephone, telex, facsimile, cable, television. User choice rather than carrier choice or regulatory ruling must be the prevailing principle. The sender should be able to use voice, video, text, freeze frame, or graphic or data transmission singly or together according to the function. Use should not be limited by legal restrictions that inhibit technological development. In the United States the Federal Communications Commission recently acted to remove the unnatural legal barrier between computers and communications, thus allowing technological development to proceed in whatever direction the marketplace dictates in terms of consumer choice, economic viability, and message need.

Universality is, of course, the ultimate extrapolation of availability, interconnectivity, and transparency. Universal availability of some modes of transmission has been achieved in several of the more developed nations, but only in Japan do policy analysts claim to have reached a saturation point of information delivery when, in 1965, 75 percent of the households had television and 40 percent, telephones. Nevertheless, some Japanese scholars argue that a saturation point can never be reached because the appetite for information increases exponentially with the availability of new communication technologies. Thus, the United States sees no saturation point in sight despite 95 percent of households with telephone service and 98 percent with television; home computer terminals, an entirely different mode of message transmission and use, represent a new market to satisfy.

To demonstrate these developing principles of communications policy, which might be more fruitfully pursued than the more politically charged information policy issues, I shall review recent operational and experimental satellite systems and data networks that illustrate the principles proposed.

OPERATING SATELLITE SYSTEMS AND DATA NETWORKS

The international satellite system known as INTELSAT is providing common carrier service to 137 nations, with 67 percent of international messages traveling via its transponders. The primary use is telephone traffic. The vast majority of participating countries are developing nations. This global system has carved new world communication paths: heretofore, messages traveled via point-to-point cable facilities, which connected only the wealthiest, most developed countries by underwater cables. INTELSAT is a multipoint, rather than a point-to-point, service that by its very nature provides more equitable access. It is distance-insensitive and volume-insensitive, so small users are not penalized by higher rates. Each participating country controls its own connection to the global system. (INTERSPUTNIK is a similar common carrier serving the Eastern European countries.)

The international navigational satellite system called INMARSAT provides positioning information to all ships at sea anywhere on the globe. Such navigational assistance is incredibly precise. The U.S. Navy also has its own navigational satellite system, NAVSAT, that is accurate to an average error of less than ten meters, sufficient for virtually all purposes. Such technology benefits international maritime transportation by realizing savings in time as well as by providing a high degree of safety for crew and cargo.

While INTELSAT offers a public, global common carrier service with access controlled at the national level, various special-purpose satellites and satellite systems also have emerged. The U.S. worldwide defense communication system is so sophisticated that those with access to it become frustrated when encountering the interruptions, delays, and distortions inevitable with more primitive, land-based wire and radio transmission systems. Military surveillance and communication needs stimulated the research and development that produced these specialized space communication services. Although satellite technology is not controlled on an international basis, reconnaissance satellites provide the necessary information to maintain peace. An international monitoring program could be administered on a global basis to insure that arms control agreements were being honored.

Probably next in line of significance and sophistication is NIMBUS, a weather satellite operated by NOAA, the National Oceanic and Atmospheric Administration. NIMBUS provides, on a cooperative basis, information on weather fronts, hurricanes, and so on. The morning television news has been altered radically by real-time satellite pictures that permit us graphically to analyze on our television monitors the rain clouds and sunshine so that we can plan our day accordingly. Cost alone limits the availability of these weather pictures, which could be made available via satellite directly to saucers anywhere on the globe.

LANDSAT, a NASA-operated satellite, remote-senses earth surface conditions and seabed resources, retrieving information on the geological wealth of nations and foreseeing climatic and topographical changes. Although this system is owned and operated by the United States, LAND-SAT information has been disseminated widely. However, remote-sensing technology is controversial in information policy contexts: who has access to and control over these economically valuable data? Can or should a country be able to prohibit the remote-sensing of its territory? Technologically such control would require violent, destructive, and prohibitively expensive means. Practically, access can be encumbered by political and legal protocols. On the other hand, access to all nations with an interest in the subject matter—whether it be agricultural, geological, or environmental—can be guaranteed. Prudent global resource management suggests that international protocols or management devices should be developed. At present, the International Telecommunication Union allocates frequencies for remote-sensing satellite use and the United States takes the position that the raw data from LANDSAT will be made freely available to all countries but that proprietary rights in the processed data should be retained. Yet, global access could be assured by shared economic investment, management, and distribution of the processed data.

Satellites are also being used in educational projects. SITE brought instruction to remote Indian villages and PEACESAT links up widely dispersed South Pacific islands for purposes of broadcasting entertainment and educational programs. Control Data's PLATO system provides hundreds of sophisticated educational software programs worldwide over their CYBERNET. Anywhere a customer has access to a telephone and satellite linkup, the technology offers on-line, instantaneous, individual, computer assisted learning. Cost limits such usages much more than does availability.

The entertainment and informational uses of satellite systems are proliferating primarily on the domestic front. In the United States, RCA and Western Union satellites are being employed extensively to provide television programming across a wider range of uses (pay TV; religious and foreign language broadcasting) and modes (teleconferencing, teletext, facsimile, remote editing). The global impact of the instantaneous, worldwide distribution of television signals was dramatically demonstrated during the 1969 moon landing. Transmitting pictures for twenty-two hours to an estimated audience of 538 million required cooperation among a half dozen entities, including NASA and Eurovision. Thus the moon landing was made available in a transparent manner to the viewer through interconnecting many different technologies into an almost universal system.

The business uses of international satellite systems are also proliferating. Although most of these rely on privately leased facilities in the United States, in Europe and elsewhere, government agencies such as PTTs are moving to provide public data networks for both public and private sector consumers. The functional international systems that have received the greatest exposure and use are the banking system known as SWIFT (Society for Worldwide Interbank Financial Telecommunications) and SITA (Société Internationale de Télécommunications Aeronautiques), the reservation system used by most airlines providing international service. SWIFT has effected a global revolution by opening up the international money market to on-line, real-time, twenty-four-hour banking. Money is in constant motion around the globe, and international bankers must and can respond promptly to currency fluctuations worldwide. The airline reservation system, which uses SITA, knows neither national boundaries nor political animosities: although most countries maintain a national airline, many—for example, Poland, Hungary, and Bulgaria—process their reservations through a computer located in Atlanta, Georgia.

Finally, multinational companies are developing their own computer-communication facilities. IBM, for example, has several worldwide data networks. The multi-mode communications service offered by Satellite Business Systems provides businesses with internally managed communication systems that could technically, if permitted, bypass the PTTs if they were permitted to offer such services internationally. Such private, intra-company communications offer great flexibility, diversity, and interactivity; what they do not offer is interconnectivity.

POLICY ALTERNATIVES

Yet interconnectivity is needed if new satellite systems are to be used most productively. Moreover, transparency must be achieved if such interconnected systems are to be cost-effective. Thus, interactivity is also necessary, especially if individuals are to exercise choice in the individualized educational environment provided by systems like PLATO.

Those who would like to encourage a world in which information may flow freely across national boundaries would be wise to concentrate their efforts on the building blocks which can insure that global communications systems develop in a manner which can accommodate and encourage such flows.

Translated into common sense, action-oriented policy, these building blocks mean:

—developing satellite systems which can be economically used by the largest number of users
—developing protocols and standards which permit diverse technical

systems to be pieced together to form integrated international public networks
—encouraging the development of cable television and home computers which put interactive responsive telecommunications into the hands of users
—developing mechanisms for shared use of facilities where individual needs cannot justify the efficient and cost effective use of advanced communications systems
—designing telecommunications systems with random access switching rather than centralizing authority and control in a tree branched head-end.

Finally, and most importantly, it means public investment in publicly available computerized communications facilities which will provide universal access to the public switched integrated international networks.

Information technology is benevolent or malevolent only according to its use. The potential for ill should not be permitted to impede progress toward positive goals. The technology can provide instantaneous and equitable access to information. We can make this process apolitical only if we concentrate on building the system rather than fighting over the content. Responsibility for how the system is used will devolve upon the users whether they be individuals, business entities, institutions, or nation-states.

Twenty-Three

Transnational Data Flow: An International Policy Survey

G. Russell Pipe

The computer has introduced boundless possibilities for the storage, integration, transfer, and accessibility of vast quantities of information. The convergence of computing and telecommunications has removed earlier technical constraints of distance and transmission costs in setting up international information networks. Even these developments may be outpaced by concurrent advances in semiconductor and laser technologies, ushering in the micronization of computer power and transmission possibilities with seemingly limitless applications. The automated office, briefcase computers with sizeable memories, interactive home communication systems, a plethora of voice and video cassette equipment, and many other innovations are coming into use in the major industrialized countries, giving rise to new industries in information equipment and services.

Many corporations which have been involved in manufacturing industrial products or data processing equipment are expanding into this high growth sector. The annual reports of Exxon, Xerox, Chase Manhattan, General Electric, Aetna Insurance, Columbia Broadcasting Corp., Inc. and dozens of other Fortune 500 American-based multinationals illustrate an expansion into information industries: A cadre of small entrepreneurial endeavors have also emerged, such as Aspen Systems Corporation, Calspan On-Line Information Service, Data Courier, Dataflow Systems Inc., Information Access Corp., and Micromedia Limited. In Europe there is a parallel trend, and expansion of the computer industry is sometimes supported by government funds. The European Computing Services Association, for example, has 500 members in Western Europe, providing services to thousands of user companies.

Traditionally, vendors of data processing and telecommunications equipment and services have restricted themselves to their respective specialties. With the blurring of the distinction between processing and transmission and the thrust of new techniques, however, a major restructuring of these organizations is in progress. Telephone companies, such as the privately owned American Telephone and Telegraph Company and the many government-run post and telecommunications monopolies in Europe, are concerned about rapid growth in private company-leased line data traffic, impending satellite services using rooftop antennas, the home video (view-data) market, electronic message switching, and other new services wrought by modern technology. Computer companies like IBM have launched Satellite Business Systems (SBS), Control Data has CYBERNET, and other companies are branching out into providing equipment to facilitate linkups and better utilize telecommunications possibilities.

Publishers and broadcasting companies are also moving into data resources as auxiliary products and services, the *New York Times Index* being an early example. Micrographics and "electronic" newspapers, periodicals, and books already show the potential to revolutionize publishing. Newspapers and press agencies rely more and more on digital communications to transmit material to editorial centers and to redistribute it around the world.

It is not surprising that this changing information communications environment has drawn the attention of national governments. Most countries are in the early stages of grappling with the political, legal, economic, and social ramifications of the "informatization of society" for their own economies. Nevertheless, because the movement of information and knowledge is not restricted by territorial boundaries, many of these issues are now under deliberation by regional, international, and intergovernmental organizations as well. International involvement (some would contend interference) tends to upstage national efforts to define and prepare communications policy in this area because, it is asserted, the stakes are too high to allow undue advantage to any one country, region, or bloc. Indeed, the concept of interdependence may be baptized by the international debates on the information/communications issues.

U.S. INTERNATIONAL COMMUNICATIONS POLICY

An official statement of U.S. policy on international communications submitted to Congress in 1979 was prepared by the Department of State (6). The provision for formulating such a policy was explained in Senate Report No. 95.842:

> Last year the International Operations Subcommittee held a series of hearings which served to emphasize the growing importance of a variety of political and technological issues relating to the transfer of information across international boundaries. Because these issues will be dealt with in a decisive way

at a number of international conferences now scheduled, and because the United States is the leading user of communications channels and information in the world, the committee believes it to be imperative that the U.S. government establish effective procedures by which to develop and maintain a comprehensive United States policy in this area. This section, which was initiated by Senators McGovern and Percy, calls upon the President to transmit to the Congress by January 20, 1979, a report detailing, first, the policy-making mechanism which has been developed for this purpose and, second, the goals and general policy (not negotiating) positions of the United States with regard to anticipated international meetings which will address communications and information issues.

The State Department document describes very clearly the U.S. interests in international communications:

The United States has national security, political, ideological, economic, and technological stakes in international communications.

Our national security is dependent on advanced telecommunications systems. Politically, we are committed to a broad exchange of information both domestically and internationally.

Our economic interest is obvious: our industrial base relies on adequate communications; large corporations have become increasingly dependent on world-wide computer circuits. Moreover, the United States is the world's largest producer and consumer of telecommunication equipment and services. (Exports of communications computers and auxiliary hardware exceed $5 billion per year.)

Technologically, the United States holds a lead in most areas of satellite communications, in fiber optic communications (along with Japan) and in very large electronic switching systems. In other areas of basic communications technology, such as microwave transmission systems or satellite earth stations, the United States, Japan, and Western Europe are roughly equivalent technologically. In computer and data communications and in their applications, the United States is commercially dominant.

The report also emphasizes that "more Executive Branch resources are being allocated to communications issues, and policy is being coordinated at higher levels of government and approved at the highest level." The framework for the coordination of communications policy includes the National Telecommunications and Information Administration (NTIA) and the International Communication Agency (ICA).

In reference to data flows, the U.S. policy statement reiterates America's preeminence in the area of computer equipment and services, and their economic importance: "Computer systems are critical to multinational corporations and the data service industry. They store, process, and transmit information, and transfer funds for aviation, banking, and other industries. Transborder data flows are thus important." A step is taken toward differentiating data flows and news, or public communication: "Although the principle of free flow of information is also applicable to transborder data flows, in contrast to DBS and UNESCO, the information involved is essentially economic and technical data or personal records rather than news or other forms of public communications."

The report then refers to an interagency task force on transborder data flows research and policy coordination chaired by the Department of State and NTIA. This task force has had an active role in formulating the U.S. position in the Organization for Economic Cooperation and Development (OECD) project to draft international guidelines for dealing with personal data flows. The task force is operating according to the following broad objectives:

1. To assure U.S. multinationals and others of nondiscriminatory access to low cost, efficient information systems.
2. To assure non-discriminatory commercial opportunity for U.S. firms that are marketing international data processing and data bank services.
3. To participate in developing international computer, data processing, software and encryption standards.
4. To protect the privacy of personal data of U.S. nationals.
5. To support general access to scientific and technical data bases.
6. To respond to international concern about U.S. domination of international computer and data processing and the reliability of access to U.S. bases.
7. To encourage U.S. access to foreign advances in hardware and software technologies.
8. To encourage foreign governments to restrict their privacy laws to coverage of natural persons.
9. To provide a functional system for government-to-government exchange of data with due regard to national security and personal privacy.

American initiatives in supporting its communications policy have thus far been relatively successful. The precepts of the international communications policy were vigorously pursued at the UNESCO 24th General Conference during the framing of a mass media declaration, resulting in a text which presented an acceptable linguistic compromise. In discussion and debate in other international forums, such as the OECD, the U.S. similarly has been able to maintain its basic position.

United States international communications policy is a useful framework for the analysis of issues involved in transborder data flows for two reasons. First, it illustrates the justification for countries to initiate national strategies and policies aimed at building stronger domestic economic and social systems. Second, in the international arena, it posits an ideological, political, economic, and social philosophy to be defended in negotiations on a bilateral and multilateral basis. The debate, but not negotiations as yet, has opened a flurry of issues and arguments.

INTERNATIONAL DEBATE

National interests in the international debate on transborder data flow have been expressed in many forms. The press has chosen to headline the sensational: the *Washington Post*'s "The Coming Information War" (Jan. 5, 1978), the *European Community Newsletter*'s "A World Information War?" (Jan.–Feb. 1979), and *Datamation*'s "Is the World Building Data Barriers?" (Dec. 1977). Some partisans for an unregulated environment have substituted the term "data" for "news" and assert the principles contained in the U.N. Universal Declaration's Article 19 or in Articles 9 and 10 of the European Convention on Human Rights. Others have introduced the language of "a free and balanced flow" of information into the debate. In these discussions, however, the effort to distinguish data flow from media interests, at least on the basis of economics, has been unsuccessful. Another group has supported the idea that international communications are necessary in an interdependent world, but has had difficulties pinpointing specific areas of local competence which should be downgraded in favor of external suppliers and cooperation.

Charged language and unsupported assertions, rather than facts or solutions, have characterized this debate, both in print and at international meetings. Empirical analysis has been lacking because proponents of measuring the quantities (bits and bytes) of data streaming across frontiers are vigorously opposed by those who claim that data flow is a qualitative matter. Those arguing the qualitative side stress that it is not how many data cross a national border but what is done with them. The organizations which opt for quantitative standards are the postal, telephone, and telegraph companies which in Europe are urging the International Telecommunication Union (ITU) to charge telecommunications tariffs based on volumes of data transmitted rather than the time used in transmission.

INTERNATIONAL POLICIES: FRANCE, CANADA, SWEDEN

The French government has initiated a number of steps to ascertain the impacts of data flow on the French economy and citizenry. The motives prompting French actions were articulated by Louis Joinet, formerly Magistrate with the Ministry of Justice and now Secretary-General of the Commission on Data Processing and Liberties, in an address to the OECD symposium on Transborder Data Flow and the Protection of Privacy in Vienna, in September 1977: "Information is power and economic information is economic power. Information has an economic value, and the ability to store and process certain types of data may well give one country political and technological advantage over other countries. This, in turn, leads to a loss of national sovereignty through supranational data flows." These steps, instituted by the French Ministry of Industry, have taken the form of a program to provide data-processing products for export, and the implementation of projects for the "informatization of French society." In addition, in December of 1978 a government task force was appointed to assess the interests of France in international movements of information (*Transnational Data Report*, December 1978, p. 16). The phrase "transborder data flow" is to be particularly avoided, says Philippe Lemoine, a consultant to the "Chef de la Mission à l'Informatique," because it "gives the impression of being a problem which is still technical and obscure. . . . To be more precise as to its potency in levels of employment in countries and their balance of payments, a simpler term would be *international information commerce*" (4). The government task force, composed of officials from the ministries of justice, foreign affairs, taxation, and customs and from private data processing companies, is assessing the impact of information commerce on the French economy.

For at least ten years, the Canadian government has also been trying to establish and maintain an information-communications policy. A number of studies have been produced on privacy, satellites, cable television, and communications in remote areas. A report entitled *Telecommunications and Canada* (1) completed in April of 1979 considers the implications of transborder data flow for Canadian sovereignty (see also 3). According to the report, Canada is increasingly reliant on foreign, primarily U.S., computing services. When 400 Canadian subsidiaries of U.S. companies were approached, it was found that in 1978 some 300–350 million dollars worth of computing services were imported from U.S. company headquarters, with an increase to about $1.5 billion estimated for 1985. Further, it was expected that, as a result, about 23,000 jobs in computer services will have been lost to the Canadian economy by that time. Such a dependence upon foreign computing services would, the committee suggested,

—reduce Canadian control over disruptions in service resulting from technical breakdowns or work stoppages
—reduce Canadian power to ensure protection against other events, such as invasions of personal privacy and computer crime
—lead to greater dependence on foreign computing staff, which would result in turn in lower requirements for Canadian expertise and a smaller human and technological resource base upon which systems specifically geared to Canadian requirements could be developed
—jeopardize the exercise of Canadian jurisdiction over companies operating in Canada which store and process their data abroad
—undermine the telecommunications system in Canada by the use of for-

eign communications satellites and roof-top receiving antennas for the importation of data into Canada
—entail the risk of publication of information that is confidential in Canada
—give access to Videotex services based on foreign databanks emphasizing foreign values, goods and services
—facilitate the attempts of the government of the United States to make laws applicable outside U.S. territory

Because a piecemeal approach to various aspects of the problem might have undesirable side effects on the Canadian economy or result in regulatory "overkill," the report suggests that "the only solution lies in the cooperative development of a national strategy to protect Canadian interests and derive the greatest benefits from the development and use of informatics technology in Canada." To this end the committee made two recommendations:

RECOMMENDATION 23: The federal government, in concert with the governments of the provinces and the private sector, should stimulate forthwith the development of plans for the creation of Canadian-owned private databanks, as well as others funded by governments. Tax and other incentives should be devised for that purpose.

RECOMMENDATION 24: The government should act immediately to regulate transborder data flows to ensure that we do not lose control of information vital to the maintenance of national sovereignty. Therefore the government should:
—Launch a national awareness campaign to explain the social, economic and cultural implications of the new electronic information society. Without a much wider appreciation of the fundamental nature of the changes now taking place it is unlikely that effective mechanisms for considering the issues will be developed, let alone the implementation of appropriate solutions. It should be the responsibility of the Department of Communications to monitor the development in this area.
—Require that data processing related to Canadian business operations be performed in Canada except when otherwise authorized.
—Consider the feasibility of extending the provision in the Bill to revise the Bank Act related to the prohibition of exporting client data for processing and storage abroad. This might be extended, for example, to the insurance and loan industries.
—Provide greater access to risk capital for Canadian corporations in data processing, to prevent foreign take-overs. Use government procurement more effectively in promoting Canadian enterprise in this area.
—Promote more effective education and training for high caliber programmers, systems analysts, and others required for developing Canadian systems. The emphasis should be on application development rather than on machine-oriented research and there should be an effort to exchange personnel between government and industry.

Some more cautious steps have been recommended by other groups, however. At a seminar organized by the Institute for Research and Public Policy in Montreal in 1978, several business executives warned Canadian government officals that "misguided regulation . . . could prematurely freeze computer technology and increase the cost of doing business in Canada" (2).

Highly automated industry and public services have made Sweden a notable example of a planned society. However, there have been negative reactions to the bounties of this computerized welfare state. Partly as a result of the zealous statisticians of the 1971 census, and as an assurance to the public that the identity-numbering system was not creating a population of non-people, the first national law to establish rules over the collection, maintenance, and dissemination of personal information was adopted in 1973. The Data Act, as it is known, established a Data Inspection Board, which had jurisdiction over public and private sector data banks, and imposed a licensing requirement on organizations maintaining personal records. Section 11 of the statute states that personal information may be exported only on the condition that there be equivalent protection wherever the information is to be kept. This stipulation of equivalency has been a force behind discussions in the Nordic Council, the Council of Europe, and the OECD to harmonize other national laws and regulations covering personal data flows.

Other fundamental issues relating to the automatization of society have since been raised. These include a decline in jobs and the quality of working life due to the use of computers, the concentration of information on the Swedish population into a few central registers and computer centers vulnerable to internal or foreign induced breakdowns, and an increasing dependence on computer systems which use imported equipment and rely on foreign data processing. A number of Cabinet-appointed commissions investigated these issues and their results were presented to Parliament in late 1979.

Parliament adopted a data policy bill that contained principles and policies for administrative data processing within the public sector. Most policies favored a decentralization of data centers, with joint development of several systems being recommended to provide uniform national operations. Following a recommendation in the 1979 bill, the government established a delegation on data policy to make it possible for political parties, industry and employer associations, and local authorities to have access to information about data flow.

The concern about foreign influence upon the operation of Swedish society has been extended to another area—that is, the storage of sensitive political, economic, and social information about Sweden outside the country. The danger inherent in this possibility prompted one member of Parliament to state that "the critical mass of data concerning the Swedish economy and its citizens should never leave the national territory." Both the government and leaders in business, labor, and other organizations are currently assessing the extent of this threat so that its implications can be incorporated into a more broadly based "data policy."

DATA FLOW IN DEVELOPING COUNTRIES

For two decades or more leaders of developing countries have complained about the imbalance in the flow of news and media products. Recently, the potentials of computerized information systems, especially as they apply to public administration and planning, have received major attention. From this discussion has come the new term "informatics." Going beyond merely the act of computerizing personal and public information, informatics encompasses the infrastructure and management techniques employed to use, apply, and integrate such information. It has been defined as "the political and economic power of information" by the Director-General of the Intergovernmental Bureau for Informatics (IBI), an international body which has been formed exclusively to focus on informatics development and national policy.

A 1978 IBI survey showed that 60 countries have already adopted some form of official informatics policy. Most have enacted legislation creating an administrative authority to direct or coordinate the procurement of data processing equipment and training of operators, and to set priorities in its use and application. A further role of such authorities is to make possible the integration of record systems for the improving of public services, especially to remote and less developed areas. The characteristics of the Japanese "National Information System," France's "Plan Calcul," and the recent report to the U.S. President on a "National Information Policy" have received press attention and are somewhat known. Less familiar may be the national informatics strategies which have been introduced in countries such as Algeria, Brazil, Cameroon, Cuba, Ghana, Iraq, Jordan, Mexico, and Zaire.

ISSUES IN DATA FLOW

A 1978 survey published in the *Transnational Data Report* (5) of respondents from business, government, and academic circles in 67 countries indicated that developing countries differed from developed countries on several issues. Such issues included whether important data banks should be kept in their national boundaries, whether data flow across borders is a threat to "national integrity," and whether national laws will slow the growth of international data flows.

The transborder data flow, then, really involves several issues, with different countries selecting different areas for focus and debate. The political, economic, social, and technical issues involved are only beginning to be recognized. However, it is clear that several important considerations may already be enumerated:

1. The many issues involved in transborder data flow are interrelated but lack a fully developed theoretical or conceptual framework.

2. Data flows provide considerable political and economic power, especially as they affect the operation of multinational corporations and the sovereign interests of nation-states.

3. The need for and use of technology—both hardware and software—have received most government attention thus far. However, as evidenced in the debate over direct broadcast satellites, content is also becoming a principal point of consideration.

4. The post-industrial period, indeed the opening decades of the twenty-first century, can be expected to be an era of information/communications. Acknowledging its far-reaching impact on countries at all levels of development will require a considerable expenditure of human and financial resources by national governments, international bodies, academic institutions, and private organizations.

5. Attempts to deal with early manifestations of data flows are mostly in evidence on a regional basis and in a few United Nations organizations. There is a pressing need for a more rational treatment of information/communication topics which cut across traditional institutional arrangements.

The rapidly changing environment in which these issues are evolving demands that a sound empirical and historical framework be constructed as a basis for enlightened public policy. This is a challenge for academic institutions as well as for those who will design and implement such policy in the future.

REFERENCES

1. Canada, National Parliament, Consultative Committee on the Implications of Telecommunications for Canadian Sovereignty. *Telecommunications and Canada.* Ottawa, April 1979, pp. 63–65.

2. Cundiff, W. F. and Mado Reid (Eds.). *Issues in Canadian/U.S. Transborder Computer Data Flows.* Proceedings of a conference at the Institute of Research on Public Policy, Montreal, September 6, 1978.

3. Gotlieb, Allan, Charles Dalfen and Kenneth Katz. "The Transborder Transfer of Information by Communications and Computer Systems: Issues and Approaches to Guiding Principles." *American Journal of International Law* 68, 1974, pp. 227–257.

4. Lemoine, Philippe. Article in *Systemes d'Informatique.* Paris, May 1979.

5. Lloyd, Andrew. "World Questions Free Flow of Economic Data." Special issue of *Transnational Data Report* 2(7), 1980.

6. U.S., Dept. of State. *Reports Submitted to Congress Pursuant to the Foreign Relations Authorization Act,* Fiscal Year 1979 (Public Law 95–426). Washington, D.C.: U.S. Government Printing Office, March 1979, pp. 67–83.

Twenty-Four

International Finance and the Information Industry

Cees J. Hamelink

The bulk of information goods and services flowing across the globe is produced and distributed by the roughly 100 large corporations that constitute the "transnational industry-information complex." These corporations, based in the United States, Japan, England, the Federal Republic of Germany, France, Italy, and the Netherlands, advocate competition but many are strongly interrelated through such mechanisms as joint ventures, mutual stockholdings, and interlocking directorates. Together these concerns control an estimated 75 percent of the global trade in the subsectors identified in Table 24.1 (1).

The core of the information-industry complex—where the greatest overlap between informatics and telecommunications occurs (see Figure 24.1)—is dominated by the largest corporations, which spend the most money on research and development and reap the highest revenues in the complex. Though the information industry overall is rapidly gaining ground on both the domestic and the international economic front, the core companies account for roughly 10 percent of world trade, an impressive figure that has enticed such entities as Volkswagen and Exxon into this arena.

The information industry is highly capital-intensive. The fixed costs for the production of goods such as films, records, and TV shows are high. Moreover, in the core of the complex, 5 percent of total revenues are directed to research and development (microelectronics, lasers, optical fibers, satellites), a greater expenditure than one finds in the chemical, mining, energy, or automobile industries. At the same time, the favorable ratio between high fixed costs and relatively low variable costs encourages concentration in the industry.

Clearly, the information industry must be financed on a massive scale. Taken as a whole this sector falls into the category of moderate to heavy users of long-term debt: the ratio of long-term debt to assets is 20 to 50

Table 24.1   Information Subsectors and the Goods and Services They Provide

Subsector	Goods and Services
Informatics	mainframe computers, minicomputers, peripherals and terminals, service and software, media and supplies, data processing and storage
Telecommunications	telephone, telex, and satellite systems (operated) telephone switching systems and telephone sets telex and message switching systems coaxial cable microwave systems satellite communication systems launch and space vehicles earth stations (manufactured)
Broadcasting	radio and TV stations, radio and TV programs
Films	feature theatrical films, feature TV films, videotapes
Publishing	newspapers, magazines, books, educational materials
News	print news, photo news, film news
Records	records, tapes, cassettes, videodiscs
Advertising	promotional messages, media campaigns
Consumer electronics	radio and TV receivers, record players, VCR equipment, tape recorders
Supporting technology	printing equipment, newsprint/paper, copiers, typewriters, film, cameras, studio equipment, radio and TV transmitters, electronic components like semiconductors

percent. As noted earlier, however, the information-industry complex invests heavily in R&D (some 30 percent of the world research and development budget) and attracts many investors on this ground.

Finance in the form of financial information is also important to the information industry. Up-to-the-minute news on the currency, stocks and bonds, and commodities markets is vital to the industry's survival.

THE IMPORTANCE OF INFORMATION TO THE FINANCIAL SYSTEM

Information and financial systems relate to each other in complex ways. First, banks need to market themselves and to fill customers' requests for

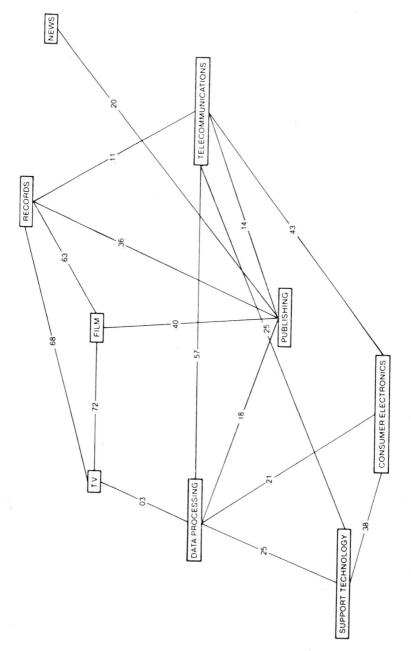

Figure 24.1 Density of Multi-Sector Activities.

information about account balances, foreign currencies, interest rates, bond markets, etc. Second, banks need to provide fund transfer services; indeed, money transfer has become information transfer. Third, banks need to follow political and economic developments worldwide (e.g., money market fluctuations, changes of government, crop failures). Thus, the operations of banks, especially large transnational banks, involve collecting, processing, storing, and disseminating information on a vast scale. These activities take various forms:

• Banks compile political and economic profiles of key trading areas throughout the world for internal or client use; such profiles are based on information from diverse sources such as national central banks, trade journals, and news services; some banks produce "country risk profiles."

• Banks publish newsletters, often quoted as authoritative sources by broadcast and print journalists.

• Some banks maintain information services departments—which may have revenues exceeding those of the international news agencies (as in the case of Chase Manhattan).

• Banks use telephone, cable, telex, and satellite services provided by private and public carriers; they also use internal computer-communication networks for transborder financial data flows.

SWIFT, GLOBECOM, and EUREX are transnational information systems serving the financial sector. SWIFT, the Society for Worldwide Interbank Financial Telecommunications, connects over 700 banks in 26 countries through European and U.S. centers. Established in 1973, SWIFT handles more than 150,000 transactions daily: customer transfers, bank transfers, foreign exchange confirmations, and loan or deposit confirmations. GLOBECOM, the network of leased channels that interconnect Citibank's overseas branches in some 60 countries, handles more than 300,000 transmissions per month via computer switches in London, Bahrein, Hong Kong, and New York. Incorporated in 1977, EUREX serves the European bond market through a network of leased lines connecting most of the European financial centers. This system has on-line links with clearinghouses and provides information, trading, and back office services to its customers.

Finally, banks recently have turned to advertising, breaking with tradition, both because competition has become stiffer and because service diversification (into insurance, for example) cannot succeed without publicity. Thus, banks have been quick to purchase the very information goods and services they help finance.

LINKS BETWEEN THE FINANCIAL SYSTEM AND THE INFORMATION INDUSTRY

Bankers are obviously interested in the equipment and services the information industry can deliver to them. Also, since the information industry can be described as big, growing and profitable business, it would indeed be rather unusual if the banking community were not interested for investment purposes. Moreover, the capital intensive information industry needs to approach the financiers for the expansion of its capital supply through credits, mergers, acquisitions and the sales of stock.

Over the past decades a strong interdependence has grown between large transnational financiers and the information industry. In a study on the converging interests between finance and information I have used indices such as stockholdings, interlocking directorates and debtholdings to establish the degree of financial control over information corporations (2). Combining the cases in which banks have the capacity to exert a significant degree of control, financial control was found in 35 percent of the information corporations. Adding to this those cases in which banks are certainly among the influential controllers, a significant to moderate degree of financial control is present in 50 percent of the world's largest information firms.

Looking at the sector where financial control is strongest the data indicate that of the corporations under significant financial control more than three-fourths are involved in the production/distribution of information hardware. This is further corroborated by the customer-supplier links that exist particularly between the banks and the dataprocessing and telecommunications corporations. In all probability the degree of financial control is significantly larger in the information industry than in other industrial branches. This is primarily due to the fact that the dataprocessing and telecommunications sectors of this industry are very expansive, capital intensive and profitable types of industrial production and distribution.

TRANSBORDER FINANCIAL DATA FLOWS

The international data flow has assumed vast proportions. Raw data, machine-readable data, and computerized information travel world-wide via different signals and media. While most data are still transported in relatively traditional ways—say, by telex or telephone—the rapid convergence of computer and telecommunication technology has resulted in computerized data networks that speedily and reliably transmit enormous volumes of information in the form of digital signals. Table 24.2 surveys various applications of these transnational computer-communication systems.

Presently, transborder data flows consist of technical or scientific and

Applications	System	Traffic	Data	Example	Benefits	Users
Coordination of operations; corporate management	Centralized processing (computer to central computer)	Bulk transfer	Production, marketing, accounting, personnel	IBM	Large volume transport and processing	Transnational firms
Banking and credit control	Distributed networks (computer to computer; people to computer)	Interactive data transmission	Customer and bank transfer, bond, stock and credit letters, foreign exchange	SWIFT	Resource sharing, volume, speed, validation, security	Banks, credit bureaus
Reservations	Distributed networks (computer to computer; people to computer)	Interactive data transmission	Customer records, ticket availability	SITA	Resource sharing	Airlines, travel agencies
Databanks	Remote access (teleprocessing) timesharing (people to computer)	Interactive data processing	Scientific, economic, and technical data; simulation models	CERN, GE, Lockheed	Resource sharing, large volume of data processing, information access	Scientists, governments, business, communities
International governmental cooperation	Distributed networks (people to computer)	Interactive data transmission	Meteorological data, criminal records	WMO, INTERPOL	Resource sharing, information exchange	Governments, intergovernmental organizations
Public tele-communications	Message switching (people to computer to people)	Message transmission	Telephone and telex messages	GLOBECOM (RCA)	Large volume transport, speed and reliability	General public

economic information. We can assume that financial data represent an important part of this traffic and that banking interests figure heavily in such information flows. The following discussion takes these assumptions further.

Transnational banks are constantly making decisions based on international developments. Management needs quick access to vital information on customers' banking activities and therefore staunchly advocates free flow. (The Western information media thus have powerful allies in the global banking community.) At the same time, the banks' need for centralized data processing and system interconnectivity brings them to the computer and telecommunication manufacturers that dominate world markets, supporting concentration in that industry. Finally, transnational banks transmit huge volumes of data over great distances. They therefore prefer leased private circuits to public carriers that charge volume-sensitive and distance-sensitive tariffs. No matter the route, banking data must be kept secure, but balancing personal privacy and national sovereignty is particularly tricky in regard to transborder flows of financial information. Regulations in this area—and the technology to circumvent restrictions—are developing side by side.

FINANCIAL INFORMATION: THE NEW INTERNATIONAL ECONOMIC/INFORMATION ORDER

Financial information traveling across the globe takes the form of computer data transmitted through banking networks and economic news transmitted through transnational news agencies and newspapers. As I noted earlier, financial data—an important portion of all transborder data flows—are in large part controlled by the transnational banks that own or operate transnational computer-communication systems. Chase Econometrics, Reuters, and AP-Dow Jones are the services that meet most of the world demand for economic news. Such information reaches the business community at large via the seven leading financial newspapers: the United Kingdom's *Financial Times*, the *Wall Street Journal*, the *Australian Financial Review*, Brazil's *Gazeta Mercantil*, the West German *Handelsblatt*, Italy's *Il Sole-24 Ore*, and the *Nihon Keizai Shimbun*.

Financial information flows follow the general pattern of international communications: there is two-way traffic among the countries of the North and between those nations and the countries of the South. However, the flow north consists primarily of raw, unprocessed data; the North then exports completed information packages to the South. Though such imbalance also exists in the North, with the United States processing a large portion of Europe's data, for example, Western Europe, the United States, and Japan all exchange information goods and services. The economic consequences of this pattern are enormous.

Although recent international debate has tended to ignore the link between world information flows and economics, many countries (including the newly industrializing nations) are rapidly becoming information economies, with information goods and services taking an increasingly prominent place in world trade. At the same time, the complexion of this trade is strongly influenced by the financial and information giants, which enjoy close mutual ties. Indeed, the information-industry complex controls access to the world's preeminent resource, financial data. The quest for a new international order thus has to focus on rectifying this situation. Unfortunately, the dizzying pace of technological developments in communications, the enormous financial stakes involved, and the convergence of economic and information power structures lessen the possibility of a prompt solution.

REFERENCES

1. Hamelink, Cees J. *The Corporate Village*. Rome: IDOC, 1977.
2. Hamelink, Cees J. *Finance and Information*. Norwood, N.J.: Ablex, 1982.

Twenty-Five

Transborder Data Flows: Competition and Regulation

Herbert S. Dordick

Transborder data flow is data transmission via computer-communication across national boundaries. Numerous computer-based telecommunications systems now span the globe, permitting the continuous and virtually instantaneous transmission of data for processing, for maintenance in files or libraries, for retrieval and updating, for remote computing and analysis, for the performance of transactions, and for any other operations that add value to the information product. The availability of relatively inexpensive terminals capable of remotely accessing powerful computers and large data bases has made the transfer of data processing tasks via telecommunications networks a common occurrence in the United States. Nora and Minc (4) noted, for example, that the proliferation of international satellite communications has made it economically sensible for a significant number of French firms to transfer part of their processing operations to the United States. Indeed, the time difference encourages European firms to conserve computer power and cut processing and data storage costs by transferring a portion of their operations during the full hours in Europe to the empty hours in the United States.

This new technology has created concern about information dependence, self-sufficiency in information processing and production, and the economic and cultural aspects of technology transfer, issues that take their place alongside earlier concern over privacy, sovereignty, and telecommunications and information industry economics. Thus, Brazil, Canada, and France are actively seeking to control foreign participation in their nations' budding information industries, by imposing selective tariffs on equipment and by discouraging local industries from purchasing foreign information products. Free trade in information products is thus under severe attack—despite inadequate empirical data on just what is happening in the world's networks and what the future is likely to hold.

210

Both developing and highly industrialized nations are concerned about their future trading prospects in an era of global computer-communication networks. Specifically, developing countries fear that once again they may be relegated to being providers of basic resources unable to form sufficient capital to become providers of higher valued information products. Inadequate capital can severely limit a nation's ability to obtain the human skills necessary to make a place for itself in the new information markets, let alone the specialized equipment required for successful participation. More developed nations, too, are concerned with the degree to which they can maintain or improve their market positions in this highly competitive and technologically sophisticated area of product manufacture and sales.

An industrial production model of transborder data flows with the computer-communication network perceived as a distributed production facility is a useful instrument in the analysis of the economic impact of transborder data flows.

THE INFORMATION NETWORK AS A PRODUCTION FACILITY

A widely distributed network of computers, software, terminals, and data bases constitutes a production facility in which new information products and services are manufactured or value is added to existing products and services. Producers pool resources to achieve economies of scale or they specialize in processes and products in which they have the competitive edge. There is even room for the small producer to tailor products and services to an individual user's specifications. The aggregation of interconnected resources constitutes a massive production facility, which enables producers to purchase only those production capabilities that they need and to change the mix easily and quickly as production demands change and markets alter.

The notion of an information good or product is relatively recent. In the past the production of information was thought of as *processing* rather than manufacturing. In legal terms a manufactured article is something made by hand as distinguished from something created naturally. But as machinery has largely supplanted this method, "manufactured" is now ordinarily applied to an article upon which labor has been expended to make a finished product. In general, the manufactured article takes a different form or serves a different purpose from the original material and is given a different name; for example, the mining of coal is not manufacturing because "the substance was coal when it was extracted from the mine and subjected to processing and it was coal at the conclusion of the processing" (*T. T. Calley* v. *Eastern Coal Corporation*, 470 S.W. 2d 338a + 340 [KY 1971]). If manufacturing requires a substantial transformation of natural products, then the process of gathering raw data, as in surveys, for example, constitutes a transformation and thus manufacturing, especially if the data product is packaged on a tape or chip.

Daniel Bell (1) argued that information is a basic resource both as raw material and as finished product and that information machines are basic tools in the manufacturing process in postindustrial society. Given the increasing sophistication of data capture methods and equipment, including the politically sensitive remote acquisition via satellite, it is difficult to conceive of low-valued raw material for the manufacture of information products; rather like oil, information—raw or processed—is inherently valuable if perceived as such by the purchaser.

By any definition, data gathering that transforms events, natural phenomena, or abstractions into information is a form of manufacturing; the output is a definable and marketable product whose value is greater than that of the unorganized material from which the information was produced. Data processing is a transforming activity producing a new product with value added every step of the way. The factors of production, capital, and labor are required here, as in the manufacture of any other good.

INFORMATION PRODUCTION AND MANUFACTURE THROUGHOUT THE WORLD

Little is known of the types and amounts of information or data flowing across national borders; however, transborder data flow is insignificant in volume compared to domestic flow. Local units of multinational companies apparently have become relatively independent of their parent companies, especially with respect to information product manufacturing and processing, but some multinationals have centralized their data processing, including employee record processing,[1] in one or a few countries. Despite these important trends, little research has been done on the economic consequences of transborder data flow.

Most transborder data flows involve economic, financial, or administrative data. Airline reservations, other travel transactions, banking, credit, insurance, information services, and several industrial and scientific exchange services constitute the major types of today's information transfer. Even a cursory examination of the rate at which terminals capable of accessing computers and data bases are multiplying and the comparable growth in international telecommunications channels indicates that the number of potential "manufacturing" locations and branch "job shops" will soon create a veritable flood of transborder data.

The rate of proliferation of data terminals in the United States is about 20 percent per year. By the end of 1980 there were somewhat more than four million terminals in the United States; in Europe there were about six hundred thousand terminals by that date. The recent French decision to expand significantly France's telephone and computer-communication terminal industries can be expected to at least double this European figure by 1985.[2]

In parallel with this growth, there is rapid proliferation of both public and private international telecommunications networks. While many of them, such as United Press International's circuits, were configured for low-speed narrow-band services, the availability of low cost digital communications techniques will allow for significant network upgrading. By installing their own switching centers, these formerly primitive networks can be developed into moderately high speed transmission facilities for data. Major banks, including Citicorp and Chase Manhattan, maintain international networks. Both SWIFT (Society for Worldwide Interbank Financial Telecommunications) and SITA (Société Internationale de Télécommunications Aéronautiques) serve numerous customers in Europe and North America.

Public networks available for international traffic include, of course, the existing submarine cables, which have been added to, rather than curtailed, with the launch of international satellites (such as INTELSAT). Finally, several commercial networks are designed for data communications: General Electric, Computer Sciences Corporation, and Control Data have long offered such services worldwide. Indeed, there are few places on the globe that cannot be reached by a telephone or terminal of one sort or another.

The network of data production and transmission is emerging throughout both the developed and the developing world. With the decreasing cost of data processing, coupled with the almost universal access to one form or another of international communications, most nations will be capable of mining the natural resource of data in a form that will be valuable to someone. This is but the first step in the manufacturing process that creates information goods and services. If competitive advantages in the production, processing, and distribution of information goods or services appear, nations will wish to benefit from these economies of specialization. Assuming that these competitive advantages appear, what are some of the barriers to profiting from them?

CONSTRAINTS ON TRANSBORDER DATA FLOW

The issue of personal privacy is crucial both to the individual and to the nation. A government that cannot protect the privacy of its citizens has lost its sovereignty. But the manner in which privacy is assured must be carefully weighed against economic loss to the nation, a loss that will be felt in jobs and national income. Additionally, a nation that locks itself out of the international computer-communication network will also lock itself out of the market for the increasingly complex technology vital to the information society.

Tariffs and other trade barriers also affect participation in the transborder data network. Japan has effectively locked out U.S. firms by means of unusually high local network costs and tight government restrictions on obtaining domestic circuits: Control Data had to wait more than two years for a circuit, only to find that government restrictions on the circuit made it almost impossible to operate. Likewise, in its 1979 report to the minister of communications, the Consultative Committee on the Implications of Telecommunications for Canadian Sovereignty (the Clyne Committee) recommended that "the government . . . should act immediately to regulate transborder data flows so that we do not lose control of information vital to the maintenance of national sovereignty."[3] Specifically, the committee called for the government to require that data processing related to Canadian business operations be performed in Canada unless otherwise authorized. Furthermore, the committee sought to extend the Bank Act, which prohibits the exporting of client data for processing and storage abroad, to the insurance and loan industries.

Such restrictions can cut both ways. For example, though the United States is currently the major provider of information services and products, an efficient data processing industry in Canada could attract processing and production work from the United States. Indeed, a major U.S. travel reservation service has recently contracted with a Toronto data processing firm to provide on-line accounting services.

As Ithiel de Sola Pool and Richard Solomon (5, p. 35) pointed out, "In all cases [of international rate setting] there is an issue as to whether tariffs should reflect carrier costs or whether they should reflect the value of the services to the consumer, i.e., what the traffic will bear." International rates tend to be high compared to domestic rates so that carriers, often (if not always) government monopolies, can earn a surplus on sophisticated services that will be used to maintain less profitable services. Furthermore, since the carrier sets rates it will do so with respect to imported business so as not to lose its own business.

Once again, these restrictions can cut both ways. Opportunities may be lost to import attractive information business that not only brings revenue but also enables the importer to learn new techniques and upgrade its own facilities or develop new facilities with which to achieve competitive advantages.

A necessary requirement for realizing the benefits promised by a network production facility is that it be transparent, allowing all forms of machine and terminal interaction with minimal need for specialized software and operating protocols. No nation wants to be locked out of the production cycle because it chose a protocol that does not meet agreed-upon international standards. But no nation wants to be forced to accept standards that are incompatible with its own interests.

There is a strong element of sovereignty in this game, particularly if proposed standards emanate from the most powerful competitor—and if the competitor is a multinational firm already deeply involved in the business of the country. As Nora and Minc (4, p. 67) pointed out, "Standardization is a cage. If IBM did not enter, its competitors rather than IBM would be locked out."

When to standardize is a critical technical issue that can become a significant political question. One might wonder why this issue should now emerge: over the years international agreements on radio and telephone standards have been, in general, easily concluded. Perhaps it is because we are dealing with standards that affect information and not merely communication.

FREE FLOW AND THE UTILIZATION OF KNOWLEDGE

Making a relatively modest capital investment, a developing country can obtain much of the equipment needed to acquire, store, and retrieve information. Satellite receive-only earth stations costs are falling rapidly; specialized minicomputer and microprocessors with high capacity bubble storage devices are becoming increasingly available. However, a nation can acquire the technology and be welcomed into the information society only to find itself falling even further behind in terms of the comparative statistics of development.

Access to and availability of information do not guarantee effective utilization; analytical skills and an infrastructure capable of using information for decisionmaking are also required. As Rita Cruise O'Brien (2, p. 43) aptly observed, "The problem is therefore not only one of international imbalance and inequality but also one of the assessment of requirements, expertise and institutional arrangements in the national context." Free flow and equality of access do not guarantee equality of results. Access and power do not necessarily equate; information is power only if it is used powerfully.

NOTES

1. Centralization of employee record processing has aroused widespread concern over privacy rights.

2. These figures refer to the public network; it is difficult to determine private capabilities, but they may almost equal the public.

3. This followed on the heels of Robinson's report (cited in 3, p. 14) which estimated that by 1985 thirty thousand electronic data processing jobs will have been created outside Canada to deal with Canadian information processing. Others fear that this is a conservative figure—the Royal Bank of Canada estimated one hundred thousand jobs!

REFERENCES

1. Bell, Daniel. *The Coming of Post-Industrial Society*. London: Heinemann, 1974.

2. Cruise O'Brien, Rita. "Specialized Information and Interdependence." *Telecommunications Policy*, March 1980.

3. Keddy, Barbara. "Transborder Data Flows: An Uncertain Threat." *In Search*, Fall 1979 (Department of Communications, Government of Canada).

4. Nora, Simon and Alain Minc. *L'Informatisation de la Société*. Paris: La Documentation Française, 1978.

5. Pool, Ithiel de Sola and Richard Solomon. "Transborder Data Flows: Requirements for International Cooperation." Unpublished manuscript, Research Program for Communications Policy, M.I.T., July 1978.

Twenty-Six

Toward an International Data Network[1]

V. A. Vinogradov, L. S. Kiouzadjan, T. V. Andrianova,
S. K. Vilenskaya, G. B. Kossov, A. M. Kul'kin, R. R. Mdivani,
A. I. Rakitov, V. R. Khisamutdinov, and L. V. Shemberko

No efficient system of socioeconomic information is possible without analyzing information needs, and how to meet those already manifest, or latent. Two approaches may be adopted to this end: as a separate research area; and as the basis for designing an information system.

Much research has pointed to the significance of a complex analysis of information needs and stressed the danger of information systems producing a mass of irrelevant data, useless in the process of decision-making.

One of the goals of the study of information needs is the identification of those principles according to which types and forms of information packaging for various categories of users are differentiated.

It is well known that those requiring socioeconomic information greatly exceed the number of its actual users. The main purpose of an information system must therefore be to cater appropriately to the main categories of users.

The most important determinant of information needs is the user's profession—scientific research, management, planning, teaching—the analysis of which allows the hierarchy and priority of information needs to be established.

Users can be divided into several basic groups; however, information needs within each are heterogeneous: (a) researchers and research teams; (b) teachers, the information needs of whom have been analyzed quite extensively by the INFROSS project of Bath University (United Kingdom); (c) statesmen, politicians and decision-makers at the governmental, organizational, national and international levels; (d) those responsible for development programs, including the construction of indicators; forecasting studies, surveys and maps; the analysis of socioeconomic and sociopolitical situations; evaluation of research projects, etc.; (e) mass media personnel; (f) information services (national and international) catering to the interests of the above categories.

National information bodies (existing and future) in developing countries cannot meet the needs of individual users, but may function, more or less satisfactorily, by dividing users into categories. One should begin an investigation of information needs and the derivation of a typology of users with an analysis of the structure of the economy. Since users in some developing countries do not always know precisely what information will advance the solution of national problems, they are compelled to consult foreign specialists (principally in industrial countries). Hence the requirement of effective methods to ascertain information needs through the collaboration of national personnel with foreign specialists. The bulk of research on information needs has been conducted at the national level, though the international significance of socioeconomic information and the importance of collaboration in information on a global scale are clearly acknowledged. The creation of an international system would both help to broaden access to information and overcome the isolation of national systems, centers and services.

The investigation of user-system interrelations must be supplemented by a study of various approaches to the creation of a language for the user's interaction with the information system (national, regional, international) and also by research into the choice of optimal search strategies allowing for the fullest satisfaction of the needs of broad segments of users. To construct an ideal or at least relatively efficient model of information needs, qualitative and quantitative methods of forecasting must be worked out, through the coordination, within the framework of UNISIST, of research projects in different countries.

THE ORGANIZATION OF INFORMATION SERVICES AND NETWORKS

National and International Services and Centers

Numerous publications deal with the organization of information services and networks. We wish to refer particularly to *Handbook for Information Systems and Services* by Pauline Atherton (2), especially Chapter IV, and to the rather comprehensive information on information services in European countries and Canada from the materials of the first European Cooperation in Social Science Information and Documentation (ECSSID) Conference held in the U.S.S.R. in June 1977 (3).

Socioeconomic information institutions include special libraries, data centers, analysis centers, service centers and general centers, providing comprehensive information services. It is next to impossible to give their total number but it is estimated that there are some 243 bodies in Europe, and 112 in the U.S.S.R.

Lately, libraries have extended their information activities: the Lenin State Library of the U.S.S.R., for example, is the information center on culture and arts, and the State University Library in Hamburg is the information center on politology.

Data centers deal with raw or semi-processed data, while, as a rule, centers handle data evaluation, dissemination, and reference services. Their activities have resulted in the creation of data banks, the efficiency of which was substantially enhanced by the availability, in the early 1970s, of specialized software packages for statistical data processing. Among the most advanced data centers are the Inter-University Consortium for Political and Social Research in the United States, the Cologne Zentralarchiv in the Federal Republic of Germany, and the Norwegian Social Science Data Services.

Information analysis centers collect data on concrete, strictly defined areas. They analyze and evaluate information, store it and diffuse it through data lists and reviews. They also provide services both in the SDI mode and as replies to queries.

Information service centers may be libraries, other information service components or independent bodies. They provide SDI using external data bases on magnetic tapes, collect, and process user information profiles. All acquisitions are examined for their compatibility with requests. Bibliographic information on documents requested is printed up and sent to the users. Services of this kind are usually rendered for a fee.

Over the past decade information institutions of a new type have emerged, combining libraries and information centers into a complex whole. Among such pioneering bodies are the Institute of Scientific Information on Social Sciences of the U.S.S.R. Academy of Sciences (INION), or the Fundamental Library Centre of Scientific Information of the Czechoslovak Academy of Sciences. INION is a combination of a large information center, a fundamental library and a publishing house, a structure creating significant advantages by facilitating the acquisition of unified holdings, and multiple uses of information from a single input. The institute has a computer center and has started automated procedures for preparing publications using electronic photocomposition, selected dissemination of information and retrospective retrieval.

National services may be considered from different viewpoints, for example according to subject coverage, to the degree of automation, to types of services rendered, to their organization or to geographical scope.

Most countries have a number of separated and isolated bodies, a rather obvious tendency towards integration and cooperation exists.

The term "national information systems" covers various types of centers. In the U.S.S.R., as in most European socialist countries and some other countries, the systems function on a nationwide basis; elsewhere cooperation is carried out by cooperative arrangements.

The INION of the U.S.S.R. Academy of Sciences is the nationwide information center on the social sciences which coordinates the work of separate information subdivisions. The system comprises central branch bodies, thirteen republic centers and a network of information divisions of scientific institutions and higher educational establishments, etc. INION is closely connected with all of them and coordinates their work.

The tasks of information centers in the U.S.S.R. are practically the same as those of INION, but local in scope. They process and forward to INION information on scientific projects, which help to feed the INION data bank. They also acquire and process the world flow of publications dealing with their own region.

At the international level, several information systems have been launched, such as DEVSIS, COMNET, EUDISED, SPINES, DARE and the international systems of the socialist countries on pedagogy and culture (Interinformculture).

Also, over the past five years several international bodies have been established for socioeconomic information, including the International Association for Social Science Information Services (IASSIST), 1974; the international social science information system of the socialist countries (MISON), 1976; the Committee on European Social Science Data Archives (CESSDA), 1976; the European Co-operation in Social Science Information and Documentation (ECSSID) Project of the European Centre for the Co-ordination of Social Science Research and Information in Vienna (Austria), 1977; and a special committee of the International Federation of Data Organizations (IFDO), 1977.

MISON is of special interest, since it is functioning successfully and has yielded practical results.

It is a multiprofile and multipurpose information system of the Academies of Sciences of Bulgaria, Hungary, Viet Nam, the German Democratic Republic, Mongolia, Poland, the U.S.S.R. and Czechoslavakia founded in July 1976 in Moscow, and based on equitable cooperation between the participating national scientific information systems. Each country has selected a national information center to co-ordinate activities within the MISON framework. Activities are guided by the MISON Council on which sits one representative from each academy of sciences; the leading MISON body is INION.

MISON has set itself the task of working out and introducing uniform approaches to designing an automated system and unified methodological, linguistic, mathematical and technical procedures. Methodological directions on abstracting and preparing bibliographical publications, exchange and premachinery formats, and a "MISON Rubricator" have been adopted. Experiments on the exchange of information on tape and through other communication channels have been started.

The ECSSID project of the Vienna center, designed to promote European cooperation, has become another catalyst. An important aspect of it is coordination of the principles and norms for the input, storage and exchange of information, elaboration of uniform linguistic and terminological approaches to information and data exchanges, etc.

Data Banks, Information Networks

The present state of technology opens up prospects for an automated information system (AIS) through the use of data banks and bases.[2] Generally, a data bank can be defined as a system for the accumulation of interrelated data from one broad area (field of knowledge, territory, organization) that provides random access to the entire accumulated stock of information.

A data bank has the following characteristics to distinguish it from the earlier information retrieval and computing systems oriented towards specific, strictly defined files and targets: (a) independence of special applications and calculations; (b) absence of data duplication; (c) multiple functions and recall; (d) feasibility of access and operation; (e) structural flexibility.

The basic technological characteristic of a data bank is the separation of content and physical structure of data files from software. An operational feature just coming into prominence is the possibility of on-line access to a data bank.

The data bank is the basis for the organization of information networks, the simplest variant of which is a complex of remote terminals connected with the host computer. Access to the latter (commands for data retrieval and processing) and the input of information into files is carried out from terminals. The latest variety of information networks are distributed data banks (bases) (DDBs). DDBs represent a new stage towards the maximum independence of substantive areas from data files and technical constraints. DDBs provide comprehensive information processing on remote computers, i.e., the information network is not a series of terminals, but of interrelated computers. An essential DDB component is special management through a set of facilities, devices and methods that relieve the user of many constraints and allow him to focus on the specifics and requirements of his particular needs.

DDBs represent the most efficient form of information exchange and processing. Data banks, information networks—especially those based on DDBs—are the most effective devices for obtaining and processing socioeconomic information which usually comes in from remote points, and consists of data that differ greatly in their semantics, structure and volume and are to be applied in various fields. The universality and logical and functional structure of data banks and their design makes it possible to use the wide experience accumulated in the process of developing data banks in other fields in the sphere of socioeconomic information.

As examples of data banks on socioeconomic information we can take the corporate data base of the Scandinavian countries on regional time series, the data bank on Italian cities, and the system of automated data banks on social, economic and political sciences which is being created under the auspices of the Centre National de la Recherche Scientifique in France. The latter has bibliographical data bases on the social sciences and a data bank on current political events. For information retrieval from these data bases, a widely known software package is used.

According to certain assessments, data bases, access to which is provided through automated information systems, at present contain about 60 million bibliographical references.

In addition, there is wide use of data bases containing quantitative information of various kinds. Their number is not known exactly, but is somewhere in the hundreds.

Social scientists have always been in need of raw (primary) data which libraries have failed to meet. Consequently, there have appeared specialized centers (archives) for the collection and analysis of voting and survey data, and social statistics by country or region.

The users of data processing systems form a large, fast-growing group. Thus, for example, in Sweden over 1 million people or 28.7 percent of the working population use such information, about 300,000 of them through computer terminals.

Access to different data bases offers fresh opportunities for the information bases of interdisciplinary research. It also makes it possible to conduct selective retrospective information retrieval from different data bases without huge initial investments for the creation of very large consolidated local data banks. But information systems can function successfully only if there are service centers.

Technical progress has required drastic changes in information control. Since there was a certain lag in this field in Europe, it was decided to organize a new service to meet the needs of scientific and business circles. Called Euronet, and functioning at the level of the European Economic Community, it was set up in the summer of 1979, and already offers direct access to bases of scientific, technical, juridical and socioeconomic data through terminals in Amsterdam, Brussels, Dublin, Copenhagen, London, Luxembourg, Paris, Rome and Frankfurt.

From the outset, Euronet has been providing access to approximately one hundred data bases, 75 percent of which are European; suppliers are fully responsible for the data selection and operation of their services.

Eighteen supplier organizations ("Telesystem," SPI, Blaise, Infoline) are interested in being switched to the Euronet network, as well as a number of internal centers, for example, within the Commission of European Communities; which will then become available to all users. Contacts have been established with private firms to obtain access to data banks.

Information is generally of a technical character, but in view of the European parliaments' preoccupation with the correction of asymmetry in the data, steps are being taken to increase the number of data banks with socioeconomic information (at present there are only five). A certain insufficiency of economic information is also evident, it being proposed to create within a few years a statistical and economic data bank of the Commission of European Communities. As yet there is no intention to establish links with North American networks, but in the future this will no doubt be done on a mutual basis.

Access to Euronet is through rented communication lines, through the state telephone networks or through state data transmission networks, in those countries where they exist.

The tariff rates reflect the main principles of the Community: unified tariffs for international transmission of data, irrespective of distance, based on the duration of linkage with the network and on the volume of communications. Special measures are being taken to lower current rates.

The extension of the European network is being contemplated: thus, in September 1979, an agreement was concluded with Switzerland to that end.

But Euronet organizers face many difficulties, particularly the automatic and semi-automatic translation of terminological data banks and multilingual thesauri to overcome the language barrier. To facilitate the use of data banks, Euronet is creating special information services which will store information in data banks to which Euronet has access. This system is called DIANE (Direct Information Across Networks for Europe). The data banks will include large United States bibliographic files on the social sciences. Also worth mentioning is the new data bank on sociopolitical problems, EUROBASE, which deals with elections to the European Parliament.

For historical reasons, different data banks use different retrieval methods, i.e., different linguistic means, methods of abbreviating terms, and logical operations. This has led to a situation where users of different data banks have to follow many different instructions, a serious problem in working with the network environment.

The service rates are high, a large part being for telecommunications. In recent years, extensive efforts to create automated systems and networks have been made in socialist countries. The MISON system is being elaborated as a network of automated systems; participating data banks will contain information on the most scientifically interesting publications appearing in these countries.

Obviously, these data banks will also interest Western countries, and the opportunities of mutually advantageous cooperation have increased thanks to the ECSSID project, which has the exchange of magnetic tapes and mutual access to data banks on its agenda.

Operational Problems of an International System

Cooperation in creating and correlating automated information bases, the integration of data banks and access to them from different countries are the most important and promising directions towards an international socioeconomic information system. However, considerable research and development will be required to resolve difficult organizational, administrative, legal, financial, political, technological, linguistic and mathematical problems.

One group of legal and administrative problems concerns safeguarding copyrights, access to existing and future networks and data banks, and payment for services. These are set out in the 1971 UNISIST report. The Conference on Security and Co-operation in Europe, at which the participating governments confirmed their readiness to further information exchange, gives hope that progress will be made.

The political problems are related to the fact that the majority of information networks and data banks are predominantly under the control of developed West European and North American countries. Even if the legal, technological, and financial problems of providing access to networks through communication channels are solved, other countries may find themselves dangerously dependent on changes in the political situation in the world arena. The creation of alternative data banks at a national or a regional level would require resources not likely to be available to developing countries in the foreseeable future. One possible solution could be the placing of all large information networks under the control of international organizations, such as UNESCO.

The technological problems include servicing several users simultaneously, including remote ones, which implies standardizing the protocols of telecommunication access to information networks, and training personnel. It is also important to tackle the problem of exchanging information in different languages and different alphabets (Roman or Cyrillic).

The alternative approach envisages the equipment of centers in the countries where the Roman alphabet is used with input-output units which make it possible to use both the Roman and the Cyrillic alphabets with due regard for diacritical marks.

Among the organizational problems are the division of labor on information processing and input, the creation of automated reference systems, directing users to data banks corresponding to their needs, and the design of management and scheduling.

There is less difficulty with mathematical problems. Practically, the programs for different systems are becoming more similar, a certain satiation of program function potential is evident, and problems of information conversion from internal to exchange formats and vice versa are being solved.

Linguistic difficulties are among the hardest. The form in which they arise is somewhat different from that which they assume in autonomous national systems.

First of all, the language barrier has to be overcome. The manner in which the content of social science documentation is extracted is not uniform, but is expressed in various natural languages, unevenly distributed around the world.

Specialists experience great difficulties in overcoming language barriers in two areas: in making it possible for users to acquaint themselves with scientific findings and in enabling the rest of the world to acquaint itself with their work. This problem is typical not only of national languages in developing countries.

Creating an international socioeconomic information system is closely bound up with problems of language compatibility which can be divided into two groups: those related to the differences in languages and those related to the creation and use of information retrieval languages, which make the functioning of multilingual systems possible.

From the point of view of language compatibility, an ideal solution would be a service giving users the full text of sources in their own language. However, at present no effective automatic translation exists; thus presenting sources in languages accessible to the user can only be done through translators. It is quite evident therefore that specialized translation and/or abstracting services constitute a necessary element in developing an information infrastructure.[3]

CONCLUSION AND PROSPECTS

An international socioeconomic information system should be a flexible, gradually developing network able to cope with an ever-growing volume of information. The greater the opportunities for a society to obtain rich and diverse information, the easier for it to make sound decisions in conformity with its evolution and aims.

Socioeconomic information is to be an international resource, and the acceleration of development depends to a greater extent on how accessible it is, how efficiently it is used, and the extent to which it corrects existing imbalances.

The preservation and strengthening of peaceful coexistence between different socioeconomic systems through détente is not only a welcome but also an indispensable factor for social progress on a global scale, as well as a key precondition for the unfolding of information processes. Recent experience has shown that, when used as an instrument of political pressure, scientific information is either stultified or voided of its scientific character. Tensions and confrontation inevitably block all the information channels, socioeconomic information in particular, while peaceful coexistence and stable détente promote the continuous circulation of scientifically grounded information.

We now propose the following three prognostic scenarios which are more complementary than alternative. The first can be called a long term scenario, for its implementation is hardly possible within the coming years: it may be regarded as an ultimate ideal. It supposes a consolidated, automated socioeconomic information system at a regional or even global level providing access to all information from all countries, branches of industry, norms and managerial situations for any user anywhere. Its establishment, however, would require such a high level of automation, investment, and special training as is hardly attainable not only at present but probably also over the first few decades of the coming century. Nevertheless if this ultimate perspective is not kept in view in the elaboration of local information systems, it may turn out that in the distant future, integration, and consolidation within a consolidated structure will prove impossible.

The second scenario can be called preparatory, being quite realistic and, if properly constructed, can even today prove widely useful. It is based on the assumption that valuable scientific and technological information is currently being produced by a relatively limited number of industrial countries. The rest of the world generally makes use of it, its form and content being the same for all. Thus, information on physics, chemistry and technology is normally consumed in the very form in which it is produced, requiring no more than a general university qualification on the part of its users.

Socioeconomic information, on the other hand, is produced everywhere but differs significantly from country to country there being no absolutely identical national situations. Such information is of value both for purposes of cross-national cooperation and contacts. The task, therefore, is to make it available in acceptable form to users of the most varied backgrounds. Its dissemination promotes trust and mutual understanding. The second scenario therefore does not propose ready-made local, regional and global information systems but concerns the preliminary steps connected with the investigation of current information needs in different contexts. It applies to institutions capable of responding to two questions: first, what types of information produced abroad can be used domestically in the attainment of local socioeconomic goals? Second, what types of information produced domestically can be useful abroad? Thus, the second scenario represents a preliminary stage involving an extensive analysis of information requests, needs and the information situation of each country.

The results can be used in constructing, projecting and linking information systems at all levels.

Finally, the third scenario calls for a detailed elaboration of methodology for the practical construction and exploitation of integrated socio-economic information systems in three stages: country-by-country, at the level of regions and worldwide. At this point the third scenario falls in line with the first one. All the stages require maximum reliance on the experience already gained in the field, as under the MISON system. Due to marked differences, such experience cannot well be mechanically transferred, but almost any country can profit from thoroughly studying and adapting it to local conditions. The complex dynamics of international relations, and differences in material, financial and human resources mean that the implementation of these scenarios in different countries will vary over time, but they should be "staged" in succession. It seems most realistic to carry out the first scenario in the majority of industrial and many developing countries. By the beginning of the next century it could be a reality almost everywhere given current or accelerated paces of social and scientific development. The second scenario can probably be carried through by a number of countries, including some developing ones over the last decade of the present century and almost certainly within the first quarter of the next century. Presumably this will be followed by the third long term scenario, although these perspectives remain shrouded in thick fog and their chronological order rather uncertain.

In any event it is clear that the identification of the major stages, the main scenarios of our information perspectives provides ample ground for reflection and cooperation in search of the most correct and radical solutions to pressing problems in the field of socioeconomic information.

NOTES

1. This chapter is excerpted from the *International Social Science Journal* 33(1). © UNESCO 1981. Reproduced by permission of UNESCO.

2. These terms are frequently used as synonyms. But for many specialists a data base is specifically organized information files (a system of subfiles) that can be utilized for various operations; a data bank is a data base together with its management system: software, communication networks, and interfaces of different types.

3. Studies carried out by ASLIB and EUSIDIC on 337 data banks in Western Europe show that 76 percent work in English; 10 percent in German; 10 percent in French and 4 percent in other languages. Of 149 data banks (including about ten terminological ones) 66 percent use English, 20 percent other languages, and only 7 percent are multilingual (1). With the Automated International Social Sciences Information System of socialist countries (AIS MISON) the working language is Russian, in which the system data bank is formed. For a more in-depth description of the linguistic problems of data bases and how the Soviet republics have dealt with linguistic problems, see (4, pp. 41–45).

REFERENCES

1. ASLIB/EUSIDIC. *Data Bases in Europe: A Directory to Machine-Readable Data Bases and Data Banks in Europe.* 1976 (European Users Series).

2. Atherton, Pauline. *Handbook for Information Systems and Services.* Paris: UNESCO, 1977.

3. *Information Processing and Management* (Oxford) 14(3/4), 1978.

4. Vinogradov, V. A. *et al.* "Towards an International Information System." *International Social Science Journal* (UNESCO) 33(1), 1981, pp. 10–49.

Twenty-Seven

The Radio Spectrum: Principles for International Policy

William H. Melody

It is often said that the best things in life are free. Historically, one of these "best things" for a select group of users of high technology in telecommunications has been the radio spectrum. But, if the WARC-79 proceedings provide any indication, radio frequencies are not likely to remain free in the future.

As a natural resource, the spectrum is more valuable than oil. High technological societies are heavily dependent upon information transmitted over telecommunication systems—telephone, television, and news and data services. Most industrial, political, and military institutions require efficient networks for information generation, classification, transfer, storage, and retrieval. Telecommunication systems—microwave, satellite, etc.—that use the radio spectrum support these operations. Indeed, loss of access to the spectrum would gravely disrupt the economic, political, and social functions of any high technology nation (see 10, 12). The spectrum is the cornerstone, and the Achilles' heel, of the so-called information society.

If this is so, why has the spectrum received little national and international attention until recently? The answer lies in the unique properties of the spectrum resource, the lack of knowledge and understanding of the significance of the spectrum outside the small technical community directly involved, and the ability of early national and international spectrum allocation schemes to satisfy a *limited* number of users. Now the spectrum has become a major international policy issue because demand for allocations has skyrocketed: the developing nations want in and the high technology nations want more. This pressure has prompted reconsideration of the traditional standards for spectrum allocation.

For perhaps the first time, there is a real possibility of absolute denial of important segments of spectrum to some future claimants. And even where new spectrum claims can be accommodated, the opportunity costs of receiving a second- or third-choice assignment are substantial and increasing rapidly. Second choices increase the costs of telecommunication equipment and services both in absolute terms and in comparison to first-choice assignments. The traditional criteria of spectrum allocation for international and, in many countries, national uses no longer satisfy.

THE SPECTRUM RESOURCE AND ADMINISTERED SYSTEMS

When valuable economic resources are allocated to users at zero or nominal cost, the system will remain viable only as long as awareness of this very favorable state of affairs is limited to its beneficiaries. Once the word gets around and a significant number of potential beneficiaries begin to make claims for the "free" good, it becomes necessary to establish a formal system for distributing the resource among claimants. Resource allocation can proceed via market systems or administered systems.

Most economic resources and products are allocated through market systems, with prices reflecting current exchange values. Administered systems employ nonmarket criteria—technical, economic, social, or political standards—in allocating resources. An administrative authority judges the compliance of applicants with the standards and selects among competing applicants. Of course, market systems and administered systems overlap. For example, all markets require a set of administrative rules, say, laws of property and contract, for their functioning, as well as a common understanding of acceptable and unacceptable market behavior. In turn, administered systems are influenced by market forces acting on the administrative process, and many include selected market criteria in the set of factors upon which administrative judgments are made.

The radio spectrum traditionally has been allocated by administrative authorities at both the national and the international level. When the spectrum is allocated and assigned, no price is charged to users for the spectrum resource obtained (the market price is zero) although the various spectrum claimants do incur the costs of participation in the administrative process. But, as we all know, someone must pay for free lunches. In fact, the economic opportunity costs of the spectrum are very high. Spectrum allocations for one service preclude valuable alternative uses. And recipients of spectrum assignments are able to realize substantial savings by access to this resource.

By definition, all administrative processes are political: the necessary judgments require a balancing of competing interests. As we have seen, the criteria specifically considered in administrative decisions may be technical, economic, social, and/or narrowly political. If the major political and economic interests affected by an administrative process remain stable in their relative power and influence over time, and the basic character of the administrative problems does not change significantly, the process will soon evolve into an apparently technical exercise. Nevertheless, the evaluation of technical trade-offs and the selection of technical standards will reflect the establishment's political and economic influences, which remain invisible to outside observers. This state of affairs insidiously preserves the status quo: resolving political and economic differences in the labyrinth of technical issues creates an enormous barrier to entry for outsiders desiring to break into the process. Outsiders must somehow phrase their broad political and economic interests in terms of complex technical issues, where they are at an overwhelming disadvantage. If outsiders pursue their political and economic interests directly, they will be accused of politicizing a technical process, ignoring technical realities, and demanding the technically impossible. Indeed, these changes have been heard.

INTERNATIONAL SPECTRUM ALLOCATION

Until recent times, spectrum allocation has responded to relatively stable political and economic influences from dominant governmental and industrial interests in the developed nations. The essential problem for the International Telecommunications Union (ITU) has been to accommodate, by means of technical standards and adjustments, the new demands for spectrum and new telecommunication technologies. Spectrum allocations have been made on a first-come, first-served basis; second and third waves of demand have been technically fitted into a system wherein the early bird got the best frequency. Indeed, soon after its establishment, the ITU took on the character of an old boys' club of engineers, the relatively stable political and economic forces growing invisible even to many of the participants (see 3).

WARC-79 marked a watershed for change in the underlying structure of political and economic influence upon which technical spectrum allocation decisions are made (see 11). The possibility of total exclusion from important portions of the spectrum and the disadvantages of low-priority allocations have been recognized as major policy issues, not simply complex technical questions. The fundamental issue of *priorities* among spectrum uses and users is now front and center, and the political and economic criteria for priority selection will no longer be submerged entirely in technical considerations.

The spectrum is a unique natural resource; in fact, it is a social resource in the broadest sense (see 4, 6, 7). Subject to neither private nor national ownership, the spectrum requires users to cooperate if the resource is to be used effectively by anyone. National, regional, and worldwide cooperation in spectrum allocation and exploitation exists now (although many nations have been excluded from the process) and has been maintained by opposing sides even during wartime. Although interference and congestion can reduce effectiveness, the spectrum cannot be exhausted, as can other natural resources. On the contrary, technological advances have steadily expanded spectrum capacity.

Spectrum rights are probabilistic, depending upon environmental conditions and the pattern of use at a particular time. Moreover, such rights are not susceptible to legal enforcement, as are private property rights, although both international law and national law in many countries recognize the spectrum as a social resource. To protect this peculiar form of social property, the global community needs a set of sharing rules that reflect the interests, values, and power of all affected parties. At present, the developing countries are pressing to change the international sharing rules established some years ago by a small group of high technology nations to further their own interests in an atmosphere of relative plenty.

EFFICIENCY IN SPECTRUM USE

One major difficulty with administrative allocation of the valuable spectrum resource is that there is little, if any, economic incentive to conserve. To the contrary, if the cost of using spectrum is essentially nil to the user, there is an incentive to waste and even to hoard spectrum. Thus, as congestion and scarcity become more serious, it is important to create strong incentives to conserve. The United States and, to a lesser degree, Canada, are contemplating proposals to impose license fees on spectrum users at sufficiently high levels to make waste and inefficiency more costly to the user (see 1, 2, 5, 9, 13, 14). Also under discussion is the principle that spectrum license fees should be set at levels that would capture for the public the economic profit from exploiting the spectrum (see 8).

In addressing these issues, nations often tend to respond differently depending on whether the problem is at the national or the international level and on whether the nation is already using spectrum inefficiently. WARC-79 and related events prompted the high technology nations to return to ITU for reallocation, significant quantities of spectrum that had been obtained in prior allocations but were not being used or planned for use in the foreseeable future. This important first step will help eliminate stockpiling and improve efficiency on a global scale.

Although WARC-79 resolved some of the most pressing technical issues and debated underlying policy issues that had not been questioned within the ITU since its creation, no long-term policy goals or directions were established (see 15), thus setting the stage for continuing WARC negotiations on spectrum allocation. WARC brought to the forefront the apparent conflict between equity and short-run economic efficiency. The developing nations can claim a greatly expanded share of the spectrum on the ground of basic equity, but for the immediate future the high tech-nology countries—with certain exceptions—have the greatest and fastest growing demands and can make more efficient use of the spectrum. Although this issue has not been confronted head-on as yet, its resolution lies in the direction of compensation payments (i.e., fixed-term leases). Benefits that the developing countries cannot achieve by their own use in the short run can be realized through rents based on the value of the spec-trum. Such a compensation scheme would permit expanded use by the high technology countries during a transition period and stimulate research and development—especially on expansion of spectrum capacity to facilitate the necessary longer term adjustments.

SPECTRUM PLANNING

The apparent conflict of spectrum planning versus no planning is misla-beled and often misinterpreted. Any administrative system requires plan-ning. There always has been system planning at both the international and the national level. The first-come, first-served principle is a plan. Its suc-cessful implementation requires acceptance, or at least acquiescence, by all parties. The only sensible interpretation focuses this debate on different kinds of planning, which means different policies and different assessments of whether the proposed policies are good or bad. The real issue is straight-forward: an immediate adoption of massive changes in spectrum rights favoring developing nations at the expense of high technology nations could result in the allocation of spectrum to the developing nations that they are not ready to use, thereby keeping this resource idle, denying real demands from high technology countries, and possibly making equipment obsolete.

But these are short-term problems to be handled through a phased adjustment process employing transition rules such as the compensation payments suggested earlier. The important policy issue is that the adjust-ment process must be pointed toward a long-term goal that reflects revised, equitable sharing arrangements. Unfortunately, WARC-79 provided very little guidance as to what these long-term goals should be. Without spec-ification of the long-term goals and the underlying principles of spectrum allocation, spectrum use will follow the lines of the existing, unbalanced world economic order. With long-term goals and underlying principles established, communication technologies and markets can be directed, through a series of adjustment policies, to achieve them. Surprisingly, the United States in particular and the high technology nations in general refuse to recognize in the international spectrum policy debates the very principles of spectrum sharing that they employ in making their domestic spectrum allocations and assignments.

CONCLUSION

The gradual enunciation of revised spectrum sharing rules and the adoption of adjustment policies are not going to satisfy many nations seeking to protect and control their information environment. International spectrum allocation policies based on equitable principles of sharing are, of course, a necessary condition, but they are by no means sufficient.

Canada provides an excellent illustration. Two generations ago for broadcast radio and one generation ago for television, Canada unquestioningly accepted the spectrum allocations adopted by the United States for its broadcast systems. Equipment was manufactured, transmission and distribution systems established, and receivers sold. In the face of this infrastructure, Canadian cultural policy, attempting to prevent the Canadian mass media from being overrun by U.S. content, has been waging a losing battle. Canada's most recent efforts in this direction are being defeated by the establishment of earth stations across Canada in ever-increasing numbers to receive U.S. programs transmitted via U.S. satellites. At the same time, Canada continues to pioneer in the development of satellite technology as well as interactive data bank systems, such as Telidon; yet, the bulk of the mass communication and information service content to be transmitted over these systems will come from the United States. Thus, Canada is developing the very technology that enables Canadians to receive U.S. messages.

Free information flows, like free trade, are justified only if the flows are balanced and no nation or interest group dominates the terms and conditions of information exchange. For a developing country, the outward flow of specialized data about its domestic resources, markets, economy, political and social structure, and citizens, in return for an endless supply of U.S. television reruns, hardly achieves a balance. A crucial first step toward the creation of an international information environment in which free flows will be balanced—in both the volume and the structure of the information exchanged—is the establishment of an equitable set of sharing rules for the radio spectrum. If this goal is to be achieved, international spectrum negotiations will have to proceed at two levels: the formulation of specific long-term policy objectives and the development of transition policies and rules that set forth the temporary adjustments needed to reach the long-term objectives. For effective participation at both levels, nations require detailed knowledge of the technology. To a major degree, spectrum policy will continue to be negotiated in the trenches of technical trade-offs and standards.

REFERENCES

1. Canada, Department of Communications. *A Proposal for Restructuring the Radio License Fee Schedule*. Ottawa, 1976.

2. Coase, R. H. "The Federal Communications Commission." *Journal of Law and Economics* 2, 1959, pp. 1–40.

3. Codding, G. *The International Telecommunication Union: An Experiment in International Cooperation.* New York: Arno, 1952.

4. Levin, H. J. *The Invisible Resource: Use and Regulation of the Radio Spectrum.* Baltimore, Md.: Johns Hopkins University Press, 1971.

5. Meckling, W. "History of International Allocation and Assignment." Paper presented at the Conference on Economics of Regulated Public Utilities, Chicago, Ill., 1965.

6. Melody, W. H. "Radio Spectrum Allocation: Role of the Market." *American Economic Review* 70(2), May 1980.

7. Melody, W. H. and D. W. Smythe. "A Study of the Feasibility of Applying the Opportunity Cost Concept to the Spectrum Allocation Process." Report to Canadian Department of Communications, Contract No. OSU77–0368, Ottawa, 1978.

8. Melody, W. H., D. W. Smythe and A. Oliver. "A Study of the Applicability of Economic Cost and Value Criteria in Establishing License Fee Schedules for Radio Spectrum Assignments, with Particular Reference to the Microwave Range 0.890 mHz to 16 GHz." Report to Canadian Department of Communications, Contract No. 02SU–36100, Ottawa, 1979.

9. Minasian, J. R. "Property Rights in Radiation: An Alternative Approach to Radio Frequency Allocation." *Journal of Law and Economics* 18, 1975, pp. 22–72.

10. Ploman, E. W. "Vulnerability in the Information Age." *Intermedia* 6, November 1978.

11. Rutkowski, A. M. "The 1979 World Administrative Radio Conference: The ITU in a Changing World." *International Lawyer*, Spring 1979.

12. Smythe, D. W. "The Electronic Information Tiger or the Political Economy of the Radio Spectrum and the Third World Interest." Paper presented at the World Communication Conference, Philadelphia, Pa., May 1980.

13. United States Congress, House, Interstate and Foreign Commerce Committee, Subcommittee on Communications. *Option Papers.* Washington, D.C., 1977.

14. United States President's Task Force. "The Use and Management of the Electromagnetic Spectrum." Parts I and II, Staff Paper No. 7, United States Department of Commerce, Washington, D.C., 1969.

15. "WARC: More Conferences Will Be Held." *Intermedia*, January 1980, pp. 5–12.

Twenty-Eight

Remote Sensing by Satellite: Global Hegemony or Social Utility[1]

Herbert I. Schiller

The late fifteenth and the sixteenth century were the era of exploration and discovery for early Western capitalism. With what now seems painful slowness, navigators and sailors charted global waters and continental coastlines. Capitalism, as a system of world enterprise, required these geographical measurements. Half a millennium later, communication satellites photograph, survey, and "sense" the earth, transmitting the data around the world to reception stations that instantaneously process the information with powerful computers. In its entirety, this activity is termed *remote sensing*. The first experimental remote-sensing earth satellite was launched by the National Aeronautics and Space Administration (NASA) in 1972.[2] A data center (EROS) that disseminates some of the information derived from the sensing satellites began operating in 1974.

The uses to which remote-sensing data already have been applied are numerous and impressive, including crop monitoring, mineral and fuel exploration, forest management, national resource inventorying, flood control, pinpointing fish concentrations for the fishing industry, and charting Gulf Stream fluctuations. As an oil company spokesperson specified, the data have been used "for locating prime uranium targets, laying out pipeline routes through mountains, extrapolating geologic models to upgrade offshore drilling locations, pinpointing hot spots of concern in our refineries, mapping ancient burnout zones in coal fields, predicting areas of intensely fractured rocks for safety control in coal mining . . . and, of course, preliminary oil and gas exploration" (4, Part 2, p. 287). As the field is still in its infancy, the uses of remote sensing doubtless will multiply. It is already clear that the potential of remote sensing for providing physical information about all areas of the globe, for human benefit, is phenomenal.

REMOTE SENSING: THE QUINTESSENTIAL INTERNATIONAL ACTIVITY OR THE SOURCE OF HEGEMONY?

As an enumeration of existing applications demonstrates, the technique of remote sensing suggests one central assumption—this technology will benefit the general public wherever it is used. Yet this crucial expectation cannot be taken for granted.

Remote sensing, utilizing orbiting space satellites, is an *international activity*. Spatially, territorially, nothing less than the earth itself is the compass of the sensing process. Consequently, unless remote sensing is treated as a global public service function, fully in accord with the needs, wishes, and aspirations of the nations the satellites pass over and survey, the process can create suspicion and discord, rather than support and appreciation. That is, the *social* use of remote sensing must be assured if this technology is to be acceptable to the world community, whose space and geography the satellites routinely trespass. Precisely because this assurance has not yet been given, remote sensing is becoming a source of international uneasiness and disagreement.

The reasons for this disappointing direction in the development of a new technology are to be found in the structure of the economy in which the process originated: from the outset remote sensing has been used for national and private advantage. The groups that occupy commanding positions in the United States have been awake, from the beginning, to the opportunities offered them by this technology, and to capitalize on these possibilities the government—representing the overall system—specific clusters of corporate power, and the military machine have been the movers and shakers in the development and deployment of the new communication and information satellites.

Remote sensing, along with other high technology, is considered a strategic factor in the maintenance of the American global business empire. U.S. officials have frankly expressed this view. For example, former President Carter's science advisor and director of the Office of Science and Technology, Frank Press, assured a congressional committee in 1979 that "so far as the Europeans are concerned, they're starting in a position so far behind us that all their activity right now is an effort just to get going. The resources that we commit to remote sensing and other applications in space far exceed all that they do together." Press assured the legislators, however, that he could not "conceive that this Administration or succeeding ones would allow remote sensing technologies of other countries to supersede our own. . . . As you know, the President's commitment to maintaining leadership includes and subsumes remote sensing as one of the many areas in space where we want to maintain our leadership" (4, Part 1, pp. 50–51).

Becoming the "primary finders and developers of the world's non-renewable resources" (4, Part 1, p. 204), a possibility linked to the utilization of remote-sensing equipment, is no small matter when the limits of the earth's bountifulness are increasingly apparent and the struggle for access to scarce resources ever more intense. "Leadership" in space, and in remote sensing in particular, can give the United States the competitive edge in this struggle by wresting information about areas from those who have first claim on such knowledge—the local inhabitants. Consequently, this claim is dismissed, as in testimony by a high-ranking official in the U.S. State Department's International Environmental and Scientific Affairs Bureau:

> One [problem] concerns the question of sovereignty over information pertaining to natural resources. We find that many developing countries guard their natural resources quite jealously and are considerably concerned that advanced countries and companies within advanced countries, might be able to exploit them to their disadvantage. That has motivated a number of countries to assert sovereign control and sovereign claims over information and data concerning their natural resources that is in the hands of others.
>
> *This is a claim that, of course, we can't agree with and it is a claim put forth strongly by a number of developing countries. . . . We do not consider the question of sovereignty negotiable. That is, the question of sovereignty over information in the hands of others* (4, Part 1, p. 172, emphasis added).

Under this interpretation, leadership in remote sensing technology permits the leader to assume rights over the information obtained by satellite while denying the nation whose territory has been surveyed the right to claim sovereignty over its national resource information. This is a neat construal of international law.

Less legalistically inclined, Senator Adlai Stevenson, Chairman of the Senate subcommittee considering remote-sensing legislation, stressed force majeur as determining: "*We* have strategic interests in the world's resources" (4, Part 1, p. 209, emphasis added). And to protect these interests the military establishment enters the picture.

Actually, remote sensing has always been a military project, affording the United States a critical advantage in global deployment of forces and in intelligence gathering. This point was nicely made by COMSAT's executive vice-president:

> Specifically, the reason for carrying out Defense Department [data] collection activities is to be prepared for some kind of a military contingency, or to know more about what adversaries are doing. Typically, the uses for data on the civil side are not in the same parts of the world (4, Part 1, pp. 208–209).

In fact, the data collecting capability of the U.S. military is so sophisticated that it creates a problem of intelligence merely to mention it. As Senator Stevenson noted: "[Remote sensing] is a difficult area to discuss because everything is classified, and *most of those on the civil side don't know what it is we're talking about. But there are some who do*" (4, Part 1, p. 209, emphasis added).

Who are these "some who do"?

REMOTE SENSING AS A PROFITMAKING TOOL

Those in the know are found mostly in the private (corporate) sector, working for or managing companies with a material stake in the earth's resources, for example, firms engaged in resource exploration and exploitation, manufacturers of communications hardware, and data processors that turn the raw information gathered by the sensing satellites into commercially usable data.

These companies have no lack of expertise. For example, the Geosat Committee, an organization "sponsored by 100 U.S. and non-U.S. international oil, gas, mineral and engineering-geological companies who produce more than half of the nation's non-renewable energy and mineral resources," advises NASA, the U.S. Geological Survey, and other government agencies on technical issues. As NASA's administrator told Congress: "We are continuing to work with the Geosat Committee to explore ways to satisfy the needs of the petroleum and mining industries" (4, Part 1, pp. 199, 45, 62).

How these needs are satisfied is suggested by practices in the petroleum industry. According to a report in *Science*: "Consortia of oil companies have entered into agreements with the federal government to drill test wells for the sole purpose of gathering geological data, *but those data are not made public until the participating companies have bid on leases to drill for oil and gas nearby*" (1, p. 627, emphasis added). We can imagine how much more effective remote sensing could be in providing these same companies with privileged information on resource locations *globally*. Additional help in this effort comes from firms that process the raw data gathered by satellites, integrating this information with relevant material stored in commercial data banks. The last elements in the corporate sector involved with remote sensing are the electronics industry, which manufactures the hardware, and the communications corporations, which carry on the business of information transmission.

Though mining and mineral interests, data processing firms, and electronics and communications corporations do have conflicts of interest, all agree on the desirability and indeed the necessity of eventually using remote sensing for profitmaking under United States corporate management.

PRIVATE CONTROL OF A PUBLICLY FINANCED TECHNOLOGY?

Since World War II, a number of new technologies, funded by huge investments of public monies and carrying the promise of great public benefit, have been diverted to profitmaking and hegemonic ends. This practice is especially evident in communications. Remote-sensing technology seems slated for a similar fate.

The federal government financed the creation and development of this remarkable technology, but an exact price is unavailable because many of the costs were inseparable from those of other communication-space projects. Taking this problem into account, one authority stated: "If one goes back over the past 15 or 20 years to determine how much the U.S. Government has spent in these areas, it is very difficult to run down that number, but it exceeds billions of dollars" (4, Part 2, p. 267).

By the end of the 1970s, remote-sensing satellites were fully operational and Congress took up the matter of what should be done with this important activity, which still enjoyed government management. The discussions are instructive for they reveal the political-economic mechanisms whereby late twentieth-century American capitalism operates. Most striking of all is the paramount role of the government in developing and supporting the profitmaking interests of the corporate sector in new areas of the economy.

In early 1979, two bills were introduced in Congress "to establish an institutional framework for an operational remote-sensing system to gather data by satellite on the Earth's resources and environment" (4, Part 1, p. 1). One bill, sponsored by Senator Stevenson, recommended that a government entity, NASA, have initial operational responsibility, which eventually would be transferred to the private sector. The other bill, sponsored by Senator Harrison Schmitt, proposed that a private entity *immediately* take over the operational service, with no transition period of government management. Both bills and sponsors assumed that private management of the system is desirable and necessary. Only the timing of the private takeover separated the two proposals. However, the reasons for deferring private management of remote sensing illuminate government-corporate relationships in the present age.

In November 1979, President Carter announced that the Department of Commerce's National Oceanic and Atmospheric Administration (NOAA) would "manage all operational civilian remote sensing activities from space." At the same time, the president, following the recommendations of Senators Stevenson and Schmitt, insisted that "the Commerce Department . . . seek ways to further private sector opportunities in civil land remote sensing activities, through joint ventures with industry, a quasi-government corporation, leasing, etc., *with the goal of eventual operation of these activities by the private sector*" (5, emphasis added).

Thus, although remote sensing will remain a government function for an indefinite number of years to come, the intention to turn the activity over to the private sector has been proclaimed.

ISSUES IN THE TRANSFER OF CONTROL OVER REMOTE SENSING

The Disposition of Public Investments

The first issue to be faced in transferring operational responsibility for remote sensing from government to the private sector is how to handle the existing plant and equipment, all of which has been publicly financed. The business community, taking innumerable precedents into account, recommends giving away the technology free of charge to the private entity assuming control of the remote-sensing function. One businessman put it this way: "Whatever plant and equipment and other related investments have been made that are determined by the new organization to be useful for its purposes should be looked upon as a contribution by the Government to start off this operation" (4, Part 2, p. 267).

Financing Research and Development

Once the existing plant and equipment have been donated by the government to the private entity, the next question relates to the heavy costs of research and development—which probably have to be increased if American capitalism is to remain dominant in this strategically important sector. Who should underwrite these expenditures? The private sector is "universally agreed that the government should continue to conduct research and development programs in remote sensing systems and applications even after private operations are established" (2, Appendix 5). This position was seconded by NASA's administrator, Robert A. Frosch: "I think there would have to be a continuing government role in R&D, partly because we need that continuing stimulus for progress which would not certainly in the initial provision of services be easily accommodated while an outside entity was building up a market" (4, Part 1, p. 73).

Building a Market for Remote-Sensing Data

The main activity of a private business in charge of remote sensing would be to sell the data secured by satellite. Who would buy these data? Indeed, who buys the information now being produced? In 1978, the LANDSAT (remote-sensing satellite run by the government) data market showed the following user breakdown: federal government, 52 percent; private industry, 12 percent; non-U.S., 27 percent; and universities, state and local governments, etc., 9 percent (2, Appendix 7). The largest user by far is the federal government. The business community, as well as other informed parties, expects this pattern of use to continue: "Indeed, one company felt the government must provide 75 percent of the market share to make private investment attractive" (2, Appendix 5). This was also the opinion of NASA's administrator:

> One of the key questions in establishing any private entity as the favored or chosen instrument . . . is the question of the establishment of the Government as, in effect, a single buyer from that single source, because I think that's likely to be the initial economic guarantee that makes such an enterprise a viable one as it gets started, and as it faces the problem of aggregating and developing for the non-Government market (4, Part 1, p. 72).

The corporate sector in effect is demanding that government give away existing facilities; guarantee future R&D expenditures; promise not to enter into any competition with a privately run remote-sensing industry; provide a fixed market for remote-sensing data; and undertake the international negotiations that global remote-sensing activities necessitate (4, Part 1, pp. 181, 211). The extent to which this agenda will be followed will ultimately be determined by the level of opposition, if any, from what is now an uninformed and therefore indifferent public.

Hidden Costs

Still, the public aspects of the remote-sensing function are so pressing that uncontested adoption of the corporate agenda cannot be considered a foregone conclusion. In truth, the terms that the corporate sector has set as preconditions for direct assumption of remote sensing are the strongest arguments for maintaining public control of the new technology. All the vital elements in the operation require both the public's financial support and government guarantees. To be sure, government oversight and operation of remote sensing *of the sort now occurring* cannot be viewed as protective of the public's interest. The present government role in remote sensing, as in many other important functions in the economy, serves a corporate, not a popular, constituency; yet the public underwrites the entire effort.

Another unsettling element in the corporate scenario for managing remote sensing is that the high profits and insurance against losses that the agenda stipulates are only the *visible* costs of private enterprise in what is essentially a public undertaking. A longer term cost is the deepening information inequality in the society at large.

INFORMATION INEQUALITY AS AN OUTGROWTH OF MARKET FORCES

The management of remote sensing turns on the paramount issue of how technology is to be used. The kind of information sought, organized, and disseminated depends ultimately on who the primary user will be. The primary user, in turn, is an artifact of the decisionmaking process of the overall institutional system. To wit, once remote sensing—or any other information technology—is the instrument of a profitmaking private entity, market factors will determine the primary user. And market criteria insist that the user be identified on an ability-to-pay principle. Insofar as remote sensing is concerned, the ability-to-pay yardstick confers decision-making authority on the mineral and mining, data processing, electronics, and communications companies—or the federal government acting as a proxy for these interests. The public is disenfranchised in this kind of voting.

Local government and public interest groups are fully aware of this dynamic, which largely excludes their participation in this technology. The National Conference on State Legislatures, for instance, informed Congress that "the needs of public-sector users would not necessarily be adequately met in an environment where profit and loss are the major considerations" (4, Part 1, p. 107). The National Governors Association elaborated on this viewpoint:

> Due to the public service nature of remote sensing, it is recommended that the system be Federally owned and operated for at least the near term. The states' major concern, particularly in regard to the ground segment, is that a privately operated system could tend to develop standardized products in response to the needs of large, aggregated markets and reduce or eliminate marginal products for limited markets in an attempt to increase profitability. Although this approach would provide very efficient and responsible service to the large markets, it may reduce the amount of very useful service to a wide range of users, such as State and local governments (4, Part 1, p. 121).

Demand, expressed through the price system in a profitmaking context, inevitably works to the advantage of the strongest forces in the market. When the product is information, this means that the strongest buyer, in addition to having priority access to the information product, largely determines as well the *kind* of information product that is made available.

MARKET DETERMINATION OF TECHNOLOGY TRANSFER

In sum, information demand, determined on an ability-to-pay basis, results in a highly specific kind of information. Another aspect of market determined information demand further exacerbates inequalities in the social sphere. This has to do with what is called *technology transfer*. Technology transfer refers both to hardware and to the entire range of expertise required to manage and use knowledgeably any technology and its related processes. In the information realm, and with remote sensing in particular, technology transfer is especially important because if it does not occur in a meaningful way, then the recipient of the information, however benefited by the data, *remains dependent on the information provider and the technology supplier.*

The more developed technology becomes and the less adequately it is transferred, the more likely the extension of dependency (both among and within nations). This is one of the central but invisible assumptions in the leadership rhetoric continually expressed by U.S. policymakers. Leadership in technology is a euphemism for maintenance of domination in the technical sphere and all related cultural and economic areas. In the domestic arena, states and municipalities accordingly have voiced the fear that they may be denied adequate technology transfer if the remote-sensing function is delivered over to private control: "The basic organizational imperatives of industry and state and local government result in the private sector (as an entrepreneur) being unsuited to provide technology transfer. After all, it is not in the interest of private firms to truly transfer technology since such an action would eliminate subsequent opportunities for business" (see 2, Appendix on State and Local Views).

In sum, a privately operated remote-sensing system would fail to provide adequate technology transfer and therefore encourage information dependence. The implications of this situation are the same domestically and internationally.

FUTURE DIRECTIONS

Responsibility for remote sensing now rests with the National Oceanic and Atmospheric Administration. This temporary assignment of responsibility was made largely because no private company expressed an interest in taking over the operation *at that time*. Profits and markets are currently uncertain, but all firms "wish the door kept open" (2, Appendix 5).

How remote sensing will be administered in the years ahead remains an open issue. The special opportunities that this technology offers to its custodians, along with the monopoly privileges it confers on those with access to its processed data, suggest strongly that control of remote sensing will not be yielded easily by those—the military and the government as trustee for the corporate sector—presently enjoying its benefits.

All the same, the technology's dependence on international agreements for its complete utilization introduces a considerable and increasingly powerful check on arbitrary usage and monopolistic advantage. Not surprisingly, United Nations bodies have been reviewing a broad set of issues—economic, legal, cultural, and technical—related to remote sensing. International sentiment, though not unanimous, heavily favors *international decisionmaking* to remove the scanning technology from national, essentially U.S., domination (3). Domestically, too, we can expect increasing public recognition of the potential for social benefit from remote sensing as well as the potential for its exploitation on behalf of corporate and political interests. It seems, therefore, that the struggle for access to and ,equality of information will continue to be waged and that pressure will mount for the genuine social development and application of remote sensing.

NOTES

1. An expanded version of this chapter appears as Chapter 6 in Herbert I. Schiller's *Who Knows: Information in the Age of the Fortune 500* (Norwood, N.J.: Ablex, 1981).
2. An environmental—as distinct from an earth-scanning, remote-sensing—satellite, for weather observation and prediction, began operating in 1966, under the jurisdiction of the National Oceanic and Atmospheric Administration of the Commerce Department.

REFERENCES

1. Kerr, Richard A. "Explorer: Can Oil and Science Mix?" *Science* 207, February 8, 1980, p. 627.
2. *Private Sector Involvement in Civil Space Remote Sensing.* Prepared by an Interagency Task Force, Washington, D.C., June 15, 1979.
3. United Nations. 17th Sess., 228th meeting. *Discussions Before the Outer Space Scientific and Technical Subcommittee of the Committee on the Peaceful Uses of Outer Space.* February 4, 1980. New York: Department of Public Information, United Nations.
4. U.S. Congress, Senate. 96th Cong., 1st Sess. *Hearings Before the Subcommittee on Science, Technology and Space of the Committee on Commerce, Science and Transportation. On S. 663 and S. 875.* Part 1, April 9, 11, 1979; Part 2, July 31, 1979. Washington, D.C.: U.S. Government Printing Office, 1979.
5. United States, The White House. *Weekly Compilation of Presidential Documents*, Monday, November 26, 1979. Volume 15, No. 47, pp. 2141–2152.

Twenty-Nine

Direct Satellite Broadcasting: Definitions and Prospects[1]

Rolf T. Wigand

In fewer than twenty years, satellites have become an integral part of the communications industry, and have been used successfully for voice, video, and data transmissions in numerous situations. Newspaper printing, medical care, peace missions, teleconferencing, Olympic games, teaching, and emergency disaster and rescue services have all been carried out successfully via satellite communication.

Satellite systems operate at the international (intercontinental) level, at the regional (continental) level, and at the domestic (national) level. In addition, there are six military systems and a handful of satellite systems designed for data relay, maritime, and aeronautical purposes. Many nations which are members of international or large regional systems are also planning national or smaller regional systems of their own (see Figure 29.1).

The largest and oldest international organization is INTELSAT, of which 106 countries are members. As of early 1983, INTELSAT functioned as the carrier for national domestic services in 23 countries, and 18 others are planning to join the INTELSAT system between 1983–1986.

One of the first regional organizations was the European Space Agency (ESA), a consortium of 17 member countries. It has its own experimental satellite, the Orbital Test Satellite (OTS), with 6,000 voice channels. Future plans include the European Communications Satellite (ECS), intended for digital communications, and Eurovision by 1984, as well as L-SAT, to be operated by ESA, marketed by EUTELSAT, and used by member countries of the European Broadcasting Union.

Other regional systems that are operational or are imminently so include the PALAPA 1 and 2 satellites which already provide communication services to Indonesia and the inhabited islands of Southeast Asia, Telesat's CTS and the Anik satellite series in Canada, the BSE 12/14 in

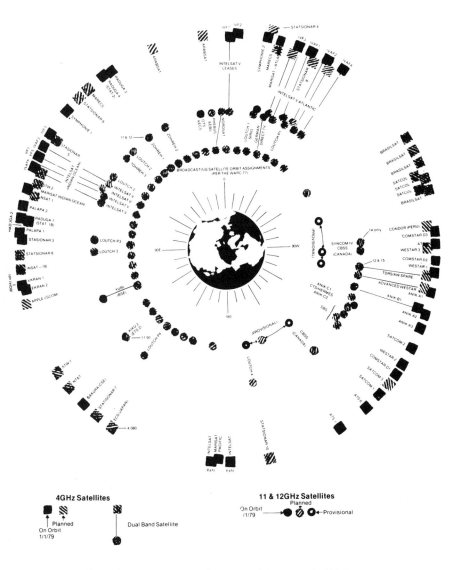

Figure 29.1   Satellites Planned on Orbit as of January 1, 1979.

Japan, Intersputnik's U.S.S.R.-built MOLNIYA 2 system linking Eastern European countries, Cuba, and Mongolia with Russia (see 1, 3, 4) as well as the U.S.S.R.'s EKRAN and GORIZONT satellites. The joint venture by the Federal Republic of Germany and France in the launching of the Symphonie 1 and 2 satellites in 1974–75 has also provided useful satellite communication service for several regions.

Other regional systems on the drawing boards include ARABSAT, an Arab regional satellite system (6), an African satellite system being considered by the 38-member Panaftel group (AFROSAT), and an Andean satellite system proposed by ASETA, a regional organization of the countries of Brazil, Chile, Colombia, Ecuador, and Peru. The five Nordic countries have been working on their own system, NORDSAT, as well, expecting this satellite system to be operational between 1990 and 1995.

DIRECT SATELLITE BROADCASTING

A clear-cut distinction between *direct* broadcasting satellites and other broadcasting satellite systems is difficult. Early definitions distinguished satellites by what function the satellite would perform. Thus a broadcast satellite system (BSS) was distinguished from a "fixed" satellite system (FSS) which was used as a relay for point-to-point or point-to-multipoint systems for telephone service, data transmission, radio links, and so on. These distinctions were used by the International Telecommunication Union (ITU) in assigning frequencies, and sufficed as long as the satellites produced were small and limited in capability, and the receiving earth station was the powerful component. However, as satellite technology improved and their antenna size, power, and sophistication increased, more and more services could be carried by a single satellite, and it became possible to reduce the power and antenna size of the earth stations receiving the signals. This redistribution of power in the communications link between satellite and earth station has made the original distinctions between "fixed" point-to-point services and direct satellite transmission difficult to maintain. For the present purpose, direct satellite broadcasting can be defined as the transmission of broadcast signals via high-powered satellites that permit direct reception of television or radio programs by means of small antennas.

In the definition adopted by the ITU at the 1977 WARC for space telecommunications, the "direct" part of direct broadcasting was defined in terms of reception, not transmission. According to the ITU, "in the broadcasting satellite service, 'direct reception' shall encompass both individual reception and community reception" (5, at 1573, n. 1). Individual reception is defined as "the reception of emissions from a space station in the broadcast satellite service by simple domestic installations and in particular those possessing small antennae" (5, at 1574). Community reception is defined as

> . . . the reception of emissions from a space station in the broadcast satellite service by receiving equipment, which in some cases may be complex and have antennae larger than those used for individual reception, and intended for use by a group of the general public at one location or through a distribution system covering a linked area (5, at 1574).

As can be seen, these distinctions between direct and other broadcast do not rely upon physically or technically distinct concepts, but rather upon how the broadcast signal is received.

Another important concept in the ITU definition is the treatment of the technology involved. By specifying in the "community reception" definition the possibility that direct broadcasting can include satellite signals with terrestrial links, the ITU definition implicitly accepts the fact that a satellite broadcasting system need not be confined exclusively to one carrier in order to qualify as direct broadcasting. One example of a hybrid broadcasting system which illustrates the potential for linking satellite broadcasting with terrestrial systems is the CATV system in the United States.

In 1976, Home Box Office (HBO), a private corporation offering television programs to subscribers via cable, had about 500,000 subscribers. Of this number only 75,000 were served by a network of 45 satellite earth stations (7). At that time the minimum diameter permitted by the FCC for a receive-only dish antenna was 9 meters. In December of 1976, when the FCC passed a new regulation allowing antennas with a diameter of 4.5 meters, the cost of a receive-only earth station was significantly decreased. Consequently, in 1979 HBO had over one million subscribers, of whom over 64 percent received their programming via local satellite earth stations. As the technology develops and the size and cost of ground installations are able to be further reduced, it might eventually be possible for individual home TV antennas to receive signals directly from a geostationary satellite. It is this potential development—direct-to-home television reception—that is most hotly debated.

DIRECT-TO-HOME TELEVISION RECEPTION

North America. Canada has a long-term interest in DBS, manifesting itself most recently in experiments utilizing its HERMES/CTS satellite. The Canadian Department of Communications is planning a direct-to-home television delivery project using the Anik-B satellite under contract with Telesat Canada (2).

In the United States, many firms have started to offer dish antennas to private individuals. One such firm, Homesat, a subsidiary of Scientific-Atlanta, is now offering such a system of satellite color reception for a variety of channels. The price for such a setup in 1983 is about $8,000 without shipping and installation costs, mostly due to the necessity of using a large dish antenna of 4.5 meters in diameter. The price includes, in addition to the antenna:

—all cable, two 12-channel amplifiers and a switch
—a remote receiver that converts the satellite signal to a television picture

—a modulator that adapts the television picture to the normal television set using a spare channel
—frequency coordination
—Federal Communications Commission license and construction permit[2]
—pay television fees.

With higher powered satellites smaller dish antennas would be adequate and would drastically reduce the cost of the required equipment.

The Communications Satellite Corporation (COMSAT) is developing a subscription television service that would be available to millions of U.S. homes using rooftop antennas. The service would offer subscribers programming on several channels simultaneously with no commercial interruptions and would emphasize first-run movies, sports events, education and cultural programs, and data and text transmission. Subscribers would pay a monthly charge that would cover the total service, including the use and maintenance of a rooftop antenna. COMSAT estimates that the monthly costs would be no more than many families now pay for a single night at the movies. The service is planned for 1986 and theirs was the first DBS proposal approved by the FCC in 1982. COMSAT has conducted demonstration experiments using a Canadian satellite and COMSAT-developed dish antennas suitable for rooftop installation (see Figure 29.2).

Western Europe. Western European nations have already developed large-scale, fixed plans for direct-to-home television and radio broadcast services, with fully operational satellite systems anticipated by the end of 1984. It is expected that the ESA's first communications satellite to carry paid transmissions, the European Communications System or ECS, will be launched sometime in 1983. The ESA will serve as a carrier's carrier and the services themselves will be marketed by EUTELSAT, the consortium of Western European PTT (post, telephone, and telegraph) ministries,

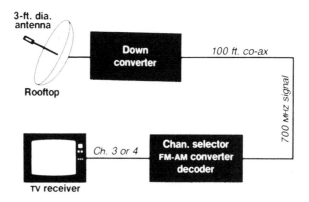

Figure 29.2 Components of a Home Terminal to Receive the Proposed COMSAT TV Subscription Service.

which include Belgium, Denmark, Ireland, France, Italy, the Netherlands, Spain, Sweden, Switzerland, the United Kingdom, and the Federal Republic of Germany. ECS is intended primarily to carry television programs, but also telephone and data transmissions. By 1980 European PTTs plan to provide service between small earth stations. The current thrust of the development of ECS is clearly toward the higher frequencies.

France and West Germany have taken the lead in proposals for both domestic and cooperative DBS systems. They cooperated in the development of Symphonie 1 and 2, experimental satellites in operation over the Atlantic and Indian Oceans, and in 1979 agreed to work jointly on a direct broadcasting satellite venture. On the national level, France has proposed TELECOM-1, 2, and 3, for the latter half of the 1980s, to serve metropolitan France (including Corsica) and her overseas *Départments*. France's broadcasting satellite TDF-1 is scheduled to be launched in 1984–1985. The Federal Republic of Germany has ordered TV-SAT, a satellite scheduled to begin direct broadcasting between 1985 and 1987. All that would be needed to receive the broadcast signals would be a parabolic antenna, exactly 69 centimeters in diameter, and a frequency converter, at an approximate cost of $280 to $560 when mass-produced.

Japan. DBS holds obvious attractions in this country with its large numbers of islands and mountainous terrain. DBS would make reception possible for Japan's citizens without regard to geographical isolation or urban shadow. Japan is scheduled to launch its first domestic communication satellite in 1984 and a domestic broadcasting satellite in 1985. The Diet is presently considering a new bill that calls for a Communications/Broadcast Satellite Organization to own and manage these satellites. This organization would be financed 50 percent by the government and 50 percent by non-governmental backers.

RELATING DBS TO THE EXISTING INDUSTRY

Given that direct-to-home satellite broadcasting is now not only a technical possibility but an economic possibility as well, the broadcasting industry may need to take a hard look at its present structure and function. A good number of important questions will have to be answered that are, in part, based on the organizational control of broadcasting in the various countries, i.e., the issuing of licenses to private operators by the government versus the functioning of the government-run PTTs. For example, will the PTTs be competing with private communication companies? Will these companies possibly exploit the lucrative business otherwise needed by the PTTs to subsidize rural services, if and when they are allowed to compete? Will the European PTTs invest their funds into cable networks, etc., because of previous heavy investment efforts in terrestrial systems, even though a rooftop-to-rooftop satellite-based system may be cheaper? Is the lack of competition in the satellite business the best route to go for PTTs and is this in the best interest of the public? As present trends indicate that DBS will most probably be nested into existing networks in an auxiliary role, it would be beneficial to the publics concerned for the broadcasting organizations to reevaluate how well they are currently serving social needs.

The picture is different for developing countries. Many do not yet operate extensive television broadcast systems. The potential of DBS is thus difficult to assess at the present time. At a relatively low cost, entire national broadcast systems could be established which would avoid the expense of terrestrial interconnections. Although the cost of direct-to-home reception might be prohibitive to individuals, community receivers installed by the government are a likely alternative. Past demonstration experiments have already shown that satellite broadcasting holds substantial promise of accelerating national development for educational purposes in such areas as literacy, family planning, health care, training in agricultural and mechanical skills, and others (7). Decisions for the implementation of such systems, however, will have to compete with other priorities.

In summary, DBS may not necessarily be a panacea which will fulfill the educational and cultural needs of developing countries in the next few years. Neither does it appear likely to dramatically change the way in which broadcasters operate in developed countries. However, the added convenience, extended geographical coverage, increase in the number of broadcast sources, and flexibility and immediacy promised by DBS offer all nations expanded technological resources if the bilateral, if not multilateral, cooperation necessary to its implementation can be accomplished.

NOTES

1. Partial support for the preparation of this paper was provided by a grant from the UNESCO International Social Science Council, Paris, France. The author acknowledges gratefully the assistance received from scholars and organizations in over 20 countries, too numerous to recognize individually.

2. On October 18, 1979, the FCC dropped its licensing requirements for satellite receiving stations to eliminate costs of the licensing process for builders and to end delays in obtaining a license. Operators of receiving stations still will have to obtain permission from the operators of the sending satellites to receive their transmissions.

REFERENCES

1. "The Global Communications Satellite Catalogue." *Satellite Communications* 2(1), January 1978, pp. 27–30.

2. Golden, D. A., Telesat Canada. Personal correspondence, July 3, 1979.

3. Grey, J. and M. Gerard. *A Critical Review of the State of Foreign Space*

New York: American Institute of Aeronautics and Astronautics, 1978.

nderson, A. T., National Communications Satellite Evaluation Sup-
, Australian Postal and Telecommunications Department. Personal cor-
e, August 6, 1979.

ternational Telecommunications Union. *Final Protocol: Space Telecom-
ns.* July 17, 1971, [1972]. 23 U.S.T., at 1573, n. 1–1574 (effective January

Kader, Salah Abdel. Secretary General, Arab States Broadcasting Union.
al correspondence, July 7, 1979.

. Topol, Sidney. "The Growth and Future of Satellite Communications."
ward L. Crispin (Ed.) *Earth Station Symposium '78.* Atlanta: Scientific
ta, 1978, pp. 2–24.

. Wigand, Rolf T. "The Process of Mass Communication: Mass Media as
of Socialization in Developing Countries."*Konferenzprotokoll der Association Internationale des Etudes et Recherches sur l'Information* 2, 1976,
pp. 7473–7486 (Leipzig, German Democratic Republic).

Thirty

Satellite Broadcasting: Cooperative Ventures in Western Europe

Edward W. Ploman

Long before satellite broadcasting was operating even on an experimental basis, it had emerged as one of those phenomena which for better or for worse serve as a catalyst for expectations and fears—both often equally exaggerated. Satellite broadcasting is, therefore, an interesting example of how individual nations and the international community react to a new technology. The following reflections will focus on the actions and reactions not of a single country nor of the larger international community but of a group of countries, and on some aspects of the continuing saga of satellite broadcasting and the Western European countries.

THE HISTORY OF POLICY-MAKING ON OUTER SPACE

Western Europe's relations to outer space have not been altogether happy, but rather ambivalent. Europe was reluctantly dragged into the space age for which it was no better prepared than anybody else. The shadows cast by the two space powers raised questions about security and independence. Some sectors of the scientific community were quick in their response to the new challenges; the linkage to military power was understood and acted on by some countries, but governments and industry seemed undecided and potential users lukewarm. The general uncertainty was reflected in the lack of clear institutional structures to deal with this new field. Most countries did not create a central authority but spread responsibilities among existing authorities and organizations—it was reported to a Select Committee of the House of Commons that in the U.K. important decisions on outer space matters had to involve some 52 different agencies. The one

---

The views presented in this chapter are those of the author and do not necessarily represent views of the United Nations University.

country that did establish a more unitary structure, France, made progress enough to claim the position of being the third space power.

Individual countries had difficulties in sorting out their priorities among the contending political, security, industrial, scientific, and communications aspects, in weighing the demands of different space "constituencies," and in defining policies. It also quickly became clear that, individually, the Western European countries were not big enough for space. Cooperation and joint ventures became a must. Many of these countries gained their first space experience through cooperation with NASA, but there was also pressure for joint European action.

The national difficulties experienced over the formation of policies and organizational structures spilled over at the regional level. It was not a good sign that the Western European countries started with two space organizations, the European Launcher Development Organization and the European Space Research Organization. The flora of committees, ad hoc groups, decisions, reversals, and delays hampered practical action and the emergence of clear organizational forms. One of the most detrimental features was the demands by a number of governments that their emerging aerospace industries should be given contracts of the same value as the national contributions to the organizations—whether they were the ones best equipped for the task or not.

The potential users were no less confused and at loggerheads. With time, the emphasis changed from scientific exploration to other more immediately practical applications. Meteorology and navigation proved in the long run to be less troublesome than the one application which attracted most interest—communications. But even though some telecommunication administrations had been quick to cooperate with the United States for transatlantic satellite communications, they concentrated their interest on a combination of submarine cables and satellites for the money-making telephone and were prepared only to tolerate television. And as to the use of satellites within Europe, they were simply not interested. The other major potential user group comprised the broadcasters, who were keen enough to use satellite facilities for novel long-distance transmission, but found tariffs prohibitive and other conditions irksome if not unacceptable.

No wonder that European organizations such as the Council of Europe called for coordination, decisions, and action. In 1966, a report to the Consultative Assembly enumerated the most important questions which had to be faced by the European governments:

- Should Europe stay in space or should it now, in view of the high and rising costs of space programs, contract out?
- Should Europe continue to develop its own major launching system or systems?

- Should Europe develop a significant independent capability in the field of communication satellites?
- Should Europe develop satellites with other possible practical applications for non-military purposes?
- Should the activities of ESRO be expanded?
- In the light of the above, what would be a reasonable level of future expenditure on the European space projects?
- What would be the best structure for the development of the European space effort of the future?
- What is the role for future cooperation in space between Europe and the rest of the world?

In answer to the first of these questions, Western Europe has stayed in space and can be considered to be an evolving third force in space with an expanding aerospace industry. The Western European countries joined INTELSAT and established a number of national or sub-regional earth stations. There is now one regional space development organization, the European Space Agency (ESA), which has replaced ELDO and ESRO. Although Europe has been dependent on NASA for launch vehicles, an independent launching system has been developed in the form of the heavy launcher, Ariane.

THE BEGINNINGS OF SATELLITE BROADCASTING

Communications satellite programs have been undertaken both at the national and at the regional level. One experimental system was successfully launched by France and Germany (Symphonie). An experimental system has also been developed within the framework of ESA; the OTS-2 has been in use for over a year for demonstrations of telephone, television, and data transmissions. In April 1979, the member states of ESA approved the development of five European Communication Satellites which would make up the regional, inter-European space telecommunications network. This system would be operated by EUTELSAT, a regional equivalent to INTELSAT, which comprises the telecommunication administrations of participating countries.

The attitudes towards satellite broadcasting remained confused. Was there any need for direct broadcast satellites at all; if so, should they be used at a regional level or only for national purposes? And in a situation where in many countries broadcasting policies were under review or transformation, how fast were the additional decisions on satellite broadcasting required? The answer to the last question became tied to the timetable of the International Telecommunications Union (ITU), which decided to convene in 1977 a World Administrative Radio Conference for the planning of the broadcasting satellite service in the currently most important frequency band for this purpose (12 GHz band).

The basic approach adopted was for national coverage only. There were a few exceptions: an extended coverage zone for the Vatican State, and a joint coverage zone comprising the entire Nordic area: Denmark, Finland, Iceland, Norway, and Sweden, including part of Greenland. Otherwise, the conference had to work out a plan providing each country with enough frequency space for five national TV channels and corresponding orbital positions. The number of countries in a relatively small geographical area and the differences in size required complex arrangements in order to define the satellite beams so that each country would get total national coverage and the unavoidable spill-over into the territory of other countries would be kept to a minimum. Still, this minimum does in certain cases extend far over neighboring countries.

Agreement was thus reached on a plan which defined the technical parameters for satellite broadcasting in Europe. Since 1977, the emerging picture comprises three main features, with a fourth looming over the horizon.

The first feature is the Bonn-Paris axis. In September 1979, President Giscard d'Estaing and Chancellor Helmut Schmidt announced an agreement to cooperate in the development of a Franco-German satellite system for direct broadcasting. Each country will supply at least one satellite with a minimum of three video channels for national television coverage.

This decision, which favors the early establishment of national operational systems, took France and Germany out of the relevant parts of the ESA program which were based on a different concept. ESA has had to restructure its plans: it abandoned the so-called H-SAT project and concentrated on the development of a space platform offering better performance, L-SAT (for "large satellite"), and allowing for directional beams intended for national coverage. ESA proceeds on the basis of a London-Rome axis which presents the second feature of the present picture and around which the other participating countries have clustered (at present Denmark, the Netherlands, Spain, and Switzerland).

The third feature represents the somewhat lopsided pentagon comprising the five Nordic countries. The NORDSAT project envisages the satellite broadcasting of the existing television and sound programs in each country for reception in all the others. NORDSAT, a multinational satellite broadcasting project, represents a formidable challenge in many fields: technical, economic, industrial-strategic, cultural, and legal. It has involved years of inquiry. The final reports were submitted to the Nordic Council of Ministers in October 1979 but as of 1982 were still not acted upon. In fact, a common decision seemed so remote that Sweden decided to focus on a national satellite (Tele-X).

The fourth feature is centered on two of the smallest countries in Europe: Luxembourg and Switzerland. In both cases, the attractive feature was not primarily national coverage, but the large audiences that could be reached in neighboring countries. In the case of the Luxembourg satellite, reactions in France, England, and particularly in Germany have been extremely negative, in view of the politically sensitive and carefully balanced national broadcasting situation.

There are additional factors. The European Economic Community so far has not had any direct role with regard to these issues. There have been attempts to act in the cultural field indirectly, mainly in such areas as copyright and the conditions and rights of performing artists. The experience of the first direct elections to the European Parliament may, however, result in new initiatives concerning common EEC action with regard to broadcasting.

REASONS FOR EUROPEAN FRAGMENTATION

The series of interlocking issues at the national and the regional level fall in many areas. They concern national security, the independence and interdependence of countries, industrial policy, cultural and media policy, and a host of tricky legal problems. All these aspects must be kept in mind in an attempt to untangle some of the issues in the communications field. A revealing factor is the difference between France and Germany, on the one hand, and the other countries working through ESA, on the other hand. France and Germany are in favor of the early establishment of operational national systems, while the other countries prefer a phased, joint approach starting with an experimental phase. However, it is not the users, in this case the broadcasters, who have been pushing for a satellite system; particularly in Germany, they are lukewarm at best. The underlying motives are different and to a large extent derive from considerations of industrial policy. Both government and industry in France and Germany want to compete in what is expected to be a boom in the provision of satellite hardware, and reckon that they need to prove their capability by establishing an operational system and not only another experimental one.

The problems of satellite broadcasting have emerged at a time when communications and, in particular, media policies have become an extremely complex and controversial issue area in all European societies. Even though the differences in approach and structure present each country with sets of specific challenges, they share some common problems. One of these common problems concerns the future of the traditional public service broadcasting which in various forms is the prevailing European model. The arrival of new technologies and services is only one dimension. All countries where broadcasting and its development have been mainly or exclusively financed by license fees on receivers face a new situation when receiver ownership has reached a saturation level and no further major increase in revenue from this source can be expected. However, inflation and other cost increases are not selective. It is, therefore, necessary to raise the license fees and this remains politically very unpopular, much more so than increases, for example, for the public services of gas and electricity or railway tariffs.

FORMATION OF NATIONAL MEDIA POLICIES

Generally, Europeans live in a more complex and abundant information environment than most Americans. In most parts of the U.S. there is no international flow of information in the form of foreign-produced materials. Europeans are used to being able to receive foreign publications and, perhaps even more importantly, foreign radio stations and foreign television programs, whether by direct reception or via cable. The case of Belgium, whose cable provides access to over ten different national television programs (two from Belgium, three from France, three from Germany, two from Holland and Luxembourg) and is involved in negotiations to obtain U.K. programs, is extreme. However, the increase in foreign information becoming available to large sections of the population in Western Europe is an accomplished fact which it would be politically impossible to reverse. Furthermore, in many cases it is actively supported—the first and basic reason for a joint Nordic satellite system is to make each Nordic country's broadcast programs available in the others. Thus, the transborder flow of information and the growing media interpenetration create a new situation where national policies, to an unprecedented degree, must take a larger environment into account.

Another issue which in recent years has emerged in almost all Western European countries is the balance to be struck between national and local broadcasting services. The most radical response has been given in Italy. Following the judgments of the Constitutional Court which broke at the local level the broadcasting monopoly of Radiotelevisione Italiana, Italy has become an extraordinary media laboratory through the largely unregulated proliferation of local "free" radio and television stations. Other countries have proceeded at a more sedate pace through extensive plans for the extension of local broadcasting (e.g., U.K., Sweden).

Thus, media policy problems, even though often shared, evolve in varied national contexts. The issues raised by the introduction of satellite broadcasting also clearly demonstrate the specific attitudes and problems of each country. The differences between France and Germany are instructive. Both telecommunications and broadcasting are operated as public monopolies, even though the unitary broadcasting structure has been broken up. In contrast to most other European countries, the French approach has provided for the broadcasting transmission network to be owned, operated, and developed by one of the present broadcasting entities, Télédiffusion de France (TDF), and not by the telecommunications administration. It is still too early to state what will be the effect of the recent decision to move TDF into the orbit of telecommunications under the Ministry of Communications.

The situation in Germany is complex in a different way. Telecommunication is a matter for the federal government, while broadcasting is the responsibility of the constituent *Länder*. The complex public service broadcasting system is therefore set up by the *Länder* governments which then have concluded agreements among themselves for the conduct of national broadcasting. In this situation, the definition of broadcasting takes on a major importance, since it will decide whether the federal government or the *Länder* governments have decision-making powers.

Germany, of course, has a well-developed terrestrial network, and the broadcasting corporations pay for its use. What will be the situation if the broadcasters will be required to provide additional payments for a direct broadcast satellite service for which they have not asked, and which is being developed by federal authorities for reasons external to broadcasting over which they have no say?

In the U.K., the use of satellite broadcasting would present another interesting situation. A direct broadcast satellite system could only reasonably be used for national broadcasting. It would thus be applicable only to the BBC, since commercial television is based on regions within the country. Would the end result be two transmission systems—a space system for BBC national programs, and a terrestrial for ITV, BBC, regional, and special (Welsh and Scottish) programs?

SATELLITE BROADCASTING ACROSS BORDERS

The situation is one of ambiguity and ambivalence, which can be clearly seen in further analysis of attitudes towards the transborder flow of programs and the international regulation of satellite broadcasting. Since the early 1970s the United Nations Committee for the Peaceful Uses of Outer Space has worked on the legal principles to govern international television broadcasts via satellites. The necessary consensus has not been achieved. There is one major stumbling block—a vast majority of countries want a principle which states that satellite television broadcasting from one country to another cannot be undertaken without previous agreements between the countries concerned. The U.S. has always opposed this principle in the name of the free flow of information, and has been more or less enthusiastically supported by some Western European countries. However, a country like Germany, which in the U.N. has defended the freedom to undertake international satellite broadcasting without prior agreements, takes a very different attitude in the ITU. In this context, it has vehemently opposed an extension of the Luxembourg satellite beam beyond the technically unavoidable, since foreign commercial television might have a negative effect on the financial basis of its own television. Also, the adoption of the plan for the satellite broadcasting service represents, if anything, a previous agreement, and Germany is far from being the only country to take different positions in different international contexts. It is equally interesting that the former Prime Minister, Sir Harold Wilson, in the House of Commons has warned against programs being beamed to Britain from the Continent. He even used the same argument as developing countries have been using against the West—"cultural invasion through the satellite." How does this square with unqualified support for the free flow of information?

European experience makes the position of the U.S. in the U.N. appear unrealistic. We can now draw upon the experience of the first case where countries have looked at the legal problems in real terms, i.e., the NORDSAT project. NORDSAT is an inter-state satellite project requiring inter-Nordic cooperation among five sovereign states in areas which have not previously been included in the cooperation between the Nordic countries. Despite their fundamental consensus in matters of social and cultural policy, there are certain contrasts and differences of emphasis between these countries in terms of language, economic affairs, and security policy which in the satellite context require special consideration.

Agreement would therefore have to be reached on the technical development and implications, financial arrangements and other economic aspects, and cultural and program policy aspects. In the legal field a close study has to be made of four major topics—copyright, broadcasting law, criminal and civil liability, and international law—and agreement has to be found on how to deal with the differences in legislation and practice. The same issues would obviously be even more difficult among countries that do not share a common legal tradition, as do the Nordic countries, or would not be used to the same continuous harmonization of laws.

The introduction of satellite broadcasting highlights a wide range of problems which the Western European countries will have to face. The solutions to be adopted will be important. The decisions on satellite broadcasting will reveal much about the European approach to the emerging electronic society.

Thirty-One

Telecommunications Alternatives for Developing Countries[1]

Ronald E. Rice and Edwin B. Parker

A large and growing body of research and reports has addressed the range of development applications a telecommunications system can support (see 7 and 11 for reviews). Some of the proposed and empirically demonstrated benefits are related to the primary function of telecommunications: to provide communication links for a geographically dispersed population. In addition, knowledge may be generated and distributed in greater and more equal amounts (18, 19), and travel or transport costs can be reduced by transmitting information instead. On the aggregate level, the economic benefits of communication have been considered in numerous studies (4, 5) indicating the high correlation between communication variables (mass media as well as telephones) and wealth variables (such as GNP). However, such measures of economic development are also limited, as they do not capture dimensions such as distribution, access, social development, appropriateness, and dependency (see 2 and 8 for a review of such studies). It is important to keep in mind that all potential benefits are conditioned (and often prevented) by local contexts, existing structure, and the lack of a "community of interest" (7, p. 23; 13; 15; 28). Access is only the first stage of the communication process and indicates nothing about exposure, content, information outcomes and, finally, social outcomes (26).

Thus we do not see telecommunications technology as a panacea for rural development. Denis Goulet calls technology the uncertain promise: it is needed for development, yet can introduce destructive values or maintain prior constraints. The goal is to manage the technology *for* people, and *by* the people affected by it. Local needs, goals, and social values must be linked with development strategies and particular technology choices. In many cases it is likely that other development or investment strategies should have a higher priority. In this context, the introduction of satellite communication technology should be considered as only one element in indigenous development.

SATELLITE COMMUNICATIONS TAILORED TO LOW-COST DEMANDS

In general, communication is more costly for poorer countries, as the relatively small message traffic costs more per circuit than heavy traffic of developed countries, which can be trunked with numerous circuits to save on material costs. This situation can be resolved by reducing the material costs of thin-route telephone systems and by coordinating national communications systems into regional systems to provide service to a number of nations. Satellite systems may play a useful role in this process.

Satellite capacity in the form of earth stations can be installed in the order of priority of need, independent of the location of previous sites, unlike terrestrial systems. This ability may reduce total cost because incremental expenses may be deferred until fully justified. In addition, satellite communication cost is insensitive to distance, so remote locations are not under cost disadvantages. Other media (such as radio or television) and additional circuits may be added later to ground stations, providing a flexibility impossible in terrestrial systems. In fact, coordinated national planning of several communication services would take advantage of this flexibility, and reduce unit costs for each service (20). For example, microwave relays must be designed for maximum end-to-end capacity, and significant rural expansion of wire lines entails high system-wide costs. Satellite systems are notably more reliable than terrestrial links, reducing remote maintenance problems and overall operational cost. The availability of satellite point-to-point service may also lessen the pressure on high frequency allocations, a bone of contention between developed and developing countries (see 27).

In terms of actual costs, our primary hypothesis is that geosynchronous[2] communication satellite systems can provide a viable alternative to traditional terrestrial telephone links and, further, that the circuit[3] cost per year of such a system can be lowered considerably *if* the satellite system is designed *specifically* to permit rural use—to accommodate a large number of thin-route circuits as well as low-cost earth stations. The trade-off for achieving such a design is, of course, higher costs for the satellite. Will the advantages from such a system design overcome the increased satellite cost?

Major factors involved in increasing the capacity and power of the satellite segment include increased bandwidth, transponder power efficiency, gain and power (EIRP), the use of frequencies, antenna diameter,[4] and demand assignment. Factors involved in lowering earth station cost include smaller ground station antennas,[5] non-tracking antennas, solid state receivers, lower power requirements, frequency use or site location which avoids terrestrial signal interference, and the mass production of hardware. Manipulation of these factors is implied in a satellite commu-

Table 31.1 Summary of Three Models for Satellite Communication Systems

	Model 1	Model 2A	Model 2B
Satellite segment	INTELSAT IVA hemispheric beam. EIRP from 26 dBW (higher at beam center). 36 MHz/ transponder channel. Capacity: 180 circuits/transponder. Lease cost: $1.2 million/ transponder/year (see 11; 16; INTELSAT Tariffs BG-30-73, BG/T-22-5E and attachments). Annualized cost per circuit per year is $6667 (PA) and $667 (DAMA). (This is the minimal cost, from INTELSAT. Carriers between INTELSAT and the end user including the national INTELSAT member mark-up final circuit charges by as much as a factor of 4 [see 7]).	This system designed for, operated by, and owned by a global or regional consortium of developing countries. Two prime satellites in orbit, one common spare in orbit, one spare on ground. Cost including launches is $200 million. Life 10 years. Syncom IV type. EIRP 36-39 dBW. G/T of 32.2 dB/K°. 1.83 Kw power. 30 MHz/transponder channel. Link calculations available upon request. Capacity: 500 circuits/transponder, 24 transponders. Fill factor 50 percent on prime satellites. Lease cost: $1.5 million/ transponder/year. Annualized cost per circuit per year is $2600 (PA) and $260 (DAMA).	The same technical system as in Model 2A would be managed by an organization such as INTELSAT. It is assumed that such an organization would make a more conservative seven-year satellite life assumption or otherwise increase lease costs. Lease cost: $2.5 million/ transponder/year. Annualized cost per circuit per year is $5000 (PA) and $500 (DAMA).
Ground segment	4.57 m. antenna G/T of 19 dB/K°.6 watts/circuit (see 16). Cost: $32,000 in quantities in the hundreds (that is, the price per	3 m. antenna. Technical specifications available. Station gain (and satellite EIRP) near optimal settings (9). Cost: very lowest cost for simplest	Same as for Model 2A.

	item for a large quantity of the item is less than the price for small quantities. Based upon what vendors call a "learning curve," it represents something like the marginal cost and includes development cost). Annualized location cost $5664 (PA) and $6018 to $9024 (DAMA).	CMI station including power source is $11,000 in quantities in the thousands. A more appropriate station with a cost of $20,000 (industry sources) will be assumed. Annualized location cost $3540 (PA) and $3894 to $7080 (DAMA).	
Advantages	Easy to initiate; technical and management support from INTELSAT; low risk; reliable; permits gradual entry into domestic and rural satellite communications.	Designed for rural applications and regional systems. Technically optimized solution and least expensive for large ground complement. Provides the impetus for the formation of a technical cadre of native personnel competent in this technology.	Designed for rural applications and regional systems. Technically optimized solution for large ground complement. Involves an experienced organization to manage system and act as buffer to political problems. Nations can lease capacity as desired or as their system grows, thus at the onset, capital outlays by user nations may be less.
Disadvantages	Not economical for large scale system because low EIRP requires expensive ground segment, although it may be an adequate means of transitioning into a full scale domestic system. These larger stations can later be used as "hub" stations in a national/domestic system.	Involves the aggregation of a large number of nations for the purpose of utilizing a common resource. Political problems need to be resolved. Requires initial investment outlays. Necessitates formation of management group to administer program.	In the long run more expensive and, because of INTELSAT or other monopoly management, potentially less responsive to needs of individual nations.

nication system designed to permit low-cost rural communication service. Martin (14, pp. 149, 361) explains these and other factors and provides several graphs which summarize the design trade-offs for both the space segment and the ground segment.

MODELS FOR APPROPRIATE RURAL TELEPHONY SERVICE

The general service model under consideration is one capable of providing thin-route (low traffic) rural telephony, probably for a global or regional consortium of countries, thus involving more than 10,000 earth stations. For any particular alternative system model, such an arrangement would allow the sharing of the space segment and the creation of a large market (with the attendant advantages of economies of scale) for ground hardware. Domestic production of such equipment could be an integral part of overall development policy, as suggested in Mexico's telecommunications policy (12). Summaries of costs, specifications, and comments on three satellite system models are offered in Table 31.1.

Model 1. The currently available space segment system is leased capacity on INTELSAT IVA satellites (hemispheric beams) which could be usable for rural telephony with 4.57 to 6 meter ground antennas. National common carriers or government entities which are INTELSAT signatories can lease small capacity (say, ¾ transponder) as it is needed without a large capital outlay. If an entire transponder is leased, the variable transponder gain setting could be set at a position more appropriate for small ground station use than the standard setting.

Model 2A. The second set of alternatives involves a higher-power satellite system and earth stations designed specifically for rural service. This second alternative involves a more costly and more powerful space segment than INTELSAT IVA which can provide more circuits per transponder while reducing earth station power and antenna size requirements (to 3 meter diameter). Like Model 1, this system could be designed for, bought by, and operated by one or several developing countries. This is a lower-bound cost estimate based on the estimated purchase price of the satellite without the expense of a large operating organization (as in Model 2B). Four higher-power 24-transponder C-band frequency (⁴⁄₆ Ghz) satellites plus three launches are assumed to cost $200 million. This provides two prime satellites in orbit, a common spare in orbit, and a spare on the ground. Global coverage can be provided except for the U.S., U.S.S.R., and some islands in the Pacific Ocean.

Model 2B. The upper-bound cost of the same technical system in 2A is associated with system management by a consortium of countries involved or by an international arrangement such as INTELSAT. This would allow countries to lease only as much of the custom-designed satellite system as they needed. In addition, such an arrangement would be congruent with current international telecommunications practice and leasing arrangements. In our calculations, typical INTELSAT operating costs are added to the equipment and launch costs included in Model 2A.

The use of permanent assignment of channels (or circuits) (PA) or demand-assignment multiple-access (DAMA) in each model is also important to consider. PA assigns fixed circuits to specific terminal pairs, and PA operation is more efficient as the amount of traffic between a given pair of terminals increases. A DAMA control system, on the other hand, assigns a circuit to a requesting terminal on demand, and then returns the circuit to the access pool when the terminal has completed its call. Its advantages are that (a) terrestrial costs may be reduced because the same equipment can provide increased connectivity and flexibility to reach all destinations with only a single transit through the satellite, (b) transponder capacity can be more efficiently used, (c) establishment of new destinations is encouraged because of the corresponding reduction in cost (3), and (d) fewer circuits can serve a given number of terminals under DAMA than PA, other things equal.

The complexity of system design, the variability and interdependence of cost calculations, and the generality of our purpose require some broad assumptions in order to compare the three system models (see Table 31.2):

- Channel capacity, lease charges and equipment costs are based upon 1977 price estimates from ORI (16), Lusignan and associates (12), INTELSAT (Tariffs BG-30-73, BG/T-22-5E and attachments), and industry sources (Hughes, IT & T, Prodelin, Andrews, and California Microwave, Inc.).
- Cost calculations do not include maintenance, operation, land acquisition, salvage or indirect costs, and are based on present value annuities.
- An interest rate or social discount of 12 percent per year is assumed. Satellite life of 7 years (except 10 years for model 2A to provide a lower-bound cost estimate) and ground equipment life of 10 years are assumed.
- Although an actual *link* involves two ground stations, and would imply a communication cost of two earth stations and the pro-rata space segment charge (19), we are only considering the incremental cost of adding one more (rural) service location to existing capacity.
- One circuit per remote ground station is implied required capacity for a rural location. This assumes single channel per carrier (SCPC) operation.
- INTELSAT IVA space charges are actual tariffs for preemptible service.

Table 31.2   Cost Comparisons for System Models 1, 2A, and 2B

Satellite Option	Circuit Space Cost/Year U.S.$	Annualized Station Cost/Year U.S.$	Location Cost/Year U.S.$
1: INTELSAT IVA			
without DAMA	6,700	5,700	12,300
with DAMA	700	6,000–9,200	6,700–9,900
2A: Syncom IV owned			
without DAMA	2,600	3,500	6,100
with DAMA	260	3,900–7,100	4,200–7,300
2B: Syncom IV managed by INTELSAT			
without DAMA	5,000	3,500	8,500
with DAMA	500	3,900–7,100	4,400–7,600

NOTE: Cost figures rounded. Cost ranges for "with DAMA" figures based upon lower and upper bound of DAMA equipment.

System alternatives of all PA or all DAMA operation are alternative maxima; a combination of PA and DAMA circuits is more realistic and usually less expensive than either extreme alternative. PA or DAMA circuit capacities are likely conservative figures, producing higher than possible costs. Models involving INTELSAT capacity may involve higher circuit costs due to intermediate carrier mark-ups.

As Table 31.2 shows, when DAMA is not used, the per-location cost is unambiguously less for a communication satellite system designed specifically for rural telecommunication than for currently available INTELSAT IVA capacity. In the case of the lower-bound alternative of buying such a system, the cost is almost half. Although the range in DAMA cost estimates[6] is wide enough to produce overlaps across configurations, for a given DAMA cost, the per location cost associated with INTELSAT IVA capacity would continue to be higher than the alternatives. However, the range in per-location costs for a 2A and 2B system *without* DAMA essentially lies in the same range as INTELSAT IVA location costs *with* DAMA. It is important to keep in mind, however, that the figures are subject to broad assumptions mentioned above and considerable approximation. In particular, the assumption of one circuit per location is a crucial condition. Costs *per circuit* (particularly for PA circuits) will be lower when more than one channel per ground station is required.

COST COMPARISON: TERRESTRIAL VS. SATELLITE SYSTEMS

As satellite circuit costs are insensitive to link distance, while the cost for terrestrial circuits is roughly proportional to their distance, there is a link

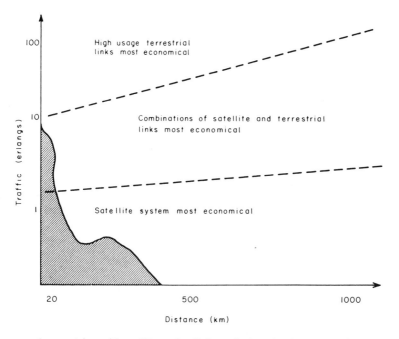

Source: Adapted from (20, section V-8; results from Iranian case study).

Note: The region boundaries are approximate and intended for demonstration only. Their placement is sensitive to changing assumptions. For example, they will shift upward *considerably* if, under the assumption of a purchased satellite system, the expenditure is considered a sunken cost. Then it would be advantageous to shift some terrestrial traffic to satellite links. No data points are available for shaded area, for *this* particular solution.

Figure 31.1   Minimum Cost Solution Regions for High Usage Terrestrial Links and Satellite Systems Links as a Function of Voice Traffic and Link Distance.

distance after which satellite communications will be less expensive than terrestrial communications. If the breakeven distance is small, then a satellite system with numerous ground stations is favored over a terrestrial system. For example, using the standard INTELSAT (30 m.) station, the breakeven distance between satellite and terrestrial circuits ranges from 500 miles to 2,000 miles, for high density routes. This last qualification leads us to two very significant points about terrestrial-satellite cost comparisons.

First, the minimum annual cost per circuit of a total telephony system depends greatly on the range of lengths and the traffic demand (present and future growth) (see Figure 31.1). Second, local conditions sometimes completely determine the most appropriate equipment: small mountains or high buildings can obstruct radio transmission and make ground stations economical; preexisting terrestrial facilities in a small town can eliminate the need for a ground station.[7] Thus, a fully optimal system involving both rural and urban service would usually involve some large and small earth stations as well as interconnection with terrestrial transmission media. In addition, as discussed previously, circuits might be optimally served by a mix of PA and DAMA operation. This "hybrid" total system can result in an overall least-cost solution which routes around 6 percent of total traffic via a satellite system (21).

In no case, especially for small nations with pockets of higher demand, would a satellite system handle a majority of the telephony traffic. Existing terrestrial facilities plus new terrestrial facilities on short distance high density routes would mean that a significant percentage of circuits would continue to be terrestrial. In fact, satellite networks are usually considered as providing supplemental capability to an existing network. The economic advantage of satellites for thin-route telephony may, however, lead to a significant number of locations being served by satellite (such as remote rural areas), possibly with a mix of PA and DAMA circuits. And, as noted above, unit costs for a variety of services would be decreased further when joint telecommunications planning produces shared facilities.

POLICY ISSUES

One problem is to demonstrate the economic and social effectiveness and benefits of rural telecommunications. The benefits of telecommunications depend heavily upon local contexts, socio-political structure, and policy goals, and must also be related more directly to alternative technologies and applications. We do not underestimate the significance of the issues involving socio-political structure; they are being increasingly discussed and analyzed throughout the literature and in international debates (see, for example, 15, 27, and 28). It is true, however, that because previous technologies have been high in cost, very few rural communities in developing countries have service. In addition, traditional economies produce investment strategies biased *against* consideration of the social benefits of a public good such as information, and *toward* technologies suitable for urban telecommunications applications. The result is lack of evidence of comparative effectiveness and benefits needed to justify any investment in any particular telecommunication system. The priority attached to investment in communication as opposed to (or in conjunction with) transportation, agriculture, etc., is not clear-cut, as we noted earlier (see, however, 4, 5, 7, and 24, among others). A series of carefully evaluated rural telecommunication projects is necessary to obtain better evidence of the benefits and of the particular constraints of prior social and political structure. Such projects must not, however, be mere transfers of sophisticated technology, and should include, for example, training components and funding to develop, test, and produce new services *for* and *by* developing countries (as in the Mexican plan).

Another problem is the difficult market aggregation issue. The high-power satellites necessary to have low per-circuit or per-location costs for thin-route applications are expensive in total cost. Few countries could afford all the capacity—many already sustain foreign debts which are too large—and none could utilize it all at the outset because of the time and cost associated with putting the ground stations in place. Excessive debts may create pressures by lending countries to reduce demand for foreign exchange in ways which may inhibit economic growth in the borrowing country, as well as curtailment of redistribution and social spending policies. The combination of low unit-cost and high total cost make it desirable to work out some kind of multinational sharing procedure, just as INTELSAT permits capacity sharing for international traffic. INTELSAT or some other comparable management facility permitting shared use of capacity (such as system 2B) will be essential if the nations most in need are to obtain the benefits.

A third problem concerns issues related to Third World access to and assistance in creating satellite services. Regional/cooperative satellite systems are one resolution to growing orbital congestion and allocation disputes. Which technologies are usable and which services and costs are appropriate for developing countries are constrained by decisions made at the international level and thus are political issues as well (see 15, 17, 27). A hybrid satellite system designed for rural telecommunications, owned or leased by developing countries, may allay those countries' fears that access to and control of communication satellite service will soon be unavailable, due to the former "first-come-first-served" approach to allocation. Such service may also reduce contrasting proposals for allocation of separate orbital positions to countries well in advance of their ability to use the resource and, in fact, provide actual access and control rather than empty orbits. Therefore, developing countries might consider issues such as pilot demonstrations, training programs, flexibility in technical specifications for rural applications (6), and arrangements for a shared satellite system. Such arrangements are not to be construed as permanent, total solutions to world information imbalances, however. As a participant in the 1976 Nairobi Conference wrote (17, p. 26), supporters of the New World Information Order "feel that various types of assistance are not enough and that what is needed is a fundamental restructuring of relationships, the elimination of all forms of inequality and foreign domination through the powerful media of contemporary communications."

A fourth problem is that of capital formation. Developing countries may well be able to finance the ground station costs and lease charges for the kind of satellite system discussed here. But they are unlikely to have the capital necessary to provide the satellite system in the first place. It may be appropriate for developing countries to request that international funding institutions provide the capital for a revolving fund that could provide initial capacity. Usage charges could be planned to make the system self-supporting from that point (including depreciation costs to raise funds for later replacement of the satellite system). It should be noted that even this source of support is controversial: Sunkel and Fuenzalida (in 28) argue that these institutions simply help maintain the system of transnational capitalism and thus, in the long run, obstruct true development goals.

Developing countries have, at one time, proposed that the International Telecommunications Union expand its budget to include communication development assistance (22). In addition, support for increased access to information resources by developing countries was a major United States promise at the November 1976 Nairobi UNESCO Conference. The U.S. commitment at the 1978 General UNESCO Conference is a start (23). Any funding plan, however, needs to take into consideration the issues surrounding the sources of funding, the proper mix of those sources, the conditions attached to such funding, and the short- and long-term effects upon national debt and foreign exchange and economic dependencies.

These policy implications indicate the potential significance of telecommunications in international debates. The New World Information Order meets head on with such technical communication issues. The implicit challenges are already on the agenda.

NOTES

1. Partial support for the preparation of this paper was provided by the Development Support Bureau of the U.S. Agency for International Development and by the Technical Cooperation Department of the International Telecommunications Union.

2. A geosynchronous satellite orbits at a height (22,282 miles at the peak of the ellipse) and velocity sufficient to allow it to remain essentially stationary over one portion of the earth.

3. By a circuit, we mean a complete *two-way* link (duplex channel) between two communicating nodes (whether it be telephone, computer terminals, etc.). This is an important distinction, as most telecommunications other than telephone are one-way, such as TV or broadcast radio.

4. Increased size of the antenna in the spacecraft will increase the effective power on the ground for a fixed level of satellite transmitter power. This permits increased satellite capacity for a fixed size of earth station, or fixed satellite capacity with *smaller* earth station antennas.

5. The standard antenna sizes for INTELSAT ground stations range from 30 meters to 6 meters (used in Saudi Arabia). For the purposes of this paper, we are considering the antenna size for INTELSAT small ground stations to be 4.57 meters. A 4.57 m. antenna can meet INTELSAT specifications. INTELSAT *has* tested these in Nigeria (2), and ORI (16) provides summary cost estimates for rural telecommunications designs which assume the smaller size. The 4.57 m. earth station antenna size may be too small for economical telephony use with the INTELSAT global beams because too much space segment capacity per circuit would be required. The smaller antenna size may be appropriate for use with the more powerful hemispheric beams which INTELSAT first offered for lease in late 1978.

6. DAMA, as considered in each model, will cost somewhere in the range of $2,000 (21) to $20,000 (industry sources) for each station. The latter number is a more realistic cost, although a larger volume market could eventually drive costs toward the lower bound. Cost comparisons use these extremes for sensitivity analysis.

7. In fact, the cost trade-offs particular to any locale are so complex that several computer programs have been developed by the Communications Satellite Planning Program at Stanford University.

REFERENCES

1. Astrain, S. "The Role of the Intelsat System in Meeting International and National Telecommunications Needs." Paper presented at International Satellite Communication Seminar, Lima, Peru, 1978.

2. Cherry, C. *World Communication: Threat or Promise?* (revised edition). New York: John Wiley, 1977.

3. Dill, G. "Comparison of Circuit Capacity of Demand-Assignment and Pre-Assignment Operation." *COMSAT Technical Review* 2(1), Spring 1972, pp. 243–251.

4. Gilling, E. "Telecommunications and Economic Development: Inter-Country Comparisons of the Catalytic Effect of Telephone Services on Development." Unpublished M.B.A. thesis, McGill University, Montreal, Canada, 1975.

5. Hardy, A. "The Role of the Telephone in Economic Development." *Telecommunications Policy*, 4(4), December 1980, pp. 278–286.

6. Hudson, H. "Implications of Development Communications." *Journal of Communication* 29(1), Winter 1979, pp. 179–186.

7. Hudson, H., D. Goldschmidt, E. Parker, and A. Hardy. *The Role of Telecommunications in Socio-Economic Development: A Review of the Literature with Guidelines for Further Investigation.* International Telecommunication Union Special Service Agreement 9-GLO-001-11-02. Palo Alto, Cal.: Keewatin Communications, 1978.

8. International Consultative Committee on Telecommunications (CCITT). *Economic Studies at the National Level in the Field of Telecommunications.* Geneva: International Telecommunication Union, 1973.

9. Janky, J. and J. Barewald. "Interference Control in Broadcast Satellite Applications: Antenna Sidelobe Patterns and Transponder Transfer Gain." In

EASCON-77 Record, IEEE 77CH 1255-9-EASCON, Arlington, Va., September 26, 1977.

10. Kiesling, J. and M. Zisserson. "Extension of Satellite Services through Low Cost Earth Stations." American Institute for Aero-Astronautics 7th Communications Satellite System Conference, April 24–27, 1978, San Diego, Cal., pp. 572–581.

11. Klees, S. and S. Wells. "Costs and Satellites: Implications of the ATS-6 Health/Education Telecommunications Demonstration." Washington, D.C., Academy for Educational Development #CHMA-147-159, 1977.

12. Lusignan, B. *et al. A Rural Telecommunications Plan for Mexico.* Stanford, Cal.: Satellite Systems Planning Center, Dept. of Electrical Engineering, Stanford University, 1979.

13. McAnany, E. (Ed.) *Communication with the Rural Poor in the Third World: Does Information Make a Difference?* Stanford, Cal.: Institute for Communication Research, Stanford University, 1978.

14. Martin, J. *Communications Satellite Systems.* Englewood Cliffs, N.J.: Prentice-Hall, 1978.

15. Nordenstreng, K. and H. Schiller. *National Sovereignty and International Communication.* Norwood, N.J.: Ablex, 1979.

16. Operations Research, Inc. (ORI). *Assessment of Candidate Communications Satellites for Developing Countries.* Silver Spring, Md.: ORI, U.S. Agency for International Development Contract AID/TA-TA-1426, 1977.

17. Osolnik, B. "UNESCO: the Mass Media Declaration." *Review of International Affairs* 690, January 5, 1979.

18. Parker, E. B. "Communication Satellites for Rural Development." *Telecommunications Policy* 2(4), December 1978, pp. 309–315.

19. Parker, E. B. "The Economic and Social Development Potential of Communication Technologies." Paper presented at the 48th Congress of Australia-New Zealand Association for the Advancement of Science, Melbourne, Australia, 1977.

20. Parker, E. B. and B. Lusignan. "Technical and Economic Considerations in Planning Radio Services." In P. Spain, D. Jamison, and E. McAnany (Eds.) *Radio for Education and Development*, Volume Two. Washington, D.C.: World Bank, 1977, pp. 443–459.

21. Pinheiro, R. "Investments and Traffic Assignment in a Hybrid Ground and Spatial Communication Network." Stanford University, Dept. of Engineering, Satellite Systems Planning Center, Technical Report No. 4, Stanford, Cal., 1976.

22. Pool, Ithiel de Sola. "The Problems of WARC." *Journal of Communication* 29(1), Winter 1979, pp. 187–196.

23. Reinhardt, J. "General Policy Statement Delivered at UNESCO 20th General Conference." November 3, 1978.

24. Shapiro, P. *Communications or Transport? Decision-Making in Developing Countries.* Cambridge, Mass.: MIT Research Program on Problems of International Communication and Security, 1967.

25. Sharma, R. "Rural Communications Planning Methodology for Integrating Satellite and Terrestrial Facilities." Stanford University, Dept. of Engineering, Satellite Systems Planning Center, Technical Report No. 66, Stanford, Cal., December 1976.

26. Shore, L. "Mass Media for Development: A Reexamination of Access, Exposure, and Impact." In E. McAnany (Ed.) *Communications in the Rural Third World: Information and Development.* New York: Praeger, 1980, pp. 19–48.

27. "U.S. Faces WARC, The." Symposium in *Journal of Communication* 29(1), Winter 1979, pp. 143–205.

28. Villamil, J. J. (Ed.) *Transnational Capitalism and National Development.* Brighton, England: Harvester, 1979.

PART 4

Mass Communications: Development within National Contexts

Thirty-Two

Communication Strategies for Social Change: National Television versus Local Public Radio

Robert A. White

In San José, Costa Rica, in 1976 the Intergovernmental Conference on Communication Policies in Latin America and the Caribbean stressed the important link between social structure and the development of communication systems. A fundamental aspect of policy is "the indissoluble relation between the phenomenon of communication and the social context in which that phenomenon takes place, and the nexus of mutual conditioning which that relation presupposes" (19). This same concern underlies most recent discussion of communications policy and represents a new trend in our understanding of communications and development.

In this chapter I examine the relation of communication systems and structural change and explore some of the practical policy implications of this relationship. The first section looks at the concept of social structure as the basis of a pattern of communication. The second analyzes one paradigm of communication structure typical of many Third World countries and summarizes the criteria for communications policy implied by this structure. Finally, I use national television and local public radio as examples of the application of structural criteria in selecting communication strategies.

THE STRUCTURAL ANALYSIS OF COMMUNICATIONS IN DEVELOPMENT

Kaarle Nordenstreng and Herbert Schiller (12) have identified "three generations" of communications research, each generation moving more explicitly toward emphasis on the structural changes implicit in national liberation movements as the dominant paradigm in development communications.

In the 1950s and early 1960s there was a tendency to see development as the transfer of technology from the developed nations to the modernized sector of the underdeveloped nations and from there to the disadvantaged hinterlands. The role of communications was to provide channels through which the techniques, lifestyles, motivations, and attitudes of the modernized sector could be diffused to the disadvantaged sector. A number of people argued that in the presence of facilities for transferring information, especially the mass media, social inequalities would gradually disappear (6, 14, 15, 16).

Few clearly perceived that a pattern of communication is constituted not by media but rather by the structure of social exchange. Those who hold commodities culturally defined as valuable are sought out for exchange and become the centers of communication networks (1). Channels of communication tend to follow the lines of social power that evolve from these lines of exchange between individuals and groups. Peasants who have nothing to offer—not even the power of organized numbers—do not get *significant* information even when the mass media are beamed at them.

Furthermore, many social commentators assumed that information is relatively culture- and value-free—that information can be transferred from one nation to another or within a nation without affecting the symbolic meaning of information. To the contrary, however, communication is a structure of meanings and fundamental integrating symbols that establish a common language among all people within a given communication network. For example, agricultural technology can be interpreted as the prestige symbol of the rural elite or it can symbolize unity and defiance against the elite among peasants forming a federation of production cooperatives. Whatever symbolic meaning is given, it serves as the signal to ministers of agriculture, extensionists, and farmers regarding the goals to be sought. These basic symbols affect the value of resources to be exchanged, power relations, and the channels of communication.

Finally, it was assumed that development is essentially a matter of increasing productivity and that there exists a relatively competitive market structure. The process of nation building was not perceived as precisely the struggle to break down internal rigidities stemming from institutionalized concentrations of social power and to eliminate the remnants of external colonial dependence. Few analysts studied the forces for structural change or the emergent social groups who were initiators of change and creators of alternative, dissident communication systems. Consequently, the formal design of communications, the selection of media, and other basic policy considerations did not facilitate the new communication and symbol systems that were taking shape.

By the early 1970s there was widespread questioning of the development model based on channels of communication from the industrialized North Atlantic nations, through the modernized elite sector of the dependent nations, to the more traditional sectors of the Third World countries. Instead of encouraging solid national political growth, creative economic adaptation, and stronger cultural identity, this approach encouraged dependence in all institutional areas. And, by ignoring structural factors, planners channeled information, technology, and other resources through existing communication channels to traditional elites, thus further concentrating power and reinforcing barriers to communication.

Recognition of this situation prompted a second-generation paradigm of communication and development advising that the centralized, top-down communication systems should incorporate the communication networks and decisionmaking of local communities and popular organizations (15). But this did not remove the basic contradiction of the old paradigm: the expectation that a modernizing elite, directly linked with and dependent on the North Atlantic nations, would be the movers of political, economic, and cultural independence. In national contexts that had not already experienced a redistribution of social power, this model simply offered a more efficient means of co-opting popular organizations into the modernization process.

Nordenstreng and Schiller have found increasing acceptance of a third-generation paradigm of communication and development research that clearly sees communication systems as an integral aspect of social structure: "Characteristic of the new perspective is an emphasis on global structure, whereby it is precisely the international sociopolitical-economic system that decisively determines the course of development within the sphere of each nation" (12, p. 6). Basic to the new paradigm is a reorganization of international communication systems to permit greater national autonomy and horizontal exchange between nations that espouse common goals of political, economic, and cultural independence. This reorganization would encourage alternative international channels and challenge the North Atlantic-modernizing elite link by permitting the growth of what are now dissident, minority communication networks within nations and the development of unifying cultural symbols distinct from those imported from the North Atlantic nations. As Karl Sauvant noted: "The impetus has to come . . . not from the leading social groups, the middle class and the professional elites . . . but from those parts of host societies that are relatively independent—especially the intelligentsia and popular movements not wedded to established structures" (12, p. 19).

This review of research perspectives suggests that the analysis of communications in national development should take into account three dimensions: (1) the underlying structure of social exchange and social power, which in effect establishes the network of information channels and allocates significant information to different groups in a national system; (2) the systems of integrating symbols, which provide cultural criteria regarding what is significant information and who should receive information; and (3) the pressure for change in the system stemming from groups experiencing a discrepancy between the information they want and the information they actually have access to (here an important aspect is the emergence of communication networks and symbol systems based on a pattern of exchange and of integrating new symbols created by dissident groups) (26, 27).

THE EMERGING STRUCTURE OF COMMUNICATIONS IN THE THIRD WORLD

I will examine the pattern of communications in light of these three structural dimensions to help identify criteria for decisions in communications policy. I will look at inequities flowing from the present structure of communications, as well as the redistribution of social power and the reorganization of communication patterns that social tensions are generating. The sociocultural background obviously varies greatly among the developing regions, but the interaction of many Third World countries with the colonial empires of the North Atlantic nations over several centuries produced a number of common tendencies.

The Establishment of the European Colonial Bureaucracies

When the trading companies and colonial bureaucracies of the European nations extended themselves around the globe, they frequently established their empires in advanced agrarian societies, creating a relatively simple, two-layered structure. There were many variations and exceptions, but essentially this pattern consisted of a sector of full-time rulers with their retinue of counselors, priests, and warriors, who constituted the decision-making group, and the semisubsistence cultivators and artisans, who provided a surplus for the maintenance of the ruling sector (5, 24). The two halves of society were linked by a hierarchy of intermediaries who performed lower-level governing functions, maintained order, and extracted the goods—and information—necessary for sustaining the decisionmaking, public order activities. It was a center-periphery pattern of communication: lower-status individuals or groups related separately to a local patron and this information was passed up the hierarchy to the center; solutions to lower-status problems were passed back down the hierarchy; finally, there was little horizontal communication between villages or at least between intervillage networks.

This hierarchical structure was explained and justified by the symbol system generated in the great (or literate) tradition of the ruling sector, with its wise men, priests, and poets. Those in the ruling sector were defined as inherently capable of decisionmaking and sustaining the existing order and those in the peasant sector, with only their little (or oral) tradition, were defined as inherently incapable of ruling.

Though the lower levels of the hierarchy resisted the extractive demands of the rulers, the system was relatively stable because of the military power of the center, the imposed beliefs, and the paternalistic concern of the rural elite for the needs of the peasant sector. The power of the center depended heavily on efficient upward channels of information and the broad capability of absorbing information. Moving down the communication hierarchy to the peasants, information was strained out. Obviously, there was no interest in transmitting *significant information* to the peasants and artisans so that they could participate in decisionmaking beyond their own villages.

The North Atlantic empires established their control over these regions either by installing their colonial representatives in the place of the ruling elites or by converting these elites into intermediaries between the metropoles and the producing peasant-artisan sectors. The effect was to move the center of the information network to the overseas metropolis and to make the resident elite the extractor of goods and information responsible to the needs of the empire but not necessarily to their own region's needs. The internal extractive demands were increased and the hierarchical communication system was strengthened so that the communication network usually became even more centralized.

The implantation of the symbol system of the literate cultural tradition of Western Europe accentuated the belief in the superiority of the ruling sector, a belief reinforced by a new or invented racial distinction between the rulers and the peasants. If the tension between the ruling and the peasant sector was increased by the greater demands coming from the empire and the denigration of native cultural traditions, the ruling elite could now count on the superior military and technical support of the metropolis. Nevertheless, humanitarian concerns (such as those expressed in the Spanish Law of the Indies) or the sheer isolation of peasant villages tempered the harshness of this configuration.

A New Phase of Empire: Technological Bureaucracies

With the advance of the industrial revolution and the impersonal efficiency of the capitalist economic system in Western Europe in the nineteenth and early twentieth centuries, a new phase of empire began. Steamships, railroads, and more rapid communications such as telegraph and then radio created vast urban markets worldwide, and extractive demands rapidly increased. National banking and credit systems were introduced, making productive capital easily available. As former colonial areas gained political independence, ministries of agriculture, industry, and education extended technological advisory systems into rural areas. Productive capital, technology, and education almost always were introduced by the traditional ruling elite—which now became an urban-technical sector—and were channeled through the existing hierarchical system to provincial and rural elites. However, the essentially extractive role of the hierarchical intermediaries meant that the new resources were not directed to the peasant-worker sector; instead they increased the power of the rural elite. This period also ushered in greatly improved living standards and the educational, health, and communication facilities associated with the liberal democratic ideal. However, these developments were appropriated by the traditional ruling elite—or the urban-technical elite—while the peasant sector benefited little.

This new phase of empire accentuated tensions that the system finally was unable to contain. Whereas before the extraction process often had been slow and inefficient, now demands were sudden and steep and lower status groups were treated as simply market factors. In many cases the new markets made land more valuable and the rural elites moved to expel peasants from land that they had held from time immemorial. Whereas before peasants could often get redress for wrongs through the paternalistic hierarchy, capitalist ideology justified their being treated as mere economic objects. This sharp new deprivation set off great peasant rebellions in many parts of the Third World: in Mexico, the Zapata movement; in China, the revolution; and so on (3, 10, 20, 25). The peasant groups, finding no support in the traditional hierarchy, cut themselves off from the dependency structure and began to establish their own independent decisionmaking and leadership, building solidary lower status linkages within and among communities and regions. They developed common unifying symbols, which provided a new language very distinct from the dependency culture maintained by traditional elites. Peasants affected by these movements came to see themselves as bearers of the authentic cultural tradition of the region or nation; they also saw themselves as the majority and the rightful claimants to the land, educational facilities, markets, and all else that the urban-technical elite controlled.

The same factors of modernization promoting the rise of peasant movements were causing profound divisions in the urban-technical sector too. As the validating symbols of the traditional ruling elites came to be increasingly dominated by the technical-scientific and capitalistic economic-financial orientations, technical and financial information became the most valuable information and the organizations supplying this information became the centers of communication networks. Humanistic, socially idealistic, and, with the secularization accompanying modernization, religious symbols lost importance and became marginal. The intelligentsia and other alienated groups tended to break away from the dominant financial-technical sector and build alliances with other aggrieved groups, notably peasant and worker movements (10, 23).

Popular movements found in these urban-technical allies the organizational, literate, and other skills necessary to transform local uprisings into a coordinated national movement. The alliance created a new, more symmetrical power relationship between alienated groups with an elite background and lower status groups because urban radicals needed the mass of peasants and workers to confront traditional elites. This exchange relationship generated new communication networks separate from the hierarchical channels of the modernizing ruling elites. Lower status groups gained access to significant information, both in the national urban sector and in the international community, sidestepping the financial-technical centers of the North Atlantic nations.

Such alliances, including peasants, urban workers, intellectuals, religious leaders, and technocrats, frustrated with government corruption and inefficiency, formulated alternative symbol systems and new sociopolitical and cultural goals for their nations. Central to the new symbols was the validation of indigenous cultures and the appreciation of lower status, less Europeanized groups as sources of national culture.

The Introduction of Mass Electronic Communications

The last fifteen years have seen the structure of international dependency relations entering a new phase. Just as the impact of empire was changed in the nineteenth century by improved transportation and communication technology, so now the institutions of mass electronic communications are significantly influencing the structure of power relations. The principal interrelated elements of the new communications institutions are the use of more direct and global communications technology, especially satellites; computerization of communication systems; development of transnational economic organizations; and centering of symbol creation in the advertising industry, with its perfection of cultural persuasion and its grounding of cultural symbols in the consumer values of capitalism. These social and technological changes have centralized communication channels and symbol creation in the North Atlantic nations to the point that the urban-technical sector of the developing nations has been almost totally absorbed or superseded. The cultural symbols of the metropoles are now transmitted directly to the public in the dependent nations without intervention from local ruling elites.

Alliances of popular movements and alienated urban based groups in the dependent nations are still protagonists in the effort to create alternative patterns of communication, but the struggle has been transferred to the international arena. Groups of nations linked in international movements such as the non-aligned bloc are providing the organizational structure of political, economic, and cultural emancipation. In so doing they are forging new horizontal communication networks and new unifying symbols.

This structural analysis of communications in Third World countries suggests the principal policy criteria to be employed if the formal planning of communications is to complement the sociocultural patterns emerging in these nations.

1. The vertical, hierarchical structure of communication channels, stretching from control centers in the North Atlantic nations to remote peasant villages is antithetical to development and new horizontal channels of communication should be encouraged at all levels. At the international level these horizontal networks could provide direct access between developing countries that have similar problems and similar social, economic, and political goals; at the national level, interchange among various popular movements; and at the local or regional level, coordination of popular movements in the area.

2. The media should provide access to the alliance of urban-technical and popular groups so that the media can be extensions of the communication structure constituted by movements seeking national independence. Since the control of the media by private enterprise in these countries generally implies the dominance of the media by transnational advertising interests and by the local elites dependent on North Atlantic centers—both hostile to independent popular movements—this goal calls for some form of autonomous or government control of the media in order to insure wider and more impartial access.

3. The content of the media should not reflect the cultural symbols of the developed nations but those new symbol systems that are being shaped by popular alliances seeking sociocultural emancipation.

4. In order to counter the deeply entrenched hierarchical pattern of communications, special efforts should be made to develop structures of participatory communication that guarantee lower status groups access to the information that is significant for their understanding of local and national decisionmaking.

APPLYING STRUCTURAL CRITERIA IN POLICY DECISIONS IN THE DEVELOPMENT OF COMMUNICATION SYSTEMS

To illustrate the significance of planning media systems congruent with and supportive of new communication patterns, I will examine two contrasting examples: introducing television and local community directed radio in developing countries.

Television at the National Level

In most developed nations television has become a medium for advertising, brief news reports, political campaigning, and popular light entertainment, placing much less emphasis on cultural and political literacy. Most developing countries have introduced some form of television, usually following the models of Britain, France, or the United States. A number of studies on broadcasting in the Third World (see 4) provide some basis for briefly reviewing the experience with television in light of structural criteria.

Encouraging the Development of Horizontal Communication Networks. The level of technology and skill that television management, production, and transmission require is high, and television systems generally have been installed directly by U.S., British, or French teams; likewise, personnel training is frequently done in these countries, which means continued dependence not only in terms of equipment preference and familiarity but also in terms of programming and production styles. Such dependence discourages experimentation in management and production, as well as in content themes that support horizontal exchange patterns between Third World countries and between popular movements within these countries.

Public Service Orientation with Autonomous or Government Direction. Many developing countries have attempted to give television a public orientation by making it partially or entirely a government function. However, television production and transmission are expensive, government budgets are limited, and it is difficult to collect user fees. There is also great pressure from international and national advertising and private enterprise interests in regard to programming. Many countries rely heavily on advertising for support, and this orients television toward audiences with purchasing power and toward bland, irrelevant content.

Moreover, given the limited number of channels and hours of television, few countries have created a flexible format that combines the intense debate of public issues characteristic of a country in the process of social change, the development of cultural and political literacy, and the promotion of national integration.

Projecting a New National Cultural Synthesis. Once television is installed, there is pressure to extend broadcasting around the clock. However, it is hard to provide attractive, worthwhile programs with local talent and low budgets, so the hours are filled out with inexpensive programs imported from the United States or other countries. Accordingly, tastes in television viewing are rapidly become oriented to such fare. Moreover, to meet the demand for technical skills, there is a tendency to recruit personnel with an urban, Western background who are less familiar with their own indigenous—often rural based—national culture.

Promoting Participatory Communications. In most developing countries rural areas do not have electricity, and even in urban areas the cost of a television receiver is too great for the majority of people. Television develops into an elite medium directed toward the urban middle class, and mass communication systems are oriented to the interests and tastes of that privileged group. In addition, the centralized, urban location of television studios and the limited numbers of hours and channels of broadcasting have developed a medium that lends itself to enhancing the images of a few dominant entertainment personalities or political figures. This encourages the feeling that one must be a demigod to use the media and reinforces the existing hierarchical pattern of communication.

This is not to argue that the institutional setting of television cannot be planned so as to support structural changes occurring in Third World countries. However, the technical limitations of television and the institutional models introduced have tended to reinforce the external dependence and internal rigidity that are the basis of the problem.

Local Public Service Radio

First-generation discussions of communication and development put great stress on large national radio and television systems as a key to integrating a new nation and mobilizing it for development. Wilbur Schramm (17) added to the analysis of these big media an emphasis on the importance of the little media, small and inexpensive modes usually employed in face-to-face group settings. However, there has been scant mention of the development role of what might be termed "intermediate media," one example of which is local public service radio.

Attention has turned to public service radio at the community level and to community controlled programming in radio and television in Canada (9), the United States (18), and Britain (7, 8). In the African and Asian countries that adopted the very centralized British and French models of national communications of thirty to fifty years ago, local radio is generally not found. Latin America has seen the major development of local public service radio in the Third World.

One of the first such organizations was Radio Sutatenza, established in 1949 to broadcast programs on basic education and to promote community development and improvements in health and agriculture. As Radio Sutatenza evolved into Accion Cultural Popular (ACPO), it began to train local community leaders to support the educational programs and other development oriented campaigns in community and regional organizations. Thus, radio was inserted into a structure of rural organization at the municipal and regional levels, serving as one part of the communications network linking these levels. ACPO has grown into a national rural education institution with relatively centralized broadcasting so that it may no longer be characterized as local radio (11).

However, the relative success of ACPO influenced the establishing of some seventy-five to one hundred educational-cultural radio stations in virtually all countries of Latin America (2).[1] These generally have remained small local stations oriented toward development and social change. To analyze the significance of local public service radio in the Third World we will return to the four structural criteria for communications policy.

Encouraging the Development of Horizontal Communication Networks. Most of the radio stations in question are small (one- to five-kilowatt) units covering the service area of a market town (a radius of thirty to fifty kilometers) and thus constituting a regional intervillage system. The market towns in which the stations are usually located are the centers of regional road systems, bus lines, commercial trading, and provincial government; they contain health, education, and agricultural services, as well as religious-cultural organizations. In other words, these towns are the focus of established, self-contained communication networks. Such official communication systems tend to follow the hierarchical lines of traditional social structure: from regional offices to local rural elites (larger landholders, merchants, political leaders, and so on).

The educational-cultural radio stations enter this communications pattern at a different level because they frequently get off the ground as part of a literacy campaign aimed at semisubsistence peasants. Most of the stations were initiated by or cooperate with socially oriented Catholic priests or lay leaders; the radio school programs have been promoted through an existing structure of neighborhood religious leaders. The combination of religious-social idealism, the emphasis on community development in Latin America in the 1960s and 1970s, and especially the rapidly worsening socioeconomic situation of semisubsistence cultivators, in comparison with that of rural elites, have provided a strong impetus to this medium.

On the basis of this motivation and the structure of religious leadership, which in the cultural context of Latin America exists in virtually every rural neighborhood, radio schools usually were rapidly extended into every part of the market region. The radio school programs gradually evolved into a lower status communication network embodied in a series of neighborhood organizations, direct broadcasts to the participants in these organizations, visits by paraprofessional peasant promoters of neighborhood organizations to isolated communities, monthly meetings of neighborhood leaders, and a regional training center in the market town for short courses in community organization, cooperatives, health, and agriculture. In time such networks came to form the basis for credit unions, consumer or marketing cooperatives, small-farmer special-interest organizations, and rural women's organizations. The radio schools and training courses often have used some form of the Freire *"concientisation* method," and this, combined with the sheer momentum of organization, has generated a type of lower status regional movement for land reform, better public services, and a greater voice for peasants in regional political decisions (21, 22).

The radio station serves as a central communication exchange within the regional system of peasant organizations; each type of organization or audience has an allotted broadcast time period. Prime time usually is devoted to a broad-ranging cultural and community service program focusing on current peasant problems in the area. Frequently, local leaders, with some help from the station's technical staff, prepare their own programs, or they are interviewed at the station or in the community. In this case the radio is a medium whereby peasant leaders can stay in contact with their organizations in remote communities and with each other.

News programs specialize in local events, often stressing local advocacy or peasant pressure group activity that ordinarily would not be reported. Since lower status groups in rural areas of Latin America do not have telephones, newspapers, or door-to-door postal service, local radio fulfills this information function.

Public Service Orientation with Autonomous or Government Direction. The majority of local stations following this model in Latin America were started by either the church or people associated with the church and this has afforded them a measure of protection. But the logic of the participatory ideology in lower-status movements is creating pressures for greater peasant and worker control of these stations. In Guatemala, Bolivia, and Ecuador where the constituency is a more solidary Indian tribal group or a peasant-worker organization, some of these groups own and administer these radio stations. The broadcasting is often done in the native Indian language and is a support of indigenous cultures.

Some governments, such as Peru's, have moved to set up regional radio stations for educational-development purposes; this offers a variant of the general model. A major problem is maintaining at low wages good local managers with a public service orientation.

Much of the initial installation costs have come from international aid organizations. Operating expenses are covered by some selective advertising, although this can be uncertain because of the inevitable hostility of local merchants; popular contributions; continued assistance from international or local church organizations; and, for some educational programs, national government. These small stations can operate on relatively modest budgets because salaries and other expenses in provincial towns are low, and much of the programming—even management—relies on volunteers or part-time help. Low budgets leave these stations no alternative but community participation.

In spite of modest budgets and competition from local commercial radio, many public service stations gain wide, loyal audiences precisely because they are directed to the large lower status rural or urban population. Stations with good management, such as Radio Santa Maria in the Dominican Republic, have achieved an unusually high level of technical skill in producing cultural and educational programs.

Projecting a New National Cultural Synthesis. Peasant-worker movements constitute an informal communication system outside of and in opposition to the communication channels dominated by elites. As this alternative communication network develops, peasant and worker groups generate a perception of themselves and the causes of their problems that is radically different from elite ideologies. In so far as the radio stations become a medium for these lower-status communication networks, the audience loyalty derives from the frank airing of lower-status problems and a treatment of these problems from a peasant or worker point of view. The stations pick up the language, perspectives, and values of the popular movements, give a public, objectified validity to this lower-status culture and solidify the social acceptance of this alternative culture. The opposition of local elites to these radio stations is precisely the fear that peasant or worker groups will no longer accept the elite ideology that has been imposed for centuries. The constant harassment from local elites, bomb threats or actual bombings, occasional station closings by the authorities, and other forms of restrictions are a measure of the hostility to the formation of a lower-status cultural synthesis.

Many of the stations have taken a resolute stand in favor of national or regional cultures—refusing to play English-language music from the United States and featuring instead local folk or popular protest music; indeed, some stations sponsor some form of annual folk music festival.

Promoting Participatory Communication. In their review for UNESCO of Latin American development projects with a dimension of participatory communications, Jeremiah O'Sullivan-Ryan and Mario Kaplún found that most projects were initiated and at first supported by international agencies but ceased when outside assistance was withdrawn (13). This is not surprising. My earlier analysis of the process of structural change indicated that truly independent lower status organizations generally are not started by outside agencies but by lower status groups spontaneously in a moment of intense conflict with the hierarchical structure. The evidence suggests that media such as a lower status oriented local station do not initiate popular participation. Instead, lower status groups formulate their message independently and begin to build their own horizontal communication networks; local radio is an accessible communication instrument that can enable them to build support within the local area.

Local stations with alert management and good contacts with popular organizations know how to spot peasant or worker actions with social change significance, seek out the people involved, encourage them to speak out, and, most important, train representatives to use radio effectively. Local stations can become participants in a local pattern of events much more easily than can national media, and many activities that are important to popular organizations will never gain access to national media because they are regional or because there simply is not time to cover all regional events. Obviously, it is much easier for peasants or workers to gain access to a nearby station than to make contact with national media. Local educational-cultural stations also provide the long-term educational and "concientisation" services that are essential in building popular organizations (health and agricultural problems, for example, tend to be relatively regional, and it is much more appropriate to address these problems at the local level than in programs at the national level).

Of course, local public service radio is just one element in a general design of communications policy for development purposes. Local radio must be complemented by rural newspapers, inexpensive books for rural families, different folk media, national media, and even appropriate forms of community or family television. The important point, however, is the analysis of how local radio—or any other medium—relates to the emerging structure of communications in a developing country. The model described in this chapter reflects the social and political context of Latin America; careful examination of structural conditions in other parts of the world would suggest how local radio could be adapted to varied contexts.

NOTE

1. The figure of seventy-five to one hundred educational-cultural radio stations of the type discussed here is a conservative estimate. Dr. Franz-Josef Eilers, director of the Catholic Media Council in Aachen, West Germany, estimated that there are more than two hundred such stations in Latin America.

REFERENCES

1. Blau, Peter M. *Exchange and Power in Social Life*. New York: John Wiley and Sons, 1964.

2. Braun, Juan. *Visión global de la investigación sobre escuelas radiofónicas*. Bogotá: Asociación Latinoamericana de Educación Radiofónica (ALER), Centro Internacional de Investigaciones para el Desarrollo (CIID), 1977.

3. Huizer, Gerrit. *The Revolutionary Potential of Peasants in Latin America*. Lexington, Mass.: D. C. Heath, Lexington Books, 1972.

4. Katz, Elihu and George Wedell. *Broadcasting in the Third World*. Cambridge, Mass.: Harvard University Press, 1977.

5. Lenski, Gerhard E. *Power and Privilege*. New York: McGraw-Hill, 1966.

6. Lerner, Daniel. *The Passing of Traditional Society*. Glencoe, Ill.: Free Press, 1958.

7. Lewis, Peter M. *Different Keepers: Models of Structure and Finance in Community Radio*. London: International Institute of Communications, 1977.

8. Lewis, Peter M. *Whose Media?: The Annan Report and After: A Citizen's Guide to Radio and Television*. London: Consumer's Association, 1978.

9. McNulty, Jean M. *Other Voices in Broadcasting: The Evolution of New Forms of Local Programming in Canada*. Government of Canada, Department of Broadcasting, 1979.

10. Migdal, Joel S. *Peasants, Politics and Revolution*. Princeton, N.J.: Princeton University Press, 1974.

11. Musto, Stefan A. *Los medios de comunicación social al servicio del desarrollo rural*. Bogotá, Colombia: Editorial Andes, 1971.

12. Nordenstreng, Kaarle and Herbert I. Schiller. *National Sovereignty and International Communication*. Norwood, N.J.: Ablex, 1979.

13. O'Sullivan-Ryan, Jeremiah and Mario Kaplún. *Communication Methods to Promote Grass Roots Participation for an Endogenous Development Process*. Caracas, Unpublished report, 1979.

14. Rogers, Everett and F. Shoemaker. *Communication of Innovations: A Cross-Cultural Approach*. New York: Free Press. 1971.

15. Rogers, Everett M. *Communication and Development: Critical Perspectives*. Beverly Hills, Cal.: Sage, 1976.

16. Schramm, Wilbur. *Mass Media and National Development*. Stanford, Cal.: Stanford University Press, 1964.

17. Schramm, Wilbur. *Big Media, Little Media*. Beverly Hills, Cal.: Sage, 1977.

18. Thomas, Thomas. Personal conversation, 1979.

19. UNESCO. *Intergovernmental Conference on Communication Policies in Latin America and the Caribbean, Final Report, San José* (Costa Rica) July, 1976.

20. White, Robert A. "Mexico: The Zapata Movement and the Revolution." In Henry A. Landsberger (Ed.) *Latin American Peasant Movements*. Ithaca, N.Y.: Cornell University Press, 1971.

21. White, Robert A. *Mass Communication and the Popular Promotion Strategy of Rural Development in Honduras*. Stanford, Cal.: Institute for Communication Research, 1976.

22. White, Robert A. *An Alternative Pattern of Basic Education: Radio Santa Maria*. Paris: UNESCO, 1976.

23. White, Robert A. *The Role of a Radio Station in the Process of Social Change in the Dominican Republic*. Unpublished report, 1977.

24. Wolf, Eric. *Peasants*. Englewood Cliffs, N.J.: Prentice-Hall, 1966.

25. Wolf, Eric. *Peasant Wars of the Twentieth Century*. New York: Harper and Row, 1969.

26. Young, Frank W. "A Proposal for Cooperative Cross-Cultural Research on Intervillage Systems." *Human Organisation* 25, Spring 1966, pp. 46–50.

27. Young, Frank W. and Ruth C. Young. *Comparative Studies of Community Growth*. Rural Sociological Society Monograph No. 2. Morgantown: West Virginia University, 1973.

Thirty-Three

Communication for Political Change: The Iranian Revolution

Hamid Mowlana

The postwar period has seen nationalism, anti-imperialism, and revolution in many parts of the world and diverse nationalities in quest of self-determination and a new world order as militarily weak nations confront the major powers with increasing success. In response, the great powers have moved from territorial conquest to establishing, restoring, or maintaining governments that are politically reliable and compatible with their strategic, military, and economic interests. This period also has witnessed the development of new technology and weapon systems and the worldwide spread of modern communications. With the articulation of new norms and institutions in the Third World and a sudden decline in distance favoring the rapid mobilization of power in different parts of the world, foreign policymakers must proceed cautiously. Internal and regional instability, a high level of transnational influence, and frequent resort to coups and other covert operations have encouraged a moralistic and intellectual approach to foreign policy, alongside intense concern with communication and persuasion.

The battlefield of international politics has shifted from the geographical and the physical to the ideological and the cultural level. The Iranian revolution in general and the U.S.-Iranian crisis in particular embody the latter type of conflict and, with communication as the new ingredient, foreshadow conflicts yet to come. In this chapter I examine various aspects of the connections between communication and political change and demonstrate the international significance of the Iran coverage.

THE ROLE OF COMMUNICATION IN THE IRANIAN REVOLUTION

A New Strategy and Development

To be sure, the Iran coverage has provided evidence of the demise of the model of modernization through industrialization, but its most profound impact will be the impetus it has given to selecting indigenous development strategies. In many ways the revolution was a direct response to an imposed development model laying heavy emphasis on industrialization and the consumer society at the expense of agricultural and middle-level technology based on Iranian tradition and resources. This clash of development strategies led to a conflict between two opposing Iranian institutions: the official culture, represented by government and ruling elites promoting Western solutions through electronic media and the press, and the popular culture of the masses, rooted in centuries of Iranian political and religious traditions and transmitted by highly efficient indigenous channels of communication.

Amidst the torrent of information flowing from both sides we see indisputable evidence of a renewed reappraisal of how communication, culture, and national development interact. Indeed, the issue of communication and cultural integrity was a dominant theme in the Iranian revolution and continues to be a major element in postrevolutionary Iranian foreign policy (6). Present Iranian ideology views development as wider than just economic and political change: to Iranians development must include the people's aspirations to move from a perceived unsatisfactory life condition toward a better life.

Reeducation as a Political Objective

The demands for the deposed shah's extradition and the return of his wealth rested on an explicit assumption that the world, particularly the United States, must learn about the true nature of the shah's regime and about U.S. foreign policy toward the shah. Iran progressed toward this goal through many approaches. By exploiting the appetite of American news personnel and by supporting the United Nations commission, Iranians succeeded in revealing secret information on the shah's assets and on his torture of dissidents. Additionally, nongovernmental organizations, church groups, and individuals have played important roles in this reeducation.

The purpose of this campaign was the rewriting of twenty-five years of U.S.-Iranian relations. Iranian leaders were demanding intangibles: apology and rethinking—hard things to come by in a world that aspires to power and wealth. These cost-free demands raised the conflict to a new level of international confrontation.

The Use of Traditional Channels of Communication

If the substance and strategy of the Iranian revolution were new, so too was the realization that, in old societies such as Iran's, control of the modern communication media does not guarantee political control. Modern media must achieve the power and penetration of traditional channels of communication if they are to be useful social tools. The Iranian leaders, it is true, utilized the most sophisticated mass communication infrastructure then available in the Third World, but traditional channels proved a more effective means to articulate and disseminate revolutionary policy and to mobilize the population. Particularly potent means of communication were the bazaar and the mosque, both rooted in Iranian political and religious traditions. Both before and after the revolution, Iranian leaders relied heavily on these and other traditional channels to effect political-social communication (5). The unity of religion and politics in the Islamic tradition, which is the rallying point of the Iranian revolution, gave further support to a comprehensive view of communication and politics in which traditional religious institutions must be integrated with modern political structures in the process of revolutionary change. In sum, the Iranian revolution underlines the importance of appreciating the total communication system of a culture when offering explanations of past events or predicting the future.

Electronic Communication and Access to the Masses

Electronic communication has increased the access of leaders to the masses. This immediate contact with the people has created a potent feedback mechanism between political leaders and their constituencies that has a direct impact on day-to-day decisionmaking. In the U.S., of course, government leaders have easy access to millions of listeners and viewers nationwide. Indeed, the entire U.S. population can be mobilized into an audience in a few hours. In the same way, Iranian leaders have benefited from a highly sophisticated network of big media and small media which by 1979 connected all parts of Iran to the capital and to the rest of the world.

During the 1970s inexpensive transistor radios and tape recorders inundated the Iranian market. Even among the poor and illiterate, transistors became a status symbol. Every tenth Iranian, regardless of class or education, owned a portable telecommunication receiver—an unanticipated tool of revolution. Thus, the exiled Khomeini had access to the people through cassettes and radio broadcasts, and written communiques, photocopied or mimeographed, were widely disseminated by all political groups in the tumultuous period before and after the revolution.

THE IRANIAN REVOLUTION AND THE MEDIA

World Communication Imbalance

The issue of the world communication imbalance crystallized in the Iranian revolution and the U.S.-Iranian crisis. The revolution and the taking of the American hostages can be attributed in no small measure to the inequality of information flow that has characterized the world for decades and that continues to affect the course of diplomatic maneuvering between the United States and Iran.

As Iranians confront a communication system that seeks to use their country as a news commodity, the norms of international news gathering have changed. Thus, students holding the hostages treated American TV producers not as journalists on a fact-finding mission but as customers for newsworthy items; they exchanged unedited films of hostages for maximum exposure of their position in the United States. In the students' view, American media were fascinated with revolutionary excesses but little concerned with legitimate Iranian grievances. Iranians rightly recognized that this lack of attention was the result of obstacles to communication. Accordingly, they reasoned that if Western media would not cover a revolution, they would heed a dramatic event. Thus, this approach was one way Iranians sought to redress the communication imbalance.[1]

In both Iran and the United States, instant access to the masses through electronic communication has had the same effect: it has created a condition of instantaneous demand for, and supply of, information and has forced a measure of accountability on political leaders. In short, even minor policy decisions are highly susceptible to immediate reaction from the masses.

The Role of the Media in Diplomacy

Diverse nongovernmental organizations such as political parties, the press, universities, and churches play varying communication roles in every society. Their impact is as different as the status and function that societies accord these bodies. But their collective contribution to the flow of communication across national boundaries has grown so vast that these institutions have become an increasingly important part of the international relations process. Particularly during crisis, media and international relations become tightly intertwined.

The role of the media in international relations has grown in response to at least four factors: (1) the broadened conception of journalists' role in the reporting of foreign affairs; (2) the ability of television to provide live, on-site reporting and the interactive, instantaneous communication made possible by satellite technology; (3) the increasing involvement of individuals and nongovernmental organizations in international relations and their reliance on the media in this effort; and (4) the use of media by government officials to signal their intentions or to disseminate propaganda, especially when customary channels are blocked. To these factors—all manifest in the U.S.-Iranian crisis—one might add the hope that the media can serve to advance international understanding and conflict resolution.

The media's capacity to create new attitudes is greatest during periods in which international tension is relatively low. In the initial period of internal struggles in the Iranian revolution, the United States through its media could have manifested acceptance of, or at least neutrality toward, the new government and Iranian grievances. This did not take place; by the time the hostages were seized, an atmosphere of confrontation existed on both sides. The mass media could have chipped away at hardened perceptions not so much by creating a mood conducive to conflict resolution but by not evoking a mood of impending crisis.

It is difficult to clarify all the issues in the American-Iranian crisis but, regarding the involvement of the media, several salient questions arise. Did the media—through greed, incompetence, or even ignorance—allow themselves to be manipulated by political leaders? Did the media create sensational news and deliberately heighten the feeling of crisis, thereby exacerbating the conflict?

Acting Foreign Minister Abolhassan Bani-Sadr's statement to the foreign press on Thanksgiving Day, 1979, underlined the crucial and delicate role the media were playing in the U.S.-Iranian confrontation: "We need to convey our message to the world. For this we must use the media. . . . What we want from you is nothing but revelation of the truth in the world. . . . Diplomats cannot solve this problem. We want to solve it through 'newspaper diplomacy.' Wouldn't you like this to be the first problem solved by journalists?" (3,8). However, the United States government apparently favored the traditional approach toward negotiations and frowned upon any attempts at negotiation that would have involved private citizens and nongovernmental organizations.

Under such highly charged circumstances, the media could play an important role as an alternative and independent source of information. They could serve, for example, to increase international understanding and to reduce tension in conflict situations. Unfortunately, news coverage of the Iranian revolution contributed to the creation of a crisis mood in which dedication to journalistic independence and neutrality appeared to be at odds with national loyalty.

The Media, Public Opinion, and Foreign Policy

One cannot deny that media on both sides were active participants in, and at times advocates for, policy decisions. From the onset, it was clear that American media and American government shared a framework of assumptions about Iran as a people and as a revolution (2). Thus, the press early on openly mobilized the American public—having experienced the defeat in Vietnam, the national humiliation of Watergate, the energy crisis, runaway inflation, and large-scale unemployment, the United States was ripe for such mobilization. And American media, particularly television, undertook to shape the public's preferences and expectations for policy purposes.

Yet this joint media-government view of the U.S.-Iranian crisis is problematic: just as media and officialdom have to maintain the public's perception of threat, they also have to be careful not to overemphasize the threat because a highly mobilized populace can limit the government's freedom to make decisions. Thus, a major result of the daily outpouring of information about the hostage seizure, often from competing or conflicting centers of power, was a sense of confusion.

NEWS COVERAGE OF THE U.S.-IRANIAN CONFLICT

Cultural Values and Ideological Orientation

News gathering is a fundamentally biased process. Relative emphasis in news selection reflects an ideological perspective rooted in the unique social and cultural circumstances of the news gatherer. In short, all news is views, and there is no such thing as facts.

Coverage of the Iranian revolution and of the U.S.-Iranian conflict show that reporting across cultural boundaries is extremely difficult since communicators and audiences must interpret unfamiliar kinds of events unfolding in unfamiliar contexts. The past experiences and cultural categories of the communicator may be inappropriate to the task of interpretation. For example, in reporting on a revival of Moslem fundamentalism in Iran, Western observers borrowed the label of fundamentalism from the history of Catholicism; this designation referred to the use of religion to resolve all social, economic, and political problems and at the same time to the restoration of dogma and rites. In the Islamic world religious laws governed social organizations for centuries. While Christianity always coexisted with the state and its legal, social, and cultural structures, there traditionally was no separation between church and state in Islam and thus, unlike the European situation, no challenge to religious institution, dogmas, and rites. Thus, the sophistication and complexity of Iran's social context was overlooked as the Western media decried "fanatic clergy," "extremist Shi'ism," and "martyr-hungry masses" (4). Islam became the menace. No attention, let alone credibility, was given the Iranian view of justice and vision of society, and modernizing progress was judged primarily by the development of American or Western European political institutions.

Socialization is a major factor in the way journalists interpret events and try to overcome cultural obstacles (9). One analysis showed that Eric Rouleau's *Le Monde* series of December 1979 was so different from American coverage that Rouleau appeared to be describing an entirely different country from the Iran in U.S. media (7). On the other hand, the failure of many American correspondents to understand Iranian culture and language, along with their cold war image of international relations, limited their ability to interpret Iranian policy. Protests and riots were written off as inevitable, though insignificant, by-products of a system ruled by a single leader. American journalists continued to believe despite all indications to the contrary that the revolution and the crisis in Iran were inspired by Communist forces on the outside who were trying to take over the country. In short, American media conceived the U.S.-Iranian crisis as a black-white event: this us-them polarity allowed Americans to turn the Iranian people into a faceless, diabolical, and dehumanized menace.

Communication in Political Crisis

A common assumption is that the volume of communication sharply decreases during a crisis. What occurred in Iran, however, was not a decrease in flow but a shift to indirect, symbolic forms of communication. In analyzing crisis communication we must distinguish between volume and effectiveness of communication since communication can flow at a high volume and at the same time suffer reduction in quality through physical and cultural distortion. Furthermore, protagonists may disagree about the fundamental dimensions of the conflict, even debating whether the channels of communication should remain open.

In the U.S.-Iranian crisis the shift from direct to indirect forms of communication had a considerable deleterious effect on the bargaining process. Positions have to be formulated in a simple, symbolic way to ensure understanding. Yet highly complex messages thus rendered could ill bridge the physical and cultural distance between Iran and the United States.

NOTE

1. In the early days of the crisis Bani-Sadr, then foreign minister, argued that Iran's first request for a Security Council meeting was made not because he thought the Security Council would support Iran's demands but because the U.N. would focus international attention on Iran's grievances (1).

REFERENCES

1. Bani-Sadr, Abolhassan. "On the UN Security Council." *Kahyan* (Tehe-ran), 6 Azar, 1358, p. 9.
2. Cottam, Richard. "Goodbye to America's Shah." *Foreign Policy* 34, Spring 1979, pp. 3–14.
3. "Dateline Teheran." *Newsweek*, December 3, 1979, p. 87.
4. Dorman, William A. and Ehsan Omeed. "Reporting Iran the Shah's Way." *Columbia Journalism Review*, January/February 1979, pp. 27–33.
5. Mowlana, Hamid. "Technology versus Tradition: Communication in the Iranian Revolution." *Journal of Communication* 29(3), Summer 1979, pp. 107–112.
6. Mowlana, Hamid. "U.S.-Iranian Relations, 1954–1978: A Case of Cul-

tural Domination." Paper presented at the annual conference of the Middle East Studies Association, Salt Lake City, Utah, November 8, 1979.

7. Said, Edward W. "Iran." *Columbia Journalism Review*, March/April 1980, pp. 23–33.

8. "Teheran's Reluctant Diplomats." *Time*, December 2, 1979, p. 64.

9. Tresize, James, James G. Stovall and Hamid Mowlana. *Watergate: A Crisis for the World—A Survey of British and French Press Reaction Toward an American Political Crisis*. Oxford: Pergamon Press, 1980.

Thirty-Four

Mass Line Communication: Liberation Movements in China and India

Kusum J. Singh

Few national leaders have differed as strikingly as Mahatma Gandhi and Mao Zedong. Gandhi led a nationalist movement that was supported by many of India's richest people, deeply infused with religious sentiments, and based on calculated nonviolence. Mao led a socialist revolution that was staunchly opposed by wealthy Chinese, infused by a new form of (nonreligious) historical materialism, and based on the calculated use of violence by the Red Army.

Despite these differences, careful study reveals interesting similarities (See 8).[1] Both Gandhi and Mao spearheaded liberation movements against imperialism—in India against the British and in China against the Japanese and other foreign interests. Both mobilized millions of illiterate peasants in fierce struggles against sometimes overwhelming odds. Even though the major channels of communication—press, radio, government agencies, and schools—were in the hands of their opponents, Gandhi and Mao succeeded in getting their messages to the masses: this was mass communication without mass media.

If Gandhi and Mao had not developed intimate communication with the people, their movements would have been doomed to bloody failure. They succeeded in large measure because they relied on mass line communication, which is based on nonelitist leadership: action is initiated on many fronts and levels, vital messages are communicated by personal example, and leaders are—and are seen as—nondivine human beings with a common, not a charismatic, touch. Using this mass line approach, Gandhi and Mao developed huge mass followings that won Indian independence from the British in August 1947 and in October 1949 gave birth to the People's Republic of China.

Today the world is far different from what it was more than three decades ago. Yet careful scrutiny of Gandhi's and Mao's achievements may help people invent more human approaches to communication than the elitist, oligarchic, and carefully contrived charismatic styles often the product of modern communicators.

THE MASS LINE: NONELITIST COMMUNICATION

In 1927 Mao first used the term "mass line." At that time the Chinese Communist party had been decimated by Chiang Kai-shek. Mao believed that the warlords and the imperialists could be overthrown only by a genuine mass movement that included the great majority of peasants, as well as urban workers, students, and intellectuals. The idea of mass line, fundamentally related to the party line, crystallized slowly: after many defeats Mao and his associates developed the mass line as a nonelitist form of leadership that would bring all party members closer to the masses.

The mass line began to take shape during the arduous Long March from southern China to the northwest in 1934. Bursting out of Chiang's blockade on October 16, 1934, Mao and one hundred thousand Chinese Communist men and women began a circuitous trek that was to last for a whole year and take them six thousand miles across China; the survivors of the march settled in Yenan. In 1943, when Yenan had become a powerful island of socialism, Mao described the mass line:

> In all practical work of our Party, correct leadership can only be developed on the principal of "from the masses, to the masses." This means summing up (i.e., coordinating and systematising after careful study) the view of the masses (i.e., views scattered and unsystematic), then taking the resulting ideas back to the masses, explaining and popularising them until the masses embrace the ideas as their own, stand up for them and translate them into action by way of testing their correctness. Then it is necessary once more to sum up the views of the masses, and once again take the resulting ideas back to the masses so that the masses give them their wholehearted support. . . . And so on, over and over again, so that each time these ideas emerge with correctness and become more vital and meaningful (3, p. 113).

Reading between the lines, one can see that Mao was inveighing against party leadership that is arrogant, authoritarian, elitist, oligarchic, voluntaristic, parasitic, and bureaucratic (see Table 34.1). The mass line alternative was to develop leaders who were self-disciplined, self-critical, democratic, willing to take initiative, and receptive to learning from the masses.

Although Gandhi never used the term "mass line," he followed this doctrine. Working with the Indian Congress party and a variety of formal and informal organizations, Gandhi opposed all forms of bureaucratic routine and hierarchical elitism. Discipline was important—but the discipline that comes from within rather than from external authority.

Table 34.1   The Essence of Mass Line Communication

Creation of New Leadership Styles	Rejection of Old Leadership Styles
Understanding. Leaders study problems with and learn from the masses. *Education.* Leaders patiently explain problems, proposals, and decisions. *Democracy.* Leaders provide for genuine decisionmaking at the lowest levels. *Leadership development.* Leaders encourage leadership at all levels. *Initiative.* Leaders take initiative. *Humility.* Leaders live simply. *Self-discipline.* Leaders set an example of self-discipline and self-criticism.	*Nonarrogant.* Leaders reject the idea that leaders know best and masses are ignorant. *Nonauthoritarian.* Leaders reject the practice of simply giving orders and overseeing execution. *Nonelitist.* Leaders reject the formalism of ritualistic participation. *Nonoligarchic.* Leaders fight against inherent tendencies toward oligarchy. *Nonvoluntaristic.* Leaders do not simply wait for the masses to act. *Nonparasitic.* Leaders do not seek or accept perquisites. *Nonbureaucratic.* Leaders minimize externally imposed rules.

For both Gandhi and Mao the mass line was not merely a personal way of life; it also meant developing thousands of other leaders who had rapport with ordinary people. Both Gandhi and Mao learned how to select colleagues who would help in realizing the potential of the masses. While seeking the support of educated elites, they also tried to transform the latter into mass line leaders. They developed techniques of encouraging and even manipulating colleagues and supporters to give their best to the movement. Groups of people with conflicting interests found themselves working together in reaching larger groups. At the same time a steady flow of communication through small elite newspapers was maintained. Paradoxically, this elite press provided indispensable communication links among formal and informal leaders of the party and the many nonparty organizations that finally took root among the masses. Finally, both Gandhi and Mao relied on a circular flow of messages to achieve mass line communication; that is, messages moved from leader to specialized spokespersons to party activists to the masses, while also moving directly from leader to masses, from masses to leaders at all levels, and, above all, among the people.

MASS LINE COMMUNICATION FOR ACTION

Mass line communication was an instrument of action and organization. To historians and activists all over the world, Gandhi's and Mao's actions outside the government machinery—organizing strikes and boycotts, convening mass meetings, leading marches and demonstrations, mobilizing the peasantry, living austerely—have been of consuming interest. Yet analysts have tended to forget that Gandhi and Mao were also involved in inquiry and advocacy, as well as in representative government—formulating strategy, engaging in theoretical and historical investigation, encouraging education, demanding system change, disseminating propaganda, mobilizing foreign support, in the first instance; lobbying, participating in political organizations, serving on government committees, and meeting with officials, in the second. Gandhi would have agreed with Mao that "without investigation, no right to speak." In other words, under Gandhi and Mao, medium and message were combined into specific forms of action and advocacy. To borrow one of Mao's metaphors, the mass line leaders walked on two feet—they engaged in more than one form of action.

Through their activism both Gandhi and Mao rejected the elitist idea that leaders merely develop models and theories. Also, they rejected the crude anti-intellectual idea that leaders merely organize protests and demonstrations without also trying to achieve some degree of intellectual hegemony. In this way, they bound leadership to the people's real needs and potential. The masses, in turn, played a key role in identifying their problems rather than serving as passive objects of research and externally imposed change.

"MY LIFE IS THE MESSAGE"

Gandhi was often asked to record his wisdom for posterity. He would answer by saying, "It is not what I say that is important but what I do. Action is my domain." For those who persisted in trying to build him into a great theoretician, Gandhi summed up his life in five simple words: "My life is the message."

> It is possible for a teacher situated miles away to affect the spirit of his pupils by his way of living. It would be idle for me, if I were a liar, to teach boys to tell the truth. A cowardly teacher would never succeed in making his boys valiant, and a stranger to self-restraint could never teach his pupils the value of self-restraint. I saw, therefore, that I must be an eternal object-lesson to the boys and girls living with me. They thus became my teachers, and I learnt I must be good and live straight, if only for their sake (1, p. 114).

In a sense, this might be called image making. And indeed both Mao and Gandhi set out to create powerful images of themselves, but in neither case was the image designed to embellish or hide reality: the reality *was* the image. For Gandhi as well as Mao, the essence of the mass line was expressed in the clothing they wore, the food they ate, the words they wrote and spoke, and even the way they traveled. Yet quite a few years of trial and error elapsed before they succeeded in adjusting to a life of austerity. And then they had to face the equally difficult task of converting their key associates, most of whom were Western trained intellectuals with little respect for the uneducated peasant (7).

In an atmosphere of austerity, courage, humility, self-discipline, and dedication, Gandhi and Mao built their movements from the bottom up, block by block. Mao did so in Yenan, where the land was poor and food scarce: Gandhi in his Sabarmati ashram at Ahmedabad. Both men spoke and wrote in the humblest of words—no flights of rhetoric or elaborated discourse in the manner of Jawaharlal Nehru or Chou En-lai. They never talked either above the heads of their audiences or down to them (10). Mao maintained contact with the masses by using "earthy, colorful" language (5, 8). Gandhi worked toward "simplifying life and doing some concrete act of service to my fellow men." In their different ways, both took on the formidable task of bringing down imperial rule in their countries.

Many of Gandhi's and Mao's actions served as inspiration to millions of people. For instance, Gandhi's rejection of Western technology, boycott of all foreign goods (particularly British textiles, which had destroyed India's cottage industries), insistence on the use of Indian languages, and wearing of *khaddar* (coarse, handspun cotton) were to become in the minds of all Indians symbols of their country's freedom. Likewise, China's and India's liberation movements came to be symbolized by Mao's Long March of 1934 and Gandhi's Salt March of 1930. The savage ordeal of the Long March looms very large in the history of China and indeed of the world. Gandhi's Salt March—241 miles across India in the summer heat to pick up a fleck of forbidden salt on the beach—protested an unjust British law that bore down on the poor. Through these dramatic actions, Mao and Gandhi expressed their identification with the people, enlisting their countrymen in a mass effort to achieve liberation.

The Common Touch, Not Charisma

Max Weber defined charisma as "a certain quality of an individual personality by virtue of which he is set apart from ordinary men and treated as endowed with supernatural, superhuman qualities, and regarded as of divine origin" (11). For Weber, the only alternatives to charismatic leadership were traditional (or feudal) and bureaucratic leadership, a classification that has gone virtually unchallenged. Indeed, not only the theoreticians but also the media seem to yearn for charismatic leaders who by force of magical qualities will lead mankind out of the wilderness of alienation, inflation, and nuclear proliferation. But neither Gandhi nor Mao had charisma. They were not "apart from ordinary men" but part of them; not "divine" but remarkably human.

"Gandhi was more deeply rooted," noted J. D. Sethi, an astute observer, "in the reality of the life of the Indian masses than any known leader" (6, p. 179). Of Gandhi, Prime Minister Nehru said, "He did not descend from the top; he seemed to emerge from the millions of India, speaking their language and incessantly drawing attention to them and their appalling condition." Indeed, Gandhi succeeded so well in becoming a part of the ordinary people that the aristocratic Nehru remarked, "Some of Gandhi's phrases sometimes jarred upon me. . . . But I was powerless to intervene, and I consoled myself with the thought that Gandhi used the words because they were well known and understood by the masses. He had an amazing knack of reaching the hearts of the people"(4).

Mao viewed the masses as the "real heroes" and the "makers of history." He cautioned that excessive centralism, which he defined as "commandism," "bureaucratism," and "warlordism," implied that "only [leaders] are good enough and everyone else is of no use" (2, p. 247). Mao's practice of criticism and self-criticism sought not only to remove barriers between leaders and led but also to emphasize that leaders make mistakes and are therefore not above reproach.

Although Gandhi and Mao were by no means charismatic in the Weberian sense of the term, their popular influence was indeed extraordinary. If for this reason some insist on calling them charismatic, their charisma was not the kind associated with such contemporary heroes as Churchill, de Gaulle, and Franklin Roosevelt. It stemmed, rather, from their success in identifying themselves with ordinary people. This is the message sent to us in the eighties by the example of Gandhi and Mao.

NOTE

1. This research was based on (a) content analysis of all Gandhi's and Mao's speeches, editorials, articles and letters during the 1942–1944 period, and of selected statements by Gandhi and Mao during the much longer period from the end of World War I to the end of World War II, and (b) tacit premises which are inferred from the more general statements. Some of the findings are summarized and interpreted further in (9).

REFERENCES

1. Gandhi, M. K. *An Autobiography or The Story of My Experiments with Truth.* Ahmedabad: Navajivan, 1927.
2. Mao Tse-tung. *Selected Works. Volume II.* New York: International Publishers, 1954–1956.

3. Mao Tse-tung. *Selected Works. Volume IV.* New York: International Publishers, 1954–1956.

4. Nehru, Jawarharlal. *The Discovery of India.* New York: Free Press, 1947.

5. Ricket, Allyn. *Prisoners of Liberation.* New York: Anchor Press, 1973.

6. Sethi, J. D. *Gandhi Today.* New Delhi: Vikas Publishing House, 1978.

7. Singh, Kusum J. "Elite Control and Challenge in Changing India." In George Gerbner (Ed.) *Mass Media Policies in Changing Cultures.* New York: Wiley Interscience, 1977, pp. 147–157.

8. Singh, Kusum J. "Gandhi and Mao as Communicators: A Comparative Study of Practice and Theory." Unpublished doctoral dissertation, University of Pennsylvania, Philadelphia, 1978.

9. Singh, Kusum J. "Gandhi and Mao as Mass Communicators." *Journal of Communication* 29(3), Summer 1979, pp. 94–101.

10. Snow, Edgar. *Red Star Over China.* New York: Grove Press, 1961.

11. Weber, Max. *The Theory of School and Economic Organizations.* New York: Free Press, 1947.

Thirty-Five

Mass Media Reform and Social Change: The Peruvian Experience

Rita Atwood and Sérgio Mattos

In October of 1968, a military junta headed by General Juan Velasco Alvarado overthrew the Peruvian civil government of President Fernando Belaunde Terry. The "Revolutionary Government of the Armed Forces" guided by Velasco Alvarado was dedicated to a transformation of Peruvian society—a transformation designed to promote the participation of vast numbers of lower socioeconomic class citizens in the national development process. Reorganization and redirection of the mass communication system in Peru became one of the central concerns of the Velasco Alvarado government, and a number of radical media reform strategies were implemented (12, 26, 33, 36).

However, according to a number of critics, these media reform measures essentially failed to accomplish their objectives. They cite as evidence the shift of the military government of General Bermudez Morales in 1975 away from most reform strategies and the elimination by the civilian government of President Fernando Belaunde Terry of the important reform measures (29, 36, 38). While a definitive assessment of the successes and failures of media reforms initiated during the 1968–1975 period in Peru is not possible, the Peruvian experiment does provide a valuable opportunity for the examination of various arguments regarding the role of mass media in revolutionary strategies.

THE ROLE OF MASS MEDIA IN REVOLUTIONARY STRATEGIES

Among those concerned with the role of mass media in the development of Third World nations, the need for substantial change in existing media structures is one of the most important topics. In general, it is widely recognized that mass communication systems and policies must be consistent with reforms attempted in other economic, political, and social sectors of developing societies. The reform strategies that have been suggested include a significant reduction of dependence on communications software and technology imported from developed nations, and a redistribution of the control over and participation in national media systems (8, 20, 23, 24, 35, 39, 47, 49, 54).

Support for these strategies and the objectives associated with them has been adequately justified. However, those strategies that focus primarily on structural or organizational changes alone often ignore the information needs of citizens who constitute the very essence of the development process (2, 25, 28, 34, 48, 50). Other critics extend this challenge further, contending that even structural changes emphasizing citizens' information needs may not be sufficient to insure the optimal use of mass communication in national development. They argue that revolutionary attempts at changing mass communication systems require revolutionary changes in thinking about human communication behavior in mass media environments (5, 6, 7, 15, 16, 17, 18, 19).

These scholars recognize that structural changes may be necessary for meeting citizen information needs, and that system constraints do exist. However, they stress that such structural or organizational changes cannot be assumed to be sufficient to guarantee the existence of mass communication systems for that purpose.

What is needed, they suggest, is an entirely different conceptualization of what information is and how people seek and use it. Information is not, in their view, a commodity to be constructed and transferred either in a top-down or lateral fashion, but is uniquely constructed by each individual.[1] Mass communication systems designed to promote national development should not only be responsive to citizen information needs and uses but should, in fact, be based on such needs and uses. The fundamental difference, then, distinguishing the perspectives of those supporting a revolutionary conceptual shift from those who argue for various forms of structural change is that the former advocate receiver-based mass communication systems, whereas the latter are concerned with alterations in the existing sender-based mass systems.

A corollary of the arguments for conceptual change is the suggestion that contemporary revolutionary strategies aimed at mass media reform may be related more to idealistic than realistic expectations. The expectations are based on two assumptions about the efficacy of mass media reform:

1. The reduction or elimination of dependence on foreign communications software and technology will result in media systems that adequately meet the information needs of citizens in developing nations.
2. The transfer of control of mass media enterprises from the hands of a few elite groups to the hands of those representing larger segments of

lower socioeconomic classes will ensure greater citizen participation, and will result in media systems that adequately meet the information needs of citizens in developing nations.

While the strategies resulting from these assumptions may have some utility in the reorganization of media systems, some scholars argue that such utility is limited by an unrealistic reliance on sender-based mass communication systems (6, 18).

MASS MEDIA REFORM IN PERU

History of the Mass Media

For the purpose of assessing the efforts at mass media reform conducted in Peru during the period of recent military rule, it is useful to understand how the media structure developed prior to the 1968 military coup, and why the media system was conducive to testing revolutionary strategies of reorganization.[2]

The development of mass media in Peru depended on foreign supply of capital, communications technology, and media software. Media were owned and controlled by wealthy, powerful families who had close connections with foreign enterprises. The evolution of *El Comercio*, the second-oldest newspaper in Latin America, illustrates this pattern. *El Comercio* was founded in 1839 in Peru by immigrants from Chile and Argentina with the technical assistance of advisers from the United States. Forty years later, *El Comercio* was purchased by the powerful Miro Quesada family, which continued to control the newspaper until expropriation by the recent military government occurred. The foremost allegiances of the Miro Quesada family were to maintaining the privileges of the upper-class coastal sector and the international economic powers active in Peru. Such allegiances were reflected in both the news coverage and editorial stances of *El Comercio* (1, 3, 21, 22, 37, 44).

Other newspaper owners in Peru had similar allegiances. Prior to the military coup of 1968, two of the eight main dailies in Lima were owned by a group of farm barons; two were owned by a consortium of merchants and industrialists; one belonged to a family that was also involved in banking, real estate, and petroleum; one belonged to a fish-flour industry magnate who also owned a chain of provincial newspapers and specialized magazines. Some newspaper owners also had television and radio station holdings (27).

The development of radio and television broadcasting in Peru paralleled that of newspapers, with concentrated elite control and dependence on foreign influences. The first radio station in Peru, for example, was established in 1925 by a group of wealthy Peruvians and Henry Ford. The first television station in Peru began broadcasting in 1958 as a result of an agreement between the Peruvian Ministry of Education and UNESCO. While it was controlled by the government and was intended to be primarily for educational broadcasts, the station was rapidly overshadowed by wealthy entrepreneurs in radio broadcasting who started commercial television stations in Peru (3, 22, 30). In 1971 the state owned only two percent of the existing radio stations and only five percent of the existing television stations; the remainder were owned primarily by wealthy families and allied groups. In fact, in 1968 five Peruvian families owned at least 13 of the 19 television channels (3, 30, 32, 36).

The mass media system that developed in Peru was largely modeled on the structure of media in developed capitalist nations. The primary source of revenue for print and broadcast media was advertising, especially by multinational corporations headquartered in the United States. The format and content of print media and commercial broadcasting outlets were not only patterned after U.S. media; they contained a substantial amount of content imported from the U.S. and other developed nations (32, 56).

The Media and the Peruvian Military

Peru, like many nations in Latin America, has a long history of government instability characterized by military coups and somewhat ineffective civilian governments that retained power only as long as the military backed them.[3] However, several factors distinguish the Peruvian military as somewhat unique in Latin America, and help to explain why the military embarked on a program of revolutionary reform in 1968.

Peruvian military leaders have come primarily from middle-class families, in contrast with military leaders who have upper-class backgrounds in many other Latin American nations. In addition, the Peruvian military has had a long history of exposure to contemporary sociopolitical ideologies. In 1950, the Center for Higher Military Studies (CAEM) was established to prepare military officers for a more enlightened participation in national defense and national development. As officers graduating from CAEM evidenced a growing concern with socioeconomic and political problems, their fragile sense of alliance with the elite power group shifted rapidly to a sense of commitment to national development goals of redistribution of wealth and power (3, 4, 27).

As the military leaders became increasingly sensitive to the need for social and economic reforms during the 1950s and 1960s, the nation experienced significant urban migration, expansion of rural education, extension of highways, a more widespread proliferation of radio stations and receivers, and increased activity in labor union organization and political mobilization of rural peasants (10, 14). These factors helped create the climate in which Fernando Belaunde Terry was elected president on a liberal reform platform in 1963. However, his reform programs were thwarted by a coalition of political opponents; the Peruvian economy deteriorated; and a military junta seized control of the government in 1968—setting the stage for a military rule unique in Latin American history.

The First "Press Law" of 1969

Revolutionary strategies for media reform developed by the former military junta governing Peru were guided, in part, by unrealistic expectations regarding the outcomes of structural reorganization. While the revolutionary military government of General Velasco Alvarado did not initially include the mass media in its industry reform plans, evidence of its concern with media reform came in 1969 with the first "Press Law." This statute articulated press obligations to "respect for the law, truth and morality, the demands of national security and defense, and the safeguard of personal and family honor and privacy"(55). Some observers have charged that the Press Law of 1969 was aimed primarily at stifling press criticism of the new regime, but others have argued that the military government was attempting to encourage the press to assist in productive national development objectives (9, 55).

Although the creation of the 1969 Press Law was not directly based on the assumptions described here, a number of subsequent military government decrees were. These decrees were enacted largely because the military leaders believed that reduction of dependence on foreign communication imports and foreign communication enterprises would result in a significant increase in citizen participation. In addition, they believed that greater national self-sufficiency would contribute to a mass media system that could adequately meet the information needs of a far greater number of Peruvian citizens (13, 36, 46).

The Telecommunications Law of 1971

One of the most important laws designed by the Peruvian military junta to restructure the mass communication system was the Telecommunications Law of 1971. This law stipulated that telecommunications services were to operate in the service of the socioeconomic development of the country. More specifically, the objectives of the telecommunications enterprises were required to be consistent with "public necessity, utility, and security, and of preferred national interest" (40, 55).

In an attempt to diminish elite and foreign influences on broadcast media, the government expropriated 25 percent equity of existing radio stations and 51 percent equity of existing television stations. The Telecommunications Law of 1971 also dictated that "all stations were to be placed in 'worker's communities' in which employees were to receive 25% of all profits . . . and were to share in managing their stations" (55). All owners and employees of broadcast stations had to be Peruvian nationals; foreign entertainers could be involved in media broadcasts only with the approval of government authorities (23, 30, 55).

The Telecommunications Law of 1971 included specific requirements for broadcast media content deemed acceptable for national development goals. For example, 60 percent of broadcast programming was to be of national origin, consisting of Peruvian cultural and educational material. A limit was also imposed on the amount of advertising generated by foreign agencies that could be aired (22, 23, 30, 40).

In spite of the Telecommunications Law of 1971, the content of Peruvian broadcasting changed little during the several years that followed. Reasons suggested for this lack of change include inadequate facilities for the production of film and video materials pertaining to cultural and educational subjects, insufficient alternative sources of advertising revenue, and ineffective administrative and regulatory agencies within the government structure (23, 30).

The Creation of the National Information System

In response to these problems, the military government created the National Information System (SINADI) in 1974. It was designed to provide the necessary administrative framework for managing and supervising all aspects of mass media reform. Included within this framework were five public enterprises: the Cinematography Enterprise; the Publishing House Enterprise; the National Advertising Corporation; National News Service; and the National Broadcasting Corporation of Peru (22, 40, 52). These public enterprises were intended primarily to foster national production of mass communication content and train mass communication personnel, thereby diminishing the need to import media software and technology from developed nations.

In addition to forming SINADI, the military government of Velasco Alvarado moved to reorganize and redistribute control of all major newspapers. The official rationale for the promulgation of the Press Law of 1974 was to transfer control of national newspapers from the hands of a few elite groups to an ownership structure in which "the worker's right to participate in the ownership, management, and benefits of enterprises was recognized"(29). Based on this rationale, the military government expropriated all newspapers with major circulations and transferred their ownership and management to existing representative groups of lower- and middle-class segments of the population. For example, *El Comercio* went to rural organizations; *Expreso* to educational groups; *La Prensa* to labor organizations; *Correo* to professional associations; and *Ultima Hora* to service organizations (29, 40, 46).

The Velasco government was severely criticized by members of the Peruvian elite and foreign commercial enterprises for implementing the Press Laws of 1969 and 1974. Peruvian journalists who participated in reforms during this period, on the other hand, defended the ideology and utility of such changes (20, 31, 41).

The Rule of Morales and Reversal of Press Reform

The need for debate was cut short, however, when General Bermudez Morales assumed leadership of the military junta in 1975, and enacted a decree that paved the way for return of the expropriated newspapers to their former owners. Among the reasons given for this policy reversal were that the popular representative groups were not prepared for administration of the newspapers; that increased government control and censorship had eroded journalistic quality of newspapers; and that economic recession and stagnation had made newspaper management by popular groups unfeasible (29, 31, 46).

It is more appropriate to view the strategy reversal of press reform in the context of the larger issues accounting for the change in military governments. These issues include charges of increased corruption in the Velasco Alvarado regime; unmanageable popular political demands associated with land reform; and a deteriorating economy suffering from the collapse of several major industries, lack of capital investment, and a general crisis on the international economic scene (22, 46). Thus, the shift toward returning the major newspapers to their former owners was consistent with a move to dismantle many of the redistribution and participationist elements of Velasco Alvarado's programs. However, the military government of Bermudez Morales was also more authoritarian in nature and maintained state control of the primary television and radio stations, as well as control of other mass media functions under the auspices of SINADI (42).

The second phase of military rule in Peru under the leadership of Bermudez Morales was characterized by economic difficulties and increased dissatisfaction with reform promises. Concerned by the worsening economic conditions and the apparent "failure" of participatory reforms, Bermudez Morales steered the country toward a return to civilian rule and reinstatement of the power and control of some of the former elite and foreign commercial groups (46).

Military rule in Peru came to an end in May of 1980, with the popular election of Fernando Belaunde Terry as president. Belaunde has returned all newspapers formerly expropriated by the military government in 1974, but he has tightened government press controls in other ways by creating tax laws relating to newspapers, control over newsprint and printing equipment importation, and government advertising contracts. Direct government control over key television and radio stations has been a strategy continued by Belaunde, despite the efforts of his government to transfer numerous other enterprises back to the private sector (45, 53).

THE SUCCESSES AND FAILURES OF MASS MEDIA REFORM

This historical overview provides an opportunity to explain the successes and failures of military reform endeavors in terms of their relation to the assumptions about the results of structural reorganization. With regard to possible successes, it can be argued that the revolutionary media reform strategies accomplished a number of potentially long-lasting benefits for national development. For example, for the first time in Peruvian history, a cohesive set of regulations and regulatory bodies was created to guide mass media operations. This regulatory system resulted in reduced advertising time allocated by broadcast media, and increased citizen exposure to cultural, educational, and discussion programming. This national approach to reducing dependence on the importation of foreign media software and technology also stimulated the growth of print and broadcast production facilities.

While the reforms failed to produce a lasting private sector redistribution of control over mass media outlets, the employees of broadcast stations and print media operations experienced a role of greater involvement in decision-making—albeit a role curtailed by government supervision. In fact, the concept of employee ownership and editorial input continues to be popular among media professionals in Peru, and several print and broadcast outlets maintain a system of employee stockholding and participation (42).

Finally, while the concept of greater citizen participation in the determination of media structure and content has been considered largely a failure, there may be repercussions from a population sensitized to more active media participation. Conversely, the failures of the revolutionary attempts at mass media reform diminish the optimism that can be articulated regarding long-lasting effects. For example, the revolutionary reforms failed to alter the basic capitalistic, commercial nature of the mass media system in Peru—a failure permeating many of the reform measures tried in other sectors of Peruvian society. This failure was evidenced by the inability of the government to sustain print media ownership and control by representatives of popular organizations; to accomplish decentralization of broadcast media ownership and control in Peruvian territory; and to stimulate popular support for mass media reform that encouraged citizen participation.

EXPLAINING THE FAILURES OF PERUVIAN MASS MEDIA REFORM

There are several levels at which the failures of the Peruvian mass media reform can be explained. On one level, the failures of the revolutionary strategies attempted by the military radicals can be attributed to the economic and political constraints of the national system within which they were introduced. Philip (46) argues that the Peruvian military governments never had the broad base of popular support to effect their redistributive and participatory policies. He suggests that the military radicals engaged in numerous compromises in order to maintain both internal unity and external support—compromises that undermined their ability to institute effective systems of participation.

On another level, it can be argued that the structural changes made by the military government of Velasco Alvarado in the mass media sector were prematurely thwarted by Bermudez Morales. One can only speculate on how the media might have evolved had the revolutionary reforms been pursued longer and more vigorously.

A third level of explanation of the failures of revolutionary media reform strategies in Peru relates to the argument that the military were operating under idealistic assumptions about the effectiveness of structural changes in the mass media. While the successes of the reform measures are most certainly associated with structural changes, the failures are linked to the fact that structural changes alone are not enough to ensure citizen participation and the satisfaction of citizen information needs. Jaworski (29) offers a related criticism of Peruvian mass media reform:

> Structural reform in the area of information cannot be in isolation. It has to fit into a receptive social setting. As has been shown, in Peru there was effective representative support for earlier reforms: on the land, in business, in education and advertising. . . . Reform of information suggests something more than transforming the conditions of ownership and management. . . . [it] also means a change of mentality by the professionals.

Peirano, a Peruvian scholar who was active in the reform attempts, asserts that while the military government tried to solve the political problems of mass media structure before it solved the economic ones, it completely abandoned the possibility of creating a new communication order based on the information needs of the citizens. He suggests investigating why a truly democratic mass communication system cannot be created solely by enabling popular participation (43).

THE NEED FOR AN ALTERNATIVE CONCEPT OF INFORMATION

The view presented here extends the argument that alternative concepts of information are needed. We contend that one of the main reasons the revolutionary communication policies and practices in Peru failed to accomplish their goals is that information was treated as a tangible commodity to be delivered to the public—and the reform of information delivery enterprises was treated just like the reform of other economic sectors involving land, goods, and services. This concept of information is associated with sender-based communications systems—systems that function on the premise that suppliers of information determine both what information will be available to the public and the ways in which the public will use it. Strategies that attempt only to reshuffle the structure of sender-based communication systems will necessarily focus attention on the information senders—primarily those operating and influencing mass media enterprises. It is not surprising, then, that such strategies have aimed both to reduce dependence on foreign communication imports and to redistribute national media ownership.

However, if information is conceived of as something people create from their message environment and put to use in ways they find most appropriate, then the focus of media reform strategies must shift from message senders to message receivers. Such a shift allows one to envision alternative media reform strategies designed to create receiver based communication systems.

Thus, structural changes in mass media and attempts to take citizen information needs into consideration may be necessary for realization of national development goals, but such efforts alone will never be sufficient to attain those goals. Revolutionary strategies of mass media reform must be constructed on the basis of revolutionary changes in the conceptualization of human communication processes.

NOTES

1. Dervin (e.g., 16, 17, 18) has developed a theoretical and empirical framework for looking at how individuals make sense out of their environments; Atwood and Dervin (7) have examined how people seek and use information to bridge the gaps or discontinuities they encounter in their movement through time and space (see also 11).

2. A comprehensive historical review is untenable for the purposes of this paper. For an excellent description of early Peruvian history see (51).

3. Peru was ruled exclusively by military leaders until 1872, when Manuel Prado became the first civilian leader. Military intervention in the Peruvian government has been frequent (see 3, 51).

REFERENCES

1. Alisky, M. "The Peruvian Press and the Nixon Incident." *Journalism Quarterly* 35(4), 1958.

2. Ascroft, J. and G. Gleason. "Communication Support and Integrated Rural Development in Ghana." Paper presented at the 30th International Conference on Communication, Human Evolution and Development of the International Communication Association, Acapulco, Mexico, May 1980.

3. Astiz, C. *Pressure Groups and Power Elites in Peruvian Politics,* Ithaca, N.Y.: Cornell University Press, 1969.

4. Astiz, C. "The Catholic Church in the Peruvian Political System." In D. Chaplin (Ed.) *Peruvian Nationalism: A Corporatist Revolution.* New Brunswick, N.J.: Transaction, 1973.

5. Atwood, R. "Communication Research in Latin America: Cultural and Conceptual Dilemmas." Paper presented to the Intercultural Division, International Communication Association, Acapulco, Mexico, 1980.

6. Atwood, R. "Los impactos de tecnología nueva en relación de las necesidades de información humana." Paper presented at a symposium for graduates of the Universidad Regiomontana, Monterrey, Mexico, 1981.

7. Atwood, R. and B. Dervin. "Challenges to Socio-cultural Predictors of Information Seeking: A Test of Race vs. Situation Movement State." In M. Burgoon (Ed.) *Communication Yearbook* 5. New Brunswick, N.J.: Transaction, 1981.

8. Beltrán, L. R. "Alien Premises, Objects, and Methods in Latin American Research." *Communication Research* 3(2), 1976.

9. Beltrán, L. R. and E. Cardona. "Latin America and the United States: Flaws in the Free Flow of Information." In K. Nordenstreng and H. Schiller (Eds.) *National Sovereignty and International Communication.* Norwood, N.J.: Ablex, 1979.

10. Borque, S. C. and D. S. Palmer. "Transforming the Rural Sector: Government Policy and Peasant Response." In A. Lowenthal (Ed.) *The Peruvian Experiment: Continuity and Change under Military Rule.* Princeton, N.J.: Princeton University Press, 1975.

11. Carter, R. F. "Theory for Researchers." Paper presented to the Theory and Methodology Division of the Association for Education in Journalism, Carbondale, Illinois, August 1977.

12. Chaplin, D. "The Revolutionary Challenge and Peruvian Militarism." In D. Chaplin (Ed.) *Peruvian Nationalism: A Corporatist Revolution.* New Brunswick, N.J.: Transaction, 1975.

13. Comité de Asesoramiento de la Presidencia (Ed.) *Plan del gobierno revolucionario de la fuerza armada.* Lima: Editorial Universo S.A., 1974.

14. Cotler, J. and F. Portocarrero. "Peru: Peasant Organizations," In H. Landsberger (Ed.) *Latin American Peasant Movements.* Ithaca, N.Y.: Cornell University Press, 1969.

15. Dervin, B. "Strategies for Dealing with Human Information Needs: Information or Communication?" *Journal of Broadcasting* 20, 1976.

16. Dervin, B. "Communication With, Not To the Urban Poor." ERIC/CUE Urban Diversity Series, No. 50, Eric Clearinghouse on Urban Education, Institute

for Urban and Minority Education, Teachers College, Columbia University, New York, August 1977.

17. Dervin, B. "Sense-making as a Prerequisite for Information Equality." Paper presented at the 7th Annual Telecommunication Policy Research Conference, Skytop, Pennsylvania, 1979.

18. Dervin, B. "Communication Gaps and Inequities: Moving Toward a Reconceptualization." In B. Dervin and M. J. Voigt (Eds.) *Progress in Communication Sciences*, Volume 2. Norwood, N.J.: Ablex, 1980.

19. Dervin, B., S. Harlock, R. Atwood, and C. Garzona. "The Human Side of Information: An Exploration in a Health Communication Context." In D. Nimmo (Ed.) *Communication Yearbook* 4. New Brunswick, N.J.: Transaction, 1980.

20. Diaz-Bordenave, J. "Communication of Agricultural Innovations in Latin America: The Need for New Models." *Communication Research* 3, 1976, pp. 135–154.

21. Gargurevich, J. *Mito y verdad de los diarios de Lima.* Lima: Editorial Gráfica Labor, 1972.

22. Gargurevich, J. *Introducción a la historia de los medios de communicaciones en el Peru.* Lima: Editorial Horizontes, 1977.

23. Gerbner, G. (Ed.) *Mass Media Policies in Changing Cultures.* New York: John Wiley, 1977.

24. Guback, T. *The International Film Industry.* Bloomington, Ind.: Indiana University Press, 1969.

25. Halloran, J. D. "The Context of Mass Communication Research." In E. McAnany, J. Schnitman, and N. Janus (Eds.) *Communication and Social Structures: Critical Studies in Mass Media Research.* New York: Praeger, 1981.

26. Hamilton, N. "Possibilities and Limits of State Autonomy in Latin American Countries." Paper presented at the 8th national meeting of Latin American Studies Association, Pittsburgh, Pennsylvania, April 1979.

27. Henderson, G. *Public Diplomacy and Political Change.* New York: Praeger, 1973.

28. Hornik, R. "Communication as Complement in Development." *Journal of Communication* 30(2), Spring 1980.

29. Jaworski, C. H. "Towards a New Information Order: Rural Participation in the Peruvian Press." *Development Dialogue* 2, 1979.

30. Katz, E. and G. Wedell. *Broadcasting in the Third World.* Cambridge, Mass.: Harvard University Press, 1977.

31. Knudson, J. W. "The Peruvian Press Law of 1974: The Other Side of the Coin." *Mass Communication Review* 5, 1978.

32. Lee, C. C. *Media Imperialism Reconsidered: The Homogenizing of Television Culture.* Beverly Hills, Cal.: Sage, 1980.

33. Lowenthal, A. (Ed.) *The Peruvian Experiment: Continuity and Change under Military Rule.* Princeton, N.J.: Princeton University Press, 1975.

34. McAnany, E. *Communications in the Rural Third World: The Role of Information in Development.* New York: Praeger, 1980.

35. Mattos, S. "The Impact of Brazilian Military Government in the Development of TV in Brazil." Unpublished master's thesis, University of Texas at Austin, 1980.

36. Mattos, S. *The Development of Communication Policies under the Peruvian Military Government (1968–1980)*. San Antonio, Tex.: V. Klingensmith, 1981.

37. Merrill, J. C., C. R. Bryant, and M. Alisky. *The Foreign Press*. Baton Rouge, La.: Louisiana State University Press, 1970.

38. Neyra, J. V. General manager of Andina and board chairman of Cine Peru. Personal interview, Austin, Texas, September 1981.

39. Nordenstreng, K. and H. I. Schiller (Eds.) *National Sovereignty and International Communication*. Norwood, N.J.: Ablex, 1979.

40. Ortega, C. and C. Romero. *Communication Policies in Peru*. Paris: UNESCO, 1977.

41. Ortega, J. *La cultura Peruana: Experiencia y conciencia*. Mexico: Fondo de Cultura Económica. 1978.

42. Ortega, J. Personal interview, Austin, Texas, October 1981.

43. Peirano, L. "Relevancia de lo popular en la democratización de los medios de communicación: Apuntes para el análisis de la reforma de la prensa en el Peru." Paper presented at the seminar "Comunicación y Democracia," Santa Marta, Colombia, 1981.

44. Peirano, L., E. Ballon, L. Bartet, and G. Valdez. *Prensa: Apertura and limites*. Lima: Centro de Estudios y Promoción del Desarrollo (DESCO), 1978.

45. "Peru: The Price of Press Freedom." *Latin America Regional Report*, June 19, 1981.

46. Philip, G. J. *Rise and Fall of Peruvian Military Radicals*. London: University of London. Published for the Institute of Latin American Studies by the Athlone Press, 1978.

47. Rogers, E. "Communication and Development: The Passing of the Dominant Paradigm." *Communication Research* 3(2), 1976.

48. Roling, N. G., J. Ascroft, and F. W. Chege. "The Diffusion of Innovations and the Issue of Equity in Rural Development." *Communication Research* 3(2), 1976.

49. Schiller, H. I. *Communication and Cultural Domination*. White Plains, N.Y.: International Arts and Sciences Press, 1976.

50. Smythe, D. W. *Dependency Road: Communications, Capitalism, Consciousness and Canada*. Norwood, N.J.: Ablex, 1981.

51. Stein, J. and B. H. Stein. *The Colonial Heritage of Latin America*. New York: Oxford University Press, 1970.

52. Torres, L. R. *El gobierno militar y las comunicaciones en el Peru*. Lima: Ediciones Populares los Andes, 1975.

53. "Transferira el gobierno Peruano 26 empresas estatales a manos privadas." *Excelsior* (Mexico City), September 26, 1982.

54. Tunstall, J. *The Media Are American*. New York: Columbia University Press, 1977.

55. Weil, T. E. *et al. Area Handbook for Peru*. Washington, D.C.: Foreign Area Studies of the American University, 1972.

56. Wells, A. *Picture-tube Imperialism: The Impact of U.S. Television in Latin America*. Maryknoll, N.Y.: Orbis, 1972.

Thirty-Six

Serving Two Cultures: Local Media in Belgium

Guido Fauconnier

The development of cable television in Belgium is increasingly drawing attention not only from industry but also from the authorities and more specifically from the authorities of the two cultural communities in Belgium: the Dutch-speaking community in the north and the French-speaking community in the south.[1] After briefly sketching the Belgian national broadcasting situation, I shall review the growth of Belgian cable television with regard to both formal structure and viewing patterns. A local cable TV experiment—a recent phenomenon in Belgian media evolution—is also described.

NATIONAL BROADCASTING IN BELGIUM

The organization, objectives, and activities of Belgian broadcasting are determined largely by regulations issued by the authorities of the separate cultural communities. In Belgium, there are two independent broadcasting organizations: Belgian Radio and Television-Dutch Transmission (BRT, Belgische Radio en Televisie-Nederlandse uitzendingen) and Belgian Radio and Television-French Transmission (RTBF, Radio et télévision belge-émissions françaises). These two systems have a monopoly on radio and television broadcasts, though a political debate on breaking this monopoly is going on. In contrast to the newspapers which are privately owned but government-subsidized, BRT and RTBF are statutory bodies that are mandated to allow a variety of opinions to be aired and to respond to specific needs of the population for news, entertainment, and education. Because advertising is forbidden on radio and television, BRT and RTBF receive their income from a budget approved by the national parliament, which budget corresponds to roughly two-thirds of the revenue from Belgium's radio and television tax. Both organizations acquired a second television network in 1977 that, in contrast to the first network, provides entertainment and educational programs but no news. Because of a lack of finances, this second network broadcasts only about four hours a day, five days a week.

THE STRUCTURE OF CABLE TELEVISION IN BELGIUM

The reception by subscribers of broadcast television programs transmitted by cable from a central distribution center dates to the early sixties in Belgium; cablecasting has developed rapidly. Around 1960, a few private companies laid experimental cable networks in small communities in the south of the country, where antenna reception was poor because of the hilly terrain. Thereafter, a large number of communities not only in the south but also in the center and north of Belgium (where reception was sometimes hampered by tall buildings) followed this successful example. Some foreign stations were also offered via cable. The real boom of cable television began shortly before 1970. At that time, several electricity companies extended their activities to include cable television; new companies tried to get established in the cable market; existing radio distribution companies offered cable television distribution; and communities and groups of communities themselves expressed the desire to provide this service to their citizens. The promise of cable television everywhere, with the accent primarily on good reception of as many foreign networks as possible, was an important factor in the campaigns for the municipal elections of 1970. The installation of cable networks was also strongly stimulated by the benevolent attitude of the authorities to the importation of foreign programs and the demand of viewers for more options. Table 36.1 summarizes the evolution of the period from 1970 to 1978.

By 1981, approximately forty companies—private (50 percent), public (35 percent), and mixed (15 percent)—provided cable distribution over almost all of Belgium, making it the most cabled country in Europe. The cable companies together have over 2.4 million subscribers, or 77 percent of the total television audience. This public can now choose from a maximum of sixteen stations: the original Belgian stations (BRT-TV 1 and RTBF-TV-1), on some days two other Belgian stations (BRT-TV 2 and RTBF-télé 2), the three French channels (TF 1, A 2, FR 3), the three German stations (ARD 1, ZDF, ARD 3), the two Netherlands stations (NED 1 and NED 2), Luxembourg commercial television (RTL), and sometimes four British channels (which presently can be received directly only in the coastal area).[2]

The transmission in Belgium of television programs via cable is regulated by the royal decree of December 24, 1966, which was based on the radio legislation of 1930 and 1934. This decree regulates only the cable distribution of so-called open network television broadcasts by broadcast-

Table 36.1 Television Penetration in Belgium, 1970–1978

	Population (millions)	Households (millions)	No. of TV Sets	% of Households with TV	No. of Cable Subscribers	% of Households with Cable
1970	9.69	3.2	2,099,893	65.6	4,546	0.22
1974	9.78	3.2	2,464,201	77.0	785,216	31.9
1978	9.84	3.3	2,866,451	90.0	1,919,459	67.0

SOURCES: (2, 6, 7, 9, 10)

ing organizations authorized to transmit in the country in which they are located (the first generation, or passive phase, of cable television). Moreover, these regulations forbid distributors, or other potentially interested parties, to produce or transmit special programs. The distribution companies may not even have the infrastructure that would make the second generation, or active phase, of cable television possible. For the third generation, or interactive cable TV, no provisions exist. Thus, this legislation is concerned primarily with assuring good reception of existing programs.

The proscription on transmitting television commercials is widely ignored. The cable TV companies argue that the omission of advertising spots is not only difficult and expensive but also unfair both to subscribers, who wish to receive the programs in their entirety and without disruption, and to foreign television organizations, which wish to broadcast their programs intact to the cable viewing public (in accordance with European law).[3]

CABLE TELEVISION VIEWING IN BELGIUM

While the decree of December 1966 intended that national stations be better received via cable in less favorably situated regions, since 1970 vacant channels have been filled with foreign programming, giving Belgian viewers sixteen channels to choose from. In this context, it is relevant to examine the viewing behavior of cable subscribers and to compare this pattern with that of antenna viewers. What do subscribers do with this broad range of television programs from countries with diverse cultures? Do they now watch more or less television? Do they make use of foreign offerings? Have the selection criteria of TV consumers changed? Ultimately, what is the effect of extended contact with foreign languages and cultural patterns in a small, multilingual country such as Belgium?

Using findings from research conducted by the BRT, the RTBF, and the Department of Communication Sciences of the Catholic University of Leuven (1, 3, 4, 5, 9), I shall try to answer some of these questions.

The majority of cable viewers subscribe because they want a greater program choice. Thus, the strategy of the cable companies to capture as many stations as possible from the ether and to distribute them by cable apparently meets a specific need in the population. From the broadened offering, users most often choose programs in their own language, which is to say that the competition of the national stations comes from the wider linguistic community.[4] Flemings, in the north, prefer the BRT and the Netherlands stations; Walloons, in the south, favor the RTBF, the French, and the Luxembourg stations. Exceptions to this rule occur for soccer games, musical shows, occasional movies, and music programs for the young—the hit parade is followed on all stations.

The average Belgian TV consumer spends a good two hours in front

Table 36.2   Cable TV Viewing in 1979 by Program Category for Six French Language Stations (RTBF-TV 1, RTBis, TF 1, A 2, FR 3, RTL)

Program Category	Broadcast %	Available[a] %	Viewed %
News	31	26	24
Culture (local affairs)	15	21	7
Drama (films, plays, serials)	36	27	47
Entertainment (game and variety shows)	13	17	16
Sports	4	7	6
Religion	1	2	—
	100	100	100

SOURCE: (8)

[a] Available programs = broadcast programs − overlapping programs. For example, even though several films are transmitted simultaneously on various channels, the viewer can watch only one.

of the set each day. There is no substantial difference in viewing time between cable and antenna viewers, which implies that the time given to TV viewing has reached a saturation point. If total viewing time does not increase along with the number of channels, competition among channels must stiffen. However, the vigorous competition early in the 1970s has stabilized. The equilibrium situation reached by the various channels could be related to the slackening in the extension of the cable system.

Belgium's own stations currently lose a considerable number of viewers to foreign stations, which, according to the BRT and the RTBF, reflects the broader range of choices. Yet the national television networks still have relatively large audiences. The reason for this pattern lies in the important and even irreplaceable domestic programming core, which consists of local drama and particularly national and regional (for the RTBF) news broadcasts.[5] Nevertheless, viewer density for the national programs depends largely on what other stations are offering; audiences remain faithful only if similar programs are being broadcast simultaneously by competing stations.

The greatest success among cable viewers is achieved by entertainment programs, the most popular being light dramas, game shows, musical shows, and commercial films. Serials are popular with children. The major loser is cultural programming. As Table 36.2 shows, the assumption that the viewer watches programs in direct relation to the quantitative increase in options is not supported by data.

A study of the period 1971–1977 found similar viewing preferences, suggesting a long-range pattern. Entertainment programs have had the most success with the public, an increase of 112 percent in effective viewing time over the 6-year period. News and sports increased 28 percent and 79 percent in effective viewing time, respectively. Finally, in spite of the increase in number and type of local cultural programs, they are almost ignored (a 6 percent decrease in effective viewing time).

In summary, cable viewers seem to be better entertained and better informed but less interested in local culture and affairs. Therefore, the question arises whether some type of effort at "social conscientization" would meet with more success if another formula, namely community television, were used.

EXPERIMENTAL COMMUNITY TELEVISION IN BELGIUM

Active cable television on an experimental basis has been authorized only in the southern (French-language) portion of Belgium. On May 4, 1976, six communities were empowered to experiment with local cable television for two years (most continued to participate for three or four years). The law stipulated that a local, ideologically pluralistic production organization could offer news, sociocultural community conscientization programs, and education of a local or semiregional character; this organization was to work out the entry procedure to the local medium for both individuals and groups. Cable distributors are prohibited from participating in programming and the community-based production company, which is ultimately responsible for local transmissions, must respect the law (which forbids advertising) and the common interest (whatever that might be). This cable experiment is subsidized by the government, and the centralized production services of the RTBF sometimes give technical help in program production. The entire project stresses the expression of local culture. Almost all of the communities have since ceased to participate in the experiment, mostly for financial reasons.[6]

In the north of Belgium, Flanders, local cable television is not permitted, and local (hertz) radio stations, which broadcast illegally, are silenced by the government, sometimes with a heavy hand.[7] The Flemish cultural minister has adopted a wait-and-see attitude toward technological and communications evolution as a whole. Regulations must be drawn up before there can be experiments; some type of research should be engaged in to see how new media respond to specific needs and how they can be fitted into the existing media landscape before regulations are drawn up.

Flemish broadcasting policy—to the extent that it exists—envisions a high degree of centralization. The Walloon community is clearly taking another course; for example, local cable television experimentation is allowed and local radio stations are tolerated as interesting phenomena (the possibility is being studied of assigning these media a number of frequencies in the 100–104 MHz band). The Walloon position is simply this: first experiment, then regulate. In the meantime, cable television has emerged from a phase of technological toy to a phase that is fundamentally political. It is hoped that the consumer and culture, principally local culture, will not be lost in the transition.

NOTES

1. Since 1971 media policy has been the responsibility of Dutch-language and French-language cultural ministries; however, certain technical matters (e.g., infrastructure, cable licenses) and financial matters (e.g., determination of subscription fees for cable TV) are still controlled on the national level by the Ministry for the Post, Telegraph, and Telephone.

2. Because of copyright problems in cable television, no British programs are yet offered by Belgian cable companies.

3. In 1974, the European Court of Justice ruled that radio and TV broadcasts, including advertising messages, must be considered services. According to European legislation of 1960 and 1965, the "free traffic of services" (interstate) may not be hindered. In the controversy between consumer organizations and cable television companies about the transmission of advertising, a Belgian judge, ruling in the first instance, opined in 1979 that publicity may not be transmitted via cable. The cable TV companies appealed, and the appeals court passed the case on for interpretation to the European Court of Justice. This court ruled in March 1980 that the Belgian legislation forbidding advertising transmissions, with conditions, was not in conflict with the principle of free traffic of services. It is now for the Belgian court to issue a definitive ruling.

4. In the cable television offering, a distinction needs to be made between the great majority of public stations and the one private station, Luxembourg's RTL. While most of the stations present a balanced schedule of news, entertainment, and educational programs, the RTL is only an entertainment pipeline, carrying no cultural or educational shows.

5. The percentage share of news programs in the whole programming package was 17.51 percent for the BRT in 1977 and 39.2 percent for the RTBF. This large difference is to be ascribed to the 10 percent of regional news that the RTBF offers (the BRT gives none) and also to the methodological differences in the BRT and RTBF studies that make some of their data difficult to compare.

The percentage of their own productions included by the BRT and the RTBF in their total programming for 1978 was 63.66 percent (BRT-TV 1), 38.40 percent (BRT-TV 2), 66.82 percent (RTBF-TV 1), and 76.53 percent (RTBF-télé 2). (The RTBF percentages were based on a single week in autumn 1979.)

6. In Liège, the city with the most cable coverage in the world after Montreal, local cable television (Radio television culturelle-Canal Plus) is still active. There are concrete plans in conjunction with the city's millennial celebration to provide programs daily and not just on Saturdays.

7. In 1983, a law has been passed that permits local radio stations to broadcast in a small area under specific conditions.

REFERENCES

1. Belgische Radio en Televisie-Nederlandse uitzendingen (BRT), Research Department. Annual Reports, Permanent Inquiry, 1970–1979.
2. *Congresrapport Kabeltelevisie.* Hasselt, Belgium, 1974.
3. Fauconnier, Guido *et al.* "Televisiekijken en kabeldistributie in Leuven." *Communicatie* 7(2), 1978, pp. 14–30.
4. Geerts, C. "Die Kabelverbreitung in Belgien." *Media Perspektiven* 17(6), 1979, pp. 354–361.
5. Geerts, C. and J. Thoveron. *Télévision offerte au public, télévision regardée par le public ou les effects du cable.* RTBF, 1977.
6. Nationaal Instituut voor de Statistiek. *Statistisch Jaarboek van Belgie*, 1977, vol. 97.
7. Nielsen Research, 1979.
8. Radio et télévision belge-émissions françaises (RTBF). Permanent Inquiry on Programs, 1979 Report.
9. Regie van Telegrafie en Telefonie (RTT). Annual Report, 1979.
10. *Winkler Prins Jaarboeken.* Amsterdam, 1971, 1975, 1979.

Thirty-Seven

Communication as Complement to Development[1]

Robert C. Hornik

Communication for development crowds a dozen fields. Its practitioners have done and its investigators have written in great profusion and variety; a review of that work must choose its ground carefully, stress but a few questions and find, if it can, a central theme to organize responses to those questions.

We have focused on those applications which make some use of communication technology for providing education and information. Three questions dominate this review and serve as its outline: what roles do communication interventions play in development; what circumstances are likely to move a particular intervention toward or away from success; finally, and briefly, what do we know about the promise of specific applications.

One central theme resounds in all the most successful experiences of recent years. Communication technology works best as a complement—to a commitment to social change, to changing resources, to good instructional design, to other channels of communication, and to detailed knowledge about its users.

Communication technology has been applied to a wide variety of development problems as a component in a variety of strategies. The results of some of these projects are now in and we can begin to evaluate how well they have worked in practice. Using selected examples, we will first identify the variety of roles that communication technology has played, both expected or unexpected.

THE ROLES OF COMMUNICATIONS TECHNOLOGY

Communication as Low-Cost Loudspeaker

In Guatemala, political considerations and limited budgets constrain the number of extension agents the Agriculture Ministry can hire. The shortfall means that a large proportion of subsistence farmers are not reached with information believed to be of value to them. With support from the U.S. Agency for International Development (USAID), an experimental program of daily agricultural radio broadcasts was started in 1973 to offer farmers information about agricultural methods and practices to encourage increased yields.

The results of the project were ambiguous. Nonetheless, it remains a good example of one use of communication as loudspeaker—extending the voice of expertise where it would not otherwise go. As in this case, the loudspeaker is sometimes the only feasible information-distribution strategy (1).

In other situations, there may be an available local voice, but that voice is not considered adequate to the task at hand. In El Salvador in the late 1960s, the government implemented an instructional television system with international funding agency support so as to provide the voice of the master teacher in the classrooms of newly enrolled students and their recently retrained teachers. By the mid 1970s the enrollment in seventh through ninth grades had more than quadrupled, with the quality of instruction maintained or improved, and at a cost per student lower than in the previous system (12).

The extension of the expert voice at an acceptable cost is certainly the prime justification for the use of mass media in education informational projects. In some sectors, as in formal education, but also in agriculture or health when local reception groups with a volunteer monitor make use of radio broadcasts, the communication technology is used primarily to improve quality. In other sectors, for example, agricultural, family planning, and health projects, when rural target audiences are beyond the reach of the in-place extension network, communication technology is used to extend that network.

Communication Technology as Institutional Catalyst

As noted above, El Salvador's instructional television system (ITV) was the centerpiece of a substantial educational reform (see 12). In this and other cases, it is appropriate to view ITV as catalyst of that change in two ways. First, ITV's operational character demands concomitant change in other components of the educational system—curriculum specification and restructuring, reorganization of the school day, changes in classroom teaching styles, development of teaching material like student workbooks and teachers' guides. All may be needed to accommodate television. Second, ITV's political attractiveness can mobilize sufficient political momentum to overcome the inertia of the educational bureaucracy. Instructional television was advocated by the winning candidate for the presidency of

El Salvador in 1967, and as such, its political clout opened the way for many changes in the educational system.

Media-based projects have "star" quality and can therefore attract such support from a government. At the same time, the "star" quality holds risk. More technically appropriate strategies may be rejected in favor of politically appealing media-based strategies—a particular risk when it comes to what Wilbur Schramm (16) called Big Media, e.g., television and satellite transmissions. Also, political support may not last the course when it comes down to providing the essential infrastructure to make a communications project work effectively. Indeed, investments in communication technology can, in their worst case, provide the loud and public appearance of activity and thereby avoid the enactment of more meaningful reforms.

Communication as Organizer and Maintainer

An innovation in an educational process can be excellently conceived, and successful in affecting learning outcomes in its early use, but may not, over the long haul, maintain that success. Teacher retraining as a route to improved classroom instruction may suffer this fate. The teacher may be shown valuable new techniques, but when he or she returns to the classroom, the working environment remains unchanged. Facing the frustration inherent in trial-and-error applications of new methods that will precede their mastery, teachers will find it easy to slip back into customary practice.

Contrast this pattern of innovation with that inherent in direct instruction via mass media in the classroom. In Nicaragua, the USAID-sponsored Radio Mathematics project used thirty-minute, carefully developed radio broadcasts to teach mathematics to students in primary schools (19). Once the curriculum was complete, although modifiable, it represented a substantial deterrent against backsliding. It was there, every day, in the classroom, structuring the mathematics instruction. Once the radio was turned on, the organization of the classroom day and the probability of maintenance of the innovative educational process were enhanced.

Communication technology, when used directly in an educational process, can provide a backbone to both organize and maintain change in a resistant environment. The Tanzanian adult education authority used radio as the pivotal element in its nationwide health campaigns (5). The ten- to twelve-week "Man Is Health" campaign organized discussion and decision groups (based on smaller pre-existing political and adult education units) to listen and act upon information received via weekly radio broadcasts. Clearly, the heavy involvement of national and local political forces was instrumental to the success of these campaigns (evaluations reported the extraordinary figure of 700,000 latrines constructed). Nonetheless, the campaigns were organized around the radio broadcasts which enabled the central planners to control the pace and essential structure of the campaign activities.

A 1975 U.S. example, the Stanford Heart Disease Prevention Program, illustrates another aspect of this pacesetting function (4). This experimental program used mass media to convince its target population to change heart disease-related behavior, including diet, exercise patterns, and smoking. However, changes in such habits are not meaningful unless they are sustained. This is particularly true of personal diet and exercise patterns. In such instances, mass media campaigns can reinforce change by continually providing reminders about recommended behaviors. Thus, communication technology, used properly, may serve all three of these subfunctions—organizing an educational process, maintaining an innovative process over an extended time, and reinforcing the change of behavior when new behaviors must be repeated.

Communication as Equalizer

Whether one considers the distribution of teachers or schooling resources, agricultural extension agents or health services, history provides a close to invariant lesson—the rich get richer. More experienced teachers, better buildings, textbooks, and other instructional materials go first to the urban schools, the schools of the relatively advantaged children. Agricultural extension agents reach the larger farm owners, but rarely the mass of subsistence farmers. Health services spread only slowly from urban to rural communities.

Unequal distribution of resources is inevitable as long as such resources are limited, and the ability of particular constituencies to make claims on those scarce resources is also unequal. One partial approach to that problem is to end the limits on resources, so as to permit universal access. Communication media, in their capacity as loudspeaker, can provide such universal access.

In El Salvador, the instructional television system was the first school resource ever to approach equal distribution across the seventh- through ninth-grade population. The fact that one school made use of the broadcast signal did not reduce the ability of other schools to make use of it, given that they all were provided with television receivers. In contrast, the fact that an urban school was able to attract an experienced teacher meant that another rural school could not.

In what may seem paradoxical, the communication satellites, often viewed as the most high-technology, capital-intensive communication investment of all, can sometimes fulfill this equalizing function. The Indian Satellite Instructional Television Experiment (SITE) (15) made use of the ATS-6 communication satellite to provide instruction to villages that were beyond the range of land-based broadcast distribution networks.

The equalizing potential of the communication technology is certainly here. Nonetheless, two caveats must be entered. First, a nation must want to take advantage of this equalizing function by committing the resources necessary for such a program to exist in the first place. Second, it must be recognized that communication technology offers only the promise of equalized access or opportunity, not necessarily an equalization of benefits. While the design of both hardware and software of a communication system can affect equality of benefit, a substantial inequality will remain as a function of abilities and resources.

Communication for Improvement in Quality

Taking advantage of the special qualities of a variety of media through carefully designed software may enable the development of a different instructional process equal to or better than even high quality face-to-face instruction. The program design for the Nicaraguan Radio Mathematics project is a good illustration of maximizing the potential of the medium and not merely reproducing the voice of the master teacher. The contractors brought ten years of experience in constructing mathematics curricula for computer-assisted instruction to the creation of the radio-based curriculum. They spent one year in developing each grade: designing curricula and planning and producing programs with a complex and artful understanding of how mathematics is learned. Their experience was augmented through extensive feedback in the form of classroom observation and testing. Knowing that each program could be used in subsequent years, heavy investment in software development could be justified. Programs were produced or, more precisely, new curricula were developed that no master teacher was likely to duplicate.

The recent resurgence in distance education following the model of the British Open University illustrates the same issue (6). While correspondence education, often including television or other media, has had a long history, it has also been characterized by high dropout rates and dreary instruction. The apparent and contrasting success of the ten-year-old British effort, and of similar ones elsewhere, including Everyman's University in Israel, may be due in no small way to the care with which instructional packages have been developed. As with Radio Mathematics, each course combined some radio and television broadcasts with textbooks, exercises, and some face-to-face review. Rather than trying to duplicate the educational process carried on in traditional universities or other training centers, these institutions strike out on their own, taking maximum advantage of all the channels of communication at their disposal.

Communication Technology as Accelerator of Interaction

Rural people, for good or for evil, depend on communication with less rural areas for many aspects of their lives. Agricultural seed and fertilizer may come from outside, and cash crops are sold outside; consumer goods may be manufactured elsewhere; schools and health posts are supplied and supervised, if they are to be supplied and supervised at all, by central offices.

All of these relations with distant centers require communication. Such interaction can be accelerated substantially by the use of communication technology which will perhaps make a qualitative difference in the character of some of those interactions.

What we do not know is just what all the implications of such an acceleration would be. We do not know which center-periphery relations would be largely unaffected, which would be affected to the advantage of the rural participant (or all participants) and which to the disadvantage of the rural participant.

In Alaska, for example, small rural villages have only a health aide, a member of the community given six weeks of training, to provide ordinary health care (9). To support the limited skills and experience of those aides, the health system introduced two-way radios (eventually making use of a satellite to improve transmission quality) which provided daily contact with a physician at a regional hospital. While conceivably some slower form of communication might have been possible (mail planes irregularly arrived at the villages and might have taken messages), the character of the resulting health system would have been very different.

Communication as Legitimator/Motivator

Because it is broadcast over the mass media, it must be important and, vice-versa, if it is important surely it will be broadcast over the media. This "status conferral" function of mass media (11) is probably operative for most people in the world. Thus social advertisers use radio to sell *Super-limonada*, a rehydration formula to combat infant diarrhea, in Nicaragua (3). And while radio serves as a loudspeaker providing access to large audiences, the fact that the messages are on the radio gives them credibility for each listener. In a curiously circular logic, the advertiser buys audience-reach and because he has bought reach, he buys credibility for his product.

The credibility lent by access to mass media may extend elsewhere. The constant broadcast of a national language and other national symbols (anthems, etc.) may both teach that language and those symbols and legitimize them. A family planning campaign on radio may be no more effective per dollar investment in providing access to information than alternative channels, but its extra credibility may affect adoption. Regular television broadcasts may motivate attendance at agricultural discussion groups, even if the same content could have been presented equally well through local means.

Sensitization of policy-making elites, and their consequent involvement in policy change in such areas as population and nutrition, may affect the success of development programs more than direct actions with target audiences can. Mass media presentation may legitimize a particular problem, justifying national attention, and thereby increase access for interested groups to the policy-making process.

Communication for Feedforward

Communication technology can be used to magnify the ability of the mass of a population to speak to the central institutions which affect them. In its simplest form this involves the publication of letters to the editor of mass circulation newspapers focusing attention on one problem or another. In Senegal's "Radio Dissoo" program, the letters-to-the-editor notion was transferred to a broadcast medium (2). Seventy percent of broadcast materials were expressions of viewpoints, complaints, and questions from rural audiences. The rest were responses by government agencies to those comments, or provision of useful information. It was reported that substantial modifications of government policy were the result of the quick and large-scale peasant use of this feedforward channel.

The need for feedforward is most acute in the agriculture sector. It is often argued that the agricultural research agencies are unresponsive to the needs of subsistence farmers, in part because they have no regular means of hearing from those farmers through influential channels. In Senegal and other situations, the success of the feedforward channel in influencing policy did vary with the openness of the policy-making apparatus to such information.

Communication as a Magnifier of Dependency/Integration

That communication reinforces the links between participants is obvious; what is not so obvious is the interpretation or the valuing of that result. The potential of communication for increased exploitation has to be balanced against its benefits. What to a government broadcast authority is sharing of national language and symbols to foster nation-building, is to its critics the systematic derogation of minority cultures. In each case the optimistic view (or the view of those with control over the technology) is of beneficial integration; for those to be integrated, fearing exacerbation of already unequal status, the introduction of some specific communication technology-based programs may suggest increased dependency.

That point has been made at a more general level also. Sophisticated communication technology, it has been argued, leaves its users at the mercy of those who control that technology. At the national level that may mean that central institutions increase their dominance of national information networks. An illustration—while risking oversimplification—may make the point; the many itinerant entertainers and news carriers are replaced by the national radio station; multiple sources of information with their potential for divergence are replaced by the more efficient, more entertaining, and potentially more accurate—but often government-controlled—information sources.

The national dependence argument has its international parallel. Third World countries customarily import all of their technology, from transmitters and receivers to video tape for their ITV systems. Often only a single supplier manufactures equipment compatible with in-place systems. At least hypothetically, a shift in political winds can leave the user either stranded and faced with unexpected costs, or somehow forced to comply with what it considers interference in its own policies. This vulnerability is extreme when countries are faced with the huge capital costs of the purchase and launch of a satellite. A nation which, for example, leases time on a foreign-controlled satellite for its domestic communications network may perceive itself as risking substantial reduction in national autonomy in time of conflict. This fear of dependency has been voiced in the debates in developing countries over the appropriateness of satellites.

There are, in sum, a wide range of roles that communication technology has been asked to play or does play, regardless of whether or not it was meant to. In which of those roles has it been most successful? What has been learned from these many projects about what factors contribute to this success?

CONCLUSIONS FROM PAST EXPERIENCE

If the past two decades have taught us anything, it is the importance of ripe circumstance, of right context, of making communication activities fit as a complement to other activities. What we have gained over these years is increasing knowledge of how to recognize ripe circumstance (and not-yet-ripe circumstance) and how to specify what other activities must be going on if communication is to be an effective complement.

Foremost, we have learned that success of any communication intervention is improbable without *prior commitment to social change* in the sector by substantial political forces. In earlier, more naive times, communication enthusiasts had hoped that their awesome technologies might somehow circumvent current political interests. By changing the organization and speed of information distribution, it was argued, the distribution of power and society's goods could also be changed.

However, experience has taught us that the technologies, awesome as they may be, are under the control of those with power and will be used in ways consistent with those interests. The information that is to be transmitted and the feedback that will be heard are defined by those who control the hardware.

Mathematics education can be improved through the use of radio—but it will not be unless a real commitment to change is reflected in salaries adequate to attract and retain high-quality production personnel, time and facilities to produce good programs, encouragement and training for teachers, and availability of sufficient resources to implement and maintain the project broadly.

By the same token, agricultural radio, which informs the farmer of an innovative way to plant his crop, will have little impact if the necessary follow-up visit of the extension agent does not take place, if the fertilizer the farmer needs is unavailable or too expensive, if the market system cannot absorb his surplus, or if the cost of credit, the insecurity of land tenancy, and the vagaries of weather make the innovation too risky. The programs will fail to meet development goals if, because there is no mechanism to assure that the agricultural research and development stations are developing innovations relevant for small farmers, the innovations are suitable only for commercial farmers.

Communications interventions *must complement or be accompanied by changes in resources or environments*. There is a close fit between how people behave and the environment in which they live. This seems an obvious statement. Yet it has been implicitly denied by many past and current communication projects which assume that the transmission of information (about a new nutrition practice, for example) by itself, if only it can be phrased persuasively enough, will lead to behavior change. Perhaps, for relatively low-cost behaviors which do not invade important cultural territory, for behaviors which are easily adopted and which produce obvious rewards, information alone can produce change. However, with the economists and the anthropologists, we must assume that most behavior is not easily changed in the absence of substantial change in the environment supporting the behavior.

If new resources which change the character of the decision environment are available, communication interventions may be quite valuable in accelerating the pace and broadening the distribution of change. Similarly, if new resources are introduced into a community without complementary communication activities, projects may also fail. For example, efforts to introduce sanitary water supply systems into communities may fail to change the incidence of gastrointestinal illnesses. Families may persist in carrying and storing the pure water in open containers subject to contamination if no complementary communication campaign addressed to those practices is mounted.

New resources are only one way in which the environment can be changed. Social dislocation—caused by population pressures, new employment or schooling opportunities, deterioration of land, or changes in cost of foodstuffs or agricultural supplies—may mean that current behaviors are no longer reinforced by the environment. In such cases, new behaviors which fit well into the changed environment may be learned easily—and communication interventions may find fertile ground.

The introduction of new communication technology must also be *complemented by good instructional design*. Projects which are viewed by their sponsors primarily as investments in hardware have little probability of success. While this may be commonplace wisdom to those who are experienced in media-based instructional projects, it is not always shared by the enthusiasts who are responsible for the creation of the dozens (perhaps hundreds) of media projects which appear annually around the world. Enthused by the extraordinary reach of the medium, they may not invest sufficiently in the design of the content they transmit to have any hope of success.

While it may be stretching the analogy, the necessity for good software design extends to two-way communication systems also. The best configuration of hardware for a given country will depend on what messages need to be transmitted on the system. Location of telephones within communities, who has access to the telephones, type of transmission system, order in which communities are given access to telephones, which telephones can be used to talk with which other telephones and at what cost are, in the end, software design decisions. These organizational issues are important "software" questions, just as message content is important for one-way transmission media.

The most repeated conclusion of researchers interested in persuasion via mass media is that effectiveness is magnified by *complementing media messages with local audience groups* organized for listening, discussing, and deciding. In the abstract, we endorse that conclusion. However, perhaps because it is the oldest of the communication-as-complement principles, it no longer seems as telling as it once did.

The difficulty in executing this principle is the cost and complexity of creating and maintaining the field structures that such local groups demand. Projects find it difficult to maintain initial enthusiasm as administrative complexity grows and time extends beyond a few months. Projects which try to create field structures from scratch, so as to complement the broadcast message, are unlikely to succeed. Also, given normal social stratification in communities, some social groups do not join or are excluded from these organizations—often the poorest people are least likely to participate.

However, when they can take on more than one role, or when they have a function in the community that is separate from the use of broadcasts, or when they are not expected to serve as permanent organizations, local groups can be a powerful channel for magnifying the effects of a communication intervention. In Tanzania and in China, local groups based on political cell structures have been quite successful, as have been multi-purpose Mother's Clubs in the Republic of Korea (10).

Finally, a necessary ingredient for a successful communication inter-vention is that it complement *knowing what is going on in the field*. Com-munication projects make assumptions about what is true in the environment of their intended beneficiaries, an environment which may be at substantial geographic and cultural distance from the projects' spon-sors and staff. Because of that distance, it is likely that those assumptions are wrong, either in general or in detail. Communication projects need to know what is going well and what is not. They need efficient data gathering mechanisms and, no less, time and flexibility within their operational struc-tures to define the information which can be used, and to take full advan-tage of the information that is gathered.

OBSTACLES TO USING COMMUNICATIONS AS COMPLEMENT

Foremost among the obstacles to communication as complement are prob-lems related to the distribution of power. In the creation of any commu-nication project, there are always competing interests. Both at the level of commitment to the expressed goals of a project and at the level of par-ticular emphases within a project, those with economic and political power dominate. This may mean that subsistence farmers fail to guide agricultural research because others have first call on research institutions. Broadcast primary-school instruction may be stymied if other priorities—university education or teacher salaries—have first call on available resources. The list can go on, but the implication is clear. At the risk of repetition, project failure often is not merely a technical failure or a failure of management. Rather, technical and management failings may be symptoms of the true distribution of power in a society.

The problem of fitting communication into the existing system also stands in the way of success. Organizers of communication for develop-ment usually choose one of three administrative locations for their proj-ects. The predominant mode has been to locate communication projects within the substantive ministry concerned. A second strategy has been to locate projects within the communications ministry (post and telegraph, telecommunications, or whatever its title) or national radio or TV service. The third strategy is to create a hybrid agency by drawing on two or more institutions.

Which of the above strategies is chosen will depend on the overall character of the project and, particularly, its political genesis and support. In that context, expert advice may be irrelevant. However, when there is some flexibility in the decision, the first mode is preferable. Placing com-munication within the substantive ministry concerned recognizes that communication must complement a broader intervention. It serves to accelerate change, not instigate it.

Realistically, projects organized outside the ministry which employs the agents or controls the resources cannot count on their long-term availability, no matter how sincere the promises of cooperation at the outset. The centrifugal pull of institutional loyalties, rooted in competition for scarce resources, may be too great. In general, projects cannot succeed if they are not guaranteed such long-term support of the substantive ministry, and they are not likely to achieve that support outside of the ministry.

While a view of communication as complement necessitates this recommendation, one can recognize two powerful counterarguments. One is that a substantive ministry is not easily galvanized and while communication projects can be impressive catalysts to change, they may be insufficient to move an entrenched bureaucracy. The second is that projects organized within single ministries make rational telecommunication hardware planning difficult.

Sensible investment in production, transmission, and reception for a single substantive project will be very different from sensible telecommunication investment for a large number of projects aggregated across ministries and over time. The dilemma is real and not solved by letting things take their course. Under natural forces, the pattern of telecommunication investment is likely to reflect commercial and particularly urban interests, leaving rural development concerns in second or later place. Systems inappropriate for development communication uses may be the result.

In the abstract, a hybrid agency with representatives of all communication-using institutions advising the telecommunications ministry would be ideal. However, it is not clear how this will provide funding for development telecommunication, unless the advice is accompanied by binding commitments for budget subventions. In most nations, telecommunication agencies are expected to pay their own way; a change in that policy could require some new source of funds. Until rents from users (in this case other government institutions) are available, direct financial support from donor agencies may be necessary. User agencies may be able to pay their share of usage charges once facilities are in place, but special assistance may be required for the initial capital investment for rural systems.

PRACTICAL APPLICATIONS OF COMMUNICATION TO DEVELOPMENT

Three categories of given applications of communication to development problems can be distinguished. The first category includes two applications which have proved their worth. While there can be no guarantee, much of what is transferable from one setting to another has been learned. In-school core instruction through media represents the most successful application of communication technology to development. Substantial improvements in learning, an easing of the implementation of solutions to access problems, and effective catalyzing of broad educational reform have all been achieved. Costs can be manageable, and while the obstacles can be non-trivial—teacher reluctance, language diversity, and coordination of class schedules—the outcome is likely to be worth the effort.

A second application within this category is distance teaching of motivated young people and adults. Using some combination of broadcasts, correspondence, local tutors, and learning centers, institutions in both more and less developed countries have successfully reached physically dispersed audiences with educational programs. While most existing programs have addressed higher education, the approach has promise for the continuing education of field workers and teachers, and for primary school equivalence education for post-school-age persons. Costs are usually lower than comparable residential training programs, both because capital costs are less and because opportunity costs are reduced since participants can remain at home and working in their jobs.

Several roles for communication technology which are ready for systematic evaluation, but perhaps not for widespread application, form a second category. Mass campaigns using radio, printed materials, local group meetings, and the full attention of national and local leaders have been markedly successful in mobilizing a large number of people to take concerted action in health and other sectors. However, success largely has been restricted to countries like Tanzania and the People's Republic of China that have well-developed political infrastructures. It is an open question whether a campaign in health, nutrition, or family planning would succeed in countries where tentacles of government do not reach the most rural villages.

Media-supported discussion and decision groups as exemplified in the radio farm forums of India and the radio schools of Colombia which taught literacy and other complex skills were the communication expert's gospel ten or even five years ago. But plagued by high dropout rates, poor learning, and administrative complexity, these programs have achieved only limited success. The evidence suggests that starting from scratch to organize groups for the specific purpose of receiving, discussing, and deciding to act on broadcast messages over a long term is probably unrealistic under most circumstances. However, when local groups are already organized, whatever educational function they serve may be magnified by using broadcasts as one channel of communication.

The use of communication for the social marketing of new family planning, health, and nutrition practices has become increasingly popular. Strategies range from simple advertising campaigns to sophisticated operations including extensive pre-campaign research, product development and distribution, and carefully pretested and monitored multi-media advertising. Such programs are promising, partly because of the reflected glow from the commercial sector applications from which they derive and partly because they promise a way around the administrative and logistical nightmares associated with programs that require extensive field infrastructure. Their drawback is that they may be appropriate only for a narrow domain of development goals which our current level of knowledge does not yet permit us to define.

Finally, there are three proposed applications of communication for development which deserve further research and development. The first involves incorporating two-way communication into rural health care systems. If a health care worker had immediate access to a physician for consultation about diagnosis and treatment of patients, might not the quality of care delivered be improved, and the confidence of both health workers and clients enhanced? Are the costs (particularly if they can be shared with other rural institutions needing two-way communication) appropriate given the changes that are achieved?

Second, some observers have suggested that the great advances in agricultural technology achieved in recent decades have had minimal impact on subsistence farmers—the technology is inappropriate for them because the needs of commercial farmers have guided the activities of research centers. Some have argued that a communication system that provides timely and continuing information about the needs of the small farmer will tie the national research and extension system to that farmer's needs. Information about how such a feedforward system should be designed, and whether it will influence research priorities, will be the product of development and trial.

The third proposed application incorporates the first two—creation of an all-purpose rural telecommunications infrastructure. Optimists argue that rural telecommunications investment will facilitate rural development broadly. Two-way communication will ease management and supply problems for networks of field workers, increase access to the levers of power for rural people, enable full integration of rural economies into national market systems, and accelerate distribution of useful information to rural audiences. Skeptics worry about an exceedingly high cost investment, at best absorbing resources better spent elsewhere, at worst facilitating further exploitation of the peasantry by those who have the resources to make economic use of two-way communication. The question remains open, and can only be settled by investigation.

In sum, the history of communication as complement to social change is a tale of caution and of a field maturing. That communication and other elements of development are inextricably linked has been argued often (e.g., 17). What this chapter suggests is that we now understand that the character of those necessary links takes on a more complex hue. We understand that communication technology can take a myriad of roles in development and that its success in those roles depends on how it is done and in what circumstances. If as part of that richer understanding some additional caution is expressed, so be it.

NOTE

1. This chapter is a revised version of a paper produced as part of a review of Agency for International Development policy in communication undertaken by Stanford University's Institute for Communication Research for which Edwin Parker and the author were co-principal investigators. Others contributed heavily to earlier drafts of this paper and the background papers on which it was based (see 7, 8, 13, 14, 18). They include (in alphabetical order) Ronny Adhikarya, Eduardo Contreras-Budge, Dennis Foote, Douglas Goldschmidt, John Mayo, Emile McAnany, Jeanne Moulton, Jeremiah O'Sullivan, Edwin Parker, Everett Rogers, and Douglas Solomon. The "we" used in the text is neither royal nor editorial, but refers to some subset of the author and this list of contributors. The work was performed under contract ta-C-1472 with the Development Support Bureau (Office of Education and Human Resources) of USAID, and benefited from advice from Clifford Block, Anthony Meyer, and David Sprague of that office.

REFERENCES

1. Academy for Educational Development. "The Basic Village Education Project: Final Report." Washington, D.C., 1978.

2. Cassirer, H. R. "Radio in an African Context: A Description of Senegal's Pilot Project." In P. Spain et al. (Eds.) Radio for Education and Development: Case Studies, Volume 2. Washington, D.C.: The World Bank, 1977.

3. Cooke, Thomas and Susan Romwebber. Changing Nutrition and Health Behavior Through the Mass Media. Washington, D.C.: Manoff International, 1977.

4. Farquhar, John, Nathan Maccoby, et al. "Communication for Health: Unselling Heart Disease." Journal of Communication 25(3), Summer 1975, pp. 114–126.

5. Hall, Budd and Anthony Dodds. "Voices for Development: The Tanzanian National Study Campaigns." In P. Spain et al. (Eds.). Radio for Education and Development: Case Studies. Volume 2. Washington, D.C.: The World Bank, 1977.

6. Hawkridge, D. G. The Open University: A Select Bibliography. Milton Keynes: The Open University Press, 1975.

7. Hornik, R., B. Searle, D. Foote, and J. Moulton. "The Role of Communication in Education." Stanford, Cal., Institute for Communication Research, 1979.

8. Hornik, R. and D. Solomon. "The Role of Communication in Nutrition." Stanford, Cal., Institute for Communication Research, 1979.

9. Hudson, Heather and Edwin Parker. "Medical Communication in Alaska by Satellite." New England Journal of Medicine 289, December 20, 1973, pp. 1351–1356.

10. Kincaid, D. I., *et al. Mother's Clubs and Family Planning in the Republic of Korea: The Case of Orgubi.* Case Study No. 2. Honolulu: Ewic, 1975.

11. Lazarsfeld, Paul and Robert Merton. "Mass Communication, Popular Taste and Organized Social Action." In I. Bryson (Ed.) *The Communication of Ideas.* New York: Institute of Religious and Social Studies, 1948.

12. Mayo, John K., Robert Hornik, and Emile McAnany. *Educational Reform with Television: The El Salvador Experience.* Stanford, Cal.: Stanford University Press, 1976.

13. O'Sullivan, J., E. Rogers, and F. Contreras-Budge. "Communication in Agricultural Development." Stanford, Cal.: Institute for Communication Research, 1979.

14. Rogers, F., D. Solomon, and R. Adhikarya. "Further Directions for USAID's Communication Policies in Population." Stanford, Cal., Institute for Communication Research, 1979.

15. "Satellites for Rural Development." Symposium in *Journal of Communication* 29(4), Autumn 1979, pp. 89–144.

16. Schramm, Wilbur. *Big Media, Little Media.* Beverly Hills, Cal.: Sage, 1977.

17. Schramm, Wilbur. "Communication Development and the Development Process." In L. Pye (Ed.) *Communications and Political Development.* Princeton, N.J.: Princeton University Press, 1963.

18. Solomon, D. E. McAnany, D. Goldschmidt, E. Parker, and D. Foote. "The Role of Communication in Health." Stanford, Cal., Institute for Communication Research, 1979.

19. Suppes, Patrick, Barbara Searle, and Jamesine Friend. *The Radio Mathematics Project: Nicaragua 1976–1977.* Stanford. Cal.: Institute for Math Studies in the Social Sciences, 1978.

Thirty-Eight

The Small Media in Egyptian Village Life

Kamal El-Menoufi

Over the last few decades, the role of communication in bringing about social change in developing nations has grown tremendously. A great deal of attention has been paid in particular to the mass media, which have been expected to serve as major purveyors of modern influences (see 2, 3). In Egypt, as in most other developing countries, communication has been a one-way process used to inform villagers about development programs and policies but not to encourage them to seek information, talk over decisions, or express their needs and wishes. Accordingly, rural communication research has tended to focus on vertical communication from the national capital to the village based masses. Field studies have examined the role of mass media in diffusing innovations, promoting family planning, and raising the level of national consciousness;[1] yet there is virtually no research on horizontal communication. Important questions in this area demand answers. How and to what extent do various modes of communication further community development? How far do the media feed the forums of interpersonal discussion? How do villagers work together? How do they adopt or oppose changes? How does communication contribute to satisfying the human needs of joy, laughter, and entertainment?

In this chapter I will address these questions by examining the role of small media—tape recorders, loudspeakers, and folksingers—in Egyptian village life. Data were collected on nine villages selected for exploratory study in a research project on communication needs for rural development in Egypt.[2] Researchers gathered information from a variety of sources: official records, informants, and a questionnaire administered to a sample of 474 male respondents between December 1978 and February 1979.[3]

CASSETTE RECORDERS

During the early 1960s, audio cassette recorders made their appearance in rural Egypt, albeit on a very limited scale, when some villagers who had participated in the Yemeni Civil War (1962–1967) brought tape recorders back to their home communities. The soldiers could pay the high prices for recorders because they had been well paid. With extensive migration to the Arab petro countries and electrification of rural areas, the number of cassette recorders owned by villagers has increased. Data from the 9 villages revealed a total of 2,754 cassette recorders, or one set for every 25 persons. However, the machines were found mainly in the large and medium-sized villages, and ownership tended to be associated with both occupational status and education (see Table 38.1). The percentage of non-peasant respondents who reported having recorders was higher than that of the peasants: 31.5 percent and 18 percent, respectively. Likewise, ownership among literate interviewees exceeded that among illiterates: 29 percent versus 17 percent.

To be sure, figures on ownership do not represent an accurate index of exposure since the use of a recorder is not limited to its owner but extends to relatives, neighbors, and friends. Owners constituted around 24 percent of the interview sample, whereas listeners represented 63 percent. Cross-tabulation of ownership and exposure indicated that even non-owners had had considerable exposure (about 55 percent). Most owners listened to recorders at home (91 percent), while the great majority of non-owners listened to recorders at a neighbor's home (91 percent).

Background factors somewhat affected exposure. The percentage of recorder listeners among nonpeasant interviewees exceeded that among peasants: 72 percent versus 58 percent. However, a fairly weak statistical relationship existed between exposure and occupation. Education seemed to affect level of exposure slightly: 70 percent of literate respondents, compared to 56 percent of illiterates, were listeners. Finally, younger people were exposed more than their elders; for example, 80 percent of respondents under thirty listened to cassette recorders, whereas only 38 percent of those over sixty-five did so.

Tape recorders were used mainly for listening to Koran readings and religious talks. Sermons and religious broadcasts by leading holy men have been recorded and marketed in both rural and urban Egypt. The Koran tapes liked best by the villagers were not those made of national reciters but rather those recited by prominent local figures. The reason for this preference was simple: villagers could hear the Koran recited on the radio by any of the nationally known figures; this was not the case with local reciters. They could be heard only on certain public occasions; most villages could not easily afford to hire them for private ceremonies. Wealthy families, however, typically hire a well-known local reciter when a family member dies, and villagers owning recorders often used magnetic tape to record the Koran recitations on such occasions.

Tape recorders were used also for songs and music. As with Koran reciters, national singers, heard on radio, seldom were listened to on tape. Villagers preferred folksingers and reciters from the immediate vicinity. Finally, tapes were sometimes used to communicate with relatives or friends in Cairo and even abroad.

LOUDSPEAKERS

Loudspeakers came to the villages less recently than tape recorders. At least four decades ago, well-to-do families were hiring loudspeakers, especially for funerals. However, recent years have witnessed an increase in the number of loudspeakers, as well as a diversification of their usage.

Seven of the nine villages—the large and medium-sized ones (see Table 38.1)—had loudspeaker systems. The loudspeakers were mounted mostly on mosques (36 out of a total of 51 loudspeakers). The loudspeakers were bought by using local donations and have come to be perceived by Moslems as necessary to the practice of their religion. Craftsmen owned the remaining loudspeakers, which were either portable or mounted on cars; these could be rented for wakes or weddings.

The mosques used loudspeakers mainly for religious purposes: calling the faithful to prayer and broadcasting Friday sermons so that people who did not attend the services at the mosque, namely women and the very ill, could hear the sermon. In villages with more than one *imam*, these broadcasts tended to interfere with each other.

The loudspeakers on the mosques were sometimes used to transmit important public messages—notifying people of a death, missing children, or lost animals; broadcasting the date of fodder, fertilizer, seed, or food-

Table 38.1   Availability of Small Media

Village	Loudspeakers	Tape Recorders	Folksingers
Asfour	1	1	0
Sheikh Hassan	0	10	0
Beleida	8	201	3
Ezbat Radwan	0	50	0
Telwana	9	109	5
Abu Mosallam	5	60	7
El Zaafaran	6	23	0
Kaha	10	2,050	19
Oleila	12	250	9
Total	51	2,754	43

Table 38.2 Means of Finding Out Important Information

Type of Information	Loudspeaker		Village Crier		Notice on Door of Important Building		Staff of Institution Concerned		Word of Mouth		Valid Cases
	N	%	N	%	N	%	N	%	N	%	N
Date of distributing foodstuffs	32	10	0	0	0	0	64	20	226	70	322
Date of distributing seed, fertilizer, or fodder[a]	45	16	18	6	0	0	0	0	219	78	282
Crop rotation system[a]	9	4	0	0	51	22	21	9	154	65	235

[a] Questions were addressed only to peasant respondents.

stuff distribution; giving health care instruction; and inviting villagers to public meetings. As shown in Table 38.2, 10 percent of all interviewees said that they learned the date of foodstuff distribution via loudspeaker; 16 percent of peasant respondents reported being notified of the date of fodder, seed, and fertilizer distribution the same way.

The use of loudspeakers for such announcements may discourage word-of-mouth communication, lead to the disappearance of village criers, and diminish the influence of locally important interpersonal sources of information. On the other hand, this medium gives all villagers an equal chance to hear important information. Yet this advantage is in effect a mixed blessing since villagers may crowd together, provoking quarrels and creating disorder, on distribution days.

FOLKSINGERS

An important element of Egyptian village tradition is the folk reciter, or folksinger. Historical, anthropological, and literary writings dealing with village life have touched on their role in entertaining peasants living in a social context marked by deprivation and coercion. Until recently, most villages have had their own folksingers. According to our survey, 43 singers lived in the 9 villages. Once again, the large and medium-sized communities monopolized this medium (see Table 38.1 above).

To celebrate weddings, circumcisions, pilgrims' returns, and fulfillment of solemn pledges, families hire a folksinger from their own or a nearby village. On public occasions—the anniversaries of the prophet Mohammed and the Moslem saints—villagers usually hire a well-known singer and pay him from donations collected for this purpose.

Folksingers recite *mawawil* (poems in the vernacular), *madaih* (panegyrical religious poems), and *siar schabyyia* (biographies of heroic personalities in Arabic history). They use simple musical instruments such as rebecs, drums, whistles, and tambourines to enhance the recitations, which stress values and beliefs important to the villagers (patience, predestination, piety, and honor).

Villagers and their relatives living in urban centers attend ceremonies graced by folksingers in both their home communities and in neighboring villages. Such social occasions foster a sense of membership in a community larger than the home village, bring new information, and discourage hostility and distrust among villages. Table 38.3, which shows exposure to folksingers, indicates that about two-thirds of persons interviewed listened to folk recitations. More than one-third of listeners did so more than four times a year. The home village was the place of exposure for the majority of listeners, yet neighboring villages accounted for a significant portion (31 percent). Background factors did not explain the variation in listening habits. Nonpeasant and literate villagers were not better

Table 38.3 Exposure to Folksingers in Past Year (in percent)

Classification	Respondents Who Reported Listening	Number of Times Listened				Place Where Listened[a]	
		1	2	3	≥4	Inside Village	Outside Village
Occupation							
Peasant (N = 184)	65	28	24	16	32	87	30
Nonpeasant (N = 120)	64	22	17	19	42	85	31
Education							
Literate (N = 161)	64	24	20	18	38	89	30
Illiterate (N = 143)	66	27	23	16	34	83	31
Age group							
Under 30 (N = 65)	75	25	15	28	32	82	35
30–40 (N = 73)	66	20	25	22	33	89	34
40–50 (N = 76)	66	21	24	10	45	87	36
50–60 (N = 64)	63	33	20	11	36	91	17
Over 60 (N = 26)	48	35	23	11	31	77	35
Total sample (N = 304)	65	25	22	17	36	86	31

[a] Respondents reporting exposure in both places account for a total in excess of 100%.

351

exposed, and the distribution by age group was almost uniform (however, villagers under thirty had had more exposure than those over sixty).

CONCLUDING REMARKS

Egyptian rural communities do have local communication devices, but these media are available almost exclusively in the large and medium-sized villages. However, unlike a mass communication system that is centrally directed and used to convey national messages, the small media are not controlled from above and are used to disseminate local information. They help messages travel at the village level and help perpetuate folk culture.

The small media play almost no role in bringing about change and in encouraging popular participation in the development process. Folk recitations heard on tape or live stress values that inhibit rather than foster development. Yet these media can be employed in initiating and implementing development projects: they are effective means to infuse new ideas into rural communities in forms that are familiar, trusted, and adapted to local dialects and culture. Outside support and further study are needed to inject modern content into these now traditional forms.

NOTES

1. Empirical rural communication studies in Arabic made by Egyptian students were abstracted and compiled in (1).

2. The villages (Asfour, Sheikh Hassan, Beleida, Ezbat Radwan, Telwana, Abu Mosallam, El Zaafaran, Kaha, and Oleila) were distributed over seven rural governates. With a population of 69,701 (in 1976), the nine villages fell into three categories: three large villages, with more than ten thousand persons (Oleila, El Zaafaran, and Kaha), four medium-sized villages, between four and seven thousand persons (Telwana, Beleida, Ezbat Radwan, and Abu Mosallam), and two small villages, of fewer than three thousand persons (Asfour and Sheikh Hassan). Cairo University and the Massachusetts Institute of Technology have jointly sponsored this project.

3. Because the researchers observed no involvement on the part of women in the public affairs of the villages and because of practical research limitations, women were not included in the survey. The respondents were men from the agrarian and nonagrarian sectors, not a cross-section of each village's population. The peasant respondents were drawn from landholders according to the size of the landholding. The sample size ranged from 2 percent in the large villages to 5 percent in the small villages. As to nonpeasant interviewees, each researcher was asked to select two persons from every nonagricultural activity that existed in the village he was assigned to study. This technique yielded a sample of 286 peasants and 188 nonpeasants. The total sample consisted of 256 literates and 218 illiterates.

REFERENCES

1. *Communication and Rural Development in Egypt.* Annotated Bibliography, Arabic. Cairo University, M.I.T. Technological Adaptation Program, Report No. 5, June 1979.

2. Pye, Lucian (Ed.) *Communications and Political Development.* Princeton, N.J.: Princeton University Press, 1963.

3. Rogers, Everett, *Modernization Among Peasants: The Impact of Communication.* New York: Holt, Rinehart, and Winston, 1969.

Thirty-Nine

Satellite Instructional Television: SITE in India

Binod C. Agrawal

The singular success of the Satellite Instructional Television Experiment (SITE) in India heralded a new era in direct reception systems. In bringing television to isolated rural audiences SITE demonstrated that all parts of the globe are technologically accessible. The social evaluation of SITE must be examined in light of this achievement.

The Satellite Instructional Television Experiment was conducted by the Space Applications Centre of the Indian Space Research Organization (ISRO), in collaboration with National Aeronautics and Space Administration (NASA), USA, and Doordarshan (government-owned television authority), India. Though the center originally planned to have an outside evaluation of the experiment, commercial research would have proven too expensive. Thus, aside from a number of independent studies conducted by university departments, research institutes, the Planning Commission of India, and India's National Council of Educational Research and Training, the social evaluation of SITE was done by ISRO itself. This delayed the evaluation until May and June of 1974, many years after SITE was first conceived, a delay with important consequences for SITE. First, the experiment was conceived without adequate consideration of its social objectives (see 1). Second, lacking information about program content and coming late upon the scene, the researchers could evaluate the project only on the basis of the instructional objectives of SITE. No criteria were defined for the social evaluation. Throughout the chapter I shall indicate additional ramifications of SITE's lack of social science input.

THE SATELLITE INSTRUCTIONAL TELEVISION EXPERIMENT

The basic goals of SITE were to improve primary school education, provide teacher training, give information on agricultural practices, health, hygiene, and nutrition, and contribute to family planning and national integration. The one-year experiment (August 1975 through July, 1976) was conducted in 2,330 villages within twenty districts of six economically backward states. The states or "clusters" were Andhra Pradesh, Bihar, Karnataka, Madhya Pradesh, Orissa, and Rajasthan. In addition, 355 villages of the Kheda district of Gujarat state received satellite TV signals on conventional television receivers through a rediffusion system.

A direct reception television receiver was installed in each village. Specially prerecorded TV programs were telecast from the Ahmedabad television studio, which was connected with a nearby earth station. The TV signals were beamed to NASA's Applications Technology Satellite-6 (ATS-6). ATS-6 was capable of transmitting one video and two audio signals. Thus, Andhra Pradesh and Karnataka viewers could watch the same picture in the evening while hearing the audio portion of the show in their own language.

SITE programs were telecast for about four hours daily, 1.5 hours in the morning and 2.5 hours in the evening, in all clusters except Kheda, where only evening programming was received. Programs were produced by Doordarshan's three base production units in Delhi, Cuttack, and Hyderabad. In addition, science education programs for children and Gujarati programs for Kheda were produced by the Space Applications Centre's Ahmedabad and Bombay SITE studios. Half-hour programs (partly live) were produced by the Delhi TV unit and were transmitted from the Delhi earth station.

SOCIAL EVALUATION OF SITE

This aspect of SITE involved content, input, process, and summative evaluations before, during, and after the experiment. However, most emphasis was given to summative evaluation. The total cost of the social evaluation research represented approximately 3 percent of the total SITE budget, or the equivalent of $600,000. The SITE evaluation was a long-term effort using both qualitative and quantitative methods. Most of the evaluation research took a multidisciplinary approach, drawing on anthropology, communications, educational psychology, and sociology.

Schoolchildren

Each school day from 10:00 to 11:30 A.M. 22.5-minute programs in Hindi, Kannada, Oriya, and Telegu were telecast for children five to twelve years old (first through fifth grade or higher). Science education occupied the most content time.

The programs were shown in the classroom and seating was inadequate: the average audience size per TV set was 95, varying from 70

(Orissa) to 114 (Bihar and Madhya Pradesh). Both schoolchildren and teachers viewed TV attentively despite the cramped conditions, and the overall attrition rate was 14.5 percent (2). However, incomprehensible programs made children restless and noisy. Teachers in a majority of the schools did not hold posttelecast discussions.

SITE's social impact on schoolchildren was measured in two evaluative studies. Shukla and Kumar (6) using field experimental design interviewed and observed third-grade (630 experimental and 643 control) and fifth-grade students (631 experimental and 642 control) from six clusters in pre- and post-SITE periods. In achievement tests in three subjects—general science, social studies, and native language—students showed very little improvement. The schoolchildren (especially in third grade) did not appear to learn the appropriate lessons from the science education segments. In general, schoolchildren participating in SITE showed increased inquisitiveness, particularly in classroom instruction in general science; this effect was more prominent in younger children. Also, general understanding and information-seeking behavior apparently increased.

Teacher Training

A two-week multimedia in-service training package with nine important pedagogic messages was developed to train schoolteachers in teaching science. Presented twice during the SITE year, this program reached approximately forty thousand teachers. Statistically significant improvement was found in the science knowledge of the trainees, and most of the teachers felt that the training had been useful. Television rather than radio was preferred by the teachers for such training (see 7).

Adult Viewers

Every evening two and one-half hours of programming was telecast to adult viewers in Hindi, Kannada, Oriya, and Telegu, including a half-hour national program in Hindi. Program content, format, and range of topics differed in each language. On the whole, about 30 percent of the programs consisted of instruction in agriculture, animal husbandry, family planning, health, hygiene, and nutrition.

Initially referred to as *saleema* (cinema), television was well accepted by the villagers. After the novelty period of the first three months was over, the total estimated audience size leveled off at 245,000 per day (an average of about 100 persons per TV); in all clusters 40 percent of this audience were children of both sexes. In general, younger men (24 years or less) and middle-aged women (25 to 39 years) were the most numerous. These people were illiterate, lived in *kutcha* houses, and belonged to poorer sections of the villages. Almost one-fourth of the TV viewers had never listened to radio, seen a film, or read a newspaper. In this sense, satellite TV was a more powerful mass medium than other conventional mass media, capable of reaching previously inaccessible groups, particularly women.

Television sets were installed in public places like schools and village council buildings, making TV accessible to all who wanted to view it. As a whole, audience size and frequency of viewing increased in the last six months of SITE. One of the major reasons offered for not watching TV was work. Inappropriate use of telecast language was the single most important factor in comprehension of the TV programs (in the Hindi-speaking clusters of Bihar, Madhya Pradesh, and Rajasthan, where a common language was used, this problem was most acute because of dialect differences).

The results of SITE's social impact on adults are based on three evaluative studies (2, 3, 5). Agrawal (2) conducted holistic study in seven villages using anthropological methods and techniques in approximately 18 months of intensive field work, observation, and case study. Agrawal et al. (3) conducted an impact survey using field experimental design in 108 villages (72 experimental and 36 control villages). In each village a panel of 72 adults (about 15 years of age) was randomly selected and interviewed in pre-, during-, and post-SITE phases. The total pre-SITE sample size was 7772. The overall sample attrition rate was 16.4 percent. The Planning Commission (5) also conducted an impact survey using field experimental design in 60 villages. A panel of 30 randomly selected adults over 18 years of age was interviewed in pre- and post-SITE phases. The total pre-SITE sample size was 1686. The overall sample attrition rate was little over 15 percent.

Health and Family Planning

On the whole, more females than males gained in knowledge of health matters and family planning. The information received on health from TV changed or reinforced existing beliefs and added new knowledge. And although TV viewing did not accelerate the rate of adoption or use of family planning methods, it made this subject accessible as a topic of discussion.

Agriculture and Animal Husbandry

The farmers who participated in SITE had relatively high awareness of and knowledge about agricultural innovations before SITE. Some positive gains in awareness were found in regard to animal husbandry innovations like artificial insemination. Some indication of positive gains, though statistically insignificant, in adopting new agricultural and animal husbandry methods was also observed. When the awareness and knowledge levels were fairly high, as indicated earlier, adoption of agricultural innovations apparently was hastened by SITE even within the short span of one year. TV viewing also led to the greater use of extension services by cultivators.

Political Socialization

Effects of television viewing on political awareness, empathy, national integration, and efficacy of administrative units were evaluated. Researchers found statistically significant gains in empathy and in educational and occupational aspirations for sons (see 3). Illiterate male viewers showed greater gains than did their literate counterparts. However, the problem of subsistence remained a major concern that did not change with TV viewing.

Overall the evaluation found that TV viewing either had no effect or had positive effects in SITE. Frequency of TV viewing apparently was an important variable: a higher frequency of viewing was closely associated with changes in audience attitude or behavior (see 2, p. 13). The most striking conclusion from the study of adult viewers was that poor, illiterate women who had no access to any other media gained most from TV viewing; a lack of formal education did not keep them from comprehending new information.

IMPLICATIONS FOR THE FUTURE

Planning and Production

One of the major lessons of SITE was that software planning requires more time than hardware development (see 3).

Second, audience preferences indicated that using television in rural development efforts is a delicate art. For example, cultivators participating in SITE showed least interest in agricultural broadcasts, suggesting that innovative programming is vital to the success of such a development strategy.

Third, the most preferred and comprehended instructional programs used field, rather than studio, shots in a lecture-demonstration format. Portable video equipment gave producers remarkable flexibility. The use of such equipment cuts down initial and operating costs—a welcome savings in developing countries—and makes it easier to reach rural viewers in their own language.

Fourth, community viewing was well accepted in the SITE villages. Through Indian National Satellite (INSAT) it soon will be possible to provide community viewing on a large scale. But using television for rural development calls for greater investments in equipment and in maintenance, as well as in the training of TV service personnel.

Finally, SITE suggested that programming explicit about development goals but sensitive to traditional ways is a more effective development tool than is technologically sophisticated programming per se. The crucial ingredient is commitment among media practitioners and respect for the cultural milieu of the audience.

Social Research

Social scientists joined SITE only after most planning decisions had been made, a delay that curtailed the experiment's effectiveness. Future development projects of this kind must take a team approach, including social scientists along with producers, policymakers, and program designers from policy formulation to final evaluation. SITE also indicated that the developing countries should use both quantitative and qualitative methods of social evaluation. Additionally, in-depth studies relying on anthropological methods can elucidate the process of developmental communication. Adequate investments in preproduction research can eliminate irrelevant and ineffective programming—a waste of time and money the developing countries can ill afford.

In SITE not a single television set was damaged. However, minor clashes between rich and poor were reported, responding to televised information on the Twenty-Point Program; moreover, many landless laborers demanded higher wages, a few contemplated not repaying their debts, and others dreamed about a bright future—all to no avail. I think that television can be an effective tool in rural reconstruction given the political will for creating a just and egalitarian society. Indeed, technological innovations used consciously to attack the system responsible for rural inequality and backwardness are among the most powerful tools in development.

REFERENCES

1. Agrawal, Binod C. "SITE Evaluation Through Holistic Study." Ahmedabad: Space Applications Centre, Second Workshop, June 4–6, 1976.

2. Agrawal, Binod C. *Television Comes to Village: An Evaluation of SITE.* Ahmedabad: Space Applications Centre, 1978.

3. Agrawal, Binod C., J. K. Doshi, Victor Jesudason, and K. K. Verma. *Social Impact of SITE on Adults* (2 volumes). Ahmedabad: Space Applications Centre, 1977.

4. Chitnis, E. V. "Preface." In B. C. Agrawal *et al., Social Impact of SITE on Adults.* Ahmedabad: Space Applications Centre, 1977.

5. *Satellite Instructional Television Experiment: An Evaluation of its Social Impact.* New Delhi: Planning Commission, 1977.

6. Shukla, Snehlata and Kuldip Kumar. *SITE Impact Study on Children.* New Delhi: National Council of Educational Research and Training, 1977.

7. Shukla, Snehlata, Jagadish Singh, and Suresh Batra. "In-Service Teacher Training." In M. S. Gore, *A Critical Assessment of the Studies Relating to the SITE, India.* Bombay: Tata Institute of Social Sciences, 1979, pp. 216–228.

Forty

The Role of Communications Training and Technology in African Development

Chen C. Chimutengwende

The Third World campaign for a New International Information Order as part of economic and cultural decolonization has heightened interest in mass communication, and African officials and academics, as well as international organizations, are scrutinizing the relationship between the mass media and the development process. In this chapter I review the state of communication uses and training in Africa, focusing on the development of the field, current problems, and future prospects. The assumption from which I proceed is that mass communication media, like other social institutions, must continually change their policies, structure, personnel, and equipment to keep pace with the evolving demands of a developing society. The mass media exist within a larger sociopolitical context; thus, the society's values, political situation, and economic configuration are reflected in the content and level of training and research in this area (7, 13, 14, 18, 27). Accordingly, problems and solutions in communications will vary with the internal and external forces active within a given country (8, 10).

AN OVERVIEW OF AFRICA'S DEVELOPMENT TASK

Africa is not a monolithic entity but a continent of some fifty autonomous states that differ in political orientation, national cohesiveness and stability, and level and pace of social and economic development. However, historical features, people's aspirations, national objectives, and the nature of relations with the industrially developed countries are sufficiently similar to permit some generalizations. Thus, this chapter treats Africa as a whole, reflecting the continent's own tendency toward unity and coordination, both before and after independence, in many spheres of human endeavor, including communications.

The Media in Africa

Africa is the least developed continent in the world in terms of mass communication media: the continent had under two hundred daily newspapers in 1979 (32). Thirteen states had only one newspaper each; nine countries had no daily newspaper. Circulation per thousand of population was about 14; whereas it was 64 in Asia, 70 in Latin America, and 312 in the industrially developed nations. Growth was almost nil in the 1970s.

The press is geared largely to the educated urban elite; the rural majority is almost totally neglected. Sporadic experiments with rural newspapers have failed—in part because many governments have no defined policy on the issue.

Literacy levels in Africa remain low and the market for the printed media therefore is small. Africa has 10 percent of the world's population but accounts for only 2 percent of the books published annually worldwide. In 1976 the world average of book titles was 186 per million inhabitants annually but only 27 for Africans. Likewise, the national languages spoken by the majority of the people are not being adequately promoted as tools in development oriented communications.

In broadcasting, Africa also trails other regions of the world. The continent has about seven hundred radio transmitters and thirty million receivers. Twenty-six African states have fewer than fifty radio receivers for every one thousand people. Many people, therefore, have no access to radio. Television remains a luxury for an urban minority. There were only 2,750,000 television sets in 1976 for the entire population. Seventeen countries had no television service.

As for the cinema, for every one thousand persons there are only 4.8 seats. The figure for the rest of the developing world is 9.7. It is 52 for the developed countries. These statistics conform to other socioeconomic indicators. For instance, Africa's GNP is $365 per capita a year, which comes to only 2.7 percent of the total GNP worldwide. The development task is therefore immense. Indeed, one can say that a state of emergency exists.

The Urgency of Development

Responding to the need to develop in a hurry, Africa, like the rest of the Third World, is following national development plans that typically cover periods of one to twenty years. The aim is to achieve in a few decades what the developed countries did in two millennia. African states are at war against poverty and economic and technological backwardness: the goals of educating the people and modernizing society are too pressing to permit trial-and-error efforts. Moreover, the poverty and suffering among former colonial peoples and the post-independence crisis of rising expectations ultimately would lead to indomitable resistance among the people against slow socioeconomic advance—in the same way that opposition to colonial rule arose, eventually leading to a change of government.

THE DEVELOPMENT PROCESS AND THE MASS MEDIA

The process of development therefore has been carefully planned to achieve the speedy socioeconomic advancement of society. Whether socialist or capitalist, African nations have identified precise objectives, targets, and stages to reach this goal (1, 4, 17, 28). Clearly, mobilization of the population is essential to development, and the mass media have a crucial role to play in educating, informing, persuading, and organizing the people.

The Role of Communications in Development

The problems that led Africans to overthrow colonial rule—widespread poverty, illiteracy, unemployment, injustice, corruption, rural neglect—continue to plague post-independent Africa. Any state that does not give high priority to the speedy and progressive reduction and final elimination of these problems is likely to experience political unrest, instability, and, sooner or later, an abrupt change of government. The people naturally expect that their aspirations, which were frustrated during colonialism, will ultimately be realized after independence. Thus, the liberation struggle is a dynamic process that goes on in a different form after independence (2, 12, 19, 20, 25, 29).

In developing countries, therefore, development-oriented and campaigning journalism is essential; any other type of journalism represents a waste of resources. The notion that mass media are one of the essential auxiliary means of modern economic construction and social and cultural development was advanced by Frantz Fanon, who argued that "The Algerians must know where they are going and why a specific course has been embarked on. The politician must realize that the future will remain dim as long as people's consciousness remains dim and incomplete" (quoted in 30).

Modernizing lifestyles and changing ideas and attitudes based on ignorance, along with other practices that are not conducive to national development, are tasks the mass media could perform effectively. The mass media are an important means of achieving social control and facilitating the social process; accordingly, their ideological and socialization functions are indispensable factors in programs of national development. For example, media campaigns can promote good health practices, education, and agricultural techniques; encourage the growth of participant political institutions; promote industrial production and expansion; enforce social norms and raise aspirations; give legitimacy to values and institutions; open communication among diverse groups; expose corruption; and facilitate national integration (11, 15, 24, 26).

As the figures given earlier make clear, the mass media do not as yet directly reach the majority of Africans. But they nevertheless reach the key groups and opinion makers in the centers of modern development—the people whose political views are usually decisive at this point in time in the developing countries. But it is also part of development continually to increase the mass media audience, making direct contact with the majority of the people. Without getting to the majority through use of the mass media, quick mass mobilization for development is almost impossible. Of all agents of change, the media can most effectively complement traditional and interpersonal channels of communication, bringing the spirit and goals of development to the masses.

Control of the Media and Their Role in Development

Precisely how the media perform their role and the problems they face vary from one country to another and from one period to another as a result of differences in the larger economic and political system and in the stage of development. In certain developing countries the mass media are state owned or controlled; in others, they may be privately owned or partially state owned. Yet even privately owned media are expected to support national development programs and in one way or another to act as state directed agents of planned social change. Developing countries with privately owned media must grapple with the problem of how to make commercial operations serve development needs. Obviously, the profit motive is often at odds with the task of meeting the information requirements of a developing society.

Advocates of a Western communication model in developing countries have not resolved this problem. In a laissez-faire society, the government does not get directly involved in the media; yet in a Third World country trying to develop rapidly the government has to take an active part in the establishment and operation of the media and also in the defining of communication policies (16, 22, 23). Thus, the developing countries that originally attempted to adopt capitalist economic and political theories and strategies of socioeconomic growth have had to accept state planning and direction of the development process. This necessity has had tremendous implications for the structure, control, and role of the media, affecting the content and the pace of communication training and research.

THE EVOLUTION OF MASS MEDIA TRAINING IN AFRICA

An historical overview of media development in Africa may help clarify the current state of communication training and research.

The Mass Media Before Independence

The mass media have an elitist history in Africa. They were established in the colonial era largely to serve the information and communication needs of the European colonists (3, 7). When the power of the media as instruments of social control, socialization, and persuasion was recognized, a serious attempt was begun to direct some of the media to the "natives," especially the educated elite and the working (21).[1] Therefore, a few Africans had to be trained as journalists and broadcasters. Their training was largely on-the-job, however, and the positions they held in the media were normally subordinate to those of the colonial settlers, who remained in control of policy and content.

African nationalists who were campaigning for independence throughout the continent also realized that the media, especially the press, the medium they could afford, could be useful in countering procolonial information and ideas. The nationalists used the press to disseminate their views among literate Africans who were considered opinion makers. This group was expected to spread the nationalist perspective among the broader African population.

The African press operated under serious legal, financial, and professional constraints, however. Such independent indigenous journalism was officially discouraged and labeled subversive and extremist. Moreover, the Africans who owned the newspapers, magazines, and journals were not rich enough to compete with the white settlers' press. Finally, the journalists who worked on the African nationalist press were either self-trained or trained on-the-job.

Post-Independence Developments

Immediately after independence was achieved, the need to train African journalists in large numbers became very apparent. The white settlers who had run the mass media were leaving Africa; some of those who remained needed to be replaced because their attitudes were diametrically opposed to the new situation of African majority rule. Similarly, the inevitable expansion of the print and broadcast media and the government information services meant that African media practitioners were needed in large numbers and at all levels.

But African governments and educational institutions could not easily establish programs or schemes for training media personnel. In English-speaking Africa, for instance, the British traditional notion that journalists are born and not created was strong. Therefore, some official and educational circles resisted the idea of formal training for journalists (33). Many African journalists who had been trained on-the-job during the colonial period also argued that formal training for journalists is neither necessary nor suitable. African academics, true to their British upbringing and educational values, could not easily accept the idea of formal journalistic training, especially in the universities. They gave an elitist and antidevelopment argument to the effect that the university is a center for satisfying the academic and intellectual rather than the vocational needs of society. Mass communication studies were not seen as an academic discipline. And it was anathema even to suggest that mass communication studies be introduced in secondary schools as a long-term strategy for increasing public access to and participation in the communication process. Some of these attitudes persist today.

Lack of resources also discouraged communication training and research after independence. Manpower problems of course existed in all sectors of society, and financial constraints were formidable. This is where international agencies and organizations played and still play an important role: they had the necessary resources and experience.

UNESCO, the International Press Institute, the Thomson Foundation, the Friedrich Ebert Foundation, and the Commonwealth Broadcasting Association set up training programs for media personnel, and on-the-job training continued to produce journalists and broadcasters, but most such efforts were ad hoc and uncoordinated (31, 35). These programs depended on the availability of foreign expertise and funds. There was no serious attempt to train local instructors—a lack with far-reaching consequences. Since the international bodies were reluctant to get involved in local politics, the courses tended to be narrow in scope, aimed at giving basic communication skills: how to report, write an article, produce a newspaper, announce, and put together a radio show. The training programs neglected the social sciences, yet the trainees by and large had no background in this area; development economics, history, politics, and international affairs would have been valuable to the trainees in their future work as interpreters of society and as communicators. (Where such subjects were included, they usually were colored by the orientation of the foreign instructors, whose views and values normally were not in harmony with the political direction of the country and the aspirations of the people, including the trainees themselves.)

From the beginning of the independence era, a significant percentage of media personnel were trained in the developed countries. The trainees faced the problem of learning on equipment that was not in use at home. Likewise, the Western emphasis on professionalism led to the avoidance of questions concerning the objectives and orientation of communications work, important considerations in the context of developing societies. By the late sixties, a growing number of decision makers and academics were protesting the absurdity of turning out African media professionals who were mere carbon copies of ex-colonialist communicators. The production of uncommitted media workers whose own outlook and philosophy of life were not in harmony with the circumstances and aspirations of Africa was becoming increasingly unacceptable, as was dependence on short-term foreign consultants or training abroad, and the idea of setting up communication training, education, and research centers in Africa began to gain support.

In 1976 the African Council of Communication Education was established with the following aims:

—To assess the training needs of African communication training institutions and to generate common solutions to these needs.
—To assist in curriculum design at the request of African communication training institutions and to encourage the circulation of various curricula and course designs among the training institutions.
—To evolve a system of accreditation among African communication training institutions and universities.
—To find ways and means of student and staff exchange among African communication training institutions.
—To promote regional workshops and training courses and to initiate high-level training programs for communication trainers.
—To cooperate with international organizations in research, information exchange, and support.
—To promote awareness in the African governments of the crucial role of mass media as an instrument for national development.
—To engage in the collection and dissemination of information on media development, research, communication training, and curriculum design (31).

Each African country must have a national center or at least a regular in-service training program for basic and intermediate communication skills. There also should be regional centers capable of accommodating the specific training and research interests of a region; such centers should be mainly for advanced communication studies.

Presently, media education is available in university departments, autonomous institutions under the auspices of the ministries of information, or schools under the sponsorship of religious organizations.[2] University programs offer both professional and academic training in mass communication studies; they try to integrate the theory and practice of communications on a firm academic base in a variety of disciplines. The government-sponsored media institutions specialize in professional training. The church-funded programs have a religious bias; their primary task is the production of professionals to serve the communication needs of the church. Finally, radio and television, newspapers, and film organizations carry on some regular training programs for their staffs or for future staff members.

Problems Faced by Media Personnel

Most African governments fail to recognize communicators as professionals. Media personnel are often treated with suspicion and perhaps are persecuted more than other workers. Furthermore, they enjoy no job security because of the sensitive nature of their role in society. Media workers also are victims of changes in administration. Government also slights communication training, allocating inadequate resources to this task and failing to develop consistent policies toward mass media education. Low wages in comparison to those of other professionals also discourage would-be journalists and broadcasters. Finally, promotions are slow and based on civil service procedures, which are ill-suited to assessing merit in this field.

Accordingly, professional communicators find that they can get better wages, quicker promotions, closer attention to their training needs, greater job and personal security, and higher status in the eyes of the authorities if they use their communication training and experience in jobs outside the mass media.[3] On the surface, this tendency looks like a loss to society, but further examination suggests otherwise.

The communication professionals who leave the mass media are merely serving their countries in other capacities.[4] Communication training and education in its wider sense does not prepare people to work only in newspaper, radio, and television services, the film industry, public relations, or media research organizations; such training can improve one's performance in other kinds of work that may be equally valuable to society.

FUTURE DIRECTIONS IN MEDIA TRAINING AND THE ROLE OF INTERNATIONAL AGENCIES

Communication programs both within and outside the universities suffer serious financial hardships. For example, both classrooms and equipment tend to be in short supply. Generally, schools are understaffed and therefore unable to conduct the research they deem vital, nor are they able to train enough people to meet the ever-increasing demands of society. The financial and other assistance these institutions need could presently come most easily from the relevant international organizations (5, 9, 34). This is the kind of aid that ultimately would eliminate the need for outside help.

With adequate assistance, African media training and research institutions could carry out the tasks for which they were established. Such assistance would help them to consolidate themselves and achieve maturity and credibility; train more local media teachers, researchers, and practitioners, which would reduce and finally eliminate dependency at this level; and conduct research relevant to the development needs of society—particularly on mass mobilization for national development and the use of the mass media in literacy, education, and other development oriented projects.

The production of more and better trained communication practitioners and research of a high standard would boost the status of the media institutions, encouraging media executives, government leaders, and other relevant people with influence in society to push for increased state funding of the centers of communication training, education, and research (see 6). This would greatly reduce the need for foreign training and hasten the development of a committed media community. However, in order to eliminate dependence in communication training, education, and research, clearly defined communication policies will have to be worked out, integrating the mass media fully into the national development process.

NOTES

1. Research projects were undertaken to investigate the influence of mass media, particularly film, among Africans. For instance, during the 1922 white miners' strike in South Africa, two hundred thousand African workers were kept idle in the compounds. The Bantu Educational Cinema Experiment was set up to find out how film could be used to "prevent the spread of wrong ideas among the natives." African workers in the compounds were shown films making it clear that "rebelliousness and disrespect for authority was wrong, dangerous and evil." Other groups of Africans in South Africa were shown these films and their reactions were analyzed. A Belgian filmmaker reported on the experiment to the International Colonial Institute in Brussels in 1936. The experiment was considered successful, proving that film could be a useful ideological tool.

2. The debate as to whether professional training in mass communications is best done in a university environment, in an independent institution, or on-the-job within a media organization continues. If such studies are available outside the universities, should governments finance them or should funding be private? Indeed, can a communications school under a ministry of information freely engage in research?

3. There has always been a resistance to the introduction of new disciplines in the educational system internationally. The debate about the necessity of introducing communication education is still going on even in the industrially developed countries.

4. Because media work puts one in contact with diverse enterprises, the communications professional has been accused of opportunism and lack of commitment to the profession, a charge that can be evaluated only case by case.

REFERENCES

1. Adelman, Irma. *Theories of Economic Growth and Development.* Stanford, Cal.: Stanford University Press, 1967.

2. Allende, Salvador. Address (verbatim record) to the United Nations General Assembly, New York, December 4, 1972.

3. Ainslie, R. *The Press in Africa*. New York: Walker and Company, 1968.

4. Apter, David E. *The Politics of Modernization*. Chicago, Ill.: University of Chicago Press, 1965.

5. Bielenstein, Dieter (Ed.) *Toward a New World Information Order: Consequences for Development Policy*. (Report on an International Conference in Bonn, West Germany, December 4–6, 1978: Institute for International Relations and the Friedrich Ebert Foundation). Bonn, 1979.

6. Bordenave, Juan E. Diaz. *Communication and Rural Development*. Paris: UNESCO, 1977.

7. Chimutengwende, C. C. *South Africa: The Press and the Politics of Liberation*. London: Barbikan Books, 1978.

8. Conforth, Maurice. *Dialectical Materialism*. London: Lawrence and Wishart, 1972.

9. Duisberg, Carl Gesellschaft, V., Cologne, and the Union of Radio and Television Organizations in Africa, Nairobi. *Broadcasting Planning—Training Needs in Radio and Television*. Report of the Joint Workshop in Nairobi, January 7–13, 1979.

10. Engels, Friedrich. "Socialism: Utopian and Scientific." New York: Pathfinder Press, 1972.

11. Golding, Peter. *The Mass Media*. London: Longman, 1974.

12. Haq, Mahbub ul. *The Poverty Curtain*. New York: Columbia University Press, 1976.

13. Holland, Stuart. *The Socialist Challenge*. London: Quartet Books, 1975.

14. Hood, Stuart. *The Mass Media*. London: Macmillan, 1972.

15. Lerner, Daniel. *The Passing of Traditional Society: Modernising The Middle East*. Glencoe, Ill.: Free Press, 1958.

16. Lewis, A. W. *The Theory of Economic Growth*. Cambridge: Cambridge University Press, 1960.

17. Mboya, Tom. *The Challenge of Nationhood*. London: Heinemann, 1970.

18. Miliband, Ralph. *The State in Capitalist Society*. London: Quartet Books, 1973.

19. Myrdal, G. *The Challenge of World Poverty*. London: Penguin, 1970.

20. Nabudere, Dan. *The Political Economy of Imperialism*. London: Zed Press, 1977.

21. Nee-Owoo, Kwate. "How They Brainwash People." *Liberation Struggle* (Europe-Third World Research Centre, London), June 1972.

22. Nurkse, Ragnar. *Problems of Capital Formation in the Underdeveloped World*. Oxford: Oxford University Press, 1953.

23. Pearson, Lester B. (Chairman). Report of the World Bank Commission on International Development: *Partners in Development*. New York: Praeger, 1969.

24. Pye, L. W. (Ed.) *Communications and Political Development*. Princeton, N.J.: Princeton University Press, 1963.

25. Rodney, W. *How Europe Underdeveloped Africa*. London: Bogle L'Ouverture, 1972.

26. Schramm, W. *Mass Media and National Development*. Stanford University Press/UNESCO, Paris, 1964.

27. Siebert, Fred S. (Ed.) *The Four Theories of the Press*. Champaign: University of Illinois Press. 1973.

28. Tinbergen, January. *Development Planning*. London: Weidenfeld and Nicolson, 1967.

29. Todaro, Michael P. *Economics for a Developing World*. London: Longman, 1977.

30. Ullrich, Werner. Article in *The Democratic Journalist*. International Organization of Journalists, Prague, November 1974.

31. UNESCO. *Communication Education in Africa*. Paris, December 1977.

32. UNESCO, Experts for the 1980 Intergovernmental Conference on Policies in Africa, Nairobi Working Group. *Working Document*. Paris: UNESCO, 1980.

33. UNESCO. *Media Studies in Education*. (Report and papers on mass communication, No. 80). Paris: UNESCO, 1977.

34. UNESCO. *Tanzania School of Journalism*. Report prepared for the Government of the United Republic of Tanzania by UNESCO. Paris, September 30, 1979.

35. UNESCO. Training for Mass Communication. (Reports and papers on mass communication, No. 73). Paris: UNESCO, 1975.

Forty-One

Reaching a Rural Population: A Case Study of Malawi

Hastings Mawola Sanderson Chunga

Every country in the world, whether developed or developing, is concerned about the dissemination of information and the speed at which such information is transmitted. Policy decisions on information and communication flow may be the responsibility of either central, regional, or municipal government or the private sector, but any policymaking must rest on accurate evaluations of the technology requirements and capabilities of the particular country or locality. Especially in developing countries, decisionmakers must be clear as to whether the technology available locally is adequate in both quantitative and qualitative terms for the specific goals that have been set. Indeed, it is no longer prudent for any country to import technology wholesale without taking local conditions into consideration: technology transfer implies a broad range of tangible and intangible costs. This chapter looks at how Malawi has solved certain communication problems by using local extension workers, political party machinery, and medical radio communications, along with the tailoring of radio programs and telecommunications facilities to meet rural needs. In this way the rural environment has kept touch with the rest of the country.

MALAWI BEFORE INDEPENDENCE

Malawi is a small, landlocked, independent African state located south of the equator. Roughly a fifth of the country is taken up by Lake Malawi and other lakes, which profoundly affects temperature, land use, etc. The 1977 census reported a population of 5.5 million; the yearly growth rate is estimated at 2.6 percent. Malawi's principal urban areas are Blantyre (222,153), Zomba (21,000), Lilongwe (102,000), and Mzuzu (16,119).

Under the name British Central Africa, Malawi was declared a British colony in 1891. Early colonial history was dominated by Christian missionary activities in the wake of Dr. David Livingstone's missionary travels. The Church of Scotland and the Free Church of Scotland eventually established themselves at Blantyre in the south and Livingstonia in the north respectively; smaller groups of missionaries followed.

The influx of missionaries throughout the continent stimulated the race among European powers for the acquisition of territory—the Scramble for Africa. The African colonial empires were established for the benefit of the colonial metropolis. Thus, when protectorate status was given to British Central Africa in 1891, the new administration lacked both the manpower and the money to carry out meaningful development. The British government was reluctant to provide financial support, and Cecil John Rhodes agreed to furnish funds from his own savings to meet administrative expenses of the new protectorate, which he was eager to use as a springboard in his effort to control the vast stretch of land from Cape Town to Cairo. Rhodes's interest in British Central Africa did not last beyond 1895, when financial responsibility over the protectorate was finally assumed by the British.

Throughout the entire colonial period, the British administration concentrated on the maintenance of law and order and tax collection from the indigenous people. Socioeconomic development was relegated to the lowest rung on the ladder of priorities. Economic stagnation resulted: able-bodied men were forced to seek low-paying jobs on European-owned plantations and at church mission stations. As farming and mining expanded, the demand for cheap labor increased in South Africa and Southern Rhodesia (now Zimbabwe) at the close of the nineteenth century, and a large number of men from British Central Africa flocked to these countries for work. It is estimated that between 1904 and 1905 some ten thousand men left British Central Africa to work outside the country; in the process, many families were broken up and agricultural development of British Central Africa was neglected.

From 1907, when British Central Africa was renamed Nyasaland, to 1961, when the first general election was held in preparation for the transfer of power to the indigenous people, the economy of the country continued to stagnate. This occurred despite the inclusion of Nyasaland in the Federation of Southern Rhodesia, Northern Rhodesia, and Nyasaland, which was established in 1954 on the argument that Nyasaland was too poor to stand on its own and needed to be included in an entity with a wider economic base. The arrangement did not last long; the federation broke up in 1963. In 1964 Nyasaland was granted independence and adopted the name Malawi. The country became a republic on July 6, 1966.

MALAWI'S DEVELOPMENT TASK

The government that assumed *de facto* political power in 1961 (when the first general election was conducted in Nyasaland) was faced with formidable economic problems, among them lack of mineral resources, industry, and access to trade routes. The question was how to modernize a stagnant economy. Agricultural development was the best choice given the factors enumerated above.

The Malawi Congress party identified the new government's priorities in its 1961 election manifesto (2, p. 13):

1. To raise the living standard of ordinary people in the villages by building up basic economic institutions, modernizing agriculture, industrializing the economy, and developing mineral resources.
2. To increase economic opportunities so as to minimize unemployment and underemployment. Large-scale commercialization of agriculture and a policy of balanced regional development were to be implemented.
3. To calculate the benefits of new economic activities not so much in terms of monetary profit as in terms of social gain.
4. To promote business activity among the less privileged sectors of the community.

Thus, Malawi came on the international stage with a determination to bring about economic and social change. However, the particular development program mattered less than the country's national will to develop.

The overwhelming majority of Malawi's people live in rural areas. Agriculture is still the mainstay of the economy, employing over 90 percent of the working population. The goal of raising the standard of living of this majority through the development and commercialization of agriculture remains the foremost concern of the Malawi government.

MALAWI'S DEVELOPMENT STRATEGY

Technology as a tool of fundamental social change cannot be effective in a cultural vacuum and in order to understand its impact one must first appreciate the structure and social process of the society in which such technology is being assimilated. A transitional society such as Malawi's, unlike a purely traditional one, has had considerable exposure to outside influences over the years, acquiring new technology along with political, religious, and other imports. Thus, transitional societies are more complex than traditional societies. Mass media communication puts the transitional society in touch with the global community. Its people develop new aspirations and new needs, which in turn create new institutions. These new institutions generate new roles and opportunities, which complicate the dynamics of social change and social mobility. To oversee these developments and to insure that new needs are satisfied, government must be vigorous.

Accordingly, immediately after independence Malawi embarked on a general development program with particular emphasis on agriculture.

Studies were carried out with the assistance of external advisors and four major projects were begun in key areas (25 percent of Malawi's territory and population are involved). The projects are designed to achieve a high rate of direct return on capital invested and also to serve as a frame of reference to the small cultivator in surrounding areas. The primary objective of these programs is to increase rural incomes by stepping up the agricultural production of the small farmer through a more rapid adoption of improved agricultural practices. Extension and training services, health services, and community development efforts (road and bridge construction and extension of telephone lines, for example) are important aspects of each project. The Malawi government also has launched the National Rural Development Program (NRDP). This is a twenty-year plan for increasing crop production, improving roads, expanding markets, providing health and education facilities, and insuring water supplies in rural areas throughout the country.

THE ROLE OF COMMUNICATIONS IN MALAWI'S DEVELOPMENT

Communications has a critical role to play in Malawi's development effort since the majority of people live in scattered homesteads or villages not serviced by reliable roads. A mix of communication strategies has had good results.

Extension Services

Face-to-face contacts between an extension aid worker and a small farmer can explain new farming techniques and answer the farmer's questions. Community health nurses perform functions of a similar nature. They visit remote clinics and health centers to explain modern techniques of health care delivery. Finally, the community development assistant is the link between the community and the Ministry of Community Development.

The Ministry of Agriculture and Natural Resources uses a variety of means, besides extension workers, to provide assistance and information to farmers. One-day to four-week courses are given, instructional radio programs are broadcast on a regular basis, mobile units use films and puppet shows to provide instruction in agricultural methods, and various publications are distributed.

Medical Radio

In 1974 the Ministry of Health in Malawi invited the African Medical and Research Foundation, based in Nairobi, to examine the feasibility of introducing a medical radio communication system in Malawi to strengthen its health care delivery especially in isolated areas. The team sent by the foundation concluded that a medical radio communication system could be of value to the Ministry of Health and suggested that the ministry introduce trial service for one year in a selected area in the northern part of the country. Nine stations were created.

In 1976 an evaluation team discovered that out of the original nine radios only four were still working; staff changes made maintenance of the radios difficult. The evaluation team replaced some of the radios and relocated the base control station. In-service training on radio maintenance and use was also given. The team recommended extending the trial period in order to collect more information on the system's utility. To date the radios have been used to verify laboratory results, report on public health matters such as outbreaks of disease, and obtain assistance in obstetric emergencies.

Broadcasting

Broadcasting is probably the easiest and most effective method of reaching the rural population in a country like Malawi. There is only one broadcasting organization in Malawi, the Malawi Broadcasting Corporation (MBC), which was set up by statute in 1963.

Malawi Broadcasting Corporation is charged with providing informational, educational, and entertainment programs to listeners in Malawi. Despite limited facilities, MBC broadcasts have filled in the gap created by the absence of television services in the country. On the air nineteen hours a day, MBC radio transmits school programs, news reports in both English and Chichewa, Malawi music, health care tips, agricultural bulletins, and overviews of development efforts in the country, including interviews with local leaders of self-help projects.

Telecommunications

The telecommunications industry in Malawi is experiencing the effects of a rapidly advancing technology—specifically, satellites and earth stations. Thirty years ago the main telephone exchanges and lines covered only the southern region, with only a part-time earth return line to Lilongwe in the central region. By 1958 lines reached Mzuzu, in the north. But telephone continued to be a novelty found only in the big towns. Since independence, telecommunications technology has proliferated. The principal towns of Blantyre, Zomba, Lilongwe, and Mzuzu are linked by modern microwave systems; a satellite earth station already links Malawi to South Africa, Kenya, the United Kingdom, and the rest of the world (with updating on the horizon); and a new ultra high frequency system links Malawi with Zambia from Lilongwe.

Moreover, telephone service is now available in many remote areas; in 1978 the principal cities in Malawi accounted for only 36.5 percent of all telephones in the country (1, p. 41). Though the telephone system in Malawi grew steadily in the 1970s (by over 10 percent a year), this rate of development was inadequate to meet the demand. The outpacing of supply is very significant in a country that is largely rural. Malawi's record in telecommunications is impressive and plans are being formulated to upgrade the system by extending microwave services into neighboring countries.

The Political Party

The contributions of modern communications technology cannot be overemphasized; however, the human factor in communication systems is equally important. In Malawi, as in other developing countries, the government takes an active interest in the welfare of the community as a whole. The position of the only political party is unique: the Malawi Congress is one of the very few political parties in Africa to have a grass-roots organization. Moreover, its innovative role in socioeconomic development is unequaled. Every party functionary, whether a member of Parliament or a cabinet minister, subscribes to the country's development efforts, and party officials enthusiastically participate in community programs and other activities in rural areas. Through a hierarchy of committees the party cements the bonds of national unity as an integral part of nation building.

In conclusion, extension services, radio broadcasts, the telephone, the party machine—all have had a positive impact on Malawi's development. New techniques in crop production and animal husbandry have enabled farmers to increase agricultural output, reflected in the rising volume of exports. Indeed, the value of agricultural exports virtually doubled between 1974 and 1977, and the GNP increased nearly sixfold from 1964 to 1974 (3, p. 12). These indicators suggest that the application of modern communications to a rural nation can significantly further development goals.

REFERENCES

1. A. T. & T. *The World's Telephones: A Statistical Compilation as of January, 1978.* Bedminister, N.J.: A. T. & T., 1978.

2. Malawi, Congress Party. *Malawi Congress Party Manifesto 1961.* Lilongwe, 1961.

3. Malawi, Office of the President and Cabinet. *Malawi Government Economic Report 1979.* Lilongwe, 1979.

Forty-Two

Change within a Stable Environment: The Austrian Example

Benno Signitzer

Stability as one of the characteristics of contemporary Austria extends far beyond the realm of communications.[1] It has become a basic value in Austrian domestic and international conduct. Since the end of World War II and the treaty of 1955, which ended Austria's postwar occupation and restored national autonomy, the principal actors of Austria's political culture have stressed consensus over dissent, compromise over full expression of partisan interests. This quest for stability has helped the Socialist party, under Chancellor Bruno Kreisky, to maintain an absolute majority of seats in Parliament since 1970. Industry also enjoys a stable, contractual partnership between business and labor, which has reduced dispute to a minimum. The international equivalent of the idea of consensus and stability is Austria's neutral status.

Certainly, this stability has nurtured Austrian society since the war, but a younger generation of Austrians has come to regard such an environment with disquiet. At a time when the assumptions upon which Western industrialized society has been based are increasingly being called into question and new solutions for new problems are sought (e.g., environmental protection, conservation of natural resources), Austria would certainly appear to need creative and far-sighted policies, that only public awareness and articulation of problems can generate. Here, overemphasis on consensus at the expense of debate may be counterproductive.

Austria's media and communication systems also need to question the allegiance to stability as a national goal. With considerable delay, politicians and media professionals have come to recognize that profound structural changes are occurring in these areas. Austria faces such problems as an astounding degree of press concentration, a high measure of foreign dependence in media production and ownership, and the management of new communications technology that will alter the very nature of the mass media. In this chapter we assess some of the characteristics of the development of broadcasting, both illustrating structural problems and indicating corrective strategies.

The Austrian Broadcasting Corporation (ORF) is a publicly chartered entity that holds a legal monopoly over broadcasting in Austria. All broadcasting is under federal jurisdiction. The law defines broadcasting in a comprehensive way to include not only wireless transmission but also cable transmission; moreover, impartiality must prevail—the diverse views in society must be taken into consideration and the range of programs balanced. The Broadcasting Act of 1974 included detailed provisions on the internal structure of the ORF (which runs two TV and three radio channels), its purposes and aims, as well as the scope of programming activity. Legislation in this area followed extended controversy both between the two major political parties (the Socialist party and the conservative Austrian People's party) and between ORF and privately owned newspapers (which feared ORF's competition for advertising revenues). Unfortunately, this debate was stimulated by narrow partisan interests and did not sufficiently pursue the issues of new technology and "new legitimacy," a shortcoming reflected in the limited version of the broadcasting acts.

ORF's status as a publicly chartered corporation has shielded Austrian broadcasting from some of the more overt pressures toward commercialization and mass appeal programming. However, the organization is not trouble-free. First, the various groups entitled to a certain measure of influence over ORF operational and programming policy through their representation on the board of trustees have at times confused legitimate lobbying activities with a license to interfere in day-to-day editorial decisions. Especially guilty in this regard are the political parties and the so-called social partners (organized business and labor represented by the Federation of Chambers of Commerce and the Federation of Trade Unions), which have exercised a heavy hand in many aspects of Austrian life. ORF, like many of its western European counterparts, also has been plagued by financial problems resulting from a saturation of license ownership, on the one hand, and ever increasing production and operating costs, on the other. Possibly, too, the sheer size of the corporation (presently employing some three thousand persons) encourages bureaucratic arrangements that can stifle journalistic independence and artistic creativity. Finally, the extent of foreign program importation, especially on television (50 percent of total air time), undoubtedly discourages Austrian cultural expression in the broadcast media.

INNOVATION IN TELEVISION TRANSMISSION

As we have seen, adherence to the notion of stability has had a considerable impact on the evolution of postwar Austria, an influence manifest in broadcasting. ORF's monopoly owes its legal justification to the natural limitation of channel capacity, but technological innovations may call this rationale into question. We shall explore the implications of one of these new technologies, cable television (CATV).

Until recently CATV operations had been confined to localities in the western part of Austria to improve reception of West German and Swiss stations. This market includes a large number of West German tourists, who can watch their favorite TV programs via cable even during vacations abroad. Most of western Austria is within broadcasting range of the West German and, to a lesser extent, the Swiss stations, so cable was introduced only to create equal access to these broadcasts for all Austrians living in the west.

In the mid-seventies the possibility of extending cable service into eastern Austria (where two-thirds of the population live) was given serious consideration. An amendment to an existing law setting out technical requirements and standards for broadcasting paved the legal way for cable transmission. However, the law refers only to the distribution of conventional foreign TV and radio programs via cable; ORF alone is legally empowered to originate programs.

Despite this legal impasse, various groups have begun to organize their interests and stake their claims in present cablecasting possibilities (e.g., the distribution of foreign programs outside the ORF monopoly) and possible future CATV operations (e.g., program origination). Roughly ten more or less provincewide associations are slated to operate in Austria's nine provinces. While organizational setup and financial arrangements may differ, a closer look at one of these associations—Kabel-TV Salzburg—will reveal how different interest groups currently are represented and suggest how influence patterns may evolve.

At the end of 1978, 75 percent of the investment shares in this cable association were divided among the province (29 percent) and city of Salzburg (20 percent), along with a cable company (26 percent). The remaining shares were held by a wide range of interests—two daily newspapers, the chamber of commerce, several workers' organizations, and a private cable company. The governor of the province was chairman of the board; the mayor of Salzburg, vice-chairman; and a high-ranking civil servant in the provincial administration, executive director.

The structure of Kabel-TV Salzburg reveals that influential groups in society have seized the opportunity to gain a considerable measure of control over this new medium. The official power structure (represented by provincial and city government) and, to a lesser extent, its "social partners" (chamber of commerce, chamber of agriculture, unions of industrial workers, other employees in agriculture and farm workers) control the bulk of shares. Two companies that represent the interests of the cable installation industry hold nearly 30 percent of shares. In addition, two Salzburg dailies have token influence (5 percent of shares) over a medium that could develop into their major competitor in the local advertising market.

The future of CATV, however, will be decided in Vienna, where more than one-fifth of Austria's population lives (about 1.6 million people). In Vienna cable installation is advancing rapidly. Though in August 1979 four thousand households had cable, two hundred fifty thousand subscribers are anticipated by 1985. Current planning involves the distribution of West German and Swiss, as well as ORF, programs, but the facilities are designed both for more channels and for feedback. The city of Vienna is sole owner of the association managing the Viennese CATV operation; Phillips (holding 95 percent of shares) and the city of Vienna (5 percent) control the company doing the technical work for this project.

Organizational and technical arrangements are one side of the coin; the other is the potential audience for CATV and viewing patterns. Data on viewing behavior in western Austria, where three German channels and, in some areas, one Swiss TV station have been available for many years even without cable, could suggest future uses of CATV. Studies conducted in 1979 showed that the additional programming options generally have modified viewing behavior. For example, Austria's first TV channel (FS 1) continues to dominate in providing topical information. Two of the West German channels (ARD and ZDF) represent entertainment program competition. The more specific user interests, such as sports, culture, science, education, and political documentaries, are met largely by the two Austrian channels (FS 1 and FS 2).

Austrians devote about one-third of their daily viewing time to foreign shows (that is, two hours). The data on total daily viewing are inconclusive: some evidence points to a slight overall increase; other data suggest no change in response to an expanded number of channels. In either case, the new channels have not had a dramatic impact on viewing behavior, though entertainment ranks on the very top of the interest scale (66 percent) followed by sports (37 percent) and news (36 percent).

THE NEED FOR POLICY DECISIONS ON CABLECASTING

Austria's policy debate over communication involves the political parties, labor and business, as well as the mass media. This debate has centered around the question of the legality of the ORF monopoly, with the Conservative party and business opposing the status quo and the Socialist party and the trade unions supporting it. However, the political positions are far from clear-cut and often cross party lines. For example, in 1980 Austria's maverick chancellor, Bruno Kreisky (who is also chairman of the Socialist party), has offered a third TV channel to privately owned newspapers (which, of course, would mean the end of the ORF monopoly); the president of the journalists' union (part of the Austrian Federation of Trade

Unions) approved of such a course, which, in turn, is violently opposed by ORF journalists.

The more pressing issue—namely, the transmission of foreign TV programs via cable to population centers in east Austria—received virtually no systematic attention. The desirability of additional channel capacity is apparently taken for granted. Even the ORF, which is and will continue to be most directly affected by foreign imports, has never seriously considered resisting this development. Rather, the national broadcasting organization has begun to readjust its programming schedule in order to avoid heavy competition from foreign stations, which could relegate the ORF to a peripheral position—especially regarding entertainment programming.

The lack of debate on the desirability of TV imports via cable reflects broader tendencies in Austrian policymaking: progress has for too long been equated with implementation, rather than evaluation, of technological innovations. Consequently, a wait-and-see cable policy would have run into stiff resistance from the prevalent political culture as well as the manufacturing industry, which faces serious problems in a saturated market. Moreover, the current open-door approach is politically and ideologically supported by the free flow of information doctrine, to which Austria is formally committed at the international level. Therefore, a policy that questioned the propriety of large-scale program importation inevitably would challenge the concept of stability, which guides the conduct of Austrian affairs. Yet the quest for stability in CATV policy reduces the number of options available to a small country like Austria and in the long run might produce the very instability it was designed to avoid.

NOTE

1. The current state of communication policy in Austria is discussed in Signitzer, Benno. "Austria: Policymaking in a Small Country." *Journal of Communication* 30(2), Spring 1980, pp. 186–189.

Forty-Three

National Communications Policies: Grass Roots Alternatives

Luis Gonzaga Motta

Numerous UNESCO documents and reports have advocated the establishment of national communication policies in the developing countries (see 7, 10). This position rests on a large body of evidence indicating that the national and international information orders are unjust and on the assumption that comprehensive communication policies will correct this imbalance. UNESCO's evidence is essentially accurate: many recent studies have pointed out that international, national, and even community communication access and distribution are markedly inequitable and that communications has been associated with the exercise of political and economic power. Overall these studies have concluded that communications has both facilitated commercial and political manipulation, thereby subverting genuine democracy, and increased cultural and economic dependency rather than stimulate participation and social integration.[1]

If UNESCO's diagnosis is correct, will its prescriptions also prove accurate? It has generally been argued that national communication policies will increase democratic participation in communication production and consumption, as well as reduce centralization and verticalization. Accordingly, social development planning must provide for an entity empowered to make decisions about communication needs, access to communication systems, technological priorities, promotion of cultural values, and so on. This scheme assumes that any integrated process of social development requires rational and coordinated planning (7, special recommendations 7–10).

But what do UNESCO and communication experts in fact mean by *communication policy*? Such a policy, according to UNESCO advisors, is a series of principles and norms established to orient the behavior of a communication system (10). Communication policies also have been defined as integrated, explicit, and lasting assemblages of partial policies organized in keeping with a coherent set of principles and norms and applicable to communication processes and activities in a country (1).

However, such policies do not exist in reality. Usually, partial or provisional policies apply to specific sectors or periods of time; in other cases, functioning communication norms are not recognized as policies. This does not mean that communication policies do not exist; rather, *operational policies* govern communications everywhere on an apparently *ad hoc* basis. However, such policies if analyzed in the context of broader social concerns will reveal political meanings and underlying coherence. Analysis of a given communication procedure or norm therefore must take into consideration the implicit organizing principles linking communication practices throughout a society and not be limited to explicitly formulated plans. Nevertheless, whether explicitly formulated or informally operational, national communication policies have implied centralized decisionmaking everywhere. Vertical communication structures are justified by the need to rationalize the use of scarce resources and avoid duplication of efforts (in order to increase efficiency), for example.

The MacBride Report, attempting to change this view, defined communication policy as an instrument to give structure and consistency to overall actions undertaken at the national level and recognized the lack of unanimity concerning the role of communications in national development. The Report argues that the question is to decide what kind of development we want and then to determine communication strategies. In this sense, communication policies cannot be equated *a priori* with democratization of communications; what they imply is the defining of priorities, which vary from one country to another (8, Chapter 15).

UNESCO's new and old approaches toward national communication policies differ in two important ways.

1. The former approach assumed that centralized planning would benefit any type of society. The new approach recognizes that countries differ in the kind of development wanted; thus, the diverse objectives of various national states will produce different policies with distinct results.
2. The former approach assumed that communication imbalance is mostly a question of technological or infrastructural deficiencies and prescribed technology transfer as the cure—more media is better communications. The new approach, calling attention to the risks of saturation, cultural homogenization, and so on, suggests that modern communication technologies complement rather than replace traditional media, including interpersonal communication.

As we have seen, however, UNESCO's experts still believe that national communication policies are the answer to underdevelopment and imbalance.[2] Is this in fact the best way for developing countries to overcome conservative internal communication structures and abolish external communication dependency? If the current state of affairs is the result of private enterprise and "freedom of expression" run wild, is state control a solution to backwardness and authoritarianism? Have national communication policies actually helped democratize information access and produce an information equilibrium? Answers to these questions must recognize, first, that policies generally have been equated with national planning and planning is usually associated with concentration of decisionmaking and second, that national policies are rarely integrated and explicitly formulated plans; for the most part they are the product of partial strategies or diffuse communication practices lacking formal coherence.

NATIONAL COMMUNICATION POLICIES IN LATIN AMERICA

In Latin America, as elsewhere, state intervention in national affairs has increased overall. The modern capitalist state plays an even larger role in society as a whole. Political liberalism, along with economic liberalism based on the principle of nonintervention in the marketplace, is dead. The state interferes increasingly in the economy while widening techno-bureaucratic control over the civil society.

In Latin America this process of capitalist state intervention has produced authoritarian (mostly military) governments that have centralized decisionmaking. Consequently, many segments of civil society are excluded from participation in public affairs. The illegitimacy of these governments leads them to champion national security—which means that all sectors of society are suspect and must be strictly controlled to prevent political subversion. In these circumstances development goals take a back seat to law and order.[3]

In the interests of national security, then, virtually all sectors of society and spheres of activity are manipulated and regulated. National communication policies, whether explicitly incorporated into cultural and educational programs or informally pursued, have helped consolidate authoritarian governments in Latin America. Communication policies in these states exhibit two principal tendencies.

First, the government controls the creation, distribution, and operation of mass media, as well as the flow of messages. This control takes many forms—station licensing, broadcasting regulations, and censorship. Legislation tends to be vague in order to permit broad interpretation. Thus, the government can seize a newspaper or a radio station, claiming it offends public morality or encourages political subversion. This type of control seeks to depoliticize and demobilize society.

Second, the government widely circulates official messages in order to mobilize the population toward state ends and to legitimize itself. During elections, government media campaigns and civic appeals increase markedly.

In sum, national communication policies have not produced the desired democratization of communications in Latin America. On the contrary, policy has been translated into planning and planning has meant state intervention, characterized by centralization of communication decisionmaking, tight regulation of the media, and the use of communication media and messages to legitimize authoritarian governments.

A GRASS-ROOTS ALTERNATIVE TO A NATIONAL COMMUNICATION STRUCTURE

Is there an alternative to national communication policies? Unfortunately, creative answers are elusive and it is risky to propose general solutions for a complex problem, particularly because historical conditions change continually. A model of communications produced in a given context of social development is not applicable everywhere. Both communication and development models must be conceived dynamically in response to specific historical conditions and possibilities, including social relations, cultural aspirations, and material and technological resources. Nevertheless, some guidelines that can be translated into practical action are offered here.

What is needed are alternative media and alternative messages that decentralize and deinstitutionalize communications, thereby democratizing information flow. This process depends on the dissemination of small and medium-size media through popular organization on the local level. Such media help people interact with each other and communicate directly. Broadened access to and participation in communications implies the transfer of decisionmaking from the national to the community level. At the community level

> the real interactive, participatory communication process takes place as a small group of people work together in direct contact on various problems, discuss them, find solutions and pass decisions, and where they exchange views on general problems of the country and the world. What is specially important about this form of communication is that those smaller units have their own media by which they can express themselves and also impart information (their own newspapers, local radio and TV centers, bulletins, brochures, films, exhibitions, etc.). Those smaller units are small enough to be able to preserve the individual role of their members and they are big [social] enough to have official status and financial means to realize the right to co-create and impart information of their members (6, p. 8).

Of course, decentralization cannot take place in communications alone. To achieve horizontal communications, decisionmaking must be democratized in all spheres of society. Development must be

> geared to the satisfaction of needs, beginning with the basic needs of the poor, who constitute the world's majority: at the same time, development [must]

ensure the humanization of man by the satisfaction of his needs for expression, creativity, conviviality, and for deciding his own destiny. . . . Another development requires transformation of socio-economic and political structures [including] such fundamental steps as agrarian reforms, urban reforms, of the commercial and financial circuits, redistribution of wealth and means of production as well as the redesigning of political institutions through, inter alia, decentralization with a view to ensuring democratization of the political and economic decision-making power, promoting self-management and curbing the grip of bureaucracies (11).

Another stimulating form of alternative development is proposed by Johan Galtung. He argues that development has been treated as a way to increase material consumption, thereby causing overconsumption. This pattern of *overdevelopment* vis-à-vis material needs implies "underdevelopment where non-material needs are concerned" (4, p. 9). According to Galtung, alternative lifestyles constitute an effort to reduce material consumption and increase non-material consumption, thus achieving a better balance. The decline in interest in big society goes hand in hand with more leisure time and more togetherness.

In this alternative concept of development, communication media and messages are instruments to bring people together. Communications can promote awareness, a sense of community, and active involvement of citizens. Active participation requires that people have something to say—and this goal is furthered by public dialogue, which encourages social involvement and collective identification of social needs. Public discussion and criticism discourage alienation and direct people toward social subjects, insuring their conscious participation in local decisionmaking. In this process of conscientization, authoritarian mass media have no place.

Both small modern media and traditional media do have dynamic roles in such a development model. Public meetings, workplace discussions, and other socialization contexts are valuable sources of communication. Low cost electronic media must also be developed and their uses diversified. Such media

belong to the community and not to individuals, state or private/public industry. . . . There is no threat of cultural colonialism and foreign domination. Also, local talent and localised messages would have more credibility than those centralised ones emanating now from state capitals. . . . Folk media are egalitarian. They may prove a better outlet for egalitarian messages than the present elite press, film or radio-TV. There is a commonality about them. Acceptability, cultural relevance, entertainment value, localised language, legitimacy, flexibility, message repetitionalibility, instant two-way communication, etc., are among their virtues (3).

Emphasis on small media does not preclude changing present-day mass media, too. Increased public participation and decentralization are desirable goals. There are many ways to expand participation.

First, professional communicators need to examine thoroughly the prevailing concepts of news. This concept may be functional for the communication system as well as the social system overall or it may serve commercial ends alone. Insight into what constitutes news can illuminate the entire mass communication process, revealing whether news is treated as a commodity or a social service, a public right or a private privilege, and uncovering the criteria that determine the selection of certain information as news and the reliance on particular sources.

Second, all communication media—newspapers, radio, and television—should be co-owned by those who participate in the process of media production. This form of collective ownership allows communicators to acquire material and intellectual control over media messages and gives them access to decisionmaking. This development sets the stage for eventual community ownership of the mass media.

Third, mass media audiences must organize themselves. The organization of newspaper readers and radio audiences into pressure groups to discourage vertical mass media structures depends on individual awareness of the consumer's place in the present communication flow. Workers' unions, women's clubs, community associations, and other organizations can critically evaluate communication content, function, and access, encouraging selectivity in program choice, participation in political decisions about communications, and production of alternative messages, for example.

CONCLUSION

Though the position taken in this chapter may be utopian, it demonstrates how far we have moved from personal, interactive communication in favor of institutionalized, mass mediated information flows, inaccessible to the majority of the people. This chapter calls for cooperative social organization and participatory communications, rejecting national communication policies, which have produced centralization. Centralization has excluded people from decision making, just as vaguely articulated national security appeals have helped consolidate authoritarian regimes.

Freedom and democracy cannot be secured by law. Only effective community organization can achieve and protect these goals. If we are to realize a New International Information Order we must first establish a new community economic and communications order.

NOTES

1. Dozens of studies could be cited. Latin America, to take one Third World region, has been studied by Juan Somavia and Fernando Reyes Matta at ILET in

Mexico City (international communication and information agencies), Armand Mattelart in Chile (cultural and technological dependency) and Claudio Aguirre Bianchi at the Institute of Latin American Studies in Stockholm (international information order and communication alternatives).

2. The MacBride Report insists that communication policies (a) serve to marshall national resources; (b) strengthen the coordination of existing or planned infrastructures; (c) facilitate rational choices with regard to means; (d) help to satisfy the needs of the most disadvantaged and to eliminate the most flagrant imbalances; (e) enable all countries and all cultures to play more of a leading role on the international scene. The political option of elaborating communication models must be considered a reasonable and rational course to take (see 8, pages 355–356).

3. For an account of the ideology and practices of national security advocates see (2). On the importance of information to this doctrine see (5).

REFERENCES

1. Beltrán, L. R. Paper prepared for Experts' Meeting on Communication Planning and Policies in Latin America. UNESCO, Bogotá, January 1974.

2. Comblin, Joseph. *A Ideología da Seguranca Nacional.* Rio de Janeiro: Civilizacaõ Brasileira, 1978.

3. Eapen, K. E. "Specific Problems of Research and Research Training in Asian/African Countries." In *Communication Research in the Third World: The Need for Training.* Geneva: Lutheran World Foundation, 1976.

4. Galtung, Johan. "Overdevelopment and Alternative Ways of Life." Paper prepared for the Second Alternative Ways of Life Conference, Palermo, April 1979.

5. Mattelart, Armand. *Communicación e Ideología de la Seguridad.* Barcelona: Editorial Anagrama, 1978.

6. Pasteka, Jadwiga. "Right to Communicate: A Socialist Approach." Paris: UNESCO, 1979.

7. UNESCO. Final Report, Intergovernmental Conference on Communication Policies in Latin America and the Caribbean. San José, Costa Rica, July 1976.

8. UNESCO. *Un Solo Mundo, Voces Multiples* (MacBride Report). Mexico City: Fondo de Cultura, 1980.

9. UNESCO. Provisional Report on Communication Problems in Contemporary Society, International Commission for the Study of Communication Problems, Paris 1978.

10. UNESCO. Report of Communication Experts Meeting on Communication Policies and Planning. Paris: UNESCO, July, 1972.

11. "What Now? Another Development." Uppsala: Dag Hammarskjold Foundation, 1975.

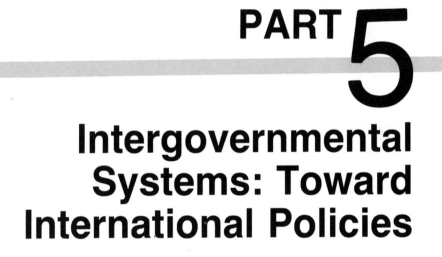

PART 5

Intergovernmental Systems: Toward International Policies

Forty-Four

International Communications Agencies: An Overview

Syed A. Rahim

The role of international communications organizations has come under increased public scrutiny in recent years, largely because of Western press coverage of several dramatic issues. They include free and balanced flow of information, equitable access to communication resources, prior consent for direct satellite broadcasting, remote sensing by satellites, protection of privacy in transborder data flow, transfer of appropriate communications technology, communications development in Third World countries, the cultural impact of such development, and the roles and responsibilities, of governments, transnational communication enterprises, and professional communicators (see 1, 3). These critical issues have been gradually unfolding against a backdrop of changes in the political, economic, and technological environment.

The developing countries took the initiative in bringing some of these issues to the international forums, particularly in reference to their call for a New World Information Order. They raised the basic political questions of inequality, unbalanced distribution of resources, infringement on national sovereignty, and persistence of dependency in an increasingly interdependent world. They used the most accessible and responsive international organizations—UNESCO and the International Telecommunication Union (ITU)—in making their voices heard by the international community. However, the debates and their implications should not be seen as just a confrontation between the developing and the developed countries. Within the developed countries both the public and the private sector are seriously discussing the implications of communications technology innovation and the need for regulatory and institutional reform (see 2, 4), as is evident from the proliferation of study commissions, congressional hearings, professional conferences, and long-range planning efforts at the national level. Indeed, all countries have a stake in formulating long-range development policies for better national and international communication systems.

COMMUNICATION POLICY AND UNESCO

The declarations and resolutions adopted in UNESCO and other international forums attempt to state internationally accepted fundamental principles governing the role, organization, and responsibility of communication systems in promoting peace, understanding, equality, and development. They also emphasize the need for organizing cooperative activities to assist in the implementation of these fundamental principles at the national and the international level, stressing the urgency of communications development in Third World countries.

Since 1948 communication issues have been discussed and resolutions adopted in the United Nations, UNESCO, and ITU. The intensity of activities in the communications arena increased sharply in the 1970s. A resolution adopted in the sixteenth UNESCO general conference in 1970 affirmed the "inadmissibility of using information media for propaganda on behalf of war, racialism, and hatred among nations." Member states were invited to take necessary action, including legislative measures, and the director-general of UNESCO was asked to assist national efforts to formulate communication policies.

In 1972 the seventeenth UNESCO general conference resolved to prepare "a draft declaration concerning the fundamental principles governing the use of the mass information media." Accordingly, a draft declaration was prepared and presented to the eighteenth general conference (1974), which discussed the proposal and then called for further study and revision. The same conference also considered other resolutions concerned with "a new information order, and the development of communication capabilities of the Third World to remove information imbalance."

The debate over mass communications reached a climax in the 1976 UNESCO general conference in Nairobi, when the Western nations vigorously opposed certain provisions in the draft declaration that implied government control over the mass media. In a tactical move the conference decided to submit the draft declaration for further negotiation and revision. UNESCO was asked to organize a comprehensive study of communication problems, which led to the formation of the MacBride Commission.

Finally, agreement on the declaration was reached in the Paris general conference, November 1978, after intense diplomatic negotiations and removal from the draft of all references to government control of the media. The Mass Media Declaration was adopted by acclamation. In a follow-up resolution the United Nations General Assembly requested that the UNESCO director-general draw up a model general plan for "cooperation and assistance in the application and improvement of national information and mass communication systems for social progress and development." The General Assembly also endorsed the need for a new, more just, and more effective world information order, based on free flow and better balance of information, for promoting international peace and understanding.

The international community thus seems to agree that the mass media have a leading role to play in promoting a fair and wide distribution of information on the goals, aspirations, and needs of all nations and cultural groups, particularly those oppressed peoples who are struggling against imperialism, neocolonialism, and racism. A new information order is necessary to insure individual, group, and national access to diverse sources of information. The media should promote understanding and solution of problems arising from prejudice, sexism, poverty, malnutrition, and disease; the mass media can also facilitate national policy formulation for the reduction of international tensions and peaceful settlement of international disputes. In order to perform this vital role the mass media need both access to information and freedom to report. Accordingly, states must protect media professionals and create favorable conditions for the operation of the mass media in conformity with internationally accepted principles.

THE 1979 WORLD ADMINISTRATIVE RADIO CONFERENCE

Another set of issues debated in the world communication forums concerns the exploitation, allocation, registration, and utilization of telecommunication resources. The main intergovernmental forum for these questions is the International Telecommunication Union (ITU). The World Administrative Radio Conference (WARC), convened by ITU in September 1979 and attended by two thousand delegates from 142 countries, adopted many resolutions, revised radio regulations, and discussed plans for the allocation, use, and registration of radio frequencies and the geostationary orbit. The radio regulations adopted by WARC-79 came into force on January 1, 1982.

ITU's traditional "first-come, first-served" principle was challenged by the developing countries. A related issue is the demand for a priori assignment of radio frequencies and the geostationary satellite orbit for future use by countries that presently lack the capacity to exploit these resources. Another important policy area concerns the rights of national governments in knowing about and/or regulating direct satellite broadcasts, the transfer of computerized data, and satellite remote sensing across national borders.

Because of the technical nature of its activities, ITU has avoided making general policy statements on these issues, but some change in ITU policy in favor of the new demands is evident. The 1979 WARC resolution on the planning and use of the geostationary orbit accepted the need for equitable access of all countries to the spectrum and orbital resources. The conference also agreed that the utilization of these resources by different countries "can take place at various points in time, based on their requirement and the availability of the resources at their disposal." The resolution (No. BP) called for a special WARC to be convened by 1984 to discuss how to provide all countries with equitable access to the geostationary orbit and the space services utilizing it (see 6). Another WARC resolution (No. DI) allocated 60 percent more spectrum for high frequency broadcasting and called for a special WARC to establish the allocation and utilization principles that would guarantee all countries a free and equal right to use high frequency bands. This special WARC will also revise the radio regulations in accordance with the principles it enunciates.

The 1979 WARC did not settle the controversial issues of access to and equitable allocation of the high frequency spectrum and the geostationary orbit. The conference accepted the general principles of equitable distribution and efficient use of these resources but left the critical tasks of planning and policy formulation to the special WARCs. Undoubtedly, difficult debates will dominate these upcoming conferences.

INTERNATIONAL PLANS AND PROGRAMS

The culture and communication sector of UNESCO is responsible for communication plans and programs, and only two out of ten units in this sector are concerned directly with mass communications. These are the Division of Free Flow of Information and Communication Policies and the Division of Development of Communication Systems. UNESCO's total budget, including outside contributions, was $481 million for 1979–1980; of this amount only $44 million, or less than 10 percent, was allotted to the culture and communication sector. The budget for programs that are directly involved with realizing some of the communications objectives is only $10.6 million, or about 2 percent of the total UNESCO budget.

The communication programs seek to promote a free and balanced flow of information, international exchanges, appreciation of the process and role of communications in society, high professional standards, policies, infrastructure, and training in the field of communications, and the use of the media for social ends. Planned activities include cooperative research on the flow of information and the role and impact of transnational communication industries, the study of national communication policymaking and planning, along with the development and testing of communication planning methods, and worldwide interchange of research findings on these problems. The problem-oriented research and action projects will focus on cooperative arrangements for the exchange of news and other broadcasting material, improvement and expansion of communication training institutions, transfer of communication technology and establishment of more effective communication infrastructures in developing countries, and improvement of professional standards and codes.

In contrast to the situation in UNESCO, ITU's financial and well-organized technical resources are available exclusively for policy formulation and planning of telecommunication systems. The organizational structure and operational methods of ITU facilitate serious examination of technical problems and international participation of telecommunication experts. However, the developing countries face considerable difficulty in contributing to ITU's technical task because they lack experts and experience in the high technology of communications.

A major function of ITU is to prepare world and regional telecommunication plans. The planning function consists basically of forecasting demands and supplies, studying technical problems, and coordinating national plans. Allocation of radio frequencies is another planning function. The 1979 general WARC authorized ITU to convene special WARCs on mobile services, planning high frequency allocations, and the use of the geostationary satellite orbit and the planning of space services utilizing it. ITU's planning activities during the eighties are concentrated in these areas.

THE MacBRIDE REPORT

Following the Nairobi conference the director-general of UNESCO constituted an international commission to study the *problematique* of communications in a global context and to make recommendations for practical action. The sixteen-member MacBride Commission included a select group of communication scholars and professionals from the United States, Canada, Ireland, France, Belgium, the Netherlands, the Soviet Union, Yugoslavia, Japan, Zaire, Nigeria, Tunisia, Egypt, Indonesia, India, Chile, and Colombia; the commission also received input from many other communication agencies and individual scholars and professionals. The MacBride Commission submitted its interim report in 1978 and the final report in 1980.

The commission's conclusions and recommendations were generally consistent with earlier resolutions and the main direction of UNESCO's programs on communications. The report made a strong case for treating communications as a crucial societal resource and, therefore, incorporating it into overall development policymaking and planning processes at the national and international levels. The various recommendations in this area clearly implied that national planning should aim at greater independence and self-reliance by paying more attention to communication policy formulation and resource allocation. Similarly, the international development assistance program for communications should be expanded and better coordinated across nations. All communication planning process should be participatory, involving all the constituencies affected by communications development. Special efforts should be made to meet the particular challenges of the worldwide shortage of paper, high tariffs obstructing the flow of information, and equitable sharing of the electromagnetic spectrum and the geostationary orbit.

The commission also called for reducing commercialism in communications and increasing access to scientific and technical information. A substantial part of the commission's recommendations dealt with sensitive matters—the democratization of communications and the integrity, responsibility, and protection of journalists. The report emphasized the media's role in promoting oppressed peoples' struggles for freedom, independence, access to information, and right of expression and reinforced these basic values. The clarity and directness of these recommendations reflected consensus among the commission members.

Looking at UNESCO's role, the commission recommended that a "distinct communication sector" be organized and that member countries increase their support of UNESCO's communication programs. Another recommendation concerned the establishment of an international center for the study and planning of information and communications. Overall the report envisaged an increasingly active and expanded role for UNESCO in the implementation of the new communications and information order.

Finally, the MacBride Commission suggested that more studies be carried out to identify specific means for the mobilization of additional financial resources for communications development. Possible sources included surplus profit on raw materials, an international duty on the use of the radio spectrum and the geostationary orbit, and an international tax on the profits of transnational communication enterprises. These bold suggestions did not generate much enthusiasm among either government-operated or private industrial and business concerns, particularly in the West.

IMPLICATIONS FOR POLICY

The world's nation-states, particularly the developing countries and the smaller developed countries, have used UNESCO and ITU forums to articulate their concerns and formulate policies for a more equitable and just international communications system. The rhetoric of political debates has dramatized the issues and shaken the complacency of the established order, and a better climate of understanding and willingness to cooperate is emerging from the storm of the 1970s.

But this does not mean that a New International Information Order is around the corner. There are many contradictions in the present situation, some of which may take years to resolve. The MacBride Commission report and the 1979 WARC proposals posed new issues for another series of debates in UNESCO and ITU in the 1980s. However, this time the issues will be more specific and the participants are likely to have done their homework before coming to the forums because of the heightened level of consciousness about communication problems and their ramifications.

Communications scholars, policymakers, and practitioners seem to agree that national and international communication policies and programs are a priority of the highest order. According to one view gaining popularity, bilateral and international aid programs for transferring technology, building communication infrastructures, and training personnel in the developing countries will automatically bring about the new order envisioned by the Third World. To this claim one need only point out that similar prescriptions for economic development have not worked well in reducing national and international economic inequality and imbalance. After two decades of development efforts, the results are so disappointing that the developmentalists are now talking about a new paradigm of development based on the concepts of equality, participation, self-reliance, appropriate technology transfer, and integration of traditional and modern systems (see 5).

The rich developing countries are investing substantial capital in modernizing their communication systems, but they are nowhere near the goals of the New World Information Order. The poor Third World countries are unable to make large capital investments in modern communication infrastructure, and the possibility of mobilizing sufficient international aid seems remote. Even if such assistance were forthcoming, however, a more equitable communication order would not follow automatically. The assumption that the new order is a function solely of technical capability for communications has not yet been tested, but some Western nations with highly modern communication systems are as concerned as the developing nations about an unbalanced flow of information to and from their countries. The real problems are very complex; some of them derive from the existing communications order, dominated by a few developed countries.

Intensive development efforts will not eliminate the technology gap between the developed and the developing countries, but this gap is not the central problem; rather, the gap lies in the absence of an institutional arrangement to incorporate diverse technological communication capabilities into a more equitable and just system of world communications. The new communications order will begin to develop when the high and low technological communication systems around the world are integrated around the goals for which the new order stands. Technological development should take place in that framework, and for this reason international organizations like UNESCO and ITU have a vital role to play in promoting a new order based on democratic values.

A major consequence of debates held and decisions made in the 1970s is that the responsibility and legitimacy of UNESCO and ITU as the leading international institutions promoting communications development have been enlarged and reinforced; the director-general of UNESCO called this a landmark in the history of that body. However, UNESCO's communication sector presently lacks the organization, staff, budget, programs, and operational strategy to meet the challenges of the eighties. The MacBride Commission made a few recommendations on this point and UNESCO is expected to begin working on its own reorganization.

Another matter of great importance is better collaboration between UNESCO and ITU. The complementary nature of their work requires close cooperation—noticeably absent in the past—in designing communication programs.

Better research on the socioeconomic and institutional problems of communication systems, and rigorous application of this knowledge in policymaking, will greatly benefit future communication programs. The research record of UNESCO and ITU is not satisfactory; and studies initiated or supported by them have not produced a coherent body of knowledge that can be utilized in planning new order programs. Moreover, the academic communication research institutions in the West and in the Third World have contributed very little to help these organizations (indeed, both the quantity and the quality of policy-oriented research done by the developing countries on their own communication problems are insignificant). While the immediate program planning for the new order cannot be delayed until better research results are available, UNESCO and ITU must identify long-range research needs, secure more research funds, involve independent study organizations in problem-oriented projects, and promote research in the Third World, if the communication needs that have been identified are to be met.

REFERENCES

1. Gunter, J. F. et al. "The United States and the Debate on the World Information Order." Washington, D.C.: Academy for Educational Development, Inc., 1979.

2. Homet, Roland S., Jr. *Politics, Cultures and Communication*. New York: Praeger, 1979.

3. Masmoudi, Mustapha. "The New World Information Order." *Journal of Communication* 29(2), Spring 1979, pp. 172–185.

4. Robinson, Glen O. (Ed.) *Communication for Tomorrow: Policy Perspectives for the 1980s*. New York: Praeger, 1978.

5. Rogers, Everett M. "Communication and Development: The Passing of the Dominant Paradigm." *Communication Research* 3(2), April 1976, pp. 213–240.

6. U.S. Department of State. "World Administrative Radio Conference: Summary Report No. 9." Washington, D.C., 1979.

Forty-Five

INTELSAT: An International Satellite System[1]

Marcellus S. Snow

The response of the nations of the world to technologies having commercial, political, or military potential has been characterized by competition rather than cooperation. Later imposition of international agreements or organizations has served to codify or attenuate that competition to mutual advantage rather than to eliminate it. This article is an attempt to understand and to evaluate the international institutional matrix that arose after a particular telecommunications technology, that of communications satellites, attained technical realization and commercial promise about twenty years ago. Particular attention will be focused on the International Telecommunications Satellite Organization (INTELSAT), an international organization formed in 1964 along commercial operating lines to provide international public telecommunications by satellite.

As is often the case with new technologies of strategic importance, military development came first in the satellite field. At this early stage, of course, the "technology" in question was primarily that of launch vehicles to place what were originally small and rudimentary communications devices into highly elliptical orbits. The early development of rocketry capable of placing increasingly massive, sophisticated, and high-capacity satellites into synchronous orbit made the commercial promise of satellites more immediate. Anticipating their commercial usage between the United States and points abroad, the U.S. Congress in 1962 chartered the Communications Satellite Corporation (COMSAT) (9).

COMSAT was set up as a private corporation and awarded a monopoly in conducting international commercial public telecommunication by satellite for American users. Congressional factions favored a body of a wholly public or wholly private nature; the hybrid corporation that emerged was a political compromise. COMSAT's shares were originally owned half by the major U.S. overseas communications carriers and half by the public at large.

In the period immediately following the formation of COMSAT, only the United States and the Soviet Union had the technological wherewithal to design, and particularly to launch, communications satellite systems into synchronous orbit. Yet for political reasons, these two countries did not communicate commercially by satellite. It is not surprising, therefore, that the United States took the initiative in laying the institutional groundwork for an organization to provide commercial public telecommunications by satellite between the United States and other countries. Fortunately, the Early Bird satellite and a number of earth stations on both sides of the Atlantic had already been used experimentally and could now evolve into commercial operations. Thus the signing, in August 1964, by a number of countries of the INTELSAT Interim and Special Agreements (10) established by multilateral treaty an international organization (which did not assume the name INTELSAT until sometime later) whose purpose was to conduct international commercial public communications by satellites among its members. Commercial operation began across the Atlantic in 1965, and followed in the Pacific region in 1967. Service across the Indian Ocean in 1969 made the system a global one.

Many nations felt that the interim or initial INTELSAT treaties were one-sided in favor of the United States, which held most of the technology at the time. Thus, provision was made for the renegotiation of INTELSAT's treaties at such time as the developed nations in Europe and elsewhere had reached more of a technological balance, and when the distribution of traffic was not so heavily skewed toward the United States. INTELSAT's definitive or permanent agreements (11) were negotiated at a large international conference held at Washington, D.C. from 1969 to 1971. They entered into force in 1973.

ORGANIZATION AND REGULATION OF INTELSAT

Legally, the 1965 and 1971 general agreements were concluded among the governments of those nations acceding and dealt with general principles and policies underlying INTELSAT. The operating agreement of 1965 and the special agreement of 1971 were signed by operating entities designated by the governments which were parties to the respective general agreements. The 1965 interim agreements provided for major policy decisions regarding INTELSAT's operation to be taken by an Interim Communications Satellite Committee (ICSC), composed of members and groups of members comprising more than 1.5 percent of INTELSAT's traffic. Voting was on the basis of investment shares, and in the early years the share of COMSAT, designated as the U.S. operating entity, was upwards of 50 percent, although it has declined gradually to between 20 and 30 percent in recent years. The ICSC had advisory subcommittees on financial, technical, and contracting matters to provide specialized input, and met six times a year, generally at INTELSAT headquarters in Washington, D.C., to transact business. COMSAT, during the interim regime, was Manager of the INTELSAT system, meaning that COMSAT personnel were loaned to INTELSAT on a cost-reimbursable basis to handle the day-to-day financial, technical, legal, secretariat, and other functions necessary for the operation of INTELSAT.

In essence, INTELSAT regulates itself. This is at substantial variance with the norm in the United States, where public regulatory commissions generally regulate private firms entrusted with public utility monopolies, or in many other countries, where operating government entities such as post and telegraph ministries directly implement policies determined by legislative or administrative action. While other international organizations composed of representatives of sovereign governments must also govern themselves according to some kind of multilateral treaty or other agreement, INTELSAT was until recently the only such organization that involves the operation of an enterprise along commercial lines, a fact which makes its financial principles of particular interest. INMARSAT, the global maritime satellite consortium, is now operating along commercial lines patterned consciously after those of INTELSAT.

Economically, INTELSAT is a cooperative of owners and users.[2] That is, each member has a dual personality—as an investor or part owner, it provides funds for the capital and operating expenses of INTELSAT and receives a return or interest on its net investment; as a user of the system, it pays a fee for its usage based on the basic "unit of utilization," which is a one-year lease of a telephone-grade half-circuit. Thus, the basic financial parameters of INTELSAT are the rate of return it pays its members as investors, and the usage fee it charges its members as users. It should be noted here that the rate of return has been and continues to be set at a level of 14 percent per annum on net investment, as a reasonable return reflecting risk (although perhaps not international inflation in recent years). Furthermore, the usage fee for the annual lease of one unit of utilization is required to be set at a level that recovers operating and investment costs, depreciation, and return on capital. This means that INTELSAT's basic tariff is cost-based.

It might appear that INTELSAT's members have a conflict of interest in their roles as owners and users of the system. That is, as owners (investors), they favor the highest possible return on their investment, which can only come, ceteris paribus, from higher usage fees. Higher fees, in turn, would be against their interest as users. It turns out, however, that when ownership and usage shares are exactly equal, so are the INTELSAT members' incentives as owners and users; at that point, the level of the return on investment and usage fee become superfluous, since the one exactly repays or counter-balances the other.

During the interim regime, there was not sufficient provision for the periodic realignment of investment quotas with recent past usage shares, and serious imbalances did in fact occur. Net users of the system, whose actual usage shares came to exceed the investment quotas originally assigned on the basis of anticipated usage, fought in INTELSAT for a low rate of return, which meant a low usage charge. Net owners, including many with little or no system usage due to slippages in operational dates of their earth stations, favored a high rate of return, which meant a high usage charge. Both groups, however, had an incentive to favor low operating and capital outlays. To correct these imbalances, the definitive arrangements of 1971 provide for periodic realignment of investment quotas to reflect recent past utilization shares, so that investment and use are always approximately in balance. The level of rate of return, however, continues to be of significance to users of the system who are not INTELSAT members and therefore have a zero investment share. This group includes a number of Eastern European countries and others.

It should be noted that the 14 percent rate of return was not captured in INTELSAT's early years of operation, but that such a cumulative rate was first attained by INTELSAT members by 1969 and has been maintained since then. In addition, the lease charge for one unit of utilization, initially at a level of $32,000 per year, is now near $6,000 per year and is still declining.

A salient technical feature of a satellite is its ability to provide service to multiple destinations—in other words, its broadcast potential—at a high level of economic efficiency. Numerous cost studies (see, e.g., 7) have shown that satellites exhibit strong economies of scale. In addition to static economies, technological progress has contributed to dynamic economies—the per-unit cost at *each* level of output is also declining with time as new generations of INTELSAT satellites incorporate bandwidth-saving and other techniques such as speech interpolation, spectrum polarization, and so forth (see 7). These economies are the basis of the fundamental argument in favor of monopoly provision of satellite services—one large system can offer circuits more cheaply than several small ones. The monopoly argument is weakened to the extent that satellite services are considered as heterogeneous and incommensurable (e.g., television, data, broadband, facsimile, basic telephone service) instead of as homogeneous and derivative from the basic telephone service.

POLICY ISSUES IN SATELLITE COMMUNICATIONS

One persistent source of difficulties in the international telecommunications arena has been differing national policies and practices regarding ownership, control, and regulation of telecommunications entities. COMSAT, while unique in its own right, bears many features similar to large national public utilities in the United States. Thrust into negotiations with foreign entities and government agencies, however, COMSAT had difficulty finding compatible opposite numbers.[3] More generally, the wide range of organizations designated as representative government entities in INTELSAT under the operating and special agreements has caused difficulties. Some are post and telecommunications ministries in countries which use relatively lucrative overseas traffic revenues to subsidize modernization of domestic facilities; others are public or private corporations with shareholders and are consequently under pressure to maximize their return on capital. Still others are divisions of foreign ministries and see INTELSAT's activities primarily in terms of international politics, development, technological advancement, and so on. These differences in the objectives of the designated government entities for the various national members of INTELSAT can in turn be traced to the differences in the ways in which international telecommunications are organized and controlled on the national level. The U.S. situation illustrates how the national institutional structure has affected U.S. relations to INTELSAT.

The two domestic developments in the U.S. that have had substantial import for INTELSAT are the evolution of U.S. domestic satellite systems and the current deregulatory, pro-competitive attitude of the U.S. public and of federal regulatory agencies, in particular the Federal Communications Commission (FCC). Applications to the FCC for authority to establish domestic satellite systems (see 2, 5) were made as early as 1965, and the increasing backlog of applications before the FCC by the end of the 1960s made a national policy highly desirable. A White House memorandum to the FCC (13) in 1970 stated the government's policy to be one of cautious evolution, with the primary initiative and system ownership coming from private corporations rather than from the federal government. The economies-of-scale argument favoring a single monopoly was found not to be compelling, given the many uncertainties involved and the diversity of needs to be satisfied by domestic satellite systems. This basically pro-competitive attitude was at variance both with the approaches that had been taken in the two then-existing satellite systems in the Soviet Union and Canada (see 1), and with the conclusions of the Task Force on Communication Policy (12), submitted to the outgoing Johnson administration in December 1968 and something of a dead letter after the change in administration a month later. A new round of applications in the early 1970s was followed by the first operational system in 1974. Several more are planned or are operating (see 3, pp. 29–30).

A second U.S. trend with a good deal of international spill-over, although one difficult to isolate in the context of INTELSAT, is the present mood in favor of deregulation, competition, and efficiency in many industries that for years had been strictly regulated. This has been most dramatically manifest in a number of administrative actions by the Civil Aeronautics Board, which has greatly increased the U.S. airlines' power to set rates and to determine routes without lengthy adversary proceedings before the CAB. In the communications area, the FCC, as noted above, has encouraged competitive entry into the domestic satellite arena for more than a decade. It has shown a much more cost-conscious and pro-competitive approach to the allocation and regulation of international tele-communications facilities, particularly across the Atlantic. Most of the FCC's recent analysis using cost-based criteria has been in favor of satel-lites and against undersea cables. A major outcome was the FCC's decision (subsequently reversed) not to allow construction of the projected TAT-7 Atlantic cable, a project heavily favored by European administrators and by major American power groups as well, notably the military and the international communications carriers. The TAT-7 uproar, and the inter-national facilities planning strains more generally during the past several years, illustrate well the difficulties involved in international telecom-munications when differences in structure and philosophy characterize the telecommunications administrations and governments dealing with each other.

In a December, 1979 statement summarizing a broad swath of pro-competitive decisions, FCC Chairman Charles Ferris said that U.S. com-munications users "should be able to choose among the greatest number of services at the lowest possible cost" and served notice on existing car-riers that "the easy and profitable life inside the cartel is over" (*Telephony*, December 24, 1979, p. 9). Although he added that the U.S. did not want to impose its views "of what was right on our foreign correspondents," it is difficult to conceive of a set of objectives and actions more at odds with the traditional PTT practice and attitude that characterize most of the FCC's "foreign correspondents." The ongoing divestiture and restructur-ing of A.T. & T. is further evidence of the seriousness with which deregula-tion and competition have been taken by U.S. regulatory authorities.

A similar mood of competition among communications systems and the differing objectives of those involved is reflected in the international communications environment by the growth of domestic and regional sat-ellite systems in competition, to some extent, with INTELSAT. Assuming that one large system is more economical than several small ones, the escalating proliferation of planned and operating regional and domestic satellite systems today may be said to derive from basically non-economic motives, indeed from motives that turn out to conflict with the criterion of cost minimization. Those motives certainly include national prestige, desire for complete control of one's own system, specialized needs, regional affinities, and so on. While these systems certainly serve legiti-mate functions in the countries and regions in which they operate, they are a direct threat to the existence of the INTELSAT system to the extent that they drain potential traffic away from it and therefore increase the unit cost of INTELSAT service to its remaining users (see 3, 8). Yet a subtler analysis is certainly required. Even in a country as large and as cost-conscious as the United States, little or no thought was given to massive or continued usage of INTELSAT facilities for domestic purposes, although a link from Hawaii to the U.S. mainland on INTELSAT satellites preceded today's domestic service for that route.

SPREAD OF DOMESTIC AND REGIONAL SYSTEMS

There is some irony in the role that INTELSAT itself played as a catalyst in promoting the emergence of domestic systems, namely by offering a concessionary transponder rate for domestic usage within the INTELSAT system. This allowed the world to observe the benefits of satellites for domestic commercial telecommunications, and perhaps more dramatically, for developmental and other non-commercial applications. In short, the genie is now out of the bottle.

A catalogue of such systems is helpful. The Soviet Union, Canada, the United States, and Indonesia (in that order) have acquired their own domestic systems apart from INTELSAT. Approximately twenty-three countries are leasing INTELSAT transponders at concessionary rates. Many other countries are actively considering their own separate domestic systems. A considerable amount of imaginative planning has gone on in Australia and Japan, two countries with needs well-suited to satellite systems, but the approach there, similar to that in the United States, is to allow commercial forces to dictate the conditions and timetable under which such systems evolve and become operational. Finally, regional systems are being planned or realized in Africa, the Andean region, the Arab countries, Europe, and the Nordic countries. Planning is particularly far advanced in the Arab and European countries. This listing is exclusive of all military, aeronautical, maritime, meteorological, and other specialized, scientific, and experimental systems.

The most important background to the current situation of INTELSAT is Article XIV of the present INTELSAT Agreement, which provides that public international (but not domestic) satellite systems established by INTELSAT members outside of the INTELSAT framework shall be such as to avoid "significant economic harm" to INTELSAT. This was perhaps the most difficult of many controversial provisions to occupy those who negotiated the permanent agreements during the two-year period from 1969 to 1971. Basically, the United States and most of the developing countries favored a stronger provision, one barring other systems that would cause any economic harm whatever, while the European and other industrialized countries wanted no restrictions on their rights to establish separate international and regional systems. The compromise, while it made no mention of domestic systems and required that the economic harm be "significant" before it was proscribed, was still basically a victory for those favoring safeguards against dissipation of INTELSAT traffic into uneconomical, premature, and politically motivated separate systems. Undoubtedly, American hegemony in synchronous rocketry exerted much of the influence leading to the ultimate outcome.

It is of interest to project the future course of the separate systems issue, because it is of such fundamental importance to the structure of public international telecommunications. Article XIV leaves wide latitude to the Board of Governors and the Assembly of Parties, which are charged with making and approving findings relating to the economic and technical effects of separate systems. It has been observed (8, p. 43) that Board of Governors members, as representatives in INTELSAT of their own national administrations, have dual loyalties[4] and therefore conflicts of interest, affecting both the welfare and integrity of INTELSAT and their own administrations' possible plans to pursue separate regional and domestic systems.

For a number of reasons, a steady increase in domestic and regional satellite systems appears inevitable, an increase to which INTELSAT will have to adapt and shows every sign of adapting. The international community is perhaps at a point not unlike the United States was when the White House memorandum of January 1970 was issued. As noted, that statement said, in effect, that while economies of scale were important, their presence did not constitute an argument sufficiently strong to justify granting monopoly powers to a single domestic system. The analogy here breaks down, however, when we observe that no such monopoly system or "domestic INTELSAT" was already functioning in the United States in 1970.

From a narrowly economic point of view, separate systems will harm not only INTELSAT but those countries opting to construct systems outside of INTELSAT, although whether such harm will be "significant" or not is an important empirical question yet to be investigated. The international community is not, however, sufficiently well-integrated to get by with a single international system. It had no choice but to do so during its early years, but advances in technology and decreases in satellite costs— brought about largely due to INTELSAT's extensive experience—have increased the options. In a perhaps comparable vein, one international currency or language would be more narrowly "economical" also, but national and regional differences are too great to permit such a radical change now or in the foreseeable future. Still, given that major decisions relating to INTELSAT have not taken place in a hothouse of dispassionate technological and economic analysis, but rather in the brutal arena of international politics, it has fared very well.

THE FUTURE OF INTELSAT

Even among those knowledgeable in international organizations, INTELSAT is not a household word, and it is even less familiar to most of the lay public. Yet its activities have had and will continue to have a profound effect on international telecommunications. Charged with a technical, operational, and commercial mission unprecedented among past international organizations, INTELSAT has consciously kept a low profile. For many years, its physical *pied-à-terre* consisted of one leased floor of the COMSAT building in Washington, D.C., and at one time its members complained that it had no entry in the Washington telephone directory. Since the permanent agreements entered into force, INTELSAT has acquired its own secretariat and other specialized staff instead of borrowing them from COMSAT; COMSAT's role as Manager and later as management services contractor for INTELSAT has lapsed; and INTELSAT has acquired its own headquarters. Above all, INTELSAT has obtained its relative absence from the public eye by avoiding political issues and other diversions from its statutory role. Even the withdrawal of Taiwan and the entry of the People's Republic of China into the organization were handled with as little rancor as one could expect.

Perhaps the efficiency of INTELSAT in achieving its objectives without excessive public exposure and notoriety has been aided by avoiding excursions into high diplomacy and politics. On many occasions, for example, it could have decided to give developmental assistance, free circuits, and so forth to various less developed countries within and outside of its membership. The commercial principles on which it is based, however—recall that both net owners and net users of the system share the common goal of cost minimization—prevented such an initiative.

This is not to say that INTELSAT is operating in a vacuum. Older organizations, such as UNESCO, the ITU, the United Nations itself, and various regional and specialized bodies have taken up a number of more controversial and less readily soluble topics than spot beam alignment, telegraph channel charging policy, and prime contractor selection. For example, United Nations committees have dealt with the issue of direct broadcast satellites; UNESCO has considered the effect of press and other information flow asymmetries in less-developed countries; the ITU has taken up the question of geosynchronous spectrum allocation; and so on. This specialization of labor has been a healthy one for INTELSAT, at least, by allowing it to carry out a more narrowly and technically defined mission more efficiently than would otherwise have been possible.

All this is not cavalierly to dismiss the legitimate concerns of the smaller members of INTELSAT. It was clear that under the interim regime, no effective forum existed for the expression of such concerns within INTELSAT, as the ICSC was composed only of relatively large users. Under the permanent agreements now in force, two newly created bodies, the Assembly of Parties and the Meeting of Signatories, are composed of all INTELSAT members (currently numbering over 100), operate on a one-person, one-vote basis, and are charged with the consideration and disposition of overall policy questions at their periodic meetings.

Although the effectiveness of INTELSAT in achieving goals of equity in the community of nations is a large and deserving question, it is clear, in terms of this analysis, that such goals have been secondary to INTELSAT's statutory goal of efficient provision, technologically and economically, of world-wide commercial satellite communications. There is consequently limited justification to expect that INTELSAT or international organizations modeled after it can achieve anything more than technical success or efficiency, although that in itself is a laudable and difficult objective. The even harder questions and challenges in the international communications policy arena, however, must be answered by efforts and qualities of the heart and mind that transcend the organizations that house them.

NOTES

1. A longer version of this paper was presented at the 1979 Advanced Summer Seminar on International Communication Policy and Organization, East-West Communication Institute, July 1979.
2. For a financial model of INTELSAT summarizing in mathematical language what follows, see (6, pp. 147–149).
3. Some foreign satellite and other operating entities do resemble COMSAT, since they are privately owned. KDD of Japan and particularly Telespazio of Italy are examples.
4. Indeed, an analogy with the early COMSAT board of directors on which members of cable-holding international carriers served who had an obligation to foster a new and competing technology is not too far-fetched.

REFERENCES

1. Drury, C. M. Minister of Industry, Canada. *White Paper on a Domestic Satellite Communication System for Canada.* March 28, 1968.
2. Nelson, Richard W. "Domestic Satellite Communications: Economic Issues in a Regulated Industry Undergoing Technical Change." In Joseph N. Pelton and Marcellus S. Snow (Eds.) *Economic and Policy Problems in Satellite Communications.* New York: Praeger, 1977.
3. Pelton, Joseph N. "Communication Satellite Proliferation: Will We Have Too Much of a Good Thing?" *Satellite Communications* 2(1), January 1978, pp. 22–30.
4. Pelton, Joseph N. and Marcellus S. Snow (Eds.) *Economic and Policy Problems in Satellite Communications.* New York: Praeger, 1977.
5. Snow, Marcellus S. "Intelsat and Domestic Satellite Systems in the United States and Abroad." *Proceedings of Fifth Annual Telecommunications Policy Research Conference* (1977). Springfield, Va.: National Technical Information Service.
6. Snow, Marcellus S. *International Commercial Satellite Communications: Economic and Political Issues of the First Decade of INTELSAT.* New York: Praeger, 1976.

7. Snow, Marcellus S. "Investment Cost Minimization for Communications Satellite Capacity: Refinement and Application of the Chenery-Manne-Srinivasan Model." *Bell Journal of Economics* 6(2), Autumn 1975, pp. 621–643.

8. Staminger, Reinhard."Intelsat vs. Regional Systems: Politics and Technology Determine the Outcome." *Satellite Communications* 2(5), May 1978, pp. 40–44.

9. U.S., Congress. *An Act to Provide for the Establishment, Ownership, and Regulation of a Commercial Communications Satellite System* (Communications Satellite Act). Public Law 87–264, 87th Congress, 2nd session, August 31, 1962.

10. U.S., Department of State. Treaties and Other International Acts Series 5646. *International Telecommunications Satellite Consortium. Agreement Between the United States of America and Other Governments, with Special Agreement and Supplementary Agreement on Arbitration.* Washington, D.C., August 20, 1964, and June 4, 1965 (interim agreements).

11. U.S., Department of State. Treaties and Other International Acts Series 7532. *International Telecommunications Satellite Organization (INTELSAT). Agreement Between the United States of America and Other Governments, and Operating Agreement, with Annex Concluded by Certain Governments, and Entities Designated by Governments.* Washington, D.C., August 20, 1971 (permanent agreements).

12. U.S., Office of the President. Task Force on Telecommunication Policy. *Final Report.* Washington, D.C., December 7, 1968.

13. U.S., Office of the White House. "Memorandum for the Honorable Dean Burch, Chairman of the Federal Communications Commission." Mimeo. Washington, D.C., January 23, 1970.

Forty-Six

INTELSAT and Initiatives for Third World Development

Joseph N. Pelton

The "North" and "South" countries of the world are separated by an enormous gap in communication capabilities: nine African countries and territories have no daily newspaper and twenty nations have no television; in Asia twelve countries have daily newspaper circulations of less than ten per thousand, while eight countries have no television; Japan alone has far more telephones in service than the 159 remaining nations and territories of Asia, Africa, and South and Central America. Nevertheless, the unique feature of the computer-communications revolution is that quantum leaps in economic and social development can be made once a basic infrastructure has been established.

Economic and communications development proceed hand in hand. Yet, communications generally has been neglected in economic development programs. The World Bank, the Inter-American Development Bank, and other financially related international organizations have given priority to energy, roads, dams, irrigation, factories, and similar needs. These agencies, as well as governments, have expected the telecommunication sectors of developing countries to attract funds from local or foreign sources. Thus, U.S. telecommunication multinationals in South and Central America, European telecommunication multinationals in Africa and Asia, and Japanese telecommunication multinationals in Asia have supplied the capital for such development, which has tended to focus on the wealthiest urban areas because rural areas cannot economically sustain the needed investment when commercial profit must be the investment criterion.

The views expressed in this chapter are those of the author and are not intended to reflect the official views of the International Telecommunications Satellite Organization (INTELSAT).

In the 1970s many developing countries began to look at communications development with interest and concern. They are now focusing on a matrix of key questions that are increasingly interrelated—technologically, socially, psychologically, and politically:

1. Who owns and controls telecommunication and broadcasting facilities and to what end?
2. Who controls the content of telecommunications and broadcasting (telephone, data networks, radio, television, electronic mail) and for what purposes?
3. How important is communications development to economic development?
4. Are new telecommunication and broadcasting technologies a means or an obstacle to the effective and widespread delivery of social services (education, health care, job training)?
5. What is the multiplier effect of investment in communications as opposed to investment in other sectors?
6. What communication technologies and services are appropriate in the urban and rural areas of various countries? Are these technologies and services available and, if so, from whom and at what cost?
7. What are the serious objectives and key priorities encompassed by the New World Information Order? Is the central goal low-cost, effective telecommunications? Control of content? Ownership of facilities? Preservation of future rights and options? Protection of local culture from outside influence?
8. Are existing national, regional, and international communication institutions and processes likely to produce desired results or are new approaches needed?

INTELSAT has a decisive role to play in working out solutions to the gamut of telecommunication problems faced by developing nations. A summary of INTELSAT services already available appears in Table 46.1.

INTELSAT now provides international public telecommunication services to some 170 political entities and similar domestic services to 24 countries. Besides expansion of these systems, maritime mobile service is expected soon. At the same time, advances in technology and economies of scale have enabled INTELSAT steadily to reduce charges (currently one-eighteenth of original levels when adjusted for inflation). Flexibility in leasing arrangements—choice of modulation technique, earth station size, and transmission plan—further enables developing countries to participate in this technology.

Faced with burgeoning international demand, INTELSAT is exploring new satellite services.[1] To provide for growing domestic requirements with a high degree of reliability and at reasonable cost, INTELSAT even-

Table 46.1   Available INTELSAT Services and Other Options

Sevices Allowable under the INTELSAT Agreement	INTELSAT Status	Other Options through Non-INTELSAT Systems
1. International Public Telecommunications Services (Fixed Satellite Services)(Article III(a))	Over 220 earth station antennas operational in over 150 countries and territories. Over 60 percent of the world's overseas international public telecommunications, including virtually all live TV transmissions.	Submarine cable systems, INTERSPUTNIK and, in future years, European Communications Satellite System, ARABSAT, etc.
2. International Public Telecommunications Services (Aeronautical and Maritime Mobile) (Article III(a) and Article I.K)	INTELSAT V (F-5 through F-8) satellites are equipped to provide maritime mobile service. This service is provided INMARSAT under long-term lease arrangements. Aeronautical services are under study but no firm requirements for this service have been identified by INTELSAT Signatories.	MARISAT through 1982; MARECS; LEASAT (military only); VOLNA (USSR).
3. Domestic Public Telecommunications Services (Telephone, Telex, Data, Television) (Article III(c) of the Agreement)	Operational in 24 countries, with nearly 300 domestic earth stations accessing INTELSAT satellites. Active planning for leased domestic service in 20 other countries. These services are currently over 10 percent of INTELSAT's total revenues.	Separate satellite systems such as Indonesia (PALAPA); India (INSAT); ARABSAT; Canada (TELESAT); Colombia (SATCOL); USSR and US Systems, etc.

Table 46.1   Continued.

4. Domestic Direct Broadcasting and Community Reception Specialized Services (Article III(d) of the INTELSAT Agreement)	Low-powered quasi DBS service in 14/11 GHz band being provided by INTELSAT to the United Kingdom. Service to other European countries may follow.	Separate satellite systems, as listed above, plus Germany (TV Sat), France (TDF), Japan (BS-2) and Sweden (Tele-X).
5. Domestic Telecommunications Services to Rural Areas (Article III(c) and (d) of the INTELSAT Agreement)	Tests and demonstrations of such services have been carried out with INTELSAT satellites in countries such as Norway, Saudi Arabia, Nigeria and Peru. Solar and battery powered 4.5 meter antennas need to be developed and optimized for such services to grow. Service could be provided now.	Separate satellite systems, such as listed above. France and the United Kingdom have proposed AFSAT system for Africa.
6. Separately Financed Space Segment Facilities Optimized To Meet Individual or Multi-client Requirements in a Single Country or for a Group of Countries (Article III(e) of the INTELSAT Agreement)	Several INTELSAT studies have been conducted to respond to needs of particular countries. Dedicated satellite systems have been considered by INTELSAT.	Hughes Aircraft's LEASAT Concept; European Spacecom Proposal.
7. Specialized International Satellite Services (Radio-navigation, Meteorology, Earth Resource Sensing, Direct Broadcasting) (Article III(d) of the INTELSAT Agreement)	INTELSAT is not now seriously studying this service. Would be reappraised if a Signatory or group of Signatories specifically requested such service.	Experimental projects only, primarily by ESA and NASA.

tually must make the transition from its current, largely preemptible, spare capacity domestic service to service on a planned basis with backup spare capacity. Such service inevitably would require somewhat higher charges but burgeoning customer demand dictates this shift.

Another area that INTELSAT recently has entered—the INTELSAT Assistance and Development Program—should pay dividends in the 1980s. This effort to provide technical, operational, and economic expertise includes assistance with earth station retrofit operations, particularly those associated with the implementation of new satellite technology; implementation of earth stations for both international and domestic services; assistance with site selection; and assistance with major earth station servicing requirements. Certain limited services are available free of charge, while other, more extensive services generally are provided on a cost-reimbursable basis.

A third area in which significant contributions to developing countries are expected during the 1980s is the introduction of new technologies and standards of service suited to the unique needs of the Third World. During the 1970s INTELSAT inaugurated a 10- to 11-meter Standard B earth station antenna that well serves countries with small volumes of international traffic. INTELSAT also introduced in the Atlantic Ocean region a demand access system known as SPADE that allows countries with small volumes of traffic to access other countries on a flexible, call-by-call basis. The 1980s should see new digitial communications techniques and innovative use of computers that should benefit countries at all levels of economic development. Finally INTELSAT is exploring small antennas in the 5–7 meter range that could be employed for domestic rural telecommunications services.

A fourth area of potential benefit in the 1980s involves cooperative activities with other organizations. The Agency for International Development, for instance, has a $20 million program for conducting telecommunications related test and demonstration projects in developing countries around the world. Some of these projects may be carried out on INTELSAT satellites free of charge; others will lease the minimum service (a quarter of a transponder). Most significant, the end of each test period can easily witness the transition from demonstration project to operational service.

INTELSAT is also interested in proposed telecommunications applications to serve both developed and developing nations: a global tele-library to make research and technical information available via computer terminals; telehealth information systems; and networks for linking specialized research groups together on a regional basis in such areas as agriculture and energy. Taking an even longer term view, INTELSAT has given serious consideration to technologies that may become operational in the 1990s, such as telecommunications-oriented space platforms that could combine a large number of services—space broadcasting, fixed point-to-point telecommunication services, mobile telecommunication services, meteorological services, remote data collection, and, possibly, earth resources services—providing new economies of scale for all these uses.

Clearly, major problems must be addressed and resolved in the near future if the benefits of space communications are to flow to all nations of the world. These issues include satellite proliferation; the emergence of competitive regional systems that could undercut INTELSAT's economies of scale; frequency congestion and geosynchronous orbital arc allocation; system interconnection; and institutional coordination and cooperation at the international, regional, and national levels.

For several reasons INTELSAT is especially concerned about regional satellite systems. By international agreement INTELSAT must price all services equally regardless of volume, whether for one telephone circuit or for a thousand circuits. INTELSAT is a nonprofit organization charged with providing service reliably and efficiently to all users. Thus, INTELSAT cannot cost-effectively offer global services if high-volume traffic, the cream of the market, is skimmed away; in such an environment, the developing countries, with thinner streams of traffic, stand to lose most. At the same time, the proliferation of regional satellites will create technical and operational problems.

Practical needs, technological advances, and social and political requirements tend to push in the direction of short-term solutions. International cooperation promises long-term benefits. The global community needs to establish procedures for the planning and operation of satellites and submarine cables to meet future international and domestic (especially rural) communication needs. Yet international circles presently are divided over the importance of telecommunications versus mass media. Some UNESCO members vitally concerned with issues relating to broadcasting and new services have called for a New World Information Order. Other nations have stressed technical telecommunication issues within the ITU, the WARCs, and elsewhere. This lack of dialogue between mass media and telecommunications experts not only at the international institutional level (the ITU vis-à-vis UNESCO) but also within developed and developing countries has created more confusion than understanding. Certainly the debate has yet to identify priorities in the communications field.

Progress toward more efficient and lower cost services depends on international cooperation among nations and through agencies like the ITU, UNESCO, the World Bank, and INTELSAT. Negotiations to establish formal relations between the ITU and INTELSAT, a Second United Nations Conference on the Exploration and Peaceful Uses of Outer Space (UNISPACE-82), and new World Bank interest in financing communications development projects are steps in the right direction. The challenge is great; the potential benefits of success, even greater.

NOTE

1. INTELSAT V-A (satellites to be available in 1984–85) can increase the capacity available for international service or, through electronic switching, can be reconfigured to provide higher power for domestic services. INTELSAT VI satellites (to be deployed in 1986) with capacities of up to 40,000 voice circuits, plus color television channels, are under construction. INTELSAT VI satellites will employ space-switched TDMA, a new digital communications technique, and multiple-beam antenna feeds to achieve their enormous capacities. We are also studying for the mid-1980s a smaller class of satellites that could be devoted to domestic services on a planned basis.

Forty-Seven

WARC: Some Legal and Political Issues on Space Services[1]

Stephen Gorove

The 1979 World Administrative Radio Conference (WARC-79) was convened to revise, update, and harmonize international radio regulations. Developments in space technology necessitated the adoption of new terms and procedures, particularly in the field of space radiocommunication services. While the purpose of WARC-79 was the overall revision and coordination of the radio regulations, the new regulations may be regarded as "a continuation rather than a dramatic break" inasmuch as the changes adopted by the conference are to be carried out according to a timetable that takes into account the telecommunications possibilities for all member states, especially the developing countries (see *Telecommunications Journal* 47, 1980, p. 4). In this chapter I will discuss some of the legal and political issues of WARC-79 as they relate to the use of the geostationary orbit and the planning of space services utilizing it.

THE GEOSTATIONARY ORBIT: THE DEBATE OVER NATIONAL SOVEREIGNTY

The geostationary orbit is located at a distance of approximately 22,300 miles (35,800 kilometers) about the equator. A geostationary satellite is in the plane of the equator and moves around the polar axis of the earth in the same direction and within the same period as the earth itself.

While the geostationary orbit, or corridor, in which the satellites move has obvious physical limitations, the major concern caused by geostationary satellites is electromagnetic interference with other satellites and users of the radio spectrum (2, p. 445). In 1977 about one hundred satellites were in geostationary orbit. By 1990 there will be an estimated 240 working satellites in geostationary orbit, an increase that may well create problems of overcrowding, which in turn will present hard choices with respect to the determination of priorities (2, p. 446).

The 1967 Outer Space Treaty, the fundamental charter of international space law, sought to exempt outer space from claims of national sovereignty. The equatorial countries' claim to segments of the geostationary orbit, formalized in the Bogotá Declaration of 1976 (see 4), was the first assertion of national jurisdiction over an area of outer space in which satellites orbit (this area extends from about 100–110 kilometers up and includes the geostationary orbit). The Bogotá Declaration argued that portions of the geostationary orbit above the national territories of the equatorial countries were under their exclusive jurisdiction and sovereignty and portions of the geostationary orbit over the high seas constituted "the common heritage of mankind."

While the legal and scientific arguments advanced by the equatorial countries in support of their claim were not accepted in the United Nations, there was "an undercurrent of sympathy" for consideration within the framework of the Outer Space Treaty of the development of legal principles governing the use of the geostationary orbit (see 3, p. 597).

INTERNATIONAL REGULATION OF TELECOMMUNICATIONS: WARC AND OTHER INSTRUMENTS

No country that has placed a satellite in orbit or beyond has ever asked for permission to do so and no country has filed an official protest against such action. Nonetheless, under the so-called first-come, first-served principle, subsequent users are not entitled to priority with respect to areas entered by earlier users. A review of the history of the International Telecommunication Union (ITU) indicates that ITU has operated in accordance with the first-come, first-served rule (2, p. 455).

Recognition of the limits of the electromagnetic spectrum and the geostationary orbit, as well as the increase in opportunities and demands for their use, has brought about increasing pressure from the developing nations to alter the first-come, first-served rule, which, in their view, benefits the developed countries. Third World efforts in this area are reflected in a series of legal instruments adopted by ITU bodies. For instance, the International Telecommunication Convention of 1973, very much like the 1971 WARC for Space Telecommunications, stressed that members must bear in mind that the geostationary orbit and the electromagnetic spectrum are limited natural resources and countries should have equitable access to both in conformity with the radio regulations and their needs and the technical facilities at their disposal. The same convention also emphasized that all stations, whatever their purpose, must be established and operated in such a manner as not to cause harmful interference.

Another basic principle, the equal rights of all countries, was affirmed by the 1977 WARC for the Planning of the Broadcasting-Satellite Service in Frequency Bands 11.7–12.2 GHz (in regions 2 and 3) and 11.7–12.5 GHz (in region 1). The 1977 Broadcasting WARC adopted a plan making frequency assignments in the bands and the positions in the geostationary orbit for regions 1 (Europe, Africa, the Soviet Union, and Mongolia) and 3 (Asia and the Pacific). The conference postponed the decision on an orbital position and frequency channel plan for region 2 (the Americas). Instead, it adopted an arc segmentation approach, under which alternating segments of the geostationary arc were allocated to the broadcasting satellite service and the fixed satellite service; the conference also agreed to hold a regional administrative conference to draw up a detailed plan for the broadcasting satellite and fixed services of region 2 (2, p. 458).

WARC-79 witnessed a continuing effort on the part of the developing nations to change the first-come, first-served principle in connection with the use of the geostationary orbit and the space services utilizing it. The Third World nations charged that the first-come, first-served principle does not conform to Article 33 of the 1973 International Telecommunication Convention mandating equitable access to use of the geostationary orbit and frequency bands.[2] They contended that the principle benefits only a small number of technologically advanced countries. The developing nations were concerned that all geostationary orbital slots and frequencies would be allocated elsewhere by the time they were prepared to use them; consequently, they pressed for a conference to assign certain space services and bands on an *a priori* basis—that is, to allot orbital slots and frequencies to nations in advance and reserve them for future use. The conference eventually adopted the Resolution Relating to the Use of the Geostationary Orbit and to the Planning of Space Services Utilizing It.

Marked differences of opinion surfaced at the 1979 WARC. For instance, Iraq's proposal embraced all space services in all frequency bands, whereas India's proposal related to the fixed satellite service (including feeder links to the broadcasting satellite service). The Soviet scheme to limit planning to the broadcasting satellite service feeder links differed from China's proposal that only new allocations of the fixed satellite service below 10 GHz be planned (5, p. 11).

The United States, an advocate of the evolutionary approach, under which orbital slots and frequencies can be made available on an "as needed" basis, opposed *a priori* planning on the ground that it not only would lead to a wasteful use of the radio spectrum but also would freeze the development of technology. Joined by other developed countries, the United States argued that detailed planning is unsuitable for most space services and, in particular, for the fixed satellite service. The developed countries suggested as an alternative that improvements in regulatory procedures and flexible approaches to planning be introduced to insure equitable access to all nations. The developing countries responded that planning would encourage rather than stifle the development of technology and that it would not necessarily freeze orbital assignments inasmuch as unused space allotted to one country could by mutual agreement be utilized by another.

The 1979 resolution calling for a planning conference leaned toward the position of the developing countries insofar as planning was put on the agenda. Such a conference, however, is to decide only which space services and frequency bands should be planned and to "consider other possible approaches that could meet the objective" of guaranteeing equitable access to all countries (6, Resolution BP). While the resolution stipulated that the future conference would be free to establish principles, as well as criteria and technical parameters, for planning, it included no specific reference to claims of equatorial countries to segments of the geostationary orbit but only a watered-down provision that in the planning process the conference would take into account "the relevant technical aspects concerning the special geographical situation of particular countries" (6, Resolution BP). Finally, the 1984 conference date set forth in the resolution suited the developing nations, which were concerned that after a longer period, say fifteen or twenty years, the presence of a large number of satellites in the geostationary orbit would likely impede the realization of the principle of equitable access. The developed countries ultimately went along with the proposed starting date, which gave them four years to convince Third World nations that an evolutionary approach would better satisfy their needs.[3]

The 1979 conference also made a significant change in the interim plan adopted by WARC-77 for region 2, under which the geostationary orbital arc for the Western Hemisphere was segmented between fixed satellite and broadcasting satellite services sharing the same frequency band, 11.7–12.2 GHz. In abandoning arc segmentation and adopting frequency separation in relation to the two services, WARC-79 acted in keeping with the U.S. position that such a change would provide greater flexibility for administrations to place their satellites in orbital position (6, Resolution CHI; Radio Regulation No. 3787B; cf. 4, p. 8).

CONCLUSION

WARC-79 has been called "an evolution not a revolution," a "political" conference, a "technical" conference with "zero politics," and a "footnote" conference because of the wholesale use of footnotes (*Broadcasting*, Dec. 3, 1979, p. 21).

Most of the nine hundred or so proposals submitted by the United States were adopted either in their entirety or in substantial part. The majority of the adopted changes will take effect gradually. Finally, most of the conference issues did not appear to involve strict bloc voting by the developing countries "independent" of their "national interests," and the number of U.S. reservations was relatively small (1, p. 3).

Nevertheless, the United States has expressed concern about the "unrealistic expectations" of some nations for working out assignment plans for space services and the geostationary orbit (5, p. 3). To a great extent this concern is understandable: the developing nations, with their numerical voting strength, were able to move considerably closer to their objective of *a priori* planning, thereby substantially weakening, if not eroding, the first-come, first-served principle.

Legislation in the domestic sphere or treaty making in the international arena seldom results from isolated efforts. Thus, the preceding analysis of selected issues pertaining to the geostationary orbit and the planning of space services must be seen in the light of broader trends in the world community. Such trends reflect the persistent efforts and strong determination of the developing nations to insist on rights and champion interests that would give them a greater share of the world's material benefits. The challenge facing legal technicians and policymakers is to formulate principles and procedures that serve the interests of developing and developed nations alike.

NOTES

1. I wish to express my appreciation to Wilson Dizard of the U.S. Department of State, David M. Leive of INTELSAT, Edward R. Jacobs and Anthony M. Rutkowski of the Federal Communications Commission, and Stephen E. Doyle of the Office of Technology Assessment, U.S. Congress, for providing information and materials relating to WARC-79. This presentation draws on materials from the *Zeitschrift für Luft- und Weltraumrecht* with permission.

2. No official summary records or minutes cover working group meetings. I am indebted to Anthony M. Rutkowski of the Federal Communications Commission for providing me with an unofficial, unpublished account of the meetings of Ad Hoc Group 2 of Committee 6.

3. The conference is scheduled to take place in two sessions, with the first to convene in 1984 and the second, a year to eighteen months later. The first session is to make the decisions; the second, to carry them out (see 5, p. 12).

REFERENCES

1. Federal Communications Commission. *Staff Report to the Commission on the Results of the 1979 World Administrative Radio Conference*, Jan. 15, 1980.

2. Gorove, Stephen. "The Geostationary Orbit: Issues of Law and Policy." *American Journal of International Law* 73, 1979.

3. Gorove, Stephen. "Solar Power Space Stations: Some Issues of Law and Policy." American Astronautical Society, *Advances in the Astronautical Sciences*,

Vol. 38, Part II: *The Future United States Space Program* (R. S. Johnston, Ed.), 1979.

4. International Telecommunication Union. Broadcasting Satellite Conference, Doc. No. 81-E, Annex 4 (Jan. 17, 1977).

5. U.S. Department of State. World Administrative Radio Conference. Summary Report No. 9, 1979.

6. World Administrative Radio Conference of 1979. *Final Acts*, Geneva, 1979.

Forty-Eight

WARC: Third World Positions and Achievements[1]

Nolan A. Bowie

The 1979 World Administrative Radio Conference (WARC-79) provided a golden opportunity for the United States to reestablish and enhance its credibility and to gain substantial goodwill among the developing countries. However, the United States missed that opportunity by failing to provide the type of leadership and assistance that the public record clearly demanded. Official spokespersons for the United States claimed that 95 percent of its objectives were accomplished (see 6). The actual tally of victories or successes does not really matter, however; the discussion that follows will show that both the Third World *and* the rest of the world won on some points, lost on others, and postponed the remainder for later conferences. I shall examine some of the dynamics that may have influenced various Third World positions and discuss U.S. responses.[2]

SETTING THE STAGE FOR WARC-79

There was no monolithic Third World position on any single issue at WARC. The Third World is a group of autonomous developing countries, each operating in a manner perceived to be in its own national interest. In fact, the concept of nonalignment, another label attached to this group, stresses the desire of these nations not to be viewed as satellites of the superpowers. On issues in which Third World countries perceived themselves to have a common interest, their votes coincided. So far as common interests go, the Third World came to WARC seeking spectrum assignments to meet their national needs for basic telecommunication services for both the present and the future. Third World demands for spectrum allocations that would permit development of low cost communication systems were tied to the belief that modern means of communications—

424

including access to the geostationary orbit—are critical to national economic development.

Third World nations, recognizing that they lack adequate resources, wanted assistance from developed countries both directly and through international organizations. They sought technology, technical help, and, above all, training. They wanted and needed information and investments to develop their *own* telecommunication infrastructures for their *own* requirements. For example, the Third World needed and wanted the developed countries to help them with spectrum management. The highly industrialized countries have almost an oligopoly on experts in spectrum management, with the United States and the Soviet Union holding the lion's share (this fact is not surprising since satellite coordinating procedures and space applications technology are by-products of military space technology) (see 5). The Third World also wanted to simplify the international radio regulations—their language as well as their procedures. Many of these rules were written before most of the Third World existed as independent states. The old rules were highly technical, complex, and so arcane that they were difficult to understand. Furthermore, since much of the Third World is in tropical regions having heavy and unusual rainfall, the developing countries wanted data collected and analyzed regarding the effects of rainfall and propagation phenomena in the tropics.

At the start of the conference the Third World nations were aware that the few rich industrial countries had 10 percent of the world's population but 90 percent of the spectrum, and they wanted their fair and equitable share. Furthermore, they recognized that they could vote to postpone those decisions that required concentrated analysis in order to be able to vote intelligently in their self-interest at a later date. The Third World also had most of the votes and the moral power associated with the term "equity," for who could publicly admit to being against the concept of providing equity? In addition, the Third World had articulate and effective leadership within its ranks—experts who could and did define terms and concepts as well as anyone else in the world (see 10).

In short, while the United States and other highly industrialized countries had the technology, technical and human resources, satellite parking space, and some underutilized or surplus frequencies going into WARC, the developing countries had the votes, along with an understanding of how the game would be played. The developed nations needed Third World votes and the Third World needed the assistance of the developed countries.[3]

THIRD WORLD EXPECTATIONS

The Third World's expectations of technical assistance and telecommunications technology transfer from the industrialized nations—especially the

United States—had been delineated and acknowledged prior to WARC-79 in several places. In May 1976, former Secretary of State Henry Kissinger made pledges of assistance at a U.N. conference in Nairobi on trade and development. At a UNESCO conference that same year, John Reinhardt, former director of the International Communications Agency, then chief of the U.S. delegation to the conference, pledged assistance from the U.S. government and other industrialized countries to help develop the mass media of Third World countries, both through government and private assistance.

> It is our conviction that the most effective way to reduce the current imbalance is not by inhibiting the communications capacity of some, but by increasing the communications capacity of all. . . . We believe that the United States and other nations in which are found highly developed mass media facilities and capabilities should endeavor to make available, through bilateral and multilateral channels, both private and governmental assistance to other states in helping to develop their mass media.

President Carter reiterated these pledges in 1977 in a speech before the Organization of American States.

> Our own science and technology can be useful to many of your countries. For instance, we are ready to train your technicians to use more information gathered by our own satellites, so that you can make better judgments on management of your resources and your environment.

Clearly, the Third World's expectation of U.S. assistance was justified. That expectation was not realized at WARC and U.S. credibility has been impaired.

The United States, in addition to making general pledges of assistance prior to WARC, was well aware of the overall goals of many Third World countries at WARC. For example, *African Regional Seminar on Communications Policy and the 1979 World Administrative Radio Conference*, a UNESCO report published in November 1978, summarized a four-day meeting of the Joint Economic Commission for Africa, the Konrad Adenauer Foundation, the International Institute of Communications, and the Union of National Radio and Television Organizations in Africa. This document identified the leadership roles that would be played by the administrations of Kenya and India at WARC because of their recent experience with telecommunication satellites. The report also noted the need for rural development and development of public education and agriculture, demonstrated the significance developing countries attach to high frequency fixed satellite services, and reviewed the goals of the African countries for improved communication within the continent via a network that would include satellite services, revision of ITU rules, and establishment of Africa as a separate region of the ITU.

Additional information about the needs and goals of Third World countries at WARC was gathered by U.S. officials firsthand. During the two years preceding WARC, the U.S. engaged in bilateral meetings with many nations of the world, including Third World countries. From these numerous meetings, the U.S. planners for WARC learned that most of the Third World countries did *not* have the highly skilled personnel to prepare for technical issues at WARC and thus probably would be voting in a bloc. This situation might have been avoided had the U.S. provided the technical assistance or resources that these countries required to prepare properly for the conference and to participate in a more sophisticated manner therein. However, the U.S. did virtually nothing in this regard.

The Third World's call for spectrum planning should have surprised no one. The U.S. was aware as early as the 1959 WARC of the nonaligned countries' call for a New International Information Order in connection with some sort of plan that would guarantee frequency assignments to other than those first in line. At the 1959 WARC, a Pakistani delegate noted that the first-come, first-served method of allocating station rights should be radically altered by giving all listed frequency assignments the same date for applications at successive radio conferences.

Still other direct clues concerning Third World communication needs were provided by the U.S. WARC planners in working group sessions prior to the conference and in official proposals submitted to the ITU regarding the work to be done at WARC. Working group 5, for example, was devoted to the special problems of the developing countries and recognized the need for the United States to establish credibility among Third World nations by fulfilling its pledges of assistance. In January 1979, Papua –New Guinea filed its proposals for the 1979 WARC. In March Uganda submitted its proposals. In April Egypt followed suit. India filed later that month. The beginning of WARC-79 was still five months away.

U.S.-THIRD WORLD ANTAGONISM

Thus, the United States had official notice of specific Third World goals. As Glen Robinson, head of the U.S. delegation, reportedly said (12), the New World Information Order is a "coming concept, like the North-South dialogue generally." Robinson further acknowledged the need to come to grips with this concept, though complaining of its ambiguity, and conceded that the present system of allocating spectrum space involving coordination and notification, is expensive and extremely complicated for developing nations, which lack the specialized expertise this system requires. The United States, at least as far as Robinson was concerned, recognized the legitimacy of Third World goals in early 1979.

Yet there was antagonism at WARC-79 between Third World positions and official U.S. positions. Part of the problem was that the United States approached WARC arrogantly; while recognizing the voting strength of the Third World, the U.S. was not prepared to make reasonable attempts at accommodation. Asked whether the United States should offer technical assistance to Third World countries to demonstrate our good faith and to create a favorable climate at WARC, Robinson is quoted as saying: "We are not going to buy votes" (12). In an even more telling expression of U.S. feelings, an unnamed member of the U.S. delegation said, at the first official meeting of the delegation in Washington, D.C., "These banana boat countries don't know how good they are going to have it at WARC!"

The official U.S. goals at WARC, according to releases of the Bureau of Public Affairs of the Department of State, were as follows:

1. We seek agreement on necessary, incremental changes in frequency allocations and related regulations in order to enhance U.S. economic, social, and national security interests.
2. We seek to maintain those procedures which provide maximum flexibility and adaptability to changing needs.
3. We wish to strengthen ITU's role as the international organization responsible for implementing WARC decisions, without adversely affecting U.S. sovereign rights.
4. We support changes in allocations and related frequency management procedures that will accommodate other nation's needs—consistent with our own requirements—while endeavoring to avoid or limit the impact of politically inspired efforts to impede fair and efficient use of the spectrum (11).

The very language with which we described our goals appears antagonistic to the expressed goals of many developing countries: we sought to "enhance U.S. economic [and] social . . . interests [and] to strengthen ITU's role" but only "without adversely affecting U.S. sovereign rights."

CONFERENCE OUTCOMES

By maintaining an introspective and shortsighted posture, by being concerned primarily with protecting our already substantial portion of the spectrum, the United States did not win many friends or favorably influence developing countries at WARC-79. Though the U.S. achieved perhaps up to 95 percent of its goals (which were contained in the more than 900 proposals submitted by the United States), these were technical goals that were neither controversial nor competing with the legitimate interests of others, particularly Third World nations. On controversial issues—whether there would be planning frequencies—U.S. gains in large part simply involved delay of decisionmaking. In regard to the Third World's renewed demand for a New World Information Order and equitable access, the United States acknowledged the legitimacy of the concept of equitable access but gained some time: the 1984 World Administrative Radio Conference for the Space Services will allow the U.S. to take a second bite at the apple, so to speak. On the other hand, the United States and other industrialized countries could buy a little more time by recognizing that this changing world is already a global village.

The Third World too made a number of gains. First, postponement of decisionmaking to future special conferences (particularly on space services and high frequency bands) can be viewed as a victory for the developing countries. The time gained will allow Third World nations to concentrate their limited resources, especially skilled personnel, on circumscribed issues. The frantic pace produced by the working structure and ten-week time limit of WARC-79 tended to disfavor administrations with small delegations.[4] The Third World can take advantage of the interval preceding the next conferences to monitor U.S. experiences with, and policies on, fixed satellite services to determine whether we indeed encounter crowding in the geostationary orbit and frequency congestion and how we remedy the situation.

Second, the Third World secured passage of several resolutions for increased assistance in a range of areas:

- Technical cooperation in maritime telecommunications, especially technical advice and assistance in training Third World personnel.
- Technical cooperation in propagation studies in tropical areas designed to improve and develop Third World radio communications.
- Development of national radio frequency management within the Third World countries through such means as regional seminars and training.
- Transfer of technology in telecommunications for the purpose of attaining social, economic, and cultural objectives of Third World countries.
- Expanding the role of telecommunications in rural development. These resolutions look to the United Nations Development Center as the primary source of funding.

Third, the developing nations at WARC succeeded in presenting a clear message to the developed world that the key to dealing with them is recognizing and meeting their telecommunication needs. The Third World delegates proved themselves tough negotiators and hard bargainers, winning a new respect from developed countries. They were effective, for example, in defeating a European proposal to extend citizen band radio into a band African countries use for television and in securing the election of a chairman from the Third World.[5]

An article in *New African* (June 1979) on the resentment of Third World nations toward the current system of international frequency allocation claimed that because so few Third World countries had attended the 1959 WARC, "the industrial nations seized . . . the lion's share of most frequencies." Accordingly, "in most rural parts of Africa, radio listeners often have difficulty catching their own national broadcasting stations. But they tune in with ease to foreign stations such as the BBC, VOA, Radio Moscow." This situation lays the foundation for the Third World claiming still another victory at WARC—containing U.S. spectrum space:

> The U.S.'s major disappointment at WARC was the inability to gain the desired frequencies needed by the Voice of America, Radio Free Europe, Radio Liberty and the Armed Forces Radio Service shortwave broadcasting (*Broadcasting*, Dec. 10, 1979).

In the final analysis, however, to speak in terms of victories and defeats is inappropriate. Either WARC works for everyone or it works for no one.

PROMISE VERSUS PERFORMANCE

The critical and controversial issues, such as the future of space services and high frequency band use, were not decided at WARC-79. These issues, which will determine the course of telecommunications in the world, do not lend themselves to easy solution or to easy victory for anyone's long-term interests. The U.S. discovered at WARC-79 that the Third World is not overly impressed with strictly technical or logical arguments. In fact, what the Third World wants is a plan that would guarantee equitable access for all, in both the present and the future. Without the support of the Third World, the United States may find itself in a voting minority on these crucial questions, yet the U.S. approach at WARC-79 to the Third World demonstrated a lack of integrity and goodwill.

The danger in claiming that the United States achieved a 95 percent victory is that the U.S. strategy toward WARC-79 may be interpreted as a winning game plan. We are deluding ourselves if we do not look beyond the numbers on which we based our claim of victory. If the U.S. does not assume leadership in the area of international telecommunications assistance, the United States will not regain the credibility we lost by our empty promises and the arrogant way in which we approached the Third World at WARC-79.

The United States must deliver on past promises. It is not enough to assist developing countries within the framework of international organizations. The United States must take the initiative by sponsoring multilateral and bilateral assistance programs. Moreover, the U.S. must establish its credibility by aggressively pursuing equitable access in terms of ownership and control of communications systems, nondiscrimination in employment, and, especially, equitable decisionmaking vis-à-vis Third World peoples and their descendants living in the United States, the so-called minorities.

The U.S. fails to recognize that its domestic telecommunications policy is monitored by the rest of the world and is used to assess the good faith of its international commitments. Domestic activities also represent a microcosm of what goes on in the rest of the world. For example, the free flow of information concept is an extension of the U.S. First Amendment. And the FCC, which regulates U.S. communication policies and laws internally, also plays a significant international role. FCC enforcement, ostensibly intended to protect disenfranchised domestic minorities, has not been effective, which may be taken as an indication of how the United States will deal with the disenfranchised Third World.

If the United States is to be a responsible world citizen, it needs to develop something akin to an international public interest standard. Application of an international public interest standard would help restore our credibility abroad and move us in the direction of insuring equitable access. Development assistance to the Third World, consistent with such an international public interest standard, would also help the United States from a market viewpoint. Economic aid and aggressive bilateral assistance programs create new export markets for the United States while meeting the specific needs of developing countries. Loan repayments and the dollar value of U.S. goods and services provided by aid agencies probably exceed the amount of foreign aid money we send abroad.

The twenty-odd major international radio conferences scheduled throughout the eighties will decide on assignments and uses of the high frequency bands and all space services (including the geostationary orbit). These decisions will be made by majority vote—one country, one vote. The Third World wants what domestic minorities want: the power to persuade and influence; equitable access to telecommunications technology; ownership and control of communications hardware; and the means, expertise, and opportunity to develop software and become a gatekeeper. The United States still has the opportunity to demonstrate, through vigorous affirmative action here and abroad and through robust public debate, its commitment to these goals.

NOTES

1. The author was invited by the U.S. Department of State to represent the private sector in the U.S. delegation to WARC. He participated in the conference only in an advisory capacity.

2. A comprehensive report summarizing the outcome of the 1979 World Administrative Radio Conference was completed and published by the Academy for Educational Development (4). See also 1, 3, 7, 8, 9.

3. At the time of WARC-79 communications assistance to developing countries was not a priority of the United States. A host of developments reflect U.S. commitments in the area of assistance: funding problems in the U.S. Agency for

International Development and the World Bank; the introduction of restrictive and isolationist legislation like the Helms Amendment; the priority given to projects and policies outside the communications area; the skepticism of development economists in the United States and other industrialized countries about loans for communication systems; U.S. failure to link communication issues or to analyze potential linkages among such issues (WARC and UNESCO) or between communication questions and foreign policy at large; and our paramount concern with inflation and reduced government expenditures (see 2).

4. The U.S. delegation included 106 persons—67 accredited and 39 in support. The developing countries lacked both the expert personnel and the funds to support large delegations.

5. Third World countries initially sought to elect a delegate from a non-aligned nation, India, as chairman of WARC. Western nations had privately agreed upon their choice for chairman, a New Zealander. The ultimate chairman, a compromise candidate, was nonetheless from a Third World country, Argentina.

REFERENCES

1. Armstrong, Anne A. "Was WARC a Victory for the U.S.?" *Information World* 2(1) February 1980, p. 11.

2. Aspen Institute Program on Communications and Society. "Problems in International Communications." Conference Report, August 14–18, 1978, Aspen, Colorado.

3. Federal Communications Commission. *Staff Report to the Commission on the Results of the 1979 World Administrative Radio Conference.* January 1980.

4. Hudson, Heather (Study Director). "Results and Implications of WARC 79 for Development Communications: A Report to USAID." Prepared by the Academy for Educational Development, February 1980.

5. Leister, Velnora. "Space Technology for Development: Dreams and Realities." Published for the International Institute of Space Law by the American Institute of Aeronautics and Astronautics, September, 1979.

6. Love, Thomas. "Radio Parley Went Well, FCC Told." *Washington Star,* January 10, 1980, p. D6.

7. *Mimeo,* Washington, D.C., January 1980.

8. Nelson, Sharon L. "Report on WARC 79." Consumers Union, January 1980.

9. Rutkowski, A. M. "A Structured Analysis of WARC 79." Paper presented before the Carnegie Endowment for International Peace, Face to Face Program. Washington, D.C., January 30, 1980.

10. Rutkowski, A. M. "Six Ad-Hoc Two: The World Speaks Its Mind." *Satellite Communications,* forthcoming.

11. U.S. Department of State, Bureau of Public Affairs. "GIST." August, 1979.

12. "WARC 79: The Haves vs. the Have-Nots." *Broadcasting,* January 1, 1979.

Forty-Nine

U.S. Communication Policies at Home and Abroad: Are They Consistent?

Harvey J. Levin

U.S. communication policies abroad are not consistent with such policies at home. One dramatic example is longstanding U.S. opposition to Third World demands for *a priori* planning of the geostationary orbit, space frequencies, and the shortwave (HF) spectrum. This opposition to spectrum planning abroad contrasts with U.S. domestic approval of preplanned TV and FM allocations. It contrasts also with U.S. domestic policy of long-term channel reservations to insure latecomer access for less affluent public and local community TV applicants.

A second inconsistency is continued U.S. resistance to Third World calls for a balanced information flow. "Balance" implies the right to monitor transborder data flow, to control foreign media and journalists, and to require prior consent before any advanced nation can blanket a less developed one with foreign based news service by direct broadcast satellite or other means. The United States rejects the principle of balanced flow as tantamount to government censorship and as opposed to its own commitment to a free flow of information. Yet the United States has long endorsed domestic policies that promote media balance, fairness, equal access, and output diversity—each of which qualifies the concept of free flow.

In both cases, failure to address apparent inconsistencies leaves the United States open to criticism that could undermine its credibility. The unspoken negotiating strategy is to let sleeping dogs lie, but this tactic justifies the accusation, as was made of U.S. policy planning for the 1979 World Administrative Radio Conference, that U.S. policy is "reactive, introspective [and aimed] primarily at protecting [our] already substantial uses of the spectrum" (5, p. 146). Before pursuing these matters, let me review a few more obvious sources of Third World concern over information balance and latecomer access.

SOURCES OF THIRD WORLD CONCERN

The radio spectrum is a multidimensional resource with decidedly international characteristics (13, Chapter 1). Unless third parties cooperate through the multilateral arrangements embodied in final agreements of a World Administrative Radio Conference, for example, reliable communication between any set of communicating partners cannot be guaranteed. Radio frequencies are in some ways as much a shared global resource as the oceans or the seabeds. Under current U.S. law at least, spectrum is what economists call a common property resource: being the property of no one user, like the air mantle, the watershed, or the migratory fishery, it becomes the common property of all.

To grasp the spectrum's international character, on the other hand, one has only to consider the common airwaves that non-U.S. partners use to communicate with one another. Coordination and cooperation of many third parties, as well as of the communicating nations in a given instance, are the precondition of information delivery. International factors also constrain spectrum use within national borders. Once again, cooperation is essential, say, near U.S. borders with Canada and Mexico, to coordinate the different domestic usages of domestic frequencies.

When the 154 International Telecommunication Union (ITU) delegates came to Geneva in fall 1979 for WARC-79 it was clear that the Third World presence and needs would be crucial (7, 8, 12, 17, 19, 22). First, over half the ITU members are Third World nations, some sixty of which had joined ITU subsequent to the 1959 World Administrative Radio Conference. Also visible at WARC was a classic North-South cleavage, along which players divided notably into poor-rich, low-high technology, and former colonies-former colonial powers. The delegates at WARC-79 also divided into latecomer nations lacking the technology, know-how, and capital to develop and use the spectrum and first-come, advanced nations that had long utilized the resource on a first-come, first-served basis.

These preceding lines of alliance assumed new urgency within the ITU decisional framework, wherein each nation has one vote. Whatever the equity or political wisdom of disregarding population size, per capita income, special communication needs, or existing capital investments, this voting formula raised understandable concern among advanced nations of possible bloc voting or of Third World coalitions short of that. Third World insistence on guaranteed future access perhaps reflected a further concern that latecomers to spectrum are normally shunted off to the higher spectral regions, which, while less congested, are more costly to develop and operate in. This had certainly been the U.S. experience with domestic land mobile and television services. It is presumably true in a general way for latecomer nations.

U.S. OPPOSITION TO THIRD WORLD DEMANDS FOR *A PRIORI* PLANNING

A Priori Planning Versus First Come, First Served

U.S. opposition to *a priori* spectrum planning abroad appears to derive from stated or implied concerns over economic distortions, technological retardation, and military security.

The U.S feels that any preplanned allocation that holds open short-wave frequencies (HF) for latecomer access could allegedly impair military communications flexibility. Expanded or rigid band width requirements for TV could further reduce U.S. access to VHF and UHF military mobile channels, with similar adverse effects on military requirements. Such potential constraints on military usage are indeed serious just because extra (literally redundant) channels are needed to insure instantaneous contact with far-flung security forces in the event that primary HF channels are jammed or destroyed (5, p. 140; 22, pp. S9314, 9317–18; 6).

The U.S. also believes that *a priori* reservation of space frequencies and orbital slots will impede optimal development and use of satellites for civilian (as well as military) purposes—navigation assistance; direct broadcasting; data processing; radio astronomy; space research; and the monitoring of weather, crop, and forest conditions, ocean resources, and environmental quality (11, p. 98; 23, pp. S9313, 9318; 24, p. 10). The U.S. also deplores the economic distortions, forgone outputs, and technological retardation allegedly implicit in long-term *a priori* spectrum reservation (see 19, pp. 306–309).

Nevertheless, developing nations late to acquire the technologies needed to exploit common resources like the radio spectrum will no longer automatically acquiesce to those high technology nations with the capital and know-how to proceed. Increasingly, latecomers demand their fair share, even privileged access (to the lower, congested, but less costly to use spectral regions already occupied by advanced nations) to compensate for their long-standing deprivation. The contrasting approaches to global spectrum management of developing and developed countries were nowhere more vivid than in deliberations at WARC-79 over specialized planning conferences for the geostationary orbit and the HF spectrum and preferential access to unused HF fixed assignments by Third World applicants.

SPECIALIZED PLANNING CONFERENCES

The record of WARC-79 reveals nothing tantamount to concerted bloc voting on key issues, i.e., voting on the basis of ideology rather than national interest (22). Yet after Third World delegates failed to secure election of their preferred president (Srinangan of India), their potential voting power appears to have given them new resolve (12, 19, 20, 22). Thus, the final negotiation of a resolution to convene a specialized WARC on the geostationary orbit in 1984 seems to reflect such a Third World coalition, possibly at the expense of the U.S. (see 20). This conference will consider which satellites and services should be subject to a priori planning.

The final decision on whether (and if so, to what extent) a priori orbital spectrum planning and channel reservation would effectively replace the first-come, first-served principle must await the space conference itself. However, the importance of this apparent Third World success seems underscored by skillful maneuvering of Third World delegates in the face of persistent U.S. and other First World opposition. Even Second World efforts to leave open the question of whether any part of the orbital spectrum or so-called parking slots would be planned (reserved for late-comer access) were of no avail.

In a still more definitive fashion, WARC-79 resolved that a specialized HF broadcast conference be convened sometime before 1985. This, too, would lay out an a priori plan, in this case to insure future Third World access to broadcasting frequency-hours in the shortwave band.

Both resolutions revealed U.S. inability to command decisive support for the first-come, first-served principle. Nevertheless, some circles contend that this principle is administratively more convenient, as well as more conducive to economic efficiency, than any lengthy reservation of spectrum for an uncertain future use.

Counterparts in U. S. Allocation Policies

There is a serious question, however, as to whether U.S. hostility to a priori planning abroad belies preplanned domestic allocations (and allotments) for TV and FM radio. FCC allocation tables were established to implement no fewer than five social priorities often at the expense of market efficiency and surely of first come, first served (these priorities include wide area service, local community stations, multiple service areas, multiple station communities, and a system of public as well as commercial TV licensees). Moreover, for years unused VHF channels were reserved for future public use, against the certainty that those channels would otherwise be snapped up by commercial first-comers ready and willing to proceed, and for latecomer local community applicants in small and medium markets, against the certainty that applicants in more populous areas would otherwise preempt the frequencies. As late as 1966, fourteen years after the TV plan was introduced, thirty-eight (33.3 percent) VHF channels reserved for public TV remained unused and forty-four (22.7 percent) of the VHF outlets were allocated to smaller markets—those below the top one hundred. Presumably, VHFs and UHFs reserved for public television would more likely have been activated if allocated to commercial use. By the same token, in all market sizes, the percentage of channels allocated (and reserved) for public TV that remained unused was notably higher than for commercial TV. This was true for VHF stations as well as for UHF (15, p. 354, Table 40).

In sum, the risk that a reserved channel might take a long time to activate appeared to alarm the FCC far less than the risk that prior commercial entry might preclude future access by tardy public television applicants or local community candidates. How, then, can one reconcile staunch U.S. opposition to Third World calls for guaranteed future access to orbital slots, space frequencies, and HF spectrum (rejected as inefficient and technologically damaging) with its domestic policy of long-term channel reservation to implement certain social priorities?

Preferential Access to Unused Shortwave Radio Assignments by Third World Applicants

Still another WARC dispute over the first-come, first-served principle related to latecomer access to shortwave frequencies for fixed (i.e., point-to-point) domestic purposes. Early entry by high technology nations had placed much of the occupied HF spectrum in their hands. Though Algeria proposed that developing nations be given preferential access to assignments in 70 percent of the HF fixed service bands, the United States and many other members eventually acceded to a compromise to insure equitable access to the whole band: first, unused HF assignments identified by an applicant from a developing country would be removed from the International Frequency Registration Board's master frequency register; second, remaining assignments would be reclassified "according to needs and alternative means"; third, incumbents would be reaccommodated, receiving new frequencies for HF fixed services disrupted by "allocational changes"; fourth, the IFRB would increase its assistance to developing countries trying to locate a new frequency or to identify signal interference with other users; fifth, and most important, by special resolution the developed countries were explicitly asked to "minimize their use of these provisions," leaving them mainly for the benefit of developing countries (24, pp. 12–13).

This preferential treatment of developing nations has been likened to the U.S. affirmative action program. Still more pertinent here, the proposal resembles decisional preferences that the FCC grants in comparative broadcast hearings to less affluent applicants who are local residents (rather than absentee owners), non-newspaper owners, or newcomers unaffiliated with other media (rather than members of some TV or radio empire), etc. (4, pp. 409–10; 14, pp. 11–14). In both cases—at home and at WARC—other things being equal, entities with fewer resources, less know-how, and possibly less experience have been favored. Such preferential treatment is supposed to further overriding political and social values—equity and diversity of owners and ideas, on one hand, and equity of latercomer access, on the other.

But the well-known administrative inconvenience and time-consuming character of comparative broadcast hearings make one wonder how efficacious any even crudely comparable international attempt to favor developing over developed countries would be. In seeking to forestall clashes between applicants for the same unused HF spectrum, the new procedure does attempt to favor the developing countries; yet for the process to be effective, the following conditions must hold:

1. All nations must be explicitly classified as either a less developed country (LDC) or developed country.
2. Latecomer, less affluent LDCs must be given significant technical assistance in monitoring seemingly unused assignments registered by incumbent administrations of developed countries.
3. LDCs must also be helped in demonstrating the adequate electromagnetic compatibility of their proposed HF usage with operating incumbents elsewhere.

Nevertheless, the details of preferential treatment—how and where—are unclear for competing applicants that are *both* LDCs, though at different stages of development; an LDC newcomer applicant that is shown to interfere with an incumbent from a developed country within some small (*how* small?) fraction of the latter's service area or under certain atmospheric conditions; such LDC interference within a large (*how* large?) fraction of the incumbent's service area; such interference where equipment adjustments by either party could eliminate the interference but where the LDC's adjustment costs are substantially *lower* than the incumbent's; or such interference where LDC adjustment costs are substantially *higher* than the incumbent's.

To insure equitable access to latecomer entrants, then, this modified Algerian proposal presumably requires substantial technical assistance to developing countries and hard to secure ITU funds to reimburse adjustment costs. How long an assignment must, or ought to be, monitored and found unused before being released to others is not clear.[1] Nor is it clear how the procedure would keep a paper incumbent from periodically activating an unused assignment (after notice of LDC interest) to forestall loss.

U.S. Counterparts to Proposed HF Procedures to Accommodate Latecomer Applicants

How much softening of the U.S. commitment to the first-come, first-served principle does its support of this modified Algerian proposal really represent? Related is the U.S. experience with domestic AM broadcast licensing in which radio engineers typically try to shoehorn in new entrants through an ingenious use of directional antennas, temporal sharing, horizontal and vertical polarization, etc. Insofar as latecomers normally incur costs to avoid interfering with incumbent licensees, the former suffer an economic handicap even if they do ultimately get in (the option, of course, is to operate elsewhere geographically in AM or to move up to unused FM channels, where other economic difficulties may arise).

U.S. experience in this area points up the complexity, time-consuming character, and great cost of comparative hearings of as many as thirty applicants (in a number of geographically separate communities) for the same AM broadcast frequency. The far-flung interference patterns of HF radio (and the vagaries of sunspot cycles) are paralleled perhaps nowhere better than in AM broadcasting, with its long-distance, nighttime sky wave interference. Furthermore, the painful experience in AM comparative licensing has been that it must first be determined who interferes, how much, with whom, and where, and hence a simultaneous comparative evaluation of qualifications for rights to use a desired frequency is required. The United States has found this whole procedure to be at best a costly, clumsy, and inequitable way to promote the AM licensing goals of localism, owner diversification, and program diversity.[2]

In sum, U.S. experience with AM comparative licensing, under a basic regime of first-come, first-served principle, should make quite clear that *a priori* planning could guarantee latecomer access to the crowded HF spectrum (or the geostationary orbit). The U.S has followed this route in allocating FM and TV channels, thereby safeguarding various social priorities. Opposing this approach in the international arena (for albeit different but equivalent Third World goals), the United States risks major embarrassment.

U.S. COUNTERPARTS TO THIRD WORLD DEMANDS FOR BALANCED INFORMATION FLOW

U.S. Opposition to Calls for Balanced Flow

Under the New World Information Order each nation would be entitled to monitor all its transborder data flows; control foreign media and journalists; and require prior consent for direct broadcast and remote-sensing satellite deployment. Even where Western satellite data networks claim to further balanced information flow, developing nations remain sensitive to increased information dependency therefrom. A Yugoslav proposal suggested that to achieve balanced flow all international broadcasters be required to take account of the ethnic, religious, political, and economic composition of the populations that they serve.

The contrasting U.S commitment to free flow seemingly derives from the long-standing view that freedom of expression first and foremost requires freedom from government constraint (10, 18, 25). According to this theory, direct government intrusions in the free flow, composition, and content of media output are inimical to values associated with First Amendment guarantees. Third World countries, on the other hand, are increasingly sensitive to invasion of their sovereignty by technologically advanced ITU members, to greater information dependency, and to so-called cultural imperialism.

To avoid the rhetoric of these positions and the polarization that results, U.S. delegation leaders at WARC-79 emphasized the technical character of the issue and official U.S. postconference reports reckoned the predominantly technical climate of WARC-79 a success. Yet many technical issues are intertwined with political, social, economic, and even military factors (7, 8, 9, 23). For example, the divergent U.S. and Third World positions on HF allocations involve numerous nontechnical factors. Developing countries want to expand their use of HF radio for domestic point-to-point service, eminently suited to their current stage of economic development; yet on strictly ideological grounds they oppose foreign broadcasting at those same high frequencies. The United States, on the other hand, wants those frequencies for expanded international broadcasting (to say nothing of emergency military communications).

Be this as it may, U.S. opposition to Third World calls for a balanced information flow (a major nontechnical issue implicit at WARC-79) is not fully consistent with its long-standing domestic commitment to media balance and program diversity, as represented by the fairness doctrine, right of reply, equal time rule, or the diversity standard in *Red Lion* (395 US 367 [1979]). These discrepant positions at home and abroad clearly have not been reconciled. If the U.S. fails to address this double standard directly, its credibility in Third World negotiations will suffer.

U.S. Safeguards on Fairness, Balance, and Diversity

Before rejecting Third World calls for balanced flow out of hand, the United States would do well to recall that domestic policy regulations have long professed both to sustain so-called minority interest programming aimed generally at small social, cultural, intellectual, and ethnic groups and to promote balance and diversity among informational, cultural, and entertainment program types, even if this policy sometimes requires licensees to cross-subsidize certain less popular programming over the broadcast day.

Although the stated U.S. commitment to media balance and diversity at home does not always prevail over a competing commitment to keep the government out, First Amendment guarantees surely have not stopped the United States from taking (or at least considering) steps to insure a fair, balanced, and diversified media output even when this goal requires government procedures at once awkward, costly, and counterproductive (2, 3).

Contingent versus Noncontingent Access

Fairness, right of reply, and equal time (contingent access) requirements have not gone unchallenged. One objection is that they can have "chilling" effects: by imposing economic and legal risks on licensees, the so-called triggering acts allegedly intimidate media owners at the expense of bold investigative journalism. Noncontingent access, on the other hand, associated with the structural diversity of multivoice markets, represents an attempt to forestall direct content regulation by government. Structural safeguards here refer to such new technologies as cable grids, satellite broadcasting, relay satellites, interconnected CATV systems, and even short-spaced VHF drop-ins, videodiscs, or cassettes. Advocates of structural rather than content regulation in broadcast programming underscore the new emphasis on editorial autonomy, an alleged retreat from *Red Lion* (the high-water mark of contingent access under fairness doctrine); they see the older First Amendment doctrine of freedom from government intrusion as once again coming to the fore (under *Tornillo*) rather than the primary right of the public to see, hear, and read.[3]

Ongoing Dialogue at Home, Intractability Abroad

The issues raised by the fairness and equal opportunity doctrines clearly merit careful perusal by U.S. participants in the free flow-balanced flow international debate. Ongoing dialogue on these questions reveals a continued concern and lack of consensus among U.S. scholars, legislators, judges, and journalists. U.S. refusal to debate various safeguards of media balance and diversity within other nations must harm its candor and credibility.

If inconsistencies in U.S communication policy can be justified by basic political differences in the domestic and foreign arenas, such differences must surely be identified, analyzed, and publicly defended far more than is presently the case. So, too, they must air the prospects of bolstering through technical assistance programs the same structural diversity abroad that we pursue at home.

One useful place to seek ways to reconcile Third World demands for balanced flow with the commitment to free flow may be the recent dialogue over an international right of reply (see 21, pp. 76–79). The United States has so far opposed any such initiative by UNESCO. Indeed, U.S. domestic policy has itself somewhat receded from fairness and right of reply safeguards in the wake of *Tornillo* and the emergence of multivoice markets (via cable grids, satellite relays, and videocassettes). Nonetheless, developing nations are sensitive to information dependency, and free flow rests on a two-way process in which they are not yet able to participate. Until the communication infrastructures of developing nations suffice to insure a vigorous two-way information flow, more direct safeguards on a balanced information flow seem defensible and very much in line with U.S. domestic reliance on the equal opportunity and fairness doctrines.

CONCLUSION

U.S opposition to *a priori* planning of the high frequency spectrum, the geostationary orbit, and the space services using it is inconsistent with domestic allocation plans for television and FM radio. Likewise, U.S. rejection of Third World calls for a balanced information flow contradicts its long-standing domestic commitment of fairness, balance, equal access, and diversity.

By way of extricating itself from such contradictions, the United States might consider means to combine *a priori* plans with market incentives in global spectrum management, namely, mechanisms that not only vest spectrum and orbit rights with developing nations but also permit HDCs to rent or lease those rights from LDCs for mutually agreed time periods. The U.S. must also consider ways to help develop the mass media infrastructures of Third World nations so that their demand for controlled balance could be met at least in part (as increasingly within the United States) by greater structural diversity. This goal entails a more imaginative program of direct aid from the U.S. as well as expanded ITU assistance—possibly funded by the MacBride Commission's proposed international tax on usage of orbital positions and space satellite or shortwave radio frequencies and on the manufacturers of international communications equipment.

NOTES

1. However, a practical guidepost may be the informal way in which latecomers have been accommodated in past years. Latecomers (and expanding incumbents) simply have hunted out unused HF spectrum and used it on a pragmatic basis. These frequencies may in fact have been claimed via some nation's prior notification to the IFRB, by formal registration, by first use, or by longest contin-

uous use. However, such prior "paper" claims normally have not prevented new-comers from "borrowing" the unused spectrum in the informal manner just described (15, pp. 32–34). The latest "reaccommodation" procedure appears to have formalized a long-standing process that at best provides only partial relief.

2. There are also problems in the subsequent decision to license FM and TV stations by rule rather than ad hoc principles (1). However, it is unwise for the United States to ignore the demonstrated hazards of ad hoc management of mutually exclusive requests in AM broadcasting when this country supports the modified Algerian proposal, which could entail similar complexity and cost in HF management.

3. An emerging concept of structural regulation seeks to earmark some broadcast time each week for editorial spot announcements or programming by members of the public, to be allocated in part by the first-come, first-served rule and in part "on a representative spokesperson (basis)," such time allocations to be "nondiscretionary as to content with the licensee," though with the broadcasting "still . . . required to ensure that spot messages or other forms of response to 'editorial advertisements' are broadcast" (FCC, Notice of Inquiry in BC Docket No. 78–60, in re: Fairness Doctrine and Public Interest Standards, March 2, 1978, para. 6, and pp. 2–3 generally).

REFERENCES

1. Baker, Warren E. "Policy by Rule or Ad Hoc Approach—Which Should It Be?" *Law &Contemporary Problems*, Autumn 1957, pp. 66–71.

2. Barron, Jerome A. "Access to the Press—A New First Amendment Right." *Harvard Law Review*, June 1980.

3. Barrow, Roscoe L. "The Equal Opportunities and Fairness Doctrines in Broadcasting: Pillars in the Forum of Democracy." *University of Cincinnati Law Review*, Summer 1968, pp. 447–549.

4. Barton, Margaret. "Conditional Logit Analysis of FCC Decisionmaking." *Bell Journal*, Autumn 1979.

5. Branscomb, Anne "Waves of the Future: Making WARC Work." *Foreign Policy*, April 1979.

6. Clippinger, John, "The U.S. Faces WARC—The Hidden Agenda." *Journal of Communication*, Winter 1979.

7. Codding, George A. "The New Nations and the ITU: Some Policy Implications for the Future." Paper presented at the Sixth Annual Telecommunications Policy Research Conference, Airlie, Va., April 1978.

8. Codding, George A. *The U.S. and the ITU in a Changing World*. OT Special Publication 75–6, December 1975.

9. Federal Communications Commission. *FCC Staff Report on Results of the 1979 World Administrative Radio Conference*, January 15, 1980.

10. Gunter, Jonathan. *The United States Position and the Debate on the World "Information Order."* Academy for Educational Development, 1979.

11. Hudson, Heather. *The United States and the Debate on the World "Information Order."* Academy for Educational Development, Inc., 1979.

12. Jussawalla, M. "The World Administrative Radio Conference/1979 and

Two New Global Orders." Paper presented at World Communications Conference, Philadelphia, May 1980.

13. Leive, David M. *International Telecommunications and International Law: The Regulation of the Radio Spectrum.* Oceana Press, 1970.

14. Levin, Harvey J. *Fact and Fancy in Television Regulation.* New York: Russell Sage Foundation, June 1980.

15. Levin, Harvey J. *The Invisible Resource: Use and Regulation of the Radio Spectrum.* Baltimore, Md.: Johns Hopkins University Press, 1971.

16. Lukasik, Stephen J. *What Happened at WARC.* Federal Communications Commission, January 1980.

17. "Making WARC Work." *Foreign Policy*, April 1979.

18. Masmoudi, Mustapha. "The New World Information Order." Paper presented to the International Commission for the Study of Communications Problems.

19. Rutkowski, Anthony M. "The 1979 World Administrative Radio Conference: The ITU in a Changing World." *International Lawyer*, Spring 1979.

20. Rutkowski, Anthony M. "Sixth Ad Hoc Two—The Third World Speaks Its Mind." Unpublished manuscript, 1979.

21. UNESCO. *Interim Report of the International Commission for the Study of Communications Problems.* Paris, 1978.

22. United States Congressional Research Service. *The World Administrative Radio Conference of 1979: U.S. Preparations and Proposals.* Reprinted in Congressional Record—Senate, July 12, 1979.

23. United States Congressional Research Service. *An Introduction to the Foreign Policy Implications of the 1979 WARC.* March 31, 1978. Released by Sen. Charles H. Percy.

24. U.S. Department of State. *World Administrative Radio Conference.* Summary Report No. 9, January 1980.

25. "Views on UNESCO's Mass Media Declaration" (from Moscow, London, Helsinki). *Journal of Communication*, Spring 1979, pp. 186–98.

Fifty

The MacBride Report: The Results and Response

Kusum Singh and Bertram Gross

One of the few bright spots of the eighties in the generally deteriorating international communications scene was the submission in UNESCO, early in 1980, of the MacBride Report on a New World Communication Order.[1] The Report, prepared by the International Commission for the Study of Communication Problems (generally referred to as the MacBride Commission after its Chairman, Sean MacBride), was published as *Many Voices, One World: Communication and Society Today and Tomorrow*. As various Commission members and commentators have observed, this Report was "more a negotiated document than an academic presentation" (from the Report, p. 281) and "has to be seen as a *political* document prepared by a *small group* of experts for a *large international* audience" (4, p. 18).

Its conclusions have already been debated in U.N. forums. At the meeting of the Third World oriented International Association for Mass Communication Research (IAMCR) in Caracas, the idea for a collection of articles on the MacBride Report originated and resulted in the publication of *Communication in the Eighties: A Reader on the "MacBride Report,"* edited by Cees Hamelink (4). Early in 1981, First World media leaders organized a counter-caucus and issued the Declaration of Talloires. The circle of participants in this vital debate is now widening.

As a contribution toward this dialogue, we shall review the embattled birth of the MacBride Commission, the highlights of its Report, the Hamelink reader, and the Declaration of Talloires. Finally, we offer some suggestions on a Report theme—democratic and horizontal communication.

THE MacBRIDE COMMISSION: BACKGROUND AND FORMATION

To understand the emergence of the MacBride Commission one must look back to the origin of the "Third Worldism" that arose with the dissolution of the old colonial empires after World War II. At the Bandung conference in 1956 the leaders of former colonies (with the participation of Yugoslavia) organized a "non-aligned" movement. They defined it as a third force to act as a buffer between capitalism and communism—or more specifically, between the so-called First World (or Free World) led by the United States and the Second World led by the Soviet Union (11, p. 5).

As the movement grew, the non-aligned leaders launched a two-pronged attack on "neo-colonialism" (or neo-imperialism) and "cultural imperialism." The power of this attack has rested upon a tacit and often uneasy unity between two opposing Third World groups: on one side, anticapitalists eager to revolutionize the entire social structure of their countries and, on the other, native capitalists interested in opposing domination by Western transnational corporations or getting better terms from them. From the beginning, the Soviet Union (and, in somewhat different ways, China) has supported this kind of united front effort, which helps divide the capitalist world by pitting Third World capitalists against First World adversaries. As a result, the voting line-up has over time changed radically in the U.N. and in other U.N. family members such as UNESCO. During the 1950s when most Third World countries sided with the West, the Soviet bloc was invariably in the minority. But by the 1970s, with the Soviet bloc and most of the Third World countries voting together, the First World was often in the minority.

With this stronger position in the U.N. (although not in the management of the World Bank or the International Monetary Fund), the two-pronged attack took a positive form in 1973. At their Algiers conference in 1973 the leaders of the non-aligned regimes formulated positive proposals for both a New International Economic Order and a New International Information Order. In May 1974, with the Western countries giving ground at the level of generalities, the U.N. General Assembly adopted the Declaration of the Establishment of a New International Economic Order. This statement called for replacing the existing order, which was characterized by "inequality, domination, dependence, narrow self-interest and segmentation," with a new order based on "equity, sovereign equality, interdependence, common interest and cooperation among States irrespective of their economic and social systems." Behind these abstractions lay the hope of better access to Third World markets, more financial aid, and increased access to Western technology.

By and large, these hopes were dashed to pieces by the world economic crisis of combined stagnation and inflation (often called "stagflation"). Under these conditions, the developing countries' terms of trade have generally worsened and their products have been kept out of Western markets, while financial and technical aid has become increasingly bilateral (rather than channeled through U.N. agencies) and directed toward providing more favorable conditions for private Western investment and control. By 1980, as reported by the U.N.'s Director-General for Development in an unprecedented outburst of frankness, "the processes of the United Nations system have tended to be used primarily for deliberations resulting in texts of a general character rather than a firm commitment to action" (14, p. 130).

Various Third World leaders and experts developed a strong attack on neo-colonial cultural domination. This attack was most clearly articulated by Mustapha Masmoudi, Permanent Delegate of Tunisia to UNESCO, in a report (13; see also 7) asserting that the Western concept of "free flow"—like freedom of the seas, free markets, and free trade—conceals the nature of neo-imperial control. Third World leaders also sought agreement at UNESCO meetings on a declaration paralleling the U.N. Assembly's declaration on the economic order. After two years of continuous bickering, in 1978 UNESCO delegates adopted by acclamation a Declaration on the Mass Media (see 10) that was of such a "general character" that it committed nobody to anything.

To move beyond the Declaration's generalities, both sides agreed to set up a "brain trust" that would seek a middle ground—the International Commission for the Study of Communication Problems. UNESCO's Director-General, Amadou-Mahtar M'Bow of Senegal, selected as President of the Commission Sean MacBride. MacBride was active in the Irish Republican Army in the 1920s and 1930s, and his services as United Nations Commissioner for Namibia won him both the Nobel and Lenin Peace Prizes. In rounding out the group, M'Bow sought experts who, while not officially representing governments, would be "representative of the world's ideological, political, economic and geographical spectrum." The nature of this spectrum is suggested by the following breakdown:

First World—Elie Abel (U.S.), Hubert Beuve-Mery (France), Sean MacBride (Ireland), Michio Nagai (Japan), Johannes Pieter Pronk (Netherlands), Betty Zimmerman (Canada).

Second World—Sergei Losev (U.S.S.R.), Bogdan Osolnik (Yugoslavia).

Third World—Elebe Ma Ekonzo (Zaire), Mochtar Lubis (Indonesia), Gabriel Garcia Marquez (Colombia), Mustapha Masmoudi (Tunisia), Fred Isaac Akporuaro Omu (Nigeria), Gamal El Oteifi (Egypt), Juan Somavia (Chile), Boobli George Verghese (India).

It might be noted that MacBride himself comes from a country that suffered from British colonialism for many centuries, and both Garcia Marquez and Somavia are refugees from their own countries now living in Mexico. With the possible exception of India and Tunisia, the Third World countries represented are those strongly tilted toward the First World. The task here, however, was to seek a consensus between conflicting viewpoints by trying—in MacBride's words—to "transcend conventional issues" and to study "the totality of communication problems in modern society."

THE REPORT

One of the marks of civilization is the ability to discuss conflicts frankly and resolve contradictions in a manner that contributes to, rather than obfuscates, future action and dialogue. By this high standard, the Report stands out as one of the most civilized reports yet published under U.N. auspices. It moves from the rather abstract rhetoric of the 1978 Declaration on the Mass Media to a rich analysis of global, national, and even community communication problems. It offers a series of ideas and proposals that are frankly controversial. Above all, with an openness absent from most U.N. reports, the Commission provided its members an opportunity to include dissenting opinions and additional comments. While adding spice to the volume, these also clarify some areas of conflict and air a few ideas that, while long overdue, are not feasible in the near future. Because it tackles complex and rapidly changing realities, the Report makes many references to contradictions and dilemmas, which opens it to easy criticism from those who yearn for unambiguous prescriptions.

Rights To Communicate and Receive Information

Since the beginning of the non-aligned movement, there has been a stormy conflict between First World supporters of the "free flow of information" doctrine and non-aligned leaders attacking it as a cover-up for First World domination. The two sides were eventually brought together—at a skeletal level of generality—by a UNESCO synthesis: "a free flow and a wider and more balanced dissemination of information." The MacBride Commission put flesh on this skeleton. The Report relates freedom of the press to freedom of expression generally, to the many interpretations of the newly stated rights to "communicate" and "receive information," rights of reply and correction, and the civil-political and economic-social-cultural rights set forth in the U.N.'s 1966 covenants. It points out that freedom for the "strong" and the "haves" has had undesirable consequences for the "weak" and the "have nots" (pp. 141–142). It urges greater access to the media by women, young people, and ethnic, linguistic, and religious minorities (pp. 168, 267).

With the exception of Losev, all members urge that "censorship or arbitrary control of information be abolished" (p. 266). This is backed up by an incisive list of 10 different techniques used by external censors (p. 139) and by an equally incisive awareness of "self-censorship by communicators themselves" (pp. 19, 138, 234). With mild dissents from Abel and Zimmerman, they criticize the constraints imposed by commercialization, pressures from advertisers, and concentration of media ownership (pp. 104–111, 152–155, 266). They relate the growth of transnational corporations to "one way flow," "market dominance," and "vertical flow" (pp. 145–155). They point out that some of the strongest transnational corporations, while vociferous in behalf of freedom for themselves, are reluctant to provide information on their own and "have few compunctions about hindering the free flow of news," and avoid "opening up flows to share scientific and technological information" (p. 144). They unanimously ask that these corporations operate more openly (p. 261).

With no dissents (or names of countries), they charge that under the guise of free flow of information, "some governments, transnationals, media and organized pressure groups have on occasion tried to undermine internal stability in other countries, violating their sovereignty and disturbing national development" (p. 143). They also recognize instances in which "national sovereignty has been invoked to justify restrictions on news collection and dissemination" and when "under the cloak of seemingly progressive measures to correct journalistic malpractice, media activity and journalists have been placed under the exclusive control of the state apparatus" (p. 143). Garcia Marquez and Somavia stress that this analysis "is particularly crucial in third world countries dominated by repressive minority regimes" (p. 281).

The "Technological Dilemma"

In the context of what they call "the technological dilemma," the Commission members provide copious detail on innovations entering into informatics, microinformatics, and telematics. Computers, satellites, electrostatic copying, cable television, data banks (and bases), transborder data flows, and other advances, they hold, "may one day facilitate breaking down barriers between persons and nations. That trend is without doubt irreversible" (p. 31). On the other hand, the new technologies have ambiguous or dangerous consequences: less availability to Third World countries (pp. 131–132), greater control by foreign transnationals (p. 160), more obstacles to popular control in exercising democratic activity (p. 167). Accordingly, while supporting greater Third World access to advanced communication technologies (pp. 260–261), the Commission also advises delay and caution in order to avoid distortions and "negative effects" (p. 95), and more attention to the preservation (or adaptation) of traditional modes of communication. With dissents from four members (Abel, Zimmerman, Lubis, and MacBride), the members propose a new Center "within the framework of UNESCO" to foster international cooperation on these matters.

Professional Communicators

Various sections of the Report are dedicated to professional communicators (pp. 227–232), the responsibilities and rights of journalists (pp. 233–240), and norms of professional conduct and professional integrity (pp. 241–246). Here the Commission seeks "long-term evolutionary action" toward the better training of all communicators (editors, producers, managers, and technicians, as well as journalists). Third World communicators should receive their initial training at regional centers with curricula "designed by instructors from the region, and with foreign advisors as required" (p. 232). Codes of ethics are regarded as desirable if prepared and enforced by media professionals themselves (and their employers), not by governments. While the Commission as a whole embraces the possibility of a truly international code, Abel holds that "a planetary code for journalists of all nations is neither attainable nor desirable under present circumstances" (p. 244). With further reservations by Abel, the Commission maintains that "excessive" or "exclusive" professionalization creates barriers to democratic communication (p. 229).

The Commission also notes the difficulties faced by journalists in many Second or Third World countries, particularly by "harassment, threats, imprisonment, physical violence, assassination." Although this elicited no explicit dissent, members from those countries ensured that the remedies were nothing more than "vigilance" and occasional UNESCO round tables on the subject. "To propose additional measures," they observed, "would invite the dangers entailed in a licensing system, since it would require somebody to stipulate who should be entitled to claim such protection." MacBride, however, argues that journalists "be granted a special status and protection" and that the round tables be convened annually for the next five years (pp. 264, 265).

"Democratization of Communication"

The most innovative part of the Report is its two sections on "democratization of communication." Here the Commission members unanimously agree that democratization is impeded by undemocratic political systems, bureaucratic administrative systems, technologies controlled or understood only by a few, the exclusion of disadvantaged groups, and illiteracy and semi-literacy (pp. 164–174, 265–267). To break through these barriers they recommend many steps, some of which were never heretofore a part of discussions on global communication. These include participation in media managemment by representatives of the public and various citizens' groups (p. 169), horizontal communication, counter-information (p. 170), and three forms of alternative communication: radical opposition, community or local media movements, and "trade unions or other social groups with their particular communication networks" (p. 169). Any of these, it is pointed out, "has its greatest strength in interpersonal relationships and thus has a capacity to defy or evade constraints by authority" (p. 171). In an important appendix statement, Garcia Marquez and Somavia hail these discussions. "The diffusion of power concentrated in the hands of commercial or bureaucratic interests," they add, "is a worldwide necessity." They also point out that programs of technical cooperation, operating through money and training alone, could glorify technological solutions to communication problems and "reinforce minority structures within third world countries, or serve as a vehicle for cultural domination" (p. 281).

On forms of international action other than the idea of a new UNESCO center, the Commission defers to other international organizations. Thus on East-West interface, they support the implementation of the Helsinki Final Act of 1975. On the embattled issue of the electromagnetic spectrum, they favor more equity as a principle for the decisions by the World Administrative Radio Conference (WARC). They acknowledge the importance of the U.N.'s program of "development support communication," the News Agency Pool of the non-aligned countries, and the Inter Press Service. The only truly new proposal is for a feasibility study on the U.N.'s developing "a broadcast capability of its own and possible access to a satellite system" (p. 270). In an additional comment, MacBride goes further: "The U.N. should establish a broadcasting system of its own that would broadcast 24 hours around the clock in not less than 30 different languages." In a brief finale not approved by the Commission, the Report lists various themes for future study, including an international code of ethics for both journalism and advertising, and the possible financing of communication development by levying taxes or duties on "surplus profits on raw materials," "the use of the electromagnetic spectrum and geostationary orbit space," or "the profits of transnational companies producing transmission facilities and equipment."

RESPONSE TO THE REPORT: COMMUNICATORS EXPRESS RESERVATIONS

Calling the MacBride Report a "mission impossible," Cees J. Hamelink and his 10 collaborators (4) provided an almost instantaneous commentary on a remarkably complex document. With each contributor expressing his personal views, a number of different but mutually supporting approaches result. While hailing the Report as "the first international document that provides a really global view on the world's communication problems," the authors generally feel that the Report did not go far enough to meet Third World demands. It did not relate the older and the present communication orders to general historical trends (Nordenstreng, Capriles). It did not articulate the basic features of the desired new order (Capriles, Dajani) or show how efforts to attain the new order could promote the cause of peace by lessening international tensions (Nordenstreng). It reified the idea of "communication" and used both "communication" and "information" without conceptual clarity (Opubor). More attention should have been given to communication research (Roncagliolo, Dajani); to training in, not merely for, Third World countries (Eapen); and to national planning as the context of national communication policies (Szecskö).

The danger inherent in new technologies is a powerful theme for many of the authors. While commending the Report for observing that "the new communications technology raises more problems than it solves," Schiller criticizes it for nonetheless urging international cooperation on technology transfer to Third World countries and ignoring the "structural realities of transnational business as the engine behind technology transfer." This could lead to "electronic utopias." Szecskö observes that the Report "leaves open quite a few doors for technological determinism to creep in," while Hamelink charges that it could "elevate technology to the degree of mystification." With support from Dajani and Becker, Roncagliolo reports that UNESCO was already, in the wake of the Report, developing a "Marshall Plan . . . to co-opt the idea of a new world information order by transferring it into more technology, more training, more bilateral aid, in other words, more dependency." For Hamelink, this could bring the world together in a "corporate village," thereby converting the dream of a new order into a "world order of the transnational corporations."

On the more positive side, three contributors hail the Report's call for the democratization of communication. Szecskö quotes approvingly from the Garcia Marquez-Somavia comment on the necessity of promoting access, participation, decentralization, open management, and the diffusion of power "in Third World countries dominated by repressive minority regimes." Roncagliolo hails the Commission for having legitimized this issue, observing that in Latin America "no subject could be more crucial." This theme links research with political practice and "leads directly to the material base" of the mass media. "It was not by accident," he observes, "that democratization of communications has been selected by the IAMCR for its next scientific conference to be held in Paris in 1982." Foubert emphasizes the role of documentation centers and networks in promoting "alternative channels of communication" and "participatory media." After attacking the conservative West German criticisms of the Report as "Marxist," Becker holds that when translated into German the Report would "fulfill a very important role within the political situation of the media in the FRG" by virtue of "its two central demands for democratization and decommercialization."

OPPOSITION TO THE REPORT: THE DECLARATION OF TALLOIRES

After referring the Report to its member states (without endorsing any of its conclusions), UNESCO's Belgrade General Conference then proceeded to act along two lines partially prefigured in it. First, as Roncagliolo had predicted, it approved a U.S.-originated proposal for a clearinghouse to help Third World countries by training journalists and upgrading communication infrastructures. Known as the International Program for Development of Communication (IPDC), it will operate as a separate entity within UNESCO with its own director, a 35-nation advisory council, voluntary contributions, and an orientation toward bilateral activities not controlled by the Second and Third World majorities in UNESCO. Second, in preparation for UNESCO's 1983 general conference in Venezuela, the Belgrade conference authorized a package of work programs to define more fully the New World Communication Order, investigate the influence of advertising on news media coverage, and explore the possibility of international regulation of satellite communications. Another work program led to a draft proposal by a French political scientist for a Commission for the Protection of Journalists. Beginning as a nongovernmental body and then becoming a more official institution, the proposed Commission would give journalists identity cards that could be withdrawn if they violated "generally accepted codes of journalistic ethics."

First World media leaders reacted vigorously against the licensing proposal, charging that it would interfere with press freedom. The *New York Times* (1) and *The New Republic* (5) both urged that unless UNESCO dropped this effort U.S. representatives "should simply quit" and "go home." Media leaders of Western Europe, however, made it clear they would not go this far. Instead, they gathered at Talloires, in the French Alps, where they expressed their objections not only to the ethics-licensing proposal (which was not advocated in the Report) but to many of the Report's fundamental ideas.

In its opening propositions, the Declaration of Talloires resurrected the original First World formulation of "free flow," conspicuously dropping the words "and balanced." Without specifically referring to the Report's critique of commercialization, monopoly, or bureaucracy, the signatories affirmed uncompromising allegiance to "the importance of advertising as a consumer service and in providing financial support for a strong and self-sustaining press." Without commenting on the Report's plea for the democratization of communication, they supported "the universal right to be freely informed" and opposed "any interference with this fundamental right." Without mentioning the Report's comments on self-censorship, they called for the elimination of "censorship and other forms of arbitrary control of information and opinion." On ethics and licensing, finally, they were very explicit:

> There can be no international code of ethics; the plurality of views makes this impossible . . . Licensing of journalists by national or international bodies should not be sanctioned; nor should special requirements be demanded of journalists in lieu of licensing them. Such measures submit journalists to controls and pressures inconsistent with a free press.

In a follow-up on the declaration, one of its authors, Leonard Sussman, of the World Press Freedom Committee and Freedom House, urged that the First World representatives "should state clearly that its members will provide communication technology assistance only to Third World countries that accept as a fundamental commitment the expansion of the free flow of information world-wide" (12). With these developments, in the words of Rosemary Righter as reported in the *New York Times*, "the false truce in the long campaign for the international regulation of the press is over" (6).

EXPANDING UPON THE REPORT'S THEME: DEMOCRATIZATION AND HORIZONTAL COMMUNICATION

The honorific word "democracy" has been used to refer to a multitude of different things—from direct, constitutional, and representative democracy to economic, social, grassroots, functional, plebiscitary, totalitarian, people's managerial, imperial, and corporatist democracy. Behind each of these ideas or phenomena lies a complex mixture of "fool's gold" and the true democracy that provides "the opportunity for all persons to take part—directly and indirectly, both in large and small measure—in the decisions that affect themselves, others and the larger communities of which they are a part" (3, chapter 19).

Any serious exploration of this complex theme would lead to more than (in Roncagliolo's words) the "material base" of the mass media. It would relate communication to all factors that may tend to concentrate or deconcentrate power. Some of these factors were dealt with in the documents submitted to the Commission and listed in the Report's appendix—for example, those by Somavia, Beltrán, Schwoebel, Halina. Berrigan, Cassirer, and Micovik.

Truly constructive action along these lines would recognize that the fate of any apparently democratic movement may depend on whether its leaders can avoid tendencies toward elitist hierarchy and bureaucracy and develop nonelitist styles of communication and leadership (8, 9). Further, such action would escape the "media trap" by recognizing the vital roles of interpersonal, organizational, and political communication—roles underestimated when professionals overemphasize mass media and alternative media. Finally, it would distinguish between "horizontal," "lateral," or "top-top" communication between elites and experts at the upper levels of a nation or the world community and the horizontal or lateral communication of a "bottom sideways" nature that brings ordinary people together (10). Above all, better facilities should be developed for communication among the people of a nation, region, bloc, and the world. "Wars, let us remember," in Galbraith's words (2), "come when men, single-minded in certainty and righteousness, lose the ability to communicate with each other."

NOTE

1. This article follows the terminology explained in the Report itself: "At the 1978 General Conference of UNESCO and General Assembly of the United Nations . . . consensus was reached on the term 'new more just and more efficient world information and communication order' which indicates not only the aim but also its major parameters. For conciseness and completeness, the term 'new world communication order' will be used in this report" (p. 39).

REFERENCES

1. "And 'Ethical' Censorship at Unesco." *New York Times* editorial, February 17, 1981.
2. Galbraith, John K. "Galbraith on Communicating." In Carl Marcy (Ed.) *Items on East-West Relations: Just for the Press.* Washington, D.C.: American Committee on East-West Accord, April/May 1980.
3. Gross, Bertram. *Friendly Fascism: The New Face of Power in America.* New York: Evans, 1980.
4. Hamelink, Cees (Ed.) *Communication in the Eighties: A Reader on the "MacBride Report."* Rome: IDOC International, 1980.
5. Krauthammer, Charles. "Brave News World." *The New Republic*, March 14, 1981.
6. Lewis, Paul. "Gloves Come Off in Struggle With Unesco." *New York Times*, May 24, 1981.
7. Masmoudi, Mustapha, "The New World Information Order." *Journal of Communication* 29(2), Spring 1979.
8. Singh, Kusum. "Elite Control and Challenge in Changing India." In George Gerbner (Ed.) *Mass Media Policies in Changing Cultures.* New York: John Wiley and Sons, 1977.
9. Singh, Kusum. "Gandhi and Mao as Mass Communicators." *Journal of Communication* 29(3), Summer 1979.
10. Singh, Kusum and Bertram Gross. "Alternative Communication Strategies in Third World Countries." *Communicator* (Journal of the Indian Institute of Mass Communication), January 1981. Also in *Economic and Political Weekly* (Bombay), February 21, 1981.

Fifty-One

The MacBride Report: A Soviet Analysis[1]

Yassen Zassoursky and Sergei Losev

The unanimously adopted Report of UNESCO's International Commission for the Study of Communication Problems (the MacBride Report) has become an important contribution to the struggle for the use of the mass media for strengthening international mutual understanding and the eradication of racism, apartheid, and incitement to war. Representatives of the U.S.S.R., the U.S., France, India, Mexico, Nigeria, Indonesia, Japan, and other countries took part in the Commission and prepared the Report issued in March of 1980. It was headed by Sean MacBride, laureate of the International Lenin Prize and Nobel Peace Prize. After two years of work, the Commission gathered a vast amount of material on the state of affairs in the mass media in different regions of the world. A discussion was held on problems of the development of television, radio broadcasting, and the press.

The recommendations of the Commission stress the importance of the mass media in strengthening mutual understanding in the struggle for peace and disarmament. In expanding the provisions of the UNESCO Declaration on the Mass Media, the Commission calls for "encouraging radio broadcasting and other means of international journalism to introduce, wherever possible, a more complete contribution to matters of peace and international cooperation, and abstain from propaganda of national, racial and religious hatred and calls for discrimination, hostility, violence or war."

In the Report of the Commission it is stated that "the new international procedure in the field of information must become an instrument of peaceful cooperation between nations." The Commission emphasized that "the interpretation of international events occurring in various countries in a situation of crisis and tension requires exceptional prudence and responsibility." Today one must constantly remind oneself of these words when one reads the reports of Western agencies about events in Afghanistan or in Iran, in El Salvador and in the Near East. In an atmosphere of sharp conflict the bourgeois mass media are creating a situation of tension and military hysteria, and provoke, in essence, aggressive actions against the forces of progress. These actions, which contradict the UNESCO Declaration on the Mass Media and the Final Act of the Helsinki Conference, show the unwillingness of the owners of the information-propaganda complex to heed the voice of international public opinion. . . .

The Report is centered on the problem of rebuilding international relations in the field of information on the basis of respect for national sovereignty in information and culture, liberation of the developing countries from "spiritual imperialism," and the development of national mass media. The Commission outlined an important method to combat the dominance by Western information agencies and television companies of the mass media of developing countries. It recommended the formation of national information agencies, and regional and national radio and motion picture documentary production centers.

It is known that in today's world journalism operates on an industrial basis. Newspapers, television, and radio broadcasts spread material supplied by information agencies and television and motion picture studios which are complex production enterprises. In order to create a national mass media system it is not enough to publish newspapers and conduct radio and television broadcasts in the language of a country. It is necessary to make use of one's own production facilities for television films and shorts, and information material.

The Soviet Union is extending various and effective aid to developing countries to set up national agencies and centers for the production of television films. The Soviet Union regards cooperation in this field as one of the important components in establishing new information procedures on the basis of national sovereignty in the appropriate sphere and liquidation of all manifestations of colonialism and its remnants and of imperialist dominance in the spiritual life of developing countries.

The MacBride Commission called for intensifying the role of UNESCO in strengthening the mass media of developing countries and improving their material-technical base. Attempts to make the states of Asia, Africa and Latin America scientifically and technically dependent upon the West by providing them with technology produced by transnational corporations were consistently rejected.

It is natural that the Commission turned down the solicitations of American representatives who attempted to push UNESCO aside and make the mechanism of rendering aid subordinate to a certain consultative group, in which the U.S.-controlled International Bank for Reconstruction and Development, as well as Western "regional" banks, were playing dominant roles. This, essentially, was an attempt to make the struggling national agencies and other mass media of developing countries dependent upon those very transnational corporations which are the vehicles of imperialist propaganda.

Criticism of the commercial approach to information activities occupies an important place in the Report of the MacBride Commission. It mentions the need "to reduce the negative influence of the market and of commercial considerations on the content and organization of national and international information flows." The Commission submitted a progressive proposal of financing national mass media systems by imposing taxes on commercial advertisement.

The Commission subjected to criticism the process of monopolization and concentration of journalism in Western countries. The Report contains convincing facts which show that the press, radio, and television in countries of the so-called "free world" belong to a small number of newspaper, magazine, radio, and television corporations. In the U.S., for instance, 2036 newspapers were published in 1923, of which 153 belonged to corporations; by 1976, however, the number of newspapers fell to 1765, but 1061 of them were now owned by the so-called "newspaper chains." The activities of transnational corporations are an extreme example of the subordination of journalism to the interest of monopolies. Fifteen of them have taken into their own hands the manufacture of equipment for the production, transmission, and reception of radio and television programs, and the use of electronics in the newspaper and magazine business.

The monopoly domination very acutely raises the question of the place of the journalist in the mass media system, of his responsibility to society rather than to the owner. In the section of the Commission's Report entitled "Responsibilities of the Journalist," it is stated that "for a journalist, freedom and responsibility cannot be separated." It is especially important to realize a feeling of responsibility to their own nation for employees of the press of countries freed from colonial dominance.

The Report of the MacBride Commission condemned the practice of using journalists for intelligence activities. As is known, the U.S. uses American journalists for espionage purposes, especially in developing countries. Speaking in April of 1980 at the yearly session of the American Society of Newspaper Editors, former CIA Director S. Turner admitted that U.S. special services continue to carry out plans of widespread recruiting of correspondents, despite the disclosure of espionage activities of over four hundred American journalists.

In view of the rather mixed staff of the MacBride Commission, which also included representatives from the West, its Report also contains certain concepts with which it is difficult to agree. Some of these are, in particular, attempts to interpret arbitrarily the Final Act of the Helsinki Conference.

By the efforts of the Western representatives, the idea of a new international procedure in the field of information was thoroughly emasculated. The "cultural invasion" was excluded from the Report, but the pernicious role of Western "mass culture" in the destruction of national traditions of "Third World" countries is underestimated. The success achieved by socialist and developing states in the development of the mass media was not fully reflected in the Report.

All in all, the MacBride Commission Report represents a serious contribution to the cause of placing information in the service of peace and progress. . . . Further efforts in using information exchange for the good of peace and progress, the formation of a new information procedure based on respect for national sovereignty in the field of information and culture, and the liquidation of imperialist dominance in the spiritual life of developing countries, are of great significance in strengthening the political and economic independence of developing countries, international cooperation, and mutual understanding.

NOTE

1. This paper is a translation of an article published in *Pravda* on May 5, 1980.

Fifty-Two

UNESCO at Belgrade: The U.S. View[1]

Prepared under the direction of
Sarah Goddard Power

Communication issues have been center stage at UNESCO General Conferences since 1974; the General Conference held at Belgrade in the fall of 1980 was no exception. The heart of the matter, from our standpoint, has been the effort by the Soviet Union and some Third World countries to foster government control of the media under the guise of a New World Information and Communication Order (NWIO). The U.S., while recognizing that the developing countries need help in improving their communication capacities, has resisted all approaches which would make the media subservient to governments, because such a policy conflicts with our First Amendment tradition and the doctrine of free flow of information. . . .

The U.S. had three general, interrelated objectives with respect to information and communication issues at Belgrade: (1) to continue the trend within UNESCO toward more pragmatic and less controversial approaches to communications, (2) to blur North-South divisions on these issues and consolidate a working relationship with Third World moderates, and (3) to isolate the Soviets and Third World radicals who have insisted on a restrictive approach to the press.

Specifically, we sought to ensure noncontroversial treatment of the report of the (MacBride) International Commission for the Study of Communication Problems. The U.S. was apprehensive that there might be a move for immediate implementation of the 82 recommendations of the Report, some of which we strongly oppose. We also sought the establishment of the International Program for the Development of Communications (IPDC), a new UNESCO-based clearinghouse of information about communications development assistance. . . .

We were concerned at one point because the proposed statutes did not contain two elements which had been essential to our acceptance of the recommendations: preference for the consensual decision-making process in the IPDC Intergovernmental Council and autonomy for the IPDC Program Director who was to be appointed by the Director-General of UNESCO on the recommendation of the Council. These two elements were assured by a combination of amendments to the statutes and the incorporation, as a sort of "basic law" for the IPDC, of all of the previous recommendations into the Belgrade resolution.

There remains some ambiguity about the respective roles, authority, and relationship of the constituent parts of the clearinghouse mechanism. The Intergovernmental Council is elected by and "responsible to" the General Conference, meaning that it does not have to depend on the Director-General as a policy intermediary. The Director-General is to "administer" the IPDC program, which could entail nothing more than administrative support but might engage him in some substantive policy direction. The Program Director will have to devise a way to divide his responsiveness between the Council and the Director-General. Everyday practice, more than anything else, will determine how well these checks and balances sort themselves out.

The establishment of the IPDC marks the successful realization of a U.S. initiative first announced at the 20th General Conference in 1978. It expresses in concrete form an active sympathy for the communications and information disabilities of the developing world, and a desire to turn UNESCO's attention away from divisive rhetoric towards unifying works of practical construction.

Two caveats bear mentioning. If the U.S. is to maintain its leadership in this area, useful and substantial contributions must be seen to come from both public and private sectors in this country; to falter now in our support of the IPDC could see it fall into the hands of our adversaries and distorted to serve anti-free press purposes. It may take a long time for the rhetorical thirst of the Third World to abate. We are dealing with entrenched attitudes and deeply felt frustrations. These can only be changed over time and by demonstrating that the U.S. approach to communications development and a free press are delivering real benefits to the Third World. The key words for us are patience and persistence. . . .

THE MacBRIDE REPORT

The MacBride Report is a mixed bag as far as the United States is concerned. It contains a strong affirmation of freedom, diversity, and other libertarian values, but exhibits a clear bias against the involvement of the private sector in communications. The Director-General's comments on the MacBride Report were on the Belgrade agenda although the Report itself was not. The Director-General did not propose any specific follow-up, observing that the Secretariat will reflect on the Report and comments about it but that there was "no need for immediate actions at this stage." The U.S. welcomed this conclusion and quoted the Director-General frequently in opposing any move favoring immediate implementation of the MacBride recommendations. The Director-General's approach to the Report was indispensable to a constructive outcome on this issue. Had he chosen to endorse some or all of the MacBride recommendations or to call for immediate implementation, there is no doubt that the General Conference would have been engulfed in a serious fight and one that the U.S. would have lost.

The major troublesome aspect of the Director-General's comments was a paragraph implying that more work needs to be done on such questions as "the relationship between the sovereign rights of a nation and the rights of citizens to communicate or journalists to conduct investigations," as well as on "professional ethics," aspects of "protection of journalists," and "an increasing concentration of media in the hands of a few private or public enterprises." Further pursuit of these concepts by UNESCO is unacceptable to the U.S. We will be carefully monitoring this work.

The resolution on the MacBride Report is largely what we had sought. . . . It calls for widespread dissemination of the Report, for study and reflection, but little concrete action as far as implementation is concerned. It stresses "the fundamental need to safeguard freedom of opinion, of expression and information." The U.S. joined the consensus with certain reservations and an explanation of its interpretation of several ambiguous concepts in the resolution. . . .

The 1981–1983 UNESCO program and budget includes items in the section on communications which are viewed by the U.S. as ranging from unhelpful to totally unacceptable. Some of the more objectionable provisions are for studies and conferences on protection of journalists, journalistic standards, freedom and responsibility in communications, international right of reply and rectification, advertising content and management of media, and contribution of media to the establishment of a NWIO. Since experience has shown that it is almost impossible to excise individual items once set in the budget and work plan, the U.S. tried another approach at Belgrade. We proposed that the $1.5 million start-up costs of the IPDC be taken *en bloc* from the communications sector of the 1981–1983 work plan, knowing that some programs, including some we opposed, would have to be dropped if money was no longer available. We called on the Secretariat, with member state input, to determine which programs should be eliminated. When we failed to generate much support for this tactic, we submitted a resolution which argued that the advent of the IPDC raised so many organizational questions and so altered the Organization's priorities that action on existing communication activities should be suspended pending post-conference review and evaluation. This resolution was defeated 56 to 3.

We also made two strong interventions explaining U.S. objections to individual items in the communications work plan, detailing our fundamental opposition to work which encroaches on the freedom of the press, as well as a separate strong intervention concerning a project to improve the communication capabilities of national liberation movements (including the PLO). Our motion to put this item to a vote was ruled out of order. Despite these setbacks, we believe our initiatives were useful in putting UNESCO on notice as never before about our . . . concerns and . . . determination to continue the fight for our views.

Our Permanent Delegation in Paris has been instructed to work closely with the Secretariat following the General Conference to see if we can avoid the implementation of some programs which are controversial. We have some grounds for cautious optimism here; the Director-General has said he is flexible and that he will welcome comments from the U.S. media and government with respect to implementation. . . .

POLICY: FUTURE WORK PLANS AND PRIORITIES

Launching the process to develop UNESCO's Second Medium-Term Plan, which will provide an overall policy framework for work plans during the period 1984–1989, was one of the most important activities of the General Conference. We view the Second Medium-Term Plan as a major opportunity to influence the content of future work plans and, thus, to avoid the kind of unacceptable content and conflict which characterize the current plan. UNESCO's communication priorities have not developed in a coherent way and are moreover in a fluid state, with new direction being suggested by the MacBride Report and the establishment of the IPDC. The U.S. statement on the Second Medium-Term Plan stressed the need to sharpen UNESCO's focus on pragmatic developmental aspects of communications questions and to continue the de-emphasis of restrictive, ideological approaches to the mass media. We said that UNESCO's expanding responsibilities for communications development and its move to new institutional arrangements require a fresh look at how it is spending its limited resources. UNESCO cannot afford the luxury of doing all it would like to do; it must concentrate on essentials. This mandates careful evaluation of existing programs to ensure that they truly serve the Organization's developmental priorities, emphasizing work which enjoys consensus support, and prioritizing of new proposals in terms of cost effectiveness and practical application. We will be pursuing this line in our continuing contacts with the Secretariat.

An old lesson relearned at Belgrade is that offense is often the best defense. A case in point was the tactic of introducing a U.S. counter to a Soviet resolution on the Mass Media Declaration, thus necessitating a negotiating group to reconcile the two drafts. We were able to obtain the deletion of all objectionable parts of the Soviet draft except a call for an international meeting and that was watered down. Similarly, the European countries (the Nine) introduced a resolution on MacBride to counter the Soviet and G-77 (non-aligned nations) versions; this European resolution, endorsed by the U.S., was drawn upon by Commission IV Chairman Thiam in assembling the synthesis used as the working paper for the MacBride drafting committee.

The most successful demonstration of the importance of offensive tactics is represented by the IPDC—a U.S. initiative at the 1978 General Conference that symbolizes our affirmative attitude toward the improvement of the technical/professional capacities of the developing countries. This was basically a U.S idea carried through forcefully in a series of UNESCO meetings and successfully defended at Belgrade. . . .

One of the most important elements in the State Department's preparations for the General Conference was the establishment of a close working relationship with the U.S. media. Prior to the Conference, the Department consulted frequently with media leaders about such matters as the choice of a media representative on the Delegation and their reaction to proposed strategies. A group of media leaders met with Secretary of State Muskie to discuss UNESCO issues. The Department held two large formal meetings to exchange views on issues expected to arise at Belgrade. The U.S. National Commission for UNESCO, in cooperation with the World Press Freedom Committee, held a similar luncheon briefing in New York at which both public and private sector spokesmen participated. . . . There is no doubt that the Director-General is highly sensitive to the political power of the U.S. media, and that the continued involvement of the private sector is vital to the attainment of long-term U.S. objectives in UNESCO. . . .

OVERALL ASSESSMENT

The U.S. can take satisfaction in an overall positive assessment of the 21st General Conference: the recommendations of the MacBride Report were not endorsed or rushed into implementation; the IPDC was established in a form which meets our criteria of offering concrete development opportunities while defusing ideological rhetoric; and the Soviet-inspired resolution on implementing the Mass Media Declaration was drastically watered down, leaving only a call for another meeting.

On the negative side, several very objectionable programs were approved in the 1981–1983 work plan. We will have our work cut out for us to have these reduced or dropped in the implementation stage. . . .

Significantly, the conference atmosphere in which communications issues were played out was demonstrably less unfriendly to us than at previous such meetings and showed that the UNESCO focus has shifted somewhat away from normative, restrictive philosophical approaches to pragmatic action programs. The debates at the General Conference underscored the mainstream Third World desire to concentrate on communications development work and, in addition, provided an important forum for us to reiterate our First Amendment principles. The Soviet Union remained in the main outside the flow of events, and was defeated or sidetracked in most of its propaganda efforts. . . . We see a continuing effort ahead to sustain these hard-won results and to restrain our adversaries.

The practical problems of communications development were paramount at Belgrade. The awakening self-assurance of the Third World, which enabled many of the developing country leaders to see through and reject Soviet efforts to polarize the issues, augurs well for a balanced dialogue on increased Third World access to communications and information technology. However, it is essential that we remain closely engaged with the issues in UNESCO, as well as increasingly responsive to legitimate Third World communications development aspirations, if we are to retain these new links with Third World moderates. Having won a bridgehead in hard fighting in three successive General Conferences (Nairobi 1976; Paris 1978; Belgrade 1980), we are in a good position to make further gains. With close public/private sector cooperation, we should be able to exploit our advantage.

However, this is only one side of the coin. Matching private sector preparations will be necessary, particularly in such areas as the identification and evaluations of candidates for UNESCO positions and the stimulation of public/private sector support for useful work in the communications field. Consultations with private sector colleagues overseas can be a key factor in developing consensus positions in the industrialized countries. We are encouraged by reports that private sector personalities are discussing the possibility of establishing a private sector consortium to bring together all the strands of international information and communication issues. We see such a vehicle as one way to ensure the kind of systematic attention which the issues deserve from the private sector and to make the most effective collaborative contribution to the total national effort needed in this field.

NOTE

1. This article is excerpted from the complete report, "Assessment of Information and Communications Issues," 21st General Conference of UNESCO, Belgrade, September 23–October 28, 1980, which was prepared for the U.S. Department of State.

Fifty-Three

UNESCO and the International Program for the Development of Communications[1]

William G. Harley

The creation of the International Program for the Development of Communications (IPDC) at the 21st General Conference of UNESCO in Belgrade in 1980 marks the successful outcome to what was primarily a U.S. initiative begun at the 20th General Conference two years earlier. The task now is to ensure that it maintains the proper direction, that it does the job it was created to do.

Essentially, the IPDC is to be an international clearinghouse for communications development needs, resources, and priorities that will permit public and private sectors in both developing and developed countries to cooperate more effectively in this field. Its primary functions will be to gather and exchange information and arrange consultations in respect to improving communications systems and services in the developing countries.

This initiative represents a sympathetic response by the developed nations to the recognized needs of the less developed countries for the means to help themselves in expanding and strengthening communication capacities. As such, it is hoped that it will also divert attention and energies away from divisive ideological preoccupations.

Whether this happens will depend on the good faith and competence of those involved and their ability to resist demands for extraneous activities and ideological intrusions. It will also depend on their ability to focus upon a comprehensive survey and better understanding of communication needs, resources, and priorities with respect to communication infrastructures, equipment, and training—and then to match those needs to expanded resources stimulated from both the private and government sectors.

THE FIRST PROPOSALS FOR DEVELOPMENT ASSISTANCE

At a meeting of 35 delegates from representative member states convened in 1979 by UNESCO in Washington, two specific proposals were on the agenda. Both were amplifications of draft resolutions introduced at UNESCO's 20th General Conference the preceding year by Roland Homet (U.S.) and Mustapha Masmoudi (Tunisia).

The twofold objectives of the U.S. proposal for a Communications Development Consultative Group were to encourage and emphasize self-reliance, so that technical cooperation in the field of communication would reflect a genuine partnership between developed and developing countries; and to upgrade the status of communications development to afford access to the general pool of resources.

Tunisia's proposal for an International Institute for Information and Communication Planning called for the establishment within UNESCO of an autonomous center administered by a Board of Directors of 16 members serving in a personal capacity and headed by a director to be appointed by the Director-General of UNESCO. This Institute would combine the concepts of an international fund, a body for planning, implementation, and training, and a center for applied research on communication development.

The most significant difference between the two proposals was that the Institute would be solely sponsored by UNESCO and would establish and manage an international fund, whereas the Consultative Group would have multi-agency sponsorship, with administrative costs underwritten by the sponsors and project funding via voluntary contributions from governments, international agencies, foundations, industry, and other private sources.

After three days of inconclusive argument at the Washington meeting, no endorsement of either proposal was made. Third World participants were adamant on the centrality of UNESCO in any mechanism, while the U.S. urged multi-agency management and greater emphasis on bilateral aid coordination. The consensus was that a need did exist for an international institutional mechanism to promote and coordinate activities in the field of communications development, and that exploration of possible arrangements for this purpose should be continued. Principles that should guide this exploration were listed, and it was recommended that the Director-General establish a small ad hoc advisory group to prepare a document based on points of agreement and disagreement for the guidance of an Intergovernmental Meeting to be held by UNESCO to formally consider such an international mechanism.

Meanwhile, at the final meeting of the MacBride Commission on November 30, 1979, Masmoudi proposed that the Commission support establishing within UNESCO an International Center for the Study and

Planning of Information and Communication—the same proposal he had introduced at the Washington conference. Despite objections of the committee members from the U.S., France, and Canada, the Masmoudi proposal was adopted as Recommendation 78 in the Commission's Report.

At the UNESCO Intergovernmental Meeting on Communications Development Assistance, held in Paris in April of 1980, the debate that had begun in Washington continued. It became clear fairly soon that the U.S. proposal for an autonomous operation—inspired in part by a wish to dilute UNESCO's dominant role—was not going to win support even from the West. The Third World nations, which regard UNESCO as their spiritual home, were insistent that the mechanism be housed there. It also became evident that there was little support for the U.S. argument that the new body must guarantee that the United Nations Development Program, the International Telecommunications Union, and other specialized agencies be able to join as full partners.

After testing, the U.S. realized that there was no chance of getting its proposal adopted. Accordingly, the U.S. turned to working closely with its allies and moderates in the group of non-aligned countries (known as the G-77) to seek a formula that would preserve as many of its other key points as possible. In this it was remarkably successful.

THE ESTABLISHMENT OF THE IPDC

The consensus document that finally emerged called for establishing an International Program for the Development of Communications within the framework of UNESCO. A number of provisions of importance to the U.S. were included:

1. Participation is provided for U.N. agencies, intergovernmental and nongovernmental organizations, and professional groups to be "closely associated with the UNESCO program" in an "institutional framework." (An interagency group is to be established.)

2. The Program will be directed by an Intergovernmental Council composed of 35 member states elected by and responsible to the General Conference. (This council gives the program some degree of autonomy.)

3. Priority is to be given to seeking a consensus in deliberations of the Intergovernmental Council. (This means that the council will not act by simple majority rule, and provides some guarantee for protection of minority interests, i.e., the West's.)

4. The director of the program will be appointed by the Director-General of UNESCO, on the recommendation of the Intergovernmental Council. (This was a key provision, for it means the council has the power to nominate the candidates from among whom the Director-General must make the appointment.)

5. An appropriate system of resources and finances should be estab-

lished and the Director-General is requested "to mobilize the resources needed for the Program and to seek contributions from Member States and other parties concerned." (No mention is made of an international fund or even a pledging conference.)

The U.S. alone conducted the prolonged negotiations with the Director-General that finally resulted in the formula for choosing the program director, but it was joined by its Western allies in taking the position that their governments could not accept any new financial obligations, either assessed or voluntary. Though the non-aligned countries sought a special fund and/or pledging conference, the exclusion of any such provision was made the condition of the United States' joining in the consensus.

At the 21st UNESCO General Conference the U.S. delegation in Belgrade was concerned that nothing occur to upset the careful balance of interests established in Paris. This balance was largely maintained to the U.S.'s satisfaction, although the non-aligned countries, supported by the Soviets, were adamant on the necessity for establishing an IPDC international fund, and in the end made this the price of its joining a consensus.

THE DEVELOPMENTAL GOALS OF THE IPDC

Initially, the IPDC should inventory the communication needs and priorities of the developing countries. In the opinion of developing countries, international cooperative action is required for needs such as those listed in Table 53.1.

If the IPDC is to avoid being stymied by UNESCO's attachment to political objectives, it must exclude any mandate for normative activities. There must be no provision for media accountability to the state or to international organizations. In particular, it should not undertake research or other programs that can lead to establishing by UNESCO of a code of journalistic ethics, measures for protection or licensing of journalists, or any form of monitoring or judging behavior in any aspect of the communications sector.

Moreover, the IPDC's basic developmental thrust must not be diluted by saddling the mechanism with a host of other responsibilities. At Belgrade, numerous Third World delegates expressed the view that many or all of the communication programs of UNESCO should be transferred to the IPDC, apparently perceiving it as a new cornucopia from which riches will flow to gild all the communication activities of UNESCO. The IPDC must focus entirely on development—first, last, and always.

In this regard, research should be carefully controlled. Clearly a major responsibility of the IPDC is to inventory communication needs and priorities; but, other than that survey and a few specific studies not otherwise procurable, it should not allow itself to be bogged down in research. In this connection, the IPDC secretariat should remain small, since only a

Table 53.1 Communication Needs of Developing Countries That Could Be Served by the IPDC

Development of Infrastructures

- assistance in surveying communication needs and preparation of plans for appropriate and essential communication systems
- help in developing composite systems of telecommunications and postal and information services
- devising of ways to maximize use of existing and often under-utilized infrastructures, e.g., radio, telephone
- encouragement of indigenous infrastructure production capacity, e.g., newsprint, broadcast reception equipment, integrated circuits
- help in meeting the need for coherent, realistic, and creative planning of national communication systems
- creation of infrastructures that allow countries in the developing world to extend their own capabilities rather than rely on outside sources
- development of the capacity of less developed countries to gather, process, and distribute their own news and information and to articulate their own cultural values and views
- strengthening or establishing of national and regional news services
- expansion of rural press and community radio
- promotion of regional exchanges of broadcast and print news
- establishment of regional radio-television program exchange centers
- setting up of regional data bases for development flow

Professional Training

- assignment of specialists to design curricula for training programs for production, technical, and management personnel
- provision of scholarships for study in countries with advanced communication capacities and learning opportunities
- organizing of seminars at international, regional, and national levels to upgrade skills of in-service personnel
- provision of training materials and information on communication techniques and their adaptation to development needs
- strengthening of viable national and regional institutions that can extend and invigorate indigenous means of training
- fostering of training programs that will develop self-reliant skills for installation, operation, and maintenance of communication systems

Equipment and Technologies

- help in identifying appropriate equipment to fit indigenous requirements and national communications development plans
- assistance in relating technology transfer to alternative forms of technology and to local manpower and production capacities
- help in exploiting new technological approaches adapted to local needs
- adaptations of technologies originating in industrialized countries to suit local conditions and capabilities
- development of regional consortia to design more appropriate electronic communication technologies, e.g., small-gauge video cameras and recording systems

Table 53.1 Continued.

- identification of modifications in modern broadcasting equipment that will simplify maintenance and help solve production problems
- assistance with equipment requirements for printing, telephone, postal service, and computer communications

---

minimum amount of superstructure is needed to coordinate the activities of member states in initiating their own projects and seeking cooperative partners.

The IPDC must not be exploited as a "pork barrel" to curry favor with nations by passing around little grants for everyone, regardless of priority needs. UNESCO has a history of making numerous small isolated grants that often are so minuscule that they fail to stimulate anything of consequence. The IPDC should avoid this scattershot approach in its project funding. There is nothing wrong with small grants, however, if they are integral parts of an international cooperative project. The U.S. and like-minded countries should never hesitate to insist that proposed projects exceeding the limitations cited above be referred to the regular program of UNESCO.

Finally, the international fund strongly advocated by the developing countries and as strongly opposed by the U.S. and its allies would almost guarantee IPDC's growth into a monstrous bureaucracy, place inappropriate power in the hands of UNESCO, and make the IPDC into a highly centralized secretariat-controlled enterprise. A pledging conference, while entirely voluntary, would if convened place a sort of moral obligation upon member states. With the developed countries already experiencing economic difficulties, the last thing they need is a situation contrived to make them outbid one another in seeking Third World favor.

The U.S. and its friends should explore whatever aspects of their existing or planned aid programs could be fitted into the IPDC framework. In this way the maximum credit for their support for the IPDC can be derived from ongoing related assistance activities. Among these for the U.S. would be the Agency for International Development's bilateral agreement with three less developed countries to provide rural satellite services and the International Communication Agency's agreement with two regional training centers to provide senior U.S. professionals in teaching positions.

Conversations should be undertaken with media organizations that might be prepared to fund modest research, training, or technical support projects. Similar conversations should be initiated with relevant elements of the information industries—newspaper and book publishers, film and television producers, advertising and public relations firms, news services, data processors, telecommunication and computer firms, and equipment manufacturers. Such projects could be developed via industry contacts with individual countries or with private organizations in those countries.

In all of the foregoing, continuing consultations by the U.S. and like-minded governments are vital. The U.S. and its allies must move to focus collaborative efforts around concrete tasks. Since the Western countries are in the minority, it is important that they mobilize all the firepower possible out of common positions and unified strategies.

IMPLICATIONS FOR THE U.S. AND OTHER DEVELOPED COUNTRIES

For the U.S., this enterprise is the fulfillment of an idea that it conceived, steered through difficult negotiations, and finally brought into being. More importantly, the U.S. and like-minded nations are putting a high percentage of their policy commitments into this basket. The IPDC is a concrete manifestation of a principle long articulated by the U.S. and its allies in international communication debates, i.e., the way to redress imbalances is not by restricting communication activities of the countries with advanced communications but by raising the communications capacities of the developing countries. The IPDC was designed as a mechanism to implement that philosophy.

The U.S. and its allies must see to it that this mechanism moves from the start in positive and constructive channels and is seen as a means for promoting the free flow of information that is crucial to the development of developing countries, the maintenance of peace, and the improvement of the human condition. If the developed countries are to exert leadership in international communications, useful and substantial contributions must be seen to come early on from the public and private sectors in these countries. Contributions announced as of 1982 include: Netherlands, $600,000; India, $100,000; Iraq, $100,000; and Mexico, $500,000. Failure by the U.S. to support the IPDC will be seen as proving hypocrisy in its public statements, lack of sympathy for developing countries, and a determination to protect and maintain a dominant role for Western commercial communication interests. Thus the IPDC concept might well fall into the hands of those who would destroy it to serve anti–free-press purposes. In particular, perception by the Third World of reluctance to support the IPDC may well lead to further efforts within UNESCO to enact international restrictions and restraints on the media of the West, as well as similar responses at national levels.

It is hoped that the IPDC, through serious and realistic discussions between the developed and the developing countries on its purpose and potential, can be tailored to make a real contribution to the pressing communication needs of these countries. If this new mechanism can focus on these pressing problems in a workable and realistic manner; if it can be directed toward a quest for practical solutions to concrete problems; if it can maximize the cooperation of other U.N. agencies, as well as nongovernmental entities; and if all this can be done without impairing the concept of free flow, the IPDC can bring needed order as well as efficiency and effectiveness to the presently confusing and uncoordinated field of international communications development.

The first IPDC organizational meeting did not change this general appraisal of useful IPDC goals. The meeting in Paris, held June 15–22, 1981, got off to a bumpy but basically satisfactory start. The 35-member Intergovernmental Council elected officers, adopted rules of procedure, initiated steps to assess needs and establish priorities for development assistance, and called upon the Director-General of UNESCO to undertake a worldwide fund-raising effort.

The meeting took place against a background of growing suspicions in the U.S. and other Western countries of UNESCO's intentions regarding the press. Even the IPDC, which was conceived by the U.S. as a mechanism for focusing UNESCO communications activities into constructive channels, has aroused skepticism. Activities in the press preceding and during the meeting angered the Secretariat and G-77 members and led to outbursts against the press in the corridors as well as in the final day's session.

Overall, however, there was a marked decrease in the level of rhetoric at this meeting and, considering that the Western members came to the christening of a new development program with very little money in hand, they did remarkably well. The U.S. fulfilled most of its objectives and where its expectations were not fully realized, it has opportunities for further pursuit of these objectives.

NOTE

1. This article is an abridged version of a working paper that appeared in *Voices of Freedom: A World Conference of Independent News Media* (Edward R. Murrow Center of Public Diplomacy/World Freedom Committee, 1981). It was one of the background papers for the Talloires conference.

Fifty-Four

Instituting the International Program for the Development of Communications

Clifford H. Block

The International Program for the Development of Communications (IPDC) held a milestone meeting in January of 1982, hosted by the Mexican government in Acapulco. The meeting, composed of IPDC's 35-nation Governing Council, moved this new program from planning into operations by taking critical decisions relating to projects, funding, criteria, and the choice of a director. This article will assess what happened, how it affected the tone of the continuing North-South dialogue on communications, and what the future may bring.

The Acapulco meeting was a test of the implicit agreement struck at the 1978 UNESCO General Conference, an agreement that gave rise to the creation of the IPDC: if the Third World would moderate its rhetoric on issues such as licensing of journalists and adoption of worldwide journalistic codes, viewed by many in the West as dangerous to basic freedoms of speech and press, the industrialized world would assist the poorer nations in developing more rapidly their communications capabilities. Throughout the evolution of the IPDC idea, each side has been assessing the other's degree of commitment to this bargain.

THE MAJOR EXPECTATIONS FOR THE ACAPULCO MEETING

The developing nations were seeking tangible signs of Western support for the new institution: contributions, acceptance of projects proposed by the Third World, and agreement on substantial control of the new entity by the poorer nations. The Third World was looking particularly closely at the U.S. posture. The U.S. had proposed the concept of the IPDC under the Carter administration. Since then, a new administration, U.S. federal budget-cutting, and negative press reaction after the Talloires Conference in mid-1981 all raised questions about what the U.S. position on the IPDC would be.

The Western nations, on the other hand, were somewhat warily waiting to see if there would in fact be a toning down of the rhetoric that had so alarmed the Western press and others. They were looking at the degree to which Third World ideological positions would intrude on the character of projects and on organizational decisions. The fundamental question for them was whether the IPDC would be accepted as a mechanism for practical programs or whether it would be turned into another forum for the New World Information Order debate. Most Western delegations arrived with the hope of showing support for Third World aspirations while defending Western freedom-of-information principles.

Both groups had well-organized caucuses. The "Group of 77" (or G77) developing nations and the "Western Group" (U.S., Canada, West Germany, Great Britain, The Netherlands, France, Austria, the Nordic bloc, and Japan) met and negotiated throughout.

There were other key actors in addition to the developing nations and the West. UNESCO, in particular Director-General M'Bow, had a major stake in guiding the communications debate into constructive channels and seeing a practical structure set up to aid the Third World. The Director-General was in Acapulco for some days and was actively involved. The more militant New World Information Order advocates, led at Acapulco by some Latin American delegates, were there to advocate their points of view. This group was usually supported by the socialist bloc, with particularly vocal encouragement from the Cuban and East German delegations. The international telecommunications community, led by the Deputy Director-General of the International Telecommunication Union (I.T.U.), and top executives from INTELSAT and INTERSPUTNIK, were there to explore opportunities for constructive involvement. At the same time, they were a bit wary of the new institution and of its sponsor, UNESCO, both of which represented a new element in international telecommunications affairs. In addition to these groups, the Mexican government was active in seeking a successful follow-up to the earlier Cancun meeting of heads of state. President Lopez Portillo opened the meeting to emphasize its import.

The Western press had a number of observers. The press had come from the April 1981 Talloires Conference with a sharpened wariness of international actions in the field, particularly those associated with UNESCO. The U.S. media community was particularly well represented, with observers or reporters from the *New York Times, Time*, the World Press Freedom Committee, and the American Society of Newspaper Editors. They were particularly interested in the positions of the U.S. delegation; most hoped the delegation would give no ground on the freedom of information principle in supporting the new program.

In an earlier meeting, the Council had agreed to base its decisions on consensus to the maximum feasible extent, resorting to a vote on policy matters only when essential. Acapulco was a major test of whether, in so contentious an area, consensus could really be maintained.

ACCOMPLISHMENTS OF THE MEETING

The substantive work of the meeting addressed four areas: listing nominees for the directorship of the IPDC, determining priorities and criteria for future projects, discussing financing mechanisms and the collection of pledges, and deciding on the first projects to be funded.

The Directorship

It had long been agreed that the director should be from the Third World. (The chairman of the Council is from the West, Gunnar Garbo of Norway.) It was left to the Group of 77 to arrive at a list of nominees.

The choice of the director is of crucial importance, since he will imprint his style on the new organization. Would he be a pragmatic communications professional looking for ways to build the capacity of the developing world, or would he instead be a person likely to use the IPDC as a forum for continuing political and ideological confrontation?

The Group of 77, in caucus, produced a list of seven candidates from which Director-General M'Bow was to make a choice. (The candidate from Iraq withdrew after concern was expressed over his late nomination.) The final list was made up of experienced, effective communications professionals; the one selected could be expected to give the IPDC strong professional leadership. The candidates were Korshed Alam, Bangladesh (Secretary, Minister of Information and Broadcasting), Sarath Amunagama, Republic of Singapore (Secretary-General, Asian Mass Communication Research and Information Center), Goodwin Anim, Ghana (communication consultant), Albino Alberto Gomez, Argentina (newspaper correspondent), Jose Antonio Mayobre, Venezuela (Division of Development of Communications Systems, UNESCO), Parayil Unnikrishnan, India (Deputy General Manager, Press Trust of India), and T. Nelson Williams, Liberia (Director, Public Affairs Department, Lamco Joint Venture).

Sarath Amunagama has since been selected by Director-General M'Bow. He is the 42-year-old sociologist who, before directing AMIC in Singapore, was the Minister of Information and Broadcasting for Sri Lanka. Amunagama is highly regarded as a moderate but assertive spokesman for Third World communications development and as a pragmatic and energetic administrator.

Priorities and Criteria for Projects

The Council was required to set up criteria against which future projects could be judged. Priority was finally given to projects for:

- national planning for communications development;
- creation of infrastructures, particularly using indigenous technologies;
- institutional arrangements to facilitate free flow and a more balanced exchange of news and culture;
- training in research, planning, management, technology, production, and dissemination;
- regional and international cooperation, especially among developing countries;
- enhancement of "development communications" in support of education, agriculture, health, and rural development; and
- increased access to the latest technologies, such as satellites and data banks.

It also was agreed that regional projects should be given priority over national ones in the early activity of the IPDC and that among the regions Africa, least developed in its communications capacity, should have highest funding priority.

As finally agreed upon, the lists of priorities and criteria are unlikely to cause contention; they stress practical measures. Achieving this, however, involved some vigorous debate about ideological issues and evoked a few sharp confrontations. The most intense conflict centered on the concept of "social participation" in the control of media, a proposed criterion advanced by Yugoslavia and supported by Venezuela and others.

The U.S. led the objections, arguing that the concept opens the door to government control of independent media. The principle had, in fact, been so used to justify the takeover, by an earlier Peruvian government, of ten newspapers in the 1970s, a bit of history eloquently confirmed at the meeting by a Peruvian delegate. The "social participation" concept also has been the subject of bitter debate in Mexico for several years, with certain elements pressing hard for an inclusion of the concept in Mexican law.

The concept, like so many, has different connotations for different people. The Yugoslav delegate argued that it simply asserts the right of individuals and groups to send, as well as to receive, messages. In the end the text read, "projects should increase the communications capacity to receive and transmit messages of individuals and groups." The original sponsors objected but did yield to maintain consensus on the alternative language.

Debate also arose on the connotations of other phrases: as a result, encouragement of the "balanced exchange of news" was modified to also enhance "the free flow of information"; "communication to serve other public interest sectors" was rewritten "to serve other development activities," to avoid inferential agreement to a government's right to "use" the media for its political ends.

These confrontations provided a few sparks and gave the international press some stories. However, in comparison with past debates on communications issues, this was pale stuff; the relatively easy resolution of these issues was one of many evidences of a widely felt desire by all to move from rhetoric to constructive action.

The Debate on Bilateral versus Multilateral Financing Mechanisms

Funding mechanisms became the most difficult area on which to reach agreement. The developing nations, in many different forums, are consistently focusing their attention on two themes: new financing to be set aside for special purposes, and regimes for the control of that financing that reflect increased developing country influence. These issues dominated debate at the 1979 U.N. Conference on Science and Technology in Development, to the exclusion of technical discussions; the Law of the Sea negotiations centered on the same themes, as have recent meetings on trade, environment, and many other matters. The industrialized nations have tended to resist the establishment of new lending mechanisms, preferring the use of either bilateral programs or established agencies such as the World Bank or the United Nations Development Program, which have well-developed project and fiscal review procedures as well as a substantial Western influence.

In the debate on communications, the same issues have been reflected in the IPDC discussion from the beginning. For example, in the initial 1978 U.S. proposal, the IPDC was conceived primarily as a clearinghouse for funding from other sources, serving as a broker and facilitator between developing countries and existing funding institutions. At the insistence of the developing countries, the IPDC has evolved more direct funding mechanisms and a Special Account has been set up to accept contributions.

The Group of 77 at Acapulco pushed hard for all contributions to flow into the Special Account, which is controlled by the IPDC Council, with its G77 majority. The argument is that a flow of resources directly through the Special Account is basic to the growth of the IPDC as a distinct institution. It also would strengthen the G77 regional groups, since they have great influence over IPDC funds allocated for their regions.

On the other hand, most Western nations, including the U.S., Austria, the Federal Republic of Germany, Great Britain, and Japan, argued strongly for multiple funding mechanisms, including provisions for support to specific IPDC-approved projects through bilateral means. This Western preference for a bilateral "window" has several sources. Management responsibility is one; the IPDC will have a very small staff, and its procedures for providing fiscal and technical monitoring remain to be developed. Second, bilateral funding of course can be focused on specific projects, rather than being allocated to the whole spectrum of approved activities.

The issue of bilateral versus multilateral funding has been a particularly key matter for the U.S. In the value-laden area of communications, it is certainly possible that some IPDC projects will become ideologically contentious. Direct U.S. government funding for such projects would simply be unacceptable to the U.S. media as well as to the Congress and the executive branch. U.S. support for the overall concept of the IPDC would be short-lived.

The U.S. media community is remarkably united in this area; major conservative and liberal voices concur that the U.S. government must actively defend international freedom of information against any threat of international restriction. The Talloires Conference, for example, elicited broadcast commentary by Dan Rather of CBS on potential UNESCO threats to press freedom; similar editorials have come from the *Washington Post* and the *New York Times* as well as from numerous conservative organizations. Given the intensity of feelings on this issue, U.S. government support for the IPDC simply could not withstand the potential problems arising from U.S. funding of ideologically distasteful projects, even if they were rare.

Bilateral funding is a way out: U.S. funds can go to those projects that are fully consistent with its views, as a nation, of the central importance of freedom of information to a society. In this way a solid basis of U.S. support for the objectives of the IPDC has a chance to grow, with an expectation of private sector as well as governmental support.

At Acapulco, the issue was resolved only on the final evening of the conference. Since Austria, Australia, and the Netherlands had pledged bilateral support for specific IPDC-approved projects, and the U.S. also had pledged its aid bilaterally, the issue's resolution was crucial to successful meeting. The final determination was to open the system to all major sources: cash contributions to the Special Account; services such as experts and equipment; funds-in-trust (funded by a specific donor in a particular account but managed by the IPDC); and bilateral sponsorship of projects previously approved by the Council. Indeed, it was agreed that "no source of funding should be excluded." In the view of some, it expands immeasurably the potential impact of the IPDC on world communications, while admittedly making the management task a trickier one.

For the developing world, contributions to the IPDC were, of course, the most fundamental test of the sincerity of Western support. Beginning on the first day of the conference, disappointment was expressed by many Third World representatives at the caution and parsimony shown by most Western nations.

Numerous pledges, however, were recorded, the most impressive

Table 54.1   Contributions to the IPDC (in U.S. $)

To the IPDC Special Account	
Arab gulf states	2,000,000
Bangladesh	2,000
Benin	10,000
Canada	200,000
China	100,000
Egypt	10,000
France	2,000,000
Indonesia	100,000
Mexico	500,000
Tunisia	5,000
U.S.S.R.	500,000 (rubles)
Venezuela	250,000
Donations for bilateral support of specific IPDC projects	
Australia	200,000
Austria	258,000
Netherlands	250,000
U.S.	100,000
"In kind" contributions of experts, fellowships, and equipment	
Argentina	250,000
Cuba	50,000–100,000
German Democratic Republic	1,500,000 (marks)
Netherlands	24 person-months
U.S.S.R.	1,500,000 (rubles)

being France's $2 million multi-year pledge to the Special Account.[1] Subsequently, the Arab gulf states' Program for U.N. Organizations pledged $2 million to the support of the Pan African News Agency. Overall contributions are shown in Table 54.1. Over $6 million has been pledged, providing a basis for getting started on projects.

Projects

Some 54 projects were proposed: 24 regional, 3 worldwide, and 27 national. In the three-day review process, major emphasis was placed on regional or worldwide projects, and ultimately only they received funding from the Special Account. The funded projects, with their initial funding allocations, are shown in Figure 54.1.

A glance at the six most highly funded projects reveals the initial IPDC priority: each supports an effort to exchange either news dispatches or television, film, or radio programs with a region. This, of course, is a basic strategy for redressing the lack of media materials produced from the perspective of developing nations, i.e., through sharing materials. Also

Figure 54.1 IPDC-Funded Projects and Initial Funding Allocations

AFRICA

- Pan African News Agency (PANA)—$100,000 (also $2 million to be negotiated from the Arab gulf states' Program for U.N. Organizations)

  Regional project for development of communication technologies (funding to be negotiated with the government of Austria)

  ACCE Institute for Communication Development and Research—$10,000 for further study

  Establishment of a network for the exchange of economic news among the press agencies of the CEAO countries—$10,000 for further study

  Determination of needs, project preparation, and training in Africa—$125,000

ARAB GULF STATES

- Arab Project for Communication Planning and Exchange (ACPE)—$56,000 (additional funding from Arab sources)

  Arab gulf states' regional broadcasting training center—$30,000 (additional funding from Arab sources)

ASIA AND THE PACIFIC

- Asia-Pacific News Network—$80,000

  Pacific radio news exchange (funding to be negotiated with the government of Australia)

- Regional bank of films and television programs in Asia and the Pacific—$100,000

LATIN AMERICA AND THE CARIBBEAN

- Caribbean regional project for broadcasting, training, and program exchange —$45,000

- Creation of Latin American Special Information Services Agency (ALASEI)—$70,000

  Center for communication research and application (Mexico)—$40,000

  Center for automated publishing and translation (ASIN)—$10,000

  Training of technicians for the development of communication at the community level—$15,000

NATIONAL PROJECTS

Zimbabwe Broadcast Training Department, Institute for Mass Communication (funding to be negotiated with the government of the Netherlands)

INTER-REGIONAL PROJECTS

I.T.U. study of communications in rural development—$30,000

Feasibility study for international exchange of information by global satellite systems—$20,000

Center for the Study of Communications, Energy, and Space Technologies (UNESCO to provide funds for further study)

Note: Those projects receiving the largest funding are marked with bullets to give some sense of where priorities lay.

important are the regional centers in the Arab states and in Latin America; additional funding, from within each region, may make these significant centers.

The inter-regional or worldwide projects focus on telecommunications. One would experiment with the use of the INTELSAT satellite system (and other systems such as INTERSPUTNIK if appropriate) to provide a lower-cost worldwide news exchange system. A second supports the I.T.U. to continue its studies of the role of telecommunications in rural development. These studies may go far to enhance the priority placed on communications investments by international lenders and national governments, for they are compiling data on the economic payoff of such investments.

Finally, various technological developments received attention in the projects. An African center will be funded, with aid from Austria, to build on Kenya's work in indigenously produced, low-powered, low-cost radio transmitters, appropriate for widespread rural use. Satellite communications, including rural telephony using solar-powered small earth stations, was the centerpiece of a proposed Sri Lanka center supported by Arthur Clarke, who first conceived of communications satellites; it is being further studied.

On the whole, the review process had remarkably little ideological dispute; there were only a few serious concerns, and each was satisfied after sufficient discussion. A major concern of the U.S. was that the new regional news exchanges not in any way exclude access by local media to the international wire services. The Africans were very clear on that point with regard to the Pan African News Agency and received warm endorsement. However, a lengthy discussion arose about the operations of the Asia-Pacific News Network before clarification led to agreement to go ahead with the project. Finally, the concept of "social participation" reappeared in a Mexican proposal and regenerated the earlier dispute on the topic.

CONTINUING FINANCIAL AND POLITICAL SUPPORT FOR THE IPDC

For the first year of funding, a total of $910,000 was allocated, $741,000 for projects. Another $169,000 will go toward helping countries design future projects as well as for training and for publicizing the IPDC. While $741,000 is a small percentage of the life-of-project cost of approved projects (about $7 million), it is enough for significant initial work. Pledged contributions are sufficient to continue the same rate of expenditure for several years, and of course additional contributions are expected. Bilateral funding will also pick up several projects in their totality.

The United States pledged $100,000 from the bilateral aid resources of the U.S. Agency for International Development (A.I.D.) The intention is to supplement that pledge, particularly with contributions from the U.S. private sector—communications corporations, professional associations, foundations, and perhaps universities and their faculties. The effort to generate private sector participation has begun. A consortium to aid programs endorsed by the IPDC is being organized, with high-level support from the Reagan administration.

The future of the "IPDC strategy," substituting practical programs for ideological debate, will require a much more substantial U.S. response. They shared perception is that the developing world has been accommodating; the industrialized world must now keep its bargain, if the compact is to last. The prospect for sustained U.S. support is better since Acapulco; many in the U.S. press are newly supportive and some in government view communications aid with higher priority.

The allocation of the $100,000 A.I.D. contribution will have to be made within the framework of existing "economic development aid" authority, which is now specifically limited to programs that affect the economic well-being of people in the developing world, in particular the very poor. U.S. aid is required, by Congressional directive, to be supportive of development in areas such as food production, health, education, family planning, and institutional development. A.I.D. support to the IPDC will thus be for activities in the area of "development communications," rather than for news exchange and the like.

There remain basic value differences in the issues surrounding communications, in particular on the issue of governmental control of communications versus the individual's right of access to a free flow of information. Many developing nations still argue in favor of governmental influence on the media in order to maintain cultural integrity against Western influences, to sustain national unity, or to have the media directly serve development. The Western press and governments continue to stress instead the individual's right to know and to communicate as the foundation of free institutions, and insist that governmental influence can only stifle that right.

While these positions have not changed—they are derived from fundamental economic, cultural, and political situations, as well as self-interest—Acapulco marked a welcome reduction in the sort of posturing that suggests that the other point of view must be wholly malicious. This is perhaps the best we can do for a while, at the same time moving forward with common actions on which there is agreement. Curiously, actions are often far less controversial than words.

NOTE

1. Mitterrand's France is making major commitments to the new electronic technologies and to their role in global development; in late 1981, France also inaugurated a "World Center in Computers and Social Development," funding it at $20 million per year and attracting leading U.S. computer scientists and educators; work in Senegal has begun. Mitterrand made technology the centerpiece of the Versailles summit in June 1982.

Selected Bibliography for Further Reading in World Communications

The following bibliography has been selected to amplify and extend the references to particular topics which follow each individual chapter. Items in this bibliography correspond to the five sections of the book and have been chosen on the basis of their availability, breadth of coverage, and authority. In general, we have emphasized books, special issues of periodicals, and other published collections.

The foremost reference book in this area is UNESCO's *World Communications: A 200-Country Survey of Press, Radio, Television, and Film* (New York: Unipub, 1975). This survey offers useful summaries of national media activities and organizations around the world and is updated every ten years.

For the text of documents mentioned in the book we would recommend two published collections, *International Law Governing Communications and Information: A Collection of Basic Documents* edited by Edward Ploman (Westport, Conn.: Greenwood, 1982) and *Documents in American Telecommunications Policy* (two vols.) edited by John M. Kittross (New York: Arno, 1977). Also of use are the United Nations and UNESCO documents referred to in Appendix 2. Copies of many of them can be ordered directly from the United Nations, UNESCO, or Unipub and complete citations are listed in UNESCO's *Documents and Publications in the Field of Mass Communications* (Paris, 1980).

Periodicals that regularly publish material on world communications include the *Journal of Communication* published by the Annenberg School of Communications, University of Pennsylvania, *Intermedia* published by the International Institute for Communications, London, the *International Social Science Journal* published by UNESCO, the *Democratic Journalist* published by the International Organization of Journalists, Prague, *Third World Quarterly* published by the Third World Foundation, and *Media Development* published by the World Association for Christian Communication, London. A complete listing of international organizations and periodicals in communications can be found in William Rivers, *et al. Aspen Handbook on the Media* (1977–79 ed.) (New York: Praeger, 1977).

I. GLOBAL PERSPECTIVES ON INFORMATION

Bagdikian, Ben H. *The Information Machines.* New York: Harper & Row, 1971.

Balle, Francis (Ed.). *Médias et Société.* Paris: Editions Montchrestien, 1980.

Bell, Daniel. *The Coming of Post-Industrial Society.* New York: Basic Books, 1973.

Berrigan, Francis J. (Ed.). *Access: Some Western Models of Community Media.* Paris: UNESCO, 1977.

Bowes, John E. "Japan's Approach to an Information Society: A Critical Perspective." Reprinted in G. C. Wilhoit and Harold de Bock (Eds.). *Mass Communications Review Yearbook,* Vol. 2. Beverly Hills, Cal.: Sage, 1981.

Burke, Thomas J. M. and Maxwell Lehman. *Communication Technologies and Information Flow.* Elmsford, N.Y.: Pergamon Press, 1981.

Bushkin, Arthur A. and Jane H. Yurow. "The Foundation of United States Information Policy." A United States Government Submission to the High-Level Conference on Information, Computer, and Communications Policy. Organization for Economic Cooperation and Development, October 6–8, 1980, Paris National Telecommunications and Information Administration Special Publication (NTIA-SP-80–8). Washington, D.C.: Department of Commerce, 1980.

Casmir, Fred L. (Ed.). *Intercultural and International Communication.* Washington, D.C.: University Press of America, 1978.

Cherry, Colin. *World Communication: Threat or Promise?* Revised edition, New York: John Wiley, 1978.

Cornish, Edward (Ed.). *Communications Tomorrow: The Coming of the Information Society.* Bethesda, Md.: World Future Society, 1982.

Council on Learning, *The Communications Revolution and the Education of Americans.* New Rochelle, N.Y.: Change Magazine Press, 1980.

Dizard, Jr., Wilson P. *The Coming Information Age: An Overview of Technology, Economics, and Politics.* New York: Longman, 1982.

Edelstein, Alex S., John E. Bowes, and Sheldon M. Harsel. *Information Societies: Comparing the Japanese and American Experience.* Seattle: University of Washington Press, 1978.

Edward, Kenneth. "The Electronic Newspaper." *The Futurist* 12(2), 1978, pp. 79–84.

Edward, Kenneth. "Information Without Limit Electronically." In Michael Emery and Ted Curtis Smythe (Eds.) *Readings in Mass Communication: Concepts and Issues in the Mass Media.* Dubuque, Iowa: Wm. C. Brown, 1980, pp. 202–216.

Ellul, Jacques. *The Technological Society.* Trans. John Wilkinson. New York: Vintage Books, 1967.

Ellul, Jacques. *The Technological System.* Translated by Joachim Neugroschel. New York: Seabury Continuum, 1980.

Enberg, Ole. "Who Will Lead the Way to the 'Information Society'?" *Impact of Science on Society* 28(3), 1978, pp. 283–296.

Fisher, Glen. *American Communications in a Global Society.* Norwood, N.J.: Ablex, 1979.

Ganley, Oswald H. and Gladys D. Ganley. *To Inform or to Control: The New Communications Network.* New York: McGraw-Hill, 1982.

Haigh, Robert W., George Gerbner, and Richard B. Byrne. *Communications in the Twenty-First Century*. New York: John Wiley, 1981.

Harms, Leroy Stanley and Jim Richstad (Eds.). *Evolving Perspectives on the Right to Communicate*. Honolulu: East-West Communications Institute, 1977.

Harms, Leroy Stanley, Jim Richstad, and Kathleen A. Kie (Eds.). *Right to Communicate: Collected Papers*. Honolulu: University Press of Hawaii, 1977.

Harsel, Sheldon. "Communication Research in Information Societies: A Comparative View of Japan and the United States." Reprinted in G. Cleveland Wilhoit and Harold de Bock (Eds.) *Mass Communications Review Yearbook*, vol. 2. Beverly Hills, Ca: Sage, 1981.

Homet, Roland S., Jr. *Politics, Cultures, and Communication: European vs. American Approaches to Communications Policymaking*. New York: Aspen Institute for Humanistic Studies/Praeger Special Studies, 1979.

Horton, Philip C. (Ed.). *The Third World and Press Freedom*. New York: Praeger Special Studies, 1978.

International Association for Mass Communication Research. *Mass Media and National Cultures. A Conference Report and International Bibliography*. Leicester: 1980.

Journal of Communication. "The Information Society." Symposium of seven articles. *Journal of Communication* 31(1), Winter 1981, pp. 131–194.

Mattelart, Armand. *Multinational Corporations and the Control of Culture: The Ideological Apparatuses of Imperialism*. Atlantic Highlands, New Jersey: Humanities Press; Sussex: Harvester Press, 1979.

Mattelart, Armand and Seth Siegelaub (Eds.). *Communication and Class Struggle*, Volume 1: *Capitalism, Imperialism*. Volume 2: *Liberation, Socialism*. New York: International General, 1979; 1982.

Mattelart, Armand and Jean-Marie Piemme. *Télévision: enjeux sans frontières. Industries culturelles et politique de la communication*. Grenoble: Presses Universitaires de Grenoble, 1980.

McGarry, K. J. *The Changing Context of Information*. London: Clive Bingley, 1981.

McPhail, Thomas L. *Electronic Colonialism: The Future of International Broadcasting and Communication*. Beverly Hills, Cal.: Sage, 1981.

Media Development. Issue devoted to the "New International Information Order (NIIO)." *Media Development* 27(4), 1980.

Melody, William H., Liora R. Salter, and Paul Heyer (Eds.). *Culture, Communication and Dependency: The Tradition of H. A. Innis*. Norwood, N.J.: Ablex, 1981.

Middleton, Karen P. and Meheroo Jusawalla. *The Economics of Communication: A Selected Bibliography with Abstracts*. New York: Pergamon Press, 1981.

Oettinger, Anthony G. *Elements of Information Resources Policy: Library and Other Information Services* (revised edition). Program on Information Resources Policy, Center for Information Policy Research. Cambridge, Mass.: Harvard University Press, 1975.

Oettinger, Anthony G. "Information Resources: Knowledge and Power in the 21st Century." *Science* 209(4), 1980.

Oettinger, Anthony G., Paul J. Berman, and William H. Read. *High and Low Politics: Information Resources for the 80s*. Cambridge, Mass.: Ballinger, 1977.

Parker, Edwin B. and Donald A. Dunn. "Information Technology: Its Social Potential." *Science* 176, January 30, 1972, pp. 1392–1399.

Pelton, Joseph N. *Global Talk.* Alphen ann den Rijn, The Netherlands; Germantown, Md.: Sijthoff & Noordhoff, 1980.

Porat, Marc U. "Communication Policy in an Information Society." In Glen O. Robinson (Ed.) *Communications for Tomorrow: Policy Perspectives for the 1980s.* New York: Praeger, 1978, pp. 3–60.

Porat, Marc U. "Global Implications of the Information Society." *Journal of Communication* 28(1), Winter 1978, pp. 70–80.

Rivers, William L., Wallace Thompson, and Michael J. Nyham. *Aspen Handbook on the Media* (1977–79 ed.). New York: Praeger, 1977.

Robinson, Glen O. (Ed.). *Communications for Tomorrow: Policy Perspectives for the 1980s.* New York: Praeger, 1978.

Rochell, Carlton C. (Ed.). *An Information Agenda for the 1980's.* Chicago: American Library Association, 1981.

Rohrer, Daniel M. *Freedom of Speech and Human Rights: An International Perspective.* Dubuque, Iowa: Kendall/Hunt, 1979.

Schiller, Herbert. *Mass Communications and American Empire.* Boston: Beacon Press, 1971.

Schiller, Herbert. *Communication and Cultural Domination.* White Plains, N.Y.: International Arts & Sciences Press, 1976.

Schiller, Herbert I. *Who Knows: Information in the Age of the Fortune 500.* Norwood, N.J.: Ablex, 1981.

Smith, Anthony. *The Geopolitics of Information: How Western Culture Dominates the World.* New York: Oxford University Press, 1980.

Smythe, Dallas W. *Dependency Road: Communications, Capitalism, Consciousness and Canada.* Norwood, N.J.: Ablex, 1981.

Somavia, Juan. "The Transnational Power Structure and International Information." *Development Dialogue* (Uppsala, Sweden) 2, 1976.

Thunberg, Anne-Marie, Kjell Nowak, Karl Erik Rosengren, and Bengt Sigurd. *Communication and Equality: A Swedish Perspective.* Stockholm, Sweden: Almqvist & Wiksell International, 1982.

Toffler, Alvin. *The Third Wave.* New York: William Morrow, 1980.

Tomita, Tetsuro. "Japan: The Search for a Personal Information Medium." *Intermedia* 7(3), May 1979, pp. 36–38.

Tunstall, Jeremy. *The Media Are American: Anglo-American Media in the World.* New York: Columbia University Press, 1977.

Westin, Alan. *Information Technology in a Democracy.* Cambridge, Mass.: Harvard University Press, 1971.

Wiley, Richard E., and Richard M. Neustadt. "U.S. Communications Policy in the New Decade." *Journal of Communication* 32(2), Spring 1982, pp. 22–32.

Williams, Frederick. *The Communications Revolution.* Beverly Hills, Cal.: Sage, 1982.

II. TRANSNATIONAL COMMUNICATIONS

Adams, William C. (Ed.). *Television Coverage of the Middle East.* Norwood, N.J.: Ablex, 1981.

Adams, William C. *Television Coverage of International Affairs.* Norwood, N.J.: Ablex, 1982.

Atwood, L. Erwin, Stuart J. Bullion, and Sharon M. Murphy. *International Perspectives on News.* Carbondale, Ill.: Southern Illinois University Press, 1982.

Boyd-Barrett, Oliver. *International News Agencies.* Beverly Hills, Cal.: Sage, 1980.

Branan, Karen. "Downplaying the Victims: The U.S. Press Covers Lebanon." *Topic* 3, September 1982, pp. 2–4.

Compaine, Benjamin (Ed.). *Who Owns the Media? Concentration of Ownership in the Mass Communications Industry* (second edition). White Plains, N.Y.: Knowledge Industry Publications, 1982.

Compaine, Benjamin M. *The Newspaper Industry in the 1980's: An Assessment of Economics and Technology.* White Plains, N.Y.: Knowledge Industry Publications, 1980.

Curry, Jane Leftwich and Joan R. Dassin (Eds.). *Press Control Around the World.* New York: Praeger, 1982.

da Costa, Alcino Luis, Yehia Aboubakr, Pran Chopra, and Fernando Reyes Matta. *News Values and Principles of Cross-cultural Communication.* Reports of Papers on Mass Communication No. 85. Paris: UNESCO, 1979.

Diaz Rangel, Eleazar. *Pueblos sub-informados.* Caracas: Monte Avila Editores, 1976.

Dorfman, Ariel and Armand Mattelart. *How to Read Donald Duck: Imperialist Ideology in the Disney Comic.* New York: International General, 1975.

Fascell, Dante (Ed.). *International News: Freedom Under Attack.* London: Sage Publications, 1976; Beverly Hills, Ca.: Sage Publications, 1979.

Fejes, Fred. "The Growth of Multinational Advertising Agencies in Latin America." *Journal of Communication* 30(4), Autumn, 1980, pp. 36–49.

Gauhar, Altaf. "Free Flow of Information: Myths and Shibboleths." *Third World Quarterly* (London) 1(3), 1979, pp. 70–71.

Gerbner, George and George Marvanyi. "A Bibliography of Studies on World News Flow across National Boundaries." *Journal of Communication* 27(1), Winter 1977, pp. 61–66.

Hachten, William A. with the collaboration of Marva Hachten. *The World News Prism: Changing Media, Clashing Ideologies.* Ames, Iowa: Iowa State University Press, 1981.

Hamelink, Cees. *The Corporate Village: The Role of Transnational Corporations in International Communications.* Rome: IDOC International, 1977.

Hopple, Gerald W. "International News Coverage in Two Elite Newspapers." *Journal of Communication* 32(1), Winter 1982, pp. 61–74.

Horton, Philip (Ed.). *The Third World and Press Freedom.* New York: Praeger, 1978.

Institute of Social Studies. *Communication Research in Third World Realities.* Report of Policy Workshop, February, 1980. The Hague: Institute of Social Studies, 1980.

Instituto Latinoamericano de Estudios Transnacionales. *Informes ILET.* Mexico: ILET, División de Estudios de la Comunicación, 1977.

The International Flow of Information: A Trans-Pacific Perspective. The Center for the Book Viewpoint Series, no. 7. Washington, D.C.: Library of Congress, 1981.

Journal of Communication. "Third World News and Views." Symposium of ten articles. *Journal of Communication* 29(2), Spring 1979, pp. 134–198.

Journal of Communication. "Transborder Data Flow: New Frontiers—or None?" Symposium of eight articles. *Journal of Communication* 29(3), Summer 1979, pp. 113–155.

The Kent Commission. *Report of the Royal Commission on Newspapers.* Hull, Quebec: Ministry of Supply and Services, 1981.

Lanispero, Yrjo, Ibrahim Shahzadeh, and Luke Ang. *Television News Exchange in Asia: A Case Study.* Singapore: Asian Mass Communication Research and Information Center, 1976.

Lasswell, Harold D., Daniel Lerner, and Hans Speier. *Propaganda and Communication in World History.* Three Volumes. Volume I: *The Symbolic Instrument in Early Times*, 1979. Volume II: *Emergence of Public Opinion in the West*, 1980. Volume III: *A Pluralizing World in Formation*, 1980. Honolulu, Hi.: University Press of Hawaii.

Lee, Chin-Chuan. "The United States as Seen through the People's Daily." *Journal of Communication* 31(4), Autumn 1981, pp. 92–101.

Lendvai, Paul. *The Bureaucracy of Truth: How Communist Governments Manage the News.* London: Burnett; Boulder, Co.: Westview, 1981.

Lent, John A. "Foreign News in American Media." *Journal of Communication* 27(1), Winter 1977, pp. 46–51.

Lindahl, Rutger. *Broadcasting Across Borders: A Study on the Role of Propaganda in External Broadcasts.* Göteborg, Sweden: C W K Gleerup, 1978.

Mayobre Machado, José. *Información, dependencia y desarrollo: La prensa y el nuevo orden económico internacional.* Caracas: Monte Avila Editores, 1976.

Medios de difusión masiva, tecnología, dependencia y mobilización. Havana: Centro Regional de Superación de Periodistas de América Latina, 1978.

Mitra, Asok. *Information Imbalance in Asia.* Singapore: Asian Mass Communication Research and Information Center, 1975.

Nordenstreng, Kaarle and Herbert Schiller (Eds.). *National Sovereignty and International Communication.* Norwood, N.J.: Ablex, 1979.

Nordenstreng, Kaarle and Tapio Varis. *TV Traffic—a One-way Street? A Survey and Analysis of the International Flow of Television Programme Materials.* Reports and Papers on Mass Communication No. 70. Paris: UNESCO, 1974.

Nouira, Hedi. *Information et communication.* Tunis: Secretariat d'Etat à l'Information, 1978.

Read, William. *America's Mass Media Merchants.* Baltimore: Johns Hopkins University Press, 1976.

Rice, Michael with James A. Cooney (Eds.). *Reporting U.S.-European Relations: Four Nations, Four Newspapers.* Aspen Institute Book. New York: Pergamon, 1982.

Richstad, Jim and Michael H. Anderson (Eds.). *Crisis in International News: Policies and Prospects.* New York: Columbia University Press, 1981.

Robinson, Gertrude Joch. *New Agencies and World News in Canada, the United States and Yugoslavia: Methods and Data.* Fribourg, Switzerland: University Press of Fribourg, 1981.

Said, Edward W. *Covering Islam: How the Media and Experts Determine How We See the Rest of the World.* New York: Pantheon, 1981.

Schramm, Wilbur *et al. International News Wires and Third World News in Asia.* Hong Kong: Chinese University, Center for Communication Studies, 1978.

Schramm, Wilbur and Erwin Atwood. *Circulation of News in the Third World: A Study of Asia.* Seattle, Wash.: University of Washington Press, 1981.

Singham, A. W. (Ed.). *The Non-aligned Movement in World Politics.* Westport, Connecticut: Lawrence Hill, 1977.

Smith, Anthony. *Newspapers and Democracy: International Essays on a Changing Medium.* Cambridge, Mass.: MIT Press, 1980.

Tunstall, Jeremy. *The Media Are American: Anglo American Media in the World.* London: Constable, 1977.

Twentieth Century Fund. *A Free and Balanced Flow.* Report of the Task Force on the International Flow of News, with a Background Paper by Colin Legum and John Cornwell. Lexington, Mass.: D. C. Heath, 1978.

Varis, Tapio. *The Impact of Transnational Corporations on Communication.* Tampere, Finland: Tampere Peace Research Institute, 1975.

Varis, Tapio, Raquel Salinas, and Renny Jokelin. *International News and the New Information Order.* Tampere, Finland: University of Tampere, Institute of Journalism and Mass Communication, 1977.

Weaver, David H. and G. Cleveland Wilhoit. "Foreign News Coverage in Two U.S. Wire Services." *Journal of Communication* 31(2), Spring 1981, pp. 55–63.

Wessel, Andrew E. *Social Use of Information: Ownership and Access.* New York: John Wiley & Sons, 1976.

III. TELECOMMUNICATIONS

Aspen Institute for Humanistic Studies. *Control of the Direct Broadcast Satellite: Values in Conflict.* Palo Alto, Cal., 1974.

Benton, John B. "Electronic Funds Transfer: Pitfalls and Payoffs." *Harvard Business Review* 55(4), July-August 1977, pp. 16–17.

Bowers, Raymond, Alfred M. Lee, and Cary Hershey. *Communications for a Mobile Society: An Assessment of New Technology.* Beverly Hills, Cal.: Sage, 1978.

Brock, Gerald W. *Telecommunications Industry: The Dynamics of Market Structure.* Cambridge, Mass.: Harvard University Press, 1981.

Brooks, John. *Telephone: The First Hundred Years.* New York: Harper and Row, 1976.

Chu, Godwin C., Syed A. Rahim, and D. Lawrence Kincaid (Eds.). *Institutional Exploration in Communication Technology.* Communications Monograph No. 4. Honolulu: University Press of Hawaii, 1978.

Collins, Hugh. "Forecasting the Use of Innovative Telecommunications Services." *Futures* 12(2), 1980, pp. 106–112.

COMSAT. *Comsat Guide to the Intelsat, Marisat, and Comstar Satellite Systems.* Washington, D.C.: Office of Public Affairs, COMSAT, n.d.

Dordick, Herbert S., Helen G. Bradley, and Burt Nanus. *The Emerging Network Marketplace*. Norwood, N.J.: Ablex, 1981.

Elliot, David and Ruth Elliott. *The Control of Technology*. London: Wykeham Publications, 1976.

Ferkiss, Victor C. *Technological Man: The Myth and the Reality*. New York: George Braziller, 1969.

Firestone, Charles M. (Ed.). *International Satellite Television: Resource Manual for the Third Biennial Communications Law Symposium*. Los Angeles, University of California, UCLA Communications Law Program and the International Bar Association, 1983.

Gerbner, George, Larry P. Gross, and William H. Melody (Eds.). *Communications Technology and Social Policy: Understanding the New "Cultural Revolution."* New York: John Wiley & Sons, 1973.

Helmer, Olaf. *Social Technology*. New York: Basic Books, 1966.

Hetman, F. *Society and Assessment of Technology*. OECD, 1973.

Hiltz, Starr Roxanne, and Murray Turoff. *The Network Nation: Human Communication via Computer*. Reading, Mass.: Addison-Wesley, 1978.

Irwin, M. R. *The Telecommunications Industry: Integration vs. Competition*. New York: Praeger, 1971.

Journal of Communication. "Satellite Broadcasting and Communications Policy." Symposium of eight articles. *Journal of Communication* 30(2), Spring 1980, pp. 140–202.

Journal of Communication. "The 'New Technology': Who Sells It? Who Needs It? Who Rules It?" Symposium of ten articles. *Journal of Communication* 32(4), Autumn 1982, pp. 55–178.

Journal of Communication. "Computers, Education, and Public Policy."*Journal of Communication* 33(1), Winter 1983, pp. 92–173.

Kimbel, Dieter. "An Assessment of the Computer-Telecommunications Complex in Europe, Japan, and North America." In George Gerbner, Larry P. Gross and William H. Melody (Eds.), *Communications Technology and Social Policy: Understanding the New "Cultural Revolution."* New York: John Wiley & Sons, 1973, pp. 147–164.

Kittross, John M. (Ed.). *Documents in American Telecommunications Policy* (2 Vols.). New York: Arno, 1977.

Lancaster, Kathleen Landis (Ed.). *International Telecommunications: User Requirements and Supplier Strategies*. Arthur D. Little Book Series. Lexington, Mass.: Lexington Books, 1982.

Lawrence, Shelton and Bernard Timberg (Eds.). *Fair Use and Free Inquiry: Copyright Law and the New Media*. Norwood, N.J.: Ablex, 1980.

Lewin, Leonard (Ed.). *Telecommunications: An Interdisciplinary Survey*. Dedham, Mass.: Artech House, 1979.

Lewin, Leonard (Ed.). *Telecommunications in the United States: Trends and Policies*. Dedham, Mass.: Artech House, 1981.

Martin, James. *Future Developments in Telecommunications*. Englewood Cliffs, N.J.: Prentice-Hall, 1977.

Martin, James. *Telecommunications and the Computer*. Englewood Cliffs, N.J.: Prentice-Hall, 1969.

Martin, James, and Adrian R. D. Norman. *The Computerized Society*. Englewood Cliffs, N.J.: Prentice-Hall, 1970.

Mosco, Vincent. *Pushbutton Fantasies: Critical Perspectives on Videotex and Information Technology*. Norwood, N.J.: Ablex, 1982.

Mattelart, Armand. "Modern Communication Technologies and New Facets of Cultural Imperialism." *Instant Research on Peace and Violence* 1, 1973, pp. 9–27.

McLuhan, Marshall, and Bruce Powers. "Electronic Banking and the Death of Privacy." *Journal of Communication* 31(1), Winter 1981, pp. 164–169.

Meyer, John R., Robert W. Wilson, M. Alan Baughcum, Ellen Burton, and Louis Caouette. *The Economics of Competition in the Telecommunications Industry*. Cambridge, Mass.: Oelgeschlager, Gunn & Hain, 1980.

Mumford, Lewis. *The Myth of the Machine: Technics and Human Development*. New York: Harcourt, Brace and World, 1966.

Nilseen, Svein Erik. "The Use of Computer Technology in Some Developing Countries." *International Social Science Journal* 31(3), 1979, pp. 513–528.

Oden, Teresa, and Christine Thompson (Eds.). *Computers and Public Policy, Proceedings of the Symposium Man and the Computer*. Hanover, N. H.: Dartmouth College, 1977.

Ploman, Edward W. and L. Clark Hamilton. *Copyright: Intellectual Property in the Information Age*. London: Routledge & Kegan Paul, 1980.

Pool, Ithiel de Sola. "International Aspects of Computer Communications." *Telecommunications Policy*. December 1976, pp. 31–51.

Pool, Ithiel de Sola. *The Social Impact of the Telephone*. Cambridge, Mass.: MIT Press, 1977.

Pool, Ithiel de Sola. *Forecasting the Telephone: A Retrospective Technology Assessment*. Norwood, N.J.: Ablex, 1982.

Quenney, Kathryn. *Direct Broadcast Satellites and the United Nations*. Alphen aan den Rijn: Sijthoff & Noordhoff, 1978.

Rice, Ronald E. "Computer Conferencing." In B. Dervin and M. Voight (Eds.) *Progress in Communications Sciences*, vol. 2. New Jersey: Ablex, 1980.

Schiller, Dan. *Telematics and Government*. Norwood, N.J.: Ablex, 1982.

Schramm, Wilbur. "Some Possible Social Effects of Space Communication." In *Communications in the Space Age: The Use of Satellites by the Mass Media*. Netherlands: UNESCO, 1968, pp. 11–29.

Seipp, David J. *Issues and Options in Telecommunications Competition: A Survey*. Cambridge, Mass.: Harvard University Program on Information Resources Policy, 1978.

Short, John, Ederyn Williams, and Bruce Christie. *The Social Psychology of Telecommunications*. New York: John Wiley & Sons, 1976.

Sigel, Efrem et al. *The Future of Videotext: Worldwide Prospects for Home/Office Electronic Information Services*. White Plains, N.Y.: Knowledge Industry Publications, 1983.

Signitzer, Benno. *Regulation of Direct Broadcasting from Satellites: The U.N. Involvement*. New York: Praeger, 1976.

Silberman, Alphons. "Communications Systems and Future Behavior Patterns." *International Social Science Journal* 29, no. 2, 1977, pp. 337–341.

Slack, Jennifer Daryl. *Communications Technologies and Society*. Norwood, N.J., Ablex, 1983.

Smith, Anthony. *Goodbye Gutenberg: The Newspaper Revolution of the 1980s*. New York: Oxford University Press, 1980.

Smith, Ralph Lee. *The Wired Nation. Cable TV: The Electronic Communications Highway*. New York: Harper & Row, 1972.

Soma, John T. *Computer Industry*. Lexington, Mass.: Lexington Books, 1976.

Sterling, C. K. and T. R. Haight. *The Mass Media: Aspen Institute Guide to Communication Industry Trends*. New York: Praeger, 1978.

Szuprowixz, Bohdan O. "The World's Top 50 Computer Import Markets." *Datamation*, January 1981, pp. 141–142, 144.

Teich, Albert H. (Ed.) *Technology and Man's Future* (2nd ed.). New York: St. Martin's Press, 1977.

UNESCO. *A Guide to Satellite Communication*. Reports and Papers on Mass Communication, No. 66. Paris: Department of Mass Communication, UNESCO, 1972.

Woolfe, Roger. *Videotex*. London: Heyden & Son, 1980.

IV. MASS COMMUNICATIONS: DEVELOPMENT WITHIN NATIONAL CONTEXTS

Academy for Educational Development. "The Basic Village Education Project: Final Report." Washington, D.C., 1978.

Agency for International Development/NASA. "*AID-SAT*" *Spaceage Technology for Development*. Washington, D.C.: Agency for International Development, 1977.

Blau, Peter M. *Exchange and Power in Social Life*. New York: John Wiley and Sons, 1964.

Block, C., D. Foote, and J. Mayo. *A Case Study of India's Satellite Instructional Television Project (SITE)*. Washington, D.C.: Agency for International Development, January, 1977.

Boyd, Douglas A. *Broadcasting in the Arab World: A Survey of Radio and Television in the Middle East*. International and Comparative Broadcasting Series. Philadelphia: Temple University Press, 1982.

Braun, Juan. *Visión global de la investigación sobre escuelas radiofónicas*. Bogatá: Asociación Latinoamericana de Educación Radiofónica (ALER), Centro Internacional de Investigaciones para el Desarrollo (CIID), 1977.

Cassirer, H. R. "Radio in an African Context: A Description of Senegal's Pilot Project." In P. Spain *et al*. (Eds.) *Radio for Education and Development: Case Studies*, Volume 2. Washington, D.C.: The World Bank, 1977.

Chu, Godwin C. and Alfian. "Programming for Development in Indonesia." *Journal of Communication* 30(4), Autumn 1980, pp. 50–57.

Clippinger, John H. *Who Gains by Communications Development? Studies of Information Technologies in Developing Countries*. Working Paper 76–1, Program on Information Technologies and Public Policy. Cambridge, Mass.: Harvard University, 1975.

Cooke, Thomas and Susan Romwebber. *Changing Nutrition and Health Behavior Through the Mass Media.* Washington, D.C.: Manoff International, 1977.

Daniel. J. S., M. L. Cote, and M. Richmond. "Project Report: Educational Experiments in Canada with the Communications Technology Satellite (CTS)." In *The Telephone in Education, Book II.* Third Annual International Communications Conference, University of Wisconsin-Extension, April 1977.

Dannheiser, Peter. "The Satellite Instructional Television Experiment: The Trial Run." *Educational Broadcasting International* 8(4), December 1975, pp. 155–159.

Farquhar, John, Nathan Maccoby, *et al.* "Communications for Health: Unselling Heart Disease." *Journal of Communication* 25(3), Summer 1975, pp. 114–126.

Filep, R. and P. Johansen. *A Synthesis of the Final Reports and Evaluations of the ATS-6 Satellite Experiments in Health, Education and Telecommunications.* Redondo Beach, Cal.: Systems 2000, February 1977.

Filep, R. and P. Johansen. *Communications Satellites and Social Service: Analysis and Annotated Bibliography.* Redondo Beach, Cal.: Systems 2000, October 1977.

Fuglesang, Andreas. *Applied Communication in Developing Countries: Ideas and Observations.* Uppsala, Sweden: Dag Hammarskjold Foundation, 1973.

Haberman, Peter and Guy de Fontgalland. *Development Communication: Rhetoric and Reality.* Singapore: Asian Mass Communication Research and Information Center, 1978.

Hall, Budd and Anthony Dodds. "Voices for Development: The Tanzanian National Study Campaigns." In P. Spain *et al.* (Eds.) *Radio for Education and Development: Case Studies,* Volume 2. Washington, D.C., The World Bank, 1977.

Hawkridge, D. G. *The Open University, A Select Bibliography.* Milton Keynes: The Open University Press, 1975.

Hedebro, Göran. *Communication and Social Change in Developing Nations: A Critical View.* Ames, Iowa: Iowa State University Press, 1982.

Hindley, Patricia, Gail M. Martin, and Jean McNulty. *The Tangled Net: Basic Issues in Canadian Communications.* Vancouver, B. C.: J. J. Douglas, 1977.

Hornik, R., B. Searle, D. Foote, and J. Moulton. "The Role of Communication in Education." Stanford, Cal.: Stanford University Institute for Communication Research, 1979.

Hornik, R. and D. Solomon. "The Role of Communication in Nutrition." Stanford, Cal.: Stanford University Institute for Communication Research, 1979.

Howkins, John. *Mass Communication in China.* New York: Longman, 1982.

Hudson, Heather and Edwin Parker. "Medical Communication in Alaska by Satellite." *New England Journal of Medicine* 289, December 20, 1973, pp. 1351–1356.

Hudson, Heather E., Douglas Goldschmidt, Edwin B. Parker, and Andrew Hardy. *The Role of Telecommunications in Socio-Economic Development: A Review of the Literature with Guidelines for Further Investigations.* Report prepared for the International Telecommunication Union. Keewatin Communications, May 1979.

Huizer, Gerrit. *The Revolutionary Potential of Peasants in Latin America.* Lexington, Mass.: D. C. Heath/Lexington Books, 1972.

Jamison, Dean T. and Emile G. McAnany. *Radio for Education and Development.* Volume 3: *People and Communications.* Beverly Hills, Cal.: Sage, 1978.

Jaworski, Helan. "Towards a New Information Order: Rural Participation in the Peruvian Press." *Development Dialogue* (Uppsala, Sweden) 2, 1979, pp. 115–149.

Journal of Communication. "Communication in the Far North." Symposium of ten articles. *Journal of Communication* 27(4), Autumn 1977, pp. 120–190.

Journal of Communication. "Satellites for Rural Development." Symposium of seven articles. *Journal of Communication* 29(4), Autumn 1979, pp. 90–144.

Katz, Elihu and George Wedell. *Broadcasting in the Third World.* Cambridge, Mass.: Harvard University Press, 1977.

Kincaid D. L. *et al. Mother's Clubs and Family Planning in the Republic of Korea: The Case of Orgubi.* Case Study No. 2. Honolulu: East-West Communications Institute, 1975.

Lazarsfeld, Paul and Robert Merton. "Mass Communication, Popular Taste and Organized Social Action." In L. Bryson (Ed.) *The Communication of Ideas.* New York: Institute of Religious and Social Studies, 1948.

Le Duc, Don R. "West European Broadcasting Policy: Implications of New Technology." *Journal of Broadcasting* 23(2), Spring 1979, pp. 237–244.

Lenski, Gerhard E. *Power and Privilege.* New York: McGraw-Hill, 1966.

Lent, John. *Topics in Third World Mass Communications.* Hong Kong: Asian Research Service, 1979.

Lent, John A. (Ed.). *Newspapers in Asia: Contemporary Trends and Problems.* Hong Kong: Heinemann Asia, 1982.

Lerner, Daniel. *The Passing of Traditional Society.* Glencoe, Ill.: Free Press, 1958.

Lerner, D. and W. Schramm (Eds.). *Communications and Change in Developing Countries.* Honolulu: East-West Center, 1967.

Lewis, Peter M. *Different Keepers: Models of Structure and Finance in Community Radio.* London: International Institute of Communications, 1977.

Lewis, Peter M. *Whose Media: The Annan Report and After: A Citizen's Guide to Radio and Television.* London: Consumer's Association, 1978.

Mattelart, Michèle and Armand Mattelart. "'Small' Technologies: The Case of Mozambique." *Journal of Communication* 32(2), Spring 1982, pp. 75–79.

Mayo, John K., Robert C. Hornik, and Emile G. McAnany. *Educational Reform with Television: The El Salvador Experience.* Stanford, Cal.: Stanford University Press, 1976.

McAnany, Emile (Ed.). *Communications in the Rural Third World: The Role of Information in Development.* New York: Praeger, 1980.

McNulty, Jean M. *Other Voices in Broadcasting: The Evolution of New Forms of Local Programming in Canada.* Government of Canada, Department of Broadcasting, 1979.

McQueen, Humphrey. *Australia's Media Monopolies.* Melbourne: Visa, 1978.

Meyer, Manfred (Ed.) *Health Education by Television and Radio: Contributions to an International Conference with a Selected Bibliography.* Munich: K. G. Saur Verlag, 1981.

Migdal, Joel S. *Peasants, Politics and Revolution.* Princeton, N.J.: Princeton University Press, 1974.

Musto, Stephan A. *Los medios de comunicación social al servicio del desarrollo rural.* Bogatá: Editorial Andes, 1971.

Nasser, Munir K. *Press, Politics, and Power: Egypt's Heikal and Al-Ahram.* Ames, Iowa: The Iowa State University Press, 1979.

Nordenstreng, Kaarle and Herbert I. Schiller. *National Sovereignty and International Communication.* Norwood, N.J.: Ablex, 1979.

O'Sullivan, J. E., E. Rogers, and E. Contreras-Budge. "Communication in Agricultural Development." Stanford, Cal.: Stanford University Institute for Communication Research, 1979.

Peers, Frank W. *The Public Eye: Television and the Politics of Canadian Broadcasting, 1952–1968.* Toronto: University of Toronto Press, 1979.

Rogers, Everett M. *Modernization Among Peasants: The Impact of Communication.* New York: Holt, Rinehart & Winston, 1969.

Rogers, Everett M. *Communication and Development: Critical Perspectives.* Beverly Hills, Cal.: Sage, 1976.

Rogers, Everett M. and F. Shoemaker. *Communication of Innovations: A Cross-Cultural Approach.* New York: Free Press, 1971.

Rogers, E., D. Solomon, and R. Adhikarya. "Further Directions for USAID's Communication Policies in Population." Stanford, Cal.: Stanford University Institute for Communication Research, 1979.

Schramm, Wilbur. *Mass Media and National Development.* Stanford, Cal.: Stanford University Press, 1964.

Schramm, Wilbur. *Communication Satellites for Education, Science and Culture.* Reports and Papers on Mass Communication, No. 53. Paris: Department of Mass Communication, UNESCO, 1967.

Schramm, Wilbur. *Big Media, Little Media: Tools and Technologies for Instruction.* Beverly Hills, Cal.: Sage Publications, 1977.

Schramm, Wilbur. "Communication Development and the Development Process." In L. Pye (Ed.) *Communications and Political Development.* Princeton, N.J.: Princeton University Press, 1963.

Schramm, Wilbur and Daniel Lerner (Eds.). *Communications and Change: The Last Ten Years—and the Next.* Honolulu: University Press of Hawaii, 1976.

Schramm, Wilbur, Lyle M. Nelson, and Meret T. Betham. *Bold Experiment: The Story of Educational Television in American Samoa.* Stanford, Cal.: Stanford University Press, 1981.

Solomon, D., E. McAnany, D. Goldschmidt, E. Parker, and D. Foote. "The Role of Communication in Health." Stanford, Cal.: Stanford University Institute for Communication Research, 1979.

Suppes, Patrick, Barbara Searle, and Jamesine Friend. *The Radio Mathematics Project: Nicaragua 1976–1977.* Stanford, Cal.: Stanford University Institute for Math Studies in the Social Sciences, 1978.

Tehranian, Majid. "Development Theory and Communications Policy: The Changing Paradigms." In Melvin Voigt and Gerhard Hanneman (Eds.) *Progress in Communication Sciences,* Vol. 1. Norwood, N.J.: Ablex, 1979.

Tehranian, Majid, Farhad Hakimzadeh, and Marcello L. Vidale (Eds.). *Communications Policy for National Development: A Comparative Perspective.* Tehran: Iran Communications and Development Institute; London: Routledge & Kegan Paul, 1977.

Ugboajah, Frank Okwu. "Developing Indigenous Communication in Nigeria." *Journal of Communication* 29(4), Autumn 1979, pp. 40–95.

United Nations, Department of Economic and Social Affairs. *Multinational Corporations in World Development*. New York: United Nations, 1973.

UNESCO. *World Communications: A 200-Country Survey of Press, Radio, Television, and Film* (5th ed.). New York: Unipub, 1975.

UNESCO. Division of Statistics on Culture and Communication. *Statistics on Radio and Television 1960–1976*. Paris: UNESCO 1979.

UNESCO. *Documents and Publications in the Field of Mass Communications*. Paris: UNESCO, 1980.

UNESCO. *Informatics: A Vital Factor in Development*. Paris: UNESCO, 1980.

UNESCO. *Statistical Yearbook*. Paris: UNESCO, 1981.

Villamil, José J. (Ed.) *Transnational Capitalism and National Development*. Atlantic Highlands, N.J.: Humanities Press, 1979.

White, Robert A. "Mexico: The Zapata Movement and the Revolution." In Henry A. Landsberger (Ed.) *Latin American Peasant Movements*. Ithaca, N.Y.: Cornell University Press, 1971.

White, Robert A. *Mass Communication and the Popular Promotion Strategy of Rural Development in Honduras*. Stanford, Cal.: Stanford University Institute for Communication Research, 1976.

White, Robert A. *An Alternative Pattern of Basic Education: Radio Santa Maria*. Paris: UNESCO, 1976.

Wolf, Eric. *Peasant Wars of the Twentieth Century*. New York: Harper and Row, 1969.

Young, Frank W. "A Proposal for Cooperative Cross-Cultural Research on Intervillage Systems." *Human Organisation* 25, Spring 1966, pp. 46–50.

Young, Frank W. and Ruth C. Young. *Comparative Studies of Community Growth*. Rural Sociological Monograph No. 2. Morgantown: West Virginia University, 1973.

V. INTERGOVERNMENTAL SYSTEMS

Ayar, Farid. *Preliminary Ideas on the Foundations for the New International Information Order*. Beirut: Federation of Arab News Agencies, 1978.

Becker. Jörg (Ed.). *"Free Flow of Information": Informationen zur Neuen Internationalen Informationsordmung*. Frankfurt/Main: Gemeinschaftswerk der Evangelischen Publizistik, 1979.

Bielenstein, Dieter (Ed.). *Towards a New World Information Order: Consequences for Development Policy*. Bonn: Institute for International Relations/Friedrich-Ebert-Stiftung, 1979.

Bourges, Hervé. *Décoloniser l'information*. Paris: Éditions Cana, 1978.

Bulatovič, Vladislava. *Non-alignment and Information*. Belgrade: Federal Committee for Information/Jugoslovenska Stvarnost, 1978.

Christol, Carl Q. *The Modern International Law of Outer Space*. New York: Pergamon, 1982.

Codding, Jr., George A. and Anthony M. Rutkowski. *The International Telecommunication Union in a Changing World*. Dedham, Mass.: Artech, 1982.

Communications Media Center, New York University. *The New World Information Order: Issues in the World Administrative Radio Conference and Transborder Data Flow*. New York: Communications Media Center, New York Law School, 1979.

Edward R. Murrow Center of Public Diplomacy. *Voices of Freedom.* Working Papers for Conference of Independent News Media, Talloires, May 15–17, 1981. Medford, Mass.: Edward R. Murrow Center of Public Diplomacy, 1981.

Gerbner, George (Ed.) *Mass Media Policies in Changing Cultures.* New York: John Wiley, 1977.

Gonzalez Manet, Enrique. *Descolonización de la información.* Prague: International Organization of Journalists, 1979.

Gunter, Jonathan. *The United States and the Debate on the World "Information Order."* Washington, D.C.: Academy for Educational Development, 1978.

Hamelink, Cees. *Towards a New World Information Order.* Geneva: World Council of Churches, 1978.

Hammarberg, Thomas. *New Information Order: Balance and Freedom.* Stockholm: Ministry of Education and Cultural Affairs, 1978.

Harris, Phil. *Putting the NIIO into Practice: The Role of Inter Press Service.* Rome: IPS Research and Information Office, 1979.

Heacock, Roger. *UNESCO and the Media.* Geneva: Institut Universitaire des Hautes Etudes Internationales, 1977.

International Organization of Journalists. *Current Views on the World Information Order.* Prague: IOJ, 1977.

International Organization of Journalists. *Reflexions Around UNESCO.* Presented by Kaarle Nordenstreng. Prague: IOJ, 1978.

International Press Institute. *UNESCO and the Third World Media: An Appraisal.* Zurich: IPI, 1978.

Journal of Communication. "World Communication. The Great Debate Begins." Symposium of five articles. *Journal of Communication* 28(4), Autumn 1978, pp. 140–193.

Journal of Communication. "The U.S. Faces WARC." Symposium of ten articles. *Journal of Communication* 29(1), Winter 1979, pp. 143–207.

Journal of Communication. "Satellite Broadcasting and Communications Policy." Symposium of eight articles. *Journal of Communication* 30(2), Spring 1980, pp. 140–202.

Journal of Communication. "The Press, the U.S., and UNESCO." Symposium of ten articles. *Journal of Communication* 31(4), Autumn 1981, pp. 102–187.

Journal of Communication. "IPDC in Mexico: U.S.-UNESCO Turning Point?" Symposium of three articles. *Journal of Communication* 32(3), Summer 1982, pp. 53–85.

Kandil, Hamdy. "Developing Countries and the New Order in the Field of Information." *The Democratic Journalist* 2, 1980, pp. 8–11.

Kroloff, George and Scott Cohen. *The New World Information Order.* Washington, D.C.: U.S. Senate, Committee on Foreign Relations, 1977.

Lee, John A. R. *Towards Realistic Communication Policies: Recent Trends and Ideas Compiled and Analysed.* Reports and Papers on Mass Communication, No. 76. Paris: Department of Mass Communication, UNESCO, 1976.

Legum, Colin and J. Cornwell. *A Free and Balanced Flow.* Lexington, Mass.: Lexington Books, 1978.

Lopez-Escobar, Esteban. *Análisis del "nuevo orden" internacional de la información.* Pamplona: Ediciones Universidad de Navarra, 1978.

Mankekar, D. R. *One-way News Flow: Neo-Colonialism via News Media.* New Delhi: Clarion Books, 1978.

Mankekar, D. R. *Media and the Third World.* New Delhi: Indian Institute of Mass Communications, 1979.

Mattelart, Armand and Seth Siegelaub (Eds.). *Communication and Class Struggle,* Vol. I: *Capitalism, Imperialism.* New York: International General, 1979.

Miller, James. "Policy Planning and Technocratic Power: The Significance of OTP." *Journal of Communication* 32(1), Winter 1982, pp. 53–60.

Nordenstreng, Kaarle. *Struggle around "New International Information Order."* Tampere, Finland: University of Tampere, 1979.

Nordenstreng, Kaarle. *The Mass Media Declaration of UNESCO.* Norwood, N.J.: Ablex, 1982.

Osolnik, Bogdan. *Objectifs et stratégies d'un nouvel ordre international de la communication.* Paris: UNESCO Commission Internationale d'Etude des Problèmes de la Communication, No. 32, 1979.

Ploman, Edward. *International Law Governing Communications and Information: A Collection of Basic Documents.* Westport, Conn.: Greenwood, 1982.

Pronk, Jan. *Quelques remarques sur les rapports entre Nouvel ordre international de l'information et Nouvel order economique international.* Paris: UNESCO Commission Internationale d'Etude des Problèmes de la Communication, No. 35, 1979.

Reyes Matta, Fernando (Ed.). *La información en el nuevo orden internacional.* Mexico: Instituto Latinoamericano de Estudios Transnacionales, 1977.

Righter, Rosemary. *Whose News: Politics, the press and the Third World.* London: André Deutsch, 1978.

Roach, Colleen. "Annotated Bibliography on the NIIO." *Media Development* 27(4), 1980, pp. 47–49.

Salinas, Raquel. *Communication Policies: A Crucial Issue for the Accomplishment of the New Information Order. The Case of Latin America.* Stockholm: Institute of Latin American Studies, 1978.

Theobald, Robert. *Beyond Despair: A Policy Guide to the Communications Era.* Cabin John, Md.: Seven Locks Press, 1981.

Tunis, Secretariat of State for Information. *The New World Order for Information.* Tunis, 1977.

UNESCO. *Intergovernmental Conference on Communication Policies in Latin America and the Caribbean, San José, Costa Rica. Final Report,* July 1976.

UNESCO. *Advisory Group of Experts in Informations (AGI). Final Report.* Paris: UNESCO, September 17–19, 1979.

UNESCO. *Intergovernmental Conference on Communication Policies in Asia and Oceania, Kuala Lumpur, February 5–14, 1979. Final Report,* June 1979.

UNESCO. *Many Voices, One World.* (MacBride Commission Report). Paris: UNESCO, 1980.

UNESCO Courier. "A World Debate on Information: Flood Tide or Balanced Flow?" *UNESCO Courier,* April 1977.

Appendix Two

International and Intergovernmental Events and Documents Concerning World Communications

1944   UNITED NATIONS. Following World War II, the U.S., Great Britain, China, and the U.S.S.R. draft proposals for a United Nations charter at Dumbarton Oaks Conference.

1945   UNITED NATIONS. Founding meeting of the organization with 51 member nations. Charter accepted at this meeting.

1946   UNESCO. United Nations Educational, Scientific and Cultural Organization established, with the goal to further world peace by removing social, religious and racial tensions, encouraging interchange of ideas and achievements, and improving and expanding education. Article 1.2 of its Constitution includes a statement supporting the promotion of the free flow of information within and between countries.

1947   INTERNATIONAL TELECOMMUNICATION UNION (ITU). Adopted the International Telecommunication Convention, effective in 1949, which gave the U.N. agency responsibility for alloting radio frequencies, furthering low rates, and perfecting communications in rescue work. (Established in 1934.)

1948   UNITED NATIONS. General Assembly adopted the Universal Declaration of Human Rights which stated that everyone has the right to freedom of opinion and expression. Article 19 guarantees freedom to hold opinions without interference and to seek, receive and impart information and ideas through any media and regardless of frontiers.

1955   NON-ALIGNED COUNTRIES. Bandung Conference of Asian-African Countries gave rise to the Non-Aligned Movement.

1959   UNITED NATIONS ECONOMIC AND SOCIAL COUNCIL (UN ECOSOC). Requests UNESCO to conduct world survey on mass media.

ITU. Radio Regulations adopted. Regulation 423 states that broadcasting stations shall not employ power exceeding that necessary to maintain effective national service within the frontiers of the country.

1961   UN ECOSOC. Council passes the Resolution on Mass Media in Developing Countries recommending that governments of developed countries cooperate with less developed countries in meeting the needs of these countries for the development of independent national information media (Paragraph 5). Also recommends that governments of underdeveloped countries review tariff and fiscal policies to facilitate the development of information media and the free flow of information within and between countries (Part VI).

1962   UNITED NATIONS. General Assembly passes the Resolution 1802 on Communication by Satellite. Part IV states that communication by satellite offers great benefits to mankind in permitting the expansion of radio, television and telephone transmission thus facilitating contact among peoples of the world.

UNESCO. General Conference authorizes a study of the consequences of the use of satellites on a world scale upon the achievement of UNESCO objectives.

1963   ORGANIZATION OF ASIAN NEWS AGENCIES created.

1964   UNESCO. General Conference authorizes Director-General to convene a meeting of experts on space communication.

INTELSAT. Consortium founded. INTELSAT I (Early Bird) was orbited over the Atlantic Ocean in 1965. (TELSTAR I, the first commercially built communication satellite, had been orbited in 1962 and SYNCOM II had successfully demonstrated the practicality of synchronous communications satellites in 1963.)

1965   UNESCO. At Expert Meeting on Space Communication, UNESCO is urged to undertake a study of problems for the free flow of information, the spread of education, and cultural exchange posed by space communication.

1967   UNITED NATIONS. Outer Space Treaty provides that all nations shall have equal access to outer space (Article 1).

1968   UNESCO. Broadcast Organizations on Space Communications meet in Paris.

UNESCO. General Conference authorizes intergovernmental meeting on space communication; the findings of this meeting were to provide the basis for a Declaration.

UNESCO. General Conference requests research on mass media.

1969   UNESCO. Intergovernmental Meeting on Space Communication meeting attended by government representatives from 61 countries.

1970   UNESCO. General Conference passes Resolution 4.21 which authorizes the Director-General to assist Member States in formulating policies with respect to the mass communications media.

UNITED NATIONS. General Assembly formulates international development strategy for the Second United Nations Development Decade which stresses mobilization of public opinion in both developed and developing countries in support of objectives and policies (Paragraph 84).

NON-ALIGNED COUNTRIES hold summit in Lusaka to discuss the role of information in developing countries.

1971   ITU. World Administrative Radio Conference (WARC) for Space Tele-communications passes an Amendment to Radio Regulations (428 A) which states that nations will do all in their power to reduce their broadcasting across borders via satellite unless they have reached a prior agreement with those countries.

1972   UNESCO. General Conference passes Resolution 4.113 requesting the Director-General to prepare and submit a draft of a Declaration on the Use of Mass Media.

UNESCO. General Conference adopts the Declaration of Guiding Principles on the Use of Space Broadcasting for the Free Flow of Information, the Spread of Education and Greater Cultural Exchange. Article II states that, in using space broadcasting for the free flow of information, all nations should respect the sovereignty and equality of others. Article V affirms the need for a balanced flow of information between all countries.

UNITED NATIONS. General Assembly approves UNESCO Declaration on Space Broadcasting.

1973   NON-ALIGNED COUNTRIES. Fourth Conference of Heads of State and Government of the Non-Aligned Countries formulates a Programme for Action for Economic Development which stresses that action should be taken to promote greater interchange of ideas among developing countries and to reorganize existing communication channels.

CONGRESS ON INTERNATIONAL TELEVISION BROADCAST EXCHANGES is held in Finland.

INTERNATIONAL BROADCAST NEWS WORKSHOP is held in Cologne.

1974   UNESCO. General Conference considers the Draft of a Declaration on the Role of Mass Media. Draft 18 C/35 stresses the responsibility of the mass media in disseminating information and opinions in a manner compatible with the rights and dignity of States and peoples (Article I, 1), the importance of two-way flow of information and the rights of states and information media in transborder diffusion of information (Article III), and the responsibility of states for the activities of mass media under their jurisdiction as governed by customary international law and agreements (Article X).

In the General Conference, amendments were proposed to the Draft to modify the paragraphs on the responsibility and duties of states for the activities of national mass media and to state that UNESCO should give priority to building up the information infrastructure in developing countries to correct the existing imbalance.

Agreeing that Draft and Amendments require further study, General Conference Resolution 4.III authorizes intergovernmental meeting on Draft 18C/35 to prepare a Draft Declaration for submission to the General Conference at its 19th session in light of these documents.

UNITED NATIONS. General Assembly passes Resolutions 3201 and 3202 calling for the Establishment of a New International Economic Order based on equity, sovereign equality, interdependence and cooperation among all States.

1975   AMIC holds Regional Conference on Information Imbalance in Asia.

CONFERENCE ON SECURITY AND COOPERATION IN EUROPE. In Helsinki, Conference passes Final Act which aims, in the spirit of détente, to facilitate freer and wider dissemination of information and encourage cooperation in information and information exchange.

UNESCO. Intergovernmental Meeting on Use of Mass Media discusses Draft 19 C/91 which stresses support for the establishment and furthering of national mass media in developing countries to correct the existing disequilibrium (Article IV) and the responsibility of states for the activities in the international sphere of all mass media under their jurisdiction (Article XII).

NON-ALIGNED COUNTRIES meet in Lima with Foreign Ministers of Information.

1976   UNESCO. Intergovernmental Conference on Communication Policies in Latin America held in Costa Rica. The Final Report stresses the urgent regional need to replace the criterion of the "free flow of information" with that of "balanced circulation." The conference recommends that member states define and implement policies, plans and laws that will facilitate more balanced communication relations (Recommendation No. 1) and requests the Director-General of UNESCO to call a high-level meeting for the purpose of facilitating the establishment of a Latin American news agency (Recommendation No. 27, 2).

UNESCO. General Conference passes Resolution 4.143 which authorizes the Director-General to hold further consultations on 19 C/9 in order to prepare a final Draft Declaration on "Fundamental Principles Governing the Use of the Mass Media" and also authorizes Director-General of UNESCO to appoint an international commission to study communication problems.

UNESCO. General Conference adopts the Medium-Term Plan 1977–1982 which urges members to attain a greater understanding of international information flows and formulation of strategies likely to achieve a more equitable two-way flow of information.

NON-ALIGNED COUNTRIES hold a Symposium on Communication Policies in Tunis which concluded that it is the duty of nonaligned and other developing countries to change the existing disequilibrium in world information, to obtain the decolonization of information, and to initiate a new international order of information.

NON-ALIGNED COUNTRIES hold a meeting of Information Ministers in New Delhi which notes that the existing global information flows were marked by serious imbalances and decides to endorse the agreed constitution for the Non-aligned Press Agencies Pool.

NON-ALIGNED COUNTRIES hold Summit at Colombo at which was discussed their concern with the growing gap between the communications capabilities of non-aligned countries and those of developed countries and stressed that "a new world order of information is just as important as a new international economic order."

OAU adopts Cultural Charter for Africa. Article 22 of the Charter states that African governments should ensure the total decolonization of the mass media and should establish joint cooperation in order to break the monopoly of non-African countries.

1977   WARC passes the Final Acts for the planning of the Broadcast Satellite Service.

U.S. SENATE. The Subcommittee on International Operations of the Committee on Foreign Relations on Rule and Control of International Communications files a report upon and U.S. assessment of WARC 1977, which reaffirms principle of free flow of information.

COUNCIL OF EUROPE considers a Draft Report on the International Aspects of Information which supports the principle of free flow of information.

OAU. The First Session of African Information Ministers in Kampala supports efforts being made by non-aligned countries to establish a new international information order in consonance with the interests of Third World countries.

NON-ALIGNED COUNTRIES. First Conference of Non-Aligned Broadcasting Organizations is held in Sarajevo.

SECOND INTERNATIONAL BROADCAST NEWS WORKSHOP is held in Cairo.

1978   UNESCO. General Conference adopts the Draft Declaration on Fundamental Principles governing the Contribution of the Mass Media to Strengthening Peace and International Understanding and to Combating War Propaganda, Racialism and Apartheid. Article I states that strengthening peace and understanding necessitate a free, reciprocal and balanced flow of accurate, complete and objective information. Article VI states that in order to establish a new equilibrium and greater reciprocity in the flow of information, it is necessary to correct the inequality in flow of information to and from the developing countries.

UNESCO. Draft Programme and Budget 1979–1980 (20 C/5) gives high priority to measures intended to reduce the communication gap existing between the developed and developing countries.

UNESCO. International Commission for the Study of Communication Problems is established, consisting of 16 members from the capitalist, socialist, and non-aligned nations. Sean MacBride is chosen to head the Commission.

1979   UNESCO. MacBride Commission Report, which stresses the importance of a new, more just and more efficient world information and communication order, is submitted to UNESCO.

UNESCO. The first meeting of the International Program for the Development of Communications (IPDC) is held.

ITU. General WARC in Geneva is attended by 2,000 delegates from 142 countries. The Third World presses its claims for equal access to spectrum and orbital slots.

1980   UNESCO. General Conference at Belgrade does not formally consider MacBride Commission Report, but draws upon it to form the basis of the New World Information and Communication Order resolution adopted.

1981   IPDC. Intergovernmental Council consisting of 35 member states constituted.

WORLD PRESS FREEDOM COMMITTEE (WPFC). Conference in Talloires, France, produces the Talloires Declaration which pledged "cooperation in all genuine efforts to expand the free flow of information" and called upon UNESCO to "abandon attempts to regulate news content and formulate rules for the press."

1982   IPDC. Second Meeting of the Intergovernmental Council is held in Acapulco and adopts priorities for spending and projects.

ITU. Plenipotentiary Conference is held in Nairobi and revises the ITU Convention, giving heavy emphasis to technical assistance to the Third World.

UNESCO. Extraordinary (Medium Term Plan) Conference is held in fall, at which communications issues are heavily debated.

Sources: In addition to the chapters in this book, sources of information for this appendix include the *Journal of Communication*, Edward W. Ploman's *International Law Governing Communications and Information: A Collection of Basic Documents* (Westport, Conn.: Greenwood, 1982), and "The Establishment of a New International Information Order," Chart from the Institut für Internationale Begegnungen, Bonn (*Journal of Communication* 29(2), Spring 1979, p. 134).

Appendix Three

Acronyms and Other Terms Cited

This appendix is composed of acronyms and other key terms in world communications that are cited in the text. More extensive listings in various categories can be found in the following sources:

National news agencies and broadcasting organizations: UNESCO. *World Communications: A 200-Country Survey of Press, Radio, Television, and Film.* New York: Unipub, 1975.

International communications research organizations: William Rivers *et al.* (Eds.). "Part 8." *Aspen Handbook on the Media* (1977–1979 edition). New York: Praeger, 1977.

Teletext and videotext systems: Efrem Sigel. "Table 1." *The Future of Videotext: Worldwide Prospects for Home/Office Electronic Information Services.* White Plains, N.Y.: Knowledge Industry Publications, 1982.

Online databases: Ruth N. Cuadra, David M. Abels, and Judith Wanger (Eds.). *Directory of Online Databases* (published quarterly). Santa Monica, Cal.: Cuadra Associates, 1979–

ABC (*American Broadcasting Company*) Commercially owned U.S. communications and broadcasting conglomerate including radio and television networks.

ACPE (*Arab Project for Communication Planning and Exchange*).

ACPO (*Acción Cultural Popular*) Latin American organization established to promote educational and other development programs.

AED (*Academy for Educational Development*) Non-profit organization aimed at promoting educational programs in developing countries.

AFP (*Agence France Presse*) French news agency.

AFRAM Films Association of American film companies which develops and expands distribution of American films in French-speaking sub-Saharan Africa.

AFROSAT An African regional satellite system being considered by the 38-member Panaftel group.

AMIC (*Asian Mass Communication Research and Information Center*) Research organization headquartered in Singapore.

AMPECA (*American Motion Picture Export Company*) U.S. joint-trading association for developing the African market for American films.

ANTIOPE   French teletext system.

AP (*Associated Press*)   A commercially owned U.S. news agency.

AP-Dow Jones   Transnational computer communications system which provides economic information.

ARABSAT   An Arab regional satellite system currently being planned.

ASETA   A regional organization of South American countries which is currently planning a regional Andean satellite system.

ASLIB (*Association of Special Libraries and Information Bureau*)   Merged with British Society for International Bibliography in 1949 and has since been referred to as Aslib.

AT & T (*American Telephone and Telegraph*)   Privately owned corporation that is responsible for, among other things, national telephone service in the U.S.

BBC (*British Broadcasting Corporation*)   Government run broadcasting service including radio and television services along with external services for international broadcasting.

BRT (*Belgische Radio en Televisie-Nederelands uitzendigen*)   One of the two independent broadcasting organizations in Belgium which have effective monopoly of radio and television broadcasts. Programming is broadcast in Dutch.

BSE 12/14   Regional satellite system in Japan.

CAB (*Civil Aeronautics Board*)   U.S. board that regulates air travel.

CAPTAINS (*Character and Pattern Telephone Access Information Network System*)   Japanese viewdata system project.

CATV (*cable television*)   Internationally used acronym for cable television system.

CB Radio   Generally used term for low frequency interactive radio.

CBS (*Columbia Broadcasting System*)   A commercially owned U.S. communications and broadcasting conglomerate including radio and television networks.

CBS-Newsfilm U.S.   A commercially owned worldwide newsfilm distributor.

CCIS (*Coaxial cable information system*)   Teletext system in Japan.

CEAO (*Communauté Economique de l'Afrique de l'Ouest*)   West African Economic Community, formerly UDEAO.

CEEFAX   British teletext system.

CIBS   Japanese teletext system.

CIESPAL (*Centro Internacional de Estudios Superiores de la Comunicación para América Latina*)   Latin American research institute headquartered in Quito, Ecuador, and Lima, Peru.

COMNET (*Communications Network*)   An international information system.

COMSAT or **COMSATCORP** (*Communications Satellite Corporation*)   A private U.S. corporate satellite system which was awarded a monopoly in conducting international commercial public telecommunication by satellite for U.S. users.

CTS (*Communications Technology Satellite*)   Regional satellite system owned/operated by TELESAT.

CYBERNET   Worldwide satellite network of Control Data Corporation, a U.S. company.

DAMA (*Demand-assignment multiple-access*)   A control system for assignment of satellite channels or circuits. A DAMA system assigns a circuit to a requesting terminal on demand and then returns the circuit to the access pool when the terminal has completed its call.

DARE   An international information system.

DBS (*Direct broadcast satellite*)   Term used internationally for satellites which could be used to beam television signals directly to private homes or across national borders.

DDB (*Distributed data banks [bases]*)   Information networks which provide comprehensive information processing on remote computers. The information network is a series of interrelated computers (not terminals).

DEVSIS (*Development Sciences Information System*)   Canadian-based international information system/service.

DIANE (*Direct Information Across Networks for Europe*)   A system developed to facilitate the use of data banks which stores information in data banks to which EURONET has access.

DPA (*Deutsche Presse-Agentur*)   West German news agency.

DPA-ETES   West German newsfilm distributor.

EBU (*European Broadcasting Union*)   Organization of Western European broadcasters.

ECS (*European Communications Satellite or System*)   European Space Agency's communication satellite carrying paid transmissions.

ECSSID (*European Cooperation in Social Science Information and Documentation*)   A project of the European Centre of Social Science Research and Information, Vienna, which was designed to promote European cooperation in the area of social science information. Conference held in the U.S.S.R. in June 1977.

ELDO (*European Launcher Development Organization*)   European satellite organization superseded by the European Space Agency.

EROS (*Earth Resources Observation System*)   U.S. Department of the Interior. [Also stands for the satellite of the same name operated by the National Environmental Satellite Service.]

EROS-A NASA (*U.S.*)   Affiliated data center that disseminates information derived from remote-sensing earth satellites.

ESA (*European Space Agency*)   A regional space development organization which is a consortium of 17 member countries in Europe. It has already launched an experimental satellite, OTS (Orbital Test Satellite) with 600 channels.

ESRO (*European Space Research Organization*)   Superseded by the European Space Agency.

EUDISED (European Documentation System for Education).

EUREX   Transnational information system serving the financial sector. Serves the European bond market through a network of leased lines.

EUROBASE   A new data bank on sociopolitical problems which deals with elections to the European Parliament.

EURONET (*European On-Line Information Network*) (Commission of European Communities)   A European information network set up by the European Economic Community (EEC) in 1979 to provide access to bases of scientific, juridical, and socioeconomic data.

EUSIDIC (*European Scientific Information Dissemination Centers*).

EUTELSAT   The consortium of Western European PTT ministeries which comprises the telecommunication administrations of participating countries.

FCC (*Federal Communications Commission*)   U.S. regulatory agency responsible for domestic communications.

FSS (*Fixed Satellite System*).

G-77 (*Group of 77*)   A group of non-aligned developing nations, usually referred to within the context of UNESCO.

GATT (*General Agreement on Tariffs and Trade*)   Organization concerned with the adjustment of tariffs between 87 member nations.

GLOBECOM   Transnational information system serving the financial sector through a network of leased channels that interconnect Citibank's overseas branches.

HBO (*Home Box Office*)   A private U.S. corporation offering television programs to subscribers via cable.

HERMES/CTS   Canadian satellite.

H-SAT   Satellite project of ESA which was abandoned and replaced by the L-SAT project.

IAMCR (*International Association for Mass Communication Research*)   Research organization headquartered in Leicester, England.

IASSIST (*International Association for Social Science Information Services*)   An international information system for socioeconomic information.

IBI (*Intergovernmental Bureau for Informatics*)   An international body which was formed exclusively to focus on informatics development and national policy.

IBM (*International Business Machines*)   U.S.-based multinational corporation.

ICA (*International Communications Association*)   U.S.-based scholarly association. Also stands for International Communication Agency, U.S. agency which supervises the distribution of U.S. information and entertainment abroad. Superseded the USIA.

IDOC (*International Documentation and Communication Center*)   Research organization located in Rome.

IFDO (*International Federation of Data Organizations*).

IFRB (*International Frequency Registration Board*)   Subunit of the International Telecommunication Union.

IIC (*Institute for International Communication*)   Research institute headquartered in London, England.

ILET (*Instituto Lantinoamericano de Estudios Transnacionales*)   Research institute headquartered in Mexico City.

INION (*Institute of Scientific Information on Social Sciences*)   Research institute at the U.S.S.R. Academy of Sciences, Moscow, and the leading body of the MISON system.

INMARSAT   An international navigational satellite system which provides positioning information to ships worldwide.

INSAT (*Indian National Satellite*)   Satellite owned and operated by Indian government that carries on work of experimental use of SITE.

INTELSAT (*International Telecommunications Satellite Consortium*)   An international satellite system which provides common carrier service to 130 nations, primarily Western and developing nations.

INTERSPUTNIK   An international satellite system providing common carrier service to Eastern European countries.

IOJ (*International Organization of Journalists*)   Organization of journalists of the Eastern bloc countries headquartered in Prague.

IPDC (*International Program for the Development of Communications*)   A UNESCO-based international clearinghouse for information about communications development needs, resources, and priorities established at the 21st General Conference of UNESCO in Belgrade in 1980 and located in Paris.

IPS (*Inter Press Service*) An information service which has the goal of offering an alternative source of information and news about the Third World.

ISRO (*Indian Space Research Organization*) Organization responsible for the day-to-day operation of SITE.

IT & T (*International Telephone and Telegraph Corporation*) Commercially owned U.S.-based multinational corporation.

ITU (*International Telecommunication Union*) International body concerned with international telecommunications policy and regulation.

ITV Generally used name for instructional television systems in a number of developing nations. [Also commercial television network in the United Kingdom.]

LANDSAT A NASA-operated satellite which retrieves information on earth surface and seabed conditions and resources and monitors climatic and topographical changes.

LDC (*Less-developed countries*) Commonly used term for developing nations.

L-SAT (*"large satellite"*) Satellite project being developed by the European Space Agency.

MCA, Inc. U.S.-based conglomerate communications corporation.

MISON The international social science information system of the socialist countries. A multiprofile and multipurpose information system of the Academies of Sciences of Bulgaria, Hungary, Viet Nam, the German Democratic Republic, Mongolia, Poland, the U.S.S.R. and Czechoslovakia founded in July 1976.

MOLNIYA 2 INTERSPUTNIK's regional satellite which the U.S.S.R. proposes to link Eastern European countries, Cuba, Mongolia and Russia.

MPEAA (*Motion Picture Export Association of America*) Association of U.S. commercial film producers organized to facilitate joint marketing of their products to foreign countries.

MPT (*Ministry of Post and Telecommunications*) Japanese agency which has the responsibility of regulating broadcasting, telephone and postal services. Communications services themselves are not government controlled or operated.

NASA (*National Aeronautics and Space Administration*) U.S. government agency created in 1958 to be responsible for space exploration, training of astronauts, astronomical observations, and communications.

NAVSAT (*Navigation Satellite*) Navigational satellite system of the U.S. Navy.

NBC (*National Broadcasting Company*) A commercially owned U.S.-based communications and broadcasting conglomerate including radio and television networks.

NIIO (*New International Information Order*) Term sometimes used in place of New World Information Order.

NIMBUS A weather satellite operated by the National Oceanic and Atmospheric Administration, U.S.

NOAA (*National Oceanic and Atmospheric Administration*) Under the auspices of the U.S. Department of Commerce, the administration manages all operational civilian remote sensing activities from space.

NORDSAT A regional satellite system being planed by the five Nordic countries.

NTA (*Nigerian Television Authority*) Only authority charged with broadcasting in Nigeria.

NTIA (*National Telecommunications and Information Administration*) U.S. Department of Commerce agency for the coordination of communications policy.

NTT (*Nippon Telephone and Telegraph Corporation*) Japanese telecommunications corporation.

NWIO (*New World Information Order*) Generally used term for call of developing nations within UNESCO for a more balanced flow of information among all nations.

OECD (*Organization for Economic Cooperation and Development*) Consortium of 24 member nations, primarily European, headquartered in Paris. Superseded the OEEC (Organization for European Economic Cooperation).

ORACLE British teletext system.

ORF (*Oesterreichischer Rundfunk*) Publicly chartered broadcasting organization which holds a legal monopoly over all broadcasting in Austria.

ORTF (*Office de Radiodiffusion Télévision Française*) State-owned radio and television network of France.

OTA (*Office of Technology Assessment*) U.S. agency whose function is to provide Congressional committees with information for the formulation of telecommunication and other technological public policy decisions.

OTS, OTS-2 Satellite systems developed by European Space Agency.

PA (*Permanent assignment*) A control system for the assignment of satellite channels or circuits in which fixed circuits are assigned to specific terminal pairs.

PALAPA 1 and **2** Satellites of the regional system providing communications services to Indonesia and the inhabited islands of Southeast Asia.

PANA (*Pan-African News Agency*)

PEACESAT (*Pan-Pacific Education and Communications Experiment Using Satellites*) (*U.S./NASA*) Satellite linking widely dispersed South Pacific islands broadcasting entertainment and educational programs.

PLATO (*Programed Logic for Automatic Teaching Operations*) Satellite owned by Control Data Corporation (U.S.) which provides educational software programs worldwide over their CYBERNET.

PTT (*Post, telephone and telegraph*) PTTs are the European ministries of post, telephone and telegraph which control technical and and financial aspects of these services on the national level.

PTTI (*Postal, Telegraph, and Telephone International*).

QUBE Interactive cable television system owned by Warner-Amex in Columbus, Ohio, U.S.

RCA (*Record Company of America*) Commercially owned U.S. firm involved in broadcasting, recording, and the development of new communications technologies.

R & D (*Research and development*) General term used to denote the "creative" aspects of corporate enterprise.

REUTERS A European-based commercially owned news agency.

RTBF (*Radio et télévision belge-émissions françaises*) One of the two independent broadcasting organizations in Belgium which have effective monopoly of radio and television broadcasting. RTBF is the system which broadcasts programming in French.

RTC (*Radio, Television and Cinema Board*) Mexican ministry in charge of all communications policies in Mexico.

SBS (*Satellite Business Systems*)   International Business Machines' (IBM/U.S.) international telecommunications satellite system.

SINADI   National Information System established in Peru in 1974 by the military government to provide the administrative framework for managing and supervising all aspects of mass media reform.

SITA (*Societé Internationale de Télécommunications Aéronautiques*)   International aeronautical satellite system.

SITE (*Satellite Instructional Television Experiment*)   Indian experiment in bringing television to isolated rural audiences. The experiment was conducted by the Indian Space Research Organization in collaboration with NASA (U.S.) and the Indian government-owned television authority, Doordarshan.

SOFIRAD   French international broadcasting organization.

SPINES   An international information system.

SWIFT (*Society for Worldwide Interbank Financial Telecommunications*)   International satellite banking system.

TA (*Technology assessment*)   Research tool used primarily in the U.S. for assessing the relationship between technology and society as a guide for generating public policy.

TAGOT Network (*Talking, Going and Thinking Network*)   Computer network of services deliverable to the home, such as electronic mail and newspapers.

TANJUG   Yugoslavian-based news agency of the non-aligned countries.

TASS   News agency of the U.S.S.R.

TAT-7   Proposed transatlantic cable.

TDF (*Transborder data flows*)   Term generally used to denote the movement of information through computer networks over national boundaries. [Also, TDF (Télédiffusion de France) French broadcasting organizations involved in telecommunications under the Ministry of Communications.]

TELECOM-1, 2, 3   Proposed French satellite for direct satellite broadcasting to metropolitan France and her overseas departments.

TELEDON   Canadian teletext system.

TELETEXT   System for providing updated information services to cable television subscribers.

TPEA (*Television Program Export Association*)   1959–1970, association of U.S. television producers to promote sales of U.S. television programming abroad.

TVSAT   Proposed West German (Federal Republic of Germany) direct broadcast satellite.

U.N. (*United Nations*)   International body of over 100 members established by charter in 1946, headquartered in New York City, U.S.

UNESCO (*United Nations Educational, Scientific and Cultural Organization*)   An agency of the U.N. devoted to promoting peace through education and the diffusion of information.

UPI (*United Press International*)   A commercially owned U.S. news agency.

UPITN   Worldwide news agency of joint U.S. and British ownership which also distributes news film.

USAID (*U.S. Agency for International Development*)   U.S. State Department agency responsible for projects to assist developing countries.

VIDEODISC   Technology that allows for both audio and visual recording and playback on a disc similar to an audio long-playing record album.

VIDEOTEX   A system similar to teletext which provides information to subscribers over a cable television hookup and also allows for interactive capability with the originating source of information.

VOA (*Voice of America*)   U.S.-based international broadcasting organization.

WARC (*World Administrative Radio Conference*)   Convened by the International Telecommunication Union (ITU) every twenty years.

Appendix Four: Global Satellite Systems

1. International Satellite Systems

	Members	Current Status
INTELSAT Global Satellite System	109 members	Operational (currently 16 satellites)
INMARSAT Maritime Mobile Satellite System	37 members	Operational (4 satellites)
INTERSPUTNIK Satellite System	12 members	Operational (leased capacity from U.S.S.R.)

2. Regional Satellite Systems

	Members	Current Status
Arabsat Satellite System	18 members	1985 launch
African Satellite System (AFSAT)	Most African nations	Under consideration only
EUTELSAT Satellite System	Most European nations	To be fully operational 1983–84
Palapa Satellite System	Asian countries	Indonesia domestic system, regional services to Asian members—operational

3. Domestic Satellite Systems—Dedicated Systems

	Services[a]	Current Status
Australian National Satellite Systems (AUSSAT)	FSS, CATV, DBS	Under construction for 1985 launch
Brazilian Domestic Satellite System (BRAZILSAT)	FSS	Under construction for 1985 launch
Canadian Domestic Satellite System (ANIK A–D)	FSS, DBS, domestic service to U.S.	Operational
China Domestic Satellite System		Project cancelled
Colombia Domestic Satellite System (Satcol)	FSS	Contract award under consideration

System	Type	Status
French Domestic Digital Satellite System (Telecom)	FSS	Under construction for 1985 launch
French DBS Satellite (TDF)	DBS	Under construction for 1986 launch
Germany (Fed. Rep.) Deutsch Federal Satellite (DFS)	FSS	Under construction for 1986 launch
Germany (Fed. Rep.) DBS Satellite (TV-Sat)	DBS	Planned for 1986
Indian Satellite System (INSAT)	FSS, DBS	Operational (temporarily out of service)
Indonesian Satellite System (Palapa A & B)	FSS	Operational
Iranian Satellite System (Zahreh)		Project cancelled
Italian Satellite System (Italsat)	FSS	Planned for 1986
Italian DBS Satellite System (SARIT)	DBS	Planned for 1985
Japanese Domestic Satellite System (CS-2a, 2b)	FSS	Planned for 1983
Japanese Domestic Broadcast System (BS-2a, 2b)	DBS	Planned for 1985
Luxembourg Domestic Broadcasting System (LUXSAT)	DBS	Planned for 1986
Mexican Domestic Satellite System (SATMEX)		Status uncertain
Saudi Arabian Broadcast Satellite System (SABS)	DBS	Planned for 1986
Swedish Domestic Satellite System (Tele-X)	FSS, DBS, mobile	Planned for 1986
Switzerland Domestic Broadcast Satellite (Helvesat)	DBS	Planned for 1986
United Kingdom Domestic (UNISAT)	DBS, FSS	Planned for 1986

United States Domestic Satellite Systems

System	Type	Status
Advanced Business Communications, Inc. (ABCI)	FSS, DBS	Planned for late 1980s
American Satellite Company System	FSS	Operational
Comstar Satellite System	FSS	Operational
CBS Satellite Systems	DBS	Planned for mid-1980s
Direct Broadcast Satellite Corporation	DBS	Planned for mid-1980s
Graphic Scanning Satellite System	DBS	Planned for mid-1980s
GT & E Satellite System (G-Star)	FSS, DBS	Planned for 1984
Hughes Galaxy Satellite System	FSS	Planned for 1983
Oak Satellite System	DBS	Project cancelled
Rainbow Satellite, Inc. (14/11 GHz)	FSS	Planned for 1986

RCA DBS Satellite System	DBS	Planned for mid-1980s
RCA Satcom Satellite System	FSS	Operational
Satellite Business System (IBM/Comsat/Aetna)	FSS	Operational
Southern Pacific Communications Corp. (SPACENET)	FSS	Planned for 1985
Satellite Television Corp. (Comsat)	DBS	Planned for 1985
Telstar Satellite System (AT & T)	FSS	Planned for 1984
Tracking, Data, Relay Satellite/Advanced Westar (NASA/Western Union)	Data relay, FSS	Planned for mid-1983
United Satellite Services Broadcasting (Hubbard)	DBS	Planned for mid-1980s
U.S. Satellite System, Inc.	FSS	Planned for mid-1980s
Video Satellite System	DBS	Planned for mid-1980s
Western Union Satellite System	FSS	Operational
Western Union DBS Satellite System	DBS	Planned for mid to late 1980s

U.S.S.R. Domestic Satellite Systems

Ekran Broadcast Satellite System	TV, DBS	Operational
Loutch Satellite System	FSS	Operational
Molnya Satellite System	FSS	Operational
Raduga Satellite System	FSS, military	Operational
Volna Satellite System	Maritime mobile ser.	Planned for 1984

4. Domestic Satellite Systems—(Leased/Shared Use Systems)

	Space Segment Facilities	Current Status
Algerian Satellite Systems	INTELSAT Lease	Operational
Angolian Satellite System	INTELSAT Lease	Planned for 1983
Argentina Satellite System	INTELSAT Lease	Operational
Australia Satellite System	INTELSAT Lease	Operational

System	Type	Status
Bangladesh Satellite System	INTELSAT Lease	Planned for 1984
Bolivian Satellite System	INTERSAT Lease	Planned for 1984
Brazilian Satellite System	INTELSAT Lease	Operational
Cameroon Satellite System	INTELSAT Lease	Planned for 1984
Chilean Satellite System	INTELSAT Lease	Operational
China Satellite System (P.R.C.)	INTELSAT Lease	Planned for 1983
Colombian Satellite System	INTELSAT Lease	Operational
Denmark (Greenland) Satellite System	INTELSAT Lease	Operational
Ecuadorian Satellite System	INTELSAT Lease	Planned for 1983
France Overseas Territory (Réunion, Martinique) Satellite System	INTELSAT Lease	Operational
Germany (Fed. Rep.) Satellite System Spot Beam 14/11 GHz	INTELSAT Lease	Planned for 1984
Indian Satellite System	INTELSAT Lease	Operational
Korean (Rep. of) Satellite System	INTELSAT Lease	Planned for 1986
Libyan Satellite System	INTELSAT Lease	Operational
Malaysian Satellite System	INTELSAT Lease	Operational
Mali Satellite System	INTELSAT Lease	Planned for 1983
Mauritanian Satellite System	INTELSAT Lease	Planned for 1983
Mexican Satellite System	INTELSAT Lease	Operational
Moroccan Satellite System	INTELSAT Lease	Operational
Niger Satellite System	INTELSAT Lease	Operational
Nigerian Satellite System	INTELSAT Lease	Operational
Norwegian Satellite System	INTELSAT Lease	Operational
Oman Satellite System	INTELSAT Lease	Operational
Pakistan Satellite System	INTELSAT Lease	Planned for 1983
Papua New Guinea Satellite System	AUSSAT/INTELSAT Lease	Planned for 1985
Peruvian Satellite System	INTELSAT Lease	Operational

Philippine Satellite System	INTELSAT/Palapa Lease	Operational
Portugal (Azores) Satellite System	INTELSAT Lease	Operational
Saudi Arabia Satellite System	INTELSAT Lease	Operational
South Africa Satellite System	INTELSAT Lease	Planned for 1983
Spain (Canary Islands) Satellite System	INTELSAT Lease	Operational
Sri Lanka Satellite System	INTELSAT Lease	Planned for 1985
Sudan Satellite System	INTELSAT Lease	Operational
Thailand Satellite System	INTELSAT Lease	Planned for 1983
United Kingdom Domestic Video Service (BTI)	INTELSAT Lease	Planned for 1983
Venezuelan Satellite System	INTELSAT Lease	Planned for 1983
Zairian Satellite System	INTELSAT Lease	Operational

5. Military Satellite Systems

	System Names	Current Status
NATO Military Satellite Communications Project	Phase I, II, III	Operational
U.K. Skynet Defense Communications Network	SKYNET	Operational

U.S. Military Satellite Communications Network

U.S.A.F. Communications Satellite System	AFSATCOM	Operational
U.S. Defense Satellite Communications System	DSCS Phase I, II, III	Operational
U.S. Naval Satellite Communications System	Marisat/Leasat	Operational
U.S. Fleetsatcom Communications System	FLTSATCOM	Operational

U.S.S.R. Military Communications Satellite System

Cosmos Military Satellite System	Cosmos	Operational
GALS Military Satellite System	Gals	Operational
Volna Naval Communications Satellite System	Volna	Planned for 1984

6. *Experimental Satellite Systems*

	Sponsors	Current Status
Applications Technological Satellites	U.S. NASA	Operational
Canadian Experimental Mobile Satellite Program (MSAT-X)	Canadian govt.	Planned for 1988
Communications Technology Satellite	U.S./Canada	Out of service
European Mobile Communications Satellite	E.S.A.	Planned for 1987
Japanese Experimental Broadcast Satellite	NASADA /GE)	Planned for 1987
Japanese Experimental Communications Satellite	NASADA (FACC)	Operational
Lincoln Experimental Satellite Project	U.S. DOD	Out of service
U.S. Mobile Satellite Experiment Program	NASA	Planned for late 1980s
NASA Advanced Technologies Satellite Experiment (ACTS)	20/30 GHz	Planned for late 1980s
NASA Experimental/Prototype Space Platform		Planned for late 1980s
Orbital Test Satellites (OTS)	ESA experimental sat.	Operational-2nd planned for launch
Sirio Experimental Communications Satellites	Italian	Operational
Symphonie Experimental Communications Satellite	French/German	Operational
TACSATCOM Experimental Military Satellite	U.S. Military	Out of service

[a]FSS = Fixed Satellite System; DBS = Direct Broadcast Satellite.

Index